THE NATURE AND FUNCTION OF

INTERNATIONAL ORGANIZATION

The Nature and Function of
International Organization

Stephen S. Goodspeed

ASSOCIATE PROFESSOR OF POLITICAL SCIENCE
UNIVERSITY OF CALIFORNIA, SANTA BARBARA

NEW YORK

OXFORD UNIVERSITY PRESS

1959

© 1959 by Oxford University Press, Inc.
Library of Congress Catalogue Card Number: 58-7992

Printed in the United States of America

TO

GRACE FRANCES

PREFACE

In this volume the attempt is made to explain the role of international organization, keeping constantly in mind both the strength and weaknesses which have been voiced by the critics and admirers of the existing and earlier systems.

It is my earnest hope that the reader will be confronted with a picture of the ageless endeavor of sincere men to lessen the insecurity of international life through the creation of institutions designed to bring some measure of political, economic, and social stability.

No organization, regardless of its nature, can be understood unless its objectives, its procedures, its competence, and the setting in which it must function are explained and evaluated. I have tried to do just this, with enough illustrative case material to provide a point of departure for additional exploration. Recognizing also that any organization must continually adapt itself to new conditions, new problems, and demands for change, I have sought, whenever appropriate, to indicate major issues, evolutionary trends, progress, and failure.

To many friends, colleagues, and students go my profound thanks for guidance and assistance. A distinguished and greatly revered mentor, Professor Frank M. Russell of the University of California, Berkeley, inspired in me an early desire to express my thoughts in written form. I cannot forget the faithful services of my loyal assistants, Mrs. Josephine Green, Mrs. Frances LaBarbara, and Mrs. Grace Piper as well as the many courtesies extended by Mrs. Violet Shue and others in the Library of the University. Special thanks are due those who kindly gave of their wisdom and limited time at the United Nations. I am grateful also to Francis W. Carpenter, formerly a correspondent at the United Nations; William R. Frye, United Nations correspondent of the *Christian Science Monitor;* Thomas J. Hamilton, *New York Times* correspondent at the United Nations; James N. Murray, Professor of Political Science at the State University of Iowa, Iowa City; and R. W. Van Wagenen, Dean of the Graduate School, American University, Washington, D.C., who examined all, or portions of, the manuscript, and made suggestions at the request of the Publishers. They are, of course, in no way responsible for the views that I have expressed here.

To those on the Oxford University Press staff who provided stimulation and guidance I am likewise grateful. Finally, the most sincere gratitude must be reserved for my wife — companion and critic — whose devotion, encouragement, and scholarship have been most tangible contributions to this work.

S. S. G.

Santa Barbara, Calif.
October, 1958

CONTENTS

IV. WELFARE AND TRUSTEESHIP

V. THE FUTURE

ILLUSTRATIONS

I

THE DEVELOPMENT OF

INTERNATIONAL ORGANIZATION

1

INTRODUCTION

In an address at Paris about a century ago, Victor Hugo predicted:

> A day will come when the only battlefield will be the market open to commerce and the mind open to new ideas. A day will come when bullets and bombshells will be replaced by votes, by the universal suffrage of nations, by the venerable arbitration of a great sovereign senate, which will be to Europe what the Parliament is to England, what the Diet is to Germany, what the Legislative Assembly is to France. A day will come when a cannon can be exhibited in public museums just as an instrument of torture is now, and people will be astonished how such a thing could have been.

Similar hopes can be discovered centuries before this. Various plans and ideas have arisen out of the political, economic, and social conditions of different eras because there has been a persistent longing for peace, a continuous search for some alternative to the use of force as a means of settling disputes.

There are those who believe that there is no solution to the problem of the unorganized world of nation-states. There are others who have envisaged, perhaps as an outgrowth of the memory of the Pax Romana, a situation wherein one nation may somehow become strong enough to dominate all others and, in the course of such domination, establish an empire founded on justice and wisdom. But benevolent despotisms are indeed rare and continuity is never guaranteed.

A third choice is a form of world government, based upon either the unitary or the federal model. As later discussion will reveal, the arguments for world government are persuasive and full of appeal since the goal is a warless world of peace and plenty. But again, the immediate prospects for the accomplishment of 'one world' in the governmental sense are no more encouraging than in past centuries.

What remains, then, is the need for devising a concept which falls between an unorganized world and a system of government on the universal level. It is here that the developing theory and practice of international organization makes its entrance as a mechanism for encouraging a better functioning of the system of nation-states.

National states have been willing to join in building various types of international organization primarily because they see in them the opportunity to obtain advantages which can be gained from treating some matters on an international level. In the technical field, for example, postal, communications, and meteorological services transcend purely national frontiers and are of concern to all. In recent decades there has been emphasis upon the need for international action on questions of health, labor standards, human rights, technical assistance, and other economic and social items. Either separate organizations or specific organs have been created to foster international co-operation in these fields.

The major powers have been more reluctant to depend upon international organizations for the treatment of purely political problems, but now they are aware of the potentialities inherent in an international body for the expression of views before a world public. The medium-sized and smaller states, in turn, welcome the existence of an international system that not only guarantees them a forum, not otherwise available, to which they can bring their problems freely, but also permits them voting equality on many questions. The greater measure of security afforded by an organization broad in scope and membership and dedicated to the preservation of peace has prompted many smaller states to seek to strengthen the peacemaking facilities of such an international organization so that it will ultimately (1) possess a superiority of organized force permanently on the alert to guard against a breach of the peace; (2) work toward a reduction in social and economic evils which contribute to international tension and instability; and (3) bring about a concerted effort by all states to effect peaceful change and the settlement of international disputes by conciliation.

THE OBJECTIVES OF INTERNATIONAL ORGANIZATION

International organizations are created to further political and national security on the one hand, and economic and social welfare on the other. The development of political and national security involves the organization in the prevention of armed conflict, or the suppression of it if it does arise, and in the peaceful settlement of disputes. Activity directed toward economic and social welfare is undertaken whether problems in these areas are related to the peace or not.

Depending upon its type, an organization may or may not have both of these objectives as its goals. The extent of its representation and the nature of its objectives will determine the type of organization. The Organization of American States, to pick an example, is a regional organization having a membership limited to the states that comprise a delineated area. The United Nations, however, is a universal organization, open to all nations presumably meeting certain requirements of membership. At the same time, both organizations have objectives which encompass matters of security and welfare. This has been true of all universal organizations, but there are some regional arrangements that are concerned only with the objective of security while others have goals restricted to questions of economic and social welfare. The latter are of the more functional variety and are normally constructed along universal lines, although there are some which are purely regional in scope (e.g., the Organization for European Economic Co-operation). The various specialized agencies within the United Nations system, such as the International Labor Organization and the World Health Organization, are the outstanding examples of the universal functional organization.

Important as international organizations are in themselves for welfare purposes and the contributions they may make toward international co-operation, they cannot alone advance political security. The hope that these organizations might develop habits of co-operation which would extend to the political sphere has not been realized, and their benefits have not yet become so indispensable that states would be unwilling to sacrifice them by going to war. Some have argued that the international quest for welfare policies, pursued together with appropriate educational efforts, would divert peoples and governments from their primary concern for increasing national power. In this way, there might come a moral regeneration of peoples and governments which would prove to be a solution for the problem of security. But the essential requisites of such a plan — permanence and universality — have been virtually impossible to achieve. If the majority of nations neglect security for nonsecurity matters, they become weakened in direct proportion to the few bent on aggression. Until all nations participate in giving priority to welfare policies within some system that guarantees the continuance of such a program, the primary concern will be with security and the building of organizations that concentrate upon this goal.

THE STRUCTURE AND FUNCTION OF INTERNATIONAL ORGANIZATION

The government of a national state serves and is presumably representative of its citizens whereas an international organization is composed of sovereign, independent states voluntarily joining in a common pursuit of certain goals. In the national state, the various branches of government, together with their powers, are laid down in a constitution, the provisions of which are binding upon the individual citizen. With the exception of authoritarian regimes, the establishment of a rule of law provides the individual with a protection against the arbitrary acts of government while, at the same time, obligating him to respect the fundamental laws of his land and the duties of citizenship.

An international organization, on the other hand, rests upon foundations which are much less secure. A charter or constitution must be created and agreed to by the states that wish to pursue objectives within a formal organization. While there may be considerable difficulty in resolving political differences when drafting a national constitution, the problems involved in reaching agreement among individual states on the details of an international document are greater still. The utmost care is exercised to guard against an infringment of the national sovereign interests of each member so that there will not be an invasion of 'domestic jurisdiction.' Differences in political, economic, and social systems must be reconciled in some fashion. Shall there be numerical equality of voting for all or a system of weighted voting to reduce the inequality between the physical and financial contributions of large and small states? Should the major powers be given a privileged voting position in a realistic appreciation of their greater responsibilities for maintaining peace and security? Who are to be members — just 'good' states or 'good' and 'bad' alike? What are to be the criteria for determining eligibility or expulsion? How many and what type of organs are needed to accomplish the objectives? Shall security depend upon collective action with the possible use of force or shall reliance be placed upon persuasion? What is to be the role of law and what legal devices are to be employed to bring about the security and welfare of mankind?

These are but a few of the more significant constitutional problems involved in constructing an international organization. To be successful, it is obvious that there must be permanent institutions which will enable all members to participate in free contact with each other and which will be so ready of access that any state, large or small, without fear of restraint, may at any time bring up a problem deemed vital to peace and security. Even more compelling is the need for all who participate to co-operate in a full understanding of the objectives of the organization. Above all, every member must respect his solemn obligations contained in the constitution. History has proved conclusively that an international organization, in a fashion similar to a national government, can succeed only when supported by those it is to serve. But a national government may punish those who violate its laws, while an international organization can do no more than depend upon the good faith of its members to respect its policies and decisions.

The customary separation of power on a national level into executive, legislative, and judicial branches is only roughly approximated in an international organization. To begin with, there is no executive organ, properly speaking. Certain organs are assigned special duties and are permitted to act in specific situations. In the realm of administration, however, the permanent secretariat of an international organization has an extremely important function. The Secretary-General is the executive head solely of the secretariat and can speak for the organization only when so instructed by other organs. He may, nevertheless, be given significant responsibilities involving a discretionary use of power, as has been the case with Mr. Dag Hammerskjöld of the United Nations in the Middle East crisis of 1956–57. A secretariat performs a wide variety of necessary services and concentrates its activities at the permanent seat of the organization.

International organization does not possess a legislative body in the ordinary sense although the diplomatic conference bears some resemblance to it. Ordinarily the organization meets in regular annual session with an equal representation from all members. Occasional *ad hoc* conferences are held for special purposes. The annual conference is essentially a policy-making body, performing in addition various financial and supervisory duties. It carries out certain constituent functions such as admitting new members and amending the constitution. Occasionally, as with the United Nations, the constituent power is held jointly by two organs: the General Assembly and the Security Council.

The annual conference acting as a policy-making body comes closest to the role of a national legislature but differs in two fundamental respects. In the first place, there are certain procedural distinctions. The members of an international organization, since they are states, select as representatives government officials who are carefully instructed in all activities they participate in, from general debate to how to vote on each item before them. On only the most routine questions is there permitted a decision by a simple majority vote. A two-thirds vote is the ordinary custom and, in some instances, there must be unanimity of either certain or all members. As a rule, there are standing committees to examine certain types of questions and recommend action to the plenary body. But it is not uncommon to have each member represented on such a committee, making it large and frequently unwieldly. No national legislature has even a remotely similar composition or voting procedure. While legislatures are subject to many forms of political pressure, there is nothing quite comparable to the diplomatic maneuvering and tactics of obstruction which can be exhibited by sovereign states.

The second major difference is the final product of a conference. The agenda of the General Assembly, for example, ranges from the most complex problems of a purely political nature to questions of trusteeship to a wide variety of economic and social items, all of which require a policy decision. In a comparable situation, the legislature would enact specific laws to cover these matters but the conference can only make recommendations. Implementation is left primarily to the good faith of the member-states. It is common for a conference to formulate a treaty which is the product of diplomatic negotiation. But the treaty does not become operative until legally ratified by a certain number of states through their own domestic processes. Furthermore, the treaty is binding only on those states that have performed this purely national act.

The differences between the judicial functions of national and international tribunals are even more apparent. To begin with, international tribunals do not possess compulsory jurisdiction over all disputes between states. If both parties have consented beforehand to permit the hearing of legal disputes before the International Court of Justice, the jurisdiction of that body is compulsory. But the character of disputes which can be brought before it is strictly limited. Furthermore, there is no distinction between civil and criminal cases in an international hearing since there is no international criminal law applicable to states, nor do international courts possess criminal jurisdiction.

The customary methods employed by international bodies to settle disputes peacefully involve procedures that are ordinarily quite different from those of national courts. The use of adjudication by the latter is the normal course but the processes utilized in international settlement usually involve other means. There is less dependence upon arbitration and judicial settlement than on the methods of negotiation, enquiry, mediation, and conciliation. Some smaller organ of the international organization, such as the Security Council of the United Nations, is customarily charged with employing these means although the plenary body can also do so. All members of the organization are obligated to settle their disputes by peaceful means.

But international organs can only recommend and cannot compel states to use pacific settlement. Similarly, the World Court or an arbitration panel may hand down a decision but it does not possess the means enjoyed by national courts of obtaining compliance.

The picture which materializes from this very brief survey of the functions and structure of international organization is one that reveals only an imperfect government at the most. There is no executive organ or officer to shape policy or enforce decisions. A fairly extensive administrative body is always present to perform the many services required by any permanent organization. The plenary body of all the members, which resembles a legislature only in a limited sense, does make policy but solely in the form of a recommendation and not an enactment. The settlement of disputes is a primary concern of the organization and special organs are provided to perform this necessary function, but they are not equipped to force compliance with their recommendations.

Since resort to force is a distinct possibility on the part of those who violate the solemn obligations of membership, universal organizations, as well as some regional ones, have sought to develop an international order in which the security of each state is expected to come from the combined forces of all. This is the theory of collective security which, in essence, involves the promise by sovereign states joined together by the constitution of the organization that, under certain circumstances, they will come to the aid of a state which is threatened, or actually attacked, by another. It is a system designed to provide protection for all by co-operative effort. Action can be taken against those who pose a threat to the peace, or commit an actual breach of the peace or act of aggression, through collective measures or sanctions of an economic or military nature. No international organization possesses a police force standing at the ready to come to the aid of a victim of aggression although the Charter of the United Nations envisaged the possible development of such a force. In practice, however, the United Nations has had to rely upon improvised arrangements as the occasion warranted.

Collective security represents a middle ground between a completely unregulated international order and a world government in which the war-making power of states would be eliminated. In theory, collective security assumes that war can be prevented by the bringing to bear of overwhelming power against a state with the implication of inevitable defeat for the offender. It depends for its success upon the willingness of all states to recognize that an act of aggression against one state must be considered an act of aggression against all members of the organization. All must respond to this violation of the international status quo with swiftness and determination. Most important is the need for the major powers, who possess the primacy of power, to participate in the collective action against the transgressor.

THE SETTING FOR INTERNATIONAL ORGANIZATION

The international status quo is the system of nation-states wherein there continues to exist a constant struggle for power. Since international organization is a mechanism designed to encourage a better functioning of the state system, it must, of necessity, contend with this ceaseless struggle and the forces which shape it. Despite the ideals and objectives of international organization, with the exception of the most technical matters, politics and conflict are always present, and will continue to be, as long as the national state is the basic unit of representation. What must be examined, then, are the forces underlying the state system if there is to be an understanding of the difficulties confronting the development, function, and successful operation of an international organization. These include the legal notions of sovereignty and equality, as well as the elements which make for national power and the explosive force of nationalism.

Sovereignty. One of the most compelling problems of national and inter-state organization is the legal concept of sovereignty. The idea is as old as Aristotle, and the word itself probably entered the vocabulary in its current usage in feudal times. It then represented a relationship between persons, an individual subservient to his sovereign overlord. Jean Bodin in 1576 first introduced the term into the literature of political science and defined it as 'the supreme power of the state over its citizens and subjects, unrestrained by law.' The essential features of this definition have persisted down to the present with certain modifications and interpretations. When one observes that a state is sovereign he usually means that the activities of the state are not legally subject to the control of any higher or external authority. This means that there is no legal power within the state that is superior to it, that there can be but one sovereignty in the state, and that every person and organization or group is subject to the sovereign will of the state. Put somewhat differently, sovereignty may customarily be characterized by absoluteness, universality, permanence, and indivisibility.

As applied to international relations, the legal theory of sovereignty has been considered to mean the right of a state to manage all its affairs, whether external or internal, without control from other states. This right of independent action is a natural result of sovereignty. When a state is entirely its own master, it is sovereign as regards itself, independent as regards others.

To many, this idea of the sovereign state stands as a rigid barrier against the spread of internationalism and peaceful relations between states. Unquestionably the concept of sovereignty which is characterized by the unlimited authority of the state to exercise its will unchecked by any superior or external control, is a fundamental condition of international politics. It is a problem which lies at the heart of the development of true international organization. Consequently it has been argued: that state sovereignty has been restricted by the growth of international law and agreements legally contracted with other states; that it is a legal fiction, no longer corresponding to the facts of international life; that properly speaking, sovereignty deals with the internal relations of a state to its inhabitants and is, therefore, a term of constitutional law and not applicable to international relations.

Such a line of reasoning is immediately attacked by the proponents of the strict juristic theory of sovereignty which maintains that the limitations imposed by international law and treaties and conventions are not legally binding since they are voluntary limitations, self-imposed, unenforceable by any higher authority, and can be denounced by the sovereign state at its leisure. Thus it is argued that such restrictions cannot be enforced by the state upon its citizens since it is not the product of the sovereign power in the same sense as national law.

The facts of present-day international life make it appear that despite the need for good faith in interstate relations and the development of complex interrelations among states, each state, in the final analysis, seeks to be its own interpreter of international obligations and maintains the right to determine its own standards of international conduct. In its most extreme form, such a reliance upon the greatest freedom of sovereign action is the very negation of international co-operation and destroys the fundamental obligations of membership in an international organization. Happily, most states recognize the need for a standard of international conduct based upon respect for the tenets of international law and the requirements of comity and good faith. Nevertheless, should a vital national interest be seriously threatened, a state, particularly if it is a major power, may still pursue a unilateral course of action, supported by the popular belief of its citizens that as a sovereign entity, it cannot be legally restricted in its external as well as internal acts.

Equality. Reinforcing the legal notions of absolute sovereignty and independence has been the doctrine of state equality. From the time of Grotius there has been the claim that all independent states are equal before the law. Chief Justice Marshall over a century and a half ago observed concerning the case of *The Antelope:* 'No principle of general law is more universally acknowledged than the perfect equality of nations. . . . A right, then, which is vested in all by the consent of all, can be divested by consent. . . . As no nation can prescribe a rule for others, none can make a law of nations.'

There can be no denial of the need for a system of law which affords equal protection to all and which requires all to fulfill their obligations equally. This was the meaning of the view expressed by a delegate to the Second Hague Conference in 1907 in these words: 'Each nation is a sovereign person, equal to others in moral dignity, and having, whether small or great, weak or powerful, an equal claim to respect for its rights, an equal obligation in the performance of its duties.' But, as Professor Edwin Dickinson has ably demonstrated, there is not an 'equal capacity for rights' possessed by all and such a concept is not essential to the reign of law.[1] In other words, the United States and Haiti are equally entitled to be recognized as states but they cannot claim to be accepted as equal states. In 1935 the Permanent Court of International Justice made a similar distinction when it referred to equality in law and equality in fact as follows: 'Equality in law precludes discrimination of any kind; whereas equality in fact may involve the necessity of different treatment in order to attain a result which establishes an equilibrium between different situations.'

Although the doctrine of equality before the law has validity in any respectable system of law, meaning that once the law is made it will be applied impartially, there persists the confusion over the meaning of equality of rights. Small states in particular interpret the latter to mean equality of influence, especially in such matters as voting privileges. The Charter of the United Nations, in Article 2, refers to 'the sovereign equality of its members.' But it is obvious, in fact, that all members of the United Nations are not equal in their capacity for rights and the Charter recognizes this by granting permanent membership on the Security Council to certain large states. Furthermore, although there are six nonpermanent members on the Council, their voting position may be destroyed unless there is unanimity among the Big Five. It appears, therefore, that current practice dictates that all states are equal for some purposes but not for all purposes.

Power Politics. Both national and international politics contain the forces inherent in any quest for power. National foreign policy seeks to gain security and prosperity for the state in much the same sense as domestic policies attempt to enhance material well-being and stability for peoples and groups within the state. The accomplishment of these goals depends upon the action and interaction of pressures upon the makers and executers of policy. Within the national state, capital, labor, and agriculture, for example, try to win favorable legislative and administrative action to satisfy

[1] *The Equality of States in International Law,* Cambridge, 1920, p. 335.

their group demands. Similarly, on the international scene, where nations replace individuals and groups within the arena of contesting power, pressures are brought to bear to solidify alliances, to weaken economic competition, or to threaten reprisals for acts deemed prejudicial to the national interest. However, the character of the forces which can be employed by political pressure within the state and that which is used between states stand in marked contrast. The favors sought by national groups from their government are channeled through political organs whose continuance depends upon the support received from these groups. Political favors become objects bartered for the sake of the holding of political power. Only on rare occasions is there a resort to physical violence. The game is played according to certain rules and is supervised by the entire body politic through its government, namely the agency in whose trust has been placed ultimate power. The conflicts of interest which separate groups are reconcilable by peaceful means within a superior order based upon law and justice. It is the police function which, centuries of experience demonstrates, is essential for effective administration of justice and the maintenance of peace.

In the arena of world politics there has developed a complicated system of relationships between independent states without, however, the establishment of a superior authority, based upon law and justice and possessed of the sanction of the police function which can restrain a state that has the power to enforce its will upon the minds and actions of other men. In essence, national political power in democratic countries is associated with the process of winning minds by persuasion or appeal to reason. Similarly, on the international scene, the ways in which power is most frequently evidenced are through the leadership and the persuasion of a few major states. International relations are not necessarily determined exclusively by force. But when considerations of law and justice stand challenged, when rival aspirants for leadership find no common ground, when compromise and reason have been exhausted, the ultimate decision will be determined by the amount of power possessed by the competing states. The actual use of armed strength in wartime substitutes military for political power, but even the threat of force is a very real element of the latter. Power politics viewed as a vital attribute of the national-state system is, therefore, the continuous relationship between independent states, each recognizing no superior authority. There are periods of war and peace in the relationship which are determined by the extent to which a state or group of states is willing to venture beyond the use of political and economic means and employ forceful methods to gain the desired objectives of security and prosperity. Indeed, the policy of a nation may proceed further than these goals and utilize force to gain regional, continental, or even intercontinental, hegemony.

The makers of foreign policy are confronted by a series of basic elements or factors which need constant assessment when deciding upon a given course of action. These constitute the bases of national power and largely predetermine the nature and the content of national policy. Within the limits of these elements, foreign policy can be devised, remaining flexible between the power available at home and the support to be found abroad among those nations having similar aims and interests. The ends and means of policy must be brought into balance if dangers and ultimate failure are to be avoided. These ingredients of national power may vary in strength and change from time to time. Some are more or less stable and subject to scientific measurement while others are not. All must be assessed in their relationship to each other and in the proper context of time and circumstance. Finally, these bases of national power, in policy determination, should always be considered from the standpoint of military strategy. War is seldom an instrument of national policy and, in fact, represents in large measure the failure of policy. But the various alternatives and power factors available in policy formulation inevitably enter the calculations of national strategy. It is the job of the statesman to marshal power to accomplish his policy goals peacefully but at the same time to gauge accurately the risks involved from a military standpoint and to prepare for the possible military consequences associated with the failure of his policy.

The following list contains the fundamental elements or factors which constitute the bases of national power.

1. *Geography.* The most basic and permanent although not necessarily the most important of the elements is geography. The size, location, and nature of the land surface will govern the structure and the character of the national economy and the character of national defense.

2. *Economic elements.* The type of primary economic production will characterize a state as agricultural, industrial, or balanced. The economic category to which a state belongs has an important influence upon foreign policy. Technological development can determine the success or failure of a state's quest for security and will largely shape the outcome of sustained military action.

3. *Natural resources.* To industrialize, a state must possess or have ready access to certain important raw materials, such as coal and iron. In addition, raw materials and other natural assets or resources such as fertile land and abundant water supply, are virtually worthless unless adequately exploited by technology. It follows that the most powerful states are those that actually possess the greatest abundance of total resources provided by nature and that can extract, grow, and produce from them the goods required of an industrial society.

4. *Demography*. Human geography or demography has an important bearing upon national power, since human beings are necessary for production at all times and are one of the bases of military strength. Such quantitative factors as the size of the population, its density per square mile, its trends, and its quality inevitably enter into the calculation of policy planners.

5. *Character and morale of population*. Less tangible, and hence more difficult of measurement, are the qualities which characterize the attitudes, the traditions and customs, the education, the general culture, and the morale of a state. The staying power of a nation during hostilities, the ability to absorb new technical skills, the influence of tradition on morale in an emergency play a significant part in building and maintaining national power. Some peoples appear to have inner drives that enable them to overcome great handicaps in reaching national goals. Unquestionably such attributes should be taken into consideration by those who formulate policies with or against states possessing them.

6. *Governmental institutions*. The various elements just noted become virtually meaningless unless the quality of government as a whole and the character of its leadership and diplomacy are such that there is a capable employment of all its resources. Government in democratic countries, at least, must inspire confidence among the citizenry and encourage the spokesmen for the basic interest groups — business, labor, agriculture — to follow its lead in both domestic and foreign policy. A nation poorly led will exhibit lack of resolution in its foreign policy, and morale at home can become diluted if not destroyed.

Qualified statesmen will construct foreign policy on the basis of the elements of national power available. Goals will not be set too low, indicating too great a caution and an improper evaluation of the national power potential; nor will the objectives sought be too high as a result of overestimating certain power elements and neglecting the significance of others. History is replete with instances in which a nation aspired to the role of a great power without the necessary requisites of strength. Statesmanship is required in diplomacy to the end of protecting and advancing the goals of policy. The competence of those engaged in the diplomatic service may be able to overcome deficiencies in other elements of power.

Finally, demonstrable ability in financial, economic, and military affairs can be of inestimable value in providing national strength. Traditions associated with competence tend to influence national policies and affect the attitudes of other states. The sum total of governmental and military talents as reflected in the success or failure of political institutions, policies, and ideology cannot help but provide a necessary element of national power.

Successful foreign policy is of long-range value, involving careful planning and analysis of the basic elements of power. Other factors belonging primarily in the realm of short-term phenomena should not be excluded as, for example, an isolated but strong personality or an unexpected national catastrophe. But the elements of power do not serve as constants operating with the same force for all states, nor can they be measured with positive accuracy. Some are more important than others at various times and hold more significance for some states over a long period than might be true for other nations. All are interdependent and assume importance when considered as ingredients of a whole. A large population without raw materials lacks significance. Morale and character are intangibles and can be extremely fluid. Capable government and adequate leadership, from the standpoint of power, are relatively meaningless without the other elements serving as complementary factors. Changes in power are continually taking place. The modern aircraft has brought formerly isolated areas within relatively easy access. The development of atomic energy has revolutionized military thinking. Uranium ore, virtually unknown less than two decades ago, is now an invaluable raw material. Its possession in large quantities within the borders of a state increases the power potential of that state. Again, however, the interdependence of power elements becomes evident. The physical possession of uranium is of far greater significance if the state has the technological ability to process it into atomic power for both peacetime and military uses and if government leadership can capitalize upon this new addition of power by skillful domestic programs as well as international negotiation for purposes of security and prosperity.

The term 'power' is often used interchangeably with nation and state, indicating the close indentification of power with state action. Furthermore, states are frequently differentiated according to their strength, influence, and capacity by grouping them as 'Great Powers' and 'Small Powers.' Size and numbers are the primary elements which distinguish these two categories. It is obvious that most states have small populations and territorial size and can never be regarded as great powers. A small power, because of its weakness, is always prey for the great powers and sometimes retains its independence only because a great power would never permit another to absorb it. Smallness does not indicate inferiority in all respects, however. The stability and freedom enjoyed, for example, by the Scandinavian countries, Belgium, Holland, and Switzerland are advantages not necessarily enjoyed by larger and greater states. The constellation of great powers has varied constantly since the development of the modern state system because of the shifting, changing character of national power. After the Peace of Westphalia in 1648, France and Sweden were the two dominant powers, followed by England, Spain, and Austria. Spain and Sweden lost their pre-eminent positions in the eighteenth century, leaving Russia, France, Austria, and Great Britain the leaders. The nineteenth century saw the rise of Japan, Germany, and the United States as great powers, with Russia and Austria weakening. The First World War produced the temporary eclipse of Germany, the destruction of Austria-Hungary, the diminishing power of

Britain and France, and a greatly improved position for Japan and the United States. During the interwar period, Italy assumed an important position under Mussolini, Germany and Russia recaptured their former stature, while Great Britain and France continued to weaken. The Second World War devastated Japan, Germany, and Italy, and left France prostrate.

What might be termed legal recognition of a great power first occurred with the Council of the League of Nations. Article IV of the Covenant specified that 'The Council shall consist of Representatives of the Principal Allied and Associated Powers' which, according to the Preamble of the Versailles Treaty were the United States, Great Britain, France, Italy, and Japan. These were to have permanent seats by virtue of their greater resources, responsibilities, and interests. The defection of the United States reduced the number of permanent members to four until 1926, when Germany was voted to the vacant seat. In 1934 Soviet Russia became the sixth permanent member of the Council, but in 1935 the figure dropped to four again with the withdrawal of Japan and Germany. Italy withdrew in 1937 and the Soviets were expelled in 1939 leaving but two, France and Great Britain, to uphold the position of great power status against the non-permanent middle and small nations.

The Charter of the United Nations continued the legal recognition of great powers by providing, in Article 23, that the United States, Soviet Russia, France, Great Britain, and China 'shall be permanent members of the Security Council.' Despite this award of great power status, at the present time only three nations — the United States, Soviet Russia, and, further behind, Great Britain — can be truly classified as great powers. Grievously weakened by two world wars, financially weak, and divided internally, France is a great power in name only. Nationalist China is but a fiction of a state. Communist China has become a major force in Asia and may eventually be accorded the status of a great power.

In the final analysis, anything that provides strength for a nation will add to its power. There being no single or simple formula to determine with exactness the power potential of a state in all circumstances, reliance must be placed upon careful estimates constantly re-evaluated by specialists in foreign affairs. Harold and Margaret Sprout offer the following useful series of questions which attempt to determine the dependable criteria for judging the capabilities of all states:

1. What is the state's capacity to define feasible foreign policy objectives?
2. What is the state's capacity to combine the tools and techniques of statecraft into an effective strategy for the attainment of its foreign policy objectives in view?

3. What is the state's capacity to provide the tools of statecraft required by the strategy adopted?

4. What is the state's capacity to employ effectively the tools provided and the techniques selected? [2]

Nationalism. Inseparable from the concept of sovereignty in the building of the modern national state has been the development of the sentiment of nationalism. Certainly most contemporary states were established as a result of a determination to create a separate political entity, free from alien control, for the preservation and cultivation of common ideals, loyalties, and traditions. At one time, the state and the monarch were considered as one and a glorification of the latter carried with it an inseparable support for the state. Beginning particularly in the eighteenth century, writers began to distinguish between monarch and state, ascribing to the latter certain characteristics and virtues quite apart from the former. No more potent force exists today than nationalism for incurring tensions, inflaming hatreds, and augmenting the sovereign ideal of a strong, independent, national state. Nationalism has become such a commonplace in the thoughts and actions of modern peoples that it is taken for granted and is assumed always to have been in existence.

A group of people convinced that they possess certain distinguishable characteristics associated with the feeling of belonging to one nation is the commonly accepted definition of nationality. Nationalism represents the feeling of belonging, the spirit or sentiment of loyalty, the group-consciousness of the nationality. The nation is the holder of the nationality, the physical rampart which defends the nationality from attacks launched by the foreigner and which must be supported at all costs if the unity of the nationality is to be preserved. As one noted authority states, 'Nationalism is first and foremost a state of mind, an act of consciousness . . . , permeating the large majority of a people and claiming to permeate all its members; it recognizes the nation-state as the ideal form of political organization and the nationality as the source of all creative cultural energy and of economic well-being. The supreme loyalty of man is therefore due to his nationality, as his own life is supposedly rooted in and made possible by its welfare.' [3]

Nationalities are born when certain positive characteristics evolve which serve to differentiate one nationality from another. There are elements which contribute to the formation and delineation of a nationality, such as religion, language, customs and traditions, common origin, territory, and

[2] *Foundations of National Power*, 2nd ed., New York: D. Van Nostrand Co., Inc., 1951, p. 106.

[3] Kohn, Hans, *The Idea of Nationalism*, New York: The Macmillan Co., 1945, pp. 10, 16.

political form. All nationalities contain some of these elements, but rarely do they possess all of them. Each has its particular significance. Religion is most effective when there is a certain ancient state religion that permits a national church to interpret the ecclesiastical and, frequently, the political views of the nation. Language is both a divisive and a cementing element and sets one nationality off from another. A foreigner does not speak the tongue that is common to the nationality and, arbitrarily, becomes an alien. At the same time, the gloried origins, customs, and traditions which are the hallmarks of a nationality can be carried from father to son verbally and in written form. Delimited territory and identifiable political institutions serve as tangible evidences of the nationality and become hallowed in legend, song, and verse.

In addition to these elements, according to Professor Hans Kohn, 'the most essential element is a living and corporate will. Nationality is formed by the decision to form a nationality.'[4] Latent elements, particularly in a time of stress or conflict, suddenly become fused into a consciousness of kind, a desire to manifest themselves in a single, unified, national whole. Certainly this was true of the American, English, and French nationalities. Revolution is frequently the result of a nationality cognizant of its identity and determined to solidify its oneness in an independent, political community. Nationalism, thus, is exhibited by the spirit of the awakened nationality bent upon achieving exclusive control over its own destiny, a consciousness of self nurtured by the coalescence of the elements of nationality.

Loyalty to the nationality and the nation is a necessary and a natural element of citizenship. Without the support of its nationals, no state can protect itself from anarchy for any length of time. Nationalism has become a unifying force in democratic countries, materially assisting the realization of democratic aims. The eighteenth century — the age of enlightenment — witnessed the development of modern nationalism, particularly in France and the New World. Free and enlightened citizenship, the rights of man, the benefits of democratic governments, became the gospels for later national awakenings in Europe and the Americas during the following century. The writings of Rousseau and Thomas Jefferson and the ideas of the American and French revolutions provided nascent nationalities with the spark which generated action. While revolutionary in practice, nationalism came to be associated with the entrenchment of the middle class, which viewed it with sympathy as a doctrine that encouraged peoples to cast out the foreign oppressor and build national states on the principle of self-determination.

[4] *Ibid.,* p. 15.

But nationalism can become compulsive and aggressive, leading to autocracy and paternalism in government and conflict and imperialism in international affairs. It may drive peoples apart by overemphasizing national differences and raising the nation above all others on the basis of these differences. Coupled with an extremist interpretation of unlimited national sovereignty and stimulating exclusive and indiscriminate devotion to the nation, it stands, in the final analysis, as a barrier to international cooperation and thereby makes the task of international organization more difficult. The emotional fusion and exaggeration of nationality and patriotism is by no means losing its force. The nationalisms of Asia, Africa, and the Middle East attest to its strength at the present time. The halls of the United Nations ring with its jingoism, which demonstrates that the twentieth century has not yet become truly the age of internationalism.

INTERNATIONAL LAW

Sometimes called the law of nations, *Droit des Gens,* or *Volkerrecht,* international law has developed through the ages as a system of rules and guides for interstate action. In the fullest sense, it is a product of the modern period and is associated with the rise of the European state system. Some of its principles can be traced to the customs of antiquity, such as matters relating to diplomatic immunities and procedures of negotiation between states. But it was the influence of the Reformation and Renaissance and the development of the modern state which caused writers to distinguish legal from ethical and theological questions and to argue for a separate system of international law.

The object of all law is to define the interests of the parties concerned in a controversy and then to provide adequate procedures for settlement on the basis of rational argument. International law also serves to facilitate the coexistence of many states with different cultures and governments. For several centuries, rules have been developed which seek to determine the conduct of states in their mutual dealings. Just as men cannot live together in a society without laws and customs to govern their actions, so states have discovered that there must be some system of law to regulate their conduct. Here again the difficulty encountered in the observance of international law is associated with the fact that the person in international law is a state. Within the state, law is generally obeyed because it is comparatively simple to define the interests of individuals and punish violators through the ordinary channels of law enforcement. But the family of more than eighty nations presents a far different situation. The obvious difficulty of delimiting the interests of national states is complicated by the concentration of power in only a few. It is virtually impossible for the remaining states to compel obedience to the law by coercive measures. The procedures available to secure adherence to the rules of international law depend only upon the willingness of states to use them.

As a whole, the body of international law is respected and observed far more than it is violated. Most states have discovered that it is to their interest to respect rules of conduct in order that certain rights may become more or less guaranteed without the employment of force. Careful analysis suggests, however, that occasional violations of accepted international conduct concern matters of far graver concern to international society than the quantitatively more numerous areas of obedience, since under current state practice, a large field for political action still lies open.

Despite the absence of any extensive codification, the student of international law has certain definite sources to which he can refer when seeking rules and principles that might apply to a given set of circumstances. Leading jurists as well as Article 38 of the Statute of the International Court of Justice designate four general categories of sources. Briefly stated, they include agreement, custom, reason, and authority, listed in the order of their importance. Some have claimed that the last two are not, properly speaking, sources of law. But those who drafted the Statute believed that there should be sources other than agreement or custom since, otherwise, there might be gaps in international law. The Court, it was argued, should not refuse jurisdiction in a case because there was no law on the subject. If custom or agreement revealed no rule, the Court should then resort to 'general principles of law recognized by civilized nations' which refers to 'maxims of justice' or juristic principles common to all systems of law.

The best sources of international law are those which have been drawn up in various written agreements. Treaties and other similar documents contain rules which, if properly ratified by the various signatories, are legally binding. Such instruments, particularly the multilateral variety, offer concrete and tangible evidence of intent to regularize certain actions. Significant for international law has been the increased use of the law-making treaty, one whose object is to formulate positive rules of conduct for specific matters recognized by all signatories. Conspicuous examples are the Conventions of the Hague Conferences of 1899 and 1907, the Covenant of the League of Nations, the Charter of the United Nations, and various Conventions drafted by the United Nations, such as the Convention on the Privileges and Immunities of the United Nations. It might be said that such treaties, creating international legislation as they do, perform tasks similar to those of a national state legislature. Important too are the hundreds of bilateral treaties of commerce, navigation, extradition, consular privileges and immunities, and arbitration.

The basic source of practically all law is custom. Intrinsically it forms a vitally important foundation for international law and is comparable to Anglo-Saxon common law. Custom is actually imitation and consent growing from the deeply rooted interest and sentiments of mankind. It develops out of some specific practice or form of conduct which has demonstrated its usefulness or convenience. Gradually usage solidifies and records the practice and it gains strength through observance. Finally, the course of conduct may be said to have become a customary rule of international law when nations follow it to the extent that they assume a legal obligation of obedience. Justice Strong of the United States Supreme Court observed in the case of *The Scotia,* that customary law '. . . is of force, not because it was prescribed by any superior power, but because it has been generally accepted as a rule of conduct.' In the case of *The Paquette Habana,* the Court held '. . . the period of one hundred years . . . is amply sufficient to have enabled what originally may have rested in custom or comity, courtesy or concession, to grow, by the general assent of civilized nations, into a settled rule of international law.' Despite its importance, it should be remembered that customary law suffers from two principal handicaps, namely the difficulty of proof, and the time required for its development into an authoritative force.

When agreements and general custom fail to offer a satisfactory rule in a case before the International Court of Justice, the Court is instructed by its Statute to apply 'the general principles of law recognized by civilized nations.' What the Statute refers to in this passage is the application of judicial reason, whereby there is a logical deduction made from established principles of law in order to arrive at a decision where no previous rule exists. No two cases are necessarily identical and novel situations arise where there are no clear precedents so that new rules must be developed to guide the conduct of states. Justice Marshall once observed that 'Exploring an unbeaten path, with few, if any, aids from precedents or written law, the court has found it necessary to rely much on general principles, and on a train of reasoning founded on cases in some degree analogous to this.' Such a method of seeking new rules has for centuries been a common practice for tribunals in arriving at decisions and for the conduct of relations between states.

Authority, in the words of the Statute of the International Court of Justice, consists of 'the judicial decisions and the teachings of the most highly qualified publicists of the various nations.' While Anglo-Saxon countries attach great importance to judicial precedents established by their courts, there were relatively few international adjudications of substance prior to the League of Nations system and the Permanent Court of International Justice. With the International Court of Justice, there is every expectation that a substantial number of judicial precedents can be accumulated to expand the body of international law. There can be no denying the fact that judicial decisions are influential and do serve as guides in similar cases, although the decisions of the International Court of Justice have 'no binding force except between the parties and in respect of that particular case.'

A long series of distinguished writers, from the time of Gentili and Grotius to the present, have affected the conduct of states through their published works, and their opinions are frequently consulted and quoted.[5] A nation which disregards the general consensus of these publicists is certainly placed in an unfavorable position before world public opinion. Treatises devoted to international law and exhaustive digests of state papers and documents present a ready source of information, not only in presenting evidence of what the law is generally agreed to be but in stating, in some instances, what it should be. In the latter role, publicists can aid indirectly in shaping state policy and can eventually add to or modify existing law.

Although it is considerably more precise in form, international law is concerned with much of international organization. The establishment of an international agency to perform some function is the result of multistate action seeking treatment of a problem or problems along the lines of mutual benefit. Such an international organization, whether it is a Postal Union or the United Nations, is created by a treaty binding upon its adherents as international law. Immediately, then, an international organization is responsible for creating international law through its organic statute. The wider the membership the more general the law becomes in its application. The Charter of the United Nations, in Article 2, paragraph 6, even appears to assume authority over nonmember states when it provides that it 'shall ensure that states which are not members of the United Nations act in accordance with these Principles so far as may be necessary for the maintenance of international peace and security.'

International law identifies and defines the powers of such international institutions as commissions and courts. At the same time it is an instrument or tool of international organization, useful in the efforts of the latter to secure pacific settlement of disputes through legal procedures. But it must be noted that entire sections of international law, such as those dealing with citizenship and nationality, have little relationship to international organization. On the other hand there are many aspects of international organi-

[5] In the last century, among the more prominent are, from France: Bonfils and Fauchille; Austria: Kelsen; Great Britain: Brierly, Lauterpacht, Schwarzenberger, Hall, Oppenheim, Lawrence, Westlake, Phillimore, and Lorimer; Germany: Bluntschli, Triepel, and Strupp; United States: Moore, Hyde, Hershey, Dickinson, Fenwick, Jessup, Wilson, Wright, and Eagleton.

zation, chiefly political and procedural questions, that have no legal foundations and therefore are not associated with international law.

One of the tasks of international organization is to develop and expand international law and a universal organization such as the United Nations is thereby provided with immense opportunities. Article 13 of the Charter authorizes the General Assembly to 'initiate studies and make recommendations for the purpose of . . . encouraging the progressive development of international law and its codification.' With practically all nations within its membership, such an organization could make an everlasting contribution to the rule of law in international relations. Through the procedure of the convention or treaty, international law could be expanded to meet new conditions and needs.

It should be noted here that despite the opportunities, the United Nations has not been greatly concerned with the development of international law. In spite of the need for a substantial revision of entire divisions of international law, many of the members of the United Nations exhibit impatience with so-called legal problems. An International Law Commission has been created to further the aims of Article 13 of the Charter but its recommendations and reports, inadequate as they sometimes are, have been received with a lack of enthusiasm by the General Assembly, which has done little more than merely report them to its membership. The United Nations is a political organization but it is founded upon the Charter, its legal constitution, which presupposes the operation of the rule of law. Although the solution of grave conflicts often depends upon the adjustment of political issues, no solution can endure unless it is reached on the basis of justice and the consideration of procedures established and upheld by law. Secretary Byrnes cogently observed this as he retired from the Department of State:

> The struggle for peace is the struggle for law and justice. It is a never ending struggle. Law and justice can be developed and applied only through living institutions capable of life and growth. And the institutions must be backed by sufficient force to protect nations which abide by the law against nations which violate the law. . . .
>
> And we must realize that unless the Great Powers are not only prepared to observe the law but are prepared to act in defense of the law, the United Nations Organization can not prevent war. . . .
>
> History informs us that individuals abandoned private wars and gave up their arms only as they were protected by the common law of their tribe and their nation. So I believe that in the long run international peace depends upon our ability to develop a common law of nations which all nations can accept and which no nation can violate with impunity. . . .

2

THE LEAGUE OF NATIONS — ORIGIN, STRUCTURE, FUNCTIONS

MUCH has been written in recent years about the League of Nations, with the emphasis placed upon its shortcomings and its failures. Today, it is much easier to be derogatory than to measure the contributions made toward the goals sought. The League has been discredited by many who either failed to appreciate the underlying causes of its unhappy demise or were impatient with the natural course of history and struck out in any direction that might appear to offer a quick and simple solution to the problem of world peace. The truth is that the League of Nations was abandoned by its friends, who failed to abide by their solemn obligations.

The League of Nations was the first attempt to build a universal social and political order transcending the traditional barriers of national, economic, and racial differences. In this sense it was an experiment, even a revolutionary one, when one observes the character and organization of international relations prior to the First World War and the changes which occurred following the creation of the League. In other respects, the League of Nations represented the partial fruition, at least, of ideals and principles which men had discussed and advocated for centuries, some of which had even found expression in rudimentary forms of international co-operation. In this sense it attempted to advance the progress already made in interstate relations and to supplement the methods of co-operation in existence. This the League did and, despite its failure to prevent aggressive war, it contributed immensely to the science and procedure of international organization.

The evolutionary process of developing international organization continues with the United Nations, itself a sort of revised League, a voluntary combination of nations representing not a clear-cut break from the past but a segment of the gradually developing institutional side of interstate relations. The framers of the Charter were able to avoid some of the admitted errors of the Covenant. New problems have had to be appraised in the light of past experiences. But the success of the United Nations will be measured, as in the case of the League, by the degree of support granted by its members.

ORIGINS OF THE LEAGUE OF NATIONS

Theoretical Internationalism. Efforts to reduce conflict and violence in interstate relations through organized procedures have consumed the interest of thinkers and statesmen from earliest times. Nearly thirty centuries of thought reveals the rather startling conclusion that by the outbreak of the First World War, virtually every principle and method of modern international organization had been discussed and recorded for posterity. To be sure, details were lacking, procedures remained to be developed, modern technology added complexity to or simplified older precepts and approaches to the problems of previous eras. But these earlier blueprints all represent a slow, tortuous effort to provide some measure of peace and security for mankind and form a portion of the evolutionary development of international organization of which both the League of Nations and the United Nations are a part.

Outstanding prior to the nineteenth century were the contributions of Dante, Marsiglio of Padua, Pierre Dubois, Erasmus, Emeric Crucé, Henry IV (Sully), William Penn, the Abbé de Saint-Pierre, and Immanuel Kant. The idea of a covenant joining nations together in a group and binding the members not to make war on each other, with economic or physical penalties or sanctions for those who violate their solemn obligations, has been the basic principle passed on through the centuries. Other fundamental precepts, some even dating back to the days of the Greek city-states, include the following: resort to arbitration and conciliation through permanent or *ad hoc* panels; disarmament; world federation and European federation; an international police force; an executive council and a general assembly with proposals for both unanimous and majority or weighted voting; equitable financial and military contributions by all to the central authority; self-determination for nationalities; a world court; various technical, economic, and welfare activities within the framework of a general organization; peaceful change in order to adjust territorial and political inequalities; and the abandonment of secret diplomacy. Some writers based their system upon an appeal to the reason, good will, and inherent justice of mankind. Others urged that Christian teachings be the sole guide for nations organized for peace. There were those who were convinced that any world or European authority could succeed only if it were composed of small-sized states, or Christian states, or republics. Free trade was held by many to be indispensable for the success of nations united for collective action.

Most of the early projects were ignored at the time of their publication and their authors are remembered in history primarily for achievements in other fields. Monarchs and statesmen were too preoccupied with national and dynastic ambitions to pay much attention to suggestions which would, in effect, curb their freedom of action. However, the nineteenth century, ushered in by the Napoleonic era and largely as a reaction to it, was to witness an unprecedented surge of internationalism and pacifism which was a continuation of the great body of intellectual speculation of preceding centuries. The significance of such activity lay in its intensity through a well-organized peace movement in ten or more countries. Notable among pacifist contributors were the English Quaker, Jonathan Dymond, and Americans such as Noah Worcester and William Ellery Channing. William Ladd, Victor Hugo, John Noble, Constantin Pecquer, and others revived the idea of a congress of nations, together with a world court. Some limited the scope of their projects to a United States of Europe. Elihu Burritt, John Stuart Mill, and Richard Cobden argued the case for free trade as a stimulus for international understanding and exchange of peoples and ideas.

The Concert of Europe. This quasi-institution, without permanent organization or rules, grew out of the Holy Alliance and the Congress of Vienna in 1815. In essence, it constituted a series of diplomatic conferences convened sporadically by the major European states. At the beginning, the Concert concerned itself with preventing dynastic and imperial interests from destroying the European balance of power. After the Congress at Aix-la-Chapelle in 1818, the Concert ceased to concern itself so much with the peace of Europe and concentrated upon suppressing the spread of liberal and revolutionary movements in certain countries. Following the conference at Verona in 1822, however, the Concert system was abandoned, primarily because of the refusal of Great Britain to support the reactionary policy toward governmental change advocated by the other major powers.

The Concert was revived in the second half of the century and it returned to its original principle of seeking to replace force with diplomatic negotiation. All the great powers of Europe were present at the Congress of Paris in 1856 which terminated the Crimean War. They signed the 'Declaration of Paris' which called for the protection of neutral trade in time of war. A Congress at Geneva in 1864 adopted a convention aimed at humanizing warfare and ameliorating suffering by providing for the neutralization of military hospital units in the field. Red Cross societies throughout the world were eventually established to implement the objectives of the convention.

Although the Concert was unable to prevent the Russo-Turkish War in 1877, it did manage at the Congress of Berlin in 1878 to keep it from spreading beyond these two major participants. At the same time, Serbia was informed that unless it permitted religious liberty within its borders, it could not participate in European diplomatic councils. The Concert was able to localize the Serbo-Bulgarian War of 1885, the Cretan War of 1897, and the Balkan War of 1912–13.

Although the contributions of the Concert system to international organization should not be overemphasized, certain significant developments can be noted. The system of multilateral diplomacy resulting from the various conferences of the nineteenth century represented a distinct departure from the practice of earlier centuries. The Concert assumed that there were certain interests of European states held in common which could best be treated by collective consideration and decision by agreement. No longer were the conferences concerned solely with terminating wars and signing peace treaties. The matters discussed became more varied and, for a time, through mutual consultation, peace was made possible between the great powers.

The experience gained through multilateral negotiation cannot be measured accurately but it is real, nonetheless. The decisions reached were not always just; there were no formal rules established or agencies developed to provide a continuing means of peaceful discussion. Yet in the techniques originated for collective negotiation and the atmosphere surrounding the consultations of the great powers one can discover the rudimentary elements so essential for the functioning of a universal international organization. More than anything else, possibly, the Concert system laid the groundwork for the creation of the executive organ of an international organization which was to come in the form of the League Council and the Security Council of the United Nations.

The Hague Peace Conferences of 1899 and 1907. While not momentous in terms of their specific accomplishments, the two Hague Conferences represent a further contribution to the system of international organization developing in the nineteenth century. For the first time, virtually all states in the world (twenty-six in 1899, forty-four in 1907) met on equal terms to consult together on mutual problems of international concern. Unlike most earlier assemblages, the conferences were not convened by the major European powers to decide particular problems resulting from a specific war or impending conflict. What was sought, instead, was the reform of the various rules and methods of the system of nation-states and the improvement in the general relations between states. Clearly established was the principle of multilateral consideration of global problems of peace

and the expectation that such consultation would continue at regular intervals in the future. Much experience was gained in the procedures required for holding such a conference and in the familiarization of the
participants with the protocol of a truly international conference engaged
in by states from other continents in addition to Europe. Important, too,
whether there was agreement or not, were the problems which were discussed and, on occasion, fully aired. In all these respects, the Hague Conferences were the prelude to the building of the League of Nations, a sort
of interim stage in the development of international co-operation designed
to bring about a greater measure of security within the system of nation-
states.

Public International Unions. A wholly different type of international
co-operation made its appearance in the nineteenth century, particularly
after 1850. This was the development of collaboration in nonpolitical fields
arising primarily from the needs of a rapidly expanding industrial society.
Treaties calling for the collective administration of certain economic and
social matters had been concluded for some years. Eventually, however, it
became obvious that something beyond the treaty was needed and there
arose a growing number of international bodies, composed of states, which
have generally been referred to as international public unions.

Virtually every field of human endeavor has been represented, at one
time or another, by a public union. Such diverse fields as science and art,
communications and transit, economics and finance, and health and morals,
with their numerous subcategories, now have agencies working to achieve
objectives beneficial to national states. Some of these bodies, such as the
Universal Postal Union and the International Telegraphic Union, have become specialized agencies of the United Nations. Others have been as-
similated with such specialized agencies as the Food and Agriculture Organization and the World Health Organization.

Antedating the public union but nonetheless representing a form of
international administration were the international river commissions of
Europe. The Central Rhine Commission dates back to 1804 and has served
to ensure that the river shall remain open to all nations for commercial
purposes. It also provides regulations for navigation, hears complaints for
alleged violations of its rules, and serves to maintain the technical facilities
necessary for full navigation at all times. In 1804 the original agreement
between France and Germany called for the joint appointment of a director-
general 'to direct and supervise the establishment and the collection of
navigation tolls . . . and to watch over the execution of the present agreement,' together with a commission to hear appeals on problems relating to
the administration of the river. The present arrangement is much the same.

A somewhat similar agency called The European Commission was established by the Treaty of Paris in 1856 for the Danube River. Although the
Commission still continues to function, it is now under Soviet control and
does not recognize, as it did originally, equal treatment for riparian and
nonriparian states.

The public union has served as a central, focal point for collecting information and discussing mutual problems as well as for establishing
minimum or uniform standards and co-ordinating common policies. Valuable experience was gained in developing procedures for handling the
many conferences and for perfecting the multilateral treaty or convention
which established the union and assigned it duties and functions. The
sovereign state thus recognized in the nineteenth century, however halt-
ingly, that there were certain areas within the nation-state system that
required co-operation. International agencies were needed to obtain the
necessary co-operation and the public union was the result. Permanent
staffs were needed to carry on the daily work and prepare for future conferences. An intermediate body between the general conference and the
permanent staff became necessary and there arose the council or executive
committee composed of a selected number of the participants. In this way
there developed the model for the structure of the modern international
organization: the assembly or conference, as the policy-maker; the council
or governing agency as executor of policy; and the secretariat or permanent
staff to serve the needs of the agency in a variety of ways.

Private International Associations. Mention should be made of the many
nongovernmental or private international organizations which were established in increasing numbers as the nineteenth century drew to a close.
Even more so than the public union, these associations reached into every
aspect of human activity. They have been organized to further the interests
of a particular industry, group, or profession, to promote a cause or movement such as calendar reform or world federation, or to carry out a special
task in the form of promoting religion or administering relief. Still others
confine their attention to disseminating information or engaging in scientific
research. Their number today totals many hundreds and their existence and
significance has been recognized by the United Nations to such an extent
that some of the more important groups have been brought into consultative status with the Economic and Social Council of that organization. Some
private associations eventually received official status and were transformed
into public unions.

Many of the earlier private groups were associated with religious and
humanitarian endeavors and worked primarily through international conferences which met irregularly. Since they were noncontroversial in nature

and fulfilled certain needs, this type of association developed more rapidly than others and today constitutes the largest percentage of nongovernmental organizations. The World Alliance of YMCA's, founded in 1855, has been considered to be the first modern private international organization. Examples of organizations established in other fields were the Institute of International Law (1873), the International Union of Tramways, the Inter-Parliamentary Union (1888), the International Commission of Agriculture (1891), the International Peace Bureau (1892), the International Olympic Committee (1894), the International Bureau for the Suppression of Traffic in Women and Children (1899), and the International Association for Labor Legislation (1900).

The variety and number of the nongovernmental organizations increased rapidly after 1900. Their activities were reduced to a minimum during World War I but, since 1919, there has been a steady growth in all directions. Prior to 1900, their structure and organization had not been perfected but the essential outlines of future development had been established. Periodic conferences were held, study and advisory committees were established, and gradually there came into being the permanent bureau or secretariat. Membership generally consisted of national organizations, from two or more countries, whose members were private citizens. A constitution governed the activities of the association on an international level.

Private international organizations served as early agents of international understanding and molders of public opinion. While still in their infancy in the nineteenth century, these associations nevertheless contributed to an expanding concept of international co-operation and world interdependence. Private citizens began participating in international groups which only indirectly paid attention to the boundaries of national sovereignty. The international committees and secretariats which were created served to foster a spirit of internationalism and, in their own way, were and still are the prototypes of official intergovernmental organizations. The international conference brought together many persons of like interest from a number of nations and the contacts established contributed, in some measure, to mutual understanding among peoples of diverse national traditions.

Wartime Allied Co-operation. The practice of joint deliberation established in the nineteenth century was continued in a more concise and meaningful fashion during World War I. As early as 1915, Allied government heads were meeting in conferences to determine military and diplomatic policy. These meetings eventually led to the establishment of the Supreme War Council in 1917. It was equipped with a permanent secretariat and served as the highest Allied policy-co-ordinating agency. A number of special committees working through the Inter-Allied Maritime

Transport Council procured and allocated necessary food and raw materials, munitions, and maritime cargo space. Representatives from Italy, France, Britain, and the United States jointly administered the Transport Council.

The interstate co-operation during the war lent encouragement to many who envisioned the establishment of some form of postwar organizational collaboration. The Allies had been able to pool their wartime efforts without infringing upon their individual status as independent nations. If such machinery could be devised to win a war, it was argued that similar institutions could be set in motion for the purpose of preventing war and facilitating peaceful relations between states.

Wartime Peace Plans. The First World War had progressed but a few months before internationalists were at work devising projects for a world organization. Various groups and individuals in the United States and Great Britain were the most active but others in France, Holland, Switzerland, the Scandinavian countries, Italy, and even in Germany gave thought to the problem. A great many questions were raised involving the character and role of a permanent international organization. Should nations retain their individual sovereignty or should the organization be a superstate? Would public opinion be sufficient to secure obedience to its decisions or should there be physical sanctions and an international police force? Was the membership to be controlled by the large states through a revised Concert of Powers or could the smaller states be permitted to participate on equal terms with the more powerful members? Should the enemy states be excluded permanently or for an indeterminate period? The answers to these and similar questions aroused much speculation and spirited discussion among the Allies and neutrals alike.

By the end of the War, all of the principal Allied nations, under Anglo-American leadership, were committed to some form of world organization. Woodrow Wilson had announced his peace program to the United States Congress on January 8, 1918. He declared in the important fourteenth point that 'a general association of nations must be formed under specific convenants for the purpose of affording mutual guarantees of political independence and territorial integrity to great and small powers alike.' David Lloyd George, the British Prime Minister, shortly before had presented a peace program that included a number of similar proposals. Colonel E. M. House was authorized by Wilson to consolidate the various ideas and drafts of British and American plans. Official committees were hard at work in Britain and the other leading Allied countries. Although some important differences remained by the time the Peace Conference convened, there was general agreement between the leading Allied statesmen upon a number of the principles which were to become the fundamental provisions of the Covenant of the League of Nations. Thus, the work of many individuals and organizations, tracing back through centuries of thought and activity, was embraced in the launching of the first world organization devoted to the preservation of peace by means of the collective action of its members.

DRAFTING THE COVENANT AT VERSAILLES

Unquestionably the most enthusiastic advocate of the League of Nations among the heads of governments was Woodrow Wilson. It is entirely possible that had it not been for his determined efforts, the idea of the League might have become lost amid the mad scramble to 'make Germany pay' at the Peace Conference. On several occasions deliberate attempts were made by certain delegates to sabotage the League. The French Premier, M. Clemenceau, exhibited no enthusiasm for the type of organization envisaged by Wilson. The attitude of the French press was openly antagonistic. Influential members of the United States Congress were hostile throughout the entire Conference and, of course, eventually managed to secure the defeat of the Versailles Treaty in the Senate and prevent American membership in the League. Wilson was unable to prevent the incorporation of certain damaging and vengeful provisions in the Peace Treaties. In spite of these handicaps and disappointments, he clung to his beliefs with stubborn determination. He demanded that the drafting of the Covenant have priority over other business at the Conference, fearing that if this timetable was not kept, the strained atmosphere surrounding the work of the delegates would result in a hasty, if not empty, attempt to build the League following the conclusion of the territorial settlements. His quiet insistence upon this point was rewarded by the Conference's early adoption of the resolution to create a League which 'should periodically meet in international conference, and should have a permanent organization and secretariat to carry on the business of the League in the intervals between the conferences.' The Covenant produced at Versailles was thus the direct result of his inspiration and leadership, together with the faithful and creative support of Lord Cecil and General Smuts.

Despite his authoritative position, Wilson was forced to compromise some of his major policies. The British did not agree with his principle of 'guaranteeing territorial integrity.' The much disputed Article 10 of the Covenant provided that 'The members of the League undertake to respect and preserve as against external aggression the territorial integrity and existing political independence of all members of the League.' The much stronger word 'guarantee' was replaced by the weaker phrase 'undertake to respect and preserve.' The article was further weakened by the addition of the following clause: 'In case of any such aggression or in case of any threat or danger of such aggression the Council shall advise upon the means by which this obligation shall be fulfilled.' What was meant by 'advise' is not clarified anywhere in the Covenant.

Congressional opposition in the United States forced Wilson to insert measures in the Covenant which further reduced its effectiveness and, ironically, failed to satisfy his American critics. Paragraph 8 of Article 15 thus prevented the Council from taking action in a dispute which one of the parties claimed lay within its 'domestic jurisdiction.' Domestic policy, of course, may include a number of elements damaging to peaceful international relations if not constituting outright aggression. Elsewhere, in Article 21, Wilson was compelled to place in the Covenant the statement that 'Nothing in this Covenant shall be deemed to affect the validity of international engagements, such as treaties of arbitration or regional understandings like the Monroe Doctrine, for securing the maintenance of peace.' It was incongruous that mention should be made in the Covenant of any national foreign policy. Resentment at Versailles was particularly strong and Wilson was forced to agree to French security demands in Europe and Japanese requests in Asia in order to have the Monroe Doctrine placed in the Covenant.

France was particularly disappointed over the steadfast Anglo-American refusal to provide the League with an effective military arm, either in the form of an international force or of an army comprised of national contingents. Other European countries supported this and the additional French demand for the development of an international general staff to organize League forces and command them should military sanctions be voted against an aggressor. Some elements of the original French proposals were retained in Article 9 of the Covenant which stipulated that 'A permanent military commission shall be constituted to advise the Council on the execution of the Provisions of Articles 1 and 8 (provisions for disarmament) and on military, naval and air questions generally.'

Italy had an ambitious plan for a League of Nations which, while requiring the usual machinery for the settlement of international disputes, went much further in other directions. There was a proposal for an international legislative assembly equipped with sufficient power to modify or extend international law when necessary. The Italians also believed that the League should undertake the job of distributing raw materials and foodstuffs and guarantee international social and economic justice. Such a scheme met with little enthusiasm from American and British delegates and found no place in the Covenant.

The contribution of Japan to the building of the League was minor, but her delegates managed to inject the vital issue of racial equality into the deliberations of the Commission drafting the Covenant. The Japanese proposed the following resolution: 'The equality of nations being a basic principle of the League of Nations, the High Contracting Parties agree to accord, as soon as possible, to all . . . nations or States members of the League, equal and just treatment in every respect, making no distinction, either in law or fact, on account of their race or nationality.' Members of the British Commonwealth joined the United States in successfully opposing such a provision and even argued against the expression of racial equality becoming a part of the Preamble of the Covenant. Ironically, when Wilson spoke eloquently in favor of the inclusion of a clause calling for freedom of religious beliefs, the Japanese agreed. They observed somewhat caustically that similar logic would justify the assertion of racial or national equality. Nevertheless, the result was the elimination of both these basic civil rights, so prized in Anglo-Saxon countries, from even a passing mention in the Covenant.

THE NATURE OF THE COVENANT

The Covenant of the League of Nations was a multilateral treaty creating a rather loose association of states with the twofold objective of preserving international peace and security and promoting international co-operation. Justice and international law were to be the guideposts of conduct between states. As can be seen from surveying the antecedents of the League, neither the machinery nor the procedures contained in the Covenant for the accomplishment of its objectives were entirely original. Instead, the Covenant sought to strengthen and expand those previous international practices, many rudimentary in nature, which lacked the sanction of a world organization. In no instance was there interference with the sovereign independence of the League members. No organ or agency was granted the authority to order a member to take action of any kind. Less emphasis was placed upon legal obligations and procedures than might have been expected. The great powers were granted a position of primacy in a realistic attempt to place the responsibility for maintaining peace upon those who could decide the political course of events. The principal organs of the League, the Council and the Assembly, were essentially political bodies. Diplomacy by conference was the cardinal rule of the Covenant, guaranteeing all nations fair and equal treatment and the right to argue a case before the public opinion of the world.

The Covenant was composed of 26 articles arranged in a simple plan. Following a short Preamble, the first seven articles provided for the membership and constitutional framework of the League, including the character and powers of the Assembly, the Council, and the Secretary-General and his staff. Articles 8–17 dealt with the preservation of peace, while Articles 18–21 were concerned with treaties, peaceful change, and regional arrangements. The remainder, with the exception of Article 26, the amending clause, involved the problems of welfare and international co-operation.

Original membership was given to the thirty-two states that signed the Treaty of Versailles and to thirteen neutrals. New members could be admitted by a two-thirds vote of the Assembly after providing sufficient evidence of a desire to accept the Covenant and the international obligations required by it. Withdrawal was permitted a member after giving two years' notice. At one time or another sixty-one different states were members. The maximum reached at any one time was fifty-nine. Four states withdrew from membership before 1938 and only one (Soviet Union) was ever expelled, but the goal of universal membership envisaged by some framers of the Covenant was never achieved. The absence of the United States and the entry of the Soviets fifteen years late contributed to the problems encountered by the League.

Preservation of Peace. There were a number of courses of action outlined which might lessen the possibility of war and aggression. National armaments were to be reduced and limited with the aim of preventing the harmful effects associated with the private manufacture of munitions and implements of war. The members of the League also were expected to exchange information concerning the amount of their armaments and the condition of industries able to manufacture implements of war.

The Council was required to offer a course of action in case actual or imminent aggression threatened the political independence or territorial integrity of any member of the League. Any war or threat of war automatically became a 'matter of concern to the whole League.' In the event of such an emergency, the Secretary-General was to call a meeting of the Council when a member so requested. Each member had the right to raise any question concerning a threat to international peace before either the Council or the Assembly. Should a serious dispute arise between any members, they were obligated to submit it to three methods of peaceful settlement: arbitration, judicial settlement, or inquiry by the Council. There could be no resort to war until three months had passed following the decision arrived at by the agency or organ chosen for pacific settlement of the dispute. Any member violating such procedures became subject to financial and economic sanctions by the entire League, and to military, naval, and air measures recommended by the Council. Such a violator could be expelled from the League by the Council.

A Permanent Court of International Justice was established to hear and rule upon a dispute submitted to it or to offer an advisory opinion upon any question requested by either the Council or Assembly. All treaties concluded by members were to be registered with the League in an effort to eliminate secret alliances. Provision was made for reconsideration by the Assembly of situations which might endanger the peace of the world if allowed to continue and of treaties which, in the passage of time, might become inapplicable.

It should be emphasized that these various measures designed to preserve peace were not all-embracing in nature nor was the phrasing of the various articles adequate to prevent loopholes for those seeking to avoid their obligations of membership. As was noted earlier, the weaker term 'undertake' was substituted for the more positive word 'guarantee' in Articles 10 and 16. Elsewhere, the Council was empowered only to 'advise' or 'recommend' action to restrain aggression, a term also not clearly identified or defined. Nowhere was compulsory arbitration or compulsory judicial settlement provided for. After waiting for a three-month interval to expire following a decision arrived at by arbitration, judicial settlement, or Council action, a state could resort to war and not violate an obligation of membership. Should the Council fail to agree upon a decision by unanimous vote, or if its decision had not been reached within a prescribed six-month period, a state again could undertake forceful action without having violated the Covenant. Finally, if a dispute was claimed to fall within the 'domestic jurisdiction' of a state, League jurisdiction immediately became unclear and action paralyzed. Nowhere could be found an absolute ban on war 'as an instrument of national policy.'

Promotion of International Co-operation. While it attracted less attention, the League effort to secure co-operative action in many nonpolitical fields was far-reaching and recorded some definite accomplishments. Article 22 established the mandates system in an attempt to treat the question of underdeveloped peoples as an international problem. Territories formerly belonging to the defeated Central Powers in the First World War were entrusted to various 'advanced nations' exercising responsibility for their development and eventual independence under League supervision.

The various welfare activities of the League were contained in the rather extensive provisions of Article 23. Reference was made to the general objectives of the International Labor Organization, which actually was created by Part XIII of the Treaty of Versailles. Other sections directed the members of the League 'to take steps in matters of international concern for the prevention and control of disease.' Attention was also directed toward the advancement of world communications and transit. International agencies already working in such fields were encouraged by Article 24 to participate co-operatively in the work of the League or be placed under its direction.

THE PRINCIPAL INSTITUTIONS OF THE LEAGUE

Article 2 of the Covenant stated that 'The action of the League shall be effected through the instrumentality of an Assembly and of a Council, with a permanent Secretariat.' A number of technical and auxiliary agencies, commissions, boards, committees, and semiautonomous organizations developed after 1920 to supplement this central machinery. The various technical agencies working with the Secretariat served the League as its administrative branch. The Permanent Court of International Justice and the International Labor Organization were integral parts of the League system envisaged by the Covenant but they actually maintained a separate existence.

The Assembly. The Assembly functioned as the general conference of the League and consisted of national delegations from each member-state. Each member-state could have three representatives but only one vote. Beginning in November 1920, the Assembly held annual meetings at Geneva, the seat of the League. Extraordinary sessions could be convened at any time if so decided by the Assembly itself or the Council. Individual delegates were selected by their own governments and were accompanied by a host of technical experts. Over the years most states adopted the practice of sending the same delegates to each session, frequently utilizing premiers or foreign ministers for this purpose. Some even maintained permanent delegations at Geneva in order to keep in close touch with the League activities during the intervals between meetings.

The Assembly elected its own president and traditionally chose the presiding officer from a smaller state not represented on the Council. The agenda for each session was prepared by the Secretary-General some months in advance, although any member could add an item to the list not less than one month prior to the convening of the delegates. The rules of procedure and internal organization were determined by the Assembly and remained fairly constant after the first several meetings. The principal business was accomplished through committees upon which each state was entitled to place a delegate of its own choice. New committees could be created for each session but the following six eventually developed into what might be called permanent standing committees: Legal and Constitutional Questions; Technical Organizations; Reduction of Armaments; Budget and Financial Questions; Social and General Questions; Political Questions. Items for consideration were assigned to each one of them according to subject matter. Each elected its own chairman and rapporteur. The General Committee, a sort of steering group, was composed of the President, the six Vice-Presidents, and the chairmen of the Agenda, Credentials, and Permanent Committees.

As the League developed over the years and encountered a variety of problems, the Assembly gained stature and gradually became the central organ of the entire system. It was by no means a legislative body in any sense but served as an international forum with the very broad power to 'deal at its meetings with any matter within the sphere of action of the League or affecting the peace of the world.' Its exclusive and specific powers were much more limited. Among them were the power to admit new members; to elect the nonpermanent members of the Council; to elect its own officers and establish its rules of procedure; to control the League finances; to consider disputes referred to it by the Council; 'to advise the reconsideration by members of the League of treaties which have become inapplicable.' In concurrence with the Council, the Assembly selected a Secretary-General, increased the membership of the Council, amended the Covenant and elected the judges of the Permanent Court of Justice. Either could request the Court for an advisory opinion, as well as consider 'any circumstances whatever' which might be a threat to international peace.

A brief reference to the most significant activity of the Assembly has been made already. This was the function of serving as an international forum where international affairs could be discussed by the representatives of large and small nations alike. Significant pronouncements upon a variety of topics could always be expected during the general debate which occurred at the beginning of each session in September. The annual meetings of the Assembly, particularly in later years, attracted many of the world's leading statesmen and diplomatists who could speak with the authority surrounding their high governmental offices. For the first time there was available a regular annual conference, so to speak, where the major issues confronting all states could be aired publicly. The great debates over the Japanese invasion of Manchuria and Italian aggression in Ethiopia provided the members of the League every opportunity to express themselves fully. The opinions offered, particularly in the Ethiopian case, demonstrated the desire of the overwhelming majority of League members to apply the Covenant in order to resist aggression. The fact that Britain and France neglected their obligations cannot obscure the fact that the public opinion of the world was reflected in the positive conduct of fifty nations acting to uphold the principles of collective security in the Assembly.

The Secretary-General compiled the annual budget and then submitted it to the Supervisory Committee for checking and revision. The budget was then forwarded to the individual members for their comments prior to its submission to the Assembly for action by the Fourth, or Finance, Committee. Here the budget was again scrutinized carefully and finally submitted to the entire Assembly for final adoption. The position of principal influence lay with the Supervisory Committee which had the first opportunity to amend the provisional estimates offered by the Secretary-General. Its five members were originally appointed by the Council but in 1928 the power of appointment passed to the Assembly.

In addition to these two functions, the Assembly sought to enact international legislation in the form of draft treaties or conventions. Except in the nonpolitical field, such attempts at international lawmaking were unsuccessful. Three conventions were drafted to plug the loopholes in the Covenant and strengthen the security arrangements of the Covenant but they (Treaty of Mutual Guarantee, 1923; Geneva Protocol, 1924; General Act for the Peaceful Settlement of Disputes, 1928) failed to secure the necessary ratifications of individual governments.

Finally, it should be emphasized that the Assembly undertook general supervision over the work of the League. Any item contained in the annual report of the Secretary-General could be referred to the appropriate committee for critical examination and recommendation. Most decisions arrived at by the Assembly were in the form of resolutions which required no further ratification by individual members. A number of these dealt with an expression of approval over some League policy or offered guidance upon some phase of internal operation for the various League organs and agencies. Less frequent was a resolution instructing the Council to call international conferences devoted to special problems, such as the Geneva Disarmament Conference of 1932.

The Council. The originators of the Covenant expected the Council to be the pivotal organ of the League, a sort of revitalized yet disguised Concert of Europe operating under the majority will of the United States, Great Britain, France, Italy, and Japan. It was to perform the role of a modified executive committee and, as such, to administer League policy.

In addition, it was to serve as the principal mechanism for the peaceful settlement of disputes and the collective security of the League. The four nonpermanent members of the Council, selected by the Assembly, could in no way endanger the majority position of the 'principal Allied and Associated Powers,' but would provide representation to satisfy the lesser nations. The existence of both the Assembly and the Council represented another indication of the compromise between the preponderant influence of the great powers and the principle of state equality. Both were intended to be complementary and interdependent organs. The Assembly would become stronger as the Council improved its functions by efficient and responsible action, resulting in greater authority and respect for the League as a whole.

As the League system developed, however, the Council failed to measure up to some of the hopes for it. Its life was handicapped from the start by the defection of the United States. Recurring demands for representation on the Council resulted in the very worst type of political maneuvering, which was unbecoming at best and certainly incompatible with the obligations of League membership. The inevitable result was a gradual increase in the number of nonpermanent members from four to eleven. Spirited contests developed as vacancies or new memberships were available. Some League members sponsored others in return for questionable support to satisfy special interests. The repeated failure of all the permanent Council members to accept their responsibilities under the Covenant weakened the position of the Council and eventually destroyed the League. The Assembly, in turn, gained respect and succeeded in shaping a major share of League policy. In so doing, it became increasingly critical of the Council, directing the latter to undertake measures that it should have initiated itself. In the final analysis, however, the great prestige surrounding the Council tended to offset some of its shortcomings. The great powers dominated world affairs both inside and outside of the League. Their permanent status provided them the opportuniy to block any unwanted Council activity. While the Covenant did not specifically differentiate between the functions of the Council and the Assembly, the powers of the Council were scattered throughout its provisions and greatly outnumbered those of the Assembly. Treaty stipulations added further prestige and duties to the work of the Council itself.

The Council was given the specific power to approve a number of appointments in the Secretariat, maintain League property, and even move the seat of the League if necessary. It was supposed to formulate plans for the reduction of national armaments, control any individual increase once the scale of armaments had been established, and oversee the work of the Permanent Advisory Commission on armaments. The Council had to act as a conciliator in the pacific settlement of disputes and propose the action to be followed by the League in the event of aggression. The application of military sanctions was a matter for its decision and it could expel a member of the League which had violated its obligations under the Covenant. The Council established the conditions which made it possible for a nonmember to appear before the League in a dispute and had the authority to recommend 'such action as may seem best and most effectual in the circumstances.' The Council supervised League control over the mandate system with the advice of its subsidiary agency, the Permanent Mandates Commission. Instructions were also given to other technical agencies within the League system. Finally, by the terms of the Paris Peace Treaties, the Council was made responsible for the government of the Saar from 1920 until 1935 when it administered a plebiscite which returned the territory to Germany. The High Commissioner for Danzig governed under authority of the Council. The Peace Treaties and later minorities conventions gave the Council the additional duty of guaranteeing various international obligations on behalf of racial, religious, and linguistic minorities in Austria, Czechoslovakia, Hungary, Turkey, Yugoslavia, Greece, Poland, Bulgaria, and Rumania. The Council heard complaints from minorities and sought to bring about remedial action by the offending state. The Locarno Treaties also required Council action in case of frontier violations of any of the signatories.

This survey of the Council's powers and responsibilities serves to explain its separate functions and the wide scope of its activities. Flexible procedure became mandatory for the performance of its several and somewhat unrelated tasks. At one moment, as executor of certain treaty provisions, it would be involved with political matters of high policy similar to those handled by the former Concert of Europe. The next issue might transform it into the role of conciliator between disputants. Yet another problem would be in the nature of an emergency involving the Council in some threat of war, the application of sanctions, or advising methods necessary to preserve the territorial integrity and political independence of a League member. On top of all this were the constant administrative duties related to the Secretariat, the technical agencies, the Armaments and Mandates Commissions, or perhaps some request for information or advice from the Assembly. To perform all these functions the Council had to rely heavily upon the Secretariat for assistance. The use of committees was held to a minimum but each Council member was assigned a particular item of recurring business on an annual basis. Such items (e.g. Mandates, Minorities, Disarmament) totaled at least fifteen and each member responsible for a particular matter was required to report upon it and make recommendations to the entire Council. There was no permanent executive head, but an alphabetical rotating system provided a presiding officer for each session. The unanimity rule prevailed during Council meetings which permitted any member, large or small, the right of veto. Much of its official business was conducted in private although the proceedings of such meetings were published eventually in the *Official Journal* of the League. Public meetings usually were held following the private sessions. But there was frequent use made of the unofficial secret meeting, particularly between the representatives of the great powers on the Council when vital political issues were under discussion.

The Secretariat. Until the establishment of the League, there was no stability or continuity to the discussion of international affairs in occasional international conferences. The Assembly and the Council remedied this situation to a certain extent, in that they met at least once a year at a given place and with a growing measure of procedural regularity. It was the Secretariat of the League, however, which gave substance and permanence to the League system. The experience of the various official and unofficial international unions which had been developing in technical and nonpolitical fields before the war established certain precedents for the eventual work of the Secretariat. But, for the most part, the Secretariat had to break new ground and develop its own administrative routine as it expanded together with the several League organs and agencies.

The more fundamental and specific duties of the Secretariat included those of record-keeping, research, and publicity. The accumulation of statistical data for various agencies and the development of reports and analysis was a continuous job. It maintained the League archives and served as a general clearing house for all business. Treaties concluded by every League member and even those of some nonmembers were registered and published. Innumerable pamphlets, articles, films, and communiqués were issued from time to time, explaining the work of the League and encouraging support for its many activities. Official periodicals and regular annual reports were issued for the principal League organs and technical agencies.

Less tangible but equally important was the Secretariat's close association with League policy formulation. It prepared the data for all League conferences and committees and furnished secretarial assistance to League organs and agencies. Inasmuch as their permanent status gave them intimate familiarity with all aspects of the League and its complicated procedure, Secretariat officials were in a strategic position to influence policy determination. Such questions as agenda preparation, the drafting of resolutions and reports, and committee procedure and discussion involved the constant advice and assistance of such officials. These officials, acting as a connecting link between the various organs of the League and between them and the individual League members, supplied the Secretariat with information unavailable elsewhere. Various League decisions had to be made by the Secretariat during the intervals between Assembly and Council sessions. Negotiations begun during an Assembly meeting on some League problem had to be continued after an adjournment in order to secure the proper ratification on a League agreement. Work of this nature had to be assumed by the Secretariat and inevitably involved it in certain aspects of diplomacy. Such activities were of priceless value in providing continuity for the League system as a whole, and represented a signal advance over the intermittent and disconnected conference system of pre-League years. At the same time, the close relationship of the Secretariat to League diplomacy and the indirect but vital influence it had over the work of all parts of the League gave the Secretariat a unique and unexpected position of power.

The Secretary-General was the highest permanent official of the League. Sir Eric Drummond, the first Secretary-General, was named in the Annex of the Covenant to serve for an indefinite period. His successor was appointed by the Council with Assembly approval for a term of ten years. The duties of the office were twofold. The external powers of the Secretary-General were essentially those of a statesman and diplomat, and he served the entire League in this capacity. In addition, he was the chief assistant for both the Council and the Assembly, furnishing advice and counsel which invariably came to influence certain of their decisions. The friction which eventually developed in the League, principally between the permanent members of the Council, forced him to become engaged indirectly in such rivalries, despite the restrictions in the Covenant aimed at preventing him from intervening in the affairs of League members. He also had the authority to summon the Council into special session and make the necessary arrangements to investigate disputes which might threaten the peaceful relations between League members.

In his capacity as administrator of the Secretariat, his internal powers of appointment, supervision, and control were extensive. Council approval was necessary for his nominations of the Deputy Secretary-General and Undersecretaries-General and the higher staff positions, although his choice of candidates was rarely questioned. Many additional appointments were made on his own authority with the assistance of a Committee on

Appointments and Promotions. All members of the Secretariat were pledged to discharge their functions and conduct their affairs solely in the interest of the League without instructions from their own governments. There was no system of examinations for appointment, due in part to the great variety of qualifications required for the different staff positions. The fact that qualified nationals from all League members were eligible for appointment was an additional handicap to a uniform entrance examination. The Secretary-General sought to recruit the best applicants available without regard for nationality, but on occasion he came under pressure from individual governments that demanded the appointment of their own nationals to key offices. Such a development was unfortunate in that it not only exposed the Secretariat to political intervention but also jeopardized its status as an international civil service.

The work of the Secretariat was organized into sections along functional lines, each serving the entire League in general as well as a particular agency or activity. The total mumber or sections reached fifteen by 1938 but was later reduced as budgetary deficiencies became acute. They were divided into two categories: the General, and the Special, Sections. The General Sections served primarily the Secretariat itself and included the Legal, Central, Information, and Political Sections. Added to these were the Library and the Treasury. The Special Sections were created to handle certain subjects, such as minorities, opium, and mandates. However, some questions by their global nature necessitated treatment by several different sections. This was particularly true of the social and humanitarian field. A problem falling within this field might have required the work of the Mandates, Political, and Intellectual Sections in addition to that of the Social Questions Section. In some instances, the technical work of a section could be largely independent of the Secretary-General. The Secretariat of the semiautonomous Organization for Transit and Communications, for example, was the Communications and Transit Section. Most of its technical orders same from the Organization for Transit and Communications and not from the primary League organs.

The Secretary-General depended heavily upon the individual section directors for the successful functioning of the Secretariat as a whole. The organization of the Secretariat upon the principle of international loyalty placed upon each section director the heavy responsibility of encouraging devotion to the ideals of the League among his own subordinates. To them belongs much of the credit for the general success achieved by this first major experiment in international administration. The procedures developed within the individual sections, together with those originated in the burdensome office of the Secretary-General, have provided invaluable precedents for those now performing similar tasks within the United Nations.

As soon as the League got underway, it became necessary to establish additional agencies in order to augment the work of the three primary organs and fulfill the obligations imposed by the Covenant and the Peace Treaties. These auxiliary institutions divided themselves into two categories which corresponded with the twofold objectives of the League: political and legal agencies, designed to assist in the prevention or settlement of disputes; and those of an economic, humanitarian, or social nature, which were intended to develop and expand international co-operation in welfare fields. Some of the agencies in each group were linked closely to the Council and the Secretariat, while others enjoyed a semiautonomous or even an independent status. All of them, however, must be considered as parts of the over-all League system. Many were successful in accomplishing difficult assignments with relatively few precedents to follow. From their varied experiences and organizational framework have come the numerous specialized agencies of the United Nations.

Political and Legal Institutions. Within this group were the Commissions assigned to military affairs, disarmament, and the mandates system, the Committees concerned with minority problems, as well as supervision of the Free City of Danzig and the Saar. The Permanent Court of International Justice is considered to be a part of this group although it was not an auxiliary body of the League.

One of the first acts of the Council was to establish the Permanent Advisory Commission on Military, Naval, and Air Questions which had been specifically provided for in Article 9 of the Covenant. Its composition was technical and consisted of military, naval, and air service officers. Each state represented on the Council could appoint three of its members. The usefulness of the Commission was restricted by the character of its membership and, consequently, it was unable to do more than advise the Council along limited, technical lines. The more basic questions related to the task of furthering disarmament had to be investigated and reported on by other agencies. Outstanding among these was the Temporary Mixed Commission for the Reduction of Armaments, established by the Council at the request of the Assembly after its first meeting. It consisted of experts from the Permanent Advisory Commission, the International Labor Office, and 'recognized authorities on political, social and economic subjects.' Among its valued contributions to the League was the preparation of materials on disarmament for the Treaty of Mutual Assistance of 1923, the Geneva

Protocol of 1924, and the Locarno Treaties of 1925. After 1925, its work was taken over by the Preparatory Commission for the Disarmament Conference.

The Permanent Mandates Commission was called for in Article 22 of the Covenant and was established in 1921. Certain territory originally belonging to the defeated states in the First World War was surrendered to the Principal Allied and Associated Powers by the terms of the several Peace Treaties. The Supreme Council of the Allies in turn designated the states which were to act as mandatories over the territory and so informed the Council of the League. It then became the duty of the League Council, acting through the Permanent Mandates Commission, to supervise the administration of these areas in order to facilitate their well-being and development.

The degree of control exercised by the mandatory state was determined in effect by the Allies when awarding the mandate, although it differed considerably 'according to the stage of the development of the people, the geographical situation of the territory, its economic conditions' and other similar considerations. Eventually three different classes of mandates were developed. A number of former Turkish possessions were sufficiently advanced to warrant only administrative assistance and advice from the mandatory and were classified as 'A' mandates. These included Iraq, Syria, Palestine, Lebanon, and Transjordan. It was expected that they would secure eventual independence (which has been achieved) under the tutelage of the mandatory and the League. The 'B' mandates came from Central Africa and necessitated more assistance and control from the mandatory state. Included in this category were the Cameroons, Tanganyika, Ruanda-Urundi, and Togoland. The mandatory was required to guarantee freedom of religion and was prohibited from permitting such abuses as the traffic in slaves, arms, or liquor, nor was it allowed to use the mandate for overt military purposes. Trade and commerce with all members of the League was to be encouraged. Finally, certain other territories located in South-West Africa and some islands in the South Pacific area became 'C' mandates. Their remoteness and lack of development made it necessary that they be 'administered under the laws of the Mandatory as integral portions of the Territory.' It was not expected that either the Class B or C mandates would prosper sufficiently to enable them to become sovereign states. Today they remain under international supervision through the Trusteeship Council of the United Nations.

The members of the Mandates Commission were nominated by the League Council and were selected so that a majority were from the states which held no mandates. The Commission served the Council in an advisory capacity, receiving annual reports from the mandatories based upon questionnaires provided by the Council. It conducted hearings to determine whether the mandatory state was adhering to its obligations although it did not possess the authority either to conduct investigations within the mandated territory or to compel a mandatory to follow its suggestions. The Commission gradually came to be respected by all parties for its competence and objectivity in dealing with highly complex problems. Its general success serves as a useful precedent for its counterpart in the United Nations.

The duty of protecting various Minority Groups was forced upon the League Council by provisions in the Peace Treaties, special agreements, and a series of Minority Treaties. More than a dozen states eventually agreed to the Council as guarantor of such rights for their minorities as acquisition of citizenship, life, liberty, freedom of religion, use of language, civil and political equality, and equality of opportunity in public, professional, and industrial employment. The minorities continually sought to have the Council establish a permanent Minorities Commission. However, such a step would have gone beyond the powers of the Council established by the various treaties and agreements and none of the treaty signatories were interested in making the necessary amendments. Hence, the Council had to devise a somewhat circuitous procedure which never proved to be entirely satisfactory to either the several minorities or the states containing them. A Minorities Section was established in the Secretariat, not only to gather information concerning the conditions surrounding all minorities, but to receive petitions from minorities claiming violations of their rights. The acceptability of the petition was determined by the Secretary-General of the League, on the basis of certain criteria drawn up by the Council. If the petition was accepted, it was turned over to a committee of three Council members for study and a report. The Council then undertook the unhappy role of conciliator between a state and its petitioning minority subjects, with no authority to go beyond a recommendation. A dispute over fact or law had to be referred to the Permanent Court of International Justice.

The Treaty of Versailles called for a High Commissioner for the Free City of Danzig to supervise the relationship between Danzig and Poland and adjust disputes which might arise between them. He was appointed by and responsible to the League Council which heard appeals from his decisions or referred them to the Permanent Court of International Justice. Inspired by Hitler, Nazis gained control of Danzig and destroyed the effectiveness of the High Commissioner's office prior to the return of the city into Germany in 1939.

The government of the Saar, by the terms of the Versailles Treaty, was to be vested in a commission of five appointed by the Council to represent the League. At the conclusion of a fifteen year period, a plebiscite was to decide whether the citizens of the territory preferred annexation to Germany or France. In 1935, an impartially-conducted plebiscite determined that the Saar should be incorporated into Germany.

A Permanent Court of International Justice was called for in Article 14 of the Covenant and the League Council appointed a committee of jurists to draft a statute for the Court. Following approval by the Council and the Assembly, a sufficient number of ratifications brought the Statute into effect by September, 1921. Although the Court was established as an independent organ with its own charter, it was linked to the League in several respects. Its budget, though an independent unit, formed a part of the over-all League budget. The judges were selected by the Council and the Assembly and their number could be increased by the Assembly.

Few other organs of the League could match the success and universal respect enjoyed by the Court. Its fifteen judges, sitting in annual session at The Hague, were carefully chosen and included a number of the finest legal minds available. While its work was brought to a close by World War II in 1939, the new Court created for the United Nations is practically a replica of the original, depending almost exclusively upon the Statute for its own organic law. No greater testament to its workability and value than this can be accorded the older Court.

Economic, Social, and Humanitarian Institutions. Various provisions of the Covenant and the Treaty of Versailles called for the establishment of a number of technical advisory agencies to assist the League in promoting international co-operation. Their activities formed an integral part of the League system and provided material assistance to the peoples of the world in a great variety of ways. Heading the list were the semiautonomous Economic and Financial Organization, the Health Organization, and the Organization for Communications and Transit. In addition, there was the High Commissioner for Refugees as well as the Committees on the Drug Traffic, Traffic in Women, the Protection of Children, and Intellectual Co-operation. Working closely with the League but independent of it was the International Labor Organization which continues today as a specialized agency of the United Nations. The work begun by the other bodies has been continued by the United Nations or by newly created specialized agencies. Their activities during the years of the League will be examined in the next chapter.

3

THE LEAGUE OF NATIONS IN ACTION

BEFORE reviewing some of the efforts made by the League of Nations to realize the twin objectives of peace and security and the promotion of international co-operation, it is essential to arrive at an understanding of the general setting in which the 'great experiment' was launched. The Peace Conference at Paris in 1919 produced untried international institutions based upon new standards and a new morality. At the same time, the Conference, in spite of its respect for the Wilsonian principles of political freedom and self-determination, created a peace settlement which contained the seeds of future national rivalries. Certainly the attitudes and policies toward the League by France and Britain, its primary members, were in marked contrast to the League's goal of collective security. There were other implied conditions inherent in the building of a new international order which, if not realized, would make the functioning of such a system infinitely more difficult. That the League worked at all, in the face of tremendous obstacles, is a testament to the many loyal and persevering men and women who labored in support of an ideal. They never tired of seeking to devise methods and procedures for the solution of new problems.

At no time did the major powers at Geneva fully subordinate the individual aims of national policy to the universal goals of the League when it became a matter of choice between national or League policy. The unfortunate link between the peace settlements in 1919 and the League inevitably resulted in the view held by some that the League should be the guarantor of those settlements. Others, however, were by no means so anxious to preserve the territorial status quo, and believed that the League should work to rectify certain injustices perpetrated in 1919. France belonged to the former group and was determined to use the League as a means of preventing German resurgence. To France, the primary duty of the League was to prevent aggression in Europe which meant a protection

50

against Germany destroying the provisions of Versailles. Aggression elsewhere was not considered to be of vital importance. France had insisted
during the drafting of the Covenant that the League be provided with
some form of international police which would serve as an added bulwark
to defend the status quo of Versailles. Without this military arm, the
League became only a second line of defense for France after 1919, serving
as a support to the French system of alliances designed to encircle Germany.

In contrast to this view was the position held by Great Britain that the
primary aim of the League was to make available the machinery required
for the peaceful settlement of disputes. British public opinion had the
tendency to regard the mediative functions of the League as the most important, with far less emphasis upon the use of sanctions as a means of supporting the principle of collective security. According to this view, the
League could best serve as a 'moral deterrent' to aggression. In addition,
the statesmen who charted British policy after 1918 were concerned with
protecting what they considered to be the vital interests of the Empire and
were loathe to involve Britain in League affairs that did not directly include
these national concerns. Most Conservative Party leaders refused to abandon the strategies of the balance of power and believed in older concepts
of a European Concert instead of the multilateral diplomacy of Geneva.
They were not interested in holding Germany down indefinitely, particularly because a strong German economy served to complement British
trade policies. Moreover, those in Britain who were supporters of the
League, did not agree with the French interpretation of the Covenant.
There was little sympathy for the French concern over treaty violations
but great interest in making the League an effective agency against all
aggressors.

Another factor which complicated the relationship between the wartime
allies and their policies toward the League was the failure of the United
States to become a full partner in the new international organization. This
is not the place to debate the responsibility of the United States for the
collapse of the League system. Certain facts that had a definite bearing
upon Franco-British policies and the League situation in general are relevant, however. Britain was determined to avoid action that might unneces-
sarily antagonize the United States. Should military sanctions against an
aggressor involve a naval blockade, the British fleet most certainly would
be called upon. With the United States not bound by League sanctions,
the blockade maintained by British ships would be forced to interfere with
American vessels, a situation full of danger to amicable Anglo-American
relations. The British Dominions had grown close to the United States, and

Britain could not risk alienating them by incurring the enmity of the United States in the course of some League commitment.

The refusal of the United States to ratify the Treaty of Versailles had other serious effects upon the European political situation. Much against her will, France had agreed at the Paris Conference to waive the demand for the west bank of the Rhine in return for an Anglo-American military guarantee of her frontiers. But not only did the United States turn down the Versailles Treaty but the proposed military guarantees as well, leaving France's only protection that afforded by the League. Moreover, it was a League without the prestige and support which could have come from United States membership. With the United States on the sidelines, Britain proceeded to weaken the crucial Articles 10 and 16 by interpretation and refused to grant France any assurance of aid in the event of German aggression.

Wilson had managed at the Conference to have the vexing problem of German reparations left to a Reparations Commission. Great Britain was of a like mind, not wishing Germany to be left with the burden of huge payments which would destroy her economy. Anglo-American pressure forced France to yield and assumed that French demands could be controlled in the Commission. The withdrawal of the United States, however, allowed France to dominate the Commission and invade the Ruhr in 1923 to force Germany to pay the reparations dictated by France. France was thereby given a free hand on the Continent and at Geneva, insisting upon the preservation of the status quo. Germany suffered ruinous inflation and endured the stigma of Versailles as an outcast. Although Germany entered the League in 1926, irreparable damage had been done to the German morale, a factor which later provided support for Hitler's nationalist appeal. For nearly a decade following the Armistice, France and Britain were at loggerheads. France believed she had been betrayed not only by the United States but by Britain as well. Great Britain, in turn, became convinced that France represented a threat to European security. In the meantime, the Weimar Republic gradually weakened, and with its collapse came the ruin of French policy and the inevitable demise of collective security.

One final observation on the defection of the United States should be noted. It was assumed in 1919 that the League would rapidly become an organization universal in scope and membership. The refusal to join by its greatest advocate at the Peace Conference came as a blow from which the League never fully recovered. Collective security demands the support of the most powerful nations available. Not only security but welfare measures as well, to be fully effective, must assume worldwide proportions. From the moment of the defeat of the Versailles Treaty in the Senate of the

United States until the end of the League, every action of importance at Geneva had to be made with special reservations for the position of the United States. No system of international co-operation designed to encompass the world can be an unqualified success without this powerful state a willing participant. The abstention of such a state, of course, lent encouragement to others who later sought to escape from their solemn obligations.

Outside Geneva, there did not develop the indefinable but extremely important favorable state of mind which is so essential for the beginning and successful operation of a new political experiment. Arising out of community needs and interests has come a formidable body of law in the western world. The law is customarily obeyed not only because the power of the state lies behind it but also for the reason that the great body of citizens recognize its need, understand its function, and demand its protection. But in 1920 when the League of Nations was launched, there was no such understanding among the peoples of the member-states. There was no sense of belonging to a community wider than the national state, no feeling of obligation or deep respect for the League as a political or welfare institution or to the Covenant as a basic law to be cherished on at least an equal plane with comparable national constitutions. The makers of the League took it for granted that there would develop 'among all peoples a sense of their duties as members of a corporate society . . . superior in importance to every question of political predominance or historical claims.' [1] Nationalistic fervor, given impetus by the First World War, successfully blocked the growth of this necessary state of mind just as it appears to have done after the Second World War. Without this amorphous support the League had to flounder along, depending upon the sufferance of statesmen, the tolerance of the informed, and the indefatigable spirit of the idealist.

PRESERVATION OF PEACE AND SECURITY

During its lifetime, the League of Nations became involved with sixty disputes, of which it managed to settle thirty-five through its own methods. The remainder were left to independent settlement by the parties concerned. A brief survey of some of the more interesting or important of those terminated by the League, and some that League efforts failed to resolve, will reveal the working procedures evolved within the framework of the Covenant. It should be emphasized again that the primary organs of the League which were involved on these occasions had to organize, at the

[1] Article 1:2 of the Draft Covenant quoted in Schwarzenberger, George, *Power Politics,* New York, 1951, p. 292.

beginning, with few precedents upon which they could depend. After the formative years in which much spadework was required, there followed a period of relative stability coinciding with a growing international economic prosperity. The major tests of League machinery and allegiance did not come until the fateful 1930's when, in each instance, the members failed to live up to their responsibilities. No two disputes were treated in the same fashion, although tactics and procedures were improved upon with experience.

Formative Years. The first meeting of the Council took place in Paris on January 16, 1920, six days after the League of Nations officially came into being. It was a troubled world that witnessed the start of the noble experiment in universal international organization. Civil war raged in Russia and was of immediate concern to the major powers of Europe. The United States was absent from the place reserved for her at the Council table. Turkey under Mustafa Kemal was endeavoring to consolidate a strong position in Asia Minor by force of arms. Eastern Europe was in the grip of severe epidemics and plagued by the insoluble refugee problem. In the Far East, Japan was intent upon adding to her Empire at the expense of Russia. China refused to sign the Treaty of Versailles which gave the Japanese important rights in the Shantung Peninsula. Elsewhere, tensions and disorders worsened between Rumania and Hungary, between Italy and Yugoslavia in Fiume, in Teschen between Poles and Czechs, and in Upper Silesia where Poles and Germans were ready to destroy each other. The economic condition of most of Europe was precarious.

The first serious dispute involved the contested sovereignty of the Aaland Islands in the Baltic by Sweden and Finland. Brought before the Council on July 11, 1920, by Great Britain under Article 11, paragraph 2 of the Covenant, a Committee of Jurists was appointed to determine whether the problem was a domestic question. Accepting the negative finding of the Committee, the Council then established a Commission of Inquiry to investigate the entire matter. Some months later the Commission submitted its report which was accepted by the Council and both parties to the dispute. Finland was permitted to retain sovereignty over the disputed islands, but was forbidden to fortify them in any fashion. Special guarantees for the local autonomy of the Aalanders were to be provided by the League.

The Vilna dispute involving Poland and Lithuania was never resolved despite a variety of procedures undertaken by the Council. First submitted in September, 1921, by Poland under Article 11 of the Covenant, the contested city was eventually occupied by Poland through military action. Attempts at mediation by the Council President failed as did efforts to hold a plebiscite. The Council was unwilling to take a strong stand and push its recommendations with the result that its role in this affair was largely ineffective, although hostilities were held to a minimum.

Again in 1921 the Council had to contend with a border problem which threatened to develop into war. The matter involved was the final decision on the frontiers of Albania. Although Albania claimed that her borders had been violated by Yugoslavia and that sporadic fighting was in progress, the Council refused to act since the Conference of Ambassadors was considering the entire problem.[2] The League Assembly then requested the Council to send a Commission of Inquiry to investigate the activities of the Ambassadors. The request was complied with and in November, 1921, the Conference of Ambassadors announced its decision to set the frontiers of Albania as of 1913, with certain minor changes in favor of Yugoslavia. At this time, however, the British became alarmed at the danger to peace in the Balkans and requested an immediate meeting of the Council to decide on invoking economic sanctions against Yugoslavia unless her troops were withdrawn at once. However, before the Council could be summoned, the Yugoslavs agreed to the decision of the Conference of Ambassadors.

The Corfu episode was the most serious one occurring during the formative period of the League and it directly challenged the competence of the Council. An Italian member of a boundary commission of the Conference of Ambassadors sent to establish the Albania-Greek border was assassinated, whereupon Italy issued a stern ultimatum to Greece. Mussolini then ordered units of the Italian navy to bombard the undefended Greek island of Corfu and then occupy it. Greece then placed the matter before the Council under Articles 12 and 15 of the Covenant, but Italy claimed that the Conference of Ambassadors was the sole agency competent to act. A settlement was finally arranged through the Council of Ambassadors whereby Greece indemnified Italy and Italian forces were removed from Corfu. Although the Council eventually determined its powers and vindicated its competence, the case nevertheless was handled by the Conference of Ambassadors and Italy escaped censure for its warlike acts.

The Period of Stability. By the end of 1924, there was a new spirit of confidence at Geneva. The League had weathered a number of serious storms in its formative years and had emerged without too much damage to its reputation and the hopes placed in it. To be sure, the Council had not deported itself in a fashion calculated to inspire unquestioned respect. But it had taken several stands and in one way or another managed to put out some fires which might have spread. The Assembly had begun to assume

[2] The Council of Ambassadors was a flexible postwar arrangement designed to execute the peace treaties. It consisted of the Ambassadors to Paris from the United States, Great Britain, Italy, and Japan, and of a French representative.

new and encouraging responsibilities. Its annual sessions provided the lesser nations an opportunity to speak out on all questions on an equal footing with the great powers. The welfare activities of the League had been started and a World Court established. In addition, the political complexion of Europe was improving. Intransigence in Germany and France was slowly receding, and a more reasonable attitude toward mutual problems was expressed by new leaders.

The most serious threat to peace in this period was the Greco-Bulgarian affair of 1925. The Council acted with the greatest dispatch and its clearcut stand has been considered to represent the classic example of the Covenant functioning as its drafters expected it to do. Upon receipt of a telegram from Bulgaria protesting a Greek invasion of its territory, the Council President, Briand of France, requested both parties to cease hostilities and withdraw behind their own frontiers. By the time the Council had convened, hostilities were at an end, but a commission was sent to the area to confirm the cease-fire and determine responsibility and a final decision. Greece agreed to pay $210,000 indemnity.

The year 1929 probably represented the highest point of the League and the confidence placed in its expanding efforts to improve the lot of mankind. Germany had become a faithful and respected member in 1926. The efforts of Gustav Stresemann were finally rewarded with the agreement reached outside the League to evacuate the occupation forces from the Rhineland by the summer of 1930. This was five years earlier than the date established in the Treaty of Versailles. Even German reparations were scaled down. Such arrangements could never have developed without a spirit of European unity which pervaded the sessions at Geneva.

But within three short years, the confidence of 1929 was shattered. The great depression had swept over the world by late 1930, bringing economic dislocation, financial disaster, reborn nationalism, and suspicion. The unity that was felt in Europe in 1929 disappeared. The accomplishments of the World Economic Conference of 1927 were lost. The Tariff Agreement, calling for reductions in tariff rates failed, as did the Conventions on the equal Treatment of Foreigners and the Abolition of Import and Export Prohibitions and Restrictions. The entire movement for free trade was swept away by the rising tide of economic nationalism. Briand's plan for a United States of Europe quickly died. Franco-German relations rapidly deteriorated with the rise of National Socialism and consequent fears of resurgent German militarism expressed in France. Antagonism between Germany and Poland increased over minorities in Upper Silesia and Memel. The attempt to improve the worsening economic situation in Austria and Germany through the conclusion of a customs union in 1931 raised the specter of *Anschluss* between the two states and immediately was contested by France. The Council decided to submit the case to the Court where, by an eight to seven vote, it was termed a violation of the Treaty of St. Germain and hence illegal. While the Council handled the very delicate affair with precision, the entire question increased the tensions of Europe. It was inevitable that in an atmosphere of recrimination and fear, the League would come in for increasing attacks, however unwarranted, from those who opposed its very being and from others who saw in it a possible deterrent to their ambitions. The period of stability and progress vanished, to be replaced by the total breakdown of collective security.

The Years of Collapse. The actual turning point in the history of the League came in the autumn of 1931. The Twelfth Assembly was quietly finishing its work, concerned primarily with preparations for the start of the Disarmament Conference the following year when news came on September 19 that the Japanese army had occupied Mukden, the capital of Manchuria. The Manchurian Affair was not considered at first to contain the elements of real danger, but soon the members realized that they were faced with a positive challenge to the whole League system of collective security.

China at once appealed to the Council for action under Article 11 of the Covenant. The Council responded by calling upon Japan to withdraw her troops and invoking the Kellogg-Briand Pact which had no sanctions behind it.[3] None of the major powers at Geneva nor the United States was willing to risk full-scale war by setting in motion any of the sanctions called for in Article 16 of the Covenant. At the suggestion of Japan, the Council appointed a special Commission of Inquiry, headed by Lord Lytton, with powers restricted solely to investigating and reporting upon a threat to the peaceful international relations between Japan and China. By the time that it finally arrived in the Far East in April, 1932, the Japanese had declared that Manchuria was now Manchoukuo, an independent state, and had extended the fighting to include an attack upon Shanghai. Later efforts by the League Assembly, acting under Article 15 of the Covenant resulted in condemning the actions of the Japanese and the adoption of the 'Stimson Doctrine' with respect to Manchuria, which, in effect, signified the refusal of the League to recognize a change in a legal situation engineered by force in contravention to treaty obligations. The Japanese reply was withdrawal from the League.

The League unquestionably was handicapped by the absence of any concerted leadership on the part of the major powers in the Council. The fact that the United States was not a member was a complicating feature

[3] For a consideration of the Kellogg-Briand Pact, see below, pp. 64-5.

in the negotiations. Left to pursue a methodical and judicial course without ever debating the possibility of assessing actual responsibility for the conflict and for repeated violations of the Covenant, the League could offer little in the way of a just settlement. Hitler and Mussolini could not help but receive encouragement from this evidence of League unwillingness to act firmly and with resolution against an obvious aggression perpetrated by a major power.

Even more challenging to the League's system of collective security was the Italo-Ethiopian War. An armed clash between the disputants occurred in December, 1934, and after months of fruitless negotiations, Ethiopia appealed to the Council under Article 15 of the Covenant. Efforts at conciliation were engaged in through committees appointed by the Council and, while Ethiopia co-operated faithfully with such activity, Italy pursued a policy of defiance. The next course of action called for by Article 15 was to have the Council 'make and publish a report containing a statement of the facts of the dispute and the recommendations which are deemed just and proper in regard thereto.' If Ethiopia accepted the report and Italy proceeded to attack her, it would be the solemn duty of all League members to apply sanctions against Italy. The Council's report of October 5, 1935, absolved Ethiopia of responsibility in the affair and denied Italian claims. The reply from Italy actually came before the issuance of the report in the form of a full-scale military invasion of Ethiopia. The next step was to declare Italy an aggressor and set in motion the sanctions provided for in Article 16. This was done on October 7 and the entire Council proceedings were transmitted to the Assembly where fifty nations out of fifty-four present voted to accept the decisions of the Council. It was quickly agreed to halt the export of certain commodities to Italy, to institute an arms embargo, prohibit imports from Italy, and to refrain from granting her any financial assistance. Oil was not embargoed nor was there any attempt to institute military measures. Diplomatic relations were not severed with Italy nor was the Suez Canal closed.

The mild nature of the sanctions, the backstage maneuvering of Britain and France as evidenced by the 'Hoare-Laval' plan to surrender most of Ethiopia to Italy, plus the failure of the United States to co-operate, doomed the efforts of the League. The war was over in May, 1936, and all that remained was to decide on the continued use of sanctions and whether to recognize the Italian annexation of Ethiopia. The Assembly voted in July to raise sanctions and failed to adopt the policy of nonrecognition affirmed earlier in the Manchurian Affair. To all intents and purposes, collective security was dead and the path was cleared for the Second World War.

The rest of the story down to 1939 and the start of World War II can be told quickly and briefly. Even before the Italo-Ethiopian war had ended, Hitler on March 17, 1936, ordered his troops to enter the demilitarized zone in the Rhineland. This act expressly violated not only the Treaty of Versailles, but also the Treaty of Locarno. The signatories of the latter — Belgium, Britain, France, Germany, and Italy — agreed that a violation of the demilitarized zone was to be equated with an attack on Belgium and France.[4] Furthermore, the League Council was selected as the agency to determine the obligations of the parties under the treaty. In this instance, all the Council did was to note that Germany had violated Locarno. Similarly, in the Spanish Civil War, the Council took no action on the appeal of the Spanish government against foreign assistance offered to Franco other than to express the view that states are obligated not to intervene in the affairs of others.

The renewal of hostilities in the Far East came in July, 1937, when Japan attacked China. China appealed to the League with no expectation of receiving more than moral support, possibly some material assistance, and a promise from the League members not to assist Japan in this latest aggression against a member of the League. China did receive considerable moral support, particularly from the Assembly, and some financial and military assistance from individual League members. The Council in 1938, at the instigation of China, did invoke Article 16 of the Covenant to the extent that Japan was declared 'to have committed an act of war' against all League members by virtue of refusing to attempt a pacific settlement of the Sino-Japanese War. But there was no favorable action upon the Chinese request that the League members refrain from providing aid to Japan.

Virtually on the eve of the Czechoslovak crisis, the Council in May, 1938, had to face a British request for League recognition of the Italian conquest of Ethiopia; Spain's plea to assist in ending nonintervention; China's appeal for League help; and Emperor Haile Selassie's calm reminder to the Council of its obligations and its repeated failures to respect them. The shadow of Austria, a member of the League now incorporated within the German frontiers, hung mightily over the proceedings. With such a situation, it is little wonder that the German-Czech controversy in the fall of 1938 never came before the League. As the dispute unfolded and war became a distinct possibility, one member after another announced a position of neutrality in any forthcoming call to arms. A debate in the Assembly recorded an overwhelming majority in favor of remaining free of any obligation to resist aggression. Article 16 of the Covenant ceased to exist. The months of 1939 came and went with the League never considered as an agency for

[4] For a consideration of the Locarno Treaty, see below, pp. 63–4.

preventing or ending the Second World War. It is a tragic irony that when war came in September, 1939, the countries attacked were the very ones that might have used the League to save themselves. This they could not do, for they had sacrificed it in earlier years to the forces which now sought to destroy them.

ATTEMPTS TO EXPAND THE SECURITY PROVISIONS OF THE COVENANT

The disheartening story just related of the rise and fall of the League's efforts at pacific settlement of disputes would not be complete without some reference to the sincere efforts made to improve certain inadequacies or gaps in the Covenant. Chief among the latter was the opportunity for a state to resort to arms after the failure of the machinery of the Covenant providing for peaceful settlement.

Draft Treaty of Mutual Assistance. In the first years of the League, questions of disarmament and security were joined together. A Temporary Mixed Commission of civilians was appointed by the First Assembly to study the problem of disarmament and it submitted a Draft Treaty of Mutual Assistance to the Fourth Assembly in 1923.

The Treaty began by denouncing 'aggression as an international crime' which the contracting parties agreed not to commit. While affirming the principle of general assistance, there was provision for the possibility of 'supplementary defensive agreements' of a regional character. The League Council would have the authority to examine these agreements to determine if they were in conflict with the Covenant. Extremely important was the authority given to the Council, which far exceeded that granted by the Covenant. It could order sanctions even before war broke out; request military and financial assistance from the members and determine the nature of the military contingents believed necessary; appoint a high command; decide who was the aggressor if war broke out; negotiate demilitarized zones; and propose an armistice. A state declared to be an aggressor was to bear all the costs of military operations conducted by the League and all reparations for damages resulting from the war. All the benefits of these provisions were made contingent upon the adoption of disarmament measures proposed by the Council. No state would be entitled to the protection afforded by the Treaty, unless it complied with the requirements established for disarmament. In determining which states would participate in halting aggression, the Council was to call upon only those who were located in the same continent in which the aggression had occurred.

In effect, the Draft Treaty superimposed a regional system upon the general provisions of the League, a feature particularly acceptable to France and most distasteful to Great Britain and the Dominions. Other critics claimed that the plan was too complicated, that the powers of the Council were too great and that aggression was nowhere defined. Eighteen states affirmed the Draft Treaty in principle, but the opposition of Great Britain and a number of lesser states prevented its adoption.

The Geneva Protocol. The Protocol for the Pacific Settlement of International Disputes, or more commonly, the Geneva Protocol, resembled the Draft Treaty in some respects, but the major difference lay in the emphasis upon the theory of general security in the Protocol and its abandonment of regional arrangements.

The Protocol sought to prevent a state from exercising the right to go to war after the machinery established by Article 15 of the Covenant had failed. All parties to a dispute were bound to submit it to arbitration if the Council could not negotiate a settlement. If the disputants could not agree on the composition or powers of the arbitration board, the Council was given the right 'to settle the points remaining in suspense.' Substantially the same procedure was to be applied when the Council failed to reach a unanimous decision. Controversies could also be settled by the Permanent Court of International Justice. In any case the procedures of pacific settlement had to be utilized: a decision by the Council or the Court, or a decision through an arbitral award. In the event that the Court or the Council declared a question to be within the domestic jurisdiction of a state, 'this decision shall not prevent consideration of the situation by the Council or by the Assembly under Article 11 of the Covenant.' A violation of any of these procedures would constitute an act of aggression and bring into force the sanctions laid down in Article 16 of the Covenant. Finally, should the Council fail to reach a unanimous decision, it was empowered by the Protocol to establish an armistice. A belligerent refusing to accept the armistice, or violating its terms, automatically would become an aggressor.

Arbitration became the test of aggression and the procedure to insure the adoption of pacific settlement in all cases. Obligatory military sanctions were not called for but the League was directed by the Protocol 'to consider and report as to the nature of the steps to be taken to give effect to the economic and financial sanctions and measures of cooperation contemplated in Article 16 of the Covenant.' As in the Treaty of Mutual Assistance, the aggressor was required to pay the costs of military sanctions and damages resulting from the act of aggression. Each signatory was to agree to resist any act of aggression 'in the degree which its geographical position and its particular position as regards armaments allow.' While a dispute was under consideration, no party could 'make any increase of their armaments or effectives . . . nor take any measures of military, naval, air, industrial or economic mobilization.' To cap the entire plan was the provision calling for all signatory states to participate in a general disarmament conference which was to convene on June 15, 1925. The Protocol was to become effective only after the conclusion of the conference.

However, the Geneva Protocol never received sufficient ratifications, opposition again coming from Great Britain and the Dominions who disliked what they believed to be its 'coercive' features. Others appeared to have suddenly realized what they had agreed to in 1919. The League, as far as its political features were concerned, may very well have died in 1925 with the rejection of the Geneva Protocol. A number of its features, however, have been incorporated into the Charter of the United Nations.

The General Act of 1928. Another attempt was made to augment the machinery of peaceful settlement with the unanimous acceptance by the Ninth Assembly of a General Act for the Pacific Settlement of International Disputes. One of its objects was to supplement the Briand-Kellogg Pact on the outlawry of war. Although but twenty-three states including Britain, France, and Italy acceded to it, the usefulness of the Act is attested to by the fact that its provisions have been included in the Charter of the United Nations.

Three chapters were devoted to various procedures of pacific settlement to make possible a solution to all types of controversies. The first provided the machinery for conciliation, while the second chapter detailed a procedure for the settlement of legal disputes by the Court or arbitration. In chapter three, the principle of arbitration was extended for disputes not appropriate for the methods of the Court. A final chapter made it possible for states to adhere to all three procedural chapters or as many as was desired. No one had to be committed to compulsory arbitration in all cases. Reservations were permitted and if one party to a dispute had indicated a certain type of reservation, the other parties would be entitled to enjoy similar reservations.

The Convention To Improve the Means of Preventing War. Germany had suggested in 1927 that the League might adopt a treaty in which the principle was laid down that states would agree to be bound, in advance, by any recommendations that the Council might deem necessary for the handling of a dispute. A Convention was drafted and presented to the Twelfth Assembly in 1931 for discussion. Although it was never acceded to, it should be noted in passing because certain of its features have been made a part of the Charter of the United Nations.

Included in its provisions was the obligation of the signatories to put into effect nonmilitary measures recommended by the Council for the purpose of avoiding actions which might aggravate a controversy. Among the recommendations of the Council might be the creation of a demilitarized zone, the evacuation of territory, and the acceptance of armistice terms. These decisions of the Council could be made by a majority vote. The Council would have been empowered to send inspectors to the scene to check on the execution of its recommendations. A violation of the Council's decisions might be sufficient evidence to indicate that 'the party guilty thereof has resorted to war within the meaning of Article 16 of the Covenant.' This Convention might have been of value in the Manchurian Episode and the Italo-Ethiopian War had Japan and Italy been bound by its provisions.

SECURITY ARRANGEMENTS OUTSIDE THE LEAGUE

The search for security was not restricted solely to the framework of the League. Following the failure of the Geneva Protocol in 1924, there remained the belief in European diplomatic circles that additional guarantees were essential to safeguard the peace of Europe. The revival of a strong Germany was regarded as inevitable and many believed that the League might not be able to provide machinery adequate to cope with Franco-German difficulties. Effective disarmament would be impossible unless French security could be gained through some protective agreement which would be consistent with the principles of the Covenant. The result was the consummation of the Locarno agreements in 1925. Later, in 1928, the Kellogg-Briand Pact was signed, designed to 'outlaw war as an instrument of national policy.' Both the Locarno and Kellogg-Briand treaties were hailed as 'milestones of progress' in the quest for a peaceful world but, as with the Covenant, they fell short of their aims primarily through the defection of the major powers. However, each merits further examination because the principles embodied in them were new at the time and have not been abandoned today.

Locarno. The agreements reached at the Swiss town of Locarno in 1925 emphasized regional understandings instead of the general commitments laid down in the Geneva Protocol. The territorial status quo of the Franco-German-Belgium frontier was collectively guaranteed by Belgium, Britain, France, Germany, and Italy. France and Germany, and Belgium and Germany agreed 'that they will in no case attack or invade each other or resort to war against each other' except in 'the exercise of the right of legitimate defense' or in the event of a 'flagrant breach of Articles 42 or 43 of the Treaty of Versailles, if such breach constitutes an unprovoked act of aggression.' Each party further agreed, in case of a flagrant breach, 'to come to the help of the party against whom such a violation or breach has been directed as soon as the said Power has been able to satisfy itself that this violation constitutes an unprovoked act of aggression.' It was required that the League Council determine the validity of the action undertaken and all parties were 'to act in accordance with the recommendations of the Council provided that they are concurred in by all the members' except the disputants.

In addition, various arbitration conventions were concluded between Germany on the one side, and France, Belgium, Poland, and Czechoslovakia on the other. These called for the submission of all disputes not susceptible to settlement by ordinary diplomatic procedures to the Permanent Court of International Justice or an arbitral tribunal. There was also a Franco-Polish and a Franco-Czechoslovak treaty of mutual assistance in the event of German aggression. Significantly, however, there was no British guarantee of the frontiers of Eastern Europe. The British Dominions and India were exempted from any of the Locarno obligations, unless specifically accepted.

Some measure of limited security was provided by the Locarno arrangements and the way was paved for the entry of Germany into the League. For a time, Locarno was, as claimed by Sir Austen Chamberlain, 'the real dividing line between the years of war and the years of peace.' Tensions in Europe were eased and some comfort could be gained by both France and Germany through the British guarantee of their borders. There was little speculation upon the ability or willingness of the British to honor their obligations. In effect, Locarno was a much more limited agreement than its supporters would admit. Its success depended upon the broader strengthening of security arrangements which would bind all the major powers to resist aggression in areas beyond the Rhineland frontiers.

Kellogg-Briand Pact. An entirely different and perhaps more visionary approach to the problem of war was to be found in the Kellogg-Briand Pact of 1928. It arose out of an exchange of ideas between Foreign Minister Aristide Briand of France and Secretary of State Frank B. Kellogg of the United States. Known more formally as the General Treaty for the Renunciation of War (also as the Pact of Paris), it was almost universally ratified and gained wide public acclaim throughout the world. It consisted of three articles, the first two of which reveal both its objectives and its shortcomings. Article 1 solemnly called upon the parties to 'declare in the names of their respective peoples that they condemn recourse to war for the solution of international controversies, and renounce it as an instrument of national policy in their relations with one another.' The high contracting parties in Article 2 agreed 'that the settlement or solution of all disputes or conflicts, of whatever nature or of whatever origin they may be, which may arise among them, shall never be sought except by pacific means.'

While the pact unquestionably echoed the fervent desires of mankind for peace, in reality it was little more than an ethical statement with no machinery of enforcement. Secretary Kellogg even was forced to admit that wars of self-defense were beyond the scope of the Pact. Critics immediately jumped upon this confession and rightly so, since very few nations will ever admit that their role in warfare is more than a defensive action aimed at protecting the Fatherland. The failure to distinguish between wars of aggression and action purely of a defensive nature gave substance to the charge that the Pact stood ready to end all wars except those most likely to occur. Furthermore, there was no definition of what was meant by 'pacific means' of settlement.

Reservations added by several important states further weakened the Pact. The Senate of the United States declared, for example, that the United States viewed the maintenance of the Monroe Doctrine as falling within the scope of 'national defense.' Similarly, Great Britain claimed that the right of self-defense included 'certain regions of the world, the welfare and integrity of which constitute a special and vital interest for our peace and safety.' France also emphasized the need for recognizing the right of self-defense, particularly as it related to her treaty commitments. Despite these reservations and the obvious shortcomings of the Pact, President Calvin Coolidge stated in his annual message to Congress in 1928 that 'the observance of this covenant, so simple and so straight-forward, promises more for the peace of the world than any other agreement ever negotiated among the nations.' In fact, however, it was little more than a symbol and a gesture, both morally and diplomatically, which later events were to prove so emphatically.

WELFARE AND TECHNICAL ACTIVITIES OF THE LEAGUE

Much emphasis has been placed in recent years upon the failure of the League's political machinery to avert war. Too frequently the detractors of the League have omitted from their conclusions the fact that there was an incredible growth of international co-operation during the twenty years of the League's welfare activities. If nothing more, for the first time in history, a central place was provided where specialists could meet to discuss and analyze some of the major problems outside the political arena. Regular committees of the Assembly, together with special League agencies, systematically applied their skills and experience to a variety of problems. The Secretariat became a repository of information, with a limited but highly competent and loyal staff ceaselessly endeavoring to collect information and distribute it to those in need. While by no means as extensive as that engaged in by the United Nations, the activity of the League in the essentially nonpolitical field was remarkably broad. The examples which follow are illustrative of the types of activity in which the League engaged and indicate motivation and objectives.

Health. The general effort to obtain international co-operation in this field was accomplished through the League's Health Organization, the Secretariat, and the various narcotics bodies. The problem of epidemics of typhus, smallpox, and cholera was of concern immediately following the end of World War I. Even before the Health Organization was formally established, emergency assistance by the League managed to blunt the spread of these serious diseases. Special sanitary training conferences were held and methods were agreed upon for combatting specific epidemics. In later years, attention was directed to reducing the spread of syphillis, leprosy, malaria, sleeping sickness, rabies, and tuberculosis. A major contribution was the establishment of a worldwide epidemiological intelligence service to warn peoples in advance of epidemics and permit governments to undertake precautionary measures.

A number of governments sought the aid of the Health Organization in developing their own health authorities and facilities. The League's Health Committee toured Greece in 1928 in response to a request from that country for assistance in reorganizing its sanitary services. A lengthy report contained specific recommendations for the development of certain technical services, a revamped public health system, and a school of hygiene. The Greek government responded by enacting legislation to implement these suggestions. Similar assistance was provided China and several Latin American countries. Frequently, a country would request a League agency to convene a conference to discuss health problems of particular concern to it. Thus, in 1932, a regional conference was held to study methods of preventing the spread of yellow fever. The Health Organization, through the granting of scholarships, made it possible for health officials to travel abroad and obtain the benefit of the most recent scientific research and practices.

The control of narcotic drugs entered a new phase under the League. Prior to the League, some agreements had been concluded in an effort to control the production and distribution of certain narcotics, but no international organization existed to supervise these arrangements. The League Covenant, however, specifically entrusted the League with the general supervision 'over the execution of agreements with regard to the traffic in opium and other dangerous drugs.' Several new agreements were concluded under the auspices of the League, and the Advisory Committee on the Traffic in Opium and Other Dangerous Drugs was the first agency assigned the task of supervising their execution. This was done by gathering specific information on the production, distribution, and consumption of narcotic drugs and thereby revealing the extent of international compliance with agreed-upon regulation. A Permanent Central Opium Board was created in 1925 to receive national reports on exports and imports. Another agency, the Supervisory Body, was established in 1931 by a convention which sought to limit the manufacture of narcotic drugs to strictly legitimate needs. These broad features of narcotic drug regulation proved to be of great value and have been continued and expanded through various agencies associated with the United Nations.

Economic Co-operation. Although seriously handicapped by a lack of funds, the League did make efforts to improve world economic conditions. Probably the major contribution came from activities centered around the encouragement of broader and more regular consultation between nations. Large-scale technical assistance to underdeveloped countries was not attempted, primarily because of limited budgets and the absence of co-ordinated planning among the various agencies operating in the economic field. Some isolated instances of technical assistance could be noted, however, and the League Assembly considered such items as financial reconstruction, customs formalities, access to raw materials, and tariffs. Considerable progress was made in arriving at some uniformity in statistics on economic and financial matters. A Convention on Economic Statistics was concluded in 1928 which requested its signatories to publish a series of economic statistics, and provided a committee of experts to work out details of standardization.

The League also sponsored several world conferences to consider various financial and economic questions. While these conferences were relatively unsuccessful in producing concrete solutions for immediate problems, they did point out the need for international collaboration on many economic matters. On these occasions, in addition, experts from many countries, some not even members of the League, were able to compare views and generate ideas free from the confines of national policy and interests. The various League agencies could quietly plan in advance with great flexibility for these meetings, preparing statistical and other data without arousing political suspicions which frequently had been the case when an individual nation had been the conference host in other years. Specialists could meet regularly at a central location without the necessity of waiting for a particular state to initiate proceedings.

Although it was unable to obtain much agreement on multilateral conventions relating to such major items as monetary and trade questions, the League had more success in dealing with individual countries and small groups of nations concerned with specific problems. Of particular note was the service rendered by reconstruction loans. Through the efforts of the Financial Committee, a loan of £26 million, underwritten by ten countries, was made to Austria in 1923. Hungary received a loan of £10 million for economic reconstruction. The Financial Committee also supervised loans for Danzig and aided Estonia in establishing a new banking system. Rumania was given similar technical assistance, Greece and Bulgaria were granted loans for refugee settlement, and China was assisted in re-establishing its currency. International relief, in modest amounts, was made available in the form of clothing, food, and medical supplies to victims of floods, earthquakes, and other catastrophes. This activity was conducted by the International Relief Union which was established by individual governments under the auspices of the League.

Communications and Transit. Most nations exhibited the same reluctance to commit themselves to rigid agreements governing communications and transportation as they did with regard to economic and financial matters. In spite of this hesitancy, League agencies made considerable efforts toward bringing national communications systems into greater harmony with each other. The section of the League Secretariat devoted to communications did its best to serve as a co-ordinating agency to assist nations in planning transportation of all kinds in the most efficient manner.

The Communications and Transit Organization carried on useful research and informational activities. It provided technical assistance to China in road building and in hydraulic works. A report was compiled on navigation questions of the Danube river which offered recommendations for coordinating river and railroad transportation. Navigation on the Rhine river was also studied, particularly with respect to competition between river vessels and railroads. A recommendation was made by the League that the railroads, ports, and waterways of a country be placed under a unified governmental agency, so that a co-operative development of communications could be brought into being. Advice was given to Poland on the problem of transporting coal by waterways. Whenever called upon, the League offered its encouragement and assistance for activities within the communications field which were undertaken by non-League agencies. This was especially true with respect to the efforts of the International Commission for Air Navigation, the International Telecommunication Union, and the Universal Postal Union.

Other Activities. The League's technical and welfare efforts reached into a number of other fields which can be only briefly noted. Mention should be made at this time of the work of the International Labor Organization which will be discussed in more detail in later chapters. The ILO functioned primarily to bring to the attention of the world the need for improving labor standards and the methods by which this might be accomplished. Forty-six conventions were in force in more than fifty states by the end of 1939. A number of countries which failed to ratify these conventions observed their general principles in practice. Among the subjects covered by these conventions or by other recommendations were the following: the protection of women and children in industry; a weekly rest day for all workers; annual holidays with pay; the eight-hour day; and the hours of work in agriculture and maritime occupations. Valuable studies were made on industrial hygiene, the prevention of industrial accidents, social insurance, and many other matters of equal importance. Going far beyond the more modest role originally envisaged by its founders, the ILO thus considered not only industrial problems but the welfare of workers in all fields of employment. It survived World War II and with renewed energy continues to devote itself to the many questions bearing on labor standards and related matters.

One of the most unheralded accomplishments of the League in the technical field was the regular publication of numerous scientific and technical journals and compilations. Among the most useful publications were those dealing with economic and financial matters, such as *The World Economic Survey, Monetary Review, Monthly Bulletin of Statistics, International Trade Statistics, The Statistical Yearbook, The Review of World Trade,* and *International Trade in Certain Raw Materials and Foodstuffs.* Noteworthy also was *The Bulletin of The Health Organization.* Others in the fields of communications and transit, population, housing, and drug control were equally valuable.

The Advisory Committee on Traffic in Women and Children and the Advisory Committee on Social Questions conducted studies on the problem of human exploitation in Europe, the Americas, and the Far East. The League Secretariat maintained a Child Welfare Information Center after 1933. Working with it to investigate the immense problem of child welfare, with particular attention paid to health problems, was a special League Committee on Child Welfare. Insufficient funds retarded the scope and effectiveness of these efforts, as it did with respect to the League's limited but useful work in the field of population and migration. The small number of devoted League specialists doing pioneer work in these heretofore neglected social problem areas have been rewarded by the continuance of their activities in a greatly expanded form by the United Nations and the specialized agencies.

A High Commissioner for Refugees was appointed by the Council in 1921 for the purpose of alleviating the misery of millions of Russians, Greeks, Turks, Armenians, and others who had been made homeless by the War. Although the responsibility for such action did not rest with the League through any provisions of the Covenant or Peace Treaties, the desperate plight of so many unfortunate human beings made such an undertaking necessary. Dr. Fridtjof Nansen of Norway became the High Commissioner and managed to relieve some of the distress in spite of the fact that the funds available were negligible. An added handicap was the determination of most League members to maintain the High Commissariat on a temporary basis with no formal obligations which might entail a sizeable financial burden. Some additional funds were raised by Dr. Nansen himself besides contributions made by private philanthropy and individual governments, but they were never in sufficient amounts to take care of the need.

The High Commissioner's staff was attached to the International Labor Organization for a time, but for the most part it operated out of the League Secretariat. The introduction of the so-called Nansen passport did ease some of the hopelessness for many refugees by making travel easier between states. It consisted of a certificate issued by national governments on the recommendation of the High Commissioner which was accepted as the equivalent of a regular passport by most countries. This made it possible for many refugees to gain employment or seek the shelter of friends and relatives which had been denied because of travel restrictions upon their emigration.

After Dr. Nansen's death in 1930, the activities of the High Commissariat fluctuated due to a lack of direction and co-ordination, despite an increase in the flood of refugees resulting from Hitler's policies. Nevertheless, some work with refugees was continued on a limited scale during the Second World War.

The last of the technical, permanent bodies established by the Council was the Committee on Intellectual Cooperation, which began its work in 1922. Because it was handicapped throughout its existence by a lack of funds, it could accomplish only a small portion of the threefold objective contemplated by its sponsors. One purpose was to improve the material condition of the great body of intellectuals who had suffered through the devastation and the general chaos of the War. A second aim was to facilitate international contacts between those engaged in various cultural, artistic, and intellectual professions. The final purpose of the Committee was to develop enthusiastic support among intellectuals, and particularly those engaged in teaching on all levels, for the general objectives of the League in promoting international co-operation.

The Committee throughout its existence was composed of some of the most brilliant and prominent men and women from the arts and the intellectual professions. France aided its work by establishing in Paris an International Institute of Intellectual Co-operation which eventually became the headquarters of the Committee. Another international Institute was provided in Rome by the Italian government and was devoted primarily to the field of education and motion pictures. Both Institutes remained under the control of the League and were free from national supervision. National committees of Intellectual Co-operation were inaugurated in more than forty countries and served as connecting links between cultural and intellectual institutions in those countries and the International Committee.

The experimental and useful work begun by the Committee is now continued on a more ambitious scale and with more substantial financial backing by the United Nations Educational, Scientific, and Cultural Organization.

TERMINATION OF LEAGUE FUNCTIONS

The League was forced to make one final political decision after the onset of World War II. On December 8, 1939, the Secretary-General, Joseph Avenol, received a note from Finland which requested that the Council invoke Articles 11 and 15 of the Covenant against Soviet Russia, whose armies had invaded Finland a few days previously. Avenol called a meeting of the Council for December 9. The Assembly, to which Finland also had appealed, was convoked for December 11. While a number of European members were hesitant about provoking the Russians, Latin American delegates had no such qualms. Argentina, in particular, was determined to have the Soviet Union expelled from the League and introduced a resolution to that effect in the Assembly. On December 14 the Assembly unanimously adopted the Argentine proposal, at the same time condemning the Soviet aggression and, without specifying sanctions of any nature, called upon all members of the League to assist Finland against the unprovoked attack. On the same day, the Council voted, for the only time in its history, to expel a League member, stating that 'in virtue of Article 16, paragraph 4 of the Covenant that by its act the USSR has placed itself outside the League of Nations. It follows that the USSR is no longer a member of the League.' No previous aggressor had received such treatment, despite actions of an equally reprehensible nature on earlier occasions when the League was not dead.

After the fall of France in June, 1940, Geneva was virtually isolated from the free world. League technical activities could not continue for long under such a handicap, but other countries came to the rescue. The International Labor Organization moved to Montreal; the League Treasury, to London. A large part of the Secretariat eventually came to operate from Princeton University, leaving a skeleton staff in Geneva.

The twenty-first and final session of the Assembly met in Geneva on April 8, 1946, to liquidate the League of Nations. A total of thirty-five delegations were present. The Council was not convoked and the Assembly, by resolution, decided that 'so far as is required, it will, during the present session, assume the functions following within the competence of the Council.' Both the Assembly and the Council had the authority, under the Covenant, to deal with any matter which lay within the compass of the League. In addition, almost all the members who had composed the Council when it last had met in December, 1939, were present. On April 18, 1946, the Assembly voted unanimously that as of the following day (April 19) 'the League of Nations shall cease to exist.' The Covenant was not declared null and void nor was it abrogated in any way. The machinery was simply dissolved by decision of the League membership. On July 31, 1947, a special Board of Liquidation completed its task of distributing remaining funds to League members, settling financial accounts, and transferring its property and certain of its functons to the United Nations.

SUMMARY AND APPRAISAL

Any summary and appraisal of the structure and work of the League of Nations must center around the answers to two fundamental questions. Why did the League of Nations fail to keep the peace? Despite its failure, what contributions did the League make toward international co-operation and organization?

Failure of the League. Any simple answer to the question of why the League failed to keep the peace would be not only presumptuous but misleading. Were the framers of the Covenant too ambitious, aiming at goals which were unobtainable? Were the framers betrayed by those who assumed the burdens of statecraft in the years after 1919? Were there other contributing factors in the interwar years which resulted from general world conditions?

Those who framed the Covenant were fully aware of the fact that the fundamental principles underlying the traditional multi-state system had been preserved. The concept of the sovereign state as the unit of modern international society was retained in the Covenant as was the acceptance of the role of the great powers as the key participants in the organization. It was fully expected that the League would be called upon to function in a normal world adjusting, to be sure, to postwar strains and tensions but nevertheless a world determined that peace should be the norm. The League was believed to contain the means whereby the events leading to the outbreak of war in 1914 could be averted. But a new political system was not developed to replace the old. Instead, certain changes or reforms had been built into the old system which would permit it to continue, strengthened by procedural devices which would reduce the recourse to force in the settlement of international disputes. The Covenant was constructed in the belief and with the conviction that there had arisen a new political morality to guide the course of international politics.

It was expected that the membership of the League would be virtually universal, with all the major nations of the world active members dedicated to substituting responsibility for power. From this near-universal membership would arise the leadership necessary to modify in due course certain injustices inherent in the peace settlements of 1919, and to accept and enforce the obligations of membership equally upon all. Further, the framers recognized that while the Covenant prohibited the members from resorting to war under certain conditions, they might go to war in the absence of such conditions. It was expected, again, that responsible leadership would be able to bridge the gap and through co-operation and compromise reduce if not eliminate the loopholes in the Covenant. These are assumptions which were entertained in good faith by such men as Woodrow Wilson, Jan Smuts, and Lord Cecil. The goals they and other framers of the Covenant sought were obtainable, provided they materialized in the form of concrete action.

The tragic story of the League of Nations clearly portrays the failure of the world situation to develop as expected. The United States never became a member of the League. Soviet Russia joined at a late date. The absence of the two most powerful nations from the formative years at Geneva was a fundamental weakness the League never fully overcame. Without these nations present in the early years, no abiding, forceful leadership could materialize. Rectification of injustices and unequal treatment called for by the peace treaties came only through unilateral action and not through the efforts of League members. Requirements laid down in the peace settlements for disarmament, mandates, and minorities, to mention a few, might have been worked out through Article 19 of the Covenant, which provided the Assembly with the power to consider any treaty or agreement that had grown obsolete or any international condition that might threaten the peace of the world. But Article 19 was rarely employed. Various attempts were made to plug the loopholes in the Covenant, both within and without the League, but most of them were stillborn. Neither justice nor security was organized as had been confidently predicted in 1919.

Certainly a fundamental question concerning the failure of the League, then, centers around the betrayal of the Covenant by its members. It may be granted that the Covenant had weaknesses, faulty drafting, even structural defects which inhibited its smooth functioning. But its goals were unobtainable primarily because the will to achieve them was absent. Perhaps the framers of the Covenant were too visionary in expecting that there had arisen a new political morality, but without a reorientation of international relations the peoples of the world could not expect to remain at peace for long. The Covenant pointed in the direction of a reorientation but the members of the League shrank from their responsibilities and tacitly refused to respect the obligations solemnly undertaken. Challenges of aggression were not viewed as challenges to the future of an international organization such as the League, but were evaluated either as threats to particular national interests or as actions justified by prior events, or simply were considered to be acts which did not threaten the peace. The major powers on the Council refused to take action against Japan, first in 1931 and again in 1937 for these reasons. They did nothing to prevent the continuous violations of the Treaty of Versailles by Germany. France would not act without British aid, which the British in turn were unwilling to offer. The League debacle over the Italo-Ethiopian War and succeeding events is explainable primarily in terms of national policy and not as a sign of constitutional or structural weakness in the League.

Without an Anglo-American guarantee of her territory, France sought by all possible means to exploit the advantages gained for her security from the peace settlement of 1919. At the same time, Great Britain attempted to return to the traditional policy of a European balance of power. In British eyes, the threat to European security lay with France, and this fact, plus the weakening ties within the British Commonwealth and a lessening influence on the councils of the world, led to an essentially negative British policy. What was needed at Geneva was positive leadership which might have been provided by France and Britain. What was essential for the success of the League was the assurance to all its members that provision would be made for their security and that the obligations of the Covenant would be respected. It was also imperative that a gradual, peaceful modification of the peace settlement of 1919 be carried out so that its preservation could be made the interest of all and not the interest solely of a limited group. Imaginative leadership was required if developments of this nature were to materialize, but such leadership was not forthcoming.

Economic factors during the interwar years inevitably were of importance in the eventual dissolution of peace and the consequent destruction of the League. As has been shown earlier in this chapter, the League was fully cognizant of the role of economic and, of course, social factors in the maintenance of stable international relations. Much more could have been done, it is true, but there is much that was done, most of it for the first time in history. Yet, underlying social and economic problems and of greater, lasting significance were not only the political but also the psychological considerations in the failure to organize peace. National loyalties were far stronger than the ties to the League. Individuals were not yet sufficiently accustomed to an international organization as an institution designed to provide the security originally and customarily offered by national power. Hatreds and fears engendered by the War, the shattering effects of a worldwide economic depression, the gradual disappearance of any unifying force of universalism, the rise of new disruptive ideologies in the form of fascism, communism, and national socialism, all made for a divided world cursed by exaggerated nationalism. The League could not endure in the face of such disintegrating factors and forces which were totally incompatible with the needs of a new political morality and which, even in a more fundamental sense, put democratic society itself on trial.

Accomplishments of the League. The twenty years of the League cannot be written off solely in terms of collapse and failure. The fact that a new international organization, the United Nations, arose after the Second World War is a positive testament to the continuing ideals of the old League. If nothing else, the League was worthwhile in that it served as a major testing ground for both the substantive and procedural features of international organization.

The substance of political life is discovered through the compromise and conflict of politics itself. The League machinery was thoroughly tested and found wanting in some instances. But the League had to pioneer its way, having had no predecessor to follow, no substantive elements of law and order previously tested by the machinery of collective security to guide its actions. The League was confronted by varying forms of aggression which eventually brought about its downfall. In each instance, however, existing rules were interpreted, procedures were tested and developed; in sum, the entire system of international organization was slowly evolving. The conference method of discussing mutual problems, methods of voting and representation, budgetary procedures, committee structure, the rules of debate and parliamentary practice, these and numerous other organizational and procedural matters were developed. Problems, inadequacies, failures, and successes all contribute to the sum total of knowledge and the United Nations is a fortunate beneficiary of the League experience.

Certain features of the League system were distinct successes. This is particularly true of the Permanent Court of International Justice. It had no force to back its findings, yet it handed down a large number of decisions, all of which were accepted. Some of the decisions were against great nations in favor of lesser ones. The successor to the Permanent Court, the International Court of Justice, has an impressive backlog of jurisprudence and procedure upon which to build its future. Similarly, the International Labor Office was a success and continues to this day, the Second World War having failed to terminate its functions. In a more qualified sense, the Secretariat, too, was a success. The difficult creation of an international administration was undertaken and the result proved that such a venture not only is possible but can be highly efficient. As one specialist has observed, 'The League has shown that it is possible to establish an integrated body of international officials, loyal to the international agency and ready to discharge faithfully the international obligations incumbent upon them. It was not for lack of executive efficiency that the League system failed.' [5]

The technical and welfare agencies of the League were successful, for the most part, particularly when one recognizes the limits imposed by inadequate financing and the necessity to pioneer in fields customarily reserved for national action alone. Real advances were made in the control of white slave traffic, opium, and other narcotic drugs. Definite progress could be noted concerning problems of health, transit, communications, unemployment, tariffs, intellectual co-operation, and refugees. The international administration of the Saar by the League was largely successful, although a similar arrangement for the free city of Danzig was not. The mandates system worked rather well within the limits established by the Covenant and the Council.

As the League expanded its welfare and technical activities, it became clear that a reorganization of the agencies involved in this work was necessary if maximum effectiveness was to be achieved. Consequently, in

[5] Ranshofen-Wertheimer, Egon F., *The International Secretariat*, Washington, D.C., 1945, p. 428.

1938 the League Council appointed the distinguished Australian, S. B. Bruce, to head a small committee charged with the responsibility of recommending the necessary reforms within the League structure. Its report, under the title of *The Development of International Cooperation in Economic and Social Affairs,* was a significant milestone in the efforts toward more effective international co-operation.[6]

Among the more important recommendations of the Bruce Report were the following: (1) that a Central Committee of 24 government representatives and 8 technical experts be created to replace the Council as the supervisory agency of the League's technical organizations; (2) that the members of the Central Committee be important government officials and technical experts of the highest level; (3) that the Central Committee create the various necessary technical committees and agencies, supervise their work, draw up their budgets, and be the final authority to decide the validity of their proposals; (4) that states not members of the League be given the opportunity for the fullest possible co-operation in the work itself as well as in its direction and supervision; (5) that there be better co-ordination between all agencies working in the technical field. It was expected by the Bruce Committee that these changes would 'add fresh efficiency and vigor to the work itself, a result which may naturally be expected to follow if public knowledge in regard to it can be increased and if it becomes the primary interest of the directing organs . . .'

The Bruce Report was discussed and approved by the Assembly in December, 1939, which established a special Organizing Committee to work toward bringing into being the recommendations proposed. The Committee met in the spring of 1940 but its work was terminated by the Second World War. What might have been a fundamental reorganization of the League's social and economic work had to wait until the recommendations of the Bruce Report took form in the Economic and Social Council of the United Nations.

[6] Issued as a *Special Supplement to the Monthly Summary of the League of Nations,* Geneva (August 1939).

4

THE ESTABLISHMENT OF THE UNITED NATIONS

THE quest for peace and security through international organization did not die with the coming of the Second World War. On the contrary, statesmen, scholars, and many men and women everywhere were resolute in their determination that the lessons learned during the twenty years of the League be put to use either in a reformed and revitalized League or in a new international institution. It soon became evident that it would be psychologically unwise to attempt to rebuild the League. The experiment at Geneva was too generally held to be a failure in the opinion of the world. Planning got under way within months after the start of the war, first by private citizens and agencies and later by several of the governments united in the struggle against the Axis Powers. For more than three years, the United Nations was taking shape in rudimentary form, first in the minds of planners, then in the declarations of various states, and finally in the conferences at Dumbarton Oaks, Yalta, and San Francisco. Few agreements have enjoyed such extensive planning and preparation as the Charter of the United Nations which was finally completed and ratified in 1945.

PLANNING THE UNITED NATIONS

Private Groups. Private citizens, particularly in the United States, spent a great deal of time during the Second World War discussing the problems of peace and the future course of international organization.[1] Existing institutions and organizations devoted time and thought to these questions, and new groups were formed to study the matter and report on their conclusions. One of the most significant of the new groups was

[1] For an example of unofficial planning in Great Britain, see the Draft Pact for the Future International Authority drawn up by the Executive Committee of the League of Nations Union, London. Text in *International Conciliation*, No. 397 (February 1944), pp. 131–9.

the Commission to Study the Organization of Peace. It was sponsored jointly by several national organizations in the United States and began its work in November, 1939, under the chairmanship of Dr. James T. Shotwell.

After four years of study and analysis, which included several useful interim reports, the Commission in 1944 issued a statement on the fundamentals of international organization.[2] Previous reports had emphasized that 'international organization must furnish a continuous process for the achievement of security, justice, and welfare throughout the world.' While it was by no means a blueprint for the future, the fundamentals listed by the Commission called for the establishment of an organization based upon principles quite similar to those embodied in the Charter of the United Nations. Aggressive war was declared to be 'a crime against mankind' and it was further declared that all nations 'must be bound by the obligation not to resort to other than peaceful means for the settlement of disputes.' There should be an international police force, including an air force, to make effective the military sanctions against aggression. An International Court, with the scope of arbitration widened, a disarmament control commission, a special commission 'for safeguarding essential human rights,' should work together with a series of technical welfare agencies, a secretariat, an assembly, and an executive council to be 'composed of a limited number of states, including those nations that bear the heaviest share of responsibility for the restoration and maintenance of peace, and able to take quick decisions in cases of a threat of aggression.' In addition, there should be provisions for a trusteeship system over non-self-governing peoples and machinery for collaboration with regional international organizations.

In the summer of 1942, the Universities Committee on Post-War International Problems was organized to develop interest in problems anticipated in the postwar period. It also served to gather opinions from members of the faculties of American universities and colleges and bring their views 'to the attention of the public and of the responsible government officials.'[3] Approximately one hundred faculty groups at various institutions of higher learning co-operated with the Committee. At monthly intervals a Problem Analysis was prepared by the Committee and distributed to the participating groups for their discussion and study. The

---

[2] 'Fourth Report of the Commission to Study the Organization of Peace,' *International Conciliation,* No. 396 (January 1944), pp. 26–28. See also the Commission's 'General International Organization, Its Framework and Functions,' *ibid.,* no. 403 (September 1944), pp. 547–51.

[3] 'Universities Committee on Post-War International Problems. Summaries of Reports of Cooperating Groups,' *International Conciliation,* no. 401 (June 1944).

groups would send reports expressing their views to the Committee. The reports were analyzed by the Committee which then prepared summaries and distributed them to the participating groups, the press, and appropriate government agencies and personnel.

The fourth Problem Analysis carried the title, 'Should There Be an International Organization for General Security against Military Aggression, and Should the United States Participate in Such an Organization?' All faculty groups participating in this Problem replied unanimously in the affirmative to the questions raised. The groups also agreed, with one exception, 'that no means other than an international organization prepared to use force against aggressors is likely to be successful in preserving peace.' There was widespread agreement that a postwar international organization should have an international police force to back up moral, economic, and military sanctions and international disarmament.

Under the chairmanship of Judge Manley O. Hudson, a number of American specialists in international law and organization consulted for several months in 1944, and later joined in issuing a 'Design for a Charter of the International Organization.'[4] The Design bears a strong resemblance to the suggestions of the Commission to Study the Organization of Peace, primarily because of the reasonableness of both proposals and also because many of the same specialists participated in both groups. It was far more detailed, however, and envisaged the entire community of states joined together in the organization, with its charter 'the basic instrument of the law of that community.' While participation in welfare acitvities would be on a voluntary basis, there would be positive obligations incumbent upon all states for the maintenance of peace. Emphasis was not placed upon a series of 'ready-made solutions of international problems.' Instead, the Design created 'agencies, procedures, and methods by which solutions might be sought in the future according to the wisdom of the time.'

Other organizations, such as the United States Chamber of Commerce and the American Federation of Labor had special committees working on the problems of the postwar period. Both of these groups, representing broad sections of American business and labor, endorsed the idea of a postwar international organization of which the United States should be a member. In addition, the Federal Council of Churches of Christ in America (now the National Council of Churches of Christ in the U.S.A.) established a Commission on a Just and Durable Peace which enthusiastically supported a postwar international organization.

[4] The full text is in *International Conciliation,* no. 402 (August 1944), pp. 527–42.

Official Declarations Favoring a Postwar International Organization. The first official intimation that there might be a postwar international organization to replace the League of Nations came on August 13, 1941, several months prior to the entry of the United States into World War II. On this date, President F. D. Roosevelt and Prime Minister Winston Churchill met at sea and drafted the now famous Atlantic Charter, essentially a listing of war aims. The eighth and final point in the Charter made a general reference to a 'permanent system of general security.' While such a statement was rather vague and committed neither the United States nor Britain to anything specific in the form of an international organization, it nevertheless revealed that the leaders of both nations were thinking about the future possibility of such an institution. Informal planning had already begun in the Department of State some months before the drafting of the Atlantic Charter, as it had also in the British Foreign Office.[5]

On January 1, 1942, the United Nations Declaration was signed by Roosevelt, Churchill, Litvinov of Russia, and Soong of China for their respective governments. By this declaration, the four nations (later joined by others who entered the war on the side of the United Nations) 'subscribed to a common program of purposes and principles' embodied in the Atlantic Charter and agreed to pursue the war jointly, each employing 'its full resources, military or economic,' against the common enemy.

The first positive commitment toward a postwar organization followed the meeting of foreign ministers of the Big Three at Moscow in October, 1943. Known as the Moscow Declaration on General Security, it was signed by representatives of Britain, the Soviet Union, and the United States, and later adhered to by the Chinese Ambassador to Moscow on behalf of China. The four nations jointly declared through their signatories that 'they recognize the necessity of establishing at the earliest practicable date a general international organization, based upon the sovereign equality of all peaceloving states, and open to membership by all such states, large and small, for the maintenance of international peace and security.' In addition, they agreed that 'for the purpose of maintaining international peace and security pending the reestablishment of law and order and the inauguration of a system of general security, they will consult with one another and as occasion requires with other members of the United Nations with a view to joint action on behalf of the community of nations.' They agreed, finally, to 'confer and cooperate with one another and with

[5] For the planning carried on in the State Department, consult Department of State, *Postwar Foreign Policy Preparation,* Publication 3580, General Foreign Policy Series 15, Washington, D.C., 1950.

other members of the United Nations to bring about a practicable general agreement with respect to the regulation of armaments in the postwar period.'

About a month after the Moscow Conference, President Roosevelt, Prime Minister Churchill, and Premier Stalin met at Teheran to plan common policy in the war. It was the first time that the three chiefs of state had met in person and it established a precedent for a close working relationship. On December 1, 1943, a Declaration of the Three Powers was issued, which signified a determination 'that our nations shall work together in war and in the peace that will follow.' They recognized the 'supreme responsibility resting upon us and all the United Nations to make a peace which will command the goodwill of the overwhelming mass of the peoples of the world and banish the scourge and terror of war for many generations.' They also declared that they desired 'the cooperation and active participation of all nations, large and small, whose peoples in heart and mind are dedicated, as are our own peoples, to the elimination of tyranny and slavery, oppression and intolerance. We will welcome them, as they may choose to come, into a world family of Democratic Nations.'

By the end of 1943, therefore, the great powers were firmly committed to a policy of establishing a postwar international organization for the maintenance of peace. Particularly significant was the fact that both the United States and Soviet Russia had placed in the public record their determination to participate in a universal security organization. By so doing, they in effect eliminated the fears of some who believed that these two major nations might in the postwar years return to policies of isolation and aloofness from the affairs of the world.

The Dumbarton Oaks Proposals. Planning toward a new security organization began in earnest within the appropriate government agencies in Soviet Russia, the United Kingdom, and the United States following the Moscow Declaration.[6] The sentiment of the United States Congress was expressed by the Connally Resolution of November 5, 1943, in the Senate, which recognized 'the necessity of there being established at the earliest practicable date a general international organization, based upon the principle of the sovereign equality of all peace-loving states, and open to membership by all such states, large and small, for the maintenance of international peace and security.' Earlier in the year at Hot Springs, Virginia, forty-four nations had met and planned the future Food and Agriculture Organization of the United Nations, which finally came into existence in October, 1945. In November, 1943, the United Nations Re-

[6] Great Britain, known officially by that appellation in the days of the League of Nations, is presently titled the United Kingdom.

lief and Rehabilitation Administration began its work. Preliminary discussions were also under way in 1943 which led to the Bretton Woods Conference in July, 1944, creating the instruments for the International Monetary Fund and the International Bank for Reconstruction and Development.

In this auspicious atmosphere, the United States early in 1944 suggested that the British, Russian, and American governments exchange proposals representing their views on the future international organization. During the course of these preliminary negotiations, the United States invited Britain, Soviet Russia, and China to send delegations for the purpose of formally discussing a possible charter for the organization. It was agreed that such a meeting would be held at Dumbarton Oaks, Washington, D.C., in two separate phases. American-British-Soviet conversations took place from August 21 to September 28, 1944. The Chinese delegation participated only with the United States and Britain from September 29 to October 7. Such an arrangement was believed necessary because of the fact that Soviet Russia at the time was not at war with Japan and did not wish to endanger her neutral status in the Pacific war.

The wide range of questions discussed by the Dumbarton Oaks participants is best illustrated in the following summary prepared by the Department of State:

> Should economic and social as well as security matters be included within the scope of the projected organization? Should provision be made for withdrawal from membership, for suspension of the rights of a member, and for expulsion of a member? What should be the composition of the body to give military advice to the Council? By what vote should the Council reach decisions? Should members of the Council that were parties to the dispute — including parties that were major nations with permanent membership on the Council — have the right to vote or be required to abstain from voting in decisions by the Council on the dispute? The latter was fundamental to the rights and obligations of members of the organization, to the relation of large and small nations, and to the basic principles on which the organization would function. The British came with the view that the votes of any parties to a dispute should not be taken into account. The American position, presented at this stage, was that a permanent member, like a nonpermanent member, should not vote in connection with a dispute to which it was a party. The Soviet representatives held the contrary view. There was, however, no question concerning the general requirement of unanimity of the permanent members in reaching decisions on non-procedural matters of peace and security, since from the outset there was no disagreement among the three governments on this provision.

After lengthy discussion there was basic agreement on a number of points which was made public under the title of 'The Dumbarton Oaks

Proposals.' The Proposals were certainly not a full draft of a completed organization, but nevertheless they provided the basic foundation for the Charter of the United Nations and represented the principal views of the participants. The organization envisaged had as its primary function the maintenance of international peace and security, although it was to seek 'international cooperation in the solution of international economic, social, and other humanitarian problems.' It was based upon the sovereign equality of all peace-loving states, and would include a General Assembly, consisting of all its members, possessed primarily of the power of discussing international problems and making recommendations. A Security Council would have the chief responsibility for the maintenance of international peace and security. The Council was to be provided with a complicated machinery for 'the peaceful settlement of disputes' and the 'determination of threats to the peace or acts of aggression and action with respect thereto.'

In addition to the Assembly and the Council, the Proposals called for a Secretariat, a Court, and 'such subsidiary agencies as may be found necessary.' An Economic and Social Council, under the authority of the Assembly, was, among other things, 'to make recommendations on its own initiative, with respect to international economic, social, and other humanitarian matters.' Regional arrangements were to be permitted, 'but no enforcement action should be taken . . . without the authorization of the Security Council.'

Several important questions were left unsolved, and were to become the subjects of later negotiations. Of these problems, the most serious was the failure to agree upon the voting formula of the Security Council. No agreement could be reached upon the initial membership of the organization. The Soviets had demanded that all of the sixteen Soviet republics be included as fullfledged, original members. The question of arrangements to take the place of the League of Nations mandates system was not explored, nor was there a decision upon the future status of the League itself. Postponed also was the question whether there should be a new international court or some arrangement devised to continue the Permanent Court of International Justice.

The Proposals were circulated among those states which had signed the Declaration of the United Nations with requests for comment and suggestions. At the same time, efforts were made by each of the states represented at Dumbarton Oaks to reach an accord with respect to some of the matters which had not been resolved at that conference. It was necessary, however, to have an additional meeting of the Big Three before solutions could be reached.

The Yalta Agreements. The final wartime conference between Roosevelt, Churchill, and Stalin occurred at Yalta in the Crimea between February 4 and 11, 1945. Much went on at Yalta which is of no concern to our immediate discussion, but which has had a vital effect upon the postwar world. An examination of such questions as the Soviet entry into the Pacific War, the problem of a defeated Germany, and the territorial adjustments in the Far East and Central Europe belongs to another story. However, at Yalta three decisions were made for the future international organization, in addition to the formulation of plans for a conference at which the final structure of that organization would be established in a formal charter.

The first and most important decision had to do with the voting procedure of the Security Council. The famous 'veto' was agreed to, whereby on all but procedural matters coming before the Council, the unanimous agreement of the permanent members (the Big Five) was required for action by the Council. In decisions involving the pacific settlement of disputes, the party to the controversy was to abstain from voting. Voting upon procedural questions called for the affirmative action of any seven members of the Council, irrespective of whether they were permanent members.

The second Yalta decision concerned the question of original membership in the organization. At Dumbarton Oaks, it will be recalled, the Soviet Union demanded the inclusion of all sixteen of her federated republics as independent, initial members. Just as valid a claim could have been put forth by the United States for the admittance of each of her forty-eight states. At Yalta, however, it was agreed that the United States and the United Kingdom would support the Russian claim for the admittance to original membership of the Ukraine and Byelorussia, two of the Soviet Republics. No other federal state was granted such a great privilege. All other nations that had declared war on 'the common enemy' were to be invited to participate in a United Nations Conference on International Organization to begin on April 25, 1945, in San Francisco. The Conference would be sponsored by China and France in addition to the Big Three.[7]

A final significant decision was to establish a trusteeship system to replace the League system of mandates. Territorial trusteeship was to apply only to '(a) existing mandates of the League of Nations; (b) territories detached from the enemy as a result of the present war; (c) any other territory which might voluntarily be placed under trusteeship.' There was to be no discussion at the forthcoming San Francisco Conference of the specific territories which might become a part of the trusteeship system.

The Yalta decisions eliminated most of the gaps in the Dumbarton Oaks

[7] The Provisional Government of France later decided not to become a sponsor of the Conference but did attend and participate in its proceedings.

Proposals, but were to be debated vigorously and with some bitterness in the weeks before San Francisco and particularly at the Conference itself.

Mexico City Conference on Problems of Peace and War. From February 21 to March 8, 1945, a special Inter-American Conference was held in Mexico City to discuss postwar problems of common interest to the Western Hemisphere. All the American Republics were present except Argentina. Toward the end of the Conference, the Dumbarton Oaks Proposals were studied rather hastily. The various delegations, however, were extremely interested in the Proposals and considered them to be acceptable only as a basis for later discussion. Many delegations believed the Proposals to be inadequate and served notice that at San Francisco the Proposals would be carefully scrutinized with a view toward adding a number of features which had been either neglected or treated rather lightly.

Somewhat to the displeasure of the United States, the Mexico City Conference adopted Resolution XXX, which was entitled, 'On the Establishment of a General International Organization.' The Resolution was a clear indication of some of the fundamental doubts about Dumbarton Oaks which were shared by Latin American states. In the Resolution, the American Republics observed that the Dumbarton Oaks Proposals 'are capable of certain improvements.' The signatories stated that it would be 'useful for the United Nations not represented in this Conference to have a synthesis of the views expressed in it, and it would also be very valuable if those nations were to communicate to the Governments of the American Republics here present, prior to the Conference at San Francisco, their views regarding the Dumbarton Oaks Proposals.'

The Resolution further resolved that the views expressed by the Conference concerning Dumbarton Oaks be transmitted to the Dumbarton Oaks Powers and to the San Francisco conference itself, especially a number of points 'regarding which a concensus exists among the American Republics represented in this Conference that did not participate in the Dumbarton Oaks conversations.' These points included the following:

(a) The aspiration of universality as an ideal toward which the Organization should tend in the future;

(b) The desirability of amplifying and making more specific the enumeration of the principles and purposes of the Organization;

(c) The desirability of amplifying and making more specific the powers of the General Assembly in order that its action, as the fully representative organ of the international community may be rendered effective, harmonizing the powers of the Security Council with such amplification;

(d) The desirability of extending the jurisdiction and competence of the International Tribunal or Court of Justice;

(e) The desirability of creating an international agency specially charged with promoting intellectual and moral cooperation among nations;

(f) The desirability of solving controversies and questions of an inter-American character, preferably in accordance with inter-American methods and procedures, in harmony with those of the General International Organization;

(g) The desirability of giving an adequate representation to Latin America on the Security Council.

Attached to the Resolution were a number of documents expressing the individual views of certain American Republics. These, taken together with the opinions expressed in the Resolution, were of particular significance in that they reflected many of the views of other small nations outside the Western Hemisphere and gave an indication of the problems which arose between the large and small states at San Francisco.

THE SAN FRANCISCO CONFERENCE: ORGANIZATION

On March 5, 1945, invitations were issued to the United Nations Conference on International Organization by the United States in the names of the sponsoring states. Delegations from forty-six states were present when the Conference convened in opening session on April 25 in San Francisco. This total represented the entire list of sponsoring and invited governments. Soon after the Conference got under way, the governments of Argentina, the Byelorussian Soviet Socialist Republic, and the Ukrainian Soviet Socialist Republic received invitations and sent delegates. Denmark was represented on June 5, following the liberation of its territory from the Germans. Soviet Russia endeavored to have the Conference admit the Soviet sponsored government of Poland but was turned down. The Russians did manage, however, to have a place reserved for Poland to sign the Charter as an original member. At San Francisco, therefore, there were fifty participating delegations and, with Poland, a total of fifty-one signatories of the Charter.

The Conference was attended by 282 delegates representing the fifty participating nations. More than 1500 specialists and staff members advised the delegates. A Secretariat of over 1000 aided the delegates with technical and other assistance. As is customary at international conferences, the host country provides the personnel of the secretariat. This was true at San Francisco, except for a small number of persons serving from outside the United States. Many members of the Secretariat were recruited from the Department of State and from academic circles. Specialists in their own right, they served as secretaries of the various commissions and committees, frequently drafting important reports and making available their own skills and training to the delegates. A great deal of time was spent by many of these technicians in processing documents by the hundreds, and in performing routine but essential duties as librarians, translators, security officers, and interpreters.

The Secretariat was headed by a Secretary-General, Mr. Alger Hiss, from the Department of State. Immediately responsible to the Secretary-General were such services as protocol, cultural activities, information, security, admissions, comptroller, press relations, presentations, and photography. Other administrative activities of the Conference were divided into two major groups, headed by an Executive Secretary and an Administrative Secretary.

The Executive Secretary, Mr. C. Easton Rothwell, was responsible for such substantive aspects of the Conference as interpreting and translating, library facilities, the preparation, printing, and distribution of documents, and general secretarial services. The Administrative Secretary, Mr. William D. Wright, directed the various finance, personnel, medical, transportation, and communications services for the Conference.

English and French were adopted as the 'working' languages, and English, French, Russian, Spanish, and Chinese, the official languages. All documents were issued in each of the five official languages. Speeches in English were interpreted into French or vice versa. If a speech was presented in any other language, it was reproduced in both French and English. The amount of work involved in preparing documents in these different languages was a huge burden on the Secretariat, as can be seen from the fact that the Conference consumed seventy-eight tons of paper for documentation.

The great majority of delegates were distinguished representatives of their governments. Many nations sent their top political and diplomatic officials. Representing Britain were Eden, Halifax, Atlee, Cadogan, and Cranborne; while France sent Bidault, Paul-Boncour, and Basdevant. Molotov led the delegation from the Soviet Union. Also in attendance were such able personages as Evatt of Australia; Fraser of New Zealand; Spaak, Rolin, and DeSchryver of Belgium; Smuts of South Africa; Lie of Norway; Romulo of the Philippines; Masaryk of Czechoslovakia; Kleffens and Van Mook of the Netherlands; King and St. Laurent of Canada; Bech of Luxembourg; and Koo and Soong of China.

The seating of Argentina on April 30 completed the full representation from Latin America. The delegates from this bloc of twenty American states conducted themselves with distinction and at times were quite vocal in discussion and debate. Outstanding contributions were made by such skillful diplomats as Padilla, Tello, and Castillo Najera of Mexico; Belt of Cuba; Lleras of Colombia; González Videla of Chile; and Galo Plaza of Ecuador.

The Arab world, representing another bloc of states, was also quite active at San Francisco and rarely missed an opportunity to make suggestions on important issues. Particularly outstanding were Pasha Badawi of Egypt and Charles Malik of Lebanon.

The largest delegation at San Francisco, quite naturally, was that of the host nation, the United States. Eight official delegates had been appointed by President Roosevelt prior to his death. They included Secretary of State Edward R. Stettinius, Jr. as Chairman; Cordell Hull, former Secretary of State, as senior adviser (who did not attend, due to ill health); the chairman and ranking minority members of the House and Senate Foreign Relations Committees: Senators Connally and Vandenberg, and Representatives Bloom and Éaton; Dean Virginia Gildersleeve of Barnard College representing women; and Harold Stassen. The remainder of the more than 350-man delegation consisted of alternate delegates, special advisers from the State Department and other government departments, military specialists, political and civilian advisers, and a large administrative and technical staff. Private national organizations were invited to send representatives as consultants to the delegation, and forty-two of them responded.

While it is customary for the foreign minister of the host country to be selected as the presiding officer of an important international conference, this was not the case at San Francisco. At the insistence of the Soviet Union, it was agreed at the opening sessions that the presidency would be rotated among the four sponsoring governments. This view was supported by Britain on the ground that a sharing of the presidency would provide support for the appearance of unity among the Big Four. Consequently, there was a different presiding officer for each of the plenary sessions. Stettinius, however, became chairman of the Steering Committee and the Executive Committee.

On April 30, the fifth plenary session adopted the report of the Steering Committee and thereby established the permanent organization of the Conference. Thus, it was agreed that there should be four general committees, four commissions, and twelve technical committees. The general committees consisted of: the Steering Committee, which included the chairmen of all delegations; the Executive Committee, composed of the chairmen of the delegations from the sponsoring governments, in addition to ten other governments (Australia, Brazil, Canada, Chile, Czechoslovakia, France, Iran, Mexico, the Netherlands, Yugoslavia); the Co-ordination

Committee, made up of one representative from each state represented on the Executive Committee; and the Credentials Committee, consisting of one representative each from Ecuador, Luxembourg, Nicaragua, Saudi Arabia, Syria, and Yugoslavia, chaired by Luxembourg.

The Steering Committee was empowered to consider any major policy or procedural question submitted to it during the Conference by the co-Presidents or by the chairman of any delegation. The Executive Committee made recommendations to the Steering Committee for its consideration and served to aid the latter whenever necessary. The Co-ordination Committee served primarily to assist the Executive Committee in the performance of the latter's functions. The Credentials Committee verified the delegates' credentials and reported to the Conference in plenary session. In addition, there was an Advisory Committee of Jurists which provided legal assistance to the general committees.

The Conference itself was divided into four commissions, each with a president and a rapporteur nominated by the Steering Committee and approved by the Conference in plenary session. An Assistant Secretary-General of the Conference, chosen in a similar manner, was assigned to each of the commissions. Each commission, in turn, had a number of technical committees, with chairmen and rapporteurs nominated by the Steering Committee and approved by the Conference in plenary session. Additional subcommittees were established as needed. Each commission developed general principles to guide its technical committees and subcommittees. They considered the recommendations of their technical committees 'and the relationships of such recommendations to those made by technical committees of other commissions.' The commissions also recommended 'to the Conference in plenary session proposed texts for adoption as parts of the Charter.' All delegations were represented on each commission and on each of their technical committees. Each delegation was entitled to one vote on the commissions and committees, just as each had one vote in plenary sessions.

The commissions and their technical committees were established as follows:

Commission I: General Provisions
    Committee I/1   Preamble, Purposes, and Principles
    Committee I/2   Membership, Amendment, and Secretariat

Commission II: General Assembly
    Committee II/1   Structure and Procedures
    Committee II/2   Political and Security Functions
    Committee II/3   Economic and Social Co-operation
    Committee II/4   Trusteeship System

Commission III: Security Council
    Committee III/1   Structure and Procedures
    Committee III/2   Peaceful Settlement
    Committee III/3   Enforcement Arrangements
    Committee III/4   Regional Arrangements

Commission IV: Judicial Organization
    Committee IV/1   International Court of Justice
    Committee IV/2   Legal Problems

The various commissions and committee officers had been decided upon in most cases by the Steering Committee prior to the convening of the Conference. Selections were based primarily on the theory of awarding these positions to the smaller countries and not as a recognition of individual competence and skill. While in some instances the selections proved to be excellent, too many of these officers did not measure up to their jobs. Some had had little previous parliamentary experience, while others were not familiar with the subject matter assigned to their commissions or committees. Language difficulties were evident in some instances where committee chairmen or rapporteurs were not equipped to do business in either English or French.

The Conference decided at the beginning that the agenda was to consist of the Dumbarton Oaks Proposals together with amendments proposed by any delegation. Hundreds of changes and amendments were offered during the first days of the Conference, and far exceeded in number the items agreed to at Dumbarton Oaks. As soon as all the additional proposals could be assembled under the appropriate Dumbarton Oaks headings, each of the commissions as noted above were assigned specific portions of the agenda. The actual work of the Conference was carried on by the committees and their subcommittees. The commissions had relatively little to do and served little useful purpose other than receiving the recommendations of their committees and reporting them to the Conference for final approval in plenary sessions. The meetings of the commissions were open to the public, as were the plenary sessions of the Conference. The committee meetings, however, were restricted to those possessing official credentials.

Once in possession of the Dumbarton Oaks Proposals and the numerous suggestions for their amendment, the committees were left to work out their own methods of operation, except for the voting procedure. As was true for all bodies of the Conference, voting on procedural matters required only a bare majority, while a two-thirds vote of those present and voting was necessary for the affirmative passage of substantive matters. Much of the committee work was done by subcommittees, which prepared working summaries of all points under discussion, reported on technical matters, and drafted texts for final voting. Frequently joint subcommittees were employed to arrive at decisions concerning two or more committees. Informal meetings were held between committee chairmen and rapporteurs for purposes of correlating the work assigned a commission. Most committees met daily and toward the end of the Conference were forced to hold two sessions a day. Such a full schedule became a burden to the smaller delegations, in which individual members had to participate in the deliberations of more than one committee. Time limitations also made it difficult for delegations to meet in daily caucus for the purpose of determining the stand to be taken on important problems constantly arising during committee sessions.

Full discussion and debate was permitted on all points considered in committee. Once decisions had been reached, the texts of recommendations were forwarded to the appropriate commission where, although rarely done, debate and discussion on all points could be reopened. The Co-ordination Committee had the burdensome task of bringing consistency to various committee texts and arriving at a decision upon the arrangement of the several sections of the Charter. Problems over phraseology and style were frequent and, in some instances, there were contradictory aspects of committee texts which had to be resolved. The Co-ordination Committee could not change matters of substance, but even changes in phraseology often required original committee approval which was time consuming. The Advisory Committee of Jurists was able to assist the Co-ordination Committee on points of a legal nature, but was not utilized as much as had been expected due to the over-all competence of those individuals serving on the Co-ordination Committee.

On the whole, the organization of the Conference worked fairly well although there were certain defects which undoubtedly contributed toward making the completed Charter less technically perfect than it might otherwise have been. Overlapping committee assignments and the general over-organization of the Conference itself resulted in a lack of clarity and precision in some parts of the document. Some of the technical defects of the Charter can be attributed to the repeated demands of the Conference leadership for a rapid completion of the Charter. A more leisurely pace would have worked fewer hardships on the busy delegates and the harried Secretariat. However, the completion of a document as significant and complicated as the Charter in a little more than two months was a major accomplishment. Many of the delegates and most of the overworked Secretariat had never participated in an important international conference, much less in a conference as large and significant as the one at San Francisco. While the technical shortcomings of the Charter are evident, its major defects were due primarily to the political differences which inevitably became the compelling issues between the participating governments.

TENSIONS, ISSUES, AND POLITICS AT SAN FRANCISCO

The atmosphere at San Francisco was charged with tension directly or indirectly attributable to the fact that the war in Europe and particularly in the Pacific continued as the delegates were debating a postwar organization to maintain a peace which had not been achieved. Several of the delegations represented governments-in-exile whose countries were liberated during the course of the Conference. Some of these delegates had been out of contact with their own peoples for several years and had to proceed with Conference responsibilities not knowing whether their views represented adequately the public opinion at home. Important members of the Belgian, Dutch, and French delegations were forced to leave the Conference and return to more pressing duties in their home countries. Others were in the position of the Prime Minister of New Zealand, Mr. Peter Fraser, who had to conduct New Zealand affairs of state by long distance as well as lead his delegation at the Conference. Important military and political decisions consumed a large share of the time of the principal delegates whose countries were still waging total war in the Pacific.

Although it might appear from the foregoing that it was a mistake to hold a conference on postwar international organization while the war was still in progress, there were compelling reasons for having the San Francisco Conference convene when it did. It is entirely probable that had it not been for the insistence of the United States speaking through the late President Roosevelt, the Conference would have been postponed at least until the end of the war, if not indefinitely. Roosevelt and many Americans were convinced of the necessity of distinguishing between a peace conference and a conference devoted exclusively to the task of establishing an international organization. Informed circles pointed out the difficulties encountered by the League of Nations through having the Peace Treaties of the First World War and the Covenant tied together at the Versailles Conference in 1919. Roosevelt was determined to avoid this arrangement. He was also anxious to capitalize upon the wartime co-operation enjoyed by the United Nations against the Axis Powers and believed that there would be immeasurable benefits to a conference meeting at a period of such military co-operation.

Great Powers. Roosevelt did not live to see the wartime collaboration he valued so highly break down, but evidences of what has come to be the total collapse of East-West co-operation could be seen at San Francisco. While on the surface the Big Five presented a more or less solid front, Soviet intransigence and suspicions did not contribute to political harmony. The United States was in a peculiarly difficult position among the Big Five, chiefly because the United States could not permit the Conference to end in failure. This country, through a widespread press campaign, had committed itself so irrevocably to a policy of postwar support for a universal international organization, that the failure to establish such a body would greatly encourage a return to the more traditional American sentiment of isolationism. The United States, therefore, was forced to yield on the one hand to Soviet pressures while at the same time seeking to appease the views of the numerically powerful small states which were frequently at odds with the stand of the Big Five and the Dumbarton Oaks Proposals.

In this uncomfortable position, the United States usually found reassuring support from the British. Mr. Anthony Eden, the British Foreign Secretary, was forever mindful of the traditional role of Britain as a mediator of international conflicts, and steered the British course accordingly at San Francisco. He and his delegation were extremely active in all important deliberations and decisions of the Conference. They were anxious to establish an organization which was not too powerful, and which would place an emphasis on the machinery of mediation.

France had little influence and was concerned primarily with the problems of her liberated country. Similarly, China remained more or less on the sidelines, unwilling to take a stand which would place support firmly on either the Anglo-American or Soviet side when there were policy conflicts among the Big Five.

In addition, the position of the United States delegation was a delicate one, in that it had to create an organization, the character of which would meet with general American approval and at the same time satisfy the requirements of a sensitive United States Senate. According to public sentiment in the United States, such an organization should never possess the attributes of a superstate or endanger the sovereign independence of the nation. This was a view endorsed especially in the Senate where strong isolationist tendencies were still held by powerful members. At the same time, the American public believed that the future organization should possess power adequate to preserve the peace and abolish war, apparently unaware of the contradictions inherent in these views. An international organization possessed of sufficient coercive authority to put an end to war, necessarily must infringe upon the sovereign equality of all states, particularly that of the large powers who are the most dangerous potential aggressors.

The Soviet Union was interested almost exclusively in the establishment of an organization which would in no way limit her freedom of action. Molotov and Gromyko took the position that the big powers had won the war in Europe and should have the responsibility of supervising the postwar world. Policy should be determined in the Security Council where the middle- and small-sized nations would be prevented from binding any of the major powers to a course of action which might prove inimical to national interests. The Soviets were, therefore, committed to the preservation of the Dumbarton Oaks Proposals which, as we have seen, virtually guaranteed the principle of great-power supremacy. This position, from which they could not be dislodged, brought the Soviets into a head-on clash with the more determined of the smaller states. Furthermore, Soviet Russia capitalized upon the fears of the United States and Britain that the Soviets might leave the Conference unless their demands were met.

Small Powers. Standing in contrast to the position of the great powers as represented by the Dumbarton Oaks Proposals were various groups and blocs of smaller nations. These states were by no means unified in their views, but most of them undertook the task of weakening the privileged status granted the Big Five at the Dumbarton Oaks meeting. Some of them, such as Australia, Belgium, Canada, the Netherlands, and Brazil took the lead in attempting to better the position of the lesser states in the Charter. Indeed, the members of the British Commonwealth did not vote as a bloc with Britain, but actively opposed the British support of Big Five hegemony.

The largest bloc of states came from Latin America and while they did not vote as one on all occasions, their twenty votes proved to be formidable when a two-thirds vote was required. In addition, the United States could not afford to antagonize these neighbors in the Western Hemisphere and consequently had to listen to their problems and demands.

Numerically much smaller but strategically located in the Middle East were the Arab states. They voted regularly as a bloc on many issues, particularly with regard to trusteeship matters. The United Kingdom, with vital interests in the Middle East, was forced to heed as many of the Arab complaints and demands as possible.

Taken as a whole, the smaller nations, informally but skillfully led by Dr. Evatt of Australia, were as difficult to cope with as the Soviet Union. Ably supported by Fraser of New Zealand, Rolin of Belgium, and the Canadian and Brazilian delegations, Dr. Evatt fought to strengthen the power of the General Assembly and the International Court of Justice with a consequent weakening of Security Council authority. The small states had relatively little to lose from the creation of a truly strong international organization where their rights could not be swept aside through the unilateral action of one of the Big Five on the Security Council. Thus the battlelines were drawn between those, led by the Soviet Union, who thought in terms of great power domination in a sort of revived Concert of Europe, and the host of smaller nations, inspired by Evatt and his cohorts, who argued for an organization of freedom-loving states united in their determination to solve common problems in a democratic manner. The most crucial issue inevitably centered around the Yalta voting formula. On this and other similar controversies concerning the privileged position of the great powers, the small nations lost out. However, they did manage to gain certain compromises and a clarification and liberalization of the Dumbarton Oaks Proposals in a number of instances.

Voting in the Security Council. The smaller states were particularly upset by the authority granted each of the Big Five at Yalta to veto such matters as sanctions and general enforcement procedures, admission and expulsion of members, amendments to the Charter, disarmament measures, and the appointment of a Secretary-General. No less than seventeen delegations at the opening of the Conference offered amendments to the proposed voting procedure.

The task of working on the voting formula fell to Committee III/1, where the entire question was debated at length, and frequently with bitterness. In fact, Room 223 in the Veterans Building where the Committee held its many heated sessions was dubbed Madison Square Garden. The Australian delegate, Dr. Evatt, led the attack against the veto, seeking to narrow its applicability and widen the scope of questions which might be considered procedural. He sought particularly to prevent the veto from becoming applicable to any of the processes of peaceful settlement. As the debate progressed, it became clear that many aspects of the veto had become confused, and a subcommittee was appointed to bring about some clarification of the disputed issues. A questionnaire composed of twenty-two doubtful points and one addendum was drafted and submitted to the sponsoring governments for their views. Each important action assigned to the Security Council was noted and the question raised as to the applicability of the veto. All the principal phases of conciliation were listed. Could the veto apply to the selection of the Secretary-General and his deputies? Even the problem of the infamous double veto appeared on the questionnaire, as follows: 'In case a decision has to be taken as to whether a certain point is a procedural matter, is that preliminary question to be considered in itself as a procedural matter or is the veto applicable to such a preliminary question?'

The answer to the questionnaire came in the form of a joint and unanimous statement from the great powers. Some of the confused points were clarified while others remained unanswered. It was clear, however, that the sponsoring governments were adamant in their support of the veto. This can be gathered from Section 9 of the reply, which stated:

> In view of the primary responsibilities of the permanent members, they could not be expected, in the present condition of the world, to assume the obligation to act in so serious a matter as the maintenance of international peace and security in consequence of a decision in which they had not concurred. Therefore, if a majority voting in the Security Council is to be made possible, the only practicable method is to provide, in respect of nonprocedural decisions, for unanimity of the permanent members plus the concurring votes of at least two of the non-permanent members.

One concession was granted by the major powers. The Soviet Union, which had originally demanded that the veto cover even the consideration of a dispute by the Security Council, now relented. Accordingly, the reply observed that 'no individual member of the Council can alone prevent consideration and discussion of a dispute or situation brought to its attention . . .'

This dispensation did not satisfy many of the smaller nations. Dr. Evatt issued a printed memorandum which represented their views admirably and laid down the principal arguments against the great power veto. He observed that 'the interpretation given by the joint statement is not based upon any consistent principle [and] answers directly only one of the 22 questions, though these were asked at the suggestion of the sponsoring Governments themselves. The answer they would have given to some of the questions is reasonably clear, but in others the matter is left altogether at large. In a few instances the correctness of the answer implied is open to grave question.' After pointing out what he and others believed to be incorrect interpretations of the veto, Dr. Evatt then stated:

> The net effect of the joint statement is that 'consideration and discussion by the Council' is the only matter . . . that cannot be blocked by a permanent member. It is important to understand that the words 'consideration and discussion' are used in the joint statement in a much narrower sense than they ordinarily bear. In ordinary speech 'consideration' of a dispute would include calling for reports, hearing witnesses, or even the appointment of a commission of investigation. The joint statement, however, treats the veto as applicable to a decision to use any of those procedures. It is only 'consideration and discussion' of a very preliminary and restricted character that is free of the veto. It may be said that, without veto, the Council can only discuss

whether a dispute can be discussed, and can only investigate whether it should be investigated.

The importance of the fact that such consideration and discussion is free of the veto must not be underestimated, and the joint statement represents a substantial advance over a blanket veto. On the other hand, a system for the peaceful settlement of disputes in which everything except preliminary consideration and discussion of this limited character *is* to be subject to the veto is not an effective method of conciliation. . . .

The matter stands at present in so confused a condition that, if the present text of the voting procedure stands without amendment, steps should be taken to secure the opinion of the International Court of Justice on the question of interpretation involved.

But the simpler, and preferable, course is to make sure by amendment that the veto is clearly inapplicable to any decision of the Security Council under the section dealing with the peaceful settlement of disputes.

Dr. Evatt then proceeded to offer an amendment which would require that decisions by the Security Council which were concerned with peaceful settlement would be classified as procedural and hence not subject to the veto. In the ensuing debate, the proponents of the veto made it quite clear that there would be no alteration of the voting formula. On June 12, 1945, the voting on Dr. Evatt's amendment showed only ten states voting in its favor (Australia, Brazil, Chile, Colombia, Iran, Mexico, the Netherlands, New Zealand, and Panama), and twenty against it, with fifteen abstentions. Those who failed to vote were favorably disposed toward the amendment but were convinced that its passage would result in a break-up of the Conference. When the final vote occurred on the entire voting formula, it passed with thirty affirmative votes, two negative votes (Cuba and Colombia), and fifteen abstentions. Had the fifteen abstaining states voted in the negative with Cuba and Colombia, the Yalta formula would have been defeated because of the failure to secure the required two-thirds vote.

The defeat of the Australian amendment virtually ended the crisis over the voting formula for the Security Council. Others, however, sought to limit the great power hegemony in the Council by offering amendments designed to enlarge its size, making it more representative and thereby reducing the importance of the Big Five. Some tried to eliminate the provision for permanent membership or to cut down the number of concurring votes by permanent members.

Another attempt to narrow the use of the veto centered around the efforts of some small nations to define acts of aggression. Through various amendments there was proposed a list of eventualities in which intervention by the Security Council would be automatic, thereby removing certain actions from a possible veto. Although strongly supported, such proposals were steadfastly opposed by the sponsoring governments and their supporters, and were defeated. Some believed that modern warfare rendered too difficult the task of defining all cases of aggression. The great powers argued further that a definition of aggression 'went beyond the possibilities of this Conference and the purpose of the Charter.' They argued rather effectively that an automatic system against aggression was too inflexible and might result in the Council taking action despite disagreement over the identification of the aggressor and the steps which should be adopted.

In the course of the lengthy debate, a number of delegations indicated that they might be more favorably inclined to accept the voting formula demanded by the sponsoring governments if Charter revisions were not in the future subject to the veto. It was argued that while the permanent members of the Security Council were protected against amendments they opposed, this was not the case with the rest of the members of the proposed organization. The small states could not block an amendment which they considered inappropriate, nor could they secure the adoption of changes deemed necessary if only one of the Big Five disapproved. Some even claimed that constitutional restrictions in their countries would make it impossible for them to become members of the organization if they would be required to abide by amendments which they had refused to accept in good faith.

Sir A. Ramaswami Mudaliar of India, supported forcefully by Australia, led the spirited attack against permitting the use of the veto on Charter amendments. Most of the argument on this point occurred in Committee I/2 and continued even after the debate on the voting formula had ended in Committee III/1. The Indian delegate observed that he and several other delegations had reluctantly voted in favor of the Security Council voting formula in the belief that the veto would not apply to amendments proposed in the future. Others stated that it would be much easier to gain support at home for the Charter if there were a more flexible method of amendment. The sponsoring powers, however, fearful lest their predominant position be weakened, stood adamantly for the veto over amendments. The Report of the Rapporteur of Committee I/2 provides interesting evidence of the great power stand on this point in the following passage: '. . . representatives of the sponsoring governments declared that these powers could not enter upon the great responsibilities and obligations of membership which they were prepared to accept if forced to take the risk that these responsibilities might be increased without their consent.' The Soviet Union was especially outspoken on this issue, arguing that changes made in the Charter without protection of the veto would 'threaten the unanimity of the major powers' and eventually lead to the elimination of the veto itself.

One slight concession was granted by the sponsoring powers to off-set the demands of the small states on Charter amendments. They agreed to permit the calling of a United Nations Conference to review any portion of the Charter if two-thirds of the Assembly and any seven members of the Security Council so voted. Such a conference would be placed on the agenda of the Assembly by a similar vote in ten years if no reviewing conference had been held before that time. However, any revision of the Charter, whether proposed by a conference or through the ordinary amending procedure, would be subject to the veto by any of the Big Five.

Regional Arrangements. The question of regional arrangements outside the United Nations presented another specific problem. The Dumbarton Oaks Proposals had noted that 'nothing in the Charter should preclude the existence of regional arrangements or agencies,' and provided that 'The Security Council should encourage settlement of local disputes through such regional arrangements or by such regional agencies, either on the initiative of the states concerned or by reference from the Security Council.' These general provisions are continued in the Charter but have been broadened due to the insistence of many delegations. Committee III/4 was assigned the task of examining three categories of amendments which were concerned with various aspects of enforcement action.

The Latin American bloc, supported by the United States, sought to protect the traditional policy of nonintervention from outside the Western Hemisphere in the affairs of the Americas. The Act of Chapultepec, signed in March, 1945, at the Mexico City Conference, contained a provision for collective action by all American states against aggression, re-gardless of its source. The American delegations were particularly anxious to guarantee that the Security Council would not be in a position to pre-vent such collective action on their part.

Similarly, several other delegations, principally European, wished to safeguard the protection afforded by mutual defense pacts and guarantee their continuance without being endangered by action of the Security Council.

A third series of amendments sought to provide the right of regional agencies to act should the Security Council fail to undertake the solution of a dispute. Australia proposed that 'If the Security Council does not itself take measures, and does not authorize action to be taken under a regional arrangement or agency, for maintaining or restoring international peace, nothing in this Charter shall be deemed to abrogate the right of the parties to any arrangement which is consistent with this Charter to adopt such measures as they deem just and necessary for maintaining or restoring international peace and security in accordance with that arrangement.' The Belgian delegation cleverly sought to limit the veto power of the Security Council over regional enforcement action with the following proposal: 'Dissentient votes of permanent members of the Council which are not parties to such arrangements or agencies will not impair the validity of a decision of the Council in this respect.'

After lengthy discussion the inherent features of these amendments were embodied in the Charter. It permits 'individual and collective self-defense . . . against armed attack' and thereby satisfied the demands of American and European delegates. Dumbarton Oaks was broadened to allow regional enforcement action prior to the time when the Security Council has authorized measures necessary to maintain international peace and security. It is conceivable that the United States, with a view toward safeguarding the Americas, would use the veto to prevent Security Council action which might prejudice the agencies of American regionalism. On the other hand, it is possible for American regional arrangements to operate against the United States if the Council deemed such action to come under the heading of collective defense against armed attack.

The Charter provisions on regionalism do not, as requested by some, identify the meaning of regionalism. The Egyptian delegation proposed an amendment which would have defined regionalism as follows:

> There shall be considered as regional arrangements, organizations of a permanent nature grouping in a given geographical area several countries which, by reason of their proximity, community of interests, or cultural, linguistic, historical, or spiritual affinities, make themselves jointly responsible for the peaceful settlement of any disputes which may arise between them and for the safeguarding of their interests and the development of their economic and cultural relations.

A subcommittee of Committee III/4 considered this amendment and observed that even though it 'clearly defined obvious legitimate and eligible factors for a regional arrangement,' it nevertheless was much too limited in its scope and thus would eliminate such arrangements as mutual assistance treaties.

Use of Armed Forces of Members by the Security Council. Certain ambiguities were removed from the original Dumbarton Oaks text which led to a clarification of the method by which the Security Council would be granted the necessary armed forces should military sanctions be needed.

Agreements are to be concluded between member-states or groups and the Security Council instead of a 'special agreement or agreements concluded among themselves' as called for in the Proposals.

Noteworthy, also, was a provision added at the insistence of Canada and other smaller states which makes it possible for a nation contributing armed forces to the Security Council to participate in the decisions of the Council when there is a discussion of the manner in which its armed forces are to be employed. Canada originally requested that such a nation be made a member of the Security Council when this contingency arose. This type of arrangement was held to be unwieldly by the Committee studying the problem, and Canada agreed to the modification. In spite of the protests of some delegations, notably the Egyptians, the same right of participation was not granted to members furnishing only 'assistance and facilities.'

Economic and Social Matters. The economic and social provisions of the Proposals were greatly enlarged at San Francisco. It was made clear that the future organization would not be permitted to intervene in social or economic affairs of its members, these being matters solely within their domestic jurisdiction. The Economic and Social Council was increased in importance and its status solidified as one of the principal organs of the Organization. Its functions and duties were made more comprehensive and it was granted the important power to prepare draft conventions with respect to matters within its competence for submission to the General Assembly. It was also given the authority to call special international conferences on such matters and, with the permission of the Assembly, perform services if requested by members of the organization or the specialized agencies.

Colonial Questions. No decision was reached at Dumbarton Oaks on what should be done with the mandates system of the League of Nations or the arrangements which might have to be worked out for other colonial areas. These problems were fully explored at San Francisco, resulting in special Chapters in the Charter being devoted to non-self-governing territories and an international trusteeship system with a Trusteeship Council organized in the same fashion as the Economic and Social Council and possessing the status of a principal organ of the organization.

International Court of Justice. The governments represented at Dumbarton Oaks made no effort to build the framework for an international court. The Proposals noted that there ought to be 'an international court of justice which should constitute the principal judicial organ of the Organization.' No decision was reached on whether to continue the Permanent Court of International Justice or to create a new court along similar lines. In February, 1945, following the Yalta Conference, members of the

United Nations were invited by the sponsoring governments to send delegates to a meeting in Washington to prepare the draft of a statute for the Court. This preliminary conference created the United Nations Committee of Jurists which drafted a statute and submitted it to the San Francisco Conference for deliberation and decision.

The delegates at San Francisco were divided over the question of a new court or the continuation of the old. Some held strongly to the view that the Permanent Court of International Justice, a highly respected and authoritative body of jurists, should be retained for the sake of continuity. Others, while in general accord with this position, nevertheless believed that it would be far wiser to have a new court established to work closely with the new organization. After careful deliberation, the proponents of a new court were victorious and the Conference adopted a statute creating the International Court of Justice.

INTERIM ARRANGEMENTS

On June 26, 1945, at ten-minute intervals, the delegates of fifty nations signed the Charter of the United Nations. The Charter represents a tremendous amount of work undertaken and completed in a short space of time. Despite its length, its complicated and often repetitious features, the Charter represents a definite achievement in international organization and is worthy of the time and effort expended on its behalf. The Conference managed to succeed in spite of the tensions of a war only partially won and in spite of the inevitable suspicions, jealousies, and vagaries of politics. All of the delegates were not completely satisfied with their finished product, nor was public opinion in their home countries free from criticism. Nevertheless, a new security organization had been established, and this was the purpose of the Conference at San Francisco.

Once the Charter had been signed at San Francisco, it became imperative to have the necessary preparatory steps taken so that the United Nations could begin to function as an organization. To this end, the delegations at San Francisco on June 26, 1945, signed what were known as Interim Arrangements which created a Preparatory Commission 'for the purpose of making provisional arrangements' for the first meetings of the principal organs of the United Nations. The Preparatory Commission was also assigned such duties as recommending a site for the permanent location of the organization, transferring certain functions and activities of the League of Nations to the United Nations, and preparing a provisional agenda for the General Assembly and other principal agencies of the United Nations.

The Preparatory Commission, consisting of one member for each signatory state of the Charter, had its seat in London and was assisted by Sir Gladwyn Jebb of the British Foreign Office as Executive Secretary. An Executive Committee of fourteen (the same states represented on the Executive Committee of the San Francisco Conference) was empowered to act in the name of the Commission. All signatories were represented by full delegations at London.

Although the Charter did not receive the requisite number of ratifications until October 24, 1945, the Executive Committee first met in London on August 16, 1945, and established working subcommittees. In less than two months, the ten subcommittees completed their assigned duties and the Executive Committee was able to begin drafting a report for consideration by the full Preparatory Commission. The latter body first met on November 26, 1945, and created eight technical committees to study the report of its Executive Committee. The Commission experienced far more dissension than had the Executive Committee but managed to gain enough agreement so that a final report was adopted on December 23, 1945.

The General Assembly held its first historic session on January 10, 1946 in London. The Assembly and the other principal organs of the United Nations established in 1946 were greatly indebted to the Preparatory Commission and adopted many of the recommendations contained in its final report, particularly with respect to their internal governance and rules of procedure.

II

THE UNITED NATIONS SYSTEM

5

THE ORGANIZATIONAL FRAMEWORK

OF THE UNITED NATIONS

IT IS perhaps best to observe at the outset what the United Nations 'is not.' It is not a superstate, and it does not encompass a world government. By no means does it represent a federal type of government. It does not have the authority to legislate or tax, nor does it have the power to enforce its decisions upon individuals. The United Nations is, essentially, an association of states that, through a multipartite treaty — the Charter — have elected to follow a certain course of action in given circumstances in order to accomplish specific aims and purposes.

At San Francisco the delegates guaranteed that the United Nations be composed of independent states by stating in Article 2 of the Charter that 'The Organization is based on the principle of the sovereign equality of all its members.' The 'equality' thus provided for is a legal, juridical term that means equality in representation, in voting, in status. Irrespective of size or power, infractions of rights must be considered impartially. Wealth and strength are not to be used as an escape from the duty to observe international obligations. In practice, however, it is obvious that despite the guarantee of legal equality, the major powers have a position within the Organization far more commanding and influential than might be expected from the guarantees of legal equality in the Charter.

LEGAL CHARACTER

Although the United Nations has been described as merely an association of nations, it does possess a legal personality of its own. It has its own headquarters, staff, and insignia; periodically it receives delegations from its members. Article 104 of the Charter states that 'the Organization shall enjoy within the territory of each of its Members such legal capacity as may be necessary for the exercise of its functions and the fulfillment of its purposes.' The term 'legal capacity' refers to the ability of the Organization to act as a subject of international law, thereby possessing the attributes necessary to hold and dispose of property, make contracts, and otherwise conduct itself as a legal person.[1]

After considerable discussion, it was decided by the General Assembly in 1946 to construct permanent headquarters in New York City. Through the generosity of John D. Rockefeller, Jr., a seventeen-acre piece of land worth $8,500,000 was given to the Organization. Temporary quarters in several locations in the New York City area were utilized until the completion in 1950 of the building housing the Secretariat. Occupation of the General Assembly building and the Conference building came later. The location of the headquarters within the territory of a member state immediately raised a number of legal questions between the Organization and the host country. The United States and the United Nations had to work out jurisdictional limits satisfactory to both parties. Among the many questions involved were those of policing, problems of access and transit, fire protection, taxation, and communications. The Secretary-General was authorized to conduct negotiations on behalf of the United Nations with the host country. Final approval rested with the General Assembly.

On June 26, 1947, the Headquarters Agreement between the United States and the United Nations was signed and the General Assembly gave its approval on October 31, 1947. The Agreement established a 'headquarters district' in the Borough of Manhattan, New York State, which is placed within the restricted control and authority of the United Nations. The federal, state, and local laws of the United States are applicable within the district if they are not in conflict with the regulations of the United Nations. Should there be a conflict, an arbitral tribunal consisting of the Secretary-General, the Secretary of State of the United States, and a third person to be chosen by the two, is to hand down a decision in the matter. The Secretary-General is given American police protection for the area and although the United Nations has no sovereignty over the district, the area is inviolable and no persons can enter it to perform official duties except those authorized by the Secretary-General. In this and other respects, the Agreement closely resembles the principles governing the status of

[1] In the Convention on the Privileges and Immunities of the United Nations adopted by the General Assembly in 1946, Article 1, Section 1, provides that 'The United Nations shall possess juridical personality. It shall have the capacity: (a) to contract; (b) to acquire and dispose of immovable property; (c) to institute legal proceedings.' Following the assassination of United Nations Mediator Count Bernadotte in September 1948, the question arose whether the United Nations could bring a claim for injury to one of its agents. The problem was referred to the International Court of Justice which unanimously delivered an affirmative opinion. For more details on this case, see Chapter 10.

foreign embassies in the United States. Thus the United States cannot erect any obstacles to the transit to or from headquarters of United Nations officials or those engaged in business with them. Permanent representatives of the Organization whether residing inside or outside the district are 'entitled in the territory of the United States to the same privileges and immunities, subject to corresponding conditions and obligations, as it accords to diplomatic envoys accredited to it.' Other arrangements cover public services such as utilities and communications.

The United Nations, according to Article 105 of the Charter, is to 'enjoy in the territory of each of its members such privileges and immunities as are necessary for the fulfillment of its purposes. Representatives of the members of the United Nations and officials of the Organization shall similarly enjoy such privileges and immunities as are necessary for the independent exercise of their functions in connection with the Organization.'

Implementation of this Article has come from the Convention on the Privileges and Immunities of the United Nations approved by the General Assembly in 1946. Herein is to be found additional information concerning the legal personality of the Organization and, in particular, the international status of its representatives and staff. Under the convention, the property and assets of the United Nations, wherever located, enjoy immunity from every form of legal process 'except in so far as in any particular case it has expressly waived its immunity.' Its premises are inviolable and its property and assets are 'immune from search, requisition, confiscation, expropriation and any other form of interference, whether by executive, administrative, judicial or legislative action.' It may hold funds, gold, or currency of any kind and transfer them at any time. The assets and property of the United Nations are exempt from all direct taxes, customs duties, and restrictions on the importing and exporting of articles needed for official use and of publications. No censorship is to be exercised over its communications. It has the right to use codes and to send and receive its correspondence by courier or in bags which have the same immunities as diplomatic couriers and bags.

Representatives of members to the principal and subsidiary organs of the United Nations and its conferences, while on official business, enjoy immunity from personal arrest or detention and from seizure of their personal luggage.[2] They are immune from legal process in respect of words spoken or written and all acts done by them in their capacity as representatives. Their papers and documents are inviolable and they can use codes and receive correspondence by courier or in bags. In general, they are accorded

---

[2] By the term 'representatives' is meant all delegates, deputy delegates, advisers, technical experts, and secretaries of delegations.

such other privileges as are normally the prerogatives of diplomatic agents. It should be noted that the privileges and immunities are granted representatives not for their personal benefit 'but in order to safeguard the independent exercise of their functions in connection with the United Nations.' Consequently, a member must waive the immunity of its representative in any case where the immunity would impede the course of justice. These privileges do not apply between a representative and the authorities of the state of which he is a national or representative.

The privileges and immunities accorded the Secretariat and the members of the specialized agencies are in a different category from those enjoyed by representatives. The rights and obligations of such officials will be discussed in later chapters devoted to these aspects of the United Nations system.[3]

The Charter of the United Nations does not confer upon the Organization a general treaty-making power nor does it imply that there is an organ competent to exercise such a power. At the San Francisco Conference, the Belgian delegation proposed the following Charter provision: 'The Parties to the present Charter recognize that the Organization they are setting up possesses international status, together with the rights this involves.' However, Committee IV/2 of the Conference considered it 'superfluous to make this the subject of a text. In effect, it will be determined implicitly from the provisions of the Charter as a whole.' Had the Belgian proposal been accepted, the United Nations would have been able to make any treaties whatsoever, irrespective of whether the Charter conferred this authority upon a particular organ or provided for a particular function covered by a treaty. As it is, however, the United Nations, on behalf of the Organization, may enter into treaties (agreements) which the Charter authorizes in special provisions.

A treaty is established between a member and the United Nations when a plan submitted to it by the Security Council is accepted. The Security Council, in Article 26 is to formulate 'plans to be submitted to the members of the United Nations for the establishment of a system for the regulation of armaments.' The Security Council again, in Article 43, on its initiative, is to negotiate agreements with members or groups of members for the purpose of having at its command military forces, facilities, and assistance for the purpose of maintaining international peace and security.[4] The Economic and Social Council, according to Article 63, is authorized to enter into agreements with the various specialized agencies to define the terms on which the agency concerned is to be brought into relationship with the

[3] See especially Chapter 11.
[4] No such agreements have been negotiated. For more details, see Chapters 8 and 9.

Organization. Agreements such as these must be approved by the General Assembly. In addition, trusteeship agreements (Article 79) for the administering state or any alterations must be approved by the Security Council (Article 83) or the General Assembly (Article 85).

Finally, the United Nations has developed a distinct symbolism through the adoption of official insignia. The emblem and seal is a circular map of the world placed between two olive branches. The flag is a field of blue upon which is located the emblem. The insignia was adopted by the General Assembly in 1946. At its 101st meeting a resolution was adopted which declared 'that October 24, the anniversary of the coming into force of the Charter of the United Nations, shall henceforth be officially called "United Nations Day" and shall be devoted to making known to the peoples of the world the aims and achievements of the United Nations and to gaining their support for the work of the United Nations.'

PRINCIPLES AND OBJECTIVES

The first two articles of the Charter state the principles and aims to which the United Nations and its members are dedicated. The primary objective is the preservation of international peace and security. Peace is to be maintained through a system of collective security in which all members of the Organization co-operate in taking 'effective collective measures for the prevention and removal of threats to the peace, and for the suppression of acts of aggression or other breaches of the peace. . . .' Wherever possible, the United Nations seeks to arrive at a pacific solution of a conflict through various methods of adjustment and settlement prior to an actual breach of the peace or act of aggression.

At all times the Organization is 'to develop friendly relations among peoples' on the premise that an essential prerequisite for peaceful relations between states is the reduction of fears and suspicions. The furthering of friendly relations is to be based upon 'respect for the principle of equal rights and the self-determination of peoples.' Originating in the peace settlements of 1919 and restated effectively in the Atlantic Charter is the principle of self-determination, by which all peoples should be able to choose the form of government under which they desire to live, and have the right to express their wishes concerning territorial changes affecting them.

Paragraph 3 of Article 1 spells out additional aims of the United Nations. Economic stability and social progress are not only conditions favorable to a durable peace but are themselves worthy objectives of an international organization. Thus the members of the United Nations are pledged to co-operate not only 'in solving international problems of an economic, social, cultural, or humanitarian character,' but also 'in promoting and encouraging respect for human rights and for fundamental freedoms for all without distinction as to race, sex, language, or religion.' There is no guarantee that the United Nations will ensure the accomplishment of these lofty purposes. Implied, however, is the promise that the members will do their best to promote a climate more favorable to peace by investigating human needs and encouraging respect for human dignity. Specialized, technical agencies equipped to assist mankind everywhere, together with carefully worked out international conventions, serve to implement this promise.

Article 2 is devoted to an enumeration of a series of basic principles or directives which are to guide the conduct of both the Organization and its members in fulfilling the stated objectives contained in the Charter. After the postulate of the sovereign equality of all members is expressed, each is reminded of the importance of honoring its obligations assumed through membership in the United Nations. A fundamental stipulation is the use of pacific settlement for all disputes of an international character. Once a dangerous conflict develops, each member must utilize peaceful means to resolve it, even if the problem concerns a nonmember of the Organization. In the case of nonmembers, the United Nations 'shall ensure' that they act in accord with those principles so far as may be necessary for the maintenance of international peace and security. Although the threat or use of force is not eliminated by the Charter, due to the possible use of collective security measures and self-defense, all members are obliged to forego such action that is 'inconsistent with the Purposes of the United Nations.' In particular, no threat or use of force is to be used to infringe upon the territorial integrity or political independence of any state, whether it is a member of the Organization or not. Under no circumstances is any member to aid a state 'against which the United Nations is taking preventive or enforcement action.' Finally, the Organization is not to intervene in any matters which are essentially within the domestic jurisdiction of any state except for the possible use of enforcement measures adopted by a principal organ to carry out the purposes of the Charter.

These, then, are the fundamental procedural principles which guide the conduct of members of the United Nations. In most instances they are spelled out in later chapters of the Charter, particularly those with respect to the preservation of peace. Although the principles of justice and self-determination are specifically referred to as objectives, they are not covered in any later article. It should also be noted that there is one principle underlying the very structure and functioning of the Organization which is not mentioned in any portion of the Charter. It is the unwritten but nonetheless implicit dependence upon the unity of the great powers for the successful working of the collective security features of the Charter. In essence, the unity of the great powers is the key to the success of a universal international organization composed of sovereign states joined together by voluntary decision. This is a principle as fundamental as any that are written with noble intent in the Charter and it is recognized as such by those who would understand the elementary requirements of international organization at the present time.

MEMBERSHIP, SUSPENSION, EXPULSION, AND WITHDRAWAL FROM MEMBERSHIP

Since the entire problem of membership in the United Nations will be fully examined in the next chapter, only brief mention need be made of the matter at this time. Provision is made for two categories of members: original members and those subsequently admitted. Both classes enjoy equal privileges and obligations; however, although original members were accorded the opportunity of joining as a right, subsequent members are expected to meet certain qualifications prior to admittance. Those classed as original are the members who ratified the Charter following their participation in the San Francisco Conference in 1945 or who had previously adhered to the United Nations Declaration of January 1, 1942. A total of fifty-one are classified as original members.

A subsequent member must fulfill five conditions prior to consideration for membership: it must be a state, be peace-loving, accept the obligations of the Charter, and be able as well as willing to accept these obligations. An applicant must be approved by both the General Assembly and the Security Council before admission to the Organization.

Should the United Nations undertake preventive or enforcement action against a member, the General Assembly, upon the recommendation of the Security Council, may suspend the rights accorded it by virtue of its membership in the Organization. The recalcitrant member must still adhere to its obligations under the Charter, nonetheless. The primary aim of suspension is to forestall a great power guilty of a threat to the peace, a breach of the peace, or an act of aggression from interfering with the functioning of the Security Council. The 'rights' lost by suspension would include representation in the principal organs of the United Nations and the privilege of utilizing the Charter and the services of the Organization as a whole. However, the significance of the provisions covering suspension is greatly reduced should the guilty state be a permanent member of the Security Council, since it could block a motion for suspension through the veto.

Similarly, a permanent member can block the suspension of any other state. When the situation which called for the suspension has been clarified and the need for suspension removed, it remains the sole privilege of the Security Council to restore the rights of the suspended member.

In the event that a member has 'persistently violated the Principles' of the Charter, that member may be expelled by the General Assembly following a recommendation by the Security Council. Expulsion is presumed to be a greater penalty than suspension and hence must result from repeated violations of the principles governing membership. However, it is ironic that a member expelled from the Organization may in a sense have more rights than a suspended state. For example, a nonmember has the privilege of appearing before the organs of the United Nations, in particular before the Security Council, should that state be a party to a dispute. Such a right is not accorded a suspended member. Nevertheless, there may be a positive moral stigma attached to expulsion in the eyes of the world.

There is no formal provision which permits a member of the organization to withdraw. The delegates at San Francisco in 1945 firmly believed that a withdrawal clause in the Charter might encourage a member to threaten withdrawal unless his demands upon the Organization were met. It was also believed that withdrawal would be contrary to the conception of universality and might be a means of escape from fulfilling the obligations contained in the Charter. At the same time, the committee studying the problem at San Francisco believed it wise to include in its report the following statement of its views concerning the possibility of withdrawal:

> The Committee deems that the highest duty of the nations which will become members is to continue their cooperation within the Organization for the preservation of international peace and security. If, however, a member because of exceptional circumstances feels constrained to withdraw, and leave the burden of maintaining international peace and security on the other members, it is not the purpose of the Organization to compel that member to continue its cooperation in the Organization.
>
> It is obvious, particularly, that withdrawals or some other forms of dissolution of the Organization would become inevitable if, deceiving the hopes of humanity, the Organization was revealed to be unable to maintain peace or could do so only at the expense of law and justice.
>
> Nor would a member be bound to remain in the Organization if its rights and obligations as such were changed by Charter amendment in which it has not concurred and which it finds itself unable to accept, or if an amendment duly accepted by the necessary majority in the Assembly or in a general conference fails to secure the ratification necessary to bring such amendment into effect.

In effect this statement is of no legal value but may provide encouragement at some future date for the withdrawal of a member. It is a rather strange collection of reasons to justify withdrawal and if utilized by some recalcitrant state, could easily lead to the demise of the United Nations. Presumably, for example, a withdrawal could be made in the 'exceptional circumstances' surrounding amendments to the Charter. If a member does not approve an amendment adopted by the Organization, should it be permitted to withdraw? Who is to decide what circumstances are exceptional or when the United Nations could maintain peace only at the expense of law and justice? Obviously, the answer is that any state may withdraw whenever it deems it necessary to do so. In addition, if an amendment proposed by a state fails to pass, is this ground for demanding withdrawal? The committee at San Francisco was attempting to placate the states not possessing a veto in the Security Council because they had complained about having no protection against amendments that might be inimical to their national interests. But if the committee (and the Conference) believed that there should be no Charter provision for withdrawal, it should have stood its ground and not provided comfort to those who at some future date may very well challenge the competence of the Charter by adopting the excuses contained in the committee report and unilaterally withdrawing from the Organization.[5]

CHARTER AMENDMENTS

Amendments originate in the General Assembly where, by a two-thirds vote, a resolution can be adopted for the purpose of altering or making additions to the Charter. Should the resolution obtain the required majority, it must then be approved by at least two thirds of the Organization, including all permanent members of the Security Council. Once an amendment has been ratified by the required number, it becomes binding on all members irrespective of whether some failed to support it in the General Assembly.

Since there were a number of differences at the San Francisco Conference which were not entirely resolved through compromise, it was decided to make provision in the Charter (Article 109) for the calling of a general conference for the purpose of reviewing the Charter whenever ordered by a two-thirds vote of the General Assembly and any seven members of the Security Council. Should such a conference not be held prior to the tenth regular session of the Assembly, a proposal to call it was to be placed on

[5] No member had been suspended or expelled by 1958. The establishment of the United Arab Republic (Egypt, Syria, Yemen) in 1958 eliminated the individual membership of Egypt and Syria in the Organization and thereby reduced the total membership from 82 to 81. Several countries (France, Hungary, South Africa, USSR) have resorted to temporary withdrawal or boycott in order to achieve certain ends.

the agenda of that session. The conference then would be called if a simple majority vote of the Assembly and any seven members of the Security Council so decided. However, the Assembly postponed until 1959 a decision on whether to call the review conference.

SURVEY OF PRINCIPAL ORGANS

Since 1945 the United Nations has grown from a plan on paper to an important means of international action and exists today as a living organization reflecting the aspirations and the difficulties of world society. To implement the purposes of the Charter, six principal organs have been established: the General Assembly, the Security Council, the Economic and Social Council, the Trusteeship Council, the International Court of Justice, and the Secretariat. At this time, the structure of the Assembly and the Security Council will be discussed in some detail. Although later chapters examine the organization of the other primary organs, a brief description of each will be presented now in order to provide a general picture of the United Nations structure.

The General Assembly. A ponderous and complicated organism, the General Assembly is the central focus of the multifold activities of the Organization. It is difficult to characterize it specifically without qualifications. Generally speaking, the Assembly is a standing diplomatic conference of eighty-one states, already possessed of a tradition and acutely conscious of its responsibilities. It is not the parliament that it resembles, for it has no legislative powers. But it is a forum where the leading statesmen of the world have the opportunity to meet and consult with each other, often spontaneously, on any matter which they believe concerns international life. Regardless of the nature of the problem before it, the General Assembly provides the means whereby any member, large or small, may offer a comment, suggest a resolution, or debate an issue. In the twelve years of its existence, the General Assembly has greatly expanded its activities, sometimes through intent, at other times through the accident of the failure of certain organs of the United Nations (especially the Security Council) to function as expected. Individual members have more and more come to place reliance upon the Assembly, which is, in the last analysis, the supreme supervisory body of the United Nations.

The scope of the General Assembly is very wide. Within the range of the Charter, it may discuss any questions, including those relating to the maintenance of international peace and security and national armaments. It initiates studies and makes recommendations for the purpose of 'promoting international cooperation in the economic, social, cultural, educational, and health fields,' and assists 'in the realization of human rights and fundamental freedoms for all without distinction as to race, sex, language, or religion.' Subsidiary organs have been established under its authority to further the performance of these broad functions.

DELEGATIONS. Each member is entitled to have a delegation consisting of five representatives and five alternates who may sit in the General Assembly.[6] An alternate may act as a representative if designated by the chairman of the delegation. A delegation may also have as many advisers and technical experts as its needs require. Credentials of representatives and the names of the members of the delegation are submitted to the Secretary-General prior to the opening of a session. A Credentials Committee of the General Assembly, appointed by the Assembly upon the recommendation of the President and serving for the session, examines the credentials and reports on them to the full membership.

All representatives are appointed by their own governments who determine their qualifications. Their credentials are issued by the heads of states or ministers of foreign affairs who provide them with their instructions and may recall them at any time.

SESSIONS. The General Assembly normally meets in regular annual session beginning on the third Tuesday in September. Sessions are held at the headquarters of the United Nations or at some other location if the request is made at least one hundred and twenty days prior to the session and concurred in by a majority of the members. At the beginning of each session, the General Assembly may establish a target date for adjournment. It may decide at any session to adjourn temporarily and resume its meetings at a later date.

Special sessions can be held at the request of the Security Council or a member if a majority of the members concur. They are convoked by the Secretary-General. Under some circumstances, emergency special sessions can be convened within twenty-four hours of the receipt of such a request by the Secretary-General from the Security Council if any seven members of that organ so vote, or from a majority of the members.[7] In the case of an emergency special session, the General Assembly convenes immediately in plenary session and proceeds directly to consider the item proposed for consideration in the call for the session.

PRESIDING OFFICERS AND THE GENERAL CONDUCT OF BUSINESS. At the beginning of each session the General Assembly elects a President and thirteen

---

[6] Observers are permitted to the following nonmembers: South Korea, Switzerland, and West Germany. They do not vote but may sit in on many activities of the Organization.

[7] The provision for emergency special sessions originated with the 'Uniting for Peace' resolution adopted by the Assembly on November 3, 1950. For more details, see Chapters 6 and 8.

Vice-Presidents who serve only for the duration of the session. It has been customary to include the Big Five among the Vice-Presidents. The President selects one of the Vice-Presidents to take his place if he must be absent. If the President resigns or for any other reason is unable to perform his duties, a new President is elected to complete the unexpired term. These officers customarily are chosen with equitable geographical representation in mind.

The President of the General Assembly is an important and influential official. He presides at all plenary meetings of a session, directs the discussion, ensures observance of the rules, grants the right to speak, puts questions, and announces decisions. The President may not, however, refuse to recognize a speaker. He rules on points of order, and in general, has 'complete control of the proceedings at any meeting and over the maintenance of order thereat.' During the course of a discussion, he may propose to the Assembly a time limit on speakers, a limit on the number of times each representative may speak on each question, the closure of the list of speakers, or the closure of debate. The President may also propose the suspension or adjournment of the meeting or the adjournment of the debate on an item under discussion. Neither he nor an acting President has the right to vote although each may appoint another member of his delegation to vote in his stead.

An organ as large and unwieldy as the General Assembly cannot normally act with any decisive speed. The pace of work is deliberate and there is great care taken to provide adequate time for those who wish to be heard. Limitation of debate is an exception to the rule. Almost all important proposals go through a committee stage before being discussed in plenary session, to say nothing of consideration by subcommittees. Lengthy and frequently involved discussion occurs as a proposal makes its way through the cumbersome procedure which careful scrutiny and analysis require. These processes are governed by the Rules of the General Assembly and though amendments have been adopted to speed up the work there has been no great improvement. Parliamentary maneuvers, common to any democratic body, have been used by those seeking to obstruct business. Indeed, it is sometimes surprising that, with eighty-one different delegations representing as many nations, traditions, and interests, the General Assembly has been able to function as successfully as it has to date. On some occasions, most notably in the case of the Anglo-French-Israeli attack on Egypt in 1956, the Assembly has acted with remarkable speed.

A provisional agenda is compiled by the Secretary-General and sent to each member at least sixty days prior to the opening of a session. It must include the Annual Report of the Secretary-General on the work of the

United Nations and reports from the principal organs, subsidiary organs of the General Assembly, and any reports from the specialized agencies. In addition, the provisional agenda includes such items as those ordered by the General Assembly at a previous session; those proposed by members, the Secretary-General, other principal organs, and nonmembers; the proposed budget; and an accounting for the previous financial year. Supplementary items may be placed on the agenda by members, the Secretary-General, or the principal organs if done at least thirty days prior to the opening of a session. Items of an important and urgent character may be proposed less than thirty days prior to regular sessions or even during the session if so decided by a majority vote.

A General Committee, composed of the President, Vice-Presidents, and chairmen of the main committees of the General Assembly, has certain duties pertaining to the activities of the President and the agenda. It assists the President in the general conduct of the work of the Assembly 'which falls within the competence of the President' but does not decide any political question. It considers the provisional agenda and the supplementary list of items and recommends to the General Assembly whether an item should be included on the agenda and the priority to be granted each item. The General Committee also makes recommendations concerning the closing date of the session and occasionally during a session it reviews the progress of the General Assembly and its committees and makes recommendations for acceleration of work.

The Secretary-General provides the staff required by the General Assembly, its committees, and subsidiary organs. He or his representative attends the meetings of the Assembly and its committees, and may at any time make oral or written statements concerning any questions under consideration. General Assembly Rule 40 outlines the duties of the Secretariat when it serves the Assembly, as follows:

> The Secretariat shall receive, translate, print and distribute documents, reports and resolutions of the General Assembly, its committees and organs; interpret speeches made at the meetings; prepare, print and circulate the summary records of the session; have the custody and proper preservation of the documents in the archives of the General Assembly; publish the reports of the meetings; distribute all documents of the General Assembly to the members of the United Nations, and, generally, perform all other work which the General Assembly may require.

At the beginning of the first plenary session (and at the end of the last one) a moment of silence is observed, dedicated to prayer or meditation. Following the election of officers, the adoption of the agenda, and the establishment of committees, general debate is opened. Plenary meetings are held from time to time to consider matters which require direct action by the entire Assembly. Such meetings may be private but are almost always held in public. Final decisions upon items on the agenda are not usually made until a committee report has been received. No representative should speak without receiving the consent of the President although, on occasion, one does. Closure of debate may be moved at any time by a representative even though other speakers still have requested to be heard. If the Assembly so votes, closure is declared by the President. A similar procedure governs adjournment of debate and suspension or adjournment of the meeting, although no debate is in order in the latter case.

VOTING. Decisions of the General Assembly are made by either two-thirds or a majority of those present and voting. A two-thirds vote is required on the following important questions: recommendations with respect to the maintenance of international peace and security, the election of the non-permanent members of the Security Council, the election of members of the Economic and Social Council and the Trusteeship Council, the admission of new members, the suspension of the rights and privileges of membership, the expulsion of members, questions relating to the operation of the trusteeship system, and budgetary questions.

All other decisions are arrived at by a simple majority vote. This includes the important determination of additional categories of questions to be decided by a two-thirds majority. The phrase 'members present and voting' means members casting an affirmative or negative vote. Members who abstain from voting are considered as not voting. Voting is normally done by a show of hands or by standing but any representative may request a roll-call vote. In this latter case, the roll is taken in the English alphabetical order of the names of the members, beginning with the member whose name is drawn by lot by the President. The quorum required for plenary meetings is a majority, both for calling the meeting to order and for taking a vote. In a committee, however, work may proceed with only a third of the membership present, but a majority must be in attendance before a vote can be taken. All elections are by secret ballot, both for Assembly and committee officers. All votes in committee are by simple majority. Additional aspects of Assembly voting procedures and problems will be found in the next chapter.

COMMITTEES. A most important feature of any deliberative body is its committee system. The size of a body such as the General Assembly and the volume of business with which it must deal necessitates some division of labor. This is obtained by means of a system of committees which organize the work and prepare many items for final discussion in plenary session. Indeed, the plenary discussion is often perfunctory. Without the committee system it would be impossible to proceed with discussion and debate in full Assembly meetings with any degree of efficiency. The General Assembly is permitted to establish as many committees as it believes are necessary to facilitate its work. Four categories or types of committees have been established: the main committees, to which matters of substance are referred; procedural committees, which function to organize the work and conduct business; the standing committees, serving to perform continuing functions; and the *ad hoc* committees or commissions, similar to the select or temporary committees of legislatures that are established to work on a special problem.

Each new session of the General Assembly establishes its own main committees, of which there are seven. Among these is a Special Political Committee, which until 1956 was set up for each annual session, because of the great amount of work referred to the regular First Committee. It was known as the Ad Hoc Political Committee and in 1956 it was made permanent. Every member is represented on this type of committee and voting is by simple majority. The main committees are the most important of the four types and are divided up according to subject matter. Agenda items are referred to them and their primary task is to draft or consider resolutions and present them for discussion and final decision in the plenary sessions. Each committee elects its own chairman, vice-chairman, and rapporteur. These officers are expected to be elected 'on the basis of equitable geographical distribution, experience and personal competence.' Their selection has usually corresponded to this directive of the Rules and most of the chairmen and their assistants are extremely hard working and conscientious. They have difficult jobs to perform in presiding over and co-ordinating the work of an eighty-one-member committee. The obvious clumsiness of such a large committee is offset to a degree by the device of the subcommittee. Its usefulness stems primarily from its ability to concentrate on a problem in a more intimate and flexible manner. Most of the subcommittee work is devoted to special analyses, preparation of draft resolutions, hearing of testimony, and compiling data for use in nominations. Informal private consultations occur frequently and are, in effect, subcommittees, but are never formally constituted as such. These consultations actually accomplish a large proportion of the diplomatic work undertaken. Each of the main committees (except the Special Political Committee) is numbered as well as identified as to subject matter.

The First — Political and Security Committee — deals with political matters and questions of security which appear on the agenda; the admission, suspension, and expulsion of members of the Organization; the regulation of armaments; and any other matters associated with peaceful adjustment of disputes and international co-operation of a political nature.

The Second — Economic and Financial Committee — considers all problems of economic and financial co-operation, employment, standards of living, and related aspects of economic progress. It also deals with all such matters relating to the activities of the Economic and Social Council and the specialized agencies.

The Third — Social, Humanitarian, and Cultural Committee — is concerned with the program and activities of the Economic and Social Council, its subsidiary organs, and the specialized agencies which involve questions of health, human rights and fundamental freedoms, and social co-operation and progress.

The Fourth — Trusteeship Committee — has referred to it all problems relating to the trusteeship system and non-self-governing territories which come within the powers of the General Assembly.

The Fifth — Administrative and Budgetary Committee — works on budgetary matters, questions involving the financial contributions of United Nations members, budgetary matters relating to the specialized agencies, and administrative items which are of special concern to the Secretariat.

The Sixth — Legal Committee — examines all legal questions referred to it by members and committees. It is also concerned with the general problem of the progressive development of international law.

The two procedural committees — the General Committee and the Credentials Committee — which deal with the organization of the General Assembly and the conduct of business, have been discussed earlier.

The two principal standing committees, which perform duties of a continuing nature both during sessions and in the intervals between them, are the Advisory Committee on Administrative and Budgetary Questions and the Committee on Contributions. The Advisory Committee consists of nine members, chosen primarily on the basis of their personal qualifications and with considerations of geographical representation, who serve three-year terms. At least two of the members are recognized financial experts. It is responsible for providing assistance to the Fifth Committee in preparing the budget of the Organization and advising the specialized agencies on their budgetary problems. The Contributions Committee is composed of ten members, serving three-year terms, and is concerned with the apportionment of expenses among members, 'broadly according to capacity to pay.' It also hears appeals from members for a change of assessments and acts in cases of members who are in arrears on their payments.

Among the numerous other advisory bodies which perform duties of a continuing nature are: Board of Auditors, Investments Committee, the International Law Commission, and the United Nations Headquarters Advisory Committee.

The *ad hoc* or special committees and commissions established to deal with problems of a particular or temporary nature, have been utilized frequently. The more important of these have been committees and commissions of inquiry and conciliation, such as the Special Committee in Palestine, the Palestine Conciliation Commission, the two United Nations Commissions on Korea, and the special Committee on the Balkans (November 1947). Some, such as the Peace Observation Commission, have been established on a more or less continuing basis.

A unique type of *ad hoc* committee was established in November, 1947, when the Assembly created an Interim Committee to consist of all members.[8] Known also as the 'Little Assembly,' it has possessed indefinite tenure since 1949 although it has never functioned as intended and is now moribund. Ostensibly, it was expected to relieve the First or Political Committee of some of its burdens. The actual reason for its creation, however, was that the United States wished to devise a means to keep the General Assembly in virtually permanent session in case action was needed which the Security Council was prevented from taking by a Soviet veto or otherwise. Since the Assembly can now be called into emergency session within twenty-four hours through the adoption of the 'Uniting for Peace' resolution in 1950, this latter justification for the Interim Committee has ceased to exist.

Prior to 1950, the Interim Committee did not provide any significant relief for the First Committee nor did it create a commission of inquiry or examine a dispute on its own initiative. Included in its activities were such items as consultation with the Temporary Commission in Korea in 1948, advising it to proceed with elections 'in such parts of Korea as are accessible to the Commission,' consultation with the United Nations Commission for Eritrea, and work on the delimitation of boundaries of the former Italian colonies. Rather useful studies have been made on the establishment of a United Nations Good Offices Commission, the territorial integrity of China, and the procedures of pacific settlement. One of its most

---

[8] It is interesting to note that a similar committee was proposed in 1945 before the Preparatory Commission by the Netherlands, whose delegate suggested the creation of a Standing Committee on Peace and Security. It was agreed then that such a committee could, at a more leisurely pace, study questions of peace and security and report its recommendations to the Assembly for action at its regular sessions. There was the belief that an arrangement of this nature would permit the Assembly to have a continuous body on the alert to act on political problems when they arose and thereby provide the First Committee with a careful analysis of all such matters. The great powers, however, were uninterested and refused to give the proposal serious attention.

interesting reports concerned the use of the veto in the Security Council. Considered in detail were all ninety-eight possible types of decisions which the Security Council can make. The Committee then listed the decisions which it believed should be subject to the veto and those in which the veto should be abandoned.

FUNCTIONS. The activities of the General Assembly are extremely wide, resulting from a broad grant of authority in the Charter. All of its functions are fundamental to the working of the United Nations itself. In addition to its most important duty of discussing, if it chooses, all items and questions referred to it by members and organs alike, it must supervise much of the work of the Organization. It has responsibilities of a specific financial nature and, on its own or with the Security Council, it must elect members of various principal and subsidiary organs, as well as share the amending power with the Security Council.

Article 10 of the Charter establishes the key political role of the General Assembly when the Assembly is granted the authority to discuss 'any questions or any matters within the scope of the present Charter or relating to the powers and functions of any organ provided for in the present Charter and . . . may make recommendations to the members of the United Nations or to the Security Council or both on any such questions or matters.' Without question, this Article reveals the use which can be and certainly has been made of this important organ. Dr. Evatt, the head of the Australian delegation at the San Francisco Conference in 1945, expressed the position of the Assembly authorized by Article 10 when he observed that it grants

> the clear right of the Assembly to discuss any question or any matter within the scope of this Charter. That scope will include every aspect of the Charter, everything contained in it. It will include the Preamble of the Charter, the great purposes and principles embodied in it, the activities of all its organs, and the right of discussion will be free and untrammelled and will range over that tremendous area.

Other articles which confer power on the Assembly are for the most part confined to implementing the comprehensive provisions of Article 10. Thus, the Assembly in Article 11, considers and makes recommendations for 'the general principles of cooperation in the maintenance of international peace and security, including the principles governing disarmament and the regulation of armaments'; discusses and makes recommendations on any questions relating to the maintenance of peace and security (Article 11:2); may refer to the Security Council any situation which might endanger international peace and security (Article 11:3); recommends methods to promote international co-operation in the political field and encourages the progressive development of international law (Article 13:a); recommends measures for the peaceful adjustment of any situation (Article 14); and promotes international co-operation in economic, health, social, cultural, and educational fields, and furthers the realization of human rights and fundamental freedoms (Article 13:b).

In practice, the Assembly has made extensive use of its broad powers of discussion. Inquiry and investigation are part and parcel of the deliberative process. Many of the disputes and problems considered require special treatment in order that relevant facts and information may be gathered and the Assembly is wholly competent to establish whatever fact-finding machinery is believed necessary. It is now possible, as a result of the 'Uniting for Peace' resolution of 1950, for the Assembly to recommend enforcement measures.[9]

The second basic function of the General Assembly, that of general supervision of the activities of the United Nations, further emphasizes the key role that it is called upon to play. Article 15 of the Charter states that the General Assembly 'shall receive and consider reports from the other organs of the United Nations.' It is of vital importance to the operation of the United Nations that all members should receive information concerning the activities and functions of all organs and then be provided with the opportunity to give expression to their views. The most obvious method of doing this is through the Assembly where each member is represented and can speak freely on any subject.

The most comprehensive report received by the General Assembly, and the one which precedes debate in the regular annual session, is that of the Secretary-General. This is a survey of the activities of the entire Organization, together with items of interest to all with particular respect to the maintenance of international peace and security. Also in Article 15 the Charter singles out the Security Council and requires that it not only send annual and special reports to the Assembly but also include an account of the measures which it has taken or decided upon to maintain international peace and security. The Assembly, when it 'considers' these and the reports from other organs, not only can discuss them but may make recommendations on items contained in the reports. Dissatisfaction is expressed through recommending action on a particular subject or by calling the attention of the particular organ concerned to its treatment of a subject and the comments made on that treatment during debate in the Assembly. For example, resolutions calling the attention of the Security Council to its failure to admit new members approved by the General Assembly have been fre-

---

[9] The role of the Assembly in the handling of disputes is fully examined in Chapters 7 and 8.

quent. Similar resolutions have taken the Economic and Social Council and the Secretariat to task for actions they have undertaken or for their failure to act on certain matters.

Two organs in particular — the Economic and Social Council and the Trusteeship Council when acting for nonstrategic areas — are under the direct supervision of the General Assembly. Article 60 of the Charter specifically makes the Assembly responsible, through the operation of the Economic and Social Council, for all aspects of international economic and social co-operation which come within the purview of the Organization. Article 85 provides that the Trusteeship Council is to function 'under the authority of the General Assembly' whenever the Assembly has the power to regulate trusteeship arrangements. Furthermore, all agreements that are made to bring the specialized agencies into relationship with the United Nations are subject to the approval of the Assembly. Recommendations made by the Economic and Social Council to co-ordinate the activities of the specialized agencies also come under the close scrutiny of the Assembly.

The staff of the Secretariat is appointed by the Secretary-General under specific regulations adopted for its use by the General Assembly. Changes in the regulations can be made only by the Assembly. There is obviously no supervisory authority over the decisions and opinions of the International Court of Justice but the General Assembly does request advisory opinions from it and can authorize other organs and the specialized agencies to request the same advice.

Article 17 of the Charter gives the General Assembly the important financial power to 'consider and approve the budget of the Organization' as well as to apportion the expenses among the members. In addition, the Assembly considers and approves any financial and budgetary arrangements with specialized agencies and examines the administrative budgets of these agencies 'with a view to making recommendations.' A member of the United Nations, according to Article 19, is to be deprived of its vote in the General Assembly if it is in arrears in the payment of its financial contributions, provided the amount of its arrears 'equals or exceeds the amount of the contributions due from it for the preceeding two full years.' However, the Assembly may allow such a member to vote if the failure to pay is determined to be due to conditions beyond the control of the member.

These provisions which place the control of the budget and, in general, of finance, entirely in the hands of the General Assembly give to it an added degree of control over the Organization. Each of the principal organs must be reviewed annually to determine its financial needs. Estimates can be reduced if the Assembly believes that certain items or programs are unnecessary. Although the specialized agencies have retained the power of final determination of their budgets, the Assembly offers considerable advice through recommendation and consultation.

The annual budget of the United Nations moves through several stages. Departments within the Secretariat prepare budget estimates and submit them to the Secretary-General who, in turn, formulates a tentative budget and submits it to one of the standing committees of the General Assembly already mentioned, the Advisory Committee on Administrative and Budgetary Questions. Here the estimates are carefully reviewed and recommendations are prepared for submission to the Fifth Committee of the General Assembly when it convenes. The Fifth Committee conducts hearings to which officials of the Secretariat and principal organs are summoned and requested to defend their budgetary requests. The final budget is adopted in plenary session by the Assembly which acts on the report of the Fifth Committee.

Working closely with the Fifth Committee and the Advisory Committee on Administrative and Budgetary Questions is the Office of the Controller of the Secretariat which administers the budget under regulations adopted by the General Assembly. A three-man Board of Auditors is appointed by the Assembly to report on the expenditure of funds. Budgets adopted during the first thirteen years of the United Nations have varied, as the following figures indicate:

Year	Amount in dollars
1946	$19,390,000
1947	28,618,568
1948	39,285,736
1949	43,204,080
1950	44,520,773
1951	48,925,000
1952	50,547,660
1953	48,327,700
1954	47,827,110
1955	46,963,000
1956	48,566,350
1957	48,807,650
1958	55,062,850

All but approximately $5,000,000 of the total budget comes from contributions made by the members. The expenses are apportioned each year by the General Assembly among the member nations on a percentage basis. These percentages, known as the 'scale of assessments,' ranged in 1958 from 0.04 for such small members as Liberia, Haiti, and Iceland to 33.33 per cent for the United States. As noted earlier, the Committee on Contributions — a standing committee of the Assembly — is responsible for establishing the scale of assessments which is later approved by the Assembly. The most important factor in determining the scale is the member's capacity to pay. To learn this, the Committee uses as a basis not only the estimates of national income, but also additional factors such as per capita income, dislocation of national economies due to the Second World War, and the ability to obtain foreign exchange. Also included in the determination is the principle that no one nation should pay more than one third of the total budget.[10]

Not the least important is the General Assembly's function of electing, either with the Security Council or on its own, the membership of the principal organs of the United Nations. Acting concurrently with the Security Council, it selects the judges of the International Court of Justice from a list of persons nominated by the national groups in the Permanent Court of Arbitration.[11] The Secretary-General is appointed by the Assembly following a recommendation by the Security Council.

On its own authority, the General Assembly elects the nonpermanent members of the Security Council, all the members of the Economic and Social Council, and those members of the Trusteeship Council which are not administering trust territories or are not permanent members of the Security Council.

Finally, the General Assembly, by a two-thirds vote, must approve all amendments to the Charter. This action must also be concurred in by all the permanent members of the Security Council.

The Security Council. For a number of years, the best known organ of the United Nations was the Security Council. It probably is still true that to many people it is the United Nations. The publicity in the United States associated with this interesting and important organ has been primarily negative, resulting largely from Soviet obstructionism and the irresponsible use of the veto. Unquestionably, the Security Council has not functioned as had been expected. The simple fact is that the successful functioning of the Council depends primarily upon the degree of unity exhibited by its permanent members. In practice, no decision can be taken that might prejudice the national interest of any one of them. The Charter did not

[10] In October, 1957, the General Assembly decided that the maximum contribution of any member to the ordinary expenses of the United Nations shall not, in principle, exceed 30 per cent. The decision will be implemented gradually over the next few years. The prospective reduction did not bring the United States' share down to 30 per cent in 1958, but this goal may be reached in 1962.

[11] In the case of members of the United Nations who are not represented in the Permanent Court of Arbitration, the Statute of the International Court of Justice provides that 'candidates shall be nominated by national groups appointed for this purpose by their governments under the same conditions as those prescribed for members of the Permanent Court of Arbitration by Article 44, of the Convention of the Hague of 1907 for the pacific settlement of disputes.' (Article 4:1)

banish politics from the Security Council any more than it did from the General Assembly. Effective enforcement action involving military sanctions would be inconceivable without the concurrence of the great powers.

The Security Council should never be regarded as an executive body. It is one of the three Councils of the Organization, a coequal among all the principal organs, exercising a specific and limited function. Unlike the General Assembly which can discuss any questions or any matters within the scope of the Charter, the Security Council is designed to specialize in problems involving the maintenance of international peace and security. It is authorized to call upon states to settle their disputes by peaceful means involving negotiation, mediation, conciliation, consultation, arbitration, judicial settlement, or resort to regional agencies and arrangements. It may investigate any situation containing a possible threat to the peace and has the power to order enforcement measures if it determines that there is a threat to the peace. Decisions reached by the Council on enforcement measures are binding upon all members of the United Nations. But the Council cannot venture beyond these responsibilities which lie exclusively within the political field. It is not involved at all in the performance of the other functions of the Organization and has nothing to do with most of the other organs. Whatever relationship there is must involve, at least indirectly, the question of security. The recommendation for admission of new members, the joint selection, with the Assembly, of judges for the Court and a Secretary-General, the veto over Charter amendments, and the authority over trusteeship arrangements for strategic areas are matters which were considered by the Charter framers to have some bearing on security and consequently were placed within the powers of the Security Council.

ORGANIZATION AND PROCEDURE. The Security Council came into existence when the General Assembly elected the nonpermanent members of the Council on January 12, 1946. At its first meeting held in London on January 17, the Council adopted the provisional rules of procedure which had been drafted by the Preparatory Commission. A committee of the Council worked on the rules until June, 1946, when recommended changes were approved. Some amendments have been incorporated since 1946 but the rules are substantially the same as adopted at that time. The Charter permits the Council wide latitude in its procedure but does provide some organizational conditions.

The total membership of the Security Council is eleven, each member having one representative. Five of these (China, France, United Kingdom, United States, and the USSR) are permanent members who cannot be replaced. Realism and international politics dictated the choice of these five. The United Nations, and through it, the Security Council, was based on the assumption that these major powers could and would continue to collaborate. Secretary of State Cordell Hull had said in 1944, 'without an enduring understanding between these . . . nations upon their fundamental purposes, interests, and obligations to one another, all organizations to preserve peace are creations on paper and the path is wide open again for the rise of a new aggressor.' The nations at San Francisco were agreed that any system created for keeping the peace after World War II must include all the major powers, and particularly the United States and the Soviet Union, the two nations that would have the greatest military potential at the end of the war. The Charter represents the limit of agreement that could be reached on the extent to which nations would restrict their national freedom of action. To have gone beyond this limit would have meant that at least some and probably all of the great powers would not have become members of the United Nations. It was therefore decided to grant these five nations permanent seats in the organ which was primarily responsible for maintaining peace and security. No substantive decision can be made without their unanimous consent, or at least acquiescence.

Although the matter was discussed at San Francisco, there is no criterion to determine what is meant by a great power in case one of the five mentioned in the Charter ceases to belong in that unique category. There was some argument against specifying the exact five because future developments might result in one being less 'great' than another. A related problem, one involving representation, has already arisen and at present appears insoluble. A seat is reserved for China but there are two claimants: the Republic of China and the People's Republic of China (Communist).[12] Furthermore, no permanent member can lose its seat against its will, since no amendment of the Charter is possible without the unanimous consent of all permanent members on the Council.

The remaining six members of the Security Council are elected by the General Assembly for two-year terms, each ineligible for immediate reelection.[13] The Charter provides two general criteria to guide the Assembly in making its selection. A severe burden is placed on the Assembly in that these two considerations do not necessarily converge. The Charter states that due regard should be paid to the ability of a prospective Council member to contribute to the maintenance of international peace and security. This means granting Security Council membership to those states that, because of their strategic location, economic resources, or manpower reserves,

[12] For a discussion of this problem see Chapter 6.

[13] In the first election of nonpermanent members, three were chosen for one-year terms so that in the future there would be a staggering of terms to provide greater continuity of membership.

can make a significant contribution to security. At the same time, consideration should be given to equitable geographical distribution. This is a requirement which seeks to assure eventual representation to all states that are members of the Organization. The decision as to whether these criteria are followed is left solely to the Assembly which appears to have determined its selections more on the basis of geographical and ideological representation in recent years than on the character of a member's contribution to security. A form of unwritten agreement, at least up to 1949, governed the selection. One seat inevitably went to Eastern Europe, one to the Near and Middle East, one to Western Europe, one to the British Dominions, and two to Latin America. Since that time, Eastern Europe has been unrepresented, unless Yugoslavia's term from 1950 to 1951 is placed in that category. The Dominions have always been represented and the seats for Latin America, Western Europe, and the Near and Middle East have been constant.

Certain provisions of the Charter make it possible for a nonmember of the Security Council to participate in its deliberations but without a vote. This can occur when the Council decides to invite a nonmember whose interest in a question may be affected or when a nonmember has brought a dispute or a matter which might lead to international friction to the attention of the Council. Any nonmember of the Council so participating may submit proposals and draft resolutions but such propositions can be put to a vote only at the request of a representative on the Security Council. Iran was invited to join the deliberations of the Security Council in its dispute with the USSR and the Netherlands participated in the discussions of the Indonesian question. The Philippines believed that its interests were involved in the Indonesian case and its request to join in the Council debate was granted. Although it was not a party to the dispute and its interests were not involved, Chile was permitted to join in the discussion because it had brought the situation to the attention of the Security Council.

A nonmember of the United Nations, if a party to a dispute under consideration in the Council, can be invited to join the discussion if it follows the conditions which the Council deems just for such participation. Albania sat in with the Security Council in the Corfu Channel dispute. A representative of the Republic of Korea was asked to sit at the Council table at the beginning of the Korean War in June, 1950, and has always been present since that time whenever the subject has been discussed. Despite the efforts of Yugoslavia, the Council refused to invite a representative from North Korea. When the Soviets returned to the Council in August, 1950, after boycotting it since January, another effort was made to invite a North Korean representative but the Security Council again refused.[14] Mr. Austin of the United States expressed the general view of the majority when he observed that the Republic of Korea had been declared by the United Nations to be the only government that represents the Korean people; that North Korea had refused to heed the recommendations of or co-operate with the special United Nations Commission for Korea; and that North Korea had defied the Security Council. Such conduct plus the fact that the United Nations did not recognize North Korea made an invitation unwarranted. However, prior to being declared an aggressor by the Assembly, Communist China was asked and did send a representative in November, 1950, to participate in the discussion of Formosa and the Korean War.

Each member of the Council is represented at the meetings by an accredited representative. Credentials are submitted to the Secretary-General but the head of a government or a minister of foreign affairs of a member of the Council may sit as the representative without submitting credentials. The Council is so organized that it is able to function continuously. Each member has followed the practice of selecting a permanent representative who is in residence in New York for the purpose of attending sessions of the Council. Meetings are held at the call of the President of the Council when he deems it necessary. In theory, the interval between them does not exceed fourteen days but in practice it is often much longer. The President must call a meeting at the request of any member of the Security Council or if a dispute is brought to the attention of the Council by any member of the Organization or by the General Assembly. A meeting can also be held if the Secretary-General indicates to the Council, that, in his opinion, there is a situation which might threaten international peace and security. Meetings are normally held at the seat of the United Nations in New York City but the Council may decide to meet at another place if that is suggested by one of its members or the Secretary-General.

The presidency is held in turn by the members of the Council in the English alphabetical order of their names. This process of rotating the presidency results in each President holding office for one calendar month. Should the President believe that he should not preside during the consideration of a question with which he is directly concerned, the chair devolves, solely for the consideration of that question, on the representative of the member next in English alphabetical order. Unless special arrangements are made, the President calls upon representatives in the order in

[14] The USSR had refused to take its place in the Security Council from January 13 until August 1, 1950, in a protest against the Council's refusal to seat the representative of Communist China. The significance of the Soviet absence is explained fully in Chapter 8 in the study of the Korean War.

which they signify a desire to speak. As presiding officer, the President must decide points of order and make various rulings. Any ruling of the President may, of course, be challenged and overruled by the Council. He also has the authority to refer matters to Council committees for their consideration. The Secretary-General assists the President at meetings and provides information pertinent to questions under discussion. The President approves the provisional agenda drawn up for each meeting by the Secretary-General. No other officers are specified for the Council by the Charter.

The presidency may on occasion assume greater importance than that of a routine position held by the representative of each state at least once annually. During the India-Kashmir dispute and at the suggestion of the representative from Norway, the Council voted to have its president 'meet informally with the two parties and examine with them the possibility of finding a mutually satisfactory basis for dealing with the Kashmir problem.' To provide continuity after the presidency changed, the Council, in this case, appointed the retiring President as rapporteur and he continued to function in that capacity for a time. Similar procedures were adopted with some success in the Berlin and Palestine questions. The General Assembly in April, 1949, recommended and the Security Council in May, 1950, agreed in principle to adopt the following procedure when appropriate:

> After a situation or dispute has been brought to the attention of representatives on the Security Council . . . , the parties shall be invited to meet with the President of the Security Council; they shall attempt to agree on a representative on the Security Council to act as rapporteur or conciliator for the case. The representative so agreed upon may be the President or any other representative of the council who will thereupon be appointed by the President to undertake the function of rapporteur or conciliator. The President shall inform the Security Council whether a rapporteur or conciliator has been appointed.

The Assembly recommended that, if such an appointment is made, the Council abstain from further action on the case for a reasonable interval during which actual efforts at conciliation could be made.

An example of presidential stalling was conducted by Mr. Malik of the USSR in August, 1950. The Soviets returned to the Council table to permit Malik to assume the presidency and prevent the Council from taking any action on the Korean War. Malik successfully tied up the Council in interminably bitter procedural disputes for the entire month. He ruled (but was not sustained) that the representation of the Republic of China on the Council was illegal and argued that the Council should not invite the representative from the Republic of Korea to sit with the Council unless equal representation was granted to what the majority called the 'North Korean authorities,' and that the United States was the true aggressor in Korea. These and numerous other charges were answered with increasing vehemence by other members who were unable to break the dilatory tactics of Malik until the presidency was rotated on September 1, 1950.

The staff needed by the Security Council, such as clerks and translators, is provided by the Secretariat. Meetings are public unless otherwise decided and verbatim records are maintained of all official proceedings in the working languages (French and English). All important documents, resolutions, and records of public meetings are issued in the five official languages (French, English, Russian, Spanish, Chinese). Both simultaneous and consecutive translations of speeches normally are provided in the working languages for all representatives on the Council.

VOTING. One of the best known aspects of the United Nations is the so-called 'veto' possessed by the permanent members of the Security Council. The word 'veto' does not actually appear anywhere in the Charter, yet it has come into everyday usage because of the voting procedures involved in making two types of decisions in the Council. The crucial Article 27 of the Charter states that each member of the Council has one vote. Decisions on procedural matters are made by an affirmative vote of seven members. But decisions on all other matters, that is, on substantive questions, are to be made by an affirmative vote of seven members 'including the concurring votes of the permanent members.' This voting formula does not apply, however, when the Security Council acts in conjunction with the General Assembly to elect judges for the International Court of Justice. Article 10 of the Statute of the Court provides that the Council decides by an absolute majority of votes (any six votes) with no distinction between permanent and nonpermanent members. An extended analysis of the 'veto' problem will be found in the next chapter.

SUBSIDIARY ORGANS. The Security Council is a relatively small, compact organ and does not need many committees for its work. Two standing committees have been established, each composed of the representatives of all the members of the Council. The Committee of Experts, established in January, 1946, studies and advises on the rules of procedure. It also takes under consideration such other matters as may be placed before it by the Council. The Committee on the Admission of New Members, established in May, 1946, examines applications for membership in the United Nations if they are referred to it by the Council.

The Charter provides in Article 47 for a Military Staff Committee which consists of the Chiefs-of-Staff of the permanent members or their representatives. Meeting for the first time in February, 1946, this Committee was expected to assist the Security Council on all questions relating to the

Council's military requirements for 'the maintenance of international peace and security, the employment and command of forces placed at its disposal, the regulation of armaments and possible disarmament.' Nothing has has been accomplished by the Military Staff Committee, however, due to the basic differences between the USSR and the other members on practically all matters referred to it.

In 1946 the General Assembly established the Atomic Energy Commission and made it responsible to the Security Council. It consisted of all the members of the Council and, in addition, Canada, when that state was not a council member. The Commission was expected to make proposals for the control of atomic energy to the extent necessary to ensure its use only for peaceful purposes. The Assembly, also in 1946, recommended that the Security Council establish a system for regulating and reducing national armaments. The Council subsequently established in February, 1947, the Commission for Conventional Armaments, consisting of all members of the Council and responsible to it. It was expected to prepare and report to the Council proposals for the general regulation and reduction of armaments and armed forces and recommendations concerning studies to be undertaken by the Military Staff Committee and other organs of the United Nations. It was not to deal with matters which lay within the competence of the Atomic Energy Commission.

Both Commissions proved to be ineffective, again as the result of the wide disagreement existing between the Soviet Union and the other members. They were dissolved by the General Assembly on January 11, 1952, when the Disarmament Commission was established. The new Commission is responsible to the Security Council, and has the same membership as the Atomic Energy Commission.[15] The Assembly resolution creating the new body directed it

> . . . to prepare proposals to be embodied in a draft treaty (or treaties) for the regulation, limitation and balanced reduction of all armed forces and all armaments, for the elimination of all major weapons adaptable to mass destruction, and for the effective control of atomic energy to ensure the prohibition of atomic weapons and the use of atomic energy for peaceful purposes.

From time to time the Security Council has created a number of *ad hoc* or special subsidiary bodies. They have included the United Nations Commission for Indonesia, the United Nations Representative for India and Pakistan, the United Nations Truce Supervision Organization in Palestine, the Subcommittee on the Greek Question, among others.

---

[15] For more details on the Military Staff Committee and the other subsidiary organs, see Chapter 9.

MISCELLANEOUS ORGANIZATIONAL FUNCTIONS. The Security Council is required by the Charter to perform certain additional functions apart from its primary responsibility of maintaining international peace and security. These are essentially elective, supervisory, and constituent in nature.

New members of the Organization must first be recommended by the Council to the Assembly. Similarly, the Secretary-General is appointed by the General Assembly on the recommendation of the Council. Judges of the International Court of Justice are selected by the concurrent vote of the Council and the Assembly. A simple majority of any six votes is necessary for affirmative Council action on the selection of judges.

All the permanent members of the Security Council are members of the Trusteeship Council, but they possess no special voting privileges. The Security Council also exercises all functions of the United Nations relating to strategic areas under the trusteeship system, including the approval of the terms of the trusteeship agreements. For these areas, the Security Council utilizes the assistance of the Trusteeship Council to perform those functions of the United Nations under the trusteeship system which relate to political, economic, educational, and social matters.

If preventive or enforcement action is taken against a member of the United Nations, the Security Council may recommend to the General Assembly that the member be suspended from the exercise of the rights and privileges of membership. The Council, on its own authority, may restore the member to good standing in the Organization. In addition, if a member persistently violates the principles of the Charter, the Council may recommend to the Assembly that the member be expelled.

The Economic and Social Council. Although less spectacular than either the Security Council or the General Assembly, the Economic and Social Council (ECOSOC) has been given specific tasks to perform. Broadly speaking, its essential concern is the well-being of the peoples of the world. It makes or initiates studies and reports with respect to international economic, cultural, humanitarian, social, health, educational, and related matters and makes recommendations on such questions to the Assembly and the members of the Organization in general as well as to the specialized agencies concerned. Whenever it is requested, assistance is provided to the Security Council. The Economic and Social Council also prepares draft conventions for submission to the Assembly and calls special conferences on matters falling within its competence. It is also the connecting link between the United Nations and the specialized agencies which have been established on their own but are associated with the United Nations through special agreements. Each of these agencies, such as the World Health Organization (WHO) and the United Nations Educational, Scientific, and

Cultural Organization (UNESCO) has its own constitution, staff, budget, and separate organization.

The Trusteeship Council. The mandates system begun under the League of Nations in which authorization was granted to a mandatory state to oversee the development of an area formerly in colonial status has been continued, with certain modifications, under the United Nations. The Trusteeship Council takes the place of the old League Mandates Commission and operates under the authority of the General Assembly or, in the case of strategic trust territories, the Security Council. The trusteeship system applies to those territories which were held in 1945 as former mandates, areas detached from enemy states as a result of the Second World War, and those territories voluntarily placed under the system by colonial states. Special agreements are concluded between the state administering the trust territory and the General Assembly or the Security Council, if the territory is designated strategic.

The purpose of the trusteeship system is to promote the economic, political, educational, and social advancement of the inhabitants of these areas as well as encourage their progressive development toward self-government or independence. To achieve these objectives outlined in the Charter, the Trusteeship Council receives periodic reports from the administering state, conducts on the spot investigations of the trust territories, and hears any observations or complaints from interested persons or organizations.

The International Court of Justice. The judicial arm of the United Nations, essentially the same as the old Permanent Court which functioned during the lifetime of the League of Nations, is the International Court of Justice. Unlike its predecessor, the new Court is an integral part of the United Nations and is provided for in the Charter. The Statute governing the function and competence of the Court is an annex to the Charter and thus all members of the United Nations 'are *ipso facto* parties to the Statute of the International Court of Justice.' A nonmember of the United Nations may become a party to the Statute under conditions established by the General Assembly after a recommendation by the Security Council.

The Court has jurisdiction over disputes only when the parties involved have consented to present the case before it. The so-called optional clause is a means whereby states may elect, through acceptance in advance, to submit certain types of legal disputes to the Court. The judgments of the Court are binding on the parties. The Court can also render advisory opinions on particular legal points or questions of authority when requested to do so by organs of the United Nations and the specialized agencies.

The Secretariat. Functioning continuously to provide assistance for all organs and agencies within the United Nations system is the Secretariat or staff of international civil servants. Its members, although retaining their citizenship, are not to seek or receive instructions from any government or external source other than the appropriate organs of the United Nations. All members of the United Nations must respect the international character of the Secretariat and encourage it to serve the Organization as a whole.

The Secretary-General heads the Secretariat and is appointed for a five year term by the General Assembly upon the recommendation of the Security Council. He is the chief administrative officer of the United Nations, charged with exacting and numerous responsibilities. The staff is appointed under his authority and is budgeted by the General Assembly. He is placed in a particularly strategic position by possessing certain definite political responsibilities. The Secretary-General, in effect, is the single person who stands for the United Nations as a whole. In this role he is expected to co-ordinate the activities of the entire Organization and the specialized agencies.

6

CONSTITUTIONAL PROBLEMS AND DEVELOPMENTS

THE Constitution of the United States, in the passage of time, has expanded and developed informally through custom and usage, and legislative, executive, and judicial interpretation. In a more formal sense, change has been brought about by actual constitutional amendments. This process of expansion and development is also inevitable with an international organization. The Charter of the United Nations, up to the fall of 1958, has not been amended but it had, nevertheless, undergone considerable change at certain points, and been ignored or by-passed at others. The constitutional development which has resulted is the product of many forces and circumstances. Any new organic document needs testing, not only to determine its meaning and the scope of its permissive activity, but also to discover the existence and extent of possible ambiguities. The various organs created have to organize themselves and start functioning under their own rules of procedure, and then must be tested through actual performance. Questions of competence and jurisdiction immediately arise and need clarification. But who is to make the necessary interpretation, the members individually or collectively, or some specific agency? Perhaps equally fundamental is the question of what rules are to be followed in making the interpretation. Answers to these questions are available on the domestic scene from governmental practice as well as constitutional prescription and a national system of values. But for a new international organization as complex, unwieldly, and challenging as the United Nations, answers cannot be discovered so easily.

The Charter is basically the product of diplomatic compromise resulting from deep-seated differences that are inherent in divergent national traditions, and in legal, political, and economic systems. Diplomatic negotiation does not always make for clarity, particularly where there is disagreement, and the compromise which may be worked out can easily be in the form of an ambiguity to hide the disagreement. Presented with a lengthy, and at times unclear, constitution requiring constant interpretation, the United Nations has had to work out its constitutional development by trial and error. It has no supreme court with the authority to settle conflicts of competence arising among its organs although the International Court of Justice can point the way, when and if requested to do so, by an advisory opinion. At times each member reserves the right to do the interpreting, according to its own legal and political ideals. The General Assembly has undertaken the task on occasion, since it can discuss any questions 'relating to the powers and functions of any organs provided for in the present Charter.' Other organs have interpreted the Charter on their own and have frequently ignored, as has the Assembly, conflicting interpretations by individual members.

International law has been quoted as a guide for action. Moral standards have been employed, particularly by the United States and to a lesser extent by other Western powers. On occasion, there is put forward an appeal to the, as yet, amorphous ideal of duty to a developing international community. Above all other rules of interpretation, however, stand political considerations. Self-interest, whether enlightened or not, is the final determinant of sovereign state action. The manner and the course of the United Nations constitutional development are dictated primarily by national and not international interest. This may not be the soundest method of obtaining interpretation, but it is the one available to contemporary international organization and it must be judged in that context. On one occasion, a state may be a strict observer of the Charter's precepts and on the next it may be urging, even demanding, a loose construction. All of the major constitutional problems which will now be considered have been raised, discussed, and decided or postponed on the basis of political determination.

THE PROBLEM OF MEMBERSHIP

Until 1955, only nine applications for membership had been acted on favorably. In that year, however, sixteen new members were seated, four more in 1956, and one each in the spring and fall of 1957. The United Nations has now arrived at near universality, but the intervening years were consumed with much bitterness and frustration on the membership issue. There still remains the problem of Chinese representation and that of the politically separated entities — Germany, Korea, and Vietnam. There are also a few remaining advanced colonial areas which may in the future become eligible.

To be effective the broad objectives of the Charter require the fullest measure of support from as many nations as possible. These aims are universal in scope and, presumably, can best be achieved by an organization with a universal membership. Immediately, however, the question is raised concerning the advisability of admitting nations that, on the basis of their past records, may offer only qualified support for these objectives. Is it essential to have all nations within the fold or just those that provide sufficient evidence of intent to support the Charter? Put in somewhat different terms, should a nation that espouses a certain policy permit the admission of another that is dedicated to pursuing a conflicting policy? If this position is not resolved, the question of membership immediately becomes a battleground between contesting coalitions within the membership and the previous objectives become obscured in the contest to gain support for one or another of the coalitions. This was the record of the United Nations during its first ten years and although the great majority of nations are now members, the crucial issue of universal versus selective membership has not been fully defined.

The Charter provides some criteria for admission but they are difficult to determine objectively and the practice of observance has not been consistent. An applicant must be a state and presumably sovereign, if the accepted tests of recognition under international law are to be followed. However, several original members were not sovereign at the time they signed the Charter. Certainly India, the Commonwealth of the Philippines, the Ukrainian and Byelorussian Soviet Socialist Republics did not possess the degree of independence expected of sovereign states under international law. While India and the Philippines now possess full independence, the same cannot be said of the two Soviet Socialist Republics. The presence of the latter in the United Nations cannot be justified on any legal grounds whatsoever. Although the Soviet satellites — Albania, Bulgaria, Czechoslovakia, Hungary, Poland, and Rumania — are technically independent, their freedom of action is analogous to the two Soviet Republics just noted and their membership as sovereign states can be questioned. Certainly the status of the Republic of China is doubtful in many respects.

Each applicant must be a peace-loving state, must accept the obligations of the Charter, and must be able as well as willing, to carry out these obligations. Of these four conditions, only the second — the acceptance of the obligations of the Charter — can be determined in an objective manner. The Rules of Procedure of both the Security Council and the General Assembly require that the application of a state for membership 'shall contain a declaration, made in the formal instrument, that it accepts the obligations contained in the Charter.' Whether a state is peace-loving and is able as well as willing to carry out the obligations of the Charter is essentially a political question left solely to the discretion of the members of the Council and the Assembly.

By the end of 1955, two things had become clear concerning the problem of membership. One was the establishment of a procedure of admission. The other was that criteria in addition to those noted in the Charter were applied in determining who should be admitted. As far as the procedure of admission is concerned, Article 4 of the Charter provides somewhat ambiguously that admission 'will be effective by a decision of the General Assembly upon the recommendation of the Security Council.' Practice has shown clearly that the 'recommendation' required of the Security Council is not merely advice but a positive act which can block the admittance of new members. The recommendation of the Security Council must be a favorable one in order to permit the General Assembly to act. The General Assembly, however, need not admit an applicant favorably recommended by the Security Council. Any state seeking admission first applies to the Secretary-General of the United Nations, who then refers the application to the Security Council. There it is normally considered by a committee which reports its findings made with the assistance of the appropriate department of the Secretariat. The Security Council, if the permanent members vote unanimously in favor of the applicant, transmits the recommendation to the General Assembly. If the application is vetoed in the Security Council, or otherwise fails to obtain the requisite votes for a favorable recommendation, a special report containing the entire record of the case is forwarded to the General Assembly. A favorable recommendation from the Security Council requires a two-thirds vote in the General Assembly in order to admit the applicant. If the application is accepted, membership becomes effective on the date on which the General Assembly reached its decision. No state possesses a legal right of admittance to membership, and consequently has no further recourse if its application has been turned down by either the Security Council or the General Assembly. However, should the General Assembly desire the admission of a particular applicant either not acted upon or acted upon unfavorably by the Security Council, the General Assembly may return the application to the Security Council for further consideration. But the Security Council is in no way compelled to alter its original decision as a result of this action by the General Assembly.

Certain smaller nations under the leadership of Argentina have advanced the thesis that the General Assembly could, on its own, admit a state to membership when the Security Council had failed to make a recommendation either because the applying state had not obtained the needed voting majority in the Council or because of the negative vote of a permanent member. The International Court of Justice, called upon in 1950 to offer an advisory opinion on this matter, turned down the Argentine view. This did not deter Argentina and its supporters and they advocated the idea right up to the time that the membership impasse was broken in 1955. It appears to be quite clear that both organs must participate in the process of admission of new members and that a permanent member may block an application by its negative vote. However, it is doubtful whether the use of the veto on questions of admission is consistent with the provision that membership, according to the Charter, is to be 'open' to all who meet the criteria noted above.

Applications from states that appear to have met these criteria have been vetoed on other grounds. The Soviet Union, for example, turned down the admission of Italy and Finland in October, 1947, when it was discovered that the Western bloc was unwilling to support the Soviet sponsored applications of Bulgaria, Hungary, and Rumania, because of their repeated violations of human rights. The Soviets maintained that these five European allies of Nazi Germany formed a group that was inseparable; all should be admitted or all refused membership. The admission of Eire, Jordan, and Portugal was originally vetoed by Soviet Russia on the ground that the Soviets had not entered into diplomatic relations with these governments. Subsequently the Soviets opposed the applications of Eire and Portugal with the contention that they were sympathetic toward the aggressors in World War II. These and other similar actions in the Security Council led to a deadlock in its deliberations over the entire question of new members.

In an effort to clarify the situation, the General Assembly appealed to the International Court of Justice for an advisory opinion. On May 28, 1948, the Court, by a nine to six majority, delivered an opinion which declared that:

> A member of the United Nations which is called upon, in virtue of Article 4 of the Charter, to pronounce itself by its vote, either in the Security Council or in the General Assembly, on the admission of a State to membership in the United Nations, is not juridically entitled to make its consent to the admission dependent on conditions not expressly provided by paragraph (1) of the said Article; and that in particular a member of the Organization cannot, while it recognizes the conditions set forth in that provision to be fulfilled by the State concerned, subject its affirmative vote to the additional condition that other states be admitted to membership in the United Nations together with that State.

The opinion of the Court did not alter the fixed positions of the United States and the Soviet Union in the Council. The United States supported the view that the applications should be considered individually, on their own merit, and should not be made the subject of barter or 'package deals.' It was not necessarily coincidence that applicants classified as non-peace-loving by the United States were Soviet satellites and, if admitted, would buttress the Soviet position in the United Nations. The United States, therefore, was perfectly willing to see its own candidates turned down as long as those sponsored by the Soviet Union were rejected. The USSR, on the other hand, demanded that all applicants be admitted or none at all. While the claim was made that this supported the concept of universality, it actually represented a move to gain the admittance of Soviet candidates.

The United States reversed its position in 1955 and agreed to the admission of states formerly classed as not peace-loving along with those it had consistently sponsored. The satellite states had not altered their policies nor had they provided fresh evidence that they were any more able and willing to carry out the obligations of the Charter than before. The USSR in 1956, instead of continuing to insist that Japan should be kept out unless Outer Mongolia was admitted at the same time, dropped the latter's request and agreed to the Japanese application. This lack of consistency can be explained only by the pull and haul of great power politics which has been so characteristic of the United Nations.

The case of Chinese representation is a much more complicated manifestation of the East-West conflict. What is involved here is a problem of determining which government should represent China: the Peiping regime or that of Chiang and his Nationalist Republic of China. China is an original member of the United Nations and is a permanent member of the Security Council. But considerable confusion has resulted from the fact that some have considered the matter as a question of membership, which clearly it is not. However, the United States, which has been the chief defender of Chiang, is fearful that if the problem is considered only as a question of representation, that is, as a matter of determining which delegation possesses the proper credentials, the Council might treat it as a procedural question where the veto cannot be employed.

The position of the United States would also be more difficult to sustain now in the Assembly, with its increased membership, since only a simple majority is necessary for approval of a report by the Credentials Committee. What might conceivably develop is the unhappy situation in which the Assembly would accept one delegation and the Council, the other. Should the Assembly accept the credentials of Communist China, the United States would be forced either to rely upon the somewhat precarious possibility that a majority of seven would not vote in favor of following the decision of the Assembly or to construct a legal interpretation that would permit the use of the veto. The most logical assumption would be that the United States would make a question of representation analogous to that of membership and derive the authority for a veto from the procedure employed in that instance. However, if this interpretation were used, the United States would be placed in an extremely embarrassing position since its spokesmen have urged the elimination of the veto on membership questions. Furthermore, it would not be a simple thing to justify the use of the veto on the matter of representation and not on membership when the latter item is of greater significance and less of a procedural matter than the former.

What has actually happened in some cases is that a member of the United Nations has recognized the government of Communist China in its diplomatic intercourse but has refused it the right to represent China in the Organization. This means that the Chiang government is the legal representative of China only in the United Nations. This separation of the questions of recognition and representation produces a difficult legal situation in which a government is recognized in one instance and not in another. Yet this is the position adopted by Secretary-General Trygve Lie in his *Memorandum on the Legal Aspects of Representation in the United Nations* which he transmitted to the Security Council on May 8, 1950. There have been instances where a state has been admitted to membership in the United Nations but is not recognized by certain members, some of whom had even voted favorably on the application. The Chinese situation, however, involves two rival governments both claiming to represent China and is a unique case in the annals of the United Nations. It is conceivable though, that there could be other instances of a similar nature.

It is not possible, in the absence of an election, to determine which government — Nationalist or Communist — is the one more preferable in the eyes of the Chinese people and which could thereby present the better claim to represent China. However, if one seeks to determine which of the two governments in fact is in a position to employ the resources and direct the people of the state in fulfillment of its obligations, the only conclusion would be that the Communist regime is, at present, better qualified by virtue of its control over the mainland of China and the millions resident therein. On the other hand, it is extremely difficult to justify the seating of Red China if an attempt is made to apply certain of the criteria expected to govern the conduct of members. Considerable support can be found for the moralistic argument that if governments manage 'to shoot their way into the United Nations' or 'hold innocent prisoners as objects of barter' to obtain representation, the stature of the Organization is lowered appreciably and the high objectives of the Charter become hollow and meaningless. One can pose this question: how could the members of the Assembly command any respect for law and justice if they voted to seat the Chinese Communists when the Peiping regime still stands condemned as an aggressor by the Assembly?

In a strictly legal sense, the members of the United Nations should determine only if the Chinese Communists exercise effective authority within the territory of China and are obeyed by the bulk of the population. But because of other elements in the situation, the decision will be political as well as legal, namely a passing of judgment on the form of government and its international conduct. In this sense, it is impossible to disassociate the political act of recognition and the essentially legal act of discovering the more representative government. The whole problem is further compounded, if one attempts to pursue a consistent course, by the fact that there are states already within the United Nations whose international conduct and disregard for the obligations of membership are on about the same plane as that of Communist China.

THE PROBLEM OF VOTING

An international organization composed of independent states is immediately faced with the problem of adopting a voting procedure for its various organs that will provide a representative decision on important issues and, at the same time, not prejudice the jealously guarded rights of its sovereign members. The United Nations has been confronted with an extremely serious voting problem in the Security Council. The General Assembly has not been free of difficulties related to its voting procedures, although the problem there has not been so acute.

The Security Council. In many respects, the best known problem of the United Nations is the use of the so-called 'veto' possessed by the permanent members of the Security Council. By June of 1958, it had been employed ninety times to frustrate some action agreed to by a substantial majority of the Council members. The USSR has been the worst offender (eighty-three times) although France twice joined with the United Kingdom in using it in the Middle East crisis in 1956. France and the Soviet Union each used it in the Spanish question. China cast a veto against the admission of Outer Mongolia to the United Nations in 1955 and France employed it earlier in the Indonesian case. The ability of one of the permanent members to prevent the United Nations from performing some function prescribed in the Charter has led to widespread criticism of the Council's voting procedure and to demands, both within and without the United

Nations, for some modification in the method of voting. The entire question was so hotly debated at San Francisco in 1945 that the Conference nearly ended in disaster. Both the Security Council itself and the General Assembly have studied the problem with little success. The problem is, of course, inexorably associated with the position of special authority demanded by and reluctantly but realistically granted to the great powers. Once again, without the unanimity of the great powers who possess the means both for waging and preventing large-scale warfare, no voluntary association of states such as the United Nations can succeed in maintaining peace and security. Simply stated, this is the reason why the procedure known as the 'veto' was written into the Charter over the protests of many middle- and small-sized states.

It will be recalled that Article 27 of the Charter grants one vote to each member of the Council and provides that decisions on procedural matters are to be made by an affirmative vote of any seven members. But decisions on all other matters, that is, substantive questions, require the affirmative vote of seven members 'including the concurring votes of the permanent members.'

Inevitably the question is asked: but how does the Security Council determine which decisions are procedural? At San Francisco in 1945 it was recognized that the provisions for voting in the Security Council were ambiguous. Under heavy attack by a group of smaller nations, the sponsoring powers of the Conference prepared a statement intended to clarify certain inconsistencies. This so-called Four Power Statement, later adhered to by France, succeeded in only partly clarifying the matter by listing some items which were procedural. They include all questions under Articles 28–32, such as the time and place of meetings, the establishment of subsidiary organs, the modification of rules of procedure, and invitations to nonmembers of the Council and of the United Nations to participate in the deliberations of the Council.

The Statement also observed that no individual member of the Council can alone prevent consideration and discussion by the Council of a dispute or situation brought to its attention under the Charter. This appears to be an important rule and even extends to a challenge of the Council's authority to study a question. The Soviet Union in 1948 denied that the Council had the competence to study the Berlin Blockade but was unable to prevent the matter from appearing on the agenda for discussion. However, the principle is much less meaningful than appears at first sight. Should a permanent member object to the consideration of a dispute, a veto can prevent any concrete action from being taken.

The General Assembly has been greatly concerned with the problem of the veto and repeatedly has advised the Security Council on the necessity of limiting its use. It was first discussed at great length in the course of the second part of the first session. On December 13, 1946, the Assembly adopted a resolution which earnestly requested the permanent members of the Council 'to make every effort, in consultation with one another and with fellow members of the Security Council, to ensure that the use of the special voting privilege of its permanent members does not impede the Security Council in reaching decisions promptly.' The resolution also recommended that the Council do its best to adopt procedures and practices which would, in effect, broaden the category of procedural matters. In 1947 the Assembly turned over the entire problem to its Interim Committee for study and recommendations. The Report of the Committee was completed in 1948 and was referred to the Assembly for consideration. It consisted of four parts: a list of ninety-eight different decisions which can be made by the Security Council, with conclusions, in most cases, on whether the decision is procedural; a classification by categories of possible Council decisions; suggested methods for implementing the recommendations regarding the classification of Council decisions; and a list of four final conclusions for action by the Assembly.

The General Assembly, despite the vehement opposition of the Soviet bloc, accepted the four final conclusions of the Committee on April 14, 1949, and in its resolution attached an Annex containing a list of decisions deemed procedural. This resolution, and the Interim Committee Report which it endorsed, is of the greatest significance, for it clearly establishes a guide for limiting the use of the veto. It utilizes the procedure recommended in the Report of noting certain decisions which should be made by a vote of any seven members, regardless of whether the decisions are regarded as procedural or nonprocedural. The list of decisions regarded as procedural goes far beyond the Four Power Statement made in San Francisco in 1945. The resolution itself was sponsored by four of the permanent members who agreed beforehand to accept its provisions. Thirty-six items are listed as procedural and twenty-one carry the recommendation that they be decided by a vote of any seven Council members, whether the decisions are considered procedural or not.[1] Included among

[1] The list of 36 decisions considered procedural fall into the following categories: all decisions adopted in application of provisions which appear in the Charter under the heading 'Procedure'; all decisions which concern the relationship between the Security Council and other organs of the United Nations, or by which the Council seeks the assistance of other organs; all Security Council decisions which relate to its internal functioning and the conduct of its business; certain decisions of the Council which bear a close analogy to decisions included under the above-mentioned criteria; and certain decisions of the Council which are instrumental in arriving at or in following up a procedural question.

the latter are the following important decisions: the admission of new members to the United Nations; whether a matter is or is not procedural; the determination of whether a question is a situation or a dispute; calling upon the parties to a dispute to settle it by peaceful means of their own choice; the investigation of any dispute or any situation which might lead to international friction or give rise to a dispute, in order to determine whether the continuance of the dispute or situation is likely to endanger the maintenance of international peace and security; the recommendation that a legal dispute be referred to the International Court of Justice.

The Assembly resolution of April 14, 1949, also recommended to the permanent members of the Security Council that they 'consult together whenever feasible before a vote is taken if their unanimity is essential to effective action by the Security Council.' If there is not unanimity, they should 'exercise the veto only when they consider the question of vital importance, taking into account the interest of the United Nations as a whole, and to state upon what ground they consider this condition to be present.' The veto should not apply when new functions were assigned to the Security Council by special agreements.

On October 18, 1949, Mr. Austin, President of the Security Council, announced that, in accordance with the Assembly resolution of April 14, 1949, the five permanent members had met to discuss 'agreement among themselves on what possible decisions by the Security Council they might forbear to exercise their veto' and to arrange for consultation among themselves when important decisions were to be taken by the Council. Mr. Austin stated that the permanent members had agreed to the principle of consultation prior to an important vote. But the Soviet Union refused to accept any alterations in the voting procedure recommended by the Assembly. There has been no change since 1949.

Whenever there is a doubt whether a question is procedural there is a chance for the so-called 'double veto' to be employed. It usually occurs in this manner although there are several variations. A resolution comes to a vote and the Council President outlines the voting procedure to be followed. If he rules that the question is procedural, needing only the affirmative votes of any seven members, the ruling may be challenged in order to determine positively whether the question is procedural or substantive.[2] One negative vote of a permanent member can change the ruling

[2] The situation was reversed in the case of Greece before the Security Council. The United States offered a resolution to request the General Assembly to consider the dispute between Greece and her neighbors. The resolution was approved by a vote of 9 to 2, whereupon the President ruled that the question was substantive and had failed to pass because of the negative vote of the USSR. The United States challenged the ruling; a vote was held to determine whether the question was procedural or not. The Soviet Union

of the President, thereby making the question one of substance. A vote on the question itself can be vetoed, as it has now become nonprocedural and requires the unanimous consent of the permanent members. The USSR has employed the double veto to make certain that it can block action by the Security Council on questions that would have passed easily on a procedural vote. The essence of the double veto is to maneuver the Council into voting on whether a question is procedural or not. The veto is possible on such a vote, which thereby guarantees that the question will become substantive if so desired. Once declared substantive, the question itself can be vetoed. The Soviets successfully utilized this procedure when the cases of Czechoslovakia, Greece, and Spain came before the Council.

Without any clarification or limitation of its voting procedure, the Security Council can at present be prevented by a veto from taking any of the following important decisions:

1. The admission of new members.
2. Amendments to the Charter.
3. Expulsion of a permanent member of the Security Council.
4. The determination of whether any given situation might lead to international friction or give rise to a dispute.
5. The investigation of a dispute to determine whether its continuance is likely to endanger international peace and security.
6. The request to the parties in a dispute to settle their differences by peaceful means or the recommendation to the parties of procedures or methods of pacific settlement.
7. The referral of a legal dispute to the International Court of Justice.
8. The request for an advisory opinion from the Court.
9. The determination of the existence of any threat to the peace, breach of the peace, or act of aggression.
10. The application of diplomatic, economic, or military sanctions.
11. The conclusion of military agreements with member states or the formulation of plans for the application of armed force.
12. The adoption of plans for the regulation of armaments.

The Charter provides in Article 27 that no member of the Security Council who is a party to a dispute under consideration by the Council can vote. This is a matter of simple justice, that no state shall be judge and party in its own cause. However, on a technicality, a member of the Council can get around this provision by claiming that the matter is a situation and not

again voted in the negative, holding that it was substantive. This meant that the original resolution of the United States was substantive and had lost through the veto or negative vote of the USSR.

The Four Power Statement made at the San Francisco Conference upholds the right to employ the double veto. Part II, paragraph 2 states: '. . . the decision regarding the preliminary question as to whether or not such a matter is procedural must be taken by a vote of seven members of the Security Council, including the concurring votes of the permanent members.'

a dispute. Article 27 does not call for abstention when the Council is discussing a 'situation.' Put another way, it is possible for a permanent member to challenge the existence of a dispute and in so doing, cast a negative vote which would prevent the Council from considering the matter a dispute.[3] The member would then be free to participate in the discussion, even though a party to the situation, and block any action by the Council deemed inimical to its interests. Furthermore, the requirement of abstention applies only to decisions which involve the pacific settlement of disputes and does not apply to any action which concerns enforcement measures. A permanent member of the Council could simply abstain from voting on proposals for the peaceful settlement of the dispute and then veto any resolution to undertake enforcement action if such a procedure was under consideration by the Council.

Another aspect of the voting formula has arisen which has lessened somewhat the rigidity of the Charter provisions. This is the practice by a permenent member of the Security Council of abstaining from voting on a question. Article 27, paragraph 3 does not require the concurring votes of 'all' permanent members but simply says 'including the concurring votes of the permanent members.' Had the word 'all' been included, absence from voting except by a party to a dispute would constitute a veto. It is entirely probable that the framers of Article 27 did intend that an abstention would count as a veto. Had the intent been otherwise, the relevant passage in the Article could have been worded 'including the permanent members *present and voting*.' The addition of 'present and voting' would remove doubt and legally permit a permanent member to abstain without invalidating a decision. The Four Power Statement implies, as does the wording of Article 27, that on substantive matters all the concurring votes of the permanent members are required. However, it has

---

[3] The Interim Committee of the General Assembly made an interesting recommendation in an effort to clarify this technical point. In its Report on the limitation of the use of the veto, it concluded that the decision on whether a matter was a dispute or a situation should be made by any seven members of the Council. The Report then offered a definition of a dispute to govern the Council's handling of the question. It suggested that the Council hold that a dispute arises: '(a) If the State or States whose conduct is impugned, agree that there is a dispute. (b) Whenever the State or States bringing the matter before the Security Council allege that the actions of another State or States in respect of the first State or States constitute a breach of an international obligation or are endangering or are likely to endanger the maintenance of international peace and security, or that such actions demonstrate preparation to commit a breach of international obligations or to endanger the maintenance of international peace and security, and the State or States which are the subject of these allegations contest, or do not admit, the facts alleged or inferences to be drawn from such allegations. Further, if a State bringing before the Security Council a matter of the nature (here being considered), alleges that another State is violating the rights of a third State, and the latter supports the contention of the first State, then the third State shall also be deemed to be a party to the dispute.'

become fairly common practice for a permanent member to abstain instead of recording a veto. Occasions have occurred, as in the Indonesian case, when two or even three permanent members have abstained without preventing Council action. The Western powers frequently have abstained from voting on Soviet candidates for admission to the United Nations. Their abstention has resulted in preventing Soviet proposals from receiving the required total of seven affirmative votes without necessitating use of the veto. The President of the Security Council stated during the discussion of the Indonesian question, that 'it is now jurisprudence in the Security Council — and the interpretation accepted for a long time — that an abstention is not considered a veto, and the concurrent votes of the permanent members mean the votes of the permanent members who participate in the voting. Those who abstain intentionally are not considered to have cast a veto.'

The Security Council has adopted a similar practice with respect to the physical absence of a permanent member, as distinguished from abstention. When the Iranian case was before the Council in 1946, the Soviet Union demanded that consideration be postponed for several weeks. When the Council refused, the Soviet representative and his aides left the Council table and announced that they would not return until the date they had requested. In the interim the Council adopted resolutions which required the concurring votes of the permanent members. The Soviets again absented themselves from the Council from January until August, 1950, stating that they would 'not participate in the work of the Security Council until the representative of the Kuomintang group has been removed from the Council. At the same time, the Soviet Union delegation wishes to declare that the USSR will not recognize as legal any decision of the Security Council adopted with the participation of the representative of the Kuomintang group and will not deem itself bound by such decisions.' In their absence, the Security Council adopted several nonprocedural resolutions, one on the India-Pakistan question, one on the regulation and reduction of armaments, and the extremely important resolutions on the Korean War, including the recommendations of enforcement measures for the first time in the history of the United Nations. The USSR has contended that the Council resolutions of June and July, 1950, are illegal since two permanent members of the Council were absent (USSR and the People's Republic of China). The United States, however, denied that these resolutions had no legal face and stated: 'The voluntary absence of a permanent member of the Security Council is clearly analogous to abstention. No one of the ten members participating in the meetings of June 25 and June 27 raised any question regarding the legality of the action — not even the members who dissented on June 27.'

It is obvious that the use of the veto has had a serious effect upon the functioning of the Security Council at certain crucial moments. Had not the Soviet representative been absent from the Council in June and July, 1950, there would have been no enforcement action voted at the start of the Korean War. Illegal, inhumane, and warlike activities have been uncurbed because of the benevolent protection of its satellites by the USSR.

At the same time, the presence of the veto power must not be considered to be a fatal weakness of the Charter. If one makes an analysis of its use, several revealing conclusions become evident. In the first place, over half the vetoes cast have been on the question of admitting new members. The admission of Italy, for example, was vetoed six times by Soviet Russia. The frequent use of the veto on this issue by the USSR makes the total an impressive figure. This is clearly an abuse of the voting privilege granted a permanent member but it should not obscure the fact that a majority of the vetoes have been used, or applied to only one issue and that issue itself is not immediately related to important questions of the maintenance of peace and security. In addition, it is interesting to note that on some matters involving specific disputes, eventual settlement materialized in spite of the veto. This was true, for example, in the Syrian and Lebanese question.[4] New members have now been admitted as a result of political compromise. The double veto can be used but resort to it took place only in the early years of the Organization.

Actually, the veto could have been used more extensively than it has been in a number of instances. The procedure of abstaining has eliminated a large number of negative votes. Even the absence of a permanent member has been considered to be an abstention and not a veto. Although the United States has so far refrained from using the veto, a threat to do so has been sufficient to obtain the result desired.[5] The United States has also been able to use its influence to obtain negative votes or abstentions from nonpermanent members in sufficient number to prevent a majority of seven on a matter which it opposed. The veto can still block an amendment to the Charter but certain modifications tantamount to amendments have been brought about through action in the General Assembly.

This does not mean that the problem of the veto is unimportant. It does mean that the veto is not always an insurmountable problem, particularly

---

[4] See Chapter 7.
[5] In 1950, for example, the United States threatened to veto any replacement for Trygve Lie as Secretary-General.

when the Council majority is determined to avail itself of means provided elsewhere for continued negotiation, discussion, and possible settlement of the problem at hand. The frequent Soviet vetoes are not and cannot be an isolated phenomenon. They merely reflect and express the antagonism which has divided the world into two armed camps. Voting in the Council cannot be arranged by some special legal formula. The lengthy discussion over the veto, both within and outside the United Nations, has involved a great deal of oversimplification. It is true that at times the veto has paralyzed the work of the Council, lessened its ability to deal adequately with matters brought before it, and greatly undermined the confidence in it as an effective instrument for the maintenance of international peace and security. But it is the general political situation and the lack of confidence among the great powers and not the veto itself which has caused the difficulty. There cannot be unanimity among the permanent Council members when one of them is challenging the existing balance of power. It is clear to see, as well, that there will be no United Nations as envisaged by the Charter without this unanimity. No removal or modification of the present voting formula will bring about the necessary co-operation. The veto stands, therefore, as an ineradicable symptom of a divided world.

The General Assembly. A very great amount of time has been consumed in voting on the wide variety of matters coming before the Assembly. No issue similar in nature to that of the veto in the Security Council has arisen, although certain problems concerned with voting and voting practices have developed.

One of these involves the matter of what is an 'important question,' which requires a two-thirds vote. Important questions include the following: recommendations with respect to the maintenance of international peace and security; the election of nonpermanent members of the Security Council; the election of members to the Economic and Social Council and the Trusteeship Council; the admission of new members; the suspension of the rights and privileges of members; the expulsion of members; questions relating to the operation of the trusteeship system; and budgetary questions.

Despite the identification of these items as important, there has developed the problem of whether a question which does not fit a prescribed category but is admittedly significant requires only a simple majority. Must a new category be created for a question which is important enough to require a two-thirds vote?

The record of the Assembly is somewhat inconclusive on these points. It has been argued that there must be a new category before a question can be considered 'important' or not. All questions of this nature could not be foreseen by the framers of the Charter or makers of the Rules and therefore they prescribed the method by which specific questions could come under the two-thirds rule, that is, through the adoption of 'additional categories.' The rules specify 'additional categories of questions' and not 'additional questions.' It can also be argued, however, that in exceptional circumstances, it might be unwise or impossible to create a new category. There is nothing to prevent the General Assembly from deciding that a question is 'important' and then proceeding to apply the two-thirds rule.

While both positions are relevant, in the interest of reducing the number of two-thirds votes it is probable that there will be fewer such votes if a category is determined first. Although this might lead to an increase in the number of categories, such a development is less harmful than if there is a tendency to treat all questions labeled 'important' as requiring a two-thirds vote instead of examining each question more carefully. No conclusive interpretation is possible at the present, which leaves the matter essentially up to the members. Their intent will determine whether there is an indiscriminate use of the two-thirds rule.

Conflicting views have also been offered as to the time when the procedural question should be decided. Should it be done before or after the vote on the substantive question? Some argue that it should be done after the vote on the question itself, in the hope that statistics of this vote will decide the procedural question in many instances. That is to say, a vote on the substantive question may fail to receive a majority or might pass by two-thirds, in each case eliminating the need for the procedural question and thereby saving the time of the General Assembly. This position is disputed by those who believe that it is preferable to decide the procedural matter before instead of after the substantive vote. They argue — and their opinion reflects the majority view on this problem — that if the procedural issue is settled first, there is less likelihood of the result of the substantive vote influencing the procedural vote, which might be the case if it were necessary to decide the procedural question last.

The charge of bloc voting has frequently been leveled at the General Assembly. In a situation of this sort, certain groups of states are supposed to have been able to determine the outcome of elections and even the decisions on substantive questions. A bloc is presumed to be any group that votes together regularly either on all or on specific types of questions. Some believe that a powerful state may command the votes of a particular group. It is also claimed that on certain issues two or more groups of states combine to force a decision which they favor.

That there are definite blocs of states cannot be denied. These include the Latin American group, the Arab League which frequently joins with the Afro-Asian countries to form an Arab-Afro-Asian bloc, the members of the British Commonwealth, the Soviet bloc of Communist states, and the Western European area. The interesting study of Professor M. Margaret Ball throws considerable light upon the existence of bloc voting and how it operates on certain issues.[6] Voting on the election of officers and committee chairmen was found to be indicative of bloc voting but its existence was difficult to prove because of the requirement of Assembly Rule 92 for a secret ballot in elections. Also the requirement that geographical representation should, in general, govern the selection of these officials tends to obscure a definite answer. Nevertheless, it appears fairly certain that caucusing occurs prior to elections and as a result there are candidates selected by regional groups to guarantee their representation. This has been particularly true in selecting the nonpermanent members of the Security Council. The Afro-Asian, Latin American, and Soviet blocs most frequently engage in this process of nominating representatives for their regions. The Latin American and Arab states have joined together in elections and constitute a strong combination. Their combined votes, if regional lines hold firmly, can virtually dominate the election of any official in the General Assembly. This position of power, however, has not been greatly abused, with the possible exception of voting for the nonpermanent members of the Security Council.

Professor Ball compiled some useful data on the voting tendencies of these groups in connection with substantive issues. Certainly the major powers have not voted as a bloc. The United Kingdom does not appear to be able to influence Commonwealth voting, nor does the Commonwealth always vote as a unit. The Soviet bloc of nine countries is the one consistent group which follows the lead of the Kremlin and votes as a group on all issues. Arab-Afro-Asian countries, with few exceptions, vote as a unit on specific issues which concern them, such as matters concerning dependent areas. Western Europe presents no indication of true solidarity on most issues although the states comprising this area vote under the leadership of the United States on questions bearing on the East-West conflict.

A careful voting analysis reveals that most but not all Latin American states vote together. There is some evidence to indicate that the United States is able to obtain the support of a sizeable majority of votes from this area on East-West questions. The only notable exception to any consistency was Argentina prior to 1955 during the Perón regime. On matters involving the economic development of underdeveloped countries, Latin America has not voted with the United States with any degree of regularity.

    [6] 'Block Voting in the General Assembly,' *International Organization*, Vol. 5, No. 1 (February 1951), pp. 3–31.

There have been sharp disagreements, for example, on the question of governmental loans versus private investment for economic development. There is no positive indication of a close working alliance between Latin America and the Arab-Afro-Asian groups. However, since 1954, there has been an increasing tendency for Latin America to side with these blocs on colonial questions along with the Soviet countries. If even a loose working arrangement of this nature develops, with a potential voting strength of over fifty votes, it would be a formidable alignment. For example, should the Arab-Afro-Asian groups agree to support Latin American views on economic development in return for voting assistance on anti-colonial measures, the United States would be placed in a most difficult and embarrassing position.

Since 1954, the Soviet Union has taken up the cause of Arab nationalism and has been joined by the Afro-Asian powers under Indian leadership. While a working arrangement of this nature on this and other colonial issues is not strong enough to dominate the Assembly unless joined by Latin America, it does possess the voting strength to rob the West of the votes necessary for a two-thirds majority. This, in effect, gives the Soviet-Arab-Afro-Asian alignment a veto over measures which it may wish to defeat. In turn, the development of these various voting blocs and their tendency to join together on certain issues means that the United States and its immediate associates in the West will find it increasingly difficult if not impossible to gain the large majorities which they have enjoyed in the past.

With its great preponderance of small nations unable to make any positive contribution toward such basic questions as collective security and economic development, there have been some suggestions outside the United Nations concerning the possibility of introducing what might be termed a more realistic approach to the distribution of voting power. This would involve the introduction of some system of weighted voting to reduce the underrepresentation of the great powers. No agreement is evident as to what shall be the formula or who shall be weighted. Should population, military strength, proportion of financial contributions, and other factors capable of being 'weighed' be considered? The problem of underrepresentation of the countries whose responsibility it is, in the final analysis, to make peace, security, and economic betterment possible is very real. Yet there is virtually no likelihood that the many small powers will ever agree to give up their equality of voting privileges in the Assembly.

THE PROBLEM OF DOMESTIC JURISDICTION

Reinforcing the principle of sovereign equality of the members of the United Nations is paragraph 7 of Article 2 of the Charter which states that 'nothing contained in the present Charter shall authorize the United Nations to intervene in matters which are essentially within the domestic jurisdiction of any state.' The inclusion of this provision came primarily at the insistence of the great powers in order that they might be protected from undue interference in their domestic society and economy. This is a legal principle recognized by international law and one that has always been guarded jealously by national governments. Traditionally included within its scope have been questions of national politics and administration, constitutional law, and matters of cultural, economic, and social policy. But the borderline between questions of national versus international concern has been narrowing in recent decades until it has become extremely difficult in many instances to identify certain matters as lying solely within one jurisdiction or another. Tariff policies, immigration laws, and the treatment of minorities, are a few matters that are commonly treated as domestic but which may have grave repercussions beyond national frontiers.

The Charter makes no definition of or limitation on domestic jurisdiction except to state that the United Nations is competent to deal with a specific conflict that is a threat to the peace, a breach of the peace, or act of aggression, irrespective of whatever claims might be raised to bar action through the protective cloak of this principle. The restriction against intervention, with this exception, applies to all organs of the United Nations. The absence of a definition has placed the burden of interpretation upon the individual members of the Organization. This has resulted in a certain measure of confusion and inconsistency as well as considerable bitterness and resentment on the part of some nations. A strict view of Article 2:7 would prevent the United Nations from doing anything if a state claimed a question lay within its domestic jurisdiction. On the other hand, if one notes the broad obligations of members and the variety of matters which have been declared to be the concern of the Organization, the scope of domestic jurisdiction is narrowed considerably. Specific organs have been created not only to consider questions of international peace and security (Security Council and General Assembly), but also to 'achieve international cooperation in solving international problems of an economic, social, cultural, or humanitarian character, and in promoting and encouraging respect for human rights and for fundamental freedoms for all without distinction as to race, sex, language, or religion' (Economic and Social Council and its various commissions and other subsidiary bodies). Chapter XI is a

Declaration Regarding Non-Self-Governing Territories and the following Chapter establishes an international trusteeship system to supervise and administer trust territories.

A strict interpretation would employ essentially a legal approach to the problem, similar to the experience under the League of Nations. By and large, however, the United Nations has adopted a much broader conception of domestic jurisdiction based upon political considerations. Put somewhat bluntly, if there are enough votes, the matter will be placed on the agenda of the General Assembly, without much concern for a protesting claim of domestic jurisdiction. In employing the political interpretation, the organs of the United Nations have developed what has been termed the 'doctrine of international concern' which can be seen in the Spanish question before the Security Council in 1946.[7] The central issue here was the character of the Franco government. It was inevitable that the issue of domestic jurisdiction would be raised since the nature of a state's government has been traditionally considered to be beyond the reach of international jurisdiction. Some justification was needed for a censure of the regime. It was provided by the Australian delegate, Dr. Evatt, who offered this political reason:

> When you look at the internal affairs of a country, you start off with the postulate that it is no business of any other nation to concern itself with how the people of that country govern themselves . . . , but if the facts indicate that that regime, by its nature, by its conduct, by its operations, is likely to interfere with international peace and likely to be a menace to its neighbors, then the existence of that regime is no longer a matter of essentially domestic concern.

Since the Franco regime was considered to be, by its nature, 'likely' to threaten peace, Dr. Evatt argued that this was sufficient cause for consideration by the Council. He used the term 'domestic concern' instead of 'domestic jurisdiction,' stating, in effect, that a matter which is a potential threat to peace or a cause of international friction is thereby of concern to the United Nations. It is easier to have 'concern for' something than to claim 'jurisdiction over' a problem.

It is doubtful whether this approach is in conformity with the intentions of the Charter but it has been employed with success, particularly by those states, many of them former dependencies, that are anxious to reduce the extent of colonialism and delight in scrutinizing the affairs of colonial powers. For their part, the colonial powers find themselves in a minority position and have fought what they consider to be unjustified intervention

[7] Howell, John M., 'The French and South African Walkouts and Domestic Jurisdiction,' *Journal of Politics*, Vol. 18, No. 1 (February 1956), pp. 97–8.

in their domestic affairs with considerable vigor. In 1955, France, for example, walked out of the Assembly in protest against a consideration of the Algerian question. The Union of South Africa has engaged in a continuing struggle against the investigation of its racial policies and its administration of South-West Africa, a former League mandate. On several occasions, South Africa has left the Assembly and refused to negotiate with the United Nations on these matters. Both France and South Africa have used legal arguments to support their position.

Glaring inconsistencies are quite evident, however, with respect to the interpretation of domestic jurisdiction, revealing the political nature of the problem once again. India, for example, has been one of the leaders in demanding a consideration of colonial matters and has been determined to bring the Assembly into the racial question in South Africa. The argument has always been that these issues are of international concern and are likely to cause a threat to peace. The Soviet Union has been only too willing to join in this crusade. But India has indicated clearly that it will not permit the United Nations or anyone else to interfere in what it considers to be its own affairs.[8] The USSR led the fight against the consideration of the Hungarian situation in 1956, claiming that the problem lay wholly within the domestic jurisdiction of its satellite. The United States has been placed in an embarrassing situation, not wishing to antagonize its Western partners who have colonial holdings, yet basically in sympathy with the principle of national self-determination. A vacillating policy results from this predicament. It is further complicated by the fears of some in the United States that the actions and pronouncements of the United Nations and the specialized agencies will, in some fashion, infringe upon the sanctity of the Constitution and American sovereign rights. Adherence to certain conventions sponsored by the United Nations, it is believed, will almost certainly alter the Constitution and prepare the way for American subservience to some form of world government.

Although the tendency has been to interpret broadly the provisions of Article 2:7, the supporters of a strict, legal adherence to the concept of domestic jurisdiction have by no means abandoned their position. In addition, dependence upon Article 2:7 is a convenient mechanism for those who may wish to escape their obligations under the Charter or avoid the con-

[8] For example, *The New York Times* of June 12, 1951, reported that India would not tolerate any effort to tell its government 'what we should do in India or in any part of the Indian Union.' In January 1957 the Indian puppet premier of Kashmir, in direct opposition to a 10-0-1 vote of the Security Council, proclaimed adoption of a constitution joining Kashmir to India and stated: 'We are not bound by resolutions which are against our country and our interests.'

sideration of a question which might prove to be embarrassing. There is little probability that the conflict which has raged on this matter of international jurisdiction will abate to any considerable extent in the future.

THE ASCENDANCY OF THE GENERAL ASSEMBLY

One final major constitutional problem remains to be examined. This involves the very heart and structure of the United Nations itself and the original allocation of roles and powers to the Security Council and the General Assembly. The decline of the Security Council and the consequent rise of the Assembly to the role of the pre-eminent organ of the United Nations is probably the most striking constitutional change that has been experienced by the Organization.

The framers of the Charter at San Francisco envisaged a sort of equilibrium between the functions of these two bodies. Each was to have its own peculiar sphere of activities and responsibilities for the maintenance of world peace. As the supreme representative body, the Assembly was to establish the principles upon which world peace and the ideal of solidarity were to rest. In the words of the chairman of the committee charged with drafting the political and security powers of the Assembly at San Francisco, the Assembly was to be 'the creative body, . . . the fortress where human aspirations are going to be defended. It will not have armies at its disposal, it will not have cannon or prisons, it will instead have something which, though incorporeal, has, in the course of human history, shown itself to be stronger and more invincible than brute force: the power of thought.'

On the other hand, the Security Council was to act in accordance with those principles established by the Assembly, performing its duties as laid down in the Charter 'with the speed necessary to prevent any attempted breach of international peace and security' as the 'organ of action.' Should the Council decide to employ enforcement action, the decision to do so was to be binding on all members. Action with respect to threats to the peace, breaches of the peace, and acts of aggression, therefore, belonged only to the Security Council.

Thirteen years of practice reveal a situation entirely different from the one just posed. No longer is there an equilibrium between the Council and the Assembly. The Council started out as the leading organ of political action but a reverse trend which began in 1948 has led to a gradual decline in its importance. Before the middle of 1948, the Council was called upon to consider more political issues than the Assembly. But since that time more questions have been submitted to the Assembly and there has been a considerable decrease in the number of Council sessions. Several reasons account for this interesting shift to the Assembly and each deserves more than passing mention.[9]

One compelling factor has been the stalemate produced in the Security Council as a result of the failure of its permanent members to act in unison. The Commission at San Francisco which worked on the collective security provision of the Charter reported that the 'general scheme for future world security . . . is based on the unanimity of the great powers, which will bear the brunt of future enforcement action . . .' This fundamental principle has been destroyed by the East-West conflict and other means had to be found to avoid the impasse in the Council. The 'Uniting for Peace' resolution adopted by the Assembly in 1950 is a reflection of this situation and has made it possible for that organ to exercise collective measures, as we shall see later.[10] This device, which makes possible the use of enforcement action in the veto-free Assembly, was engineered by the United States but concurred in by an overwhelming majority of United Nations members. They sought this change, in the face of Charter provisions and implications to the contrary, so that the United Nations might perform the functions expected of it in the maintenance of international peace and security. With the climate of international relations characterized by tension and conflict between the major powers, it is perhaps inevitable that the Assembly should become the organ called upon to consider an increasing number of political questions.

The medium and small powers, while decrying the split in the ranks of the Big Five, nevertheless have welcomed the opportunity to make more use of the General Assembly. It is here that their greater number affords them the chance to influence the direction of the United Nations and press for decisions in keeping with their interests. Their displeasure with the great power veto was clearly evident at San Francisco and they accepted the voting procedure of the Security Council with great reluctance. It is entirely possible that this preponderant group of states would have worked toward an increasingly important role for the Assembly even if the disunity of the great powers had not materialized.

Credit must also be given to the great powers, for they, too, have individually contributed to the growing importance of the General Assembly. They have turned to this organ only in part as a result of the voting obstacles in the Council. The Assembly was quickly discovered to be an excellent forum where views could be presented for worldwide consumption.

[9] See Haviland, H. Field, Jr., *The Political Role of the General Assembly,* New York, 1951, pp. 168–71 and Morgenthau, Hans, 'The New United Nations,' *The Review of Politics,* Vol. 16, No. 1 (January 1954), pp. 3–7.

[10] See Chapter 8.

The opportunities for propagandizing in such an organ are positive and real. Here is the opportunity to counter at least verbally, the policies of potential or actual opponents in the game of international politics. Finally, it is in the Assembly that efforts can be made to win the support of the medium and small nations since only a very few of them can be represented in the Security Council. With the development and expansion of various alliances, within and without the United Nations in recent years, it has become imperative that the major powers devote considerable attention to gaining the collaboration of as many of the smaller states as possible. With its present near universal membership, the Assembly is the ideal place to pursue this political fence-mending.

The expanded role of the Assembly has not been restricted to political questions alone. Although it possesses definite supervisory powers over the Trusteeship Council and the Economic and Social Council, these organs were granted considerable autonomy of their own. It has become customary, however, for members to bring matters directly to the Assembly if they have failed to obtain what they believe to be satisfactory treatment before these organs. The anti-colonial powers, for example, have found it more expedient to employ the plenary body as a direct means of advancing their interests, particularly since the Trusteeship Council provides a strong voting position for colonial states.

The tendency to centralize activities in the Assembly has made it, without much question, the key organ of the United Nations. Whether this trend will extend to greater supervision over the specialized agencies remains to be seen. In any event, it seems fair to predict that there is little evidence to indicate that the scope of Assembly activity will be arrested by any foreseeable development.

SUMMARY

The various problems and changes of a constitutional nature which have just been examined reveal clearly the impact of international politics upon international organization. To begin with, the Charter was constructed through the processes of diplomatic negotiation which inevitably produced a document full of political compromise, at times unclear and ambiguous, which is a guarantee of future divergent constitutional interpretations, even in a world with tensions held to a minimum.

The thirteen years since the adoption of the Charter have seen a war-weary world struggling to return to some measure of stability but, at the same time, confronted by a whole series of developments unexpected in 1945. The advent of atomic and hydrogen weapons, the breakdown of great power unity, the pent-up nationalisms of colonial peoples, are some of the more obvious manifestations of the complexity of the post-World War II world. Given this setting, it is obvious that the question of voting procedures and privileges would assume greater proportions than might have been expected. There was the hope in 1945 that the Organization would achieve a universal membership. While this has almost become a reality, it has taken eleven years filled with bitterness and acrimony. A major problem still persists in the form of the two claimants for the seat reserved for China in the Security Council. The problem of domestic jurisdiction will remain, despite the tendency of the majority to proceed with a loose interpretation of the Charter.

The political developments which have brought about the new role of the General Assembly, have been accomplished within the framework of the Charter, which is a tribute to the flexibility and ambiguity of that document. What has taken place is the establishment of a practical relationship between the Charter and political reality. The Charter has shown that it is adaptable to change and does not stand as an obstacle to the functioning of the Organization when new and vital political challenges confront it.

III

POLITICAL, LEGAL, AND ADMINISTRATIVE PROBLEMS

7

THE ADJUSTMENT AND SETTLEMENT OF

DISPUTES AND POLITICAL QUESTIONS

A COMPELLING reason for establishing an international organization concerned with the problems of international peace and security is to offer permanent machinery for the peaceful settlement of disputes. This is reflected in the Charter of the United Nations which is concerned primarily with preventing a dispute from developing into a threat to, or actual breach of, international peace and security. Even the mere existence of such an organization equipped with the means to handle disputes is of value since nations can turn to it with the knowledge that there is a forum where their grievances can be aired.

Furthermore, under the Charter every party to a dispute is obligated to settle it by employing methods which are not a danger to international peace and security. It is not intended that the United Nations should supplant action by individual states through ordinary diplomatic channels and accepted procedures. Instead, the Charter specifically provides that the parties to a dispute should first of all try to settle it themselves through such accepted procedures, including resort to regional agencies or arrangements, or other peaceful means of their own choice. This is the Charter's basic approach to pacific settlement as evidenced in Chapter VI. However, should the parties fail to observe this obligation or be unsuccessful, the Charter empowers the Organization to take action but without authority to enforce its recommendations.

Primary responsibility is given to the Security Council for the implementation of peaceful settlement although the General Assembly can consider any questions which may bear upon peace and security. The Secretary-General of the United Nations plays an active role as a negotiator and conciliator between the parties to a dispute. Recourse to judicial settlement can be had by referring contentious questions and disputes to the International Court of Justice. Succeeding pages will cover in detail the procedures and machinery of pacific settlement that are available under the Charter and the manner in which they have been employed. Only passing reference will be made to the role of the Secretary-General and the conduct of judicial settlement, since later chapters will be devoted to an examination of these processes.

THE METHODOLOGY OF ADJUSTMENT AND SETTLEMENT OF DISPUTES

Chapter VI of the Charter (arts. 33–38) is devoted exclusively to the question of pacific settlement. The Security Council is the organ most concerned in this section of the Charter since it has been given the most specific responsibilities with respect to pacific settlement. The General Assembly is simply mentioned here as an organ to which a dispute may be referred. Other articles of the Charter (10, 11, 14), however, permit the Assembly to consider questions which have a bearing upon international peace and co-operation and considerable use has been made of its broad powers.

To gain an insight into the rather intricate provisions of the Charter and to learn what has occurred in practice, it is necessary, first, to examine the matter of bringing a question before the United Nations and the problems surrounding its consideration. The duties of the parties to a dispute must then be considered, as well as the functions of both the Security Council and the General Assembly. Selected case studies of the more significant disputes, situations, and political questions before both organs will then be discussed.

It should be noted that the Council and the Assembly have interpreted the Charter provision quite freely when considering situations and disputes. The Charter makes a distinction between disputes which are likely to endanger peace and security (Chapter VI) and those which are serious enough to constitute a threat to the peace, breach of the peace, or aggression (Chapter VII). However, the practice of the Council and the Assembly has tended to reduce this distinction and measures have been adopted which would appear to belong under Chapter VII without being so identified. Indirectly, at least, the Charter has encouraged such a development, since the Council is authorized to 'call upon' parties to do certain things under either Article 33 of Chapter VI or Article 40 of Chapter VII. In the Indonesia and Palestine questions, for example, the Council recommended certain measures without reference to either of these articles. In addition, even though hostilities broke out (Palestine and Indonesia), the Council and the Assembly continued the process of peaceful settlement.

Placement of Questions and Their Consideration. Bringing a dispute or situation before either the Council or the Assembly is a relatively simple matter. This can be done by any member or by a nonmember. The General Assembly cannot make recommendations upon any dispute which is before the Security Council but it still may consider it for purposes of discussion. The Council may refer a matter to the attention of the Assembly and vice versa. The Secretary-General is authorized to bring to the attention of the Council 'any matter which in his opinion may threaten the maintenance of international peace and security.' Finally, the Assembly and the Council may request the Court to hand down an advisory opinion.

The form of submission is equally simple. Normally a question is directed to either the Council or Assembly in written form with a request that it be placed upon the agenda. Occasionally this request is labeled 'urgent' and frequently, when a question is submitted to the Council, there is a request that a meeting be called to consider it. A procedural vote of the Council can convene a special session of the Assembly to consider an urgent matter. The Assembly can, by a majority vote of its members or by a vote of any seven members of the Council, meet in special session, as it did in November, 1956, to consider the Suez crisis.

Most of the questions submitted to the Council and the Assembly have originated from one of the parties to a dispute. Occasionally states who are not parties but have a special interest or responsibility in the question have brought the matter to the attention of one or the other of these organs. Rarely have nonmembers brought a dispute to either body although a number of communications involving complaints or charges have been received.

Both the Security Council and the General Assembly decide whether to consider a question, once it has been submitted. The primary step is the placement of the question in the agenda. Although both organs customarily have included on the agenda most questions brought to their attention, the completion of the agenda is not automatic and may frequently involve a considerable amount of discussion. Various objections have been raised concerning the inclusion of some matters on the agenda. These have included the charge of lack of competence, that no dispute or situation exists, that other procedures are available, and that a consideration of the question might interfere with procedures for settlement already undertaken and hence would serve no purpose. In the clarification of such issues as these, the general discussion permits all interested parties to state their views. It may also be necessary for both organs to appoint fact-finding committees and commissions to obtain additional information on the nature of a question which has been submitted before a decision can be reached.

Duties of Parties to a Dispute. All parties to a dispute which, if it continues, is likely to endanger the maintenance of international peace and security, are to seek a solution by negotiation, inquiry, mediation, conciliation, arbitration, judicial settlement, resort to regional agencies or arrangements, 'or other peaceful means of their own choice.' These are the customary methods of peaceful settlement and they are listed in Article 33. Any combination of these or some new arrangement agreed to by the parties is satisfactory as long as there is an attempt at peaceful settlement. If the dispute is not settled, the parties then 'shall refer it to the Security Council' (Art. 37) or may submit it to the General Assembly.

Duties of the Security Council. The Council, on its own authority, can investigate any dispute or any situation 'which might lead to international friction or give rise to a dispute, in order to determine whether the continuance of the dispute or situation is likely to endanger the maintenance of international peace and security' (Art. 34). The primary duty of the Council is to determine the extent of the problem, its general nature, and whether the dispute or situation may lead to serious consequences. No attempt is made at this time to recommend procedures for a settlement or determine who is right or wrong. The usual procedure is, through inquiry, to gather relevant facts and information. Documents and evidence are procured from the parties concerned and examined. The Council may employ a subcommittee or create an investigatory commission to gather pertinent facts. This was done in the Greek case and in the dispute between India and Pakistan. Material submitted by the parties is 'taken note of' and if the Council believes that the matter is not one likely to endanger peace, it may take no further action. This involves an important decision, however. At this stage of the inquiry, the Council may have to decide by a non-procedural vote whether the dispute, if it continues, will be a danger to international peace and security. A veto may be cast which can block Council action that might be necessary if the dispute actually has been determined, by prior inquiry, to be of a serious nature. But the matter may be kept on the agenda or referred to the General Assembly. Voting is procedural for both these acts.

In the case of a 'situation' the Charter provides that the Council must employ investigatory procedures to determine two things. If a situation is likely to lead to a dispute, the Council must study it with a view to deciding the nature of the dispute which may eventuate. The same process is involved with a situation 'which might lead to international friction.' If the situation, in the opinion of the Council, does not appear likely to lead to international friction or to a dispute, the matter must be dropped from the agenda. All decisions involved in determining the nature of the situation require, if it comes to a vote, the unanimous vote of the permanent members. If the matter that comes before the Council is identified as a situation and not a dispute, a member of the Council party to the problem can vote. It is only in instances where the matter is identified as a dispute that a party must abstain from voting.

It would appear that the distinction in Article 34 between a 'dispute' and a 'situation' would be important but it has not been in practice. The insertion of one word, 'situation,' was made because there are situations which, while not clearly disputes, may have serious implications and might endanger peace. As an example, the Polish member of the Council held that the Franco regime in Spain constituted such a situation. In most instances, matters coming before the Council have been concerned with well-defined disputes between specific parties who have put forth definite claims. When cases have come before the Council as 'situations' they have customarily been handled as disputes. The Iranian question and the Syrian and Lebanese question were both labeled 'situations' when first brought to the attention of the Council but the Council treated them as disputes without clarifying the record. The Hungarian Situation in 1956 came to the Security Council under Article 34 but Council action was thwarted by a Soviet veto.

As might be expected, a state bringing a question to the Council maintains that it is a dispute or situation likely to endanger peace and security. At the same time, those states against whom complaints have been lodged have denied the existence of such a danger. The British maintained, for example, that the Anglo-Egyptian dispute involved no such danger but the Anglo-Iranian dispute did. Through careful deliberation the Council members often have been able to avoid such a determination. The Council acted in this manner in the Corfu case by recommending reference of the question to the International Court of Justice without determining, under Article 34, that the case was likely to endanger peace and security. However, it is still possible for some permanent member to raise the problem of distinguishing between types of disputes and disputes and situations in order to protect some vital interest through a nonprocedural vote.

If the parties to a dispute that may endanger peace and security fail to utilize methods of pacific settlement the Council shall, 'when it deems it necessary, call upon the parties to settle their dispute by such means.' The Council adopted resolutions to this effect in the Iranian and Indonesian cases. The parties are not bound by such a 'call' or request but a refusal by a member of the United Nations to attempt a solution by peaceful means is already a violation of the Charter in two instances. Article 2:3 states that 'All Members shall settle their international disputes by peaceful means in such a manner that international peace and security, and justice, are not endangered.' Article 33:1 also requires the parties to seek a solution to a dispute by peaceful settlement. Should the Council determine, however, that the parties to a serious dispute are proceeding with a method of peaceful settlement, it may take no further action.

However, if the Council determines that the dispute is one which is likely to endanger international peace and security, it may recommend at any stage of the dispute appropriate procedures or methods of adjustment. It will be recalled that the parties themselves are expected to work out methods of pacific settlement and the Security Council may call the procedures listed in Article 33 to their attention. But the Council may, in addition, following a decision that the dispute is serious, intervene to recommend some specific method of settlement, even without waiting for the parties to proceed with measures of pacific settlement. By intervening in this manner, the Council is free to utilize any technique or procedure or combination of methods which it believes might prove useful. The initial resolution of the Council in the Indonesian case, for example, although leaving the choice of procedures to the parties, did point out that recourse to arbitration would be a useful means of negotiation. The Council can also make use of any preliminary measure adopted by the parties for pacific settlement or procedures included in prior treaty commitments which may be applicable. An intervention of this nature involves only a recommendation to pursue some specific method or procedure and does not include a recommendation of terms of settlement. This can be done only if the parties themselves have not arrived at a solution and therefore have referred the dispute to the Council. It is possible that a member of the United Nations may claim a problem, no matter how serious, to be a situation and not a dispute, thereby not being obligated by the Charter to seek a peaceful settlement before the Council intervenes. To avoid such a predicament, the Charter in Article 36:1 makes it possible for the Council to intervene at any time in a situation which it has determined to be a danger to international peace and security. Such an intervention by the Council can involve recommendations for pacific settlement and possible terms for arriving at a solution.

Should the dispute not fall within the serious category, that is, one not likely to endanger international peace and security, the Council may make recommendations with a view to a pacific settlement only if all the parties to the dispute request it to do so. When acting in this capacity, the Council performs in the capacity of conciliator but can only recommend a procedure to be followed or the terms of a settlement. The Council cannot intervene in a dispute of this nature on its own initiative except to determine, again, whether it is one likely to endanger international peace and security.

Procedures Developed by the Security Council. Many of these Charter provisions which have just been explained are similar to those available to the League of Nations under the Covenant. The League Council was forced to improvise and develop a certain flexibility in the face of rigid Covenant provisions and conflicting political interests. The same has been true of the Security Council since 1946. Both the League and United Nations Councils are considered to be political bodies, wherein the great powers have sought to advance and protect national interests. The minority position in which the Soviet Union has been placed in the Security Council is the result of a certain intransigence plus an abiding suspicion of Western motives. Consequently, the Soviets have conducted themselves largely in a negative fashion, exhibited through their use of the veto. In an effort to combat this attitude and further their own efforts, the other permanent members and many of the nonpermanent ones have had to devise techniques and procedures to enable the Council to function at all. At the same time, on the occasions when there has been relatively little discord, the members of the Council have liberally interpreted their duties under the Charter and devised certain definite methods to handle problems brought before them.

Despite the large number of Soviet vetoes, the Security Council has managed to proceed with its business in various ways. In all cases brought before it, there has been a considerable amount of discussion. Sometimes it has been possible to avoid a nonprocedural vote although it is obvious from the record that there has been far too much time spent on the actual mechanics of voting. At times the Council has been able to avoid the formal determination of whether a dispute is a dangerous one by engaging in full discussion of the problem when it is placed on the agenda. It will be recalled that the adoption of an agenda is a procedural matter and no veto is possible. The Iranian question was settled informally in this manner. On other occasions, such as with the Spanish and Corfu cases, subcommittees were appointed to ascertain certain facts. The use of subcommittees for this purpose has also reduced the number of occasions where it was necessary to determine the character of a dispute and they have been established by a procedural vote except in the Czechoslovak case.

Australian membership on the Council has been largely responsible for the development of the subcommittee technique which has proved to be of great benefit to all Council proceedings, particularly when nonpermanent members with fewer interests to protect have been appointed. On occasion the Council has employed subsidiary organs of mediation and conciliation in an effort to arrive at a settlement. Resort to this procedure has been taken ordinarily only after it has become obvious that the parties to a dispute are not making progress in reaching an agreement. The essential task of such organs is to assist the parties themselves to reconcile their differences. At the same time, these organs report to the Council on the nature of developments and do what they can to prevent a further aggravation of the dispute.

The President of the Security Council has been used as a conciliator in the Kashmir dispute and he or another member of the Council can perform useful services in this manner. Various mediation and conciliation commissions have been used in the Kashmir, Palestine, and Indonesian questions. Each of these efforts at conciliation was begun after hostilities had broken out, a fact which made the task far more difficult. Commissions of inquiry have been established to gather relevant facts and report recommendations to the Council. An example of this can be found in the handling of the Greek situation. The commissions usually adopt their own procedures based in part on those of the Council and engage in relatively few votes. No veto is possible in their voting procedure. Commissions are assisted by the Secretariat which furnishes expert advice and travel and subsistence expenses. Their size varies from three to eleven. Those concerned with inquiry and investigation usually have the largest number. Individual appointments are made with a view to competence, experience, and the wishes of the parties concerned.

When the Council has urged the parties to a dispute to continue negotiations, it has frequently attempted to make certain that its recommendations will be respected. It has requested the parties to report on the progress of negotiations and in so doing, has indicated that it will continue to examine the question after the parties have made an effort to arrive at a settlement. The Council has also stated that it might employ other measures if no agreement appears to be developing. In this manner, the Council seeks to bring pressure on the parties without, however, disturbing the delicate balance of negotiations underway. The best example of employing devices of this nature is the dispute between Iran and the Soviet Union.

The Position of the General Assembly. Chapter VI of the Charter refers only once to the General Assembly with respect to pacific settlement. This is the provision in Article 35 that a dispute or situation likely to endanger the maintenance of international peace and security may be referred by a member, a nonmember, or the Security Council to the Assembly. When a dispute or a situation is before the Security Council, the Assembly can discuss it but can offer no recommendations.

Other articles of the Charter, however, make ample grants of authority to the Assembly. Under Article 10, for example, the Assembly can discuss any question within the scope of the Charter. In article 14 the Assembly is empowered to 'recommend measures for the peaceful adjustment of any situation, regardless of origin, which it deems likely to impair the general welfare or friendly relations among nations.' Also, in Article 11, the Assembly 'may consider the general principles of cooperation in the maintenance of international peace and security.'

Although Chapter VI of the Charter specifically provides the way in which the Council is to proceed with serious disputes, no similar language applies to the Assembly. Since the Council was supposed to play the major role in pacific settlement, there is, in fact, very little indication of what is expected of the Assembly and no limitation is placed upon the type of dispute which can come before it. With the authority that is granted by Articles 10 and 14, the Assembly has a much wider range of activity than does the Council. No distinction is made between a dispute and a situation nor is any procedure suggested for the handling of situations. Consequently, the Assembly has been able to adopt a flexible attitude regarding the nature of questions it will consider and the character of its recommendations. It usually employs the more general term 'situation' in its resolutions instead of the more positive term 'dispute' in order to avoid the possibility of aggravating the parties concerned.

The Assembly has made wide use of its authority to recommend principles of international co-operation which should guide the conduct of interstate relations. This approach has been employed when the Assembly is considering specific disputes and situations. Pertinent sections of the Charter are singled out for emphasis, such as Articles 1 and 2, and the parties are encouraged to pursue their relations accordingly. In several instances, the Assembly has been concerned with the failure of members to observe respect for human rights and fundamental freedoms. The *apartheid* question in South Africa and Soviet activities in the Balkans, especially in Hungary, are good examples. Proposals have been made for strengthening the means by which the United Nations can maintain international peace and security. The Assembly has also directed its attention to the strained relations between the great powers.

Procedures Developed by the General Assembly. Despite its being limited to making recommendations, the Assembly has demonstrated its flexibility in adopting a particular course of action to meet the needs of a situation. In most instances, the Assembly resolutions do not 'recommend' but 'invite' the members to act or 'appeal' or 'call upon' the parties concerned in a dispute to continue negotiations or 'refrain' from acting in a particular manner. Thus, the Assembly resolution of November 2, 1956, in the Middle East crisis, 'calls upon Israel and Egypt immediately to cease fire.' In the November 4, 1956, resolution in the Hungarian situation, the Assembly 'calls upon the Government of the Union of Soviet Socialist Republics to desist forthwith . . .' and 'affirms the right of the Hungarian people. . . .'

The Assembly has repeatedly requested the parties to a dispute to settle it by peaceful means. This is especially the case in the initial stages of the dispute where the Assembly is reluctant to intervene any further than this so as not to upset any negotiations which might still be possible. A resolution of this nature is normally a compromise, since the state submitting the question usually desires more action than merely calling for continued negotiations. However, the simple request of resort to pacific settlement does not always bring the parties together. One of the parties, such as the Arab states in the Palestine question, may refuse to begin or resume negotiations until some prior conditions have been met. There have also been claims of lack of competence to act on a dispute. Most frequently heard has been the charge of interference in the domestic affairs of a state. The Soviet Union, for example, heatedly opposed discussion of the Hungarian situation in 1956 on this ground and the Hungarian delegation left the Assembly claiming, similarly, a violation of the United Nations Charter. The Union of South Africa also absented itself from the General Assembly in 1956, as it had done earlier on occasion, protesting against consideration of the *apartheid* question.

The Assembly by no means limits its efforts to the initial stages of a dispute. Resolutions are adopted repeatedly, as in the Palestine question, pointing out the continuing responsibilities of the parties to arrive at an agreement through peaceful means. The Assembly also has gone beyond this relatively mild procedure and become involved with the substantive issues of a question. In so doing, the Assembly may request one of the parties to refrain from continuing a particular act, as it did in the *apartheid* question by calling upon South Africa to terminate the enforcement of its racial segregation laws. The strongest language employed by the Assembly before 1958 was that contained in the censuring of Soviet action in Hungary in 1956. By a vote of 55-8 with thirteen abstentions, the Assembly, by this resolution '. . . condemns the violation of the United Nations Charter by the government of the USSR in depriving Hungary of its liberty and independence and the Hungarian people of the exercise of their fundamental rights. . . .'

The Assembly has repeatedly sought to implement its resolutions. In certain situations it has recommended a course of action to be taken by the members of the United Nations. It has, as in the Spanish question, suggested the responsibilities of all members and in other instances such as with the former Italian colonies, it has spelled out in some detail the duties of certain administering authorities. Special machinery is created at times to carry out its decisions. This was true with respect to Libya, for example, where a United Nations commissioner was appointed along with an advisory council. A Temporary Commission observed the 1948 elections in Korea and reported its findings to the Assembly.

Similarly, the Assembly has implemented its resolutions that have been concerned with pacific settlement of disputes. Progress reports have been requested from the parties. The Assembly has indicated its displeasure with the course of negotiations, as it did in the Palestine question, and informed the disputants that further measures might be required if there was no early agreement. Subsidiary organs are created from time to time as an added means of bringing the parties together through mediation and conciliation. A United Nations Mediator and a Conciliation Commission were appointed in Palestine. There also have been a Good Offices Commission on the racial problems of South Africa, a Special Committee on the Balkans, and several commissions in Korea.

The Assembly has acted frequently to express its views on the general conditions required for peaceful international relations by taking note of various situations and tensions which exist among its members. These opinions have been largely the product of concern over the deterioration in the relations between the Soviet Union and the West. Members from each group on various occasions have sought to go on record before world public opinion as the advocates of a pacific course of action and thereby to gain support for a particular approach to East-West problems. Some of the most historic and colorful debates have preceded these Assembly decisions, often participated in, at the beginning at least, by the outstanding diplomats and foreign office officials of the major powers.

Several resolutions have been passed which condemned 'all forms of propaganda, in whatsoever country conducted, which are either designed or likely to provoke or encourage any threat to the peace, breach of the peace, or act of aggression.' Such propaganda has been labeled 'an obstacle to the strengthening of peace and international cooperation.' Invariably such resolutions originated from Soviet bloc countries that were using the Assembly as a sounding board for their own attacks against the United States. In 1947, for example, a Soviet draft, later completely amended by the Assembly, stated in its first paragraph that 'the United Nations condemn the criminal propaganda for a new war carried on by reactionary circles in a number of countries and, in particular, in the United States of America . . .'

At the request of Mexico the Assembly unanimously appealed to the great powers in 1948, requesting that they renew their efforts to settle differences between them and establish a lasting peace within the framework of the declarations to this end made at Yalta in 1945. Included in the appeal was the hope that these nations 'in a spirit of solidarity and mutual understanding' would quickly reach an understanding on 'the final settlement of the war and the conclusion of all the peace settlements.' In 1952 the Assembly, at the request of Brazil, directed an appeal 'to the Governments concerned to make a renewed and urgent effort to reach agreement on the terms of an Austrian treaty [of peace] with a view to an early termination of the occupation of Austria and the full exercise by Austria of the powers inherent in its sovereignty.'

The USSR in 1949 sought to have the Assembly adopt a resolution which would condemn the preparation for a new war allegedly being conducted in a number of countries and particularly in the United States and the United Kingdom, prohibit the use of atomic weapons, call upon all states to settle their differences amicably, and express the wish that the Big Five conclude among themselves a 'Pact for Strengthening the Peace.' Following a tumultuous and bitter debate both in committee and in plenary session, the Assembly turned down the Soviet draft, paragraph by paragraph, and adopted a jointly sponsored resolution submitted by the United States and the United Kingdom. The 'Essentials of Peace,' as the resolution was called, laid down basic principles necessary for an enduring peace and urged all members to act in accordance with them.[1] Disregard of the principles was considered primarily responsible for the continuance of international tension. The five permanent members of the Security Council were requested 'to broaden progressively their cooperation and to exercise restraint in the use of the veto in order to make the Security Council a more effective instrument for maintaining peace.'

At the second part of the third session of the General Assembly held in the spring of 1949, three important resolutions based upon the recommendations of the Interim Committee were adopted. They concerned the promotion of international co-operation in the political field. The first was a revision of the General Act of 1928 adopted by the League of Nations and which contained procedures for conciliation, arbitration, and judicial settlement for those who desired to be bound by it. The Secretary-General was instructed to make the necessary revisions including the changes contained in the resolution and to hold it open to states for accession. The second resolution recommended that the Security Council 'examine the utility and

---

[1] These principles, in effect, restated the aims and purposes of the United Nations contained in the Charter.

desirability' of having the parties to a dispute meet with the Council President and select a Council member to act as a rapporteur or conciliator in the case. If such an appointment is made, 'it would be desirable for the Security Council to abstain from further action on the case for a reasonable interval during which actual efforts at conciliation are in progress.' The other resolution invited each member of the organization 'to designate from one to five persons who, by reason of their training, experience, character and standing, are deemed to be well fitted to serve as members of commissions of inquiry or of conciliation.' They would be available for service to the Security Council, the General Assembly, and their subsidiary organs.

In 1950, the 'Peace through Deeds' resolution was adopted, condemning intervention by force or threat of force 'in the internal affairs of another state for the purpose of changing its legally established government' and urging the regulation of 'all armaments and armed forces under a United Nations system of control and inspection, with a view to their gradual reduction.' Prompt united action should be taken to meet aggression wherever it arose. All nations should reduce to a minimum the diversion for armaments of its human and economic resources and strive toward the development of such resources for the general welfare, 'with due regard to the needs of the under-developed areas of the world.'

Another resolution — 'Duties of States in the Event of Outbreak of Hostilities' — was also passed in 1950. It was adopted to create a further obstacle to the outbreak of war, even after hostilities are under way, and 'to facilitate the cessation of the hostilities by the action of the parties themselves.' If armed conflict did begin, a state should within twenty-four hours proclaim its readiness, if the other state or states did likewise, to discontinue all military operations and through a notification of its action to the Secretary-General 'invite the appropriate organs of the United Nations to dispatch the Peace Observation Commission to the area in which the conflict has arisen.' The conduct of the states in performing these duties should be taken into account 'in any determination of responsibility for the breach of the peace or act of aggression in the case under consideration.'

QUESTIONS BEFORE THE SECURITY COUNCIL

The Iranian Question. On January 19, 1946, only two days after the Security Council had held its first meeting, the head of the Iranian delegation to the General Assembly informed the Acting Secretary-General that 'owing to the interference of the Soviet Union . . . in the internal affairs of Iran, a situation has arisen which may lead to international friction.' His request that the matter be brought to the attention of the Council in accordance with Article 35 of the Charter was complied with and it was considered at twelve meetings.

Iran specifically charged that the Soviet Union was maintaining troops in Iranian territory which were creating disturbances in the northern provinces and seriously jeopardizing Iranian sovereignty. The Council referred the problem back to the parties for continued discussion, stating that it wished to be kept informed of the progress made on negotiations. Several weeks later, Iran brought the matter up again, this time contending that it was a dispute, the continuance of which was likely to endanger international peace and security. The Soviet representative, Mr. Gromyko, maintained that there was no dispute, that negotiations were continuing, and demanded, therefore, that the Council remove the item from its agenda. This request was not granted, nor was the Soviet resolution which called for a postponement of discussion by the Council. Mr. Gromyko then left the Council chamber but the matter remained before the Council. Iran eventually requested that its complaint be removed from the agenda but the Council refused to do so and continued to discuss it despite the Soviet refusal to participate.

The Council at no time arrived at any determination of whether the question was likely to endanger the maintenance of international peace and security. The eventual withdrawal of Soviet troops in May, 1946, was influenced by the Council's repeated urging of the disputants to continue to negotiate and to inform the Council of any progress made. The Council not only was interested in learning of developments but also was quietly exerting pressure on the Soviets by its several requests for information. In this manner, both parties were made aware of the continuing concern of the Council and its determination to achieve the objective of a troop withdrawal. The Council thus established the principle that it may continue to be seized of a matter irrespective of the wishes of the parties or the refusal of one of them to participate in its deliberations.

The Indonesian Question. The dispute between the Netherlands and its colonies in the Netherlands Indies is one of the most important cases to come before the Security Council. Although this dispute was brought to the Council as a breach of the peace, the Council carefully refrained from taking action under Chapter VII of the Charter (Action with Respect to Threats to the Peace, Breaches of the Peace, and Acts of Aggression).

The Japanese surrender in the Pacific took place on August 15, 1945. Only two days later a group of nationalist leaders in Indonesia issued a Declaration of Independence for the people in the Netherlands Indies. In the ensuing weeks prior to the arrival of Allied contingents in the area, the Republican government extended its control over most of Java, Madura, and Sumatra, and to a much lesser extent over the other islands. A constitution modeled along the lines of that of the United States was drafted for the new Republic of Indonesia. Allied forces under the command of General Sir Philip Christison arrived in Indonesia in September, 1945, and were confronted with an Indonesian government determined not to permit the return of the islands to Dutch sovereignty. The Republican leaders and the Dutch began negotiations which soon collapsed when each refused to retreat from its individual position claiming total control of the area. Clashes inevitably broke out between Republican units and the British. By the end of 1945 the situation was clearly becoming dangerous.

On January 21, 1946, Mr. Manuilsky of the Ukrainian SRR brought the matter to the attention of the Security Council by charging that British as well as Japanese forces were participating in military activities 'directed against the local population' of the Indies. Claiming that the entire situation was a threat to the maintenance of international peace and security, Mr. Manuilsky called for the establishment of an investigating commission. But the Council refused to take such action since several members were reluctant to become involved in a matter believed to be within the domestic jurisdiction of the Netherlands. Attention had been called to the situation, however, and the way was prepared for later extensive intervention by the United Nations.

Negotiations were then resumed between the Dutch and the Indonesians and on November 15, 1946, an agreement representing marked concessions by both parties was signed at Linggadjati. It provided for the *de facto* recognition of the Indonesian Republic in Java, Madura, and Sumatra and the establishment of a sovereign United States of Indonesia, composed of the Republic and at least two other states to be formed in Borneo and the eastern islands. At the same time, Indonesia and the Netherlands would be joined together as equal members in a Netherlands-Indonesia Union headed by the Dutch monarch. Unfortunately, disagreement arose over interpretation of this arrangement and in July, 1947, the Dutch began military operations against Indonesia. A spokesman for the Netherlands maintained that his country wished to carry out the Linggadjati Agreement but that the Indonesians were unwilling or unable to do so. The truth of the matter was that neither side trusted the other and the Dutch claimed sovereignty until a political settlement had been fully implemented.

Australia brought the situation to the attention of the Security Council on July 30, 1947, claiming that the hostilities constituted a breach of the peace under Chapter VII of the Charter. The Council quickly adopted an Australian resolution which, after noting with concern the hostilities in progress, called upon the parties to cease their hostilities and 'settle their disputes by arbitration or other peaceful means and keep the Security Council informed about the progress of the settlement.' The Netherlands still refused to admit the competence of the Council. Other colonial powers (Belgium, France, and United Kingdom) shared this view and abstained from voting on the resolution. Cease-fire orders were issued in a few days but hostilities persisted. A resolution to establish a cease-fire commission was vetoed by France but the Council adopted a joint Australian-Chinese proposal calling on the Council members having 'career consular representatives in Batavia to instruct them to prepare . . . reports on the situation, . . . such reports to cover the observance of the case-fire orders and the conditions prevailing in areas under military occupation or from which armed forces now in occupation may be withdrawn by agreement between the parties.' [2] The Council then established a three-member Committee of Good Offices, one member each to be selected by the parties and the third member by the two so selected, 'to assist in the pacific settlement of the dispute.' The Council also issued a second cease-fire order.

The Consular Commission reported in September, 1947, that hostilities had lessened but could break out anew at any moment. A third cease-fire was voted and the Committee of Good Offices managed to obtain a truce settlement on January 17, 1948. It was signed aboard a naval vessel of the United States, the U.S.S. *Renville,* which had been selected as a neutral site. A second agreement was concluded, consisting of eighteen principles that were to provide the basis for continuing political discussions. The Council approved both agreements and called upon both parties to observe them. Negotiations based on the Renville principles were continued under the leadership of the Committee but collapsed in July, 1948. Military operations were resumed on the night of December 18–19, 1948, and Indonesian leaders, including the president and vice-president of the Republic, were taken prisoners.

The Security Council, meeting in emergency session on December 24, 1948, dispatched still another cease-fire and called upon the Dutch to release all political prisoners. On January 7, 1949, the Council met again following a brief adjournment and was informed by the Committee on Good Offices that the Dutch had not complied fully with its resolution of December 24, 1948. Sentiment was gradually shifting toward taking a strong position against the Netherlands. On January 28, 1949, the Council adopted a resolution which, in addition to repeating its requests for a cease-fire and the release of prisoners by the Dutch, reconstituted the Committee on Good Offices into the United Nations Commission for In-

[2] Council members with career consuls in Batavia at the time were Australia, Belgium, China, France, the United Kingdom, and the United States.

donesia. The Commission was granted broader powers to secure a political settlement, including the task of aiding in the establishment, by July 1, 1950, of a federal, independent, and sovereign United States of Indonesia.

At the suggestion of the Netherlands, a conference was held at The Hague from late August until November, 1949. Under the auspices of the Commission, preliminary agreements were reached between the Netherlands and Indonesia in May, June, and August, 1949, which facilitated the termination of hostilities and prepared the way for the final settlements made at The Hague. On November 2, 1949, the Hague participants agreed to the following: the transfer of sovereignty from the Netherlands to the Republic of the United States of Indonesia; the creation of a Netherlands-Indonesia Union under the Netherlands Crown for the voluntary co-operation between the Union partners, covering the fields of foreign relations, and defense, financial, and economic relations. The Council, in December, 1949, sought to congratulate the parties and the Commission for their efforts. But a Canadian resolution that embodied these sentiments was voted upon in two parts, both of which were vetoed by the Soviet Union. The Soviet viewpoint, a bitter footnote to long and tedious negotiations lasting nearly three years, was expressed by Mr. Galagan of the Ukrainian SRR when he stated that "the text of The Hague agreements makes it clear that the freedom and independence of Indonesia has been sacrificed on the altar of political and economic interests of a bloc of colonial powers, the United States, the Netherlands, the United Kingdom and others.' In spite of Soviet opposition, the transfer of sovereignty took place at Amsterdam on December 27, 1949, and the Republic of Indonesia became the sixtieth member of the United Nations in September, 1950.

The Indonesian question illustrates the point made earlier that the action of the Security Council can be successful only when there is a positive measure of agreement among the permanent members or where disagreement at a critical juncture is circumvented. In this instance, the major powers were determined to reach a negotiated settlement. The French veto was an expression of concern on the part of colonial powers for the future course of nationalist ambitions. It also represented a desire to prevent the Soviets from participating in a commission investigating colonial problems. The veto did not seriously impede Council action, nor did French policy in the Council after the veto. Although a satisfactory conclusion to the problem might have been reached without the intervention of the Council, it was undoubtedly able to hasten Indonesian independence and lessen actual hostilities. The subsidiary organs performed creditably, facing complex problems with determination. The Council adopted a course of action which did not involve a determination of a threat to or a breach of the peace as called for in Chapter VII of the Charter. This was done to avoid complex legal discussions and the possibility of aggravating the situation. However, some of the measures used implied the existence of a 'threat to the peace.'

The Syrian and Lebanese Question. This case is a good early example of the procedural wrangles engaged in by the Security Council. On February 4, 1946, Syria and Lebanon claimed that the continued presence of British and French troops in their territories after the end of World War II 'constitutes a grave infringement of the sovereignty of two States members of the United Nations which may give rise to serious disputes.' The representatives of these countries referred to the matter as a dispute and asked the Council to recommend 'the total and simultaneous evacuation of foreign troops' from their countries. When the matter came before the Council, there was a discussion concerning the authority of nonmembers of the Council to suggest resolutions, and whether to determine that the question was a dispute or a situation. The results of the debate were largely inconclusive but the Syrian and Lebanese delegates were seated and given the right to make proposals. Britain and France insisted that there was no dispute of any nature and were prepared to withdraw their troops. However, when it came to voting on several resolutions, the matter of deciding whether the question was a dispute or not arose. If it was a dispute, neither France nor Britain, as parties to it, could vote. The issue was avoided again when these two permanent Council members agreed to refrain from voting although they were still unwilling to admit that the matter was a dispute.

The Council was also faced with the problem of how far it should go in recommending that the parties continue negotiations. While France and the United Kingdom were agreeable to a resumption of negotiations, they were unwilling to do this if it would preclude negotiations on issues other than the matter of troop withdrawal. But Syria and Lebanon refused to discuss any additional issues until there was agreement on the removal of the troops. The central problem, therefore, was that of meeting the objections of one of the parties to negotiation until certain prior conditions had been met. Following the discussion of a number of proposals, a United States resolution was submitted which expressed confidence that an early withdrawal would occur and that negotiations to that end would be entered into by both parties. The Soviet Union promptly vetoed this plan, arguing that it was not strong enough. The Soviet Union was actually expressing concern over foreign troops in areas near its border. The veto was also an example of the willingness of the USSR to launch all manner of charges in colonial questions, with the twofold purpose of making the situation more difficult for the colonial powers and of attempting to act as the champion of colonial peoples.

The British and French proceeded to negotiate 'on the majority decision of the Council as expressed in the vote' and all troops were evacuated by December 31, 1946. Significantly, the objectives of the Council were obtained in spite of the Soviet veto and the discussion of the question alone had some influence in bringing about a settlement.

The Corfu Channel Question. The dispute between the United Kingdom and Albania over mine-laying operations in the Corfu Channel came to the attention of the Security Council in January, 1947. The British representative, Sir Alexander Cadogan, who brought the question before the Council, outlined the dispute as follows: the Albanian government had not objected to British sweeping of German mines from the channel between the island of Corfu and Albania in 1944 and 1945; a special international board supervising mine sweeping certified the Channel was free of mines and could be and was used as an international waterway until May, 1946; on May 15, 1946, two British cruisers were fired on by Albanian shore batteries; Albania had not explained this act satisfactorily and in October, 1946, two British destroyers struck mines in the Channel and were damaged with loss of life; British mine sweepers since that time had found new mines in the Channel which were laid at least with the knowledge of the Albanian authorities. The British demanded an apology and compensation for the damaged vessels and dead and injured seamen. An Albanian representative, invited to present his side of the incidents, reported that Albania had no knowledge of the presence of the mines or how they got there; that the Corfu Channel was part of Albanian territory and the British vessels were violating Albanian sovereignty; and that the British were merely seeking to intervene in Albanian affairs for the purpose of impeding the growth of Albanian democracy.

After discussion revealed the need for more information, the Council appointed a subcommittee. This subcommittee presented a report that was inconclusive because of disagreement among its members. The British then introduced a resolution, later amended, stating that the mines could not have been laid without the knowledge of the Albanians and recommending that the two parties settle the dispute on that basis, with the item itself remaining on the Council's agenda. The USSR promptly vetoed the resolution but abstained on an American resolution, adopted by the Council, referring the matter to the International Court of Justice. This became the first case before the Court.[3] Unquestionably the Council should have referred it to the Court without spending time debating a number of

[3] See Chapter 10.

technical and legal issues. As it was, the Council functioned well in spite of the not unexpected Soviet veto. Almost any other course of action would have required a determination of whether the dispute, if allowed to continue, would endanger peace and security.

The Egyptian Question. In July, 1947, Egypt called to the attention of the Security Council the problem concerning British troops in Egypt and the Sudan. It was charged that negotiations between the two parties had failed to reach a settlement. The continuance of the dispute was likely to endanger international peace and security, the Egyptian complaint stated, and the Council should consider it accordingly.

Both the British and the Egyptians presented lengthy arguments to justify their positions. Although the members of the Council indicated a desire to arrive at some adjustment, none of the resolutions offered could gain the required number of affirmative votes. No vetoes were cast nor did the Soviet Union necessarily block Council action. It was simply impossible to arrive at any agreement. The Council members exhibited a reluctance to express themselves positively on the issues of the dispute.

The case itself is one which illustrates the difficult position in which the Council has found itself. Wartime military arrangements and prewar privileges awarded certain great powers by weak states have plagued the Council from its very inception. This was true in the Syrian-Lebanese case and in part, at least, with the Indonesian, Iranian, Greek, and Corfu Channel questions. It was true of the Anglo-Iranian question discussed below. Nationalist ambitions in the postwar world clash head-on with colonial arrangements. Unless there is a truly serious threat to the peace which has aroused public attention, the tendency persists for the Council to avoid a decision and wait for some adjustment to be negotiated by the parties themselves. Inconclusive action has proved to be the wisest course at times. Anglo-Egyptian authorities eventually negotiated the issues which concerned them but not, however, without armed clashes and considerable unpleasantness.

The India-Pakistan Question. On January 1, 1948, the representative of India reported a situation to the Security Council between his state and Pakistan which needed urgent attention to avoid a breach of the peace. When India and Pakistan became independent in 1947, a number of smaller princely states, as they are called, were given the opportunity of joining either one of these countries or of remaining independent. Considerable trouble had resulted with the princely state of Kashmir which had a Hindu ruler but a population predominantly Moslem. Both Pakistan and India desired the accession of Kashmir but, according to the Indian complaint, Pakistan had instituted economic pressure and armed raids against

Kashmir to force it to accede to that state. Kashmir had sought the aid of the Indian government against these depredations and had acceded to India. If the Security Council did not intervene, a serious conflict might result.

Within a few days after receipt of the Indian complaint, the President of the Security Council appealed to both India and Pakistan to refrain from any action incompatible with the Charter which might aggravate the situation. Both governments readily agreed and the Council began a consideration of the situation. Pakistan denied the Indian complaint and stated that India had encouraged Sikh extremists in their slaughter of Moslems in Kashmir and in the princely states that had acceded to Pakistan. Furthermore, the Pakistani representative pointed out, India had militarily occupied states that had acceded to Pakistan, actually threatening his nation with destruction by armed attack; and the accession of Kashmir to India had been fraudulently and illegally obtained by India. He encouraged the Security Council to dispatch an investigatory commission to determine the true nature of the situation which, he believed, had been falsely portrayed in the Indian complaint.

On January 20, a United Nations Commission was established to investigate the facts of the case and to exercise, whenever possible, 'any mediatory influence likely to smooth away difficulties.' The Commission arrived in Karachi in July, 1948, and the following month called for a cease-fire, a truce agreement, and the holding of a free and impartial plebiscite in accordance with a suggestion by the Council in April. By the time a cease-fire was arranged in January, 1949, India held two-thirds of Kashmir. Admiral Chester Nimitz of the United States was chosen to be Plebiscite Administrator. But in December, 1949, the Commission reported that it could not secure agreement upon satisfactory demilitarization of the area nor could it fulfill the conditions necessary for holding the plebiscite. The Commission suggested that its usefulness was at an end and that it be replaced by a single person as mediator. The Council adopted this suggestion in December, 1949, and requested General A. G. L. McNaughton of Canada, at that time Council President, to act in this capacity. In April, 1950, Sir Owen Dixon of Australia took his place as mediator but could report no progress by September and requested that he be relieved of his duties. He was replaced by Dr. Frank Graham of the United States, who endeavored to bring the parties closer to agreement during 1951 and 1952, with relatively little success. The Council, meanwhile, repeatedly urged the holding of the plebiscite, to which only Pakistan had agreed, however.

After 1953 India steadily increased its hold on the state and an Indian sponsored Kashmiri Constituent Assembly prepared a constitution which declared in its third article that 'Kashmir is and shall be an integral part of the Union of India.' Negotiations between India and Pakistan had long since come to an impasse when on January 16, 1957, the Pakistani foreign minister appealed to the Security Council to request the withdrawal of foreign troops from Kashmir. He observed that unless a United Nations police force were dispatched at once to maintain peace, India would absorb Kashmir and disturbances would break out. On January 24, the Security Council, by a vote of 10-0 with Soviet Russia abstaining, called for a continuation of the status quo until the long-overdue plebiscite could be held. Three days later, however, on its Independence Day, India formally incorporated the two-thirds of Kashmir it had held since the 1949 cease-fire. In February, the USSR vetoed a Western proposal to send the Council president to India and Pakistan to investigate the possibility of stationing United Nations troops in Kashmir. However, the Council later voted to send its president to confer with the disputants in an effort to reach a settlement. In December, the Council again authorized Dr. Graham to make renewed efforts to achieve an agreement between the two governments.

In the more than nine years that have intervened since the question first came before it, the Security Council has been able to do little more than arrange the original cease-fire. On five occasions it has called for a plebiscite, but to no avail. The Council's role has been limited to mediation which, although it was impartial and painstaking, failed to discover a procedure to serve as a basis for a satisfactory adjustment. Both India and Pakistan have been critical of the Council's efforts for their own reasons, some of which appear unwarranted when one reflects upon the unbending attitudes of both parties. Neither of them welcomed the original Commission in a spirit which suggested a willingness to compromise their differences. Irrespective of the validity of the claims of either party, the record of mediation in later years clearly shows India to have rejected virtually all of the measures proposed. Pakistan, on the other hand, accepted practically all of them and agreed to place the problem of demilitarization before an arbitrator. The Council itself has been fairly well united on the measures it adopted and has supported the efforts of its mediators with little criticism. But mediation can be successful only if the parties concerned exhibit a determination to reach a compromise solution. Such a spirit quite obviously was not present in equal force on the part of India and Pakistan.

The Czechoslovak Question. A communist dominated government seized power in Czechoslovakia in February, 1948. Jan Papanek, who had been the permanent representative of the previous Czech government, sent a communication to the Secretary-General on March 10, 1948, in which he contended that the political independence of Czechoslovakia had been violated by a threat of the use of force by the Soviet Union. He believed that the Security Council should investigate the situation as one which threatened the maintenance of international peace and security. The Secretary-General, however, could not process this request because it did not come from a member government. But Chile took over the request and the situation was placed on the agenda of the Council in spite of the heated opposition of the USSR which claimed the matter to be an interference in the internal affairs of Czechoslovakia. Mr. Papanek was invited to participate in the discussion but the representative of communist Czechoslovakia refused to attend.

No purpose was served by embroiling the Council in such a question except for the propaganda value of placing the Soviets on the defensive. Chile submitted a resolution calling for the appointment of a subcommittee to investigate the charges. The Soviets demanded that the Council decide whether the resolution was procedural or substantive. As might have been expected, the USSR voted in the negative, its veto making the original resolution nonprocedural. The Chilean resolution, of course, was vetoed and a bitter debate ensued. The United States contended that the resolution was clearly procedural and, despite the double veto, has never recognized this act as a precedent. The British representative echoed these sentiments as did others.

Clearly the use of the veto on the establishment of a committee of investigation is unwarranted. However, nothing would have come from such an investigation. The Council neither could nor would have taken any action against the communist regime in Czechoslovakia or against the USSR which had aided in bringing it to power. To use the Security Council for overt propaganda purposes does not advance the cause of world peace.

The Question of Hyderabad. The government of Hyderabad notified the Secretary-General on August 21, 1948, that a grave dispute had arisen between Hyderabad and India which should be brought to the attention of the Security Council. It was charged that Hyderabad had been exposed to intimidation, threats of invasion, frontier violations, and an economic blockade 'intended to coerce it into a renunciation of its independence.' On September 12 and 13, 1948, Hyderabad reported actual invasion and urged the Council to consider the matter immediately under Chapter VII of the Charter.

The status of Hyderabad and the events listed in the complaint remained unclear during the Security Council's deliberations. One of the largest of the Indian native states, Hyderabad had not joined either India or Pakistan but on November 29, 1947, the Nizam of Hyderabad had entered into a one-year agreement of partial association with India. One effect of the agreement had been to place the conduct of Hyderabad's foreign affairs in Indian hands. Both parties had complained of violations of the agreement but had not resorted to the machinery of arbitration available under it. The territory comprising the state is completely surrounded by India, and although its ruler, Nizam the Seventh, was a Moslem and inclined toward Pakistan, the people were predominantly Hindus.

The Indian representative presented the view that 'Hyderabad is not competent to bring any question before the Security Council; that it is not a state, that it is not independent; that never in all its history did it have the status of independence.' India had been forced to intervene in Hyderabad, as inquiries had definitely confirmed 'harrowing tales of death, of arson, of loot, of rape, by what were called the private armies of Hyderabad, private armies nevertheless encouraged or countenanced by the government of Hyderabad.'

In the midst of the discussion, press reports indicated that the Nizam wished to remove the complaint from the Security Council. India had gained control over the territory but it was not clear whether India had forced the Nizam to request the removal of the complaint. The Council took no action despite the efforts of Pakistan and others to have the Council investigate whether there had been a violation of the Charter principles which supported the self-determination of peoples and decried the acquisition of territory by force. Some question still remains about the Council's failure to act.[4] At the same time, a policy of inaction might be supported by the legal issues surrounding the status of Hyderabad and the jurisdiction over the area maintained by India.

The Berlin Question. France, the United Kingdom, and the United States, addressed identical notes to the Secretary-General on September 29, 1948, calling attention to what they believed to be a serious situation resulting from the Soviet restrictions on transport and communications between the western zones of occupation and Berlin. It was claimed that the Soviet actions constituted a threat to the peace under Chapter VII of the Charter and violated its solemn obligations to the United Nations. According to the Western powers, the city of Berlin, deep in the Soviet occupation zone, was blockaded and the population intimidated and subject to starvation. Extended deliberations had produced no adjustment in the situation and, in their view, the Security Council should intervene in order to prevent

---

[4] See, for example, Eagleton, Clyde, 'The Case of Hyderabad before the Security Council,' *American Journal of International Law*, Vol. 44, No. 2 (April 1950), pp. 277–302.

the USSR from coercing them into abandoning their rights and responsibilities in Berlin.

The Soviet Union did its best to prevent the item from being placed on the Council's agenda, claiming that the matter lay beyond its competence. In the Soviet view, a consideration of the problem would violate Article 107 of the Charter which provided that 'Nothing in the present Charter shall invalidate or preclude action, in relation to any state which during the Second World War has been an enemy of any signatory to the present Charter, taken or authorized as a result of that war by the Governments having responsibility for such action.' The Western powers denied the applicability of Article 107 and the situation finally was placed upon the agenda, whereupon the Soviets announced that they would not participate in the consideration of the question. The Council then proceeded to devote five meetings to exploring the circumstances surrounding the restrictions on communications, transport, and commerce between Berlin and the Western zones of Germany and between the latter and the Soviet zone.

The neutral members of the Council (Argentina, Belgium, Canada, China, Colombia, and Syria) then introduced a joint resolution which, among other things, called upon the four occupation states to lift restrictions imposed after March 1, 1948, on communications, transport, and commerce between zones and to discuss the unification of the currency in Berlin. The USSR objected, however, and vetoed the resolution, claiming that under its provisions the Soviet restrictions would have to be lifted immediately while only the beginning of negotiations concerning the currency question and not the actual introduction of currency reform was called for. A mere agreement to discuss a problem, in the Soviet view, could not be balanced with an actual concession. The President of the Security Council then proceeded to encourage additional discussions between the parties and appointed a Technical Committee on Berlin Currency and Trade, composed of experts nominated by the neutral members of the Security Council, to aid them in reaching a settlement.

The Committee could report no progress toward a solution by February, 1949. But in April, informal talks began between the representatives to the United Nations of the four parties which, by May, 1949, resulted in an adjustment of the situation. Although the settlement was reached outside the Council, its efforts may have had some effect in arriving at a conclusion of the problem by focusing attention upon the various issues. It is interesting nevertheless, that three permanent members of the Security Council believed it necessary to bring before the Council a dispute between them and a fourth permanent member. It might well be asked, if they could not resolve it among themselves, how could the Security Council be expected to reach a solution?

The Anglo-Iranian Question. On May 1, 1951, the Government of Iran passed an Oil Nationalization Act which ended the concessions granted the Anglo-Iranian Oil Company in 1933 and expropriated the huge British refinery at Abadan. Negotiations between Iran and the British proved to be fruitless and on May 31, 1951, the United Kingdom instituted proceedings in the International Court of Justice against Iran, maintaining the Court had jurisdiction in the dispute on the ground that Article 22 of the Agreement between the two parties in 1933 called for arbitration of such matters. The British also requested the Court to issue provisional measures, in accordance with Article 41 of the Court's Statute, to protect the rights of the oil company to which it was entitled under the terms of the 1933 agreement.

The Court accepted the case and issued an Order on July 5, 1951, containing provisional measures to apply on the basis of reciprocal observance pending the final decision on the merits of the case. The Order requested that both parties not take any action which might prejudice the rights of the other. The operations of the oil company should continue under the management existing prior to May 1, 1951. Both parties should establish a Board of Supervision to regulate the activities of the company until a final settlement was reached. But on July 9, 1951, Iran withdrew its acceptance of the compulsory jurisdiction of the Court, claiming that the matter rested exclusively within the domestic jurisdiction of Iran. At the same time, British nationals were intimidated in Iran and eventually forced to evacuate.

On September 18, 1951, the British representative requested the Security Council to consider the dispute, claiming that the expulsion of British personnel from Iran and the refusal to honor the Order of the Court constituted a threat to international peace and security. The Soviet Union at once denied the competence of the Council to handle such a matter which, in its view, was one lying within the domestic jurisdiction of Iran, but the case was placed on the Council's agenda for discussion. The British requested the Council to call for the 'resumption of negotiations at the earliest practicable moment in order to . . . resolve the differences . . . in accordance with the principles of provisional measures indicated by the International Court of Justice unless mutually agreeable arrangements are made consistent with the Purposes and Principles of the United Nations Charter.' Iran, however, stated that such a resolution by the Council would be entirely unacceptable. Council members exhibited different views while searching for some compromise formula. Ecuador expressed the sentiments of most of the Council by observing that the Council should not become entangled in the legal intricacies of its competence but should use its moral influence upon the parties to reopen negotiations in a new attempt to settle their differences.

No compromise formula could be reached. At the suggestion of France, the Council agreed, in effect, to avoid taking any action, by voting to adjourn the discussion until the Court had ruled on the case. The Council could not bring itself to decide that the dispute was a threat to the peace. Most members were not convinced that the Council was even competent to hear the case. This should have been clear to the British beforehand and it is highly doubtful that the Council should be placed in the awkward position of having to consider this type of situation.

The Guatemalan Question. The Security Council met on June 20, 1954, to discuss the Guatemalan charge that 'open aggression has been perpetrated by the Governments of Honduras and Nicaragua at the instigation of certain foreign monopolies whose interests have been affected by the progressive policy' of Guatemala. The Guatemalan representative identified the 'foreign monopolies' as the United Fruit Company and other 'satellites' of the United States Department of State. Expeditionary forces had been sent into Guatemala, he maintained, from neighboring states at the encouragement of the United States. An observation mission should be sent to witness the irregularities perpetrated by Honduras and Nicaragua. Guatemala denied the charge of the United States that it represented 'an outpost of Soviet Communism on the American continent' and demanded that the Security Council direct Honduras and Nicaragua to take action against the 'mercenaries' who were using bases in those countries to launch an invasion.

Guatemala possessed an extreme left-wing government at the time which was communist inspired and had caused concern in the United States and elsewhere in the Americas. Honduras and Nicaragua immediately supported a resolution sponsored by Colombia and Brazil which would refer the dispute to the Organization of American States and called upon all parties involved to terminate activities which might lead to further bloodshed. All members of the United Nations were to abstain from giving any assistance to those who continued the hostilities. Guatemala, however, with the backing of the USSR, denied the existence of a dispute, claiming only that her neighbors were permitting the aggression to occur and should be stopped and that the Organization of American States was not the proper agency to handle such an affair. The Soviet delegate claimed that OAS was dominated by the United States and hence could not be expected to investigate the matter impartially.

The representative of the United States, Mr. Lodge, denied these charges and attacked what he believed to be Soviet preparations for a veto of the resolution. He then asked 'why does the representative of the Soviet Union, a country thousands of miles away from here, undertake to veto a move like that? How can this action of his possibly fail to make unbiased observers throughout the world come to the conclusion that the Soviet Union has designs on the American hemisphere? . . . I say to the representative of the Soviet Union, stay out of this hemisphere and do not try to start your plans and your conspiracies over here.' As Mr. Lodge expected, the vote on the resolution was defeated by the Soviet veto while the remaining ten members voted in the affirmative. The Council then adopted that part of the vetoed resolution which did not mention referring the matter to the Organization of American States. However, the Council did not take any further action in the matter, failing to place it on its agenda at a later date because sufficient votes to so do were lacking.

The Suez Canal Question. The incident of the Egyptian nationalization of the Suez Canal was brought before the Security Council on September 23, 1956, at the request of France and the United Kingdom. A Council meeting was necessary, they maintained, 'to consider the situation created by the unilateral action of the Egyptian Government in bringing to an end the system of international operation of the Suez Canal, which was confirmed and completed by the Suez Canal Convention of 1888.' Egypt then requested on September 24 that the Council hear of actions against Egypt which 'constitute a danger to international peace and security.' The Council met on September 26 and agreed to hear both complaints.

The Egyptian seizure of the Canal brought to an end a period of British history dating back to 1875. In that year, British Prime Minister Disraeli managed the purchase of 44 percent of the Suez Canal Company from the Khedive of Egypt. The Canal had been built six years earlier and had been owned and run by an international company with French and Ottoman interests in control. Actually, the British have never owned the Canal. It has continued to be owned and operated by the Suez Canal Company, an international joint stock concern with an Egyptian charter and a lease which was valid until 1968. At that time, the Canal was legally scheduled to be turned over, free, to the Egyptian government. Most of the stockholders are French and its directors are principally British and French. The administrative head office was located in Paris. But with 44 percent of the stock, the British government has always been the largest single shareholder and, as a result, has had a strong voice in the operation of the Canal and has received a major share of the Company's proceeds.

The status of the Canal was established by the Constantinople Convention of 1888, signed by Austria-Hungary, France, Germany, Great Britain, Italy, the Netherlands, the Ottoman Empire, Russia, and Spain. The purpose of the Convention was

> to establish . . . a definite system destined to guarantee at all times, and for all the powers, the free use of the Suez Maritime Canal and thus to complete the system under which the navigation of this canal has been placed by the Firman of His Imperial Majesty the Sultan, dated the 22nd February, 1866.

Politically, the United Kingdom's interest in the Suez Canal provided her with an entry into the entire Middle East and the consequent development of a 'special position' in that vital area. At the start of World War I, Britain deposed the pro-Turkish Khedive of Egypt, declared a protectorate over the country, and undertook the responsibility of defense of the Canal. The pre-eminent position of Britain was recognized in the post-1918 treaties and confirmed in the 1936 Anglo-Egyptian Treaty of Alliance which gave the British the right to defend the Canal until the Egyptian army was able to perform this function. In 1954, however, an Anglo-Egyptian Agreement terminated the 1936 Treaty and provided for the withdrawal of all British forces from Egyptian territory. The Agreement also bound the signatories to observe the 1888 convention. The last British troops were evacuated in June, 1956.

On July 19, 1956, the United States announced that it would not contribute to the financing of the High Dam at Aswan on the Nile. The International Bank and the British also indicated that they were no longer interested in the project. One week later, on July 26, President Gamal Abdel Nasser of Egypt announced the nationalization of the Canal and a plan to finance the dam from income derived from Egyptian operation of the Canal.

Since more than half of the oil needed for the economy of Western Europe passed through the Canal, reaction to the seizure was immediate. After France and the United Kingdom froze the assets of the Suez Canal Company, twenty-two nations met in London, all of them users of the Canal, to create 'operative arrangements under an international system designed to assure the continuity of operation of the Canal as guaranteed by the Convention of 1888, consistent with legitimate Egyptian interests.' France, the United Kingdom and the United States termed the nationalization an

> arbitrary and unilateral seizure by one nation of an international agency which has the responsibility to maintain and to operate the Suez Canal so that all . . . can effectively enjoy the use of an international waterway upon which the economy, commerce and security of much of the world depends.

Eighteen nations at the London Conference accepted an American proposal for the establishment of an international board which would operate and develop the Canal. The 'sovereign rights' of Egypt in the area were to be guaranteed, together with an assurance of a reasonable income. An alternative proposal, suggested by India, was supported by Ceylon, Indonesia, and the USSR. It would create a body of user interests possessed only with advisory, consultative, and liaison functions. The Western plan was turned down by Nasser on September 10 and his suggestion for a new conference to review the 1888 Convention was unacceptable to the majority powers at London.

Although the Egyptian complaint was placed on the Security Council agenda on September 26, the Council considered only the Anglo-French charge. This was done in nine meetings, from October 5 to 13. Just prior to this Council activity, a fifteen-member Suez Canal Users Association was inaugurated, on October 1, for the purpose of serving as a consultative group to present its case to the Security Council, to protect the rights of users regarding the Canal, and to maintain a collective body for any possible negotiations with Egypt.

After a lengthy opening debate on a British resolution which was, in effect, a restatement of the position adopted by the London Conference, the Council moved into private session. Three such meetings were held on October 9, 11, and 12. During that period direct high-level negotiations took place in the Secretary-General's office between the foreign ministers of Britain, Egypt, and France. At the same time, the eighteen nations sponsoring the London proposals held a series of meetings at United Nations Headquarters for 'the exchange of information and the maintenance of unity of views.'

The first public meeting of the Council after the private discussions was held on October 13 and a new joint British-French resolution was submitted. It contained the following six principles which had been agreed to in the private talks between the three foreign ministers:

1. There shall be free and open transit through the Canal without discrimination, overt or covert.

2. Egypt's sovereignty shall be respected.

3. The operation of the Canal shall be insulated from the politics of any country.

4. The manner of fixing tolls shall be decided by agreement between Egypt and the users.

5. A fair proportion of the dues shall be allotted to development of the Canal.

6. In case of dispute, unresolved affairs between the [dispossessed] Suez Canal Company and the Egyptian Government shall be settled by arbitration.

The Council adopted this portion of the resolution unanimously. However, the British and French pointed out that these principles called for no implementation: no sanctions, no international board, not even an agreed mode of procedure in further negotiations. Therefore, the second part of their resolution invited Egypt to negotiate anew and called on her 'to make known promptly . . . proposals for a system' of running the Canal 'not less effective' than the London proposals. Although nine members of the Council supported this position, the second part of the resolution was voted against by the USSR and Yugoslavia.

Having accepted only the six principles, the Council adjourned and did not discuss this question until it became part of the broader Middle East crisis brought on by the Israeli-Egyptian conflict and the Anglo-French invasion of the northern end of the Suez Canal zone. The Council was unable to act, due to the lack of unanimity of the permanent members, and the matter was transferred to an emergency meeting of the General Assembly under the 'Uniting for Peace' Resolution. The action taken by the Assembly in this instance will be examined in the next chapter.

QUESTIONS BEFORE THE GENERAL ASSEMBLY

The Indian Minority in the Union of South Africa. This question provides a good illustration of some of the continuing problems and frustrations to which the General Assembly has been exposed. It illustrates the difficulties encountered when members seek to avoid their obligations and employ the protective device of domestic jurisdiction. Also apparent is the patience of the Assembly and the various devices utilized in an effort to reach an understanding.

The question was originally presented to the Assembly by India during the first session in 1946 and subsequently discussed at every session but the fourth. India charged that the Union of South Africa had enacted discriminatory legislation against Indians by the passage of the Asiatic Land Tenure and Indian Representation Act of 1946, in which it was claimed that the rights of Indians were restricted in regard to residence and trade. Furthermore, said India, these measures not only violated international agreements (The Capetown Agreements of 1927 and 1932) concluded between India and the Union but also were not in keeping with the Charter principles governing human rights and freedoms. The delegation from the Union at once denied the competence of the Assembly to act and has maintained since that time that the Indian complaint was a matter essentially within its domestic jurisdiction. The Assembly, in turn, has refused to deny its competence and, instead of referring the question to the

International Court of Justice as suggested by the United States and others, has done its best to assist both parties to reconcile their differences. Nothing of note has come from the efforts of an Assembly-sponsored Good Offices Commission or from attempts to encourage direct negotiations between India and the Union of South Africa.

The Question of Race Conflict in South Africa. The problem of *apartheid* or racial segregation in the Union of South Africa is similar to the matter just noted. Despite the claim of domestic jurisdiction, the Assembly in 1952 created a special commission to study the situation in South Africa. At the same time, the Assembly condemned policies of racial discrimination and called upon all members to bring their policies into conformity with their obligation under the Charter to promote the observance of human rights and fundamental freedoms.

In 1953 the Commission reported that as a result of *apartheid,* four-fifths of the South African population were reduced to a 'humiliating level of inferiority which is injurious to human dignity and makes the full development of personality impossible or very difficult.' Furthermore, it was reported that the doctrine of racial discrimination embodied in *apartheid* was 'scientifically false, extremely dangerous to internal peace and international relations . . . was contrary to the dignity and worth of the human person,' was in conflict with the Charter, the Declaration of Human Rights and various Assembly resolutions; and was becoming 'more explosive and more menacing to internal peace and to the foreign relations of the Union of South Africa.' At no time, however, has the Union been willing to co-operate with the Commission and in protest against additional efforts to resolve the problem, it recalled its delegation from the Tenth and Eleventh and Twelfth Assemblies.

The Question of the Former Italian Colonies — Libya, Somaliland, Eritrea. The Treaty of Peace with Italy, in Article 23, stated that the final disposal of the Italian colonies of Libya, Somaliland, and Eritrea was to be determined jointly by France, the United Kingdom, the United States, and the USSR within a year following the coming into force of the Treaty (September 15, 1947). An annex to the Article provided that if the four states could not agree by September 15, 1948, on the colonies, the matter was to be submitted to the General Assembly for a recommendation which would be binding on the four powers. They were unable to agree and the problem was referred to the Assembly which considered it at the second part of the third session in April–May, 1949.

A large number of proposals were submitted with respect to each of the three regions and were debated at length. The First Committee submitted a draft resolution which was eventually turned down by the Assembly in plenary session and it was decided to postpone the matter until the fall of 1949 when the Assembly convened for its fourth session. At that time certain decisions were arrived at for each of the three former colonies.

LIBYA. It was agreed that Libya, comprising the states of Cyrenaica, Tripolitania, and the Fezzan, was to be constituted as an independent state not later than January 1, 1952. A constitution would be drafted by representatives of the inhabitants of the three states meeting in a National Assembly. A United Nations Commissioner, Adrian Pelt, was appointed to guide the people of Libya in preparing for independence and was assisted by a council of ten, consisting of representatives from six members of the United Nations, one from each of the regions of Libya plus a representative of the minorities in Libya. Technical and financial assistance was voted for the development of the area and it was provided that when independence was achieved, Libya was to be admitted to membership in the United Nations.

In 1950 a preparatory committee (later known as the Committee of Twenty-one) was established to recommend methods of representation in the National Assembly and machinery for drafting a constitution. On December 24, 1951, power was transferred to the newly created independent United Kingdom of Libya which became a federation under the monarchy of King Mohammed Idris El Senussi. A resolution for the admission of Libya to the United Nations offered in the Security Council by Pakistan and supported by an Assembly resolution that had been adopted with no opposition, was vetoed by the Soviet Union in 1951. Admittance was finally granted in December, 1955.

SOMALILAND. The General Assembly voted in 1949 that Somaliland was to become an independent State at the end of ten years from the date of the approval of a Trusteeship Agreement. Italy was made the trusteeship authority for the intervening period, assisted and advised by an Advisory Council consisting of representatives of Colombia, Egypt, and the Philippines. A detailed Trusteeship Agreement and an annexed Declaration of Constitutional Principles was adopted by the Assembly on December 2, 1950, and concurred in by Italy.

ERITREA. Differences of opinion with respect to Eritrea were far more pronounced than in the case of either Italian Somaliland or Libya. Some believed that the region should be joined with Ethiopia or partitioned, while others advocated outright or eventual independence. The General Assembly was unable to agree in 1949 to a disposition of the area, but it established a five-member commission to study the situation and to prepare a report, with the assistance of the Interim Committee of the Assembly.

Neither the Commission nor the Interim Committee could reach substantial agreement on recommendations to the Assembly. The entire question was studied by the Special Political Committee at the fifth Assembly session in 1950 and its recommendations, approved by the Assembly in plenary session, called for the establishment of Eritrea as an autonomous unit federated with Ethiopia under the sovereignty of the Ethiopian Crown. Mr. Anze Matienzo of Bolivia was appointed United Nations Commissioner to assist in the transition period, which was completed by September, 1952.

Observance in Bulgaria, Hungary, and Rumania of Human Rights and Fundamental Freedoms. At the request of Bolivia and Australia, the General Assembly at its third session in the spring of 1949 agreed to consider the problem of the treatment of Catholic churchmen in Hungary and Protestant churchmen in Bulgaria. The issue involved the question of whether the state trials in these countries violated both the Peace Treaties for these countries and the Charter. Both in committee and in plenary session, the Soviet bloc challenged the competence of the Assembly to consider such a matter, arguing that the subject was exclusively within the domestic jurisdiction of the states concerned. Representatives of Bulgaria and Hungary were invited to attend the discussion but refused. Following much heated argument, the Assembly determined that it was competent to consider violations of human rights and freedoms, even if they occurred in nonmember states, and refused to admit its lack of competence to discuss the function of the Peace Treaties. The resolution adopted April 30, 1949, expressed deep concern over the accusations made against Bulgaria and Hungary, pointed out to these states their obligations under the Peace Treaties, and retained the question on the agenda for the next regular session of the Assembly.

The General Assembly at its fourth session added Rumania to the other two states accused of violating human rights and freedoms.[5] Signatories of the Peace Treaties reported that the three states refused to respect the Treaty obligations which called for discussion of violations by special Treaty Commissions. Confronted by this situation, Bolivia, Canada, and the United States submitted a proposal, which the Assembly accepted, requesting the International Court of Justice for an advisory opinion as to whether there were disputes between Bulgaria, Hungary, and Rumania, on the one hand, and certain signatories to the treaties of peace on the other, concerning the implementation of the treaties. The Court was also asked to determine whether the Hungarian, Bulgarian, and Rumanian

[5] Rumania also refused to appear before the General Assembly in response to an invitation to explain its position.

governments were obligated to appoint representatives to the Treaty Commissions.

At its fifth session in 1950 the Assembly had before it the affirmative opinion of the Court and proceeded to condemn Bulgaria, Hungary, and Rumania for their willful refusal to 'fulfill their obligations under the provisions of the Treaties of Peace to appoint representatives to the Treaty Commissions which obligation has been confirmed by the International Court of Justice.' The Assembly observed that these states were aware of breaches of the Treaty provisions which obligate them to make possible the enjoyment of human rights and freedoms. All members were invited, and in particular those that were parties to the Treaties, 'to submit to the Secretary-General all evidence which they now hold' or which they may obtain in the future for transmittal to all members of the United Nations.

The Soviet Union and Human Rights. Chile requested that the General Assembly at its third regular session consider the problem of human rights and respect for traditional diplomatic practices involved with the refusal of the USSR to permit Soviet wives of citizens of other nationalities to leave Russia in order to join their husbands. This was done, charged the Chilean delegate, despite the fact that husbands were frequently members of foreign diplomatic missions. The question was first considered by the Sixth Committee and at that time Canada, the United Kingdom and the United States joined with Chile in complaining against the Soviet policy. The entire Soviet bloc steadfastly maintained that the item had been placed on the agenda for the purpose of attacking the USSR. The Soviet Union claimed that it was perfectly justified in refusing to permit its citizens to marry foreigners and that the Assembly had no authority to intervene in affairs which lay within the domestic jurisdiction of the USSR.

However, the General Assembly upheld the views of Chile and voted on April 25, 1949, to recommend to the Soviet Union that, in the light of the provisions of both the Charter and the Universal Declaration of Human Rights, the measures which restrict the right of Soviet citizens to travel abroad with husbands of a different nationality be withdrawn. Such measures, if continued, were likely 'to impair friendly relations among nations' and were 'contrary to courtesy, diplomatic practices and to the principle of reciprocity.'

Morocco. Egypt sought to have the question of the 'Violation of the Principles of the Charter and the Declaration of Human Rights by France in Morocco' placed on the agenda for the sixth session of the General Assembly. The Egyptian representative argued before the General Committee that the incidents in Morocco had caused considerable resentment in all Arab and Islamic countries. The duty of the United Nations was to take appropriate action before the situation endangered international peace and security. Canada suggested instead a resolution which would postpone the item 'for the time being' and it was adopted by the Committee. The Assembly debated the issue in plenary session and by a close vote approved the recommendation of the General Committee not to include the Moroccan question on the agenda for that session. The majority apparently subscribed to the view offered by the United States that France should be permitted to institute promised reforms without the embarrassment of a full debate on the matter in the Assembly.

Fourteen states brought the question to the attention of the seventh session of the General Assembly, noting that France had not put into effect the reforms as promised. French policies had resulted in the complete suppression of civil liberties and democratic rights and it was believed that the situation still threatened international peace. The matter was included on the agenda but the French delegate argued that the entire question was one within the domestic jurisdiction of his country and should not be considered. Furthermore, he stated that the Assembly was not competent to discuss a matter regulated by the Treaty of Fez concluded between France and Morocco in 1912. For these and other related reasons, France would be unable to participate in the discussion of the item. The Arab states demanded positive action by the Assembly but instead, it voted a moderate resolution offered by the majority of the Latin American bloc which called for further negotiation between France and Morocco and expressed the confidence that France would further the fundamental liberties of the Moroccans. A repeated Arab attempt for strong action at the eighth session failed in committee and a more moderate version did not win the necessary two-thirds majority in plenary session. In 1954, the Assembly voted unanimously with only four abstentions to postpone action on the matter.

Although the Moroccan question appeared on the agenda in 1955, the Assembly later voted unanimously to postpone action again, since negotiations between France and Morocco were about to begin. A satisfactory agreement followed and Morocco was admitted as the seventy-eighth member of the United Nations in 1956.

Tunisia. The Security Council refused to place the problem of Tunisia on its agenda in April, 1952. Thirteen nations invited the Secretary-General in June, 1952, to request the members of the United Nations to call a special meeting of the Assembly to study the question, but the required majority was not obtained.

The matter was placed on the agenda of the regular session of the Assembly in 1952. The Arab states contended that France was depriving the Tunisians of their right to self-government and, in general, creating a situation dangerous to international peace and security. The French delegate maintained, as he did with the Moroccan case, that the matter lay within the domestic jurisdiction of France and could not be considered by the United Nations. The Assembly proceeded to act in the same manner as it had with the Moroccan question. It did not adopt proposals calling for strong Assembly action but simply urged the parties concerned to continue negotiations and expressed the confidence that France would endeavor 'to further the effective development of the free institutions of the Tunisian people, in conformity with the Purposes and Principles of the Charter.' In 1953 the Assembly failed to adopt an Arab sponsored resolution recommending independence. The Assembly postponed action in 1954 as it had done with the Moroccan question. However, as with Morocco, satisfactory negotiations were conducted with France and Tunisia became the seventy-ninth member of the United Nations in 1956.

Question of West Irian (West New Guinea). In 1954 Indonesia brought a complaint before the Assembly which concerned the charge that the Netherlands had attempted to incorporate this disputed area into the Netherlands Kingdom. Indonesia regarded this as a unilateral and arbitrary decision contrary to the Round Table Agreement reached between Indonesia and the Netherlands on November 2, 1948. Indonesia requested that the Assembly call upon both parties to resume negotiations over West Irian with the assistance of the good offices of the Secretary-General.

Arguments offered by the Netherlands included the observation that the Round Table Agreement of November 2, 1948, merely continued the *status quo* in West Irian which, in effect, meant that the Netherlands retained sovereignty. There was no dispute and there had been no movement on the part of the people concerned for independence or affiliation with Indonesia. In addition, reported the Dutch delegate, the matter was part of the 'Indonesian Question' which was still on the agenda of the Security Council and thus could not be considered by the Assembly. A draft resolution calling for continued negotiations between Indonesia and the Netherlands failed to receive the necessary two-thirds majority in plenary session. In 1955 the Assembly unanimously adopted a resolution expressing hope that negotiations regarding the disputed area would be fruitful and that the problem would be peacefully resolved. However, lengthy negotiations have failed to produce the results desired and the Eleventh Assembly was unable to make any progress. In fact, a resolution recommended by the Political Committee calling for a good offices commission to assist the parties in their negotiations again did not receive the required two-thirds majority in the

General Assembly on March 1, 1957. During the Twelfth Assembly, a resolution which would have asked Indonesia and the Netherlands to 'pursue their endeavors' to solve the dispute also failed to be adopted.

Equal Rights and Self-Determination in Cyprus. During the ninth session of the Assembly, Greece sought to have accepted a resolution which would express the wish that the principle of self-determination be applied to the population of the island of Cyprus. The request was considered by the First Committee which voted on the recommendation of New Zealand that the Committee not discuss the matter. It was argued that the question actually involved a territorial claim by Greece to an area under British sovereignty and that the Treaty of Lausanne, agreed to by both Britain and Greece, had clearly affirmed the sovereignty of the United Kingdom. Greece disputed the British contention that efforts were being made to afford the peoples of Cyprus self-determination and believed that the Assembly should study the situation. However, the First Committee supported the New Zealand resolution, as did the Assembly in plenary session, and the matter was dropped.

In 1955, the Assembly endorsed the General Committee's recommendation against inscribing the item on the agenda. However, it was included on the agenda of the eleventh session in 1956. In spite of Greek efforts to obtain self-determination for the island, the Assembly, in February, 1957, with Panama and Afghanistan abstaining, unanimously adopted a compromise resolution calling for continued negotiations 'in accord with the principles of the Charter.' With the Middle East crisis at a critical stage, no one was anxious to become engaged in another protracted argument. At the Twelfth Assembly, a Greek resolution urging further negotiation with a view to having the right of self-determination applied to Cyprus failed to receive the necessary two-thirds majority.

QUESTIONS BEFORE BOTH THE SECURITY COUNCIL AND THE GENERAL ASSEMBLY

The Greek Question. The Security Council became involved in this problem, which actually consisted of several phases, on January 21, 1946, two days after it was confronted with the Iranian question. The Soviet Union complained that the presence of British troops in Greece following the termination of World War II was causing 'extraordinary tension fraught with grave consequences both for the Greek people and for the maintenance of international peace and security.' This was denied by the representative of Greece who maintained that British troops had not interfered with the internal affairs of his country. The Greek government, he observed, regarded the presence of British military forces in Greece as 'indispensable.' The majority of the Council did not accept the Soviet interpretation of the situation and was anxious to dispose of the matter quickly. A compromise was voted on February 6, 1946, by which the President of the Council stated the matter was closed, after taking note of the declarations made by the parties and the views of the rest of the Council.

On August 24, 1946, the matter again came to the attention of the Council at the request of the Ukrainian SSR who charged that incidents along the Greek-Albanian border, in which Greek detachments were firing on Albanian frontier guards, were the result of the continued presence of British troops in Greece. It was claimed to be a situation that might lead to international friction. Considerable argument ensued over placing the item on the agenda, with inconclusive results. The matter was dropped after the USSR vetoed a United States resolution which called for the establishment of a commission to investigate the situation.

The next and most serious phase of the question began on December 3, 1946. On that date, Greece requested the Secretary-General to bring to the attention of the Security Council a 'situation which is leading to friction' between Greece and her Albanian, Bulgarian, and Yugoslav neighbors. It was charged that armed groups from these states were crossing Greek borders for 'subversive purposes.' The Council appointed an investigating commission composed of a representative of each of the 1947 members of the Council, 'to ascertain the facts relating to the alleged border violations.' In its report submitted on May 27, 1947, the Commission reported that the Greek charges were substantially true, with Yugoslavia being a principal offender in supporting the guerrilla warfare in Greece, and recommended (1) that the four states concerned attempt to establish normal relations and reduce border tension; (2) that the Security Council establish a special commission composed of representatives of states not permanent members of the Security Council to investigate frontier violations and use its good offices to bring about a settlement. The United States submitted a resolution which included the substance of the report of the Commission but it was vetoed by the USSR. Four more Soviet vetoes, including a double veto, were cast to block all Council action. Finally, the question was removed from the agenda and all records and documents were transferred to the General Assembly which then took up the matter.

Despite the opposition of the Soviet bloc, the Assembly established a United Nations Special Committee on the Balkans (UNSCOB) to assist in bringing about a peaceful settlement of the problem. UNSCOB reported in 1948, and was upheld by the Third Assembly, that the continued support of guerrilla activity by Albania, Bulgaria, and Yugoslavia constituted 'a threat to the political independence and territorial integrity of Greece and to peace in the Balkans.' However, in 1951 the situation had clarified and large-scale guerrilla fighting had ceased, due largely to the defection of Yugoslavia from the Soviet bloc. UNSCOB was dissolved in 1951 and the following year the Peace Observation Commission (established by the 'Uniting for Peace' resolution) created a Subcommission on the Balkans at the request of the General Assembly. It continued to observe the frontier situation until its dissolution in 1954.

The General Assembly and its machinery of observation and conciliation performed adequately throughout its first real political undertaking in spite of Soviet obstructionism. UNSCOB offered multilateral comfort and support to Greece and provided substantial on-the-spot frontier reports for several years to the Assembly. Refugee problems, particularly those related to the repatriation of Greek children, have been severe and appropriate United Nations agencies have assisted the Red Cross in continuing efforts to alleviate distress.

The Spanish Question. The General Assembly on February 9, 1946, adopted a resolution supporting the contention that Franco Spain was ineligible for membership in the United Nations. All members were called upon to conduct their future relations with Spain in accordance with the earlier views expressed that the Franco regime was, as a result of its wartime activities, inimical to the interests of the United Nations.[6]

The Polish delegate on April 8 and 9, 1946, reopened the question in the Security Council by charging that 'the activities of the Franco government have already caused international friction and endangered international peace and security.' Poland then offered a resolution which repeated this charge and called upon all members to sever diplomatic relations with Spain. A special subcommittee was established to report to the Council on whether the Spanish situation had led to international friction and had endangered peace and security. The subcommittee of five found that Franco Spain did not constitute an existing threat to the peace but was 'a potential menace' and created a situation which might endanger the maintenance of peace and security. It proposed that its findings be placed before the General Assembly, where, after full consideration, a resolution should be adopted urging the severance of diplomatic relations by all members of the United Nations with the Franco government.

Australia submitted a proposal in the Security Council to this effect but it

[6] At the San Francisco Conference, it had been argued that the Charter provisions applying to the admission of new members would not apply to states whose governments had been established with the aid of the Axis. During the Potsdam Conference in 1945, the United States, the United Kingdom, and the Soviet Union agreed that they would not support the admission of Franco Spain.

was promptly vetoed by the USSR on the grounds that Spain did constitute a sufficient threat to international peace and security. The Soviet delegate also objected to the matter being turned over to the Assembly. The USSR was particularly adamant on this point, contending that the Council and no other organ had the responsibility of handling matters of peace and security. Australia, on the other hand, through Dr. Evatt, was determined to establish Council and Assembly procedures for processing cases which would if possible avoid the veto by one of the permanent members of the Council. Two more Australian resolutions phrased in similar language were vetoed, one of them involving the double veto. However, after using four vetoes, the Soviet Union reversed its stand and supported a Polish resolution which removed the question from the 'list of matters of which the Council is seized' and placed all records of the case at the disposal of the Assembly. On December 12, 1946, after considerable discussion, the General Assembly recommended that Spain be refused membership in the specialized agencies of the United Nations; that all members recall their ambassadors from Madrid; and that the Security Council consider what measures to take if the Franco regime as then constituted continued in office. There were strong objections to the resolution but these objections, which maintained that such action infringed upon the domestic jurisdiction of Spain, were defeated.

At the second session in November, 1947, Poland offered a resolution which provided that the Security Council consider the Spanish question and take enforcement measures, if necessary, in order to bring about a more democratic regime. Yugoslavia demanded the use of economic measures against Spain. But the Assembly refused to adopt such a stringent course of action and voted instead its belief 'that the Security Council will exercise its responsibilities under the Charter as soon as it considers that the situation in regard to Spain so requires.'

Peru and the Dominican Republic reopened the Spanish question at the fifth session in 1950. Various arguments were offered in favor of lifting the restrictions placed on Spain. Among them were the views that the specialized agencies were technical in nature and should be allowed to decide for themselves whether to admit Spain to membership, that the Assembly resolution of 1946 had proved ineffectual by virtue of the small number of adherents, that the resolution came close to infringing upon the domestic jurisdiction of Spain, and that Spain was no longer recognized as a threat to international peace and security. These arguments carried and the Assembly voted to eliminate the restriction against Spain joining the specialized agencies and decided to revoke the recommendation that members recall their ambassadors from Spain. This action by the Assembly, it was pointed out, only removed these two features of the 1946 resolution and left

the remainder of it intact and did not signify approval of the domestic
policies of the Franco government. Whatever objections remained ceased
to have any support by 1955 and Spain was admitted to membership in the
United Nations toward the end of the Tenth Assembly.

The Palestine Question. The dispute between the Arab and Jewish peoples has proved to be the most complex problem faced by the United Nations and the way to solution is not yet apparent. The events of late 1956
in the Middle East have entangled the Arab-Israeli problem with the Suez
Canal crisis and, as a result, have forced the United Nations to take unprecedented steps to bring about some measure of stability in the area. The
tragic story up to the Israeli attack on Egypt will be discussed at this time.

The origins of the problem go back a number of years. Palestine had been
for centuries a rather desolate part of the Turkish empire. To the Jews the
area represented a homeland from which they had been expelled, while
to Christians and Moslems, it was the land of the Holy Places. It was con-
quered by Great Britain in the First World War, at which time the British
made contradictory promises. Certain commitments appear to have been
made to the Arabs, while in the Balfour Declaration of 1917 the Jews were
told that the British government viewed 'with favour the establishment in
Palestine of a national home for the Jewish people . . .' Following the war,
the Supreme Allied Council decided that Palestine, now a matter of international concern, should be a League of Nations mandate assigned to Great
Britain.

Tensions between Arabs and Jews under the British mandate were at a
minimum until Jewish immigration began to increase sharply in the 1930's
as a result of Hitler's anti-Semitic policy in Germany. Until that time only
the Zionists, an extremely nationalistic Jewish minority, actively pressed for
an exclusively Jewish homeland in Palestine. Arabs protested against the
increasing Jewish population and were supported by the British who announced in 1939 that only 75,000 Jewish immigrants would be permitted
to enter the mandate during the next five years. The Second World War
brought additional refugee problems, and violence between Arab and Jewish
extremists became more frequent. An Anglo-American Committee of Inquiry was formed in November, 1945, to seek a compromise between the
British policy of restricted Jewish immigration and the demand of the
United States that immigration barriers be lifted. The Committee reported
its conclusions on April 20, 1946, and among its ten recommendations were
three of great significance: that 100,000 Jewish immigrants be permitted to
enter Palestine immediately; that Palestine should remain a mandate until
it became a trust area under the United Nations, the status changing only
when hostility disappeared; that Palestine should be neither Arab nor Jewish

but a state guarding the rights of Moslems, Jews, and Christians alike. These and other proposals proved to be unacceptable to the Arabs and acceptable in only a limited sense to the Jews.

The situation continued to deteriorate and the British, unwilling to take a positive stand against either contending faction and faced with an increasing economic and military burden of keeping order, requested in April, 1947, that the Assembly meet in special session to study the entire matter. In spite of the objections of the Arab states, the Assembly met on April 28, 1947, and following a considerable amount of time spent arguing over the agenda, the question was referred to the First Committee where hearings were given to two non-governmental organizations, the Jewish Agency for Palestine and the Arab Higher Committee. Discussion ranged over all aspects of the Palestine question and centered on the make-up and the powers of a special committee to investigate the problem. Finally, on May 15, 1947, the United Nations Special Committee on Palestine (UNSCOP) was established, consisting of eleven members none of which was a permanent member of the Security Council, with 'the widest powers to ascertain and record facts, and to investigate all questions and issues relevant to the problem of Palestine.' It was to report to the Assembly in its regular fall session.

On November 29, 1947, the General Assembly made the following recommendations, based largely on the painstaking report of UNSCOP: that the British mandate be terminated and Palestinian independence granted at the earliest possible date; that a short transitional period precede the granting of independence to Palestine, during which time the United Nations would administer the area; that the sacred character of the Holy Places be preserved and a system established for settling impartially any disputes involving religious rights; that the economic unity of Palestine be preserved; and that the states whose nationals had enjoyed special privileges in Palestine renounce them. In addition, a majority of UNSCOP recommended a plan of partition whereby Palestine would be divided into Jewish and Arab states, with economic union for Palestine as a whole to be supervised by the United Nations.[7] Economic union was to be achieved through a joint Economic Board consisting of three representatives appointed by both Arabs and Jews, with three additional members appointed by the Economic and Social Council. The Trusteeship Council was instructed to prepare a statute for the city of Jerusalem, which would become a separate, internationalized entity under United Nations trusteeship. A five-member Commission was also established to prepare for the British withdrawl from Palestine, which was expected by August 1, 1948. The administration of the area was to be

[7] A minority (India, Iran, and Yugoslavia) advocated a plan supported by the Arab states which would establish a single federated state with Jerusalem the capital.

gradually turned over to the Commission and it was to assist in the creation of provisional councils to govern the two new states.

But almost from its inception, the Commission encountered resistance from the Arabs and particularly from the British. Unwilling to antagonize the Arabs, the United Kingdom held up the Commission's entry into Palestine until just prior to the mandate's termination which had been advanced to May 15, 1948. While the Jews accepted partition with serious reservations, the Arabs denounced it completely and armed clashes became more frequent. The Security Council was informed of the serious nature of the situation by the Commission in February, 1948, and constituted its permanent members as a committee to recommend what course should be taken. The Committee reported that if 'the mandate is terminated prior to a peaceful solution of the problem, large-scale fighting between the two communities can be expected.' Consequently, it believed that 'the Security Council should take further action by all means available to it to bring about the immediate cessation of violence and the restoration of peace and order in Palestine.' In the midst of the Security Council's deliberations on these findings, the delegate from the United States revealed a change of policy by casting doubts on the success of the partition plan and suggesting a temporary trusteeship for Palestine, the calling of a special session of the Assembly to review the problem, the suspension of the Commission's efforts to implement partition, the issuance of a cease-fire in Palestine, and the establishment of a truce. On April 1, 1948, the Security Council acceded to the requests for a cease-fire and called upon the Secretary-General to convoke a special session of the Assembly.[8]

Meeting from April 16 to May 14, 1948, the Assembly refused to accede to the request for abandonment of the partition by the United States and, instead, appointed Count Folke Bernadotte, President of the Swedish Red Cross, as United Nations Mediator for Palestine to 'promote a peaceful adjustment of the future situation of Palestine.' He was instructed to cooperate with the Truce Commission established earlier by the Security Council. The special Palestine Commission created by the Assembly in the fall of 1947 was relieved of further duties.

Acting on a Security Council truce resolution of May 29, Count Bernadotte obtained a four-week truce, from June 11 to July 9. Attempts at mediation failed and fighting began immediately after the termination of the temporary truce. On July 15, the Security Council ordered a cease-fire, proclaiming for the first time that the situation in Palestine was a threat to international peace and security and that violations of the order would

[8] This was the first occasion that the Security Council, acting under the authority of Article 20 of the Charter, had requested a special session of the General Assembly.

result in possible enforcement action. The Mediator was to supervise the truce machinery but in spite of his ceaseless efforts, repeated violations of the cease-fire occurred. On September 17, 1948, the day before the Assembly was to consider his report, which included recommendations to alter the original partition plan in favor of the Arabs, Count Bernadotte was assassinated by an armed band wearing Jewish uniforms. He was replaced by Dr. Ralph J. Bunche of the United Nations Secretariat.

Fighting broke out again and Israeli forces managed to occupy most of the area set aside for it by the original Assembly resolution in November, 1947, which had called for partition. The third regular Assembly session in 1948 refused to revise its 1947 resolution and established a Conciliation Commission to arrange an armistice in the fighting. Much of the negotiation, however, was skillfully conducted by Dr. Bunche. By the summer of 1949, fighting had virtually ceased, armistice agreements had been concluded by the Arab States with Israel, and the Arab regions of Palestine were incorporated within the borders of Jordan and Egypt. The armistice was to be watched over by a United Nations Truce Supervision Organization.

In May, 1949, Israel became the fifty-ninth member of the United Nations but the armistice did not bring a final settlement. The city of Jerusalem remains divided since Israel moved its capital to that part of the city occupied by Israeli forces while the Arabs incorporated their portion into the State of Jordan. Nearly one million Arab refugees remain a constant problem and have had to be cared for by the United Nations Relief and Works Agency for Palestine Refugees in the Near East. Israel refuses to accept the refugees who desire to return to their homes, arguing that repatriation would pose serious security problems since the lands from which the refugees had fled were strategic border areas. Meanwhile, thousands of unfortunate people reside in tents and barracks, engaging in work projects of a limited nature and representing an ever-menacing problem.

Peace treaties were never concluded and frontier violations and sporadic violence have been continually reported by the Truce Supervisory Organization since the signing of the armistice. An illustration of this is the Kibya incident, involving an attack upon an Arab village by a force of Israeli soldiers, which came before the Security Council in 1953. The Chief of Staff of the Truce Supervision Organization, General E. L. M. Burns, reported that between January and May of 1953, seven incidents of this nature occurred, with responsibility about evenly divided. Israel has repeatedly complained to the Council about Egyptian restriction of the right of free passage of ships bound for Israel through the Suez Canal. Violations of the frontier in the Gaza area have beeen frequent. On March 29, 1955, the Council unanimously condemned an Israeli attack on Egyptian military forces inside Egyptian territory which involved a heavy loss of life and property. The following day, the Council had to request General Burns to redouble his efforts to bring about an Israeli-Egyptian agreement on measures to reduce violations along the frontiers of these countries. Again, in September, 1955, the Council was confronted with new outbursts of violence in the Gaza area and in December had to contend with a sharp Israeli-Syrian exchange of attacks at Lake Tiberias. In both instances the Council deplored the continued violence and appealed to the parties concerned, as it had done on March 30, 1955, to cooperate with General Burns in his attempts to preserve some measure of security in the border areas.

In March, 1956, the Council reviewed the extent of compliance by Israel and the Arab States with the armistice agreements and the Council's resolutions of 1955 urging co-operation with the Truce Supervisory Organization. Since compliance had been reduced to a minimum, the Council concluded that the situation was such that its continuance was likely to endanger international peace and security. The Secretary-General was requested in April to meet with the parties and arrange for the adoption of measures to reduce tensions along the armistice demarcation lines. Following a month of discussions in Israel, Egypt, Syria, Jordan, and Lebanon, Mr. Hammarskjöld reported to the Security Council on May 10 that he had found a 'general will to peace' in the Middle East and that unconditional cease-fire agreements had been re-established between Israel and her four Arab neighbors. In June, Dr. E. Ronald Walker of Australia, the President of the Council for that month, stated:

> The Security Council has adopted unanimously a resolution commending the Secretary-General and the parties on the progress already achieved in the direction of securing more complete compliance with the armistice agreements, and calling for further steps in the same direction.
>
> The resolution we have adopted is limited in its immediate objectives. Its primary concern is to secure the full performance by the parties of the undertakings already given by them when they accepted the armistice agreements, and it is a measure of the gravity of the situation in the Palestine area that the Security Council and the Secretary-General should find it necessary, several years after the armistice, to devote so much time and energy to the maintenance of this modest objective. The Security Council will certainly look to all the parties to give their full support to the Council, to the Secretary-General and to the Chief of Staff in the execution of this resolution.
>
> Today's decision by the Council may then indeed prove to be an extremely important forward step.

However, any hope engendered by the painstaking activities of the Secretary-General and the Council was soon to be shattered by new violence. In spite of the continuing efforts of United Nations authorities in the Middle

East and the Secretary-General's personal appeals and consultations, Mr. Hammarskjöld had to report to the Council in August, September, and October that the situation along the Israeli-Jordan cease-fire line was rapidly deteriorating. Constant trouble also was reported between Egypt and Israel. The Council had been debating the question of these recurring incidents when word was received that Israeli forces had crossed the Egyptian border on October 29 and were deeply penetrating the territory in the direction of the Suez Canal. The situation was further complicated by the threat of an Anglo-French invasion of the Canal Zone. The Council was unable to make any progress toward a solution and what had become a much more complicated problem passed to an emergency session of the General Assembly under the 'Uniting for Peace' resolution. This entirely new phase of the Palestine question will be considered in the next chapter.

AN APPRAISAL

It is obvious from the foregoing that the Security Council and the General Assembly have had to deal with a wide variety of questions, each with its own peculiar circumstances frequently involving deep-seated rivalries, ancient antagonisms, and problems directly or indirectly related to past wars. The handling of an international dispute is by no means a simple matter. There is no magic formula which can be applied to every instance of disagreement. What is important is that the parties to a dispute forgo hasty resort to force and employ every available means to reconcile their differences. The parties themselves may be able to do this but they often need to be reminded and encouraged to pursue the avenues of pacific settlement. The Council and the Assembly stand ready to remind and encourage the members of the United Nations of their obligations under the Charter. The Charter, in essence, does not demand that all disputes be brought before the Organization. Instead, it says that states should not bring their disputes to the Council or Assembly if they can settle them outside. At the same time, the Charter makes ample provision for disputes to be discussed and studied and facts ascertained. The Council and the Assembly can, if need be, suggest and recommend the means of settlement.

The increasing activity of the Assembly in the peace and security field has necessitated certain structural and procedural changes. No longer is it an organ meeting for a few short weeks each year. Special emergency sessions are called within twenty-four hours. The investigative and conciliatory functions have been expanded and perfected. Special commissions investigated problems in the Balkans, Eritrea, Palestine, Korea, and South Africa and reported their findings. The machinery of conciliation was improvised and employed extensively in Palestine, the Balkans, and Korea. The 'Uniting for Peace' resolution has injected the Assembly into a sphere of activity heretofore reserved exclusively for the Council. Significant as has been the increased influence of the Assembly in matters of peace and security, this development should not obscure the means employed by the Assembly and the Council in dealing with disputes and situations. Both organs have not employed a rigid approach to Charter interpretation. They have adapted their procedures to the needs of the particular question before them, liberally construing their authority to act under the Charter. This has been more the case with the Council since the powers of the Assembly are quite broad and flexible. Then, too, the Council has had to function with the threat of a veto always a latent possibility.

The Council has not always distinguished clearly between a 'dispute' and a 'situation' and it usually does not determine prior to considering a question, whether its continuance is 'likely to endanger the maintenance of international peace and security.' The criteria for such a determination are difficult to establish and, therefore, the effort to do so has usually been avoided or forgotten. Nonmembers have been freely admitted to the Council table and have had few limits placed upon their participation in the discussion of items which have concerned them. In its unwillingness to be bound by strict procedures, the tendency of the Council has been to employ the least controversial technique and to avoid taking the responsibility for determining the seriousness of a dispute. Weaker measures have been adopted when stronger ones would have been more appropriate, in order to obtain the agreement of some dissident permanent member.

Both organs have rather freely consented to discuss the great majority of matters presented to them. They have not often been deterred by claims of lack of competence and have not made a practice of seeking a clarification of their authority by resorting to an advisory opinion of the World Court. Preponderant Western voting majorities have kept some items off the Council's agenda, as was the case with the Tunisian (1952) and Moroccan (1953) questions.[9] In these cases there were grave doubts as to the competence of the Council to intervene in matters falling within the domestic jurisdiction of a country. At the same time, there has been a recent tendency in both the Council and the Assembly to postpone the consideration of some problems so that the parties concerned might have a greater opportunity to work out an adequate settlement on their own. This result has been achieved with the Tunisian and Moroccan items. It is a reasonable

[9] This was also the case with the Algerian question for a time. For details, see Chapter 15.

approach if not employed in such a manner as to prevent either organ from carrying out a definite responsibility.

While it may be wise, in general, to agree to hear most questions, both organs, and the Council in particular, have placed some items on their agendas without too careful a study of their possible ramifications. There is some doubt, for example, whether the Council should have been concerned with the Anglo-Egyptian, the Anglo-Iranian, or the Hyderabad questions. There was very little the Council could do to arrive at a settlement in any of these instances. The same could be said of the Czechoslovak question. Some method of preliminary discussion might be adopted prior to the placing of an item on the agenda. The Netherlands suggested in 1946, for example, that a three-member subcommittee be appointed to examine a complaint which had been addressed to the Council and to submit preliminary recommendations. Such a procedure could avoid a preliminary discussion on the substance of the question until it could be determined that a complaint was worthy of consideration.

Both organs have conducted most of their business in open, public discussion. While this is inevitable for the Assembly, since it has become the forum where all can freely express themselves on any matter, it does not necessarily hold for the Council. There are occasions when less publicity, certainly in preliminary discussions, might prove to be of value. The example of the Council meeting in private during the October, 1956, discussion of the Suez Canal question is an interesting development which, if continued, may provide good results through private negotiations. The Secretary-General can be of particular use, as he was in this case, by bringing the parties together in private consultation.

It should be noted, in addition, that both the Council and the Assembly have made little use of arbitration and judicial procedures for the adjustment and settlement of disputes. Only infrequent use has been made of the opportunity to obtain advisory opinions from the Court. This situation is in part due to the Charter's emphasis on a political approach to the problems of international peace and security. It is also the result of increased political tensions in the postwar world which tend to lessen the possibility of nations employing a purely legal approach to their problems.

What can be said, finally, of the effectiveness of the United Nations in the adjustment and settlement of disputes, particularly in the light of the developments just noted? With the decline in the importance of the Security Council and the consequent ascendancy of the Assembly, it might be expected that the latter has had more success with the process of peaceful settlement. However, this has not necessarily been the case. The most important function of either organ in this process is to gain an acceptance from the parties of the procedures or terms recommended for the adjustment or settlement of a question. It may be easier for the Assembly to recommend a course of action since it is not faced with a possible veto. But a solution adopted by a two-thirds vote may not represent the attitude of the major powers and hence, in the final analysis, might lack the necessary strength required for adequate implementation. Pressure brought to bear upon a major power in the Western bloc can have some effect, considering the fact that people in democratic countries will normally bow to the will of the majority. Nevertheless, a deep-seated bitterness may be the result as well as hostility to the Organization. There has developed an attitude of mind in some quarters in Britain, for example, that the decisions of the Assembly are effective only against democratic countries. Thus, the charge is made, with some justification, that democracies get punished for some of their policies, while actions by the totalitarian Soviet bloc which are injurious to peace and security cannot be controlled.

Similarly, the Assembly has rather consistently recommended principles of co-operation in the maintenance of international peace and security which have been adopted by large majorities but have not been implemented. For the most part, these proposals have been entirely unacceptable to the minority that has refused to respect the will of the majority. The most outstanding failure has been with recommendations concerned with the obligation of members to promote the observance of human rights and fundamental freedoms, notably in the Balkans and in South Africa. In some instances, members voting in the majority have not carried out their responsibilities. Thus, while it is not always difficult to adopt general principles, there is relatively little assurance that their effectiveness will be made certain through implementation.

Both the Assembly and the Council usually have been able to arrive at some agreement on the methods which should be followed by the parties in a dispute. Soviet vetoes in the Council have blocked some recommendations, notably in the Syria-Lebanon and Berlin questions. This can be expected where Soviet interests are involved. The major difficulty, however, has come with efforts to implement resolutions. Since there are no methods available to either organ to enforce compliance, much depends upon the willingness of the parties to accept, in advance, the recommendation. The Assembly, as an illustration, enjoyed considerable success in its efforts to arrive at a settlement for the former Italian colonies. In this instance, the major powers had reached prior agreement to accept the proposals of the Assembly. The least amount of success has come when the controversy involves the Soviet bloc or when there is a dispute between the major powers. The failure of implementation does not mean that a recommendation does not have some influence on the parties. In the consideration of the question, the discussion brings out relevant facts, clarifies certain issues, and consolidates support for one of the parties. Even where a recommendation has not materialized, the parties can arrive at a settlement, as was the case with the withdrawal of Anglo-French troops from Syria and Lebanon.

The most creditable achievement of the Security Council was the settlement of the Indonesian question. The use of subsidiary organs in this instance for purposes of mediation and conciliation reveals how effective such a procedure can be. Such methods, however, cannot even be undertaken, unless the parties are willing to co-operate. Success cannot result if this co-operation is lacking and the best illustration of this is the Palestine question. However, the primary function of the United Nations is to maintain international peace and security and not necessarily to settle disputes *per se*. In the Kashmir question, the controversy remains unsolved but a cease-fire was brought about and there is little likelihood that the Council or the Assembly would fail to bring pressure on the parties if further military action appeared imminent.

What appears to be clear, in conclusion, is that the major responsibility for peaceful adjustment and settlement of situations and disputes rests with the individual members of the Organization. They are obligated to settle their international disputes in such a manner that peace, security, and justice are not threatened. Although neither the Council nor the Assembly can enforce compliance with its proposals, both organs must continue in every way to assist the parties to a dispute to reach a peaceful agreement. These organs can serve to narrow areas of disagreement and keep alive whatever chance there is for further negotiations. The greatest flexibility must be employed, both in dealing with the disputants and in devising machinery which will keep them in contact with each other.

8

COLLECTIVE MEASURES AND ENFORCEMENT ACTION

IT will be recalled that in the Covenant of the League of Nations, the members were obligated 'to respect and preserve as against external aggression the territorial integrity and existing political independence' of all League members. However, each member was left to determine for himself whether an act of aggression had been committed and upon that decision rested the obligation of supporting a recommendation against the aggressor by the League Council. Sanctions were to be brought against a member if it resorted to war in violation of legal obligations contained in the pacific settlement portions of the Covenant (Arts. 12, 13, 15). Here again, each member had the right to decide when there had been a resort to war in violation of these obligations, to what extent, and the time at which he would employ military sanctions. Furthermore, the Covenant did not make an effective provision for the adoption of preventive measures to be taken before an actual breach of the peace.

The framers of the Charter sought to remedy these deficiencies in the League system. Chapter VII of the Charter (Arts. 39-51), which is devoted to collective measures and enforcement action by the United Nations, empowers the Security Council, and not the individual members, to determine 'the existence of any threat to the peace, breach of the peace, or act of aggression.' The Council also decides whether collective measures are necessary and what they should be if they are necessary to maintain or restore international peace and security. If coercive measures of a military character are decided upon by the Council, the decision is binding on all members of the Organization.

The 'Uniting for Peace' resolution has made it possible for the General Assembly to employ collective measures. If the Council, however, has failed to act on a threat to the peace, breach of the peace, or act of aggression because of a lack of agreement among its permanent members, the Assembly 'shall consider the matter immediately with a view to making appropriate recommendations to Members for collective measures.' The use of armed force is part of this process if it appears that such a course of action is required to maintain or restore peace.

THE ROLE OF THE SECURITY COUNCIL

The use of collective measures involves certain definite steps and the primary responsibility for carrying them out rests with the Council. It must determine the existence of a threat to, or breach of, the peace, or an act of aggression. If the Council makes such a determination, it must then decide whether to recommend the use of sanctions in order to maintain or restore international peace and security. Before making such a recommendation, the Council may call upon the parties concerned 'to comply with such provisional measures as it deems necessary or desirable.'

The Determination of a Threat to or Breach of the Peace. Article 39 of the Charter explicitly grants this power to the Council. Such a determination is of vital importance, since it is prerequisite to enforcement action. Thus, the members of the Organization are compelled to wait, before applying sanctions, until the Council has made the 'determination.'

As we shall see, the Council does not have the military forces at its command that are called for in the Charter and this fact has tended to weaken its authority. Nevertheless, when the Council has determined that a threat to the peace does exist and has indicated that further action might be forthcoming under Chapter VII unless there is compliance with its recommendations, the parties concerned have taken notice and altered their policies. That was the case in the Palestine question with respect to the compliance with the Council's cease-fire request. The North Korean attack on the Republic of Korea was determined to be a breach of the peace and although such a decision did not deter the North Koreans, the determination was believed to be essential so that the call for military sanctions would rest on a sound constitutional basis.

The Council has not taken lightly the grave responsibility accorded it under Article 39. Consequently, in only these two instances — Palestine and Korea — has the Council made a determination called for in Article 39. There appear to be several reasons for this. The veto has blocked such action on several occasions, notably in the Greek question and in the Middle East crisis of 1956. It is difficult to discover whether the facts justify the conclusion that there exists a threat to or breach of the peace or an act of aggression. None of these terms — so important for the functioning of the Council under Chapter VII — is given precise meaning although the task of defining aggression has been under study by the International Law Commission. Some members of the Council have been reluctant to reach a finding under Article 39 unless there is a certainty that it will be supported by the majority of the members of the United Nations and especially by the great powers. The Council has always sought to exhaust all other means of settlement before acting under Article 39, if for no other reason than to avoid the complicated aspects of making such a determination. It was not until the parties in the Palestine question had failed to agree to a cease-fire in 1948 that the Council acted under Article 39. The Council circumvented Chapter VII in the Indonesian case so as not to aggravate a delicate situation. The Western bloc in the Council has also been anxious to avoid the adoption of collective military measures which might permit the entry of Soviet bloc forces into areas such as Indonesia and Palestine where their presence might have broad political ramifications.

The Use of Provisional Measures. Designed to prevent a threat to the peace from developing into armed conflict, Article 40 enables the Security Council, before employing sanctions, 'to call upon the parties concerned to comply with such provisional measures as it deems necessary or desirable.' It may be preferable for the Council, if a procedure of peaceful settlement proves to be inadequate, to resort to measures short of sanctions, 'in order to prevent an aggravation of the situation.' The Charter does not specify what is meant by 'provisional measures' and hence the Council has wide latitude in its procedure.

The natural assumption would be that the Council is to make a formal determination under Article 39 before it employs a provisional measure. This has not always proved to be the case, however. The Council has failed to make a determination in some cases and has also called upon the parties to adopt provisional measures when it was acting under Chapter VI of the Charter. In this latter instance, the Council has interpreted the wording of Article 36, namely, the recommendation of 'appropriate procedures or methods of adjustment,' to mean the employment of provisional measures which have been deemed necessary to a peaceful settlement. The Council has also called for provisional measures at the same time that it has made a determination under Article 39 or after having made one. In addition, the Council has, at times, proceeded in one fashion in a case when hostilities had not broken out and in another when armed conflict was in progress. A brief review of some cases will reveal the procedure it has followed and the nature of measures utilized.

In the Indonesian case, there was no reference to Articles 39 and 40 in the resolutions of the Council. The parties were called upon 'to cease hostilities forthwith.' In the North Korean attack, the Council concurrently determined a breach of the peace and called for a cessation of hostilities and withdrawal of armed forces by the invaders. In the Kashmir dispute, no reference was made to Chapter VII and the Council presumably acted under Chapter VI. The parties were called upon 'to take immediately all measures within their power calculated to improve the situation and to refrain from making any statement or from doing or causing to be done or permitting any acts which might aggravate the situation.' In the Palestine question, the Council at first did not make a determination under Article 39 but employed measures which would appear to be those falling under Article 40. Thus, the Council called upon the parties 'to take all possible action to prevent or reduce such disorders as are now occurring in Palestine,' 'to cease acts of violence immediately,' 'to cease all activities of a military or para-military nature,' and to respect a four-week truce. However, after the truce had expired and hostilities resumed, the Council determined that a threat to the peace existed under Article 39 and directed the adoption of provisional measures under Article 40. Somewhat later, in this case, the Council called upon the parties 'as a further provisional measure under Article 40' to seek agreement through the United Nations mediator upon the establishment of an armistice.

Soviet vetoes have defeated resolutions bearing on this problem. In the Greek question, for example, one resolution determined that the situation on the northern borders of Greece did constitute a threat to the peace under Article 39 and called upon the parties 'to cease all acts of provocation.' Another resolution found the situation a threat to peace under Chapter VII of the Charter, called upon Albania, Bulgaria, and Yugoslavia 'to cease and desist' in aid to guerrillas, and stated that the Council remained seized of the question and would 'take such further action in connection with the enforcement of its orders and the settlement of the dispute as may from time to time be necessary.' In the Berlin question, a resolution, proposed by six members of the Council who were not parties to the dispute, made no reference to Article 39 but called upon the parties, pursuant to Article 40, to prevent any measures which might aggravate the situation and remove all restrictions on communications, transport, and commerce then in effect.

It has been necessary for the Council, on several occasions, to implement its resolutions calling for provisional measures. Quite frequently the members of the Organization are requested to support or assist the methods which have been adopted. Thus, the Council in the Korean case, after calling for a cessation of hostilities, requested all members 'to render every assistance to the United Nations in the execution of this resolution.' The Council has threatened enforcement action under Chapter VII to bring compliance with its resolutions, as it did in the Palestine question. In addition, it has been found necessary to create subsidiary machinery to give effect to measures of a provisional nature. In the Indonesian question, the Council requested the Committee of Good Offices to assist the parties in arriving at a cease-fire. Similar arrangements have been employed in the Palestine case.

Collective Measures. According to the theory of the Charter, should the Security Council fail to halt the progress of a threat to or breach of the peace, it is then expected to employ some form of enforcement action. The decision on the collective measures to be taken is binding on all members of the United Nations since they, in Article 25, 'agree to accept and carry out the decisions of the Security Council in accordance with the present Charter.' The Council may also make recomendations on the measures which should be adopted, as it did in Korea. Such a recommendation is not binding and leaves to each member the ultimate decision whether to proceed with collective measures. Articles 41 and 42 enumerate the nature of the sanctions which are available for its decision or recommendation. Korea is the only instance in which sanctions have been used. However, the Council was compelled to improvise because of the absence of military forces at its command as called for in Article 43. The Council was also stalemated after August 1, 1950, when the Soviet representative returned to the Council table and prevented any further action. As a consequence, it will be necessary only to enumerate the Charter provisions, following which the Council procedures employed in the Korean conflict will be noted. A full case study of the Korean question can be found at the end of this chapter.

First of all, measures not involving the use of force may be called for by the Council (Art. 41). The list includes 'complete or partial interruption of economic relations and of rail, sea, air, postal, telegraphic, radio and other means of communication, and the severance of diplomatic relations.' Sanctions in this category are to be exercised by the members themselves since the Council is authorized only to 'call upon the members of the United Nations to apply such measures.' These may be as effective as the use of armed force. An economic boycott can be particularly severe and destroy or seriously weaken the military establishment of a state. Once sanctions have been ordered, even if they are nonmilitary only, the duty of the Council has been fulfilled. It is not obligated to go beyond such measures.

If the Council is determined to put an end to the matter in the event nonmilitary sanctions have proved to be inadequate, 'it may take such action by air, sea, or land forces as may be necessary to maintain or restore international peace and security' (Art. 42). Indeed, the Council may order such action instead of nonmilitary sanctions if it believes that the later might be inadequate to meet the situation. The use of military sanctions does not necessarily mean involvement in actual warfare, since the Charter provides that sanctions may include demonstrations or a blockade by air, sea, or land forces. Members are expected, under Article 43, 'to make available to the Security Council, on its call and in accordance with a special agreement or agreements, armed forces, assistance and facilities, including rights of passage, necessary for the purpose of maintaining international peace and security.' The agreements referred to are to be negotiated through the initiative of the Council between it and a member or groups of members. To be specified in the agreements — actually treaties — are 'the numbers and types of forces, their degree of readiness and general location, and the nature of the facilities and assistance to be provided.' Members are also expected to hold immediately available national air force contingents in order to enable the United Nations to take urgent military action.

Should the Security Council decide to use force, a nonmember of the Council may request to appear before the Council and participate in the discussions of the Council concerning the possible employment of that state's armed forces. In this instance alone, a nonmember of the Council not only may join the discussion but may vote in the same manner as any nonpermanent member. The Council also has the discretion to determine whether certain nations should provide some or all of the military contingents or adopt specific economic measures. It may be far more useful and economical to have members located in one continent provide forces instead of bringing contingents from distant lands. Then, too, some nations can contribute more than others toward making economic sanctions effective. Credit can be stopped, strategic supplies can be cut off, or shipping to an island nation can cease. Only certain members, because of their economic structure, material resources, or geographical location on an ocean, would be apt to be involved in such activities. However, if preventive or enforcement measures are taken by the Council, any state, whether or not it is a member of the United Nations, 'which finds itself confronted with special economic problems' arising from the carrying out of such measures, has the right 'to consult with the Security Council with regard to a solution of those problems.'

Military Staff Committee. According to the Charter, when military sanctions are to be applied, the Security Council itself is expected to take action, as distinct from individual action by members under nonmilitary sanctions. This means that the Council takes charge of and directs whatever procedures of a military nature are deemed necessary. This supervisory function is to be entrusted to a subsidiary organ of the Council, the Military Staff Committee.

Article 47 calls for the establishment of a Military Staff Committee to 'advise and assist the Security Council on all questions relating to the Security Council's military requirements for the maintenance of international peace and security, the employment and command of forces placed at its disposal, the regulation of armaments and possible disarmament.' The Committee, which first met in February, 1946, is composed of the Chiefs of Staff of the permanent members of the Security Council or their representatives. Any member of the United Nations not permanently represented on the Committee may be invited 'to be associated with it when the efficient discharge of the Committee's responsibilities requires the participation of that member in its work.'

The Committee is also responsible for the strategic direction of any armed forces placed at the disposal of the Council. Consultation with regional agencies through the establishment of regional subcommittees is encouraged by the Charter. However, the Military Staff Committee has failed to function as expected. The Council asked it to examine the military requirements of the United Nations but the Committee, after working more than a year, was unable to arrive at any agreed conclusions. The military arrangements necessitated by the Korean action did not make use of the Committee and the United Nations Command in the war was established on a wholly different basis.

Collective Measures in Korea. In its resolution of June 25, 1950, which determined that the North Korean attack constituted a breach of the peace, the Council called upon all members of the United Nations 'to render every assistance' in support of this decision. President Truman announced on June 27 that he had 'ordered United States air and sea forces to give the Korean Government troops cover and support' in accordance with the Council's resolution of June 25. On the same day, the Council passed a resolution which recommended that the members of the Organization 'furnish such assistance' to the Republic of Korea as might be needed to repel the attack. On July 7, the Council recommended that military forces and other assistance be made available 'to a unified command under the United States.' Thus, at the beginning of the conflict the Council established an entirely new procedure to contend with a breach of the peace. No resort was made to either Article 41 or 42. No member was legally bound to 'render every assistance,' since the Council did not decide but only recommended under Article 39 that assistance be provided. North Korea was not formally labeled an aggressor although repeated mention was made of 'aggression having been committed.'

The decision to intervene in Korea has been hailed by some as the first example of collective security in action within the limits of the Charter. However, the United States actually decided to intervene against Communist aggression before the Council had called for military support. Subsequent action by the Council was possible *only* in the absence of the

Soviet member. It is extremely doubtful whether the Council will be able to act at all in similar cases whenever the interests of one of its permament members is directly involved.

The establishment of the Unified Command under the United States has introduced an entirely new principle as far as enforcement action is concerned. In the absence of military forces called for in Article 43, it is up to one state or group of states to act on behalf of the Council and take the lead in both organizing and providing the military forces which might be needed to restore and maintain international peace. Too much reliance, however, cannot be placed upon this procedure, unless such a course of action has at least the tacit approval of the permanent members. Employment of this type of action can come in the Assembly, as we shall see. But again, the conditions surrounding the conflict must favor the adoption of such a method, since a combination either of the Soviet and Afro-Asian blocs or the Western and Latin American blocs can prevent the required two-thirds vote.

The concept of the Unified Command, as proved by the Korean experience, has a number of complicating aspects which should be noted. There is, for example, the problem of liaison between the Command and the Council. In this connection, it is interesting to reflect upon a proposal submitted by the Secretary-General to France, the United Kingdom, the United States, and the Council President (Norway) prior to the resolution of July 7. In addition to having the United States undertake the task of organizing a United Nations command, the plan would have created a 'Committee on Coordination of Assistance for Korea,' composed of six Council members plus the United States, with the Secretary-General to act as *rapporteur*. The Republic of Korea would be permitted to have a representative in attendance. But the United States, the major contributor of forces in addition to having the responsibility of directing the Unified Command, would not accept the proposal. The American view was that there should be no interference with its heavy burdens in the conduct of hostilities. A similar attitude could be expected from some other nation placed in the same position of responsibility. The Secretary-General can be, as he was in Korea, a connecting link between the Command and the United Nations but he is in no position to offer political leadership, which is vital to a military undertaking.

Other problems arose in Korea which were essentially military in character and had a distinct bearing upon the concept of the Unified Command and its possible future use. Who is to decide what military contingents are to be accepted? What should be the optimum size of such a force? Who is to supply the units in the command? How are transport problems to be met? These few examples suggest others of like kind which arose in Korea and must be considered in the future.

THE ROLE OF THE GENERAL ASSEMBLY

There is no mention of the Assembly in Chapter VII of the Charter. It can be argued that the use of enforcement measures is exclusively the right of the Security Council if one employs a closely reasoned, juristic approach to the meaning of the Charter.[1] At the same time, however, it can be argued that even though the Assembly is directed by Article 11:2 to refer to the Council any 'question on which action is necessary,' if it has first come before the Assembly, there is nothing to prevent the Assembly from proceeding under its broad powers contained in Article 10 if the Council fails to act on the matter. The key word is 'action' and it has been interpreted to mean 'enforcement action.' Furthermore, Article 11:2 states that questions requiring action are to be referred by the Assembly to the Council 'either before or after discussion.' Prior to referring the question, therefore, the Assembly presumably would have to make a determination that 'action is necessary,' that is, enforcement action, and such a determination would be similar to that which the Council is to make under Article 39. This was the view advanced in favor of the 'Uniting for Peace' resolution when it was debated in the Assembly. Since the Assembly adopted the resolution by a large majority (52 affirmative, 5 negative, 2 abstentions) and has acted under it, current practice dictates that the Assembly does possess the authority to undertake enforcement action.

There are a few instances when the Assembly performed acts similar to those permitted the Council under Articles 39 and 40 before the passage of 'Uniting for Peace.' In its performance, the Assembly, like the Council, followed no consistent pattern and did not necessarily make a 'determination' prior to recommending provisional measures. In 1947, the Assembly established a Special Committee to investigate the Palestine situation and, at the same time, called upon 'all governments and peoples, and particularly upon the inhabitants of Palestine, to refrain, pending action by the General Assembly on the report of the Special Committee on Palestine, from the threat or use of force or any other action which might create an atmosphere prejudicial to an early settlement of the question of Palestine.' No determination of a threat to or breach of the peace had been made. Nor had any determination been made in the Greek question when, in the fall of 1947, the Assembly called upon Albania, Bulgaria, and Yugoslavia to cease providing aid to guerrillas opposing the Greek government. But the following year, the Assembly approved both the activities of its Special Committee, created earlier to investigate the matter, and the Committee's report, which

---

[1] See for example, Kelsen, Hans, 'Is the Acheson Plan Constitutional?', *Western Political Quarterly*, Vol. 3, No. 4 (December 1950), pp. 512–27.

noted that the support given to the Greek guerrillas constituted 'a threat to the political independence and territorial sovereignty of Greece.' The same resolution held that continued aid to the guerrillas endangered peace in the Balkans and was inconsistent with the purposes and principles of the Charter. Albania, Bulgaria, and Yugoslavia were called upon to cease such aid 'including the use of their territories as a base for the preparation or launching of armed action.'

On two occasions before the adoption of the 'Uniting for Peace' resolution the Assembly had recommended the use of nonmilitary collective measures of the nature envisaged by Article 41 of the Charter. In the Spanish question, the Assembly late in 1946 recommended that 'the Franco Government of Spain be debarred from international agencies established by or brought into relationship with the United Nations, and from participation in conferences or other activities which may be arranged by the United Nations or by these agencies . . .' and that 'all members of the United Nations immediately recall from Madrid their ambassadors and ministers plenipotentiary accredited there.' In the Greek case, the Assembly in November, 1949, called upon Albania, Bulgaria, and the other states concerned to 'cease forthwith' any assistance to the guerrillas and recommended that all United Nations members refrain from action that would be of assistance to armed groups in Greece, or from sending 'arms or other materials of war to Albania and Bulgaria,' as well as to consider, in their relations with these two countries, the extent to which they should 'henceforth abide by the recommendations of the General Assembly in their relations with Greece.'

The 'Uniting for Peace' Resolution. Since the Security Council did not have the military support specified in Article 43 of the Charter and had demonstrated its inability to deal with the Korean crisis after the Soviet delegate returned on August 1, 1950, the United States, with the support of France and the United Kingdom, was determined to have the United Nations provided with additional machinery to handle such a threat. Secretary of State Dean Acheson emphasized this in addressing the Assembly on September 20, 1950. After reviewing the Soviet conduct of international affairs, which he labeled as a barrier to peaceful relations, Mr. Acheson stated:

> There is only one real way the world can maintain peace and security in the face of this conduct. That is by strengthening its system of collective security. Our best hope of peace lies in our ability to make absolutely plain to aggressors that aggression cannot succeed. The security of those nations who want peace and the security of the United Nations itself demand the strength to prevent further acts of aggression.

The draft resolution to accomplish this purpose, known later as 'Uniting for Peace,' was placed before the First (Political) Committee of the Assembly where it became the subject of discussion for seventeen meetings during October. The general discussion was primarily constitutional in character and centered around the question of the actual competence of the Assembly under the Charter to undertake the functions proposed by Mr. Acheson. Opposition came primarily from the Soviet bloc led by Mr. Vyshinsky who, *inter alia*, argued that the Security Council should require the unanimous consent of its permanent members before calling an emergency session of the Assembly; that Article 11:2 of the Charter precluded the use of collective measures by the Assembly; and that the Charter should be formally amended if there was an objection to the veto possessed by the Council's permanent members. The charge was also made that the aim of the draft was to replace the Council by the Assembly, to paralyze the Council, and to transform the United Nations 'into a mere tool of the foreign policy of the United States of America.'

Following the resolution's adoption in committee, it was considered in four plenary meetings of the Assembly from November 1 to November 3, during which time eleven Soviet amendments were defeated. As finally adopted, the resolution contains five parts and introduces a wholly new approach to the collective security provisions of the Charter by formally permitting the Assembly, in addition to the Security Council, to participate in the use of enforcement measures. These salient points of the resolution should be noted carefully:

1. If not already in session, the Assembly can meet in special emergency session within twenty-four hours if so requested by a majority of United Nations members or by the affirmative vote of any seven members of the Security Council.

2. If the Security Council, due to a lack of unanimity of the permanent members, fails to exercise its primary responsibility in any case where there appears to be a threat to the peace, breach of the peace, or an act of aggression, the Assembly is to consider the matter immediately.

3. The Assembly may then consider recommendations 'to members for collective measures, including in the case of a breach of the peace or act of aggression the use of armed force when necessary, to maintain or restore international peace and security.'

4. A Peace Observation Commission of fourteen was created 'to observe and report on the situation in any area where there exists international tension the continuance of which is likely to endanger the maintenance of international peace and security.' Prior invitation or consent 'of the State into whose territory the Commission would go' is necessary. The Commission cannot be used in dealing with questions on the agenda of the Security Council.

5. All members were invited to survey their resources in order to determine the nature and scope of assistance they would be able to offer in support of any Council or Assembly recommendations. Further, it was recommended that every member 'maintain within its armed forces elements so trained, organized, and equipped that they could promptly be made available . . . for service as a United Nations unit or units' if recommended by the Council or Assembly. The Secretary-General was requested to appoint a panel of military experts available for advising members on technical matters related to the organization and training of military units for United Nations service.

6. A fourteen-member Collective Measures Committee was established to study and report on methods which might be used to strengthen international peace and security, in accordance with the purposes and principles of the Charter.

In essence then, the resolution grants to the Assembly the right to act in the place of the Council only when that body has failed to 'exercise its primary responsibility' in a case 'where there appears to be a threat to the peace, breach of the peace, or act of aggression.' The Council is still expected to exercise 'its primary responsibility' in such cases. When it does not, the Assembly can recommend — and only recommend — collective measures. In the case of a breach of the peace or act of aggression, the use of armed force can be recommended. Since a recommendation to use armed forces is worthless unless such forces are available and ready to act promptly, the resolution recommends that each member of the Organization prepare itself so that if the need arises it can make forces available.

However, some of these provisions are not clear-cut and the practice of the Assembly under 'Uniting for Peace' so far does not reveal much consistency in their application.

1. THE CALLING OF EMERGENCY SESSIONS. To call such a session, presumably the Council must have been discussing the means whereby action is to be taken on a threat to a breach of the peace or act of aggression. But in the two emergency sessions called in November, 1956, to discuss the Hungarian and Middle East crises, this was not the case. In the Hungarian case, the matter was brought to the attention of the Council under Chapter VI of the Charter, with Article 34 cited specifically. Before the Council came to a vote, the situation worsened considerably. Although such terms as 'brutal aggression,' and 'flagrant violation of all laws of decency, morality, and justice' were used during the discussion, there was no attempt to make a determination of a threat to or breach of the peace or act of aggression. Mr. Lodge of the United States in introducing his resoluton on November 4 did state: 'If ever there was a question which clearly raised a threat to the

peace, this is the question.' But his resolution did not contain similar language. It called upon the USSR 'to desist forthwith from any form of intervention, particularly armed intervention, in the internal affairs of Hungary . . . , to cease the introduction of additional armed forces into Hungary and to withdraw all of its forces without delay from Hungarian territory.'

Following the defeat of the United States resolution by a Soviet veto, the Council then voted to call an emergency special session of the Assembly to 'make appropriate recommendations concerning the situation in Hungary.' In making this decision, the Council only pointed out that a grave situation had been created by the 'use of Soviet military forces to suppress the efforts of the Hungarian people to reassert their rights.' However, in proposing this move, Mr. Lodge said that the Council could not afford to 'temporize over this cynical and brutal breach of the peace.' The Council also took note of its failure to exercise its primary responsibility for the maintenance of international peace and security 'due to the lack of unanimity among its permanent members.' Thus, the matter came to the Assembly without a formal attempt by the Council to determine a threat to or breach of the peace or an act of aggression. It must be said, however, that the majority of the Council believed the matter to be of such a character, as indicated by the remarks of Mr. Lodge and others.

A similar situation over the question of making the determination developed in the Middle East crisis and became one of the key arguments in the Council against referring the matter to the Assembly under 'Uniting for Peace.' A proposal to call a special emergency session of the Assembly was made on October 31, 1956, by Joza Brilej of Yugoslavia. At the time, the Council was discussing the Egyptian charge that France and Britain were planning an act of aggression against its territory. The complaint had been submitted on September 24, the day after France and Britain had brought the Suez Canal question before the Council. Just prior to the discussion of the Egyptian charge, Anglo-French vetoes defeated proposals for an Israeli-Egyptian cease-fire. Dr. Brilej proposed an emergency Assembly session because of the grave situation created by the Israeli invasion of Egypt and because the Council had been prevented by a lack of unanimity of its permanent members from exercising its primary responsibility for the maintenance of international peace and security.

Both the British representative, Sir Pierson Dixon, and Louis de Guiringaud of France maintained that the Yugoslav proposal was out of order and not in accordance with the provisions of the 'Uniting for Peace' resolution. They contended that a pre-condition of invoking the procedure contained in the resolution was that a lack of unanimity of the permament members of the Council should have prevented it from taking action. This presupposed that a resolution on the substance of a question before the Council had been discussed and voted upon. Until that had been done, there could be no determination that the Council had failed to make a decision because of the lack of unanimity of the permanent members. But, claimed the Anglo-French members, no such resolution had been discussed or voted upon in the question then before the Council, namely an Egyptian charge against Britain and France.

In addition, the resolutions vetoed earlier under another item — the cease-fire between Israel and Egypt — did not come within the scope of the 'Uniting for Peace' resolution, since neither the complaint nor the resolution came within the terms of Chapter VII of the Charter and, therefore, could not be invoked to support the Yugoslav proposal. The Anglo-French claim was that the 'Uniting for Peace' resolution could be employed only after the Council had determined the existence of a threat to or breach of the peace or act of aggression, and had failed to act, because of the absence of unity between the permanent members. The resolutions which had been considered contained no such finding.

Dr. Brilej refused to accept this interpretation, arguing that there existed not only a threat to the peace but a breach of the peace and that the provisions of 'Uniting for Peace' were in full accord with his resolution. He further observed that if the Assembly were convened, it would be the master of its own procedure and business. Therefore, it was unnecessary to state which specific item would be on its agenda. The Yugoslav proposal was then adopted by a vote of 7-2, with two abstentions. The full text of the resolution is as follows:

> *The Security Council*
> *Considering* that a grave situation has been created by action undertaken against Egypt,
> *Taking into consideration* that the lack of unanimity of its permanent members at the 749th and 750th meetings of the Security Council has prevented it from exercising its primary responsibility for the maintenance of international peace and security;
> *decides* to call an emergency special session of the General Assembly as provided in the General Assembly's resolution 377(v) in order to make appropriate recommendations.

The practice of the Council in calling emergency special sessions of the Assembly under 'Uniting for Peace' would indicate a broad interpretation of that resolution, as far as the conditions presumably required for its employment are concerned. In these two cases, the Assembly also ignored the absence of a determination of a threat to or a breach of the peace or an act of aggression.

2. THE USE OF COLLECTIVE MEASURES. The 'Uniting for Peace' resolution is by no means clear when it makes reference to collective measures, although the presumption is that action consonant with Articles 41 and 42 of the Charter is intended. Collective measures may be used in any case where there is a breach of the peace or act of aggression and also, 'where there appears to be a threat to the peace.' The words 'appears to be' are not included in Chapter VII and, therefore, it is possible for the Assembly to recommend collective measures in an instance which is not permitted the Council. The resolution mentions the use of armed force only where there is a breach of the peace or an act of aggression. A clear ambiguity arises here, since armed force is not ruled out specifically in a case where there appears to be a threat or there is actually a threat to the peace. If armed force can be used in a case which only 'appears to be' a threat to the peace, the Assembly is permitted action forbidden to the Council.

Some limited conclusions can be drawn on the question of collective action from the Assembly's use of the resolution. The Council was prevented from taking any action in November, 1950, on the matter of Chinese Communist intervention in the Korean War because of the Soviet Union's veto. The matter was then raised in the Assembly where it was decided to attempt to bring about an end to the hostilities and a peaceful settlement before taking direct action on the Chinese intervention. A Group of Three was appointed in December to negotiate with the Peiping government but was unable to establish any agreement with the Chinese. Consequently, largely at the insistence of the United States, the Assembly on February 1, 1951, determined that the Chinese Communists were engaged in aggression in Korea. No specific reference was made to the 'Uniting for Peace' resolution although the Assembly did note that the Security Council had failed 'because of the lack of unanimity of the permanent members . . . to exercise its primary responsibility for the maintenance of international peace and security in regard to Chinese Communist intervention in Korea.' No collective measures were recommended, although by calling upon all states and authorities 'to continue to lend every assistance to the United Nations action in Korea,' the Assembly indirectly suggested military sanctions. A committee composed of the members of the Collective Measures Committee (known later as the Additional Measures Committee) was requested to consider additional measures 'to be employed to meet this aggression.' Still intent upon bringing about a cessation of hostilities, a Good Offices Committee was established to continue negotiations.

When it was again obvious that nothing further could be accomplished toward arriving at a cease-fire, the report of the Additional Measures Committee was submitted and on May 18, 1951, the Assembly recommended the employment of economic sanctions against the Peiping and North Korean governments through the application of an embargo on the shipments of war materials and other strategic items. Each state, however, was to determine for itself the commodities which were to be covered by the embargo. The Additional Measures Committee became a co-ordinating body, since all members were to report to it the extent of their compliance with the resolution. The embargo was fairly successful, although most nations which participated to any great extent had been withholding strategic supplies before the embargo was recommended.

This first experience with collective measures by the Assembly fulfilled the basic requisites of the 'Uniting for Peace' resolution. The Council had been unable to discharge its responsibilities in a case of a breach of the peace. The Assembly, after a considerable delay, went beyond the Council and declared the Chinese intervention an act of aggression. Nonmilitary sanctions were eventually adopted and put into effect, without, however, having much influence on the course of the war.

In the Middle East crisis of 1956, the Assembly first urged an immediate cease-fire on November 2 and recommended that all United Nations members 'refrain from introducing military goods in the area of hostilities and in general refrain from any acts which would delay or prevent the implementation of the present resolution.' It was perfectly obvious that a breach of the peace, if not an act of aggression, had occurred, since Israeli troops were well inside Egyptian territory and key Egyptian installations were being subjected to Anglo-French air attacks preparatory to a landing of ground forces. No such determination was made in the resolution, however. On November 4, the parties again were called upon to cease hostilities. At the same time, the Secretary-General was requested to submit 'a plan for the setting up, with the consent of the nations concerned, of an emergency international United Nations force to secure and supervise the cessation of hostilities.'

What materialized from this is not an armed force in the sense that it has a truly military mission. It was established 'to secure and supervise the cessation of hostilities' and was to be located in 'an area extending roughly from the Suez Canal to the [Egyptian-Israeli] armistice line.' The United Nations Emergency Force (UNEF) was not instructed to enforce the cease-fire or compel Anglo-French and Israeli military units to leave Egyptian soil. It was not equipped with weapons or supporting elements which would make possible any enforcement action other than policing activities. In essence, it was not much more than a greatly expanded United Nations Truce Supervision Organization, with no clearly defined functions other than to serve in the field presumably as a deterrent to further hostilities. What is more, the permission of Egypt had to be obtained prior to its arrival on Egyptian territory. Finally, it can be argued that the powers exercised by the Assembly in establishing UNEF stemmed not from the 'Uniting for Peace' resolution but from authority already possessed through Charter provisions, since that document permits the Assembly to 'establish such subsidiary organs as it deems necessary for the performance of its functions' (Art. 22). Thus the Assembly can be said to have created UNEF as a subsidiary organ and recommended that all members assist in giving it life and substance. In this sense, all that 'Uniting for Peace' did was enable the Assembly to meet in emergency session and discuss a matter on which action had been stalled in the Security Council by a veto.

Considerable latitude has been given to the Secretary-General to organize UNEF and direct its activities. An Advisory Committee of seven (Brazil, Canada, Ceylon, Colombia, India, Norway and Pakistan), chaired by the Secretary-General, was established to undertake the necessary planning which was not specified by the Assembly. It was also to assist Mr. Hammarskjöld in his responsibilities and could request the convening of the General Assembly and report to it 'whenever matters arise which, in its opinion, are of such urgency and importance as to require consideration by the General Assembly itself.' As Chief of the Command, the Assembly appointed, 'on an emergency basis,' General E.L.M. Burns, the Chief of Staff of the United Nations Truce Supervision Organization. He was authorized to recruit from the observer corps of his Organization a limited number of officers but specifically none from any of the permanent members of the Security Council. The Secretary-General obtained the voluntary contributions of military forces and transportation facilities from individual members of the United Nations. Mr. Hammarskjöld was also given the authority to issue all regulations and instructions 'which may be essential to the effective functioning of the Force, following consultation with the Advisory Committee, and to take all other necessary administrative and executive actions.'

The broad powers conferred on Mr. Hammarskjöld and the absence of details in the Assembly resolutions to govern the purposes and functions of UNEF can be explained by the urgency to obtain adoption of the plan and get military contingents into Egypt. Had there been an attempt to be more specific, a fight on the floor of the Assembly might have ensued with the possible defeat of the entire project. However, the failure to define the ultimate objective of UNEF left the decision primarily up to the Secretary-

General. This proved to be a task of the greatest magnitude, since agreement had to be reached between the parties on where UNEF was to be stationed and when and under what conditions it would be withdrawn.

The Assembly was competent to act in the Middle East crisis under the 'Uniting for Peace' resolution, since the Security Council was not able to discharge its responsibility because of the Anglo-French vetoes. Although it was self-evident that there had been a definite breach of the peace, the Assembly made no such determination. However, owing to the urgency of the situation and the obvious fact that hostilities had broken out and were liable to spread, there was no need to make this finding. A discussion of the matter would have been time consuming and would have served no useful purpose. In any event, such a finding was implied in the Assembly resolution of November 2, which took note of the military operations conducted by the armed forces of France, Israel, and the United Kingdom.

3. ADVANCE PREPARATION OF COLLECTIVE MEASURES. The 'Uniting for Peace' resolution invited members of the United Nations to survey their resources to determine the nature of assistance that could be offered in support of Assembly or Council recommendations and recommended that members maintain special military elements which could be used by the Organization in an emergency. The Collective Measures Committee was to be informed of such action and was to decide upon the necessary principles and plans to govern the application of collective measures. A panel of military experts was created to provide technical advice to states on their military planning.

Members of the United Nations in April, 1951, were requested by the Secretary-General to provide information on methods adopted to implement the resolution. Most states indicated their support for the general principles of advance preparation but were unwilling to make specific commitments. A few did not commit themselves in any way while the Soviet bloc considered the whole idea illegal. In the meantime, the Committee studied the matter and reported its conclusions to the Assembly in the fall of 1951. The report did little more than suggest further implementation of the steps called for in the 'Uniting for Peace' resolution. While accepting the recommendation of the Committee in general, the Assembly made certain that the decision to make available specific forces to the United Nations rested exclusively with each state and that each would be able to employ these units for purposes of internal security or regional security as it saw fit.

The members of the United Nations in the summer of 1952 were requested to comment upon the Assembly recommendations. Their replies did not differ materially from those obtained the preceding year. A hard core of states reaffirmed their support and indicated that their constitutional processes permitted them to join in collective measures. Significantly, the majority of those answering in this manner were already participants in collective self-defense arrangements under Article 51 of the Charter.

The Committee has continued to function and has been directed to report to the Assembly and the Security Council whenever appropriate. The panel of military experts called for in the 'Uniting for Peace' resolution was constituted but members have not availed themselves of its services. There is not much evidence to support a conclusion that the efforts of the Committee have had much effect in encouraging states to develop special units for UN service. The various studies and reports of the Committee have been available for the Secretary-General in his development of plans for the United Nations Emergency Force in the Middle East and undoubtedly contained suggestions which have proved to be of assistance. The voluntary contributions to UNEF do not appear to have been special units designed for United Nations service as contemplated by 'Uniting for Peace' and the Committee reports.

The Peace Observation Commission has been constituted and made available for service but has not been employed except for frontier inspection in the Balkans. In 1954, Thailand said that hostilities in nearby Indo-China were a threat to her security and requested that observers be sent out, but the proposal was defeated by a Soviet veto.

CASE STUDIES

1. THE KOREAN WAR

The strategic location of Korea on the mainland of East Asia, bounded on one side by China and on the other by Russia and projecting to within 120 miles of Japan has made it a trouble spot for centuries. In the Sino-Japanese War (1894–95), Japan was able to put an end to Chinese influence over Korea, and the tributary relationship which had existed for some time between the two countries. The Russo-Japanese War (1904–05) culminated in the destruction by Japan of whatever position the Russians had enjoyed in Korea and by 1910 the country had become a Japanese colony.

Soon after the Japanese attack on Pearl Harbor, various Korean exiles made efforts in Washington to gain recognition for a Korean Provisional Government in exile. But no agreement was reached on these overtures because the Pacific Allies believed in 1942 that any move in this direction would be premature. However, at the Cairo Conference late in 1943, President Roosevelt, Prime Minister Churchill, and Generalissimo Chiang Kai-shek declared jointly that they were 'determined that in due course,

Korea shall become free and independent.' This declaration was reaffirmed at the Potsdam Conference on July 26, 1945 and the Soviet Union announced its adherence to this policy when it entered the Pacific War against Japan on August 8, 1945. A military understanding resulted in Soviet troops accepting the surrender of Japanese forces above the thirty-eighth parallel and United States units performing the same task below this line.

Immediate difficulties arose, however, as a result of this division of the country, which necessitated the meeting of the Foreign Ministers of the United States, the United Kingdom, and the Soviet Union. Meeting in Moscow in December, 1945, they concluded an Agreement, later concurred in by China, which called for eventual Korean independence and the establishment of a provisional democratic government to take all necessary steps to develop the industry, transport, agriculture, and national culture of the Korean people. A Joint Commission was to be created, consisting of representatives of the United States military command in southern Korea and the Soviet command in northern Korea, to assist in the formation of the provisional Korean government. In the preparation of their proposals, the Commission was to consult with 'Korean democratic parties and social organizations.' Whatever recommendations were proposed were to be presented to the British, Chinese, Soviet, and United States governments 'prior to final decision by the two governments represented on the Joint Commission.' It was to be the specific task of the Commission, with the participation of the provisional Korean government and Korean democratic organizations, to work out measures for assisting the political, economic, and social progress of the Korean people, the development of democratic self-government, and the establishment of the national independence of Korea. Immediate independence was not envisaged. Instead, a four-power trusteeship was planned, to last for a period up to five years. Finally, as a means of meeting the most urgent problems confronting a divided Korea, the Moscow Agreement provided that a conference of representatives of the two Commands convene within two weeks.

The preliminary conference met from January 16 through February 5, 1946, but failed to accomplish anything concrete because of the Soviet refusal to permit any economic or administrative collaboration for Korea as a whole. Equally unsuccessful was the Joint Commission. The United States was determined to see that the Korean government would be disposed favorably to American interests. Similarly, the Soviets were equally determined that any new government would be one which could be counted upon to fall within the Soviet orbit. When the United States became convinced that nothing further could be accomplished through the Joint Commission, it proposed on August 26, 1947, that the four powers directly concerned with Korea's future (Britain, China, the United States, the Soviet Union) meet to consider how the Moscow Agreement could be carried out. All agreed to this proposal except the Soviets who contended that such a conference 'does not stem from the Moscow decision of the three Ministers for Foreign Affairs concerning Korea' and lies beyond the scope of the Agreement.

THE KOREAN QUESTION BEFORE THE UNITED NATIONS (1947–50)

Since the Joint Commission had accomplished nothing in almost two years, the United States on September 17, 1947, presented the entire problem of Korean independence to the General Assembly. After considerable study and discussion, the Assembly adopted on November 14, 1947, a major policy resolution, not supported by the Soviet bloc, which included the following points:

1. To facilitate the participation of truly elected representatives of the Korean people in the deliberations upon Korean independence and make certain that they were not merely appointees of military authorities, there should be established a nine-member United Nations Temporary Commission on Korea (UNTCOK) with the right to travel, observe, and consult throughout the entire country.

2. Elections should be held not later than March 31, 1948, on the basis of adult suffrage and by secret ballot 'to choose representatives with whom UNTCOK may consult regarding the prompt attainment of the freedom and independence of the Korean people and which representatives, constituting a National Assembly, may establish a National Government of Korea.'

3. As soon as possible after the elections, the National Assembly should convene and form a National Government and notify the Commission of its formation.

4. As soon as 'the National Government is established, it should, in consultation with UNTCOK, constitute its own national security forces and dissolve all military or semi-military formations, not included therein, take over the functions of government from the military commands and civilian authorities of north and south Korea, and arrange with the occupying powers for the complete withdrawal from Korea of their armed forces as early as practicable and, if possible, within ninety days.'

5. UNTCOK should report its conclusions to the Assembly and, if necessary, consult with the Interim Committee of that body.

6. All members of the United Nations should provide all assistance to UNTCOK as well as 'refrain completely from any acts derogatory to the independence and sovereignty of Korea.'

Refused permission to enter North Korea and thereby unable to accomplish its task of encouraging elections for a unified Korea, UNTCOK was advised by the Interim Committee of the General Assembly in March, 1948 to proceed with the observance of elections in the part of Korea that was accessible to it. UNTCOK then undertook plans for an election to be held May 10, 1948, under the auspices of the United States military commander. On that date about 90 percent of all eligible voters south of the thirty-eighth parallel participated in selecting members for the two hundred member National Assembly. The new government, with its own constitution and Syngman Rhee as president, took over the administration from the American occupation forces. The General Assembly of the United Nations on December 12, 1948, concluded that

> There has been established a lawful government (the government of the Republic of Korea) having effective control and jurisdiction over that part of Korea where the Temporary Commission was able to observe and consult and in which the great majority of the people of all Korea reside; that this government is based on elections which were a valid expression of the free will of the electorate of that part of Korea and which were observed by the Temporary Commission; and that this is the only such government of Korea. . . .

The same resolution called for the appointment of a new United Nations Commission on Korea (UNCOK) to 'lend its good offices to bring about a unification of Korea,' assist the new government in the difficult task of bringing stability to the country, and 'observe the actual withdrawal of the occupying forces and verify the fact of withdrawal when such has occurred.'

In the meantime, after refusing to recognize the validity of the new South Korean authorities, the Soviet Union established another government in the northern zone of the country in September, 1948. Known as the 'Democratic People's Republic of Korea,' the new entity claimed jurisdiction over the entire Korean peninsula. Thus came into being an intolerable situation in which two competing governments, one in the north backed by the Soviets and the other in the south backed by the United States and the United Nations, contested for power and set the stage for the armed conflict beginning in 1950.

UNCOK enjoyed no more success in unifying Korea than its predecessor. It was able to report the withdrawal of United States troops from South Korea on June 29, 1949. The Soviets had announced earlier that their forces had left North Korea by the end of 1948. The Commission notified the USSR that it stood ready to verify the withdrawal of Soviet contingents but no reply was ever received. Throughout 1949 UNCOK did its best to make contact with North Korea but received no answers to its inquiries either from the Soviet Union or the government of the People's Republic. Tension began to increase between the two Koreas and UNCOK in its first report in 1949 emphasized that there was 'much military posturing on both sides' of the thirty-eighth parallel and warned of the danger of armed conflict. The General Assembly took cognizance of the seriousness of the situation on October 21, 1949, when it continued the life of UNCOK and directed it to 'observe and report any developments which might lead to or otherwise involve military conflict in Korea.'

As the two Koreas faced each other on the eve of the War, there existed between them a great disparity in military strength. From the moment the country was divided in half at the thirty-eighth parallel, the Soviet Union had subjected the people of the northern area to a consistent line of propaganda which held that 'American imperialism was preventing the reunification of Korea for the purpose of maintaining a military base in South Korea.' An army of at least 200,000 men was created and equipped with tanks, artillery, and planes. Nearly half of the troops had been battle-tested in warfare against the Nationalist forces in China. Over two million Koreans were brought back from Siberia, Manchuria, and northern China, where they had gone to escape the Japanese, and many of them returned well indoctrinated in Communist principles and techniques. All this meant that the USSR had built, by 1950, a puppet regime thoroughly answerable to its own dictates, with a strong, well-equipped, and dependable army.

In contrast, in South Korea the United States pursued a consistent policy of keeping the people weak militarily so that no charges could be made that a base was being prepared for an attack against the Soviet Union. When the forces of the United States withdrew in 1949, they left behind only light arms and a poorly trained militia capable solely of dealing with guerrilla activities within the southern area. Despite the repeated pleas of Dr. Rhee, the United States not only refused to supply him with tanks, artillery, and planes, but warned that any action of his north of the parallel would lead to a cessation of all American aid. Furthermore, despite generous economic assistance to Korea, Secretary of State Dean Acheson in a speech before the National Press Club in Washington, D.C. on January 12, 1950, announced that the 'defense perimeter' of the United States in the Pacific included the Aleutians, the islands of Japan and the Philippines, but omitted any mention of Korea.

THE INVASION OF SOUTH KOREA

In the early morning hours of June 25, 1950 (Korean time), the army of the People's Republic crossed the thirty-eighth parallel and attacked their southern neighbors. UNCOK observed the aggression and immediately reported to the Secretary-General of the United Nations that a serious situation was developing which could assume the proportions of full-scale war and endanger the maintenance of international peace and security.[2] At the request of the United States, the Secretary-General convened a meeting of the Security Council at 2:00 P.M. on June 25.

Three significant resolutions were adopted by the Security Council late in June and in July, laying the basis for United Nations enforcement action in the Korean War.

On June 25, by a vote of 9 to 0, with Yugoslavia abstaining and the Soviet Union absent, the Council noted 'with grave concern the armed attack upon the Republic of Korea by forces from North Korea.'[3] The Council also determined that 'this action constitutes a breach of the peace' and called for an 'immediate cessation of hostilities.' UNCOK was requested 'to communicate its fully considered recommendations on the situation with the least possible delay, to observe the withdrawal of the North Korean forces to the thirty-eighth parallel and to keep the Security Council informed on the execution of this resolution.' All members were asked to render every assistance to the United Nations on the execution of the resolution and 'refrain from giving assistance to the North Korean authorities.'

President Truman on June 26 stated that 'in accordance with the resolution of the Security Council, the United States will vigorously support the effort of the Council to terminate this serious breach of the peace.' On the following day, June 27, the President announced at noon that he had 'ordered United States air and sea forces to give the Korean Government troops cover and support' in accordance with the Council's resolution of June 25. At the same time, Truman ordered the United States Seventh Fleet 'to prevent any attack on Formosa.'

The Security Council met later on June 27 and received a number of cablegrams from UNCOK providing additional background on the events preceding the outbreak of hostilities. UNCOK indicated that the aggression was continuing and provided this estimate of the situation:

> Commission's present view . . . is, first, that judging from actual progress of operations Northern regime is carrying out well-planned, concerted, and full-scale invasion of South Korea; second, that South Korean forces were deployed on wholly defensive basis in all sectors of the parallel, and third, that they were taken completely by surprise, as they had no reason to believe from intelligence sources that invasion was imminent.

[2] The first official report of the North Korean attack came from John C. Muccio, the United States Ambassador in Seoul. It was received in the Department of State on Saturday night, June 24, at 9:26 p.m. eastern daylight time.
[3] The Soviet delegate had boycotted the meetings of the Security Council since January 10, 1950, in protest against the presence of Nationalist China on the Council. Those voting in favor of the resolution were China, Cuba, Ecuador, Egypt, France, India, Norway, the United Kingdom, and the United States.

The Council then adopted the second basic resolution by a vote of 7 to 1, India and Egypt abstaining and Yugoslavia voting in the negative, which recommended that 'the members of the United Nations furnish such assistance to the Republic of Korea as may be necessary to repel the armed attack and to restore international peace and security in the area.' The resolution also observed that its request for a cessation of hostilities had not been respected nor had the North Korean forces been withdrawn to the thirty-eighth parallel.

On July 7 the Security Council adopted the third significant resolution by a vote of 7 to 0 with India, Yugoslavia, and Egypt abstaining. It recommended that all members providing military forces and other assistance pursuant to previous resolutions of the Council 'make such forces and other assistance available to a unified command under the United States,' said country to designate the commander for such forces. The unified command was authorized to use at its discretion the flag of the United Nations concurrently with the flags of other participating nations in the operations against North Korea. The following day, July 8, President Truman complied with this resolution by designating General Douglas MacArthur as commanding general of the forces operating in Korea and directed him to use the United Nations flag in accordance with the wishes of the Security Council.

A total of fifty-three members of the United Nations signified their willingness to support the principle of collective security contained in these resolutions. Sixteen of them offered armed forces, which were accepted for action.[4] About thirty members contributed a great number of items, such as food, clothing, medical supplies and hospital units, raw materials, and transport facilities. The largest single offer of armed forces, other than those provided by the United States, came from Nationalist China. The United States refused the offer, however, believing that the defense of Formosa should not be weakened by the transfer of troops to Korea. It was also held that such a move would antagonize Communist China and possibly contribute to a spread of hostilities. Twenty members failed to offer any assistance whatsoever. Among them were the Soviet and Arab blocs and a few smaller Latin American countries.

The United States carried the greatest share of the military burden, at one time having 250,000 men in the field. The American contribution represented about 50 percent of the total ground forces and about 90 percent of the air and sea forces. South Korea gradually developed a sizeable

---

[4] These were Australia, Belgium, Canada, Colombia, Ethiopia, France, Greece, Luxembourg, the Netherlands, New Zealand, the Philippines, Thailand, Turkey, Union of South Africa, United Kingdom, and the United States.

fighting force which amounted to approximately 40 percent of the ground units. It was equipped and trained almost exclusively by the United States. Aside from American and Korean units, the forces fighting under the banner of the United Nations totaled less than 30,000. This disproportionate share of the military burden can be explained, in large part, by the commitments of the other major powers in Europe, Indo-China, and Malaya. It was virtually impossible for most nations to supply more troops than were offered without very seriously weakening already exposed strategic areas throughout the world. In addition, for political and military reasons, the United States refused several offers of military assistance.

It was particularly fortunate that the Council was able to proceed with its tasks supplied with objective and factual information from UNCOK. The presence of the Commission in Korea at the time of the attack precluded the need for a time-consuming special inquiry by the United Nations or the utilization of less dependable sources of information. In addition, the fact that the United States had armed forces in Japan only a short distance from Korea and was willing to use these forces and establish the Unified Command necessary for collective action was of inestimable value. Had this not been the case, there could have been no containment of the North Korean invaders. If the United Nations had been forced to assemble military units from all over the world, it is probable that all of Korea would have fallen to Communist control before these contingents could have been transported and sent into battle. The nearness and availability of American troops and sea and air units constituted a unique and positive aspect of the entire collective effort in Korea.

The Soviet world was quick to denounce the decisions of the Security Council. On June 29 and 30, the Soviet Union, Czechoslovakia, and Poland dispatched communications to the Secretary-General attacking the legality of the Council's resolutions regarding Korea. The substance of these denunciations was based upon the fact that the USSR had not participated in the voting and that China had been represented by the Chinese Nationalist delegate rather than by a representative of the Chinese Communists. The Soviet cable stated that the resolution of June 27 'was adopted by six votes, the seventh vote being that of the Kuomintang representative Dr. Tingfu F. Tsiang who has no legal right to represent China,' and that the resolution 'was passed in the absence of two permanent members of the Security Council,' the Union of Soviet Socialist Republics and China.[5]

[5] The reply of the United States regarding the voting procedure in the Council is lengthy and informative. It is contained in Department of State, *United States Policy in the Korean Crisis*, Far Eastern Series 34, Publication 3922, Washington, D.C., 1950, Document 93, pp. 61–3.

Furthermore, the Soviet Union supported the North Korean contention issued by General Kim Usung that 'South Korea, having rejected every Northern proposal for peaceful unification, had crowned its iniquity by launching an invasion force across the parallel, . . . thus precipitating North Korean counter attacks for which it would have to assume the consequences.' In response to a request of the United States that the USSR 'use its influence with the North Korean authorities to withdraw their invading forces immediately,' the Soviet Union accused the South Koreans of precipitating the conflict and stated that as the Soviet Union adhered to the 'principle of noninterference in the internal affairs of other states,' it would not interfere in the internal affairs of Korea.

On August 1, 1950, Mr. Jacob Malik, the Soviet representative, returned to the Security Council and assumed the presidency which was his by virtue of rotation. From that moment on, the Security Council ceased to be an effective organ of the United Nations as far as the conflict in Korea was concerned. At every turn the Soviet Union blocked all efforts to implement the work of the Unified Command. It thus became necessary to adopt further improvisation. Although technically the Unified Command under General MacArthur and his successors reported to the Security Council for direction and guidance, the Council was not able to provide direction and guidance with the Soviet representative present. Consequently, most of the work of co-ordination and leadership fell to the United States. The Headquarters of the Command were in Tokyo and there the Commander developed procedures for accepting military assistance and supplies. The operational control of the armed forces in the field worked satisfactorily and in effect was essentially American, and not of the United Nations, in character. That is, the Far Eastern Command of the United States was virtually identical with the United Nations Command. Each service — military, naval, and air — came under a United States service commander.

While the arrangements for military co-ordination and control worked reasonably well, the need of political guidance for the Unified Command was acute. The organization and procedures for political direction proved to be the weakest aspect of the collective action in Korea. This problem will be examined later after a survey of the military developments in the conflict and the effects of the Chinese intervention.

THE NEW WAR — THE INTERVENTION OF COMMUNIST CHINA

From the first attack on June 25 until September, the forces of the United Nations were on the defensive and, for a time, were in danger of being driven from the peninsula. The initial North Korean attack included forces numbering over 90,000 organized in approximately seven divisions and five brigades, well trained, and equipped chiefly with excellent Soviet material. They were supported by strong heavy artillery, about one hundred tanks and over one hundred combat planes. Opposing this force were elements of four South Korean divisions deployed along the thirty-eighth parallel with the remainder in the interior, without heavy artillery or tank support, and with only sixteen trainers as an air force. The only additional military assistance available for immediate use were United States and British Commonwealth occupation forces in Japan. These were rushed to Korea and, working with the limited American air contingents already in the Far East, managed to conduct a delaying action which prevented the North Koreans from overrunning the entire peninsula. Gradually a defense perimeter along the southern tip of Korea was developed while additional ground and air units were built up, together with the regrouping and resupplying of South Korean units.

After halting a major North Korean offensive in early September, the United Nations forces launched a daring amphibious assault behind the lines at Inchon on September 15. Kimpo airfield, the largest in Korea, was cleared on September 17 and put into use. Seoul was recaptured soon thereafter and within a matter of days the North Korean army was broken up and many units isolated or surrounded. As United Nations units approached the thirty-eighth parallel in pursuit of the North Koreans, a vital military decision with grave political implications had to be made. The immediate objective of freeing South Korea from the invader had been accomplished. But should the war be carried into North Korea with the aim of liberating all of Korea from communist control so that a unification of the entire country would result? This vital question had to be answered before the Unified Command could venture very far north of the thirty-eighth parallel with the assurance that such a course of action had the support of the United Nations.

In September, the Soviet Union vetoed a United States resolution which would have condemned North Korea for its continued defiance of the United Nations and would have called upon all states to stop assisting or encouraging the North Korean authorities and 'refrain from action which might lead to the spread of the Korean conflict to other areas and thereby further endanger international peace and security.' It was obvious, therefore, that no decision could be reached in the Security Council and the entire question of Korean independence was brought up in the General Assembly which fortunately was in session. On October 7 the Assembly adopted a major policy resolution which, in effect, authorized the Unified

Command to continue military operations north of the thirty-eighth parallel. Recalling the objectives of its resolutions in 1947, 1948, and 1949 to be 'the establishment of a unified, independent, and democratic government of Korea,' the Assembly recommended that 'all appropriate steps be taken to ensure conditions of stability throughout Korea,' and that 'all constituent acts be taken, including the holding of elections, under the auspices of the United Nations, for the establishment of a unified, independent and democratic government of Korea.' The resolution stated further that United Nations forces should not remain in Korea other than to accomplish these objectives plus the economic rehabilitation of the country. In addition, the Assembly created the United Nations Commission for the Unification and Rehabilitation of Korea (UNCURK) to replace UNCOK and requested the Economic and Social Council 'to develop plans for relief and rehabilitation on the termination of hostilities' and 'to expedite the study of long-term measures to promote the economic development and social progress of Korea.' [6]

Throughout October the United Nations forces pushed deeper into North Korea, reaching points near the Manchurian border. In his eighth report to the Security Council, which covered operations up to October 31, General MacArthur noted that 'for the first time in the Korean War, Chinese soldiers of the Chinese Communist forces were captured in combat in Korea. They wore North Korean uniforms, and may have been volunteers. There is no positive evidence that Chinese Communist units, as such, have entered Korea, although incomplete interrogation of these prisoners of war indicates that possibility.' The Chinese Foreign Minister had, late in September, sounded an ominous warning that China would not sit idly by while 'imperialists' threatened her security. The Peiping regime had been particularly annoyed by President Truman's order on June 27 directing the United States Seventh Fleet to prevent any attack on Formosa. Truman had said at that time that 'the occupation of Formosa by Communist forces would be a direct threat to the Pacific area and to United States forces performing their lawful and necessary functions in that area.' In August, the Chinese Communists had presented a complaint to the Security Council charging that the United States had committed 'armed aggression' against China in connection with Formosa. The Chinese also had complained of bombing incidents on the Chinese mainland by the United States Air Force. The Security Council did not take any action on these complaints and

---

[6] UNCURK was composed of Australia, Chile, the Netherlands, Pakistan, the Philippines, Thailand, and Turkey. The resolution of October 7 was adopted by a vote of 47 to 5, with 7 abstentions.

warnings at the time. The Unified Command and the United States, however, should have been prepared for what was to come.

In a special report to the Security Council dated November 5, General MacArthur stated:

> The United Nations forces in Korea are continuing their drive to the north, and their efforts to destroy further the effectiveness of the enemy as a fighting force are proving successful. However, presently in certain areas in Korea, the United Nations forces are meeting a new foe. It is apparent to our fighting forces, and our intelligence agencies have confirmed the fact, that the United Nations are presently in hostile contact with Chinese Communist military units deployed for action against the forces of the United Nations Command.

The Council then decided on November 8, to hear a representative from the Peiping regime and agreed to invite the representative from the Republic of Korea to sit at the Council table.

General MacArthur announced on November 24, the day on which the Chinese Communist delegation arrived at the Security Council, that the United Nations Command had launched a general attack which was to be the final assault of the conflict. But four days later, MacArthur had to report that the United Nations was faced 'with an entirely new war' inasmuch as 'Chinese Communist forces in significant strength have moved across the Yalu River and attacked United Nations forces.' As a result, he stated, 'the course of operations . . . has in consequence changed from that of pursuit of defeated and routed North Korean army remnants to that of a new campaign against a fresh enemy force.' From the end of November, United Nations forces were steadily pushed out of North Korea and by January, 1951, had slowed their retreat and established defensive positions, some miles below Seoul.

Meanwhile, the Chinese Communists attacked the United States in the Security Council with a violence not witnessed before even in the most bitter debates in that body. The Communist representative, Mr. Wu Hsiu-chuan blamed the Korean War on the United States and proposed that the Council should openly condemn, and take concrete steps to apply strong sanctions against, the United States as well as adopt measures to remove American units from Formosa and United Nations forces from Korea. A Soviet resolution embodying most of these objectives was soundly defeated in the Council; whereupon nine members of the Council, with India abstaining, voted to call upon those assisting the North Koreans, i.e. Chinese Communists, to withdraw at once from Korea. The resolution also affirmed 'that it is the policy of the United Nations to hold the Chinese frontier with Korea inviolate and fully to protect legitimate Chinese and

Korean interests in the frontier zone.' But the Soviet Union vetoed the resolution and the matter of Chinese intervention was shifted to the General Assembly.

Following the failure of attempts to mediate the conflict (which will be examined shortly), the Assembly adopted the second of its major policy resolutions with respect to the Korean War on February 1, 1951. After noting that the Security Council had failed 'to exercise its primary responsibility for the maintenance of international peace and security in regard to Chinese Communist intervention in Korea,' and that the Chinese Communists failed to accept United Nations proposals for a cease-fire, the Assembly proceeded to declare that

> the Central People's Government of the People's Republic of China, by giving direct aid and assistance to those who were already committing aggression in Korea and by engaging in hostilities against United Nations forces there has itself engaged in aggression in Korea.

The resolution also requested that the Additional Measures Committee, which had been created as part of the 'Uniting for Peace' resolution in November, 1950, 'consider further measures to meet this aggression and to report thereon to the General Assembly.'

Working diligently for three months, the Additional Measures Committee presented its recommendations to the Assembly and they were adopted on May 18, 1951. The resolution recommended that all members

> Apply an embargo on the shipment to areas under control of the Central People's Government of the People's Republic of China and of the North Korean authorities of arms, ammunition and implements of war, atomic energy materials, petroleum, transportation materials of strategic value, and items useful in the production of arms, ammunition and implements of war.

However, each member was allowed to 'determine which commodities exported from its territory fall within the embargo.' Most members who were able to export such materials and were engaged in the collective action in Korea had already adopted an informal embargo, usually as a result of pressure from the United States.

After January, 1951, the fighting stabilized and the United Nations forces began a counter attack. By March the Chinese and North Korean forces had been driven back into North Korea. Again the question was raised whether to pursue the fighting above the thirty-eighth parallel. Many members of the United Nations urged restraint and believed that diplomatic negotiations should precede any substantial advance into North Korea. On March 20 the United States Joint Chiefs of Staff informed General MacArthur that President Truman was planning to announce that the

United Nations was preparing a peace offer and they asked for his recommendations. On March 24, the General in a public statement of his own announced that he was ready to meet the enemy commander in the field' to try to find a way to end the War. This statement violated a directive of December 6 from the White House which established the rule that no statement concerning military policy should be released until it had clearance from Washington. Then on April 5 Representative Joseph W. Martin, Jr., the Republican leader of the House of Representatives made public a letter from MacArthur which lent support to Mr. Martin's demand that the forces of Nationalist China be used to open a second front against the Communists in Asia. President Truman thereupon removed General MacArthur on April 10 and replaced him with General Matthew B. Ridgway.'

Later severe fighting around the thirty-eighth parallel failed to dent the United Nations lines. In June, it became apparent to the Communists that they could achieve no military success since they were retreating steadily under severe pressure. Thus, Mr. Malik of the Soviet Union suggested on June 23 in a radio address that the belligerents should begin discussions for a cease-fire in Korea. The fighting front remained virtually unchanged from this time until the Armistice in 1953.

ATTEMPTS AT MEDIATION AND THE ARMISTICE NEGOTIATIONS

Efforts to mediate the Korean War began almost immediately after the beginning of the conflict. On July 13, 1950, Prime Minister Nehru of India dispatched messages to Secretary of State Dean Acheson and Premier Stalin suggesting that a solution of the Korean problem might result from giving Communist China a seat on the Security Council with negotiations to follow between the United States, the USSR, and China concerning a permanent settlement of the Korean problem. The United States, however, saw no virtue in this proposal.

After the intervention of Communist China in November, 1950, the Assembly requested its President, Mr. Nasrollah Entezam of Iran, to create a group of three persons, including himself, to determine the basis on which a satisfactory cease-fire in Korea could be arranged. Joined by Lester B. Pearson of Canada and Sir Benegal Narsing Rau of India, Mr. Entezam reported to the Assembly on January 2, 1951, that discussions had been entered into with the United Nations Command on a basis for a cease-fire but that the Chinese Communists refused to discuss the matter. However, the Assembly encouraged the Cease-Fire Group to continue its efforts and to submit information on the principles for a general peaceful settlement of all Korean and related problems once a cease-fire had been achieved. The Group recommended a five-point program on January 11 and then went out of existence. Briefly summarized, these points were included in the Group's recommendations:

1. An immediate cease-fire containing safeguards that it would not be used as a screen for developing a new offensive.

2. When the cease-fire had been consummated, immediate advantage should be taken to consider further steps for restoring peace.

3. To permit the establishment of a unified Korea, all non-Korean armed forces would be withdrawn by stages and appropriate arrangements made for the Korean people to express their wishes as to their future government.

4. Pending the completion of these steps, interim arrangements should be made for administering Korea and for maintaining peace and security in the area.

5. After a cease-fire, the Assembly should create an appropriate body, which should include representatives from the United States, United Kingdom, the USSR and the Chinese Communists, for the purpose of settling Far Eastern problems and, in particular, the questions of Formosa and the representation of China in the United Nations.

These principles were approved by the Political Committee of the Assembly on January 13 and the Chinese People's Republic was asked whether it would accept them as a basis for pacific settlement of Korean and Far Eastern problems. Peiping replied that: negotiations must be held among the countries concerned 'on the basis of agreement to the withdrawal of all foreign troops from Korea and the settlement of Korean domestic affairs by the Korean people themselves'; the People's Republic of China must be given its 'rightful place' in the United Nations at the beginning of negotiations; the problem of the 'withdrawal of United States armed forces' from Formosa must be a primary item for discussion; the negotiations should take place at a conference to be held in China and attended by the Chinese People's Republic, the USSR, the United Kingdom, the United States, France, India, and Egypt.

When the Assembly voted on February 1, 1951, to declare Communist China an aggressor, the same resolution included a provision for a Good Offices Committee. It was formed later and consisted of Assembly President Entezam, Sven Grafström of Sweden, and Dr. Luis Padilla Nervo of Mexico. But it was not able to make any progress. Mr. Chou En-Lai, the Foreign Minister of the Chinese People's Republic, denounced the Committee and stated that he would pay no attention to it.

But soon after Mr. Malik made his radio announcement on June 23, high-level diplomatic exchanges took place which emphasized that any negotiations should be restricted to purely military questions. General

Ridgway, the United Nations Commander, on June 29 offered to discuss the possibility of a cease-fire with the enemy commanders. Armistice negotiations opened on July 10 at Kaesong, which lay within Chinese-North Korean territory. An agenda was agreed to on July 26 which called for negotiations upon a demilitarized zone, the establishment of a supervising organization for carrying out the terms of the cease-fire and armistice, arrangements for an exchange of prisoners of war, and 'recommendations to the governments concerned on both sides.'

Negotiations were almost immediately suspended, however, due to Communist charges of violations of the neutrality of the conference site. After a two-month delay, negotiations were resumed on October 25 at Pan Mun Jom, not far from Kaesong. After nearly a year of endless haggling, during which time the Assembly did not consider the Korean question so as not to prejudice the negotiations in progress, the United Nations Command stated in a special report dated October 18, 1952, that a tentative draft armistice agreement had been worked out. One crucial matter remained, however, and that was the question of whether all prisoners of war should be returned, by force if necessary. The United Nations Command would turn over all except those who resisted repatriation but the Communists insisted that all should be returned, even if force had to be used. This deadlock caused a recess in the negotiations and the matter was taken up at once by the Assembly.

Working for six weeks on the basis of an Indian draft resolution, the Assembly on December 3, 1952, finally adopted a formula for the solution of the prisoner of war problem by a vote of 54 to 5 (Soviet bloc) with China abstaining. The resolution affirmed

> that the release and repatriation of prisoners of war shall be effected in accordance with the Geneva Convention relative to the Treatment of Prisoners of War, dated 12 August 1949, the well-established principles and practices of international law and the relevant provisions of the draft armistice agreement;
> that force shall not be used against prisoners of war to prevent or effect their return to their homelands, and that they shall at all times be treated humanely in accordance with the specific provisions of the Geneva Convention and with the general spirit of the Convention.

There followed a list of seventeen proposals to govern the exchange of prisoners under a special Repatriation Commission. The President of the Assembly was instructed to communicate these proposals to the appropriate Chinese and North Korean authorities. On December 20, the Assembly President had to report that the Communist authorities had flatly rejected the proposals as illegal, unfair, and unreasonable.

The deadlock continued until March 23, 1953, when the Chinese and North Korean Commanders agreed to a suggestion from the United Nations Commander that sick and wounded prisoners fit to travel be repatriated immediately. The Communists stated that a reasonable determination of this question could lead to a settlement of the entire problem of prisoners of war. Liaison groups met at Pan Mun Jom on April 6 and the exchange of sick and wounded prisoners was completed within three weeks.

The Assembly, on April 18, noted this exchange with deep satisfaction and expressed hope for an early armistice. It decided to recess at the completion of its agenda and reconvene when an armistice agreement had been arranged. On April 26 the full armistice negotiations were resumed and on June 8 agreement was reached, largely on the basis of the December 3, 1952, Assembly resolution, on the issue of the repatriation of all prisoners of war. With this contentious matter out of the way, the armistice agreement was all but completed when a most unfortunate incident occurred on June 18. The South Korean authorities, on their own, unexpectedly released some 27,000 Korean prisoners of war who had indicated their refusal to return to North Korea. Negotiations at Pan Mun Jom were immediately adjourned and the fighting fronts erupted with a violence that had not been seen for two years.

Finally, on July 10, the second anniversary of the beginning of the negotiations, the discussions were resumed. The long awaited armistice agreement was signed on Monday, July 27, 1953, at 10:01 a.m. Korean time. Lieutenant General William K. Harrison signed for the United Nations Command and Lieutenant General Nam Il signed for the North Koreans and Chinese. Hostilities ceased twelve hours later.

The General Assembly reconvened in August to discuss and plan for the political conference recommended in the armistice agreement. On August 7, a declaration was made public by the sixteen member nations whose military forces had participated in the Korean War.[7] The text of this memorable and significant declaration, which reinforced the security of the Republic of Korea, is as follows:

> We the United Nations Members whose military forces are participating in the Korean action support the decision of the Commander-in-Chief of the United Nations Command to conclude an armistice agreement. We hereby affirm our determination fully and faithfully to carry out the terms of the armistice. We expect that the other parties to the agreement will likewise scrupulously observe its terms.
>
> The task ahead is not an easy one. We will support the efforts of the United Nations to bring about an equitable settlement in Korea on the principles

---

[7] Agreement to make such a declaration was reached in January 1952, nineteen months earlier.

which have long been established by the United Nations, and which call for a united, independent, and democratic Korea. We will support the United Nations in its efforts to assist the people of Korea in repairing the ravages of war.

We declare again our faith in the principles and purposes of the United Nations, our consciousness of our continuing responsibilities in Korea, and our determination in good faith to seek a settlement of the Korean problem. We affirm, in the interests of world peace, that if there is a renewal of the armed attack, challenging again the principles of the United Nations, we should again be united and prompt to resist. The consequences of such a breach of the armistice would be so grave that, in all probability, it would not be possible to confine hostilities within the frontiers of Korea.

Finally, we are of the opinion that the armistice must not result in jeopardizing the restoration or the safeguarding of peace in any other part of Asia.

THE ARMISTICE AGREEMENT

The Armistice Agreement fixed a military demarcation line between the two opposing forces. Both sides withdrew two kilometers from the line so as to establish a demilitarized zone to serve as a buffer to prevent the occurrence of incidents which might lead to a resumption of hostilities. A Military Armistice Commission was created, consisting of ten senior officers, five from each side. Its duties were to supervise the implementation of the Agreement and settle any violations of it by negotiation. Joint Observer Teams were attached to the Commission to assist it in supervising its provisions.

Also established was a Neutral Nations Supervisory Commission of four senior officers, two nominated by the United Nations Command (Sweden and Switzerland) and two by the Chinese and Korean Commanders (Poland and Czechoslovakia).[8] Attached to and assisting the Supervisory Commission were twenty Neutral Nations Inspection Teams composed of officers selected by the members of the Supervisory Commission. The Supervisory Commission was given the task of inspecting the cease-fire arrangements. Both sides agreed not to reinforce military personnel or add to existing numbers of combat aircraft, armored vehicles, weapons, and ammunition. Rotation of personnel was permitted as well as replacement of aircraft, armored vehicles, weapons, and ammunition on a piece-for-piece basis. All new personnel and combat aircraft, vehicles, and weapons were to be introduced only through five specified ports in North Korea and five in South Korea where the Neutral Nation Inspection Teams were to be stationed.

[8] The term 'neutral nations' referred to those states who did not have combatant forces in the Korean hostilities.

Within two months after the Armistice Agreement became effective, both sides agreed to repatriate all prisoners of war in their custody, who insisted on repatriation, to the side to which they belonged at the time of capture. Those who were not directly repatriated were to be handed over to the Neutral Nations Repatriation Commission, composed of representatives from Sweden, Switzerland, Poland, and Czechoslovakia. The Repatriation Commission was to establish its headquarters in the demilitarized zone near Pan Mun Jom. It took into custody for ninety days the non-repatriated prisoners and permitted both sides to send representatives to the prisoner compounds to inform the prisoners of their countries of any matters relating to their return to their homelands, and, in particular, 'of their full freedom to return home to lead a peaceful life.' The disposition of the prisoners remaining after the ninety-day period was to be left to the political conference recommended by the Armistice Agreement. If the Conference did not dispose of the question within one hundred and twenty days after the Repatriation Commission took charge of the prisoners, the remaining prisoners were to be given the opportunity to go to the neutral nations of their choice. Following this final distribution of prisoners, the Neutral Nations Repatriation Commission was to cease its functions and declare its dissolution.

THE POLITICAL CONFERENCE

Article IV of the Armistice Agreement recommended that within three months after the signing of the armistice 'a political conference of a higher level of both sides be held by representatives appointed respectively to settle through negotiation the questions of the withdrawal of all foreign forces from Korea, the peaceful settlement of the Korean question, etc.' The reconvened Assembly considered plans for the conference and recommended on August 28 that the conference participants should be the member states which had contributed combatant forces in Korea plus the Republic of Korea. The United States was requested to get in touch with the opposing forces and arrange for a place and time of meeting, which should not be later than October 28, 1953.

The Soviet Union bitterly opposed this conception of the conference and proposed that fifteen members of the United Nations, not all of whom had contributed forces, should be participants. The Assembly finally agreed that the USSR could participate 'provided the other side desires it' but refused to include India as demanded by some. The Chinese and North Koreans refused to accept the conference plan and demanded that the eighth session of the Assembly beginning September 15 enlarge the composition of the conference to include Burma, India, Indonesia, and Pakistan in addition to the USSR as 'invited neutral nations' as well as all belligerent nations. Early in the eighth session the Soviet Union sought unsuccessfully to reopen the question of the composition of the conference.

In the meantime, the United States tried to arrange for the conference but it was not until October 10 that the Chinese and North Koreans agreed to discuss the necessary preparations. Discussions began at Pan Mun Jom on October 26 but the Communists reserved the right to raise the question of the composition of the conference. This was virtually a guarantee that the preliminary discussions would end in deadlock, as they did on December 12. On that date, the United States representative, Mr. Arthur Holson Dean, left the meeting after the Chinese and North Koreans had charged that the United Nations Command had connived with the President of the Republic of Korea in releasing the 27,000 prisoners the previous June. Mr. Dean refused to return unless the Communists retracted these 'calculated, rude, arrogant and insulting' references. The preliminary negotiations were never resumed.

However, on February 18, 1954, the Foreign Ministers of France, the United States, the United Kingdom, and the Soviet Union meeting at Berlin announced in a quadripartite communiqué that a conference would meet in Geneva on April 26 to reach a settlement of the Korean question. The problem of restoring peace in Indochina would also be discussed. The participants in the conference would be those who had combatant forces engaged in the Korean War, plus the Soviet Union. In other words, the composition would be the same as agreed to in the Assembly the previous August.

Fifty days were spent on the Korean question at Geneva with no accomplishment. As the nations contributing to the United Nations Command observed, 'it is better to face the fact of our disagreement than to raise false hopes and mislead the peoples of the world into believing there is agreement where there is none.' Two fundamental principles were adhered to by these nations, but the Soviets and their satellites rejected all efforts to reach agreement. These two principles were:

1. The United Nations under its Charter is fully and rightfully empowered to take collective action to repel aggression, restore peace and security and to extend its good offices in seeking a peaceful settlement in Korea.

2. In order to establish a unified, independent and democratic Korea, genuinely free elections should be held under United Nations supervision for membership in the National Assembly in which representation shall be in direct proportion to population.

No political settlement had been made by 1958. Military forces still guarded both parts of the unhappy peninsula. Aerial reconnaissance clearly revealed that the North Koreans were building and equipping airfields in violation of the Armistice Agreement. In retaliation for the failure of North Korean authorities to permit the requisite inspection of North Korean entry ports, the United Nations Command in 1956 ousted neutral inspection teams from South Korea but continued to honor its other agreements. However, in June, 1957, the Command informed North Korea that it would no longer be bound by that provision of the Armistice Agreement limiting the introduction of new weapons. Fearful that the balance of military power had turned against them because of the clandestine North Korean arms build-up, United Nations commanders were soon provided with modern jet fighters and up-to-date infantry weapons.

With few prospects for a political settlement, the Korean War, with its tragic cost in lives and the enormous expenditure of resources and supplies, is claimed by some not to have been worth the sacrifices made. Nevertheless, the North Korean invasion was repulsed and the United Nations, through the determination of many of its members, stood firmly against the policy and defiance of the Soviet Union. Importance must also be attached to the fact that this was the first collective action under the banner of the United Nations and the lessons learned may prove to be of positive value.

2. THE MIDDLE EAST CRISIS

On October 29, 1956, Israel invaded the Sinai peninsula of Egypt. This act and the subsequent Anglo-French attack upon Egypt not only greatly complicated the already serious situation in the Middle East but interjected the problem of the Suez Canal into the Arab-Israeli conflict.

Consideration in the Security Council. Immediately after the Israeli invasion was announced, the United States requested the Security Council to consider steps to end the military action. Jordan also asked the Council to intervene to stop the aggression 'which endangers peace in the Middle East and the peace of Jordan itself.' The Council met on October 30, placed the item on its agenda and proceeded to examine the situation after inviting representatives of Israel and Egypt to take seats at the Council table. The Secretary-General stated that General Burns, the Chief of Staff of the Truce Supervisory Organization, had reported to Israel that its action had violated the Armistice Agreement and the Council's cease-fire order of August 11, 1949, and consequently he had requested the withdrawal of Israeli troops and an immediate cessation of hostilities. Similarly, Egypt was asked to abide by the cease-fire and refrain from all hostile acts. Mr. Hammarskjöld also observed that the Truce Observation Organization was unable to investigate any of the incidents which preceded this action since the demilitarized zone under Israeli control had been mined and a United

Nations observer had been expelled from El Auja, a check-point on the Israeli side of the border.

Spirited debate centered around the following United States resolution:

The Security Council

noting that the armed forces of Israel have penetrated deeply into Egyptian territory in violation of the armistice agreement between Egypt and Israel, *expressing its grave concern at this* violation of the armistice agreement,

1. *Calls upon* Israel and Egypt immediately to cease fire;

2. *Calls upon* Israel immediately to withdraw its armed forces behind the established armistice lines;

3. *Calls u̯ ̯all members*
   (a) to refrain from the use of force or threat of force in the area in any manner inconsistent with the Purposes of the United Nations;
   (b) to assist the United Nations in ensuring the integrity of the armistice agreements;
   (c) to refrain from giving any military, economic or financial assistance to Israel so long as it has not complied with this resolution;

4. *Requests* the Secretary-General to keep the Security Council informed on compliance with this resolution and to make whatever recommendations he deems appropriate for the maintenance of international peace and security in the area by the implementation of this and prior resolutions.

The Egyptian representative charged the Israeli action to be a 'wholly unjustified attack' on his country, that 'Israel had ordered general mobilization, which constitutes an act of war and demonstrates beyond any doubt the aggressive and expansionist aims of Israel's policy.' Mr. Eban of Israel contended that the object of Israeli operations was to destroy the Egyptian *fedayeen* (commando) bases 'from which armed Egyptian units, under the special care and authority of Colonel Nasser, invade Israel's territory for purposes of murder, sabotage and the creation of permanent insecurity to peaceful life.' Before detailing *fedayeen* activity, Mr. Eban observed that his government had had to face a vital question:

Do the obligations under the United Nations Charter require us to resign ourselves to the existence of uninterrupted activity to the south and north and east of our country, of armed units practicing open warfare against us and working from their bases in the Sinai peninsula and elsewhere for the maintenance of carefully regulated invasions of our homes, our lands, and our very lives, or, on the other hand, are we acting in accordance with an inherent right of self-defense when, having found no other remedy for over two years, we cross the frontier against those who have no scruple or hesitation in crossing the frontier against us?

In the midst of the debate, Sir Pierson Dixon, the British representative, announced the issuance of an Anglo-French ultimatum to both Israel and Egypt, requesting that they cease hostilities and withdraw their military forces at least ten miles from the Suez Canal. Sir Pierson stated that Egypt had been asked to agree that Anglo-French forces should move temporarily into key positions in the Canal area. If compliance was not forthcoming by the expiration of the twelve-hour ultimatum, he observed that 'British and French forces will intervene in whatever strength to secure compliance.' The objective of the Anglo-French forces was to guarantee free passage through the Canal, which would be jeopardized, stated Sir Pierson, if hostilities continued. He argued that there was no urgency in adopting the United States resolution before the Council since that body could not take action which would more effectively terminate hostilities and keep open the Canal.

Shortly thereafter, Egypt submitted a request for the inclusion on the agenda of a new item concerning the Franco-British ultimatum which had exposed Egypt to the threat of aggression. What was involved was nothing less than the occupation of three Egyptian towns — Ismailia, Port Said, and Suez. Before placing this item on the agenda, the Council voted on the United States resolution. In the vote, China, Cuba, Iran, Peru, the USSR, the United States and Yugoslavia voted in favor; Australia and Belgium abstained. Since France and the United Kingdom, both permanent members, voted in the negative, the resolution was defeated. A Soviet resolution, identical with that of the defeated American draft except for the omission of Article 3 of the latter, was also vetoed by France and Britain. Belgium and the United States abstained, while Australia, China, Cuba, Iran, Peru, the USSR and Yugoslavia voted in the affirmative.

On October 31, the Council turned to the Egyptian complaint of contemplated Anglo-French aggression. Since the submission of that item, Anglo-French bombing attacks had begun on key Egyptian military installations. After more discussion which covered little new ground, Dr. Brilej of Yugoslavia introduced a proposal to call an emergency special session of the General Assembly. Despite the protests of Britain and France on the legality of such a move, and the serious doubts on this point by Australia, the Yugoslav resolution was adopted (7-2-2) and the matter became the concern of the Assembly.

On November 5 the Soviet Foreign Minister requested that the Council consider a proposal which would call upon all members of the United Nations and particularly the United States and his country, to provide Egypt with 'naval and air forces, military units, volunteers, military instructors' and other forms of assistance if the Israeli and Anglo-French forces failed within twelve hours after the adoption of the resolution to cease military action. All troops which had invaded Egypt were to be withdrawn within seventy-two hours. However, the Council voted against placing the matter on its agenda.

Action by the General Assembly. Summoned to its first special emergency session, the Assembly on the night of November 1–2 placed the question on the agenda by a vote of 62-2, with seven abstentions. After a general debate in which views similar to those expressed in the Council were repeated, the Assembly adopted a United States proposal by a vote of 64-5, with six abstentions. After expressing concern over the many violations of the 1949 armistice agreements, the Israeli invasion of Egypt, the Anglo-French military operations and interruption of Suez Canal traffic, the resolution contained the following points:

1. Urged an immediate cease-fire and a halt to the movement of military forces and arms into the area of hostilities;
2. Urged the parties to the armistice agreements to withdraw 'all forces behind the armistice lines, to desist from raids across the armistice lines into neighboring territory, and to observe scrupulously the provisions of the armistice agreements';
3. Recommended that all members refrain from introducing any military goods into the area of hostilities;
4. Urged that steps be taken, after the conclusion of the cease-fire, to reopen the Canal;
5. Requested the Secretary-General 'to observe and report promptly on the compliance with the present resolution.'

The Assembly reconvened in emergency session on the evening of November 3 to consider an Egyptian communication which complained of continuing violations of Egyptian sovereignty by France, Israel, and the United Kingdom. Also before the Assembly was a report from the Secretary-General that there had been no compliance with the cease-fire. Israel had also invaded the Gaza area and had captured the two Red Sea islands of Tiran and Senabahir. Debate continued into the early hours of November 4 and two more resolutions were adopted. The first was a Canadian proposal which set in motion the development of the United Nations Emergency Force. It requested the Secretary-General to submit 'within forty-eight hours, a plan for the setting up, with the consent of the nations concerned, of an emergency international United Nations force to secure and supervise the cessation of hostilities' (vote of 57-0-19). The second was a nineteen-nation Afro-Asian proposal which sought to strengthen the earlier cease-fire efforts by authorizing the Secretary-General immediately to 'arrange with the parties concerned for the implementation of the cease-fire and the halting of the movement of military forces and arms into the area.' He was to report compliance 'not later than twelve hours from the time of adoption of the present resolution' (vote of 59-5-12).

The Assembly met next in emergency session on the night of November 4–5. Egypt announced that it had accepted the Assembly's cease-fire proposal. Attention was now centered on a resolution jointly sponsored by

Canada, Colombia, and Norway which endorsed the proposals contained in a report from the Secretary-General covering a plan for an emergency force and also laid down clear directives for the establishment of such a body. Adopted by a vote of 57-0 with 19 abstentions, the resolution established a United Nations Command for the force, headed by General Burns, who was to recruit officers from the staff of his Truce Organization 'who shall be nationals of countries other than those having permanent membership in the Security Council.' In consultation with the Secretary-General, General Burns was authorized to recruit other officers with the same limitation on their nationality.[9]

The situation worsened on Monday, November 5, when Anglo-French paratroops began to drop on the north end of the Canal zone. Although Israel agreed to the cease-fire, Soviet Premier Nikolai Bulganin later in the day sent messages to the British, French, and Israeli premiers, warning them to stop hostilities or face the threat of Soviet intervention. Bulganin also invited the United States to join with him in bringing hostilities to an end. President Eisenhower immediately rejected the idea as did the Security Council. Radio Moscow broadcast the messages to the three premiers before they were actually received and implied that the USSR would rocket bomb the Allies. The broadcast quoted a sentence from the Bulganin messages which said: 'We are fully determined to crush the aggressors and restore peace in the East through the use of force.' Later a Moscow spokesman claimed the messages made no mention of 'rockets' and also that the 'we' in the messages meant the USSR in concert with the United Nations. It is entirely possible that the broadcast was intentionally made stronger than the messages in order to frighten the three nations concerned without actually committing the Soviet Union to attack.

Pressure from the Commonwealth, the United States, the United Nations, plus the Soviet threats, soon brought results. Although Anglo-French troops landed on November 6, Sir Anthony Eden announced that he and Premier Mollet of France would comply with the cease-fire at midnight. A new threat, however, added to the tension. Radio Cairo appealed for 'volunteers, arms and other forms of aid' and Radio Moscow rebroadcast the appeal. But at 2:00 A.M. Cairo time on Wednesday, November 7, fighting came to an end in the Middle East. Anglo-French forces controlled the top quarter of the Canal's 103 mile length which was now blocked at both ends by scuttled and bombed-out ships and wrecked bridges. The Assembly again called upon France, Israel, and the United

---

[9] The headquarters of UNEF in 1958 was located in the town of Gaza. The chain of command runs directly from the Commander of the Force to the commanding officers of each of the national contingents. UNEF is subject to orders and instructions only from its commander, and, through him, from the Secretary-General.

Kingdom to withdraw their troops from Egyptian territory. While Britain and France agreed to withdraw after the arrival of the United Nations Emergency Force, Israel at first balked at giving up its newly won Egyptian positions. Premier Ben-Gurion stated that 'Israel will not consent, under any circumstances, that a foreign force — no matter how called — take up positions . . . in any area held by Israel.' On November 8, Ben-Gurion reversed his stand under pressure from United States, Soviet, and United Nations quarters and agreed to a planned withdrawal after the arrival of UNEF.

Meanwhile, on November 7, the Assembly completed its directives on the establishment of UNEF. Primary responsibility for building and directing the force was turned over to the Secretary-General and a seven-nation advisory committee. The basic function given to UNEF was 'to secure and supervise the cessation of hostilities' in accordance with the Assembly's November 2 resolution. The specific disposition of the force and the duration of its stay on Egyptian territory were not spelled out although its functions were assumed by the Secretary-General 'to cover an area extending roughly from the Suez Canal to the armistice demarcation lines, established in the Armistice Agreement between Egypt and Israel.' Despite the fact that UNEF's individual soldiers are paid and outfitted by the governments in whose armies they serve, UNEF has had to supply food and equipment, transport and fuel, communications and other items, estimated to cost approximately $40,000 per day for a force of about 6,000 men. Initial financing of $10 million came from the Working Capital Fund of the United Nations. The Assembly decided in November, 1956, over the strong objections of the Soviet bloc, to replace this system of financing by assessing UN members $10 million in accord with the scale used for raising the annual budget. Later, the Assembly approved additional UNEF expenditures of $6.5 million, which was to come from voluntary contributions. The Twelfth Assembly decided that the Secretary-General could expend up to $13.5 million for UNEF costs through the end of 1957, and up to $25 million, as required, after that date, to be financed by a scale of assessments similar to that in use for the regular United Nations budget.[10]

Mr. Hammarskjöld had the arduous task of organizing UNEF and ar-

---

[10] The Secretary-General reported to the Twelfth Assembly that expenses for UNEF for the fourteen-month period ending December 31, 1957, would total between $24 and $30.5 million. Up to the end of September, however, only $6,330,000 had been paid in cash into the UNEF Special Account, $5,744,000 of this amount having been paid in connection with the initial assessment of $10 million. A total of $586,000 was made available in the form of voluntary contributions. An additional amount of $3,213,000 was pledged in voluntary contributions but was not yet paid in cash, and of this sum, $2.7 million was dependent on the receipt of matching contributions.

ranging transportation for it to Egypt. Upon the speed of its arrival and the adequacy of its performance depended the continuance of the cease-fire, the withdrawal of Anglo-French and Israeli troops, and the task of clearing the Canal. The least vexing problem was obtaining troops. Less than a week after it came into existence, UNEF had at its disposal troops from Canada, Colombia, Denmark, Finland, India, Norway, Sweden, and Yugoslavia. A staging area for the flight to Egypt was quickly established at Capodichino Airport near Naples, Italy. The United States offered to move troops from their homelands to Italy and the Swiss agreed to carry out the last leg of the journey. On Thursday, November 15, the first contingent of UNEF arrived in Egypt; it consisted of forty-five Danish riflemen wearing helmet-liners of United Nations blue and armbands lettered 'United Nations Emergency Force.' By the summer of 1957, 6,000 soldiers were in Egypt. Military contributions came from a total of ten states — Brazil and Indonesia joining the original eight — and another fourteen countries were providing hospital, food, and other supplies.[11]

In mid-November, 1956, however, serious problems faced the Secretary-General and the Assembly. When would Israel and Anglo-French forces withdraw from Egypt? How long should UNEF remain in Egypt, how would it be deployed, and what was to be its ultimate function? By whom and when should the Suez Canal be cleared? Several conflicting points of view were evident on these questions.

Egypt, supported by the Soviet and the Arab-Asian-African blocs, held that Anglo-French-Israeli forces should withdraw immediately, in accordance with the resolutions of the Assembly and that the function of UNEF was solely to monitor this withdrawal. Following this, UNEF should then leave the Canal zone and take up positions along the 1949 Egyptian-Israeli armistice line. Finally, Egypt maintained that the clearing of the Canal should not begin until all troops had been withdrawn. On the other hand, the view of Britain and France was that Colonel Nasser had illegally seized the Canal and could deny freedom of passage at any time he so desired; that he had threatened repeatedly and had been planning a joint Arab attack on Israel; and that the USSR was aiding him in these maneuvers with arms and thereby was being allowed a foothold in the Middle East. They maintained that their attack on Egypt was designed only to end Nasser's objectives. Since they had agreed to a cease-fire, the three nations believed that their troops should not be withdrawn until they could be relieved by a 'competent and effective' force from the United Nations. They also insisted that UNEF remain in Egypt until there had been a reasonable

---

[11] The total number of officers and men comprising UNEF at the end of 1957 was about 5600 due to the earlier withdrawal of the Indonesian contingent. Of this total, only slightly more than 3000 are available for regular patrol and guard duties, the remainder being engaged in support functions.

settlement of the Suez and Palestine questions. Britain and France were primarily interested in reopening the Canal and obtaining guarantees that it would remain open to all nations. Israel was determined to prevent the recurrence of raids from the Gaza and Sinai areas and to keep open the straits of Tiran leading to her new seaport of Elath on the Gulf of Aqaba. Having occupied Sharm el-Sheikh, the Egyptian stronghold blocking the Gulf of Aqaba, Israel refused to withdraw from it until guarantees could be obtained that Egyptian troops would not return and once again prevent free access to Elath.

The attitude of the United States was that the United Nations should take this opportunity to get a settlement of the Suez and Palestine questions. However, the best way to accomplish this was, first, to have Anglo-French-Israeli troops withdraw as soon as possible, and second, not to use UNEF as a military threat to force Nasser to negotiate.

The position of Mr. Hammarskjöld was particularly difficult in the face of these differing views. Britain and France were embittered because they believed that he was supporting Nasser's position. They objected most strenuously to Nasser's demand that clearing operations in the Canal wait upon the withdrawal of their forces since they had already begun to clear the Port Said entrance. On November 20 the Secretary-General requested that Britain, France, and Israel explain their failure to withdraw their forces to date, and to state what their future plans were. Two days later he revealed that all three had started a modest withdrawal but that the removal of additional forces depended upon the effective use of UNEF. Debate in the Assembly then became particularly acrimonious with bitter speeches from India's Krishna Menon and Arab, Egyptian, and Soviet delegates attacking Britain, France, and Israel for their failure to evacuate all their troops. On the 24th, the Assembly adopted an Arab-Asian sponsored resolution by a vote of 63-5 with ten abstentions which noted 'with regret' that sizeable Anglo-French-Israeli forces remained in Egypt and reiterated the call to these three states 'to comply forthwith' with the Assembly resolutions of November 2 and 7. The Secretary-General was authorized to proceed with negotiation of agreements for clearing the Canal.

However, France, Israel, and the United Kingdom continued to stall on complete evacuation, hoping that there would be some clarification of UNEF's functions and a start on Canal clearance. But when it became clear that the United States would not replenish the rapidly depleting Anglo-French oil supplies until a positive commitment on total evacuation was forthcoming, London and Paris gave in. Final withdrawal began on December 12 and the last remaining Anglo-French soldiers left Egypt on December 22.

A far more difficult problem concerned the withdrawal of Israeli forces from Egypt. Negotiations between Israel and General Burns resulted in an Israeli pull-back from the western sector of the Sinai Peninsula adjacent to the Canal late in December. On January 15, 1957, El 'Arish in the central part of the Peninsula was evacuated and most of the southern portion was cleared, leaving about one fourth of the Sinai desert in Israeli hands. However, the Assembly on January 19 again prodded Israel and adopted an Afro-Asian sponsored resolution by a 74-2-2 vote which noted 'with regret and concern the failure' of Israel to comply with previous demands for evacuation. It also requested the Secretary-General to 'continue his efforts for securing the complete withdrawal of Israel' and to report to the Assembly on the results within five days.

By the time the Secretary-General made his report — on the 25th — Israeli troops had pulled out of Egypt with the exception of Gaza, a 28 by 6 mile strip of land on the Mediterranean, and a 180 mile long coastal area guarding Israel's shipping on the Gulf of Aqaba. After noting that 'Israel has not fully complied with the requests of the General Assembly,' Mr. Hammarskjöld suggested in guarded terms that UNEF might be deployed in both the Gaza and Aqaba areas. He clearly indicated, however, that without a new resolution authorizing UNEF to assume that role, any action taken would have to be approved by Egypt. At the same time, he observed that the condition of affairs obtaining in Gaza before the Israeli attack was regarded universally as one which 'should not be permitted to return.'

On February 2 the General Assembly, for the sixth time, called upon Israel to leave Egyptian territory 'without delay' and made an effort, in a loosely worded United States resolution, to indicate the role which UNEF might play in the Gaza and Aqaba areas once they were evacuated by Israel. The suggestion was made that UNEF might occupy these trouble spots and be placed along the Egyptian-Israeli demarcation line but the arrangements were left to be worked out by the Secretary-General 'in consultation with the parties concerned.' Anything stronger and more specific, argued Mr. Lodge of the United States, would fail to gain the necessary two-thirds majority. As it was, the Afro-Asian and Soviet blocs abstained in protest against any assumption that UNEF might be stationed on Egyptian territory. V. K. Krishna Menon of India expressed this view when he said the UNEF can at no time 'become an occupying force of another country.' Israel, in turn, refused to recall her troops until 'firm guarantees' were offered to protect 'her security' in the controversial areas, arguing that 'consultations' by the Secretary-General with Egypt gave the latter a veto power over UNEF which, in effect, would allow Egypt to demand UNEF's withdrawal at any time.

Almost immediately the crisis worsened and the United States now undertook the difficult task of seeking some means by which an Israeli withdrawal would be brought about and an eventual settlement arrived at. Private negotiations in Washington and New York involving Secretary of State Dulles and Israeli officials and direct appeals from President Eisenhower to Israeli Prime Minister David Ben-Gurion met with little success. On February 22, six nations (Afghanistan, Indonesia, Iraq, Lebanon, Pakistan, and Sudan) introduced a resolution in the Assembly — it never came to a vote — which would condemn Israel for not withdrawing and urge all states to deny economic, military, and financial assistance to Israel until evacuation was completed. This threat of economic sanctions led to renewed efforts by Secretary Dulles to reach some agreement. Finally, after ceaseless discussion and several false starts, Israeli Foreign Minister, Mrs. Golda Meir, announced to the Assembly on March 4 the completion of technical arrangements for the transfer of the Gaza and Aqaba areas to UNEF.

On March 7, UNEF replaced Israeli military and civil administrators in Gaza and on the following day took stations at Sharm-el-Sheikh along the Aqaba coast. But on March 11, Egypt demanded and was permitted to have an Egyptian Governor in Gaza, which reduced UNEF's role in that area to an auxiliary to Egyptian police power. UNEF continued to implement the Egyptian-Israeli armistice agreement to safeguard peace between the two countries, as authorized by the February 2, 1957, Assembly resolution. Israel, however, strongly opposed the return of Egyptian administration of Gaza and refused to allow UNEF troops in its territory or on the Israeli side of the demarcation line.

In the meantime, the Secretary-General went forward with plans to ready the Suez Canal for navigation. Prior to the Anglo-French evacuation, some progress had been made by the British in clearing the northern end of the Canal but the Egyptian portion still remained tightly closed. Mr. Hammarskjöld appointed Lt. General Raymond A. Wheeler, U.S.A. (ret.), a former Panama Canal engineer, to supervise clearing the remainder of the Canal. The Secretary-General then completed arrangements to obtain salvage vessels and equipment for the clearance project and actual salvage operations got underway on December 28. A minimum of $10 million was needed to get the work started before permanent financing could be arranged. The United States agreed to lend between three and five million with the remainder pledged by Australia, Canada, Denmark, Italy, Sweden, the Netherlands, and West Germany.[12]

---

[12] The Twelfth Assembly authorized the Secretary-General to make the necessary arrangements for a 3 percent surcharge to be levied on regular Suez tolls as a means for repayment of loans made to the United Nations to cover the cost of Canal clearance and rehabilitation. Expenditures and obligations incurred in the clearance totalled approximately $8.4 million.

Although final obstructions were removed and normal passage resumed by May, 1957, Egypt refused to permit use of the Canal to Israel and no final decision had been reached on the disposition of the claims of the former owners. Also in doubt, in spite of renewed Security Council discussions, was the question of what rights would be permitted the users of the Canal.

The summer of 1958 had not yet seen any final settlement of the Israel-Arab conflict and none was in prospect. The significant question of what would happen should UNEF be requested to leave Egyptian territory was unanswered. Egyptian reparation demands from Israel, Britain, and France remained unsolved. An ominous note was injected into the unsettled situation with the sale of Soviet submarines to Egypt in 1957. To complicate the picture even further, the Soviet Union can be expected to continue its efforts to encourage anti-Western sentiment in the Arab world. The United Nations and the United States continue to face grave problems in this area.

3. THE HUNGARIAN SITUATION

On October 23, 1956, peaceful demonstrations took place in Budapest and one of the principal demands made was that Soviet troops leave Hungary. Police began firing on the demonstrators and the following day Soviet tanks joined with the police in inflicting heavy casualties on Hungarian citizens. By October 26, fighting had spread beyond Budapest and had reached the Austrian frontier. Hungarian authorities claimed to be negotiating with the USSR for the withdrawal of all Soviet troops but instead, heavy Soviet military reinforcements continued to pour into Hungary and intensified the fighting.

The United States, Britain, and France on October 28 requested an urgent meeting of the Security Council to discuss 'the situation created by the action of foreign military forces in Hungary violently repressing the rights of the Hungarian people,' secured by the Hungarian peace treaty of 1947. Shortly before the Council met on October 28, the Hungarian delegate to the United Nations protested against the consideration of the question, claiming that it fell exclusively within the domestic jurisdiction of his country. The Soviet Union supported this position and voted against placing the matter on the agenda.

The Council discussed the situation fully on October 28, November 2, and November 3 without having any proposal put to a vote. However, new developments were announced during the night Assembly session of November 3 and 4 on the Middle East crisis. During the debate on this issue, Dr. E. R. Walker of Australia went up to the rostrum on a point of order to inform the Assembly of a press message reporting that Hungarian Premier Nagy had declared over the Budapest radio that the Soviet army was attacking Budapest 'with the apparent purpose of overthrowing the democratic government of the Hungarian People's Republic.' Several hours later, at 3:13 A.M. on November 4, the Council met to consider a United States resolution which would call upon the USSR 'to desist forthwith from any form of intervention, particularly armed intervention, in the internal affairs of Hungary, . . . to cease the introduction of additional armed forces into Hungary and to withdraw all of its forces without delay from Hungarian territory.' It also affirmed 'the right of the Hungarian people to a government responsive to its national aspirations and dedicated to its independence and well-being.' The Soviet representative, however, cast a negative vote while all other Council members, with the exception of Yugoslavia which abstained, voted in its favor. The Council then decided by a procedural vote of 10-1 (USSR) to call a special session of the General Assembly to 'make appropriate recommendations concerning the situation in Hungary' since the Council had been 'unable to exercise its primary responsibility for the maintenance of international peace and security' because of 'the lack of unanimity among its permanent members.'

Meeting in emergency session for the second time within a week, the Assembly on November 4 adopted the United States resolution that had been vetoed by the USSR earlier in the day. The vote was 53-8 (Soviet bloc) with seven abstentions. The Secretary-General was requested to observe the situation directly 'through representatives appointed by him to report thereon' to the Assembly 'and as soon as possible suggest methods to bring an end to the foreign intervention in Hungary. . . .' On November 9 the Assembly again called upon the Soviet Union to withdraw its forces from Hungary and recommended that 'free elections should be held in Hungary under United Nations auspices, as soon as law and order have been restored, to enable the people of Hungary to determine for themselves the form of government they wish to establish in their country.' Two other resolutions set in motion plans for sending food and medical supplies to Hungary under the direction of the Secretary-General and arrangements for caring for Hungarian refugees. Individual members of the United Nations were urged to make special contributions for these purposes.

On November 10, the emergency special session of the Assembly decided to transfer the Hungarian situation to the agenda of the Assembly's eleventh regular session which opened on November 12. During both the emergency and regular sessions, the USSR continued to oppose any United Nations action on Hungary, claiming as it did before the Security Council that the entire matter was within the domestic jurisdiction of Hungary.

Despite a specific Assembly request on November 21, the Hungarian government refused to permit either the Secretary-General or a three-man observer team to enter the country. Countries bordering Hungary also refused the entrance of observers, with the exception of Austria.

A Cuban resolution on November 21 reiterated the need for prompt compliance with the Assembly's earlier calls for withdrawal of Soviet troops and urged Soviet and Hungarian authorities to 'take immediate steps to cease the deportation of Hungarian citizens, and to return promptly to their homes those who have been deported.' In December, the Assembly once again called upon the Soviets to leave Hungary. This resolution was much stronger than earlier ones, however, since it was in the form of a censure. It declared that the Soviet Union had violated the political independence of Hungary and thus should stand condemned for a violation of the Charter. Prior to this action, the Hungarian delegation left the Assembly after protesting that the United Nations had interfered in Hungary's internal affairs. Soviet troops still remained in Hungary and no way had been found to get a single United Nations observer into the country, except for a four-man team of economic experts who examined the relief needs of the Hungarian people in early January, 1957.

The Assembly also established in January a five-member committee (Australia, Ceylon, Denmark, Tunisia, and Uruguay) to investigate the Soviet-crushed Hungarian revolt. Following months of painstaking interrogation of Hungarian escapees at hearings in New York, London, Vienna, Geneva, and Rome, the Committee issued its findings in June, 1957. The Eleventh Assembly reconvened briefly in September just before beginning the Twelfth session and endorsed the Committee Report by a vote of 60 to 10 with ten abstentions. Among other things, the Assembly resolution noted that the events which took place in October and November, 1956, constituted a spontaneous national uprising; that the present Hungarian regime had been imposed upon the Hungarian people by the armed intervention of the USSR; that the present regime had violated the human rights and freedoms guaranteed by the Treaty of Peace with Hungary; and that the Soviet Union had carried out mass deportations of Hungarian citizens to the USSR. In addition, the resolution called upon the USSR and Hungarian authorities to desist from repressive measures against the Hungarian population, to respect that country's liberty and independence, and ensure the return of the deportees. The Report itself had indicated clearly that there was no evidence to support the Soviet charge that the uprising was fomented and helped by reactionary circles in Hungary and 'western imperialists.'

CONCLUSIONS

The experience of the United Nations with collective security reveals once again the necessity for unity of purpose among the great powers. The adoption of the 'Uniting for Peace' resolution was a clear recognition that in the absence of such unity, some means to deal with a dangerous situation had to be found if the United Nations was to justify its existence. Admittedly, the General Assembly is not the organ best suited for the employment of collective measures. Its large and unwieldly size, its frequently repetitious and tiresome debate, and its inability, even in a crisis, to do more than recommend action, would normally eliminate it as an agency capable of invoking the necessary measures of collective security. Yet there was no alternative to an undoubted stalemate in the Security Council if a decision required of it contravened the primary interests of a permanent member. This was the case with the intervention of the Chinese Communists in the Korean War, just as it was with the Middle East crisis in 1956. In Korea, Soviet Russia frustrated Council action on Chinese intervention, while in the Middle East, Britain and France were able to prevent the Council from performing its primary responsibility of maintaining peace and security.

The inclusion of the General Assembly in the collective security machinery of the United Nations has not altered the distribution of power in the world. It does challenge the assumption upon which the veto was predicated, which is, that no collective measures would be effective unless supported by the great powers. So far, the supreme test of this challenge has not materialized because collective measures have not been directed against one or more of the great powers. As a circumvention of the Council's veto, the 'Uniting for Peace' resolution offered hope in 1950 that some action could be taken in the Assembly to meet a crisis. In the years which have passed since that time, however, the increased membership of the United Nations and the political alignment in 1958 of the Soviet and Afro-Asian blocs means that sufficient voting strength can be obtained by these members to prevent the West from obtaining action on anything inimical to their wishes. The West can, in its turn, block any move undertaken by the Soviet-Afro-Asian members. In essence, there has developed a veto in the General Assembly. The present concentration of bipolar military power makes it impossible to coerce either the United States or the USSR.

Only when there has been some agreement among the permanent members has the Council been effective. On these occasions the Council has again employed a flexible approach to its responsiblities under the Charter.

Rarely has it sought to determine the existence of a threat to or breach of the peace and never has it determined that there has been an act of aggression. The Council has always attempted to exhaust all other means of settlement before resorting to Article 39 of the Charter. A variety of provisional measures have been employed, with some success, under Article 40, without making the determination called for in Article 39. Undoubtedly the effect of the measures recommended by the Council might have been greater if it had had possession of the military support which should have been provided under Article 43.

But the Korean War brought into the open for the first time the heart of the problem of collective security as a means of preserving peace within the framework of the Charter and the limitations on collective security imposed by great power politics. The absence of military agreements called for by Article 43 immediately made necessary a series of improvisations which were effective in combatting the invasion of South Korea. In itself, the makeshift arrangement to conduct the forces of the United Nations was an example of how the United Nations might act, given certain unique circumstances, to meet a breach of the peace. Also revealed were the complex problems associated with organizing and directing a multi-national armed force, the question of liaison between the force and the various organs of the United Nations, and the essential need of political guidance for the military command.

The unique circumstances attendant on the outbreak of hostilities in Korea must never be forgotten. First, the fact that there was a regularly constituted United Nations commission in Korea, equipped with trained military observers, was of inestimable value in providing factual information for the Security Council. Even more fortuitous was the presence in Japan, but a short distance from the scene of hostilities, of a few British, and many more American, military, naval, and air units which could be quickly and easily shifted from their bases to the battle-lines. A third feature was the absence of the Soviet delegate from the Security Council at the time when that body was called upon to act. Had Mr. Malik been present on June 25 and at later crucial meetings in June and July, it is certain that he would have frustrated action by the Council through the veto. The Assembly might have been called into emergency session but there is little likelihood that it could have reached any decision or improvised machinery to meet the emergency before the North Koreans had swept across the entire peninsula.

The claim is widely made that the United Nations decision to intervene in Korea is the first example of collective security in action within the limits of the Charter. The truth is, however, that the United States actually decided to intervene against Communist aggression before the Security Council had acted. It is quite possible that the intervention in Korea would have been made had the United Nations not been in existence. Certainly the support of the Organization gave a definite international character to the Korean adventure. On the other hand, it may also be said that the United Nations was utilized as a disguise for unilateral action by the United States whereby the policy of that nation was made to be the policy of the United Nations.

An interesting footnote to the United Nations military action in Korea was the previous development of security arrangements outside the United Nations based upon the right of individual and collective self-defense permitted under Article 51 of the Charter. While this aspect of international organization will be further developed, it is important to note at this time that the United States and virtually all other members of the United Nations contributing armed forces to the United Nations Korean Command were parties to these security agreements. Whether members of such collective arrangements or not, all military contributors were dependent upon the United States, through some agreement, for military assistance. There can be no doubt that the organization of the collective military effort in Korea was enhanced in large part by the prior existence of these military arrangements.

The adoption of economic sanctions, preceded some months earlier by the Assembly declaration that the Chinese Communists were aggressors in Korea, was the first example of resort to collective measures by that organ. The significance of this action is reduced considerably by the fact that it came over six months after the Peiping Government introduced its 'volunteers' into Korea. Furthermore, no important result could be attributed directly to this adoption of economic sanctions because the nations who could contribute effectively to the embargo had already been applying sanctions of their own for several months.

The creation of UNEF was another example of improvisation dictated by the conditions surrounding the outbreak of hostilities. The decision to create a United Nations force to 'secure and supervise the cessation of hostilities' in the Middle East is the type of implementation of a provisional measure that the Security Council might recommend under Chapter VII of the Charter if it had the military support expected under Article 43 and was not blocked by a veto. The cease-fire agreed to by both sides was made contingent upon placing UNEF in the area of hostilities. It is, however, too much to say that the Assembly, by employing armed forces, was able to restore international peace and security in the same way that military sanctions by the Council were expected to do under Article 42 of the Charter. The influence exerted by the British Commonwealth was largely responsible for the British decision to accept a cease-fire and complete withdrawal; France reluctantly followed the British lead. Pressure from the United States was also significant and was most compelling in bringing about an Israeli withdrawal some months later. The determined stand of the United States in both instances, in full support of the decisions reached by the Assembly, may well have been the decisive factor in preventing a serious weakening if not a collapse of the United Nations. Such action was consistent with the policy of the United States of upholding the Charter, even if it meant risking a full alienation of its closest partners in the Atlantic community.

Nevertheless, the establishment of UNEF must be considered one of the most vital developments since the inception of the United Nations. The Assembly moved with surprising speed and unanimity to get the force into Egypt. Considerable ingenuity was in evidence, as well as a flexible approach to a serious emergency. What actually happened in the Middle East crisis is that the United Nations entered the conflict as the greatest political face-saving device, to which Britain, France, the USSR, and even the United States should be indebted. Without the United Nations, Britain, France, and the Soviets could not have retreated so easily from their positions. However, one must also remember that the United States and the Soviet Union, voting together with the Afro-Asian bloc, composed an extremely unusual combination and it is doubtful whether there will be many repetitions of this unique political alignment in the General Assembly. Above all else, much of the credit must go to the indefatigable Mr. Hammarskjöld. His efforts and those of his immediate assistants, such as Andrew Cordier and Ralph Bunche, reveal that the role of the Secretary-General can be one of the most significant factors in the peace and security offered by an international organization.

There was little the Assembly could do in the Hungarian situation other than to bring, as it did, the virtual condemnation of the world upon the actions of the Soviet Union. Anything more would have involved forceful action which the Organization was not prepared to employ. In addition, this entire matter involved the explosive question of domestic jurisdiction and noninterference in the internal affairs of a sovereign nation. No enforcement measures were ever contemplated. It is also difficult to gauge the effect which the Middle East crisis had upon the Assembly's deliberations on Hungary. Stronger measures, such as economic sanctions, might have been envisaged if there had not been the fear that to act along these lines might have prejudiced the establishment of UNEF.

9

THE REGULATION OF ARMAMENTS

IT IS generally agreed that war is the least desirable method of settling disputes between nations. War does not always eliminate differences, and frequently creates new problems which may develop into future wars. While no conclusive answer has been discovered to the question of what causes war, there are many who believe that armament itself is a fundamental cause. It is argued that an increase of arms in one state contributes to a sense of security. As a result of this arms increase, real or potential rivals of that state then feel insecure and increase their military establishment. Eventually this becomes an armaments race which is likely to lead to war. Disarmament thus becomes an important goal for mankind so that it will not destroy or bankrupt itself in its search for security through increased arms.

The general view that an arms race causes war is an oversimplification of the problem. The basic question can always be asked: What led to the start of the arms race? Any attempt to regulate arms, the instrumentalities of power, is intimately associated with the security of states. An effective system for regulating armaments thus becomes dependent upon the absence of conflict in the foreign policies of the great powers. Arms provide the the means for maintaining or disturbing the status quo and the limitation of them is essentially a matter of politics. Arms will not be surrendered or reduced until some other method is available to guarantee the protection they afford. Given the present world of independent states, war always remains a possibility as an instrument of policy.

Disarmament has been discussed for several centuries but plans for its implementation have failed because no state whose participation was essential was willing to pay the price that is required. The problem is a far more complex one than appears on the surface. There is no ratio of limitation yet devised which can be applied fairly to all states, large and small, wealthy and poor. Some nations have more frontiers to guard than others, or have overseas possessions to protect. The supervising agency to enforce regulation is difficult to establish. The current system of sovereign states is a formidable barrier to any method of inspection established to determine compliance with agreements limiting arms. Who is to enforce a judgment against the violator of such an agreement? What can be done about the development of new weapons not covered by an agreement? These and other problems have confronted all organized attempts to regulate the use of force.

HISTORY OF DISARMAMENT

The idea of disarmament is certainly not new. It can be traced through the writings of Sully, William Penn, the Abbé de Saint-Pierre, Rousseau, and Kant. Philosophers, theologians, statesmen, pacifists, and laymen have contributed their thoughts and plans. Some have advocated general disarmament in which as many nations as possible should participate. Total disarmament has been suggested for certain groups of nations or for a geographical area. Qualitative disarmament has been suggested as a way to reduce or eliminate the use of specific weapons, such as the atom bomb. The argument most commonly advanced has been the one for quantitative disarmament, which attempts a reduction of most or all types of armaments.

What has been considered to be the first practical attempt at quantitative disarmament was the proposal of the Russian Tsar to Lord Castlereagh of Great Britain in 1816 for 'the simultaneous reduction of the armed forces of every kind.' Castlereagh was skeptical but proposed an international conference to discuss the problem. Austria and France were not seriously interested in the idea and nothing came of the Tsar's suggestion. In 1831 and on several later occasions, French monarchs made similar proposals which failed to be implemented. Great Britain and Italy also initiated projects before 1890 which had no success.

Tsar Nicholas II of Russia, with the concurrence of Queen Wilhelmina of the Netherlands, convoked an international peace conference at The Hague in 1899 for the specific purpose of limiting armaments by mutual agreement. The Tsar denounced war as a destroyer of civilization and on economic grounds as the cause of an intolerable financial burden. He claimed that 'the preservation of peace has become an object of international policy.' The Conference lasted two months and was attended by ninety-six delegates representing twenty-six states. All the major powers were present. The work was divided among three committees, of which the first, dealing with limitation of armaments and war budgets, is of concern here.[1] Specific

---

[1] The second committee dealt with the extension of Red Cross rules and the third was concerned with mediation, arbitration, and other methods of pacific settlement.

Russian proposals directed at a limitation of existing armaments received a cool reception. Two resolutions of little significance were adopted. One expressed the opinion of the Conference 'that the restriction of military charges, which are at present a heavy burden on the world, is extremely desirable for the increase of the material and moral welfare of mankind.' A move to provide for such restriction had been defeated earlier largely through the efforts of Germany. The entire subject was continued for additional study by the various governments in the second resolution.

After suggestions had been made by France and the United States, Russia summoned delegates to a Second Hague Conference in 1907. This time forty-four states were represented and met for four months and worked through committees similar to those of the 1899 Conference. The Conference had to confess that nothing could be done about the burden of armaments beyond confirming the resolutions adopted in 1899, particularly as 'military expenditure has considerably increased in almost every country since that time.' The Russian delegate who presided observed: 'If the question was not ripe in 1899, it is not any more so in 1907. It has not been possible to do anything on these lines, and the Conference today finds itself as little prepared to enter upon them as in 1899.' Viewed from the perspective of history, the resolve to meet again in 1915 was indeed ironic.

Part V of the Treaty of Versailles drastically limited German armaments. But there was an obligation on the part of the other signatories in the introduction to Part V of the Treaty. The reduction of German arms was directed 'in order to render possible the initiation of a general limitation of the armaments of all nations.' Clemenceau of France, on behalf of the victorious Allies, wrote a letter to the German representative at the Paris Conference, which stated that when Germany was disarmed they too would disarm in the same way.

Article 8 of the Covenant dealt at length with the reduction of armaments. The League Council with the assistance of a Permanent Advisory Commission was given the responsibility of formulating plans for reducing arms. The members of the League recognized in Article 8 that the maintenance of peace required the reduction of 'national armaments to the lowest point consistent with national safety and the enforcement by common action of international obligations.' Interestingly enough, the Covenant also stated that 'the manufacture by private enterprise of munitions and implements of war is open to grave objections.' The Council was to advise 'how the evil effects attendant upon such manufacture can be prevented.' The Council was to take into consideration 'the geographical situation and circumstances of each State' in formulating plans for a reduction in armaments. The League members were to 'undertake to interchange full and frank information as to the scale of their armaments, their military, naval and air programs, and the condition of such of their industries as are adaptable to warlike purposes.'

There were attempts at demilitarization and neutralization of specific areas after 1918. The Rhineland was demilitarized and Czechoslovakia agreed not to build military bases on the right bank of the Danube below Bratislava. Danzig was completely demilitarized as were the Aaland Islands. The Soviet Union signed demilitarization agreements with Turkey in Transcaucasia and with Finland and Esthonia in the Baltic area. At the Lausanne Conference in 1922–23, agreements were reached which demilitarized certain areas along the borders of Greece as well as zones on the Dardanelles.

A series of naval conferences took place between 1921 and 1930 which were of the local and qualitative type. At the instigation of the United States, representatives of Britain, France, Italy, and Japan met in Washington to discuss a reduction in their naval armaments. A treaty was signed in February, 1922, which limited capital ships to 35,000 tons with sixteen-inch guns, and aircraft carriers to 27,000 tons. Construction of vessels in these classes was terminated for ten years and the United States, Britain, and Japan agreed to scrap a number of older ships. New construction was limited to a ratio of 5:5:3:1.75:1.75 for the United States, Britain, Japan, France, and Italy respectively. Limitations in fortifications and naval bases in the Pacific were included. The Treaty did not cover submarines, cruisers, or destroyers. Two political agreements were concluded which are credited with creating the naval limitation program. A Nine-Power pact guaranteed the independence and integrity of China, while the Four-Power Treaty called for consultation between the United States, Great Britain, France, and Japan on matters of mutual concern in the Pacific.

At the time, it appeared that the Washington naval agreements were highly successful. The truth was, however, that there were no means of enforcing the limitations decided upon. Security was not involved in the matter of battleship construction, as the United States and Britain had nothing to fear from each other in this class of vessel. The ratio granted to the other nations did nothing to upset their naval security and relieved them of an expensive shipbuilding program. Security was, however, a prime consideration in the other classes of ships and France refused to be bound by any limitations unless granted a *quid pro quo* in the form of a European Security Pact.

The United States and Britain soon engaged in a 'cruiser race' which led to tensions between the two countries by 1926. President Coolidge invited the five Washington powers in 1927 to a conference at Geneva to discuss limitations in cruisers and other classes. France and Italy declined, as they believed that all phases of the arms problem were interdependent and should be considered in that light. Nothing was accomplished, owing primarily to Anglo-American differences over large versus small cruisers. A conference in 1930, however, did manage to bring some agreement between the United States and Great Britain on the cruiser problem. Japan also adhered with the other two powers to a limited building program of cruisers, submarines, and destroyers, but France and Italy refused to be bound by these limitations. France continued to make any naval limitation contingent upon general European guarantees of her security.

Meanwhile, the League sought to implement the Covenant provisions for a reduction in armaments. The Permanent Advisory Commission in 1920 could report only that an attempt at reduction 'would be premature.' In that same year, the First Assembly appointed a Temporary Mixed Commission of nongovernmental experts to prepare a plan for consideration by the Council. One suggestion of note to come up in the Mixed Commission was that of Lord Esher. He offered a plan which provided that the land and air forces of Europe should be limited by a fixed ratio similar to that governing the Washington treaty. Each country would be permitted units of 30,000 men of all ranks. France could have six such units; Poland and Italy, four each; Britain and six other nations, three each; and other states, two or one unit each. Nobody was interested in the Esher proposal, which was a good example of the direct, quantitative approach to the problem of armaments reduction. This symbolized the belief that armaments themselves are the cause of war and that their elimination can result in security for all.

The Temporary Mixed Commission was dissolved in 1924, and in 1925 the Assembly requested the Council to work upon the question of disarmament by making preparations for a disarmament conference. In December, 1925, the Council established a Preparatory Commission which began its labors in the spring of 1926. Enthusiasm surrounded its inception, and its activities were watched with interest during its several years of effort. It comprised the states that were members of the Council, six other members of the League, Germany, the USSR, and the United States. Progress was extremely slow, as can be seen by the fact that two technical subcommittees worked for nearly a year without arriving at a definition of 'armaments.' Basic differences soon became evident. France demanded international supervision and inspection, coupled with strong guarantees for security. The United States and Britain were not interested in the security question nor would they support the idea of supervision and inspection of disarmament. Germany was resentful over the Versailles provisions limiting her to an inferior status militarily. Wide differences developed over such questions as the annual budgetary expenditure for military purposes and the restriction of naval tonnage.

A preliminary report was issued in 1927, generalizing the deliberations of the Commission and noting the divergence of opinion. Additional sessions were held in 1928–29. Finally, in December, 1930, a sketchy Draft Convention was concluded that recorded no substantial unity on the fundamentals of the problem. It was a sad commentary on five years of intermittent effort. No decision was reached on the abolition of conscription. There was no agreement upon the maximum limits of armed forces, no limitation of trained reserves or of aircraft reserves. The Convention did accept, in part, the principle of the limitation of the annual budget for armed forces and certain aspects of reduction in naval armaments. It also called for the establishment of a Permanent Disarmament Commission to supervise the conditions laid down by the Convention.

Germany objected emphatically to the omissions of the Convention and, in particular, opposed a provision which would protect obligations already binding upon its signatories. This meant, of course, the disarmament section of the Versailles Treaty. The Soviets believed it to be totally inadequate. Britain, the United States, and most other nations were more restrained, hoping that the Disarmament Conference itself would be able to improve upon the Convention. While preparations for the Conference dragged on throughout 1931, the economic depression hit Europe, and Nazi rumblings were increasing in Germany. French suspicions were intensified by the conclusion of the customs union between Austria and Germany. Japan intervened in Manchuria and had other designs in the Far East. The setting was not auspicious for disarmament.

On February 2, 1932, the representatives of sixty-one states assembled in Geneva for the long-awaited Disarmament Conference. The Draft Convention was accepted as the framework for discussion but it was soon forgotten. France immediately offered a bold plan to create an international police force under the authority of the League, consisting of heavy bombing aircraft and such 'offensive' weapons as tanks, heavy artillery, submarines, and large warships. Incendiary, bacteriological, and chemical warfare were to be abolished and restrictions placed upon the bombing of civilian populations. Provisions for compulsory arbitration, a positive definition of aggression, and international control of disarmament were also included. The entire scheme typified the French approach to the problem. The League would be endowed with executive authority and thereby provide security for France, which could then permit some qualified disarmament. Few took the plan seriously, and Germany viewed it simply as a maneuver to postpone disarmament.

Great Britain introduced a proposal for qualitative disarmament, which would prohibit the use of 'offensive' or aggressive weapons. While the British had some ideas on what constituted a difference between these weapons, most others did not. Germany repeated earlier demands for equality in any agreement on armaments. Support in this came from Italy and the USSR, the latter insisting upon total disarmament. The Poles suggested the need for moral disarmament to be made effective through a program of education to influence public opinion. The various proposals were referred to technical committees for study but little progress was made. President Hoover of the United States offered a plan in June, 1932, which was a good example of the American approach to disarmament. It rested upon belief in a mathematical ratio to be applied more or less uniformly. All nations who had armies in excess of the 100,000 permitted Germany by Versailles should reduce them by one-third. Hoover also suggested the elimination of bombing aircraft, tanks, heavy artillery, and chemical weapons, and a reduction in naval tonnage. This is an oversimplified approach in that a reduction for all by the same percentage is entirely unworkable. Some forces exist for minimum defense purposes, such as those in Britain, while others are so large that they constitute a real threat to carry out aggressive designs. Existing armies thus represent a great difference in their capacity for aggression, and percentage reduction would only leave the relative positions intact. The Hoover scheme received only polite notice and was never seriously considered.

Throughout the summer the Conference wrestled with the German demands for equality. When it became evident that the Conference was hopelessly deadlocked on this issue, Germany withdrew her representative. Hopes were revived temporarily in December, 1932, after a meeting between the United States, Great Britain, France, Germany, and Italy. They agreed that 'one of the principles that should guide the Conference on disarmament should be to grant to Germany, and to the other Powers disarmed by treaty, equality of rights in a system which would provide security for all nations, and that the principle should itself be embodied in a convention containing the conclusions of the Disarmament Conference.' Germany was now willing to return to the Conference but it was certain that both France and Germany had their own interpretations of 'security' and 'equality of rights.'

The Conference, which had been in recess while the five-power talks were being conducted, was resumed in February, 1933. In the interval, two ominous events materialized: Japan signified its intention of withdrawing from the League and Hitler became Chancellor of Germany. In spite of the pessimism surrounding these events, the Conference proceeded to discuss a new French plan which, although it retained the characteristic features of strong collective security under a strengthened League, made some concessions to American, British, and German points of view. The plan suggested a general agreement to implement the Kellogg Pact (Pact of Paris) by calling for consultation and sanctions in the event of aggression. There was also to be a separate plan for Europe involving specific military and political arrangements, supervision of armaments, and an international police force. Certain weapons were to be prohibited and land forces reduced. But Germany and Italy steadfastly opposed the proposal, claiming that it did not provide for sufficient reduction of armaments, particularly in the aggressive classification of weapons. The Conference was again deadlocked and in March, 1933, it appeared as if it were at an end.

In the midst of an attitude of hopelessness, Mr. Ramsay MacDonald of Great Britain arrived in Geneva with a new plan. It suggested a method of consultation in the event of a breach or a threatened breach of the Kellogg Pact. Decisions reached would become effective when agreed to by all the great powers and a majority of the other nations. Disarmament was provided for by stages over a period of five years in which armies would be reduced according to figures submitted as a basis of discussion. Chemical and bacteriological warfare were barred and a Permanent Disarmament Commission was to be created with powers of inspection and control. The new American President, Franklin D. Roosevelt, endorsed the British plan in May, 1933, urging an elimination of offensive weapons and the adoption of a nonagression pact. Later it was announced by the American representative at Geneva that the United States would aid in organizing peace and would not undertake action which would hinder collective efforts to restore peace. Although the British plan was fully discussed, no agreement could be reached and the Conference adjourned in June.

Resuming in October, 1933, the Conference returned to the British proposal which had been modified somewhat during the adjournment. Germany still found the British suggestions unacceptable and on October 14, 1933, announced that it was leaving the Conference and withdrawing from the League. In December the German government communicated this memorandum to France:

> 1. The reduction of the armaments of other European countries can only be practically considered if such reduction be carried out by every country in the world; but nobody believes any longer in the possibility of such general international disarmament.
>
> 2. The events of the last few months make it clear that, even if the governments of certain countries were seriously contemplating the possibility of disarming, they doubtless would not be in a position to present, with any hope of success, proposals to this effect to their parliaments for ratification.

The price of Germany's return to the conference was announced as follows: a conscript army of 300,000, with all necessary weapons; Nazi units as the Brownshirts (S.A.) were not to be included in this figure; one-year military service; remilitarization of the Rhineland; and the return of the Saar. France would not stand for these proposals, which would destroy the security of Versailles. Although the Conference met for a few weeks in the early summer of 1934, it was never able to revive after the German withdrawal in October, 1933. It adjourned formally in June, 1934, never to reassemble.

The Disarmament Conference could never reconcile the French demand for security with the equally insistent German determination to regain a status of equality with the other European powers. General disarmament was impossible unless these positions could be reconciled. Any hope for compromise was destroyed by the rise of Hitler and the mounting suspicions of France. The Conference, however, did serve a useful purpose in that some of the technical problems of disarmament became clarified through the long years of study and debate. These can be summarized as follows:

1. Bombing by air and chemical and bacteriological warfare should be eliminated.

2. There should be a limitation of armaments by the qualitative method of gradually eliminating certain types as well as the quantitative method of reducing the overall number retained.

3. A system of national defense expenditures should be agreed upon and come under some control.

4. A permanent international authority should be established to supervise and inspect any disarmament agreement.

5. Some method should be devised for the supervision of both private and state manufacture of arms.[2]

The political means for obtaining agreement on these points was lacking but it became evident that security was the important requisite to guarantee any system of limiting armaments. The lesson was learned that disarmament itself must follow rather than precede security.

THE UNITED NATIONS AND THE REGULATION OF ARMAMENTS

It will be recalled that the Covenant of the League of Nations called for the reduction of national armaments 'to the lowest point consistent with national safety' and the enforcement of international obligations by common action. The Charter of the United Nations, however, does not speak

[2] Sharp, Walter R., and Kirk, Grayson, *Contemporary International Politics*, New York, 1944, p. 603.

of reduction but of 'regulation' of armaments. In Article 26, the Security Council is given the responsibility of formulating plans to be submitted to the members of the United Nations for the establishment of a system for the regulation of armaments. Security is supposed to be provided along with the regulation of armaments by granting military forces to the United Nations under Article 43. The members are expected to make armed forces available to the Security Council through the signing of special agreements which are to govern the numbers and types of forces, their degree of readiness and general location, and the nature of the facilities and assistance to be provided.[3] Article 47 establishes a Military Staff Committee 'to advise and assist the Security Council on all questions relating to the Security Council's military requirements for the maintenance of international peace and security, the employment and command of forces placed at its disposal, the regulation of armaments, and possible disarmament.' In order that the United Nations might move quickly to meet an emergency, Article 45 provides that 'members shall hold immediately available national air-force contingents for combined international enforcement action.'

The League Council could not take military measures itself nor could it compel the members of the League to do so. The United Nations Security Council can do both in theory although it should be emphasized that the military forces referred to in Article 43 do not constitute an international police force in the sense in which that phrase is generally understood. Such forces are supposed to be contingents belonging to the members and continually available to the Council. It was expected that their use would be governed by agreements concluded between the Council and the members supplying forces as well as by the general needs of the Council. The League Council had a Permanent Advisory Commission to advise it on military matters and armaments and, although its composition was not specified, it consisted of military representatives of the major powers as does the Military Staff Committee. Neither the Covenant nor the Charter gave to any organ the authority to impose a system of disarmament or regulation of armaments on members.

The Activities of the Military Staff Committee. The duties of the Committee are threefold: to advise the Council on military requirements, including the military agreements, to direct the employment and command of forces and their strategic location, and to give advice in respect to regulation of arms and disarmament. The initiative of negotiating the military

---

[3] In December, 1945, the United States Congress passed the United Nations Participation Act which authorized the President to negotiate agreements with the United Nations, subject to Congressional approval.

agreements belongs to the Council. The Charter states that these agreements 'shall be negotiated as soon as possible' but the Council has failed to conclude any nor has it taken the initiative to do so. It has referred to the Military Staff Committee the problem of the content and structure of possible agreements. The duty of employing and commanding armed forces has not materialized due to the absence of any military agreements. The Committee has not been concerned to any great extent with the question of regulating armaments. This has been the responsiblity of the Atomic Energy Commission, the Commission on Conventional Armaments, and the Disarmament Commission. Their labors will be examined later in this chapter.

On January 25, 1946, the Security Council requested its permanent members to direct their Chiefs of Staff to meet and constitute themselves as the Military Staff Committee. This they did on February 4, 1946, and on February 16 the Security Council directed the Committee to examine the duties outlined in Article 43 of the Charter. The Committee then proceeded to work on recommendations concerning principles to guide the adoption of military agreements between the Council and the members of the United Nations. Little was done, and the Assembly in the fall of 1946 adopted a resolution entitled 'Principles Governing the General Regulation and Reduction of Armaments.' Point seven recommended that the Security Council 'accelerate as much as possible the placing at its disposal of the armed forces mentioned in Article 43 of the Charter.' Taking cognizance of this reminder by the General Assembly, the Council on February 3, 1947, requested from the Military Staff Committee 'as soon as possible and as a matter of urgency, the recommendations for which it has been asked' by the Council on February 16, 1946. As a first step the Committee was to submit, not later than April 30, 1947, its 'recommendations with regard to the basic principles which should govern the organization of the United Nations Armed Force.'

The Military Staff Committee, on April 30, 1947, turned in its 'Report on the General Principles Governing the Organization of the Armed Forces Made Available to the Security Council by Member Nations of the United Nations.' The disagreement which had developed in the Security Council by that time had, of course, carried over into the deliberations of the Committee. The Report contained a total of forty-one articles on which there was agreement on only twenty-five. The sixteen articles which failed to win acceptance represented the most important phase of the entire question. While there were minor disagreements between the non-Soviet members, the most bitter divergencies appeared between the USSR and the other members of the Committee.

Agreement was reached on the following main points:

1. The armed forces available to the Security Council should be composed of units of national armed forces — land, sea, and air — 'what are normally maintained as components of armed forces of member nations of the United Nations.'

2. The armed forces would be limited 'to a strength sufficient to enable the Security Council to take prompt action in any part of the world for the maintenance or the restoration of international peace and security.'

3. The permanent members of the Security Council should make the initial contribution of the majority of the armed forces to which other contributions can be added as they materialize.

4. No member of the United Nations would have to increase the strength of its armed forces or 'create a particular component thereof' in order to make its contribution to the Council.

5. Contributions need not be restricted to armed forces. Offers of facilities and other assistance can be considered as fulfillment of a member's obligation under the Charter.

6. The degree of readiness of the armed forces shall be such as to make possible their rapid employment if urgently needed by the Council.

7. All necessary replacements in personnel and equipment, and adequate supplies and transport must accompany the offer of armed forces to the Council.

8. Satisfactory reserves to replace personnel and equipment should be maintained.

9. All armed forces made available to the Council should be 'under the exclusive command of the respective contributing nations, except when operating under the Security Council.'

10. When the armed forces are employed by the Council, 'the Military Staff Committee shall be responsible, under the Security Council, for their strategic direction.'

11. 'The command of national contingents will be exercised by Commanders appointed by the respective member nations. These contingents will retain their national character and will be subject at all times to the discipline and regulations in force in their own national armed forces.'

12. Commanders of national contingents should be able to 'communicate directly with the authorities of their own countries on all matters.'

13. A supreme commander might be appointed by the Security Council to lead the armed forces.

But a very fundamental difference arose with respect to the contributions of the permanent members. All but the Soviets agreed that the five permanent members of the Council, when making initial contributions of armed forces, should take into consideration the size and composition of the national forces of each. Consequently, 'in order to further the ability of the Security Council to constitute balanced and effective combat forces for operations, these contributions may differ widely as to the strength of the separate components, land, sea, and air.' But the Soviet Union insisted upon the principle of equality in respect to the over-all strength and composition of these forces. This principle meant that each of the five permanent members would have to make available identical forces. Every component and every element of every component contributed by the permanent members would thereby be limited so that it would not exceed in strength and composition the weakest corresponding component or element provided by any permanent member. Equality would represent a matching of gun for gun, man for man, ship for ship, and plane for plane. An armed force of this nature would be ridiculous. The Soviet motive was obvious, namely to limit in any enforcement action the air and naval superiority enjoyed by the non-Soviet world.[4]

A second bitter conflict broke out among the members of the Committee on the location of the armed forces when not employed by the United Nations. China, the United Kingdom, and the United States argued that the armed forces should 'be based at the discretion of member nations in any territories or waters to which they have legal right of access.' France objected to the general features of this view and preferred a more detailed recommendation. There was no serious difference of opinion between the non-Soviet members on the basic principle involved. This was, in essence, that the location of these armed forces should be so distributed geographically as to make it possible for the Security Council to take the promptest possible action to maintain or restore peace and security. On the other hand, the Soviets insisted that the armed forces in normal times be garrisoned within the frontiers of the contributing members' own territories or territorial waters.

No agreement could be reached on the matter of provision of assistance and facilities. Contrary to the views of the others, the Soviet Union insisted that 'facilities' did not and could not include bases.[5] There was also

[4] It is interesting to note the original Soviet position taken with respect to arming the United Nations. Arkaday Sobolev, at one time Assistant Secretary-General of the United Nations in charge of Political and Security Council Affairs and later the Soviet representative on the Security Council, was the Soviet delegate on the military subcommittee at Dumbarton Oaks. He argued that there should be a strong international force, permanently divorced from national allegiance, to be paid, equipped, and controlled entirely by the Security Council. Sobolev was emphatic about the necessity for a strong air force. When asked where such a force should be located, he replied without hesitation, 'in Central Europe—that is where wars start.' Eventually the Soviets accepted the Anglo-American plan for national contingents but insisted upon the inclusion of a statement which was incorporated into Article 45 of the Charter, that air forces be 'immediately available.' All parties appeared to accept the view that the military contingents would be constituted as an effective and well-balanced force. It was generally agreed that the United States and the United Kingdom would supply most of the naval and air forces and the Soviets the largest share of ground units.

[5] There was considerable discussion at Dumbarton Oaks over the question of the 'assistance and facilities, including rights of passage,' which, as eventually provided in the Charter, the member states would make available to the Security Council. At that time, it was assumed that 'facilities' included bases. The word 'facilities' was actually substituted for 'bases' because it provided a broader meaning.

sharp disagreement over the withdrawal of armed forces employed to implement a directive of the Security Council. The Soviets demanded that such units be withdrawn within a time limit of thirty to ninety days after completion of their duties. The others, however, stood adamantly for granting the Security Council the authority to recall the units without reference to any fixed time limit.

The Military Staff Committee on June 30, 1947, at the request of the Security Council, submitted provisional estimates of the over-all strength and composition of the armed forces to be made available to the Council. There were wide differences in the views of the Western powers. Originally refusing to submit estimates until the Council had determined general principles, the Soviets later did reveal some tentative figures. They corresponded roughly with the British estimates although there was no provision made for any battleships or cruisers.[6]

The Security Council has never been able to overcome any of the basic differences noted in the Report of the Military Staff Committee. Periodic meetings of the Committee have been held since 1947 but the deadlock has never been overcome. The General Assembly has attempted to carry on

[6] The following table reveals the estimates submitted by the non-Soviet members of the Military Staff Committee on June 30, 1947, and later Soviet estimates.

	FRANCE	CHINA & UNITED KINGDOM	UNITED STATES	USSR
AIR FORCES				
Bombers	775	600	1,250	600
Fighters	300	400	2,250	300
Reconnaissance	200	—	—	—
Miscellaneous	—	200	300	300
Total	1,275	1,200	3,800	1,200
GROUND FORCES				
Divisions	16	8–12	20	12
NAVAL FORCES				
Battleships	3	2	3	—
Carriers	6	4	6	—
Cruisers	9	6	15	5–6
Destroyers	18–24	24	84	24
Escort Vessels	30	48	—	24
Minesweepers	30	24	—	24
Submarines	12	12	90	12
Assault shipping and craft for number of divisions shown	1	⅔ (2 regimental combat teams)	6	—

where the Security Council has failed. The 'Uniting for Peace' resolution was adopted to provide in some measure for the absence of military contingents available to the United Nations. The members have not, however, maintained within their national armed forces 'elements so trained, organized and equipped that they could promptly be made available . . . for service as a United Nation's unit or units' as called for in the resolution.

THE ATOMIC ENERGY COMMISSION

On August 6, 1945, the world was told of the explosion of an atomic bomb over the Japanese city of Hiroshima. There were immediate demands on all sides after the Japanese surrender in mid-August for some method of controlling 'the absolute weapon.' Atomic scientists who developed the bomb were particularly outspoken on the need for haste in devising a system of controls. The Association of Los Alamos Scientists, for example, observed that a failure to regulate at once the use of atomic energy for military purposes would inevitably prepare 'the world for unprecedented destruction, not only of other countries but of our own as well.'

The first official notice taken of the insistence on a system of controls came in the fall of 1945. President Truman, Prime Minister Atlee of Britain, and the Canadian Prime Minister, King, meeting in Washington, issued a Declaration of November 15 which included the following passages:

> We recognize that the application of recent scientific discoveries to the methods and practice of war has placed at the disposal of mankind means of destruction hitherto unknown, against which there can be no adequate military defense, and in the employment of which no single nation can in fact have a monopoly.
>
> We desire to emphasize that the responsibility for devising means to insure that the new discoveries shall be used for the benefit of mankind, instead of as a means of destruction, rests not on our nations alone but upon the whole civilized world. Nevertheless, the progress that we have made in the development and use of atomic energy demands that we take the initiative in the matter, and we have accordingly met together to consider the possibility of international action:
> (a) To prevent the use of atomic energy for destructive purposes.
> (b) To promote the use of recent and future advances in scientific knowledge, particularly in the utilization of atomic energy, for peaceful and humanitarian ends.

The three statesmen did not believe that there should be divulged the information regarding the practical application of atomic energy before establishing 'effective, reciprocal, and enforceable safeguards acceptable to all nations.' They announced, however, that they were prepared to urge the creation of a United Nations commission which should prepare recommendations to attain the most effective means of entirely eliminating the use of atomic energy for destructive purposes and for promoting its widest use for industrial and humanitarian purposes. The work of the commission 'should proceed by separate stages, the successful completion of each one of which will develop the necessary confidence of the world before the next stage is undertaken.'

One month later at the Moscow Conference, the Foreign Ministers of the United Kingdom and the Soviet Union and Secretary of State Byrnes of the United States announced they had agreed to invite China, France, and Canada to join with them in sponsoring a resolution at the first session of the General Assembly which would establish a commission 'to consider problems arising from the discovery of atomic energy and related matters.' It was decided in Moscow that the commission should make specific proposals:

1. For extending between all nations the exchange of basic scientific information for peaceful ends;
2. For control of atomic energy to the extent necessary to insure its use only for peaceful purposes;
3. For the elimination from national armaments of atomic weapons and of all other major weapons adaptable to mass destruction;
4. For effective safeguards by way of inspection and other means to protect complying states against the hazards of violations and evasions.

The Atomic Energy Commission at Work. On January 24, 1946, the General Assembly unanimously adopted the resolution jointly sponsored by the permanent members of the Security Council and Canada, thereby establishing the United Nations Atomic Energy Commission. Its terms of reference were those laid down at Moscow and earlier by the November 15 Declaration of the Anglo-Saxon powers. It was composed of a representative from each of the Security Council's members and Canada 'when that State is not a member of the Security Council.' It was made responsible to the Council and has made its reports and recommendations to it.

The Commission did not meet until June, 1946. In the interim, United States policy toward the problem of controlling atomic energy had crystallized.[7] In January, Secretary Byrnes established a State Department Committee on Atomic Energy with Dean Acheson, Under Secretary of State, as chairman. This Committee soon appointed a Board of Consultants which issued a Report on March 16, 1946. Known later as the Acheson-Lilienthal Report, it carried the sponsorship of the State Department and,

[7] See *International Control of Atomic Energy: Growth of a Policy*, Department of State Publication 2702, Washington, D.C., 1946.

with some later modifications, became the official plan of the United States for the control of atomic energy. It was first presented to the Commission on June 14, 1946, by Mr. Bernard Baruch.

The plan of the United States, as outlined by Mr. Baruch, called for the establishment of an International Atomic Development Authority, which would cover all phases of the development and use of atomic energy. Included in its powers would be those of (1) managerial control or ownership of all atomic energy activities potentially dangerous to world security; (2) the power to control, inspect, and license all other atomic activities; (3) the duty of fostering the beneficial uses of atomic energy; and (4) research and development responsibilities of an affirmative character. Once an adequate system of international control had been created, the United States offered to dispose of its atomic bombs, to stop manufacturing additional atomic bombs, and to provide the Authority with its knowledge of these processes. Serious penalties should be assessed for such violations as (1) illegal possession or use of an atomic bomb; (2) illegal possession, or separation, of atomic material suitable for use in an atomic bomb; (3) seizure of any plant or other property belonging to or licensed by the Authority; (4) willful interference with the activities of the Authority; or (5) creation or operation of dangerous projects in a manner contrary to, or in the absence of, a license granted by the Authority.

That there should be no veto by the Security Council to prevent punishment was emphasized by Mr. Baruch. He stated eloquently:

> I want to make very plain that I am concerned here with the veto power only as it affects this particular problem. There must be no veto to protect those who violate their solemn agrements not to develop or use atomic energy for destructive purposes. The bomb does not wait upon debate. To delay may be to die. The time between violation and preventive action or punishment would be all too short for extended discussion as to the course to be followed.

At the second session of the Atomic Energy Commission, Mr. Gromyko presented the Soviet plan which actually consisted of two proposals. One concerned the conclusion of an international convention 'To Prohibit the Production and Employment of Weapons based on the Use of Atomic Energy for the Purpose of Mass Destruction.' It would be of indefinite duration, open to all states. The important features were as follows:

> *Article 1.* The high contracting parties solemnly declare that they are unanimously resolved to prohibit the production and employment of weapons based on the use of atomic energy, and for this purpose assume the following obligations:
> (a) Not to use atomic weapons in any circumstances whatsoever;
> (b) to prohibit the production and storing of weapons based on the use of atomic energy:

(c) to destroy, within a period of three months from the day of the entry into force of the present convention, all stocks of atomic energy weapons whether in a finished or unfinished condition.

Article 2. The high contracting parties declare that any violation of Article 1 of the present convention is a most serious international crime against humanity.

Article 3. The high contracting parties shall, within a period of six months from the day of the entry into force of the present convention, pass legislation providing severe penalties for violators of the Statutes of the present convention.

The second proposal concerned 'The Organization and Work of the Atomic Energy Commission.' Two committees should be established to further the work of the Commission. One would be concerned with the exchange of scientific information. The other would elaborate upon recommendations for the prevention of the use of atomic energy to the detriment of mankind.

A subsequent proposal submitted by Mr. Gromyko on June 11, 1947, expanded the Soviet position in certain positive respects and made clear the Russian concept of inspection and control. An International Control Commission composed of representatives of the states that were members of the Atomic Energy Commission would be assigned functions of control and inspection as well as duties with respect to research in the peaceful uses of atomic energy. Ownership and management of materials and facilities would be left in national hands. Control would consist of limited inspection, the requesting of information from governments regarding facilities, the checking and accounting of existing stocks of atomic materials, the adoption of rules of technological control and their observance, and the making of recommendations to governments and the Security Council.

The plan of the United States won early approval and, with later modifications, was endorsed by the General Assembly in 1948. It came to be known as 'The United Nations Plan.' At no time, however, did the Soviet Union accept the position of the majority in the Commission. Toward the end of 1947, it was clear that an impasse had been reached. Although the Commission continued its efforts, discussion was brought to an end in January, 1950, when the USSR refused to participate with the Chinese representative present.

At least four main issues could not be resolved between the majority and minority views. They can be summarized as follows:

1. *The Timing of a Convention Outlawing Atomic Weapons.* All were agreed that a prohibition was necessary. The majority demanded that atomic

disarmament come after a system of controls had been established. The minority insisted that a treaty be signed first, outlawing atomic weapons. There was no assurance that an adequate system of controls would follow.

2. *The Ownership Principle and National Sovereignty.* The majority believed firmly that the international control agency should own all dangerous facilities and all nuclear fuel. The Soviets viewed ownership of this nature as tantamount to intervention in the national economy of states and a threat to national sovereignty.

3. *International Inspection.* All were agreed that some method of international inspection was essential. The majority believed that there should be strict but not unlimited inspection by the international agency. This meant inspection of declared activities, such as mines and materials; and surveys and inspection to search out secret activities. There would be specified limitations on these powers of inspection. The minority position was never made entirely clear, although it encompassed no such comprehensive ideas as the majority. There would be periodic inspections of only those national facilities which a state reported as being in operation and which the state itself was reporting on to the international agency.

4. *Use of the Veto in the Security Council.* The majority stood firmly against the use of the veto when voting penalties against violators of the atomic energy agreement. The minority was equally insistent that all questions of enforcement be placed before the Security Council and that decisions on such matters require the affirmative votes of the permanent members.

A careful analysis of the three full years of work engaged in by the Atomic Energy Commission clearly reveals that all of its members during this period, with the exception of the USSR and the two satellites — Poland and the Ukrainian SSR — persevered in an attempt to reach an agreement that would eliminate the fear of an atomic war. The majority, however, was not always unanimous on various points which arose during these years. But it was determined that a system of controls be devised and functioning before disclosures were made or atomic weapons were outlawed and removed from use. The Soviets, on the other hand, were uncompromising, suspicious, and equally determined that the essential features of the majority proposal be replaced by their plan of outlawry which possessed no assured controls. The Soviet delegates did not join the discussions of the Commission to negotiate, but to press their ideas on the majority. When the majority refused to budge, they were attacked bitterly and consistently and their motives impugned. The United States, of course, came in for the greatest share of abuse. Gromyko in the Commission and at the Security Council, and Molotov and Vishinsky in the Assembly, repeatedly charged the United States with refusing to prohibit atomic weapons and with seeking to continue its monopoly of atomic energy. The other members, if they supported the majority view, had always been 'coerced into accepting the United States plan.'[8]

COMMISSION FOR CONVENTIONAL ARMAMENTS

On December 14, 1946, the General Assembly unanimously adopted a resolution on the 'General Principles Governing the Regulation and Reduction of National Armaments.' Its main features included the following points:

1. The need for an early general regulation and reduction of armaments and armed forces through the formulation of practical measures by the Security Council.

2. The fulfillment by the Atomic Energy Commission of its terms of reference and, in particular, the prohibition of 'atomic and all other major weapons adaptable now and in the future to mass destruction.'

3. The problem of security is closely connected with that of disarmament and, consequently, the Security Council should 'accelerate as much as possible the placing at its disposal of the armed forces mentioned in Article 43 of the Charter.'

4. The withdrawal as soon as possible by members of armed forces stationed in ex-enemy territories and in the territories of members 'without their consent freely and publicly expressed in treaties or agreements consistent with the Charter.'

5. The establishment, within the framework of the Security Council, of special organs to enforce an international system of control for the regulation, inspection, and reduction of armaments.

6. Nothing in the resolution should alter or limit the functions of the Atomic Energy Commission.

The Security Council early in 1947 was faced with implementing this resolution. The United States was determined that the deliberations concerning the adoption of measures to regulate conventional armaments would not sidetrack the question of atomic energy. It was obvious that the Assembly had in mind the establishment of a Commission on Conventional Armaments which was created by the Security Council on February 13, 1947, and consisted of the members represented on the Council. It was to prepare and submit to the Council within three months proposals 'for the general regulation and reduction of armaments and armed forces' together with suggestions for practical and effective safeguards. The terms of reference were clearly distinct from those of the Atomic Energy Commission, and reaffirmed the mandate of the General Assembly and conformed with the views of the majority in the Council.

[8] See Osborn, Frederick, 'The USSR and the Atom,' *International Organization,* Vol. 5, No. 3 (August 1951), pp. 480–98. Mr. Osborn was United States Deputy Representative on the UNAEC in 1947 and served in that capacity until January 1950.

Meeting first on March 24, 1947, the most important duty of the new Commission was to establish a work plan. Both the United States and the Soviet Union submitted proposals which were the basis of discussions lasting two months. The Soviet plan, which included the prohibition of atomic weapons, was rejected, and an amended United States proposal was adopted on June 18, 1947, and confirmed by the Council on July 8, 1947. On July 16, a Working Committee of the Whole was established, its terms of reference being the work plan adopted the preceding month. The items in the work schedule included the following:

1. Recommendations concerning armaments and armed forces falling within the jurisdiction of the Commission.
2. The determination of general principles in connection with the regulation and reduction of armaments and armed forces.
3. The consideration of practical safeguards through an international system of control operating through special organs to protect complying states against the hazards of violations and evasions.
4. The submission to the Security Council of a report or reports 'including, if possible, a Draft Convention.'

The first task of the Working Committee was that of defining the armaments and armed forces within the jurisdiction of the Commission. The Soviets attempted unsuccessfully to include atomic weapons within the work plan of the Commission. The Committee then decided that 'all armaments and armed forces, except atomic weapons and weapons of mass destruction, fall within its jurisdiction.' Weapons of mass destruction were defined to include 'atomic explosive weapons, radioactive material weapons, lethal chemical and biological weapons.' By August, 1948, the Working Committee was able to prepare a list of principles to govern 'the formulation of practical proposals for the establishment of a system for the regulation and reduction of armaments and armed forces.' The proposal was adopted by the Commission on August 12, 1948, by a vote of 9-2, with the Soviet Union and the Ukraine casting the negative votes. It included the following points:

1. A system for the regulation and reduction of armaments should include all states and initially must include those 'having substantial military resources.'
2. Such a system can only be put into effect 'in an atmosphere of international confidence and security. Measures for the reduction and regulation of armaments adopted after the establishment of the necessary degree of confidence might increase confidence and thereby encourage further regulation and reduction.'
3. Examples of conditions essential to such confidence and security would be (a) the establishment of an adequate system of agreements under Article

43 of the Charter, (b) the establishment of international control of atomic energy, (c) the conclusion of peace settlements with Japan and Germany.

4. A system of regulation and reduction of armaments, in order to make possible the least diversion for armaments of the world's human and economic resources, should limit armaments and armed forces to those which are indispensable to the maintenance of international peace and security.

5. Such a system must include an adequate method of safeguards.

6. 'Provisions must be made for effective enforcement action in the event of violations.'

The USSR objected strenuously to this resolution, repeating that atomic weapons should not be excluded from its purview. Also emphasized was the view that there should be no conditions or prerequisites laid down for the formulation or implementation of measures designed to regulate and reduce armaments and armed forces. Restated was the thesis that disarmament itself, including the prohibition of atomic weapons, would provide the world all the security that it desired. The Soviets also refused to accept the report of the Commission to the Security Council.

The Soviet arguments were continued when the General Assembly took up the question of armaments in September, 1948. At that time, the USSR introduced a resolution which would have the permanent members of the Security Council reduce their land, naval, and air forces by one-third during one year. A control body was to be established within the framework of the Security Council to supervise the reduction of armaments and the prohibition of atomic weapons. This Soviet draft received no non-Communist support, and instead, the Assembly adopted a resolution which urged the Commission for Conventional Armaments to continue its work and encouraged it to formulate 'proposals for the receipt, checking and publication, by an international organ of control within the framework of the Security Council, of full information to be supplied by member States with regard to their effectives and their conventional armaments.'

In February, 1949, the Commission began consideration of this Assembly resolution. By August, the Working Committee had completed a document with respect to the collection and verification of military data and the function and structure of an international organ of control to give effect to the census and verification measures. The proposal was adopted by the Commission over the now customary Soviet protests and forwarded in a report to the Security Council. There a resolution to approve the Report received a Soviet veto. The Assembly in 1949 requested the Commission to continue its work. When it held its first meeting in April, 1950, the USSR refused to participate in its deliberations, as it had done with the Security Council and the Atomic Energy Commission as long as the representative of Nationalist China was present.

THE DISARMAMENT COMMISSION

Origin. The fifth anniversary of the United Nations was commemorated on October 24, 1950, at its New York headquarters and in other parts of the world. The anniversary was proclaimed a national holiday in Korea, despite the war there. President Truman of the United States addressed a special plenary meeting of the General Assembly and in the course of his remarks made a point of expressing his views on disarmament. He observed that for nearly five years, two commissions had been working on the problem of disarmament and although their efforts had not resulted in agreement among the major powers, they had brought into clearer focus the following three principles upon which any successful disarmament plan must rest:

> First, the plan must include all kinds of weapons. Outlawing any particular kind of weapon is not enough. The conflict in Korea bears tragic witness to the fact that aggression, whatever the weapons used, brings frightful destruction.
>
> Second, the plan must be based on unanimous agreement. A majority of nations is not enough. No plan of disarmament can work unless it includes every nation having substantial armed forces. One-sided disarmament is a sure invitation to aggression.
>
> Third, the plan must be fool-proof. Paper promises are not enough. Disarmament must be based on safeguards which will insure the compliance of all nations. The safeguards must be adequate to give immediate warning of any threatened violation. Disarmament must be policed continuously and thoroughly. It must be founded upon free and open interchange of information across national borders.

Mr Truman then stated that useful work had been done by the two disarmament commissions but suggested that the United Nations could explore ways in which the work of these two commissions could now be brought more closely together. One suggestion, he thought, might be to combine their work into a new and consolidated disarmament commission. In response to this suggestion, the Assembly appointed a Committee of Twelve, composed of the members of the Security Council plus Canada 'to consider and report to the next regular session of the General Assembly' on ways and means whereby the work of the two commissions could be combined.

The statement of Mr. Truman represented an obvious shift from the position heretofore adopted by the United States. Up to 1950 the United States had refused to discuss the reduction and regulation of both atomic and conventional weapons at the same time. Undoubtedly, the President was motivated by certain political considerations in his change of policy, since suggestions for disarmament are always welcome at home and abroad, particularly in times of international tension. Probably the shift in position represented an attempt to gain favor with other members of the United Nations by appearing at least to accede to a point of view which the Soviets had defended as one of great importance for several years. The Korean War was proving the usefulness of conventional weapons and the need for their regulation. The Soviet peace offensive through the Stockholm Appeal had placed the United States on the defensive. The Western Allies of the United States were becoming uneasy over what they believed was a growing militarism among American leaders. They could be calmed to a certain extent by a fresh appeal for disarmament. Above all, the fact that the USSR had exploded an atomic device meant the end of the United States monopoly and, consequently, made obsolete much of the plan originally proposed before the Atomic Energy Commission by Mr. Baruch.

Acceding to the recommendation of the Committee of Twelve, the General Assembly created the Disarmament Commission on January 11, 1952. Composed of the members of the Security Council plus Canada, it was to report both to the Council and the Assembly, guided by the following principles:

(a) In a system of guaranteed disarmament there must be progressive disclosure and verification on a continuing basis of all armed forces — including para-military, security and police forces — and all armaments including atomic;

(b) Such verification must be based on effective international inspection to insure the adequacy and accuracy of the information disclosed; this inspection to be carried out in accordance with the decisions of the international control organ (or organs) to be established;

(c) The Commission shall be ready to consider any proposals or plans for control that may be put forward involving either conventional armaments or atomic energy. Unless a better or no less effective system is devised, the United Nations' plan for the international control of atomic energy and the prohibition of atomic weapons should continue to serve as the basis for the international control of atomic energy to insure the prohibition of atomic weapons and the use of atomic energy for peaceful purposes.

(d) There must be an adequate system of safeguards to insure observance of the disarmament program, so as to provide for the prompt detection of violators while at the same time causing the minimum degree of interference in the internal life of each country.

(e) The treaty (or treaties) shall specifically be open to all States, for signature and ratification or adherence. The treaty (or treaties) shall provide what States must become parties thereto before the treaty (or treaties) shall enter into force.

The Commission was directed to formulate plans for the establishment of an international control organ within the framework of the Security

Council to insure the implementation of the treaty (or treaties). It was also instructed 'to consider from the outset plans for progressive and continuing disclosure and verification . . . , to determine how over-all limits and restrictions on all armed forces and all armaments can be calculated and fixed,' and to consider methods according to which states by negotiation among themselves can agree upon the determination of these limits and 'the allocation within their respective national military establishments of the permitted national armed forces and armaments.'

Activities of the Disarmament Commission and Its Subcommittee. In the years since the establishment of the Disarmament Commission, a great number of complicated proposals covering virtually every aspect of arms reduction and control have been studied. The shift in the positions adopted by East and West has been striking and a partial agreement in principle on certain matters has taken place. Constantly in the forefront of the lengthy discussions, although not always prominently mentioned, is the close relationship between certain disarmament proposals and the adjustment of major political problems of Europe and the Far East.

The impasse which had persisted in earlier disarmament discussions characterized the proceedings of the Commission in 1952 and 1953. The positions adopted by East and West can be illustrated by a brief examination of the working paper submitted in 1952 by Britain, France, and the United States for establishing the numerical limitations on all armed forces. It was pointed out by these three states that political, demographic, geographic, and economic factors had to be considered, as well as Charter responsibilities, in arriving at any ceiling on limitations. No automatic formula could be applied in all cases. The tripartite proposal stated that the objective should be to reduce the possibility and fear of any disequilibrium of power which might be dangerous to international peace and security. The suggested ceilings for the five major powers were as follows: between 1,000,000 and 1,500,000 each for the United States, China, and the Soviet Union, and between 700,000 and 800,000 for Britain and France. Ceilings for other nations would be established in relation to those for the major powers. The three sponsors stated that reductions in armed forces such as these would facilitate the elimination of weapons of mass destruction and the adoption of a system of controls for atomic energy. The representative of the United States observed, however, that the proposed ceilings depended upon a settlement of the Korean War and indications of progress toward the establishment of peaceful international relations.

The Soviet representative, Mr. Malik, immediately denounced the entire tripartite proposal and paraded the usual objections. They included the failure to prohibit bacterial warfare and other weapons of mass destruction. The proposal, it was claimed, sought only 'to maintain and legalize inflated armed forces, particularly air and naval forces.' Mr. Malik also pointed out that there was no explanation of the distribution of armed forces among the various services nor limits on their armaments. The proposals did not offer any concrete reduction in armed forces but only arbitrary ceilings. He then urged the now timeworn formula of a one-third over-all reduction in the armaments and armed forces of the major powers. Efforts by the Commission to convince Mr. Malik that the proposal was a genuine beginning toward disarmament were fruitless. France presented suggestions regarding the schedule and timetable that would give effect to the program of disarmament but to no avail.

At the eighth session of the Assembly in 1953, however, two developments of note were recorded. One was the recommendation, implemented in April, 1954, that the Disarmament Commission establish a Subcommittee consisting of 'the powers principally concerned' (Canada, France, the United Kingdom, the United States, and the USSR) 'to seek in private an acceptable solution' to the many problems of disarmament. To facilitate the work of the Subcommittee, the Assembly proposed that it hold its private meetings when appropriate in the different countries most concerned with the problem.

The other was the dramatic statement before the Assembly made by President Eisenhower on December 8, 1953, surveying the dangers of atomic warfare and urging the need for continued negotiation toward an acceptable system of controls. He endorsed the idea of private conversations in the proposed subcommittee and stated that in the discussions of this group the United States would work toward the transfer of atomic energy from military to peaceful purposes. Mr. Eisenhower then introduced a startling approach to the question in these words:

> The governments principally involved, to the extent permitted by elementary prudence, should begin now and continue to make joint contributions from their stockpiles of normal uranium and fissionable materials to an international atomic energy agency. We should expect that such an agency would be set up under the aegis of the United Nations. The ratios of contributions, the procedures and other details would properly be within the scope of 'private conversations' I referred to earlier.
>
> The United States is prepared to undertake these explorations in good faith. Any partner of the United States acting in the same good faith will find the United States a not unreasonable or ungenerous associate.
>
> Undoubtedly, initial and early contributions to this plan would be small in quantity. However, the proposal has the great virtue that it can be undertaken without the irritation and mutual suspicions incident to any attempt to set up a completely acceptable system of world-wide inspection and control.

The Subcommittee first met in London from May 13 to June 22. The atomic energy pool suggested by President Eisenhower was followed up separately, outside the Subcommittee. Three problems, none of them new, persisted throughout the discussions: (1) the timing of prohibition in relation to the reduction of armaments and the establishment of controls; (2) the method by which conventional armaments could be reduced; and (3) the type of international controls which should be adopted.

All accepted the view that there should be one comprehensive agreement which should include questions of limitation, prohibition, reduction, and control. But the Soviets still insisted that controls should come after the initial prohibition of weapons, a position which the other powers had been resisting for years. The West maintained that reductions in conventional armaments should be made by stages which would bring the armaments and armed forces of the major powers into greater balance. The Soviets, however, continued to hold out for a one-third or major reduction within one year. On the matter of controls, nothing startlingly new was offered by either side except for diplomatic indications, particularly by the United States, that the non-Soviet members were now prepared for some modifications in the United Nations plan for atomic control. For example, the question of ownership of facilities by an international authority was quietly dropped and a less rigid system of punishment was hinted at.

On June 11, 1954, France and the United Kingdom submitted a memorandum on timing and staging which, although unacceptable to the USSR at the time, proved to be of value during the debate on disarmament at the General Assembly in the fall. Three phases were outlined: (1) the establishment and setting up of a control organ, during which time military expenditures and manpower would be frozen at specific levels; (2) when the control organ became fully operative, the first half of an agreed reduction of armed forces, conventional weapons and military expenditures would be carried out and further manufacture of nuclear weapons would be prohibited; and (3) when this had been done, the second half of agreed reductions and the total prohibition and elimination of nuclear weapons would go into effect. Since the Soviet delegate now agreed to use this proposal as a basis for further discussion in the deliberations of the Disarmament Commission and its Subcommittee, a number of Assembly delegates believed that the atmosphere of distrust and suspicion was slowly clearing. The Assembly President, Dr. E. N. Van Kleffens of the Netherlands, reflected this sentiment with the guarded observation that 'the possibility has now been opened to make progress with regard to disarmament.'

The year 1955 was marked by two lengthy meetings of the Subcommittee in the spring and early fall. In between there occurred the historic meeting at Geneva from July 18 to 23 when the Chiefs of State from France, the United Kingdom, the United States, and the USSR met to discuss the problems, including disarmament, which had been dividing East and West since 1945.

The discussions in the Subcommittee in 1955 and the exchange of views at Geneva were of the greatest significance and have been in the forefront of all succeeding disarmament negotiations. These cardinal points can be noted:

1. Stockpiles of atomic weapons and fuel produced in the past could no longer be detected with full, or even sufficient, accuracy by any known method of inspection, however complete and all-embracing the inspection might be in theory. The Soviet Union was the first, on May 10, 1955, to acknowledge that nuclear production could be carried on undetected, and the United States in August and September, 1955, was the first to draw the logical conclusion that existing bombs would have to remain indefinitely in national stockpiles.

2. Since nuclear weapons are going to remain in national stockpiles, the problem is to prevent their use and to guard against surprise attack. The USSR first proposed, on May 10, 1955, an early-warning system, based upon ground inspection through control posts within the territory of all states concerned to determine the existence of dangerous concentrations of military forces.

3. The United States in the fall of 1955 expanded this proposed warning system, improving upon ground inspection and adding the idea of unrestricted but monitored aerial reconaissance between the United States and the Soviet Union. The United States also proposed that the two countries exchange blueprints of military establishments.

4. The Soviet Union abandoned the formula of one-third reduction in armed force levels and tentatively suggested those first proposed by the West in 1952. The United States thereupon dropped its insistence on numerical ceilings and the 1952 levels and concentrated its disarmament negotiations on aerial and ground inspection.

5. The geographical concept of arms limitation was advocated chiefly by the British at Geneva. Sir Anthony Eden approached both armaments and the principal political problem of Europe simultaneously by suggesting the reunification of Germany, but with the Eastern zone demilitarized or without garrisoning troops of any nation. Coupled with this demilitarization would go mutual inspection and control, by integrated, international inspection teams, limited at first to the geographical area of Germany, and extending later, possibly, to other areas of Europe. A control organ would

have the right to make use of aerial reconnaissance in addition to ground inspection through control posts.

The General Assembly made a careful study of these ideas and after a lengthy debate, adopted a resolution late in December, 1955, which urged the states concerned to continue their efforts to arrive at a comprehensive plan for disarmament. The resolution provided that priority should be given to President Eisenhower's aerial inspection proposal, the Soviet plan for control posts, and 'such measures of adequately safeguarded disarmament as are now feasible.' Inclusion of this latter provision was a rebuke to the United States for placing all its emphasis on inspection and virtually none on arms reduction. Such an approach was referred to as 'inspection without disarmament' and was thoroughly unpopular with most of the rest of the world. The resolution, in effect, was not so much of an endorsement of the Eisenhower plan as it was a rescue operation by the United States, thereby saving itself from a much more severe rebuke. At the same time, probably the most significant aspect of the 1955 disarmament discussions was the beginning of efforts to provide for an early-warning system. This has been the core of negotiations since that time.

During the spring of 1956, the Subcommittee reconvened for nearly two months of discussion and the full Commission met for two weeks in July to discuss the report of the Subcommittee. At its July session, the Commission adopted a resolution by ten votes to one (USSR), with one abstention (Yugoslavia), which requested the Subcommittee to continue its efforts and noted that the following Western six-point declaration, first introduced on May 4 before the Subcommittee, 'sets forth the principles upon which an effective program for the regulation and limitation of all arms and armed forces can be based':

1. disarmament must proceed by stages, with progress from one stage to another depending upon the satisfactory completion of the preceding stage and upon the development of confidence through the settlement of major political problems;

2. the program should begin with reductions of armed forces to levels feasible in the present unsettled world conditions, with further reductions as world conditions improved.

3. under proper safeguards, the program must provide appropriate stages for stopping the build-up of stockpiles of nuclear weapon fuel and devoting all future production of nuclear material to peaceful uses, with a provision for imposing limitations upon the testing of nuclear weapons;

4. the program must provide for a strong control organization with inspection rights, including aerial reconnaissance, with the control measures providing particularly against major surprise attack;

5. preliminary demonstration of inspection methods on a limited scale to help develop an effective control system; and

6. provision to be made for the suspension of the program if a major state fails to carry out its obligations or if a threat to the peace, a breach of the peace or an act of aggression should occur.

Differences between East and West continued over how much disarmament could go into the early stages or phases of any plan, what provision would be made for transition from one phrase to the next, and what the final force levels would be. The USSR argued that a transition from one stage to another should be automatic, claiming that to make disarmament dependent upon the solution of political problems was 'no disarmament at all.' The way to disarm was 'simply to disarm,' Mr. Gromyko stated repeatedly. The search for an early-warning system continued and although the USSR refused to endorse aerial inspection during the Commission or Subcommittee deliberations, a Soviet proposal was introduced during November, 1956, at the eleventh session of the General Assembly, which suggested an 'open skies' plan limited to a European zone separating East and West. This, of course, was similar to the Eden plan of 1955. The French representative had made a similar suggestion during the 1956 Subcommittee discussions and the United States broadly hinted at the time that a modification of the original plan for aerial inspection might be feasible as a precondition for disarmament.

A significant point was developed during the year which concerned the build-up of stockpiles of nuclear weapon fuel. The important thing, as was emphasized by the United States, was to freeze present stockpiles of fuel. Past production of such fuel could not be detected but current production could be. If future production of fuel were prohibited, the result would be that no 'fourth countries' (other than the United States, Britain, and the USSR) could build any bombs.

More important than all previous disarmament negotiations were those which developed during 1957. The year began with a statement made by Mr. Lodge of the United States during the January 14 meeting of the General Assembly. He emphasized that his country was ready to take any steps toward arms reduction provided that they were subject to adequate inspection. He made proposals which outlined the following main objectives: (1) to reduce the trend toward larger stockpiles of nuclear weapons and to reduce the future nuclear threat; (2) to provide against large-scale surprise attack and thereby reduce the danger of a major war; (3) to lessen the burden of armaments and to make possible improved living standards; (4) to ease tensions among nations and to facilitate the settlement of important political issues; and (5) to ensure that research and development activities concerning the propulsion of objects through outer space would be devoted to scientific and peaceful purposes. This fifth point was the first mention of the need to control guided missiles and Mr. Lodge proposed that the testing of such objects should be placed under international inspection with provision made for international participation.

The Subcommittee resumed its discussions in March on a restrained note of optimism. Almost from the start, to the surprise of the West, it appeared that the Soviet delegation was intent upon serious negotiation. On April 26, Mr. Zorin of the USSR handed the American delegate, Mr. Stassen, a document, subsequently published on April 30, which required the most serious consideration, since the Soviet Union accepted, for the first time, the principle of aerial inspection of Russian territory as well as parts of Europe and the United States. All of the United States west of the Mississippi River plus Alaska would be opened to Soviet reconnaissance. This would embrace an area of 2,770,000 square miles containing the principle centers of United States aircraft industry and major air and naval bases. In return, 2,730,000 square miles of Soviet controlled territory would be opened to Western aerial inspection. The area would comprise a narrow belt along Russia's western border and the Siberian tundras of Soviet Asia. Most of the heavily industrialized region of Eastern Russia would be excluded. The plan would also apply to the bulk of Western Europe and the East European satellites.

Also included were suggestions for the restricted use of rocket missiles, the public renunciation of the use of nuclear weapons with negotiation on their liquidation to follow, a first stage reduction in force levels similar to those proposed by the West in meetings of the Subcommittee (United States, USSR, and Red China 2.5 million each; Britain and France 750,000 each), and a 15 percent cut in defense budgets and conventional armaments. It was further proposed to establish inspection posts at strategic points in the eastern half of the United States and in Russia's western border regions to watch over disarmament. These posts would be under Security Council supervision and therefore all of their activities would be subject to the veto. Two familiar proposals of the past which the West had been unable to accept, namely a complete elimination of nuclear weapons and liquidation of all foreign bases, were abandoned. Another encouraging sign was the acknowledgment that the Soviets would be satisfied with a limited agreement to begin with, a view which came close to the United States position that progress must come step by step rather than by an immediate and sweeping arrangement.

In June, the USSR proposed that all nuclear tests be halted for a period of two to three years. An international commission would observe how the agreement was being carried out and report on its findings to the Security Council and the General Assembly. Control posts, suitably equipped with scientific apparatus, would be set up in the United States, Russia, Britain, 'and the Pacific area' for the observation of the projected agreement on the ending of nuclear tests.

Faced with what appeared to be a more conciliatory Soviet approach, the United States re-examined its own position and, supported by Britain, Canada, and France, submitted six partial measures as a first step in disarmament. Rejected by the Soviet Union, causing still another deadlock in the Subcommittee, the plan was nevertheless endorsed by the Twelfth Assembly in November, 1957, and can be summarized as follows:

(1) the immediate suspension of testing of nuclear weapons with prompt installation of effective international control, including inspection posts equipped with appropriate scientific instruments located within the territories of Britain, Pacific Ocean areas, the United States, the USSR, and other points as required;

(2) the cessation of production of fissionable materials for weapons purposes and the complete devotion of future production of fissionable materials to peaceful purposes under effective international control;

(3) the reduction of stocks of nuclear weapons through a program of transfer of stocks of fissionable material from weapons to peaceful uses;

(4) reduction of armed forces and armaments with adequate safeguards;

(5) the progressive establishment of open inspection with ground and aerial components to guard against the possibility of surprise attack;

(6) joint study of an inspection system designed to ensure that the sending of objects through outer space will be exclusively for peaceful and scientific purposes.

The Twelfth Assembly adopted two additional resolutions on disarmament in 1957. One called for a world-wide information campaign under United Nations auspices to make people aware of the necessity for reaching an accord on disarmament. The other enlarged the Disarmament Commission by the addition of fourteen members. Resumption of negotiations by the Subcommittee on the basis of the Western six-point plan was also recommended. The Soviet Union objected to the revised composition of the Disarmament Commission, claiming that it should comprise all eighty-two members of the United Nations. The Soviets also announced that they would no longer participate in the deliberations of either the Subcommittee or the Commission as they were then constituted.

Despite this impasse in the Assembly and the failure of negotiations in the Subcommittee in 1957, there were some fairly wide areas of agreement between the West and the USSR. Both sides had reached agreement on what should be done. Ostensibly, at least, they wanted to stop experiments with nuclear bombs, control nuclear weapons, reduce conventional armaments, and accomplish something with respect to long-range missiles and upper-air satellites, under at least some system of control. But the question that plagued both the Subcommittee and the Assembly was precisely how these things should be done — and when, and in what pattern. Fundamentally, the differences turned around the old question of 'verification and control' — the establishment of some system to guarantee the observance of whatever conventions on disarmament were signed.

It should be remembered, nevertheless, that both the USSR and the West were finding it increasingly difficult to stand the economic strain of the armaments race. Both sides felt vulnerable and threatened at this stage in the evolution of armaments. The USSR had become vulnerable to an attack by missiles against which there was no defense. Fully conscious of the immense productive capacity of the United States, the Soviets would welcome some respite from the competitive race to improve upon and expand existing weapon stockpiles. The United States, in turn, with the memory of Pearl Harbor not yet dimmed, was fearful of surprise attack. Emphasis on aerial and ground inspection was a reflection of the American desire to eliminate the secrecy behind which a surprise attack could be launched. In this situation, it was reasoned that it might be worthwhile to engage in partial cutbacks and designate or offer some of America's western territory for inspection in return for Siberian areas which probably could reveal a surprise attack, at least until such time as the long-range bomber is outmoded by the very long-range (5000-mile) missile.

CONCLUSIONS

Effective, adequate disarmament depends primarily upon the development of a climate of trust and mutual understanding among the major powers. The long history of the efforts to achieve some reduction in arms has proved this fact time and time again. The Disarmament Conference in the early 1930's failed because there was no true spirit of compromise supported by a world public opinion free of distrust and suspicion. Despite United Nations peace-making machinery, the confidence and goodwill of its strongest members has not risen to that level that will permit a genuine acceptance of an adequate regulation of armaments.

Disarmament results from the processes of diplomacy and although an international organization can provide the institutional framework for discussion and debate, any final agreement reached depends upon the willingness of the parties concerned to negotiate. What has emerged from more than a decade of deliberation and recrimination in the councils of the United Nations is the recognition of the need to reduce tensions which have spread alarmingly in the nuclear age. This has been especially true since

1955. Such an approach centers around the idea of inspection, aerial and ground, to prevent the use of nuclear weapons and eliminate the possibility of a devastating surprise attack.

The problem faced particularly by the United States in 1958 concerns the political risks which may outweigh the political and economic advantages involved in any relaxation of tensions. If, for example, there is an agreement to limit armaments before the great political issues of Europe and the Far East are settled, the result may be, in effect, to accept the present division of the world. When armaments are fixed as to size and use, does this not mean the virtual guarantee of existing military boundaries between East and West? In turn, would not this situation remove the pressure on the USSR for the reunification of Germany and the evacuation of the Red Army from Eastern Europe? Relaxation of tensions in Europe would not only contribute to the demand of the NATO partners for a reduction of their military establishments but also lend support to those in the Congress of the United States who would cut the military and foreign aid expenditures. Furthermore, should some limited inspection arrangement be negotiated in the form of a treaty, what would be the reaction in the United States Senate to a provision which would permit Soviet aerial reconnaissance over American territory? Finally, there is the compelling problem of the possible need for the regulation of earth satellites. The American and Soviet satellites are now loaded with radio equipment. But in the future, there may be endless possibilities for the military use of these remarkable man-made astral bodies. Yet the United States has committed itself to negotiate, mindful of the risks, and the outcome of future disarmament deliberations may well have results of the greatest significance for the postwar world.

10

THE RULE OF LAW

JUDICIAL settlement as a means of resolving conflicts between states has long been a dream of mankind. From earliest times men have sought to judge one another and to punish those adjudged guilty of certain acts. Originally it was the individual who attempted to determine the validity of his fellow's actions but gradually there developed the custom of delegating to a specially designated person, often a chieftain or priest, the duty of making the decision on behalf of the group, the village, or the tribe. Judicial institutions, consisting of disinterested judges meting out punishment on the basis of accepted standards of justice, were the inevitable result of this gradual process of support for judicial settlement of disputed claims and errant acts. It was only natural that men should attempt to apply these practices to the relations between nations, the latter being, in essence, collections of individuals.

Arbitration represents the most common form of judicial settlement between states and can be traced back to the days of ancient Greece. Although falling into disuse during the supremacy of Rome, it returned to new life from the twelfth until the seventeenth century particularly among the princes of Switzerland and Italy. The Jay Treaty between the United States and England at the close of the eighteenth century brought arbitral processes to the fore again and wide use was made of them through the nineteenth century down to the First World War. With the League of Nations came a new development, namely the establishment of the Permanent Court of International Justice, which marked a departure from the more customary resort to arbitration. A court is of a more permanent nature than arbitration by individual states and can establish a consistent system of jurisprudence.

The belief in a world court has ancient origins but probably the most insistent demand for such an institution has come from the United States. The Massachusetts Senate as early as February, 1832, voted that 'some method should be established for the amicable and final adjustment of all international disputes.'[1] The United States Supreme Court, it was urged then and later, could be the model for a world institution to adjust international conflicts. Judicial settlement between the several states of the Union became successful and there has always been the belief that such a practice would also prove successful among nations. Many contend that the first world court, born in 1922, was the product of American thinking and the effectiveness of the United States Supreme Court. A leading Philadelphia publisher stated in 1925:

> The World Court is essentially our idea. We proclaimed it for years. We argued for it; we labored for it and finally it was worked out very largely by the best American brains. It is of American origin. It came into world consciousness because of American initiative; it is American in its conception and in its reflection of our strong national belief in courts of justice.[2]

People in all countries have supported the idea of applying judicial settlement to international relations whenever they have come to recognize the position and the innate strength of a dominant court system. The appeal of judicial settlement comes in large part from the nature and characteristics of a court. The procedure of a court, functioning as it does in public, hearing witnesses, supplying evidence, weighing the arguments of the contending parties, and evaluating the law, generally accepted facts, legal principles, and previous court decisions as they may apply to the case at hand has a basic appeal for those who seek order and justice in international relations. The decision reached by a court is final and represents a reasoned determination of the facts and the application of the law to them. What better method, it is argued, could be devised to adjust international conflicts than this, where legal principles weighed in the dignified atmosphere of the courtroom are substituted for the destructive implements of the battlefield?

Unfortunately, the application to international affairs of judicial settlement as understood and applied within states is not as simple as many of its advocates contend. A universal set of rules must first be adopted by all peoples to serve as a basis for determining the validity of a claim or the illegality of an act. All peoples, through their governments, must agree not only to be bound by these rules but by the judgment of the world tribunal which applies them. Then there must be the means of enforcing the judgment which lies beyond the scope of the court. This is the responsibility of a strong executive institution, for an impotent executive will reduce if not destroy the effectiveness of judicial action. The universal rules to be

---

[1] Quoted in Fleming, D. F., *The United States and the World Court,* Garden City, 1945, p. 15.
[2] Quoted in Fleming, op. cit. p. 23.

applied must be constantly examined to determine their validity and appropriateness in relation to changing conditions with the passage of time. This is the job of the legislative organ, representative of all peoples and shades of opinion. Thus, the judicial arm, to be fully effective in resolving disputes and reducing tensions, cannot exist in a vacuum. It must be supported by other co-ordinate organs possessing universal support and respect. As we shall see, the process of judicial settlement can do much to bring about justice in legal matters where the parties desire a settlement without resort to force. Where important political questions are involved, however, judicial settlement has failed to make much headway, primarily because the many nation-states of the world have been unwilling to construct and then place their faith in the required executive and legislative organs which are the necessary partners of the judiciary. In addition, judicial settlement is not considered suitable for many political questions.

PRECEDENTS FOR THE INTERNATIONAL COURT OF JUSTICE

The Permanent Court of Arbitration. As we have just noted, arbitration, once used widely as a means of amicable settlement by the Greeks, was gradually utilized to an increasing degree in the late eighteenth and the nineteenth centuries. A century and more of experiment with it was climaxed in 1899 by the establishment of the Permanent Court of Arbitration. Prior to that date, although there had been a growing number of treaties calling for limited arbitration, a multilateral treaty providing for general arbitration by a large number of states had never been adopted. The Convention of 1899, drawn up at the first Hague Peace Conference, was signed by twenty-six states and declared that:

> With the object of facilitating an immediate recourse to arbitration for international differences, which it has not been possible to settle by diplomacy, the Signatory Powers undertake to organize a Permanent Court of Arbitration, accessible at all times and operating, unless otherwise stipulated by the parties, in accordance with the Rules of Procedure inserted in the present Convention.

The Convention of 1907, adopted at the second Hague Conference, modified the earlier convention to a certain extent; both serve as the legal framework for the activities of the Court. Over forty states, as of 1958, still remain members of the Court.

Although efforts were put forward in 1907 to make it so, the Court is not a permanent institution despite its name. It is actually a panel of arbitrators who may be called upon to act as an arbitral tribunal. Its members serve only for six years and it has no regular sessions. In fact, it is really not a court because it meets only when a dispute arises and some of its members are selected to adjudicate it. The panel of arbitrators is composed of those designated by the signatories. Each nation may appoint up to four judges on the panel who must be 'of known competency in questions of international law, of the highest moral reputation, and disposed to accept the duties of arbitrator.' A Permanent Administrative Council to look after budgetary and administrative matters consists of the diplomatic representatives of the signatory states accredited to The Hague. It is presided over by the Netherlands Minister of Foreign Affairs and is located at The Hague. There is also an International Bureau at the same location composed of Dutch nationals which maintains the records of the Court and acts as a channel of communication with signatory states who finance these services for the Court.

The Hague Court has not been called upon since 1940 and prior to that date was utilized only twenty-three times, all but six of them before 1914. It has not had much influence in the development of law and has suffered from lack of support and inadequate authority. Yet it served as a precedent for the Permanent Court of International Justice which was able to profit from the limited success which the Hague Court had enjoyed before 1914.

The Central American Court of International Justice. Meeting a few weeks after adjournment of the second Hague Conference was the Central American Peace Conference of 1907. It established the Central American Court which lasted only ten years. The Court was composed of five judges, one appointed by each of the five Central American states for five year terms. The Convention establishing the Court bound the several countries to submit to it 'all controversies which may arise among them, of whatsoever nature and no matter what their origin might be, in case the respective Departments of Foreign Affairs should not have been able to reach an understanding.' Elsewhere the Convention provided that

> . . . this court shall take cognizance of the questions which individuals of one Central American country may raise against any of the other contracting governments, because of the violation of treaties or conventions, and other cases of an international character, no matter whether their own government supports said claim or not; and provided that the remedies which the laws of the respective countries provide against such violations shall have been exhausted or that denial of justice shall have been shown.

During its lifetime, the Central American Court heard ten cases, the final one in 1917 involving the Bryan-Chamorro Treaty between the United

States and Nicaragua. The refusal of the United States to accept the ruling of the Court that the treaty was illegal undoubtedly was influential in the decision not to continue the Court beyond the ten-year period for which it had been created. In 1923, the Court was recreated for another ten years with greatly reduced authority but no cases were ever brought before it.

The Permanent Court of International Justice. During the First World War a number of unofficial plans were conceived for an international organization to keep the peace and several embraced the idea of an international court. Such ideas were prevalent in the Scandinavian countries, the Netherlands, and the United States. The American Society for the Judicial Settlement of Disputes had been organized in 1910. In New York a World's Court League published a magazine called *The World Court* from 1915 to 1919.

However, few official plans by the end of 1918 contained clear statements on the provision for a court. But after the Paris Conference got underway, there developed an increasing sentiment in favor of some form of permanent tribunal. By the time the Commission on the League of Nations began its work on February 3, 1919, it had before it various official drafts which included references to a court. Suggestions from belligerent and neutral sources were also under consideration. The German and Austrian delegations, for example, submitted proposals which would establish a court and confer upon it compulsory jurisdiction in international disputes and a limited jurisdiction in disputes involving private persons.

The final draft of the Covenant incorporated a provision for a Permanent Court of International Justice but did not include a statement covering its competence and jurisdiction. It was believed that a Peace Conference, consisting of statesmen and diplomatists, did not possess the qualifications or the time necessary to devise so complex an institution as the court. This was a task which could only be successfully accomplished by jurists. Consequently, the framers of the Covenant contented themselves by defining specifically the four classes of disputes 'generally suitable for submission to arbitration' and imposed the obligation on members of the League to arbitrate such disputes and accept arbitral awards in good faith (Art. 13).[3] Then, in Article 14, it was provided that:

> The Council shall formulate and submit to the members of the League for adoption such plans for the establishment of a Permanent Court of International Justice. The Court shall be competent to hear and determine any dis-

[3] Listed in Article 13 as suitable for submission to arbitration were disputes 'as to the interpretation of a treaty, as to the question of international law, as to the existence of any fact which if established would constitute a breach of any international obligation, or as to the extent and nature of the reparation to be made for any such breach.'

pute of an international character which the parties thereto submit to it. The Court may also give an advisory opinion upon any dispute or question referred to it by the Council or the Assembly.

The League Council went to work on the problem immediately after it was organized. At its second session held in London on February 12, 1920, a report on the subject made by Léon Bourgeois was studied and it was decided to establish an Advisory Committee of Jurists to prepare and report to the Council plans for the creation of the court. The Committee consisted of ten experts who served in their private capacity from the following countries: Belgium, Brazil, Britain, France, Italy, Japan, Norway, Spain, the Netherlands, and the United States. It held a total of thirty-five meetings, the first of which took place in the Peace Palace at The Hague on June 16, 1920. As a special delegate from the Council, Léon Bourgeois addressed the first meeting of the Committee. In these words he foresaw a court which was to prove both an innovation and a success:

> The Court of Justice must be a true Permanent Court. It is not simply a question of arbitrators chosen on a particular occasion, in the case of conflict, by the interested parties; it is a small number of judges sitting constantly and receiving a mandate the duration of which will enable the establishment of a real jurisprudence, who will administer justice. This permanence is a symbol. It will be a seat raised in the midst of the nations, where judges are always present, to whom can always be brought the appeal of the weak and to whom protests against the violation of right can be addressed. Chosen not by reason of the state of which they are citizens, but by reason of their personal authority, of their past career, of the respect which attaches to their names known over the whole world, these judges will represent a truly international spirit which is by no means, as some pretend, a negation of the legitimate interests of each nation, but which is, on the contrary, the safeguard of these interests, within the very limits of their legitimacy.

Assisted greatly by the League Secretariat, the Committee submitted a draft statute to the Council on July 30, 1920. After adopting certain amendments, the Council referred the Statute to the League Assembly where, in December, 1920, a resolution was passed which called upon the members of the League to ratify it. On September 21, 1921, twenty-one of the forty-one signatories had deposited ratifications and the Statute came into force. Although a total of fifty-one of the fifty-nine signatories had ratified the Statute by 1942, the United States never did. Eighteen states had ceased to be members of the League, but five of them continued as members of the Court.

The Court first met in January, 1922, and annual sessions were held until 1936 when the Statute was amended to provide for continuous sessions. Sessions were terminated in 1940 by the Second World War although one final meeting took place in October, 1945, when administrative questions were considered in preparation for the transfer of archives and other properties to the new Court.

During its twenty years of existence, the Permanent Court of International Justice took under consideration sixty-five new cases and handed down thirty-two judgments and twenty-seven advisory opinions. A total of 550 international treaties were concluded during these years which conferred a jurisdiction on the Court. These treaties represented a large portion of the world law of the day. The cases before it were of great variety in the problems which they involved but all were of some importance. Some of them concerned the vital interests of states and were the type of case which states previously had refused to submit to arbitration on the grounds of infringement on the national honor. The methods and procedure adopted by the Court received widespread approval, both professional and nonprofessional. At no time did a state refuse to accept its judgment or opinion. Certainly this attests to its impartiality and thoroughness as well as its care not to exceed its jurisdiction. International law itself has been influenced by the jurisprudence of the Court. Its judgments, opinions, and orders have received worldwide attention and have provided direction to the theory and practice of international law. Its influence has been felt particularly in the extension of the law relating to pacific settlement of disputes.

In no specific case did the Court prevent war but it contributed, more than any other international institution, to a broadening of the reign of law. Through its advisory opinions it greatly facilitated the working of international organizations. Unquestionably an influence was exercised upon the resolving of disputes which never came before it. Settlement by direct negotiation commonly is the result of the existence of a court to which one of the parties may appeal if negotiations are not entered into or fail. Finally, and probably the greatest testament to its over-all worth as a useful legal appendage to an international organization, the new Court of the United Nations is virtually a replica of the old Permanent Court.[4] The organization and process of both are so similar that they can be discussed together.

THE INTERNATIONAL COURT OF JUSTICE

It was agreed at Dumbarton Oaks that the United Nations should have a court but no decision was reached upon the question of creating a new

[4] For a detailed comparison of both courts, see Hudson, Manley O., 'The Twenty-fourth Year of the World Court,' *American Journal of International Law*, Vol. 40, No. 1 (January 1946), pp. 1–52.

court or continuing the Permanent Court of the League. In March, 1945, soon after the Yalta Conference, the United States issued invitations to the United Nations to send representatives to a meeting of jurists that was to prepare a draft statute for the future court. This task was completed during April after, as stated in the report of the Committee, it had

> proceeded to a revision, article by article, of the Statute of the Permanent Court of International Justice. This revision consisted, on the one hand, in the effecting of certain adaptations of form rendered necessary by the substitution of the United Nations for the League of Nations; on the other hand, in the introduction of certain changes judged desirable and now possible.

The Committee of Jurists, however, came to no decision on whether or not there should be a new court or the manner of nominating candidates for election as judges.

At the San Francisco Conference, Committee 1 of Commission IV considered the draft submitted by the Committee of Jurists for several weeks. It completed a draft of the articles that later became Articles 92 to 96 of the Charter and made some revisions in the draft statute for the Court. The same committee had to recommend a decision on the question of whether to establish a new court or continue with the old. Without at any time being critical of the Permanent Court, the Committee decided upon a new court for these reasons:

> After balancing the advantages to be gained and the objections to be overcome in the adoption of either course, the First Committee decided to recommend the establishment of a new Court. This course recommended itself . . . as more in keeping with the provisions proposed for inclusion in the Charter, under which all members of the Organization will *ipso facto* be parties to the Statute and other states not members of the Organization may become parties to the Statute only on conditions to be laid down in each case by the General Assembly upon the recommendation of the Security Council. Some of the members of the First Committee regarded the maintenance of these provisions as essential to the acceptability of the Charter and the Statute by all members of the United Nations.
>
> Moreover, the creation of a new Court seems to be the simpler and at the same time the more expeditious course to be taken. If the Permanent Court were continued, modifications in its Statute would be required as a result of the discontinuance of the League of Nations. Only 32 of the 41 states now parties to that Statute are represented at the United Nations Conference in San Francisco, and the negotiations with the parties not thus represented . . . would encounter difficulties and might be very protracted. Moreover, a large number of states are represented at the United Nations Conference which are not parties to the 1920 Statute, and as it is not open to all of them for accession, some of them could have no part in the negotiations entailed by the process of modification. On the whole, therefore, though the creation of a new Court will involve important problems, this course seems . . . to create

fewer difficulties than would the continuance of the Permanent Court of International Justice, and it may make possible the earlier functioning of the Court of the future.

The Permanent Court of International Justice was dissolved by action of the Assembly of the United Nations on April 18, 1946. Shortly beforehand the judges of the International Court of Justice were selected by concurrent vote of the General Assembly and the Security Council. The new Court first met in April, 1946. The following month it adopted its Rules which were based upon the Rules of its predecessor.

Court Provisions in the Charter. Article 7 of the Charter states that the International Court of Justice is one of the principal organs of the United Nations. Article 92 refers to the Court as the principal judicial organ of the United Nations and states that it is to function 'in accordance with the annexed Statute, which is based upon the Statute of the Permanent Court of International Justice and forms an integral part of the present Charter.' Thus, the Court is now part of the Organization and is not separate and independent as was the case with the old Permanent Court. There is an implication in Article 92 that there might be other judicial organs, presumably of a functional or regional nature but there has been no move in this direction other than a suggestion for an international criminal court.

Unlike the situation which prevailed under the League, all members of the United Nations are, according to Article 93, automatically 'parties to the Statute of the International Court of Justice.' The question of access to the Court referred to in this Article will be discussed below.

Article 94 restates a fundamental principle of international law, namely that the parties before an international tribunal must accept its decision. Thus, all members undertake 'to comply with the decision of the International Court of Justice in any case' to which they are a party. The Statute in Article 60 repeats this principle and states that the judgment is 'final and without appeal' although Article 61 provides that the Court itself, under certain conditions, may revise a judgment. Article 94 of the Charter goes on to provide that: 'If any party to a case fails to perform the obligations incumbent upon it under a judgment rendered by the Court, the other party may have recourse to the Security Council, which may, if it deems necessary, make recommendations or decide upon measures to be taken to give effect to the judgment.' Just what the Security Council could do in such an event is not clear. However, it is quite unlikely that a state will refuse to abide by a decision of the Court, if the past practice of states is any indication for the future. The problem is not one of a state abiding by a judgment but of getting states to submit cases to an international court.

Members of the United Nations are in no way prevented by the Charter, says Article 95, 'from entrusting the solution of their differences to other tribunals by virtue of agreements already in existence or which may be concluded in the future.'

Finally, Article 96 provides that the Assembly and the Security Council may request the Court to give an advisory opinion on any legal question. An innovation is the provision in this Article that: 'Other organs of the United Nations and specialized agencies which at any time may be so authorized by the General Assembly, may also request advisory opinions of the Court on legal questions arising within the scope of their activities.' Under the League, only the Council and Assembly could request advisory opinions although the Council in several cases, particularly with respect to the International Labor Organization, requested advisory opinions from the Court on matters relevant to specialized agencies. Most of the specialized agencies of the United Nations, as well as the Trusteeship Council and the Economic and Social Council have been authorized by the General Assembly to ask for opinions on legal matters within the scope of their activities.

Access to the Court. There are three categories of states which may make use of the International Court of Justice. As has been noted, all members of the United Nations are *ipso facto* members of the Court and may avail themselves freely of its facilities.

A nonmember of the United Nations may become a party to the Statute of the Court on conditions which are determined in each case by the Assembly upon the recommendation of the Security Council. During the second part of the first session of the Assembly, a resolution was adopted in response to a Swiss inquiry concerning the conditions under which that state could become a party to the Statute. The resolution established these conditions:

> Switzerland will become a party to the Statute of the Court on the date of the deposit with the Secretary-General of the United Nations of an instrument, signed on behalf of the Government of Switzerland and ratified as may be required by Swiss constitutional law, containing:
>
> (a) Acceptance of the provisions of the Statute of the International Court of Justice;
>
> (b) Acceptance of all the obligations of a member of the United Nations under Article 94 of the Charter;
>
> (c) An undertaking to contribute to the expenses of the Court such equitable amount as the General Assembly shall assess from time to time after consultation with the Swiss Government.

Switzerland became a party to the Statute in 1948 following its acceptance of these conditions.

The third category involves states not members of the Statute who wish to make use of the Court. The Statute in Article 35:2 permits such a state access to the Court under conditions established by the Security Council.[5] In October, 1946, the Council determined that the following conditions should apply in such a situation:

> (1) . . . that such state previously have deposited with the Registrar of the Court a declaration by which it accepts the jurisdiction of the Court, in accordance with the Charter . . . and with the terms and subject to the conditions of the Statute and Rules of the Court, and undertakes to comply in good faith with the decision or decisions of the Court and to accept all the obligations of a member of the United Nations under Article 94 of the Charter.
>
> (2) Such declaration may be either particular or general. A particular declaration is one accepting the jurisdiction of the Court in respect only of a particular dispute or disputes which have already arisen. A general declaration is one accepting the jurisdiction generally in respect of all disputes or of a particular class or classes of disputes which have already arisen, or which may arise in the future.

States in this category may also accept the compulsory jurisdiction of the Court under Article 36:2 of the Statute. Any questions as to the validity or the effect of such declarations are decided by the Court.

Jurisdiction of the Court. Disputes come before the Court, as they did with the Permanent Court, only if the consent of the parties concerned has been obtained prior to or after the dispute has taken place. Such a situation would be unthinkable in a national court system. In the United States, for example, the accused in a criminal case must appear for trial. Similarly, in civil actions, when a court has had a complaint placed before it, the defendant must appear unless he wishes to be in contempt of the court and liable for severe punishment. In international affairs, however, individuals are replaced by sovereign states who are unwilling to appear in court without their consent. Compulsory jurisdiction by an international legal system is still far in the future and will remain so as long as there is the question of sovereign interests.

Disputes are referred to the Court by the parties concerned in three different ways: (1) if the parties agree to submit a dispute to the Court; (2) if both parties have agreed to the 'compulsory jurisdiction' provision of the Court's Statute and one of them refers the dispute to the Court; (3) if both parties have concluded a treaty which makes provision for utilizing the Court to resolve different interpretations of a treaty and one party submits the problem to the Court. A number of treaties, both bilateral

---

[5] Albania appeared before the Court in the Corfu Channel Case under the conditions laid down by the Security Council, since it was neither a member of the United Nations at the time or a party to the statute of the Court.

and multilateral, grant jurisdiction to the court on certain matters. For example, Article 22 of the Treaty of Peace between the Allied Powers and Japan concluded on September 8, 1951 provides that:

> If in the opinion of any Party to the present Treaty there has arisen a dispute concerning the interpretation or execution of the Treaty, which is not settled by reference to a special claims tribunal or by other agreed means, the dispute shall, at the request of any party thereto, be referred for decision to the International Court of Justice. Japan and those Allied Powers which are not already parties to the Statute . . . will deposit with the Registrar of the Court, at the time of their respective ratifications of the present Treaty, and in conformity with the resolution of the United Nations Security Council, dated October 15, 1946, a general declaration accepting the jurisdiction, without special agreement, of the Court generally in respect to all disputes of the character referred to in this Article.

An attempt was made under the League to provide a method whereby states could voluntarily agree to compulsory jurisdiction in certain instances. This was the so-called 'optional clause' in the Statute of the Permanent Court which has been continued by the United Nations. Thus, the present Statute provides in Article 36:2:

> The States parties to the present Statute may at any time declare that they recognize as compulsory, *ipso facto* and without special agreement, in relation to any other State accepting the same obligation, the jurisdiction of the Court in all legal disputes concerning,
> (a) the interpretation of a treaty;
> (b) any question of international law;
> (c) the existence of any fact which, if established, would constitute a breach of an international obligation;
> (d) the nature or extent of the reparation to be made for the breach of an international obligation.

This arrangement retains national sovereignty by leaving the decision to adhere to compulsory jurisdiction solely up to the individual members of the United Nations or those nonmembers who wish to avail themselves of the facilities of the Court. The decision to accept the optional clause is indicated when a state deposits a declaration to this effect with the Court. Each such declaration establishes the conditions surrounding the willingness of a state to agree to compulsory jurisdiction. All declarations have been made unconditionally or on the condition of reciprocity on the part of several or certain states. Some have time limits attached or contain distinct reservations. By 1957 a total of thirty-four states had accepted the compulsory jurisdiction of the Court in some form.[6] A large number

---

[6] Four cases have been brought to the Court on this basis: the *Morocco Case,* the *Anglo-Norwegian Fisheries Case,* the *Electricité de Beyrouth Company Case,* and the *Nottebohm Case.*

have made reciprocity a condition. This means that a state will not accept compulsory jurisdiction in a specific dispute unless the other party also accepts it. Most of the declarations have contained time limits, usually for five or ten years, or until a notice of termination which is normally one year.

The United States attached a strong reservation to its declaration of adherence to the compulsory jurisdiction of the Court deposited in August, 1946. The declaration was to remain in force until August 14, 1951, 'and thereafter until the expiration of six months after notice of abrogation.' The Court would not have jurisdiction in disputes concerned with the following matters, according to the declaration:

(a) disputes the solution of which the parties shall entrust to other tribunals by virtue of agreements which are already in existence or which may be concluded in the future;

(b) disputes with regard to matters which are essentially within the domestic jurisdiction of the United States of America as determined by the United States of America;

(c) disputes arising under a multilateral treaty unless (1) all parties to the treaty affected by the decisions are also parties to the case before the Court, or (2) the United States of America specifically agrees to jurisdiction.[7]

Organization and Procedure. The most difficult problem in establishing an international tribunal is arriving at an acceptable method of selecting its judges. The aim is to adopt a system which will guarantee, as far as it is possible, an impartial panel of jurists who are not merely nominees of governments. Judicial independence must be obtained in order that confidence can be built up in support of the judgments of the courts. At the same time, judges must be selected who will be able to represent all of the principal systems of civilized law.

The system of nominating and electing judges for the Court which was finally adopted follows substantially the same procedure as that which held for the Permanent Court of the League. According to the present Statute, the Court is to be composed of a body of independent judges, 'elected regardless of their nationality from among persons of high moral character, who possess the qualifications in their respective countries for appointment to the highest judicial offices, or are jurisconsults of recognized competence in international law.' The Court consists of fifteen members (judges are known as 'members' of the Court, states as 'parties to the Statute'), no two of whom may be nationals of the same state, who serve for nine year terms and may be re-elected. Each of the national groups

---

[7] Pakistan made almost identical reservations, while Mexico and France similarly reserved the right to determine matters lying within their domestic jurisdiction.

of jurists who nominate the members of the Permanent Court of Arbitration, can nominate up to four judges of the International Court of Justice but no more than two of the nominees can be of the same nationality as the group nominating them. Prior to making their nominations, the Statute recommends that each national group should consult its highest court of justice and its schools of law to obtain the very best candidates. In the case of those members of the United Nations who are not parties to the Permanent Court of Arbitration, candidates are nominated by national groups appointed for this purpose by those states, under the same conditions as those prescribed for states which are parties to the Court.

Following the alphabetical compilation of the list of nominees, which is done by the Secretary-General, the General Assembly and the Security Council proceed independently of one another to elect the judges. The persons elected are those who obtain an absolute majority of votes cast in both these organs. However, if two nationals of the same state receive a majority, only the elder of the two is elected as no two judges may be of the same nationality. Should this method fail to elect a full Court, detailed provisions of the Statute require that a conference be held between members of the Assembly and the Security Council. But if the joint conference fails to procure an election, then the members of the Court already elected can proceed to fill the vacant seat or seats by making a selection from 'among those candidates who have obtained votes in the General Assembly or in the Security Council.'

Five new judges are selected every three years so that the terms are staggered. A judge elected to replace another whose term of office has not expired holds office for the remainder of his predecessor's term. Despite this cumbersome method, both the Permanent Court and the present one have constituted a broadly representative world tribunal. Judges do not act on instructions from their governments; they enjoy diplomatic privileges and immunities as members of an international judiciary.

The seat of the Court is at The Hague where it is in permanent session but it may sit and exercise its functions elsewhere whenever it considers this desirable. The full Court sits on a case except in the event it forms itself into one or more chambers, composed of three or more judges each for dealing with particular categories of cases. These categories might include cases relating to transit and communications or labor. Nine judges constitute a quorum.

The Court is empowered by the Statute to elect its own officers. These are a President and Vice-President who hold office for three years and may be re-elected. A Registrar is appointed by the Court as well as any other officer believed necessary. The official languages are French and

English. A language other than French or English may be authorized if so requested by one of the parties and agreed to by both parties. Cases come before the Court upon application to the Registrar who notifies all parties concerned as well as the members of the United Nations through the Secretary-General. If it considers it necessary, the Court has the power to indicate any provisional measures which ought to be taken to preserve the respective rights of either party. All parties are represented by agents and counsel who enjoy the privileges and immunities necessary for the independent exercise of their duties. Procedure is both written and oral. The written proceedings include the communication to the Court and to the parties of memorials, counter-memorials and, if necessary, replies, as well as all papers and documents in support. The oral proceedings consist of the hearing of witnesses, experts, agents, and counsel. The hearings are public unless decided otherwise by the Court or the parties themselves demand that the public not be admitted.

All questions are decided by a majority of the judges present. Judges of the nationality of each of the parties need not disqualify themselves but can retain their right to sit in the case before the Court. If there is no judge of the nationality of one of the parties, such party may choose a person to sit as judge. The judgment rendered must state the reasons on which it is based and contain the names of the judges who have taken part in the decision. If the judgment does not represent in whole or in part the unanimous opinion of the judges, any judge may freely deliver a separate opinion. As noted earlier, the judgment is final and without appeal. Should there arise a dispute as to the meaning or scope of the judgment, the Court may construe it if so requested by one of the parties.[8] Any application for a revision of a judgment can be made 'only when it is based upon the discovery of some fact of such a nature as to be a decisive factor, which fact was, when the judgment was given, unknown to the Court and also to the party claiming revision, always provided that such ignorance was not due to negligence.' The Statute grants the Court the authority to adopt any additional and specific rules of procedure which may be required.

Article 38 of the Statute lays down the law to be applied by the Court as follows:

(a) international conventions, whether general or particular, establishing rules expressly recognized by the contesting States;

(b) international custom, as evidence of a general practice accepted as law;

[8] Following the decision of the Court in the *Colombian-Peruvian Asylum Case*, Colombia requested an interpretation of the judgment but the Court held by a 12 to 1 vote that the request was inadmissible.

(c) subject to the provisions of Article 59,[9] judicial decisions and the teachings of the most highly qualified publicists of the various nations, as subsidiary means for the determination of rules of law.

The Court may also decide a case *ex aequo et bono* if agreed to by the parties.[10]

The expenses of the Court are borne by the United Nations in the manner decided by the General Assembly. Each party in a case bears its own costs unless decided otherwise by the Court. Amendments to the Statute are effected through the same procedure as is called for to amend the Charter of the United Nations. The Court itself may propose amendments by written communication to the Secretary-General.

THE JUDGMENTS OF THE COURT

It was over a year before the first case was filed with the Court and during its first four years it received only five cases. Since 1950, however, increasing use has been made of its facilities and by the end of 1957 more than a dozen cases had come before it. There follows a short resume of the cases in which a judgment has been rendered by the Court.[11]

The Corfu Channel Case. The dispute between Albania and the United Kingdom over the damaging of British destroyers by mines in the channel between the Greek island of Corfu and the Albanian coast was first heard by the Security Council early in 1947.[12] Unable to resolve the matter, the Council recommended that the dispute be referred to the Court. In May, 1947, the British filed an application with the Court but Albania subsequently notified the Court of its belief that the Court lacked jurisdiction since there had been no agreement between the two parties to submit the case. Following additional disagreement over the question of jurisdiction, the Court in a preliminary judgment on March 25, 1948 rejected the Albanian objection by a vote of fifteen to one.[13]

After the delivery of the judgment, the agents for both parties announced the conclusion of a special agreement for the purpose of placing before the Court the following questions:

[9] Article 59 expressly forbids the rule of *stare decisis* by providing that 'the decision of the Court has no binding force except between the parties and in respect to that particular case.'

[10] In other words, the Court may arrive at its decision in a case 'according to what is just and good.'

[11] In several instances, after a case was filed with the Court, it has been dropped due to prior settlement or the unwillingness of one of the parties to appear.

[12] See Chapter 7.

[13] The one dissenting vote was cast by Igor Daxner, President of a Chamber of the Supreme Court of Czechoslovakia, who had been appointed as judge *ad hoc* since the Court did not have a judge of Albanian nationality on the bench.

1. Is Albania responsible under international law for the explosions which occurred on the 22nd of October 1946 in Albanian waters and for the damage and loss of human life which resulted from them and is there any duty to pay compensation?

2. Has the United Kingdom under international law violated the sovereignty of the Albanian People's Republic by reason of the acts of the Royal Navy in Albanian waters on the 22nd of October and on the 12th and 13th of November 1946 and is there any duty to give satisfaction?

The Court gave its judgment on April 9, 1949. By a vote of eleven to five it held that Albania under international law was responsible for the explosions which occurred in Albanian waters on October 22, 1946, and for the damage and loss of life which resulted. The judgment further held by ten votes to six that the British did not violate Albanian sovereignty by the acts of the British Navy on October 22, 1946, but the Court was unanimously of the opinion that the British mine-sweeping activities on November 12 and 13, 1946, did constitute a violation of Albanian sovereignty.

Experts were appointed to examine the figures and estimates of damages reported by the British. By a twelve to two vote on December 15, 1949, the Court awarded damages to the United Kingdom in the amount of $2,363,051.

Colombian-Peruvian Asylum Case. Colombia filed an application with the Court on October 15, 1949, against Peru concerning a dispute which had developed over the asylum granted to Victor Raul Haya de la Torre in the Colombian Embassy in Lima. The individual in question was a Peruvian citizen and head of a political party called the American People's Revolutionary Alliance. He had presented himself to the Colombian Embassy as a political refugee and had been granted asylum. But the Peruvian government refused to grant him a guarantee of safe conduct necessary for his departure from Peru.

Both parties were unable to draw up a special agreement to submit their differences to the Court but finally agreed that each should submit its application unilaterally. The Court was asked to rule upon the interpretation of the treaties of 1911 and 1928 concluded between the two parties, which concerned the question of asylum and safe passage. The Court gave its judgment on November 20, 1950. By a vote of fourteen to two the Court held Colombia had not granted asylum in accordance with the treaties. It was adjudged by a vote of fifteen to one that Peru was not required to grant a safe conduct to Haya de la Torre.

The Anglo-Norwegian Fisheries Case. The United Kingdom filed an application in September 28, 1949, instituting proceedings against Norway to decide on the validity, under international law, of the lines of delimitation of the Norwegian fisheries zone laid down in 1935 and amended in 1937. The British contended that Norway violated international law by regulating fishing beyond the accepted territorial limits of states.

On December 18, 1951, the Court declared by a vote of ten to two that the Norwegian regulations governing fishing rights were not contrary to international law. The decision substantiated the Norwegian claim to an exclusive fishing zone of four miles determined by lines connecting the outermost land points of the irregular coast. The Court upheld the Norwegian method of establishing straight baselines by a vote of eight to four and denied the British contention that the four-mile zone should follow coastal contours more closely.

Case Concerning the Rights of Nationals of the United States in Morocco. France on October 28, 1950, instituted proceedings against the United States in a dispute over the treaty rights of American nationals in Morocco. The United States had protested to France against measures adopted in Morocco which allegedly violated certain rights granted under the treaty of 1836 between the United States and Morocco and later treaties. France requested the Court to declare that American nationals had no right to enjoy preferential treatment and should be subject to the laws and regulations in force in Morocco. This case marks the first time that the United States was a party to a case before the Court.

The lengthy judgment of the Court unanimously upheld the claim of the United States that certain of its rights had been contravened by a decree issued in 1948 by the French Resident General in Morocco. However, the Court also held unanimously that the United States could not claim the right to approve laws and decrees before their application to American citizens. By a vote of six to five the Court adjudged that American treaty rights did not confer upon its citizens immunity from taxes except those specified in a treaty.

The Anglo-Iranian Oil Company Case. On May 26, 1951, the United Kingdom instituted proceedings before the Court on behalf of the Anglo-Iranian Oil Company against Iran. The British contended that the Iranian Oil Nationalization Act of May 1, 1951, annulled a 1933 agreement granting an oil concession to the company. This agreement contained a provision that disputes should be settled by arbitration. The Iranian government had refused arbitration and the British maintained that the Court should hear the case since Iran had agreed in 1932 to compulsory jurisdiction in such matters under the Statute of the Permanent Court.

In June the British requested that the Court issue provisional measures to preserve the rights of the Company and prevent its seizure by Iran prior to a decision in the case. Iran denied the competence of the Court, claiming that the dispute involved an exercise of sovereign rights. The Court, however, did issue interim measures in July, and requested both parties not to take any action which would aggravate the dispute or hinder the business of the Company.

Judgment was delivered by the Court on July 22, 1952. By a vote of nine to five, the Court declared that it had no jurisdiction in the case. Jurisdiction could only be based upon the Iranian declaration of assent to compulsory jurisdiction made in 1932, and that declaration limited the jurisdiction of the Court to disputes relating to the application of a treaty. The 1933 agreement between Iran and the Company was not a treaty but merely a concessionary contract and did not concern the relations between the two governments.

The Ambatielos Case. Greece placed before the Court on April 9, 1951, the claim of one of its nationals, the shipowner Nicolas Ambatielos against the United Kingdom. It was alleged that the claimant suffered considerable loss as the result of a contract which he concluded in 1919 with the British government for the purchase of steamships then under construction. Greece asked the Court to declare that it had jurisdiction and to rule that the claim be submitted to arbitration on the basis of treaties concluded between Greece and the United Kingdom. On the other hand, the British contended that the Court lacked jurisdiction.

On July 1, 1952, the Court held by a thirteen to two vote that it did not have jurisdiction to decide on the merits of the case but, by a vote of ten to five, had jurisdiction to determine whether the British were required to arbitrate the matter. Subsequently, on May 19, 1953, the Court voted ten to four that Britain was 'under an obligation to co-operate with Greece in constituting a Commission of Arbitration, in accordance with the Protocol of 1886, as provided in the Declaration of 1926.'

The Nottebohm Case. On December 17, 1951, Liechtenstein began proceedings against Guatemala on behalf of one of its naturalized citizens, Friedrich Nottebohm. It was alleged that Nottebohm had been illegally interned and then expelled from Guatemalan territory during World War II. Guatemala should return Nottebohm's property or compensate him for his losses as well as indemnify him for the illegal treatment. Guatemala contended that Nottebohm, formerly a German national, had acquired Liechtenstein citizenship in 1939 solely for the purpose of acquiring the status of a neutral person without a genuine intention of creating a 'durable link' between Liechtenstein and himself. Thus, he could not claim the support of that state and his claim had no basis. Both Guatemala and Liechtenstein had previously agreed to the compulsory jurisdiction of the Court, but

Guatemala had accepted jurisdiction for only a five-year period, which expired on January 26, 1952. Guatemala claimed, therefore, that following that date, the Court had no jurisdiction.

On November 18, 1953, the Court unanimously rejected the Guatemalan contention that the Court's jurisdiction expired on January 26, 1952. The judgment stated the case began before the date of expiration and 'once the Court has been regularly seized, it must exercise its powers, as these are in the Statute. . . .' Finally, on April 6, 1955, the Court ruled inadmissible the claim of Liechtenstein by a vote of eleven to three on the grounds that Guatemala was not obligated to recognize the nationality granted a person under the circumstances which held in the case of Nottebohm.

Minquiers and Ecrehos Case. Both France and the United Kingdom in 1951 claimed sovereignty over the Minquiers and Ecrehos islets which lie in the English Channel. Unable to resolve their conflicting claims, both states called upon the Court on December 14, 1951, to determine which of them held valid title. On November 17, 1953, the Court unanimously adjudged that sovereignty over the island groups belongs to the United Kingdom.

Case of the Monetary Gold Removed from Rome in 1943. On May 19, 1953, Italy instituted proceedings against France, the United Kingdom, and the United States concerning a large sum of monetary gold removed from Rome by Germany on September 16, 1943. Part III of the Final Act of the Paris conference on reparations provided that gold found in Germany should be pooled and distributed to participating countries to cover losses suffered by them at the hands of Germany. A tripartite commission was established by France, the United States, and Britain to which all states could submit their claims. To complicate an already complex situation, Albania claimed the gold was the property of the Albanian State Bank, formerly the National Bank of Albania, whose share capital was 88.5 percent owned by the Italian State. Albania had nationalized the Bank in 1945. Italy also claimed the gold as part of the assets of the original Bank as constituted prior to its nationalization.

The members of the tripartite commission could not agree upon the distribution of the gold, and an arbitrator was appointed by the President of the Court. He decided in February, 1953, that the gold belonged to Albania. The British then claimed that the gold be turned over to them in partial payment of the damages awarded by the Court in the Corfu Channel Case unless the Court held otherwise. Italy, on the other hand, requested the Court to award it the gold and rule that the Italian claim had priority over that made by the British.

The Court on June 15, 1954 unanimously agreed that there existed in fact a dispute between Italy and Albania over the monetary gold and that it lacked jurisdiction to decide the matter without the consent of Albania.

By a vote of thirteen to one the Court also declared that it had no jurisdiction to decide whether the British or the Italian claim had priority, since the Court would first have to decide whether Italy had a valid claim against Albania.

Cases Pending before the Court. Application to institute proceedings have been filed in two instances without judgment rendered by the end of 1957. These include the *Right of Passage through Indian Territory* (Portugal v. India) and the *Case of the Norwegian Loans Issued in France* (France v. Norway).

ADVISORY OPINIONS

In addition to its judgments, the International Court of Justice has the authority to hand down an advisory opinion on any legal question referred to it. Judgments are rendered only when states have entered definite claims against each other. Opinions can be offered before legal issues have become crystallized into claims. They are only advisory and do not constitute a final answer or a binding decision. States may request opinions as may all principal organs of the United Nations and most specialized agencies.

The procedure followed in rendering an opinion is quite similar to that employed by the Court in a contentious case. Members of the United Nations, the Secretary-General, or other organs or specialized agencies present their views orally or in briefs. The Court deliberates upon the evidence submitted and information which it has gathered. The opinion is then given in open court and possesses the full authority of the Court. In the ten opinions delivered by the Court by 1957, none has been challenged on legal grounds. This was also true of the twenty-seven opinions rendered by the Permanent Court. In all but one case (UNESCO) the opinions of the present Court, which are summarized below, have been the result of direct requests from the General Assembly.

The Admission of a State to the United Nations. The first request for an advisory opinion resulted from an Assembly resolution adopted on November 17, 1948, which was concerned with the conditions of admission of a state to membership in the United Nations. The problem had arisen when Soviet vetoes prevented the admission of several new members that had been certified by the Assembly. The Court was asked its opinion on two questions:

> 1. Is a member of the United Nations, when casting its vote in the Security Council or Assembly on an application for membership, juridically entitled to make its consent dependent upon conditions not expressly provided in the Charter?

2. Can a member subject its affirmative vote to the additional condition that other states must be admitted along with the state which is being voted upon?

The only requirements established by the Charter on membership were that an applicant be a peace-loving state and be willing and able to abide by the principles of the United Nations. The Court refused to recognize conditions other than these and answered both questions in the negative by a vote of nine to six. This opinion, however, did not resolve the previously discussed deadlock over admission of new members.

Reparation for Injuries Suffered in the Service of the United Nations. In December, 1948, the Assembly requested the Court's opinion on two questions resulting from the assassination of Count Folke Bernadotte while serving as United Nations Mediator in Palestine:

1. In the event of an agent of the United Nations in the performance of his duties suffering injury in circumstances involving the responsibility of a state, has the United Nations the capacity to bring an international claim against the responsible government with a view to obtaining the reparation due in respect of the damage caused (a) to the United Nations, (b) to the victim or to persons entitled through him?
2. In the event of an affirmative reply on point 1 (b), how is action by the United Nations to be reconciled with such rights as may be possessed by the state of which the victim is a national?

The Court decided unanimously that the United Nations 'has the capacity to claim adequate reparation' against a state causing damage to the Organization.[14] By a vote of eleven to four the Court was of the opinion that the United Nations could claim damages 'to the victim or to persons entitled through him.' The Court also held, by a majority of ten to five, that there was no conflict between a claim of the United Nations and such rights possessed by the national state of the victim.

Competence of the General Assembly Regarding Admission to the United Nations. On November 22, 1949, the General Assembly requested the Court to give an advisory opinion on the following question:

Can the admission of a State to membership of the United Nations . . . be effected by a decision of the General Assembly when the Security Council had made no recommendation for admission by reason of the candidate failing to obtain the requisite majority or of the negative vote of a permanent member upon a resolution so to recommend?

The question had arisen as a result of the repeated failure of the Security Council to act favorably on the recommendations of the Assembly. Argentina

[14] Israel remitted $54,628 in reparation for the damage suffered by the United Nations and expressed its sincere regret over the incident.

and other members were of the opinion that the Assembly itself should have the authority to admit new members when action in the Security Council had become deadlocked by the use of the veto.

In its opinion given on March 3, 1950, the Court by a vote of twelve to two answered the question in the negative, declaring that it was necessary to have the affirmative recommendation of the Security Council as well as that of the Assembly before a new member could be admitted to the Organization. The Court also firmly stated its competence to interpret the Charter when requested to do so.

Peace Treaties with Bulgaria, Hungary, and Rumania. In the peace treaties concluded in Paris in 1947, Bulgaria, Hungary, and Rumania had agreed to permit the enjoyment of basic human rights and fundamental freedoms to all persons within their jurisdiction. Provision was made to submit disputes arising under the treaties to settlement by certain procedures which included arbitration by treaty commissions. The treaties authorized the Secretary-General of the United Nations, if requested by the parties to a dispute, to appoint a third member of the treaty commission if the parties had not been able to agree on the selection of a third member.

Charges of violations of human rights in these countries had been raised in the Assembly and the treaty commissions were not put into effect. The Assembly then voted in October, 1949, to ask the Court for an advisory opinion on the following questions:

1. Do the diplomatic exchanges betwen the three states in question and certain Allied and Associated Powers signatories to the peace treaties 'disclose disputes subject to the provisions for the settlement of disputes' contained in the treaties?

2. If so, are the three states obligated to carry out 'the provisions for the appointment of their representatives to the Treaty Commissions?'

3. If so, and in the event that these countries do not appoint their representatives within thirty days from the date when the Court delivers its opinion, is the Secretary-General authorized to appoint the third member of the commissions?

4. Should the answer to the third question be in the affirmative, 'would a Treaty Commission composed of a representative of one party and a third member appointed by the Secretary-General . . . constitute a Commission, within the meaning of the relevant Treaty articles, competent to make a definitive and binding decision in settlement of a dispute?'

On March 30, 1950, the Court decided the first two questions in the affirmative by a vote of eleven to three. In July, 1950, the Court held that unless both parties to the dispute had appointed their representatives to the commissions the Secretary-General could not appoint the third member. In view of this opinion, there was no need to answer the fourth question.

The International Status of South-West Africa. It will be recalled that the Union of South Africa has refused to place South-West Africa, a former League mandate, under the trusteeship system of the United Nations. The Assembly decided in December, 1949, to ask the Court for an advisory opinion on the following questions:

> What is the international status of the Territory of South-West Africa and what are the international obligations of the Union of South Africa arising therefrom, in particular.
>
> (a) Does the Union of South Africa continue to have international obligations under the Mandate for South-West Africa and, if so, what are those obligations?
>
> (b) Are the provisions of Chapter XII of the Charter applicable and, if so, what are those obligations? [15]
>
> (c) Has the Union of South Africa the competence to modify the international status of the Territory of South-West Africa, or, in the event of a negative reply, where does competence rest to determine and modify the international status of the Territory?

On July 11, 1950, the Court, by a unanimous vote, declared that South-West Africa was still a mandate, and by a twelve to two vote, stated that the Union of South Africa continued to have international obligations under the mandate. The Court affirmed the right of the Assembly to exercise the supervisory functions formerly performed by the League and the obligation of the Union to submit reports and petitions to it. Supervision by the Assembly, however, should not exceed that exercised under the League Covenant. By a unanimous decision, the Court declared that the provisions of Chapter XII of the Charter were applicable to South-West Africa in the sense that they offered the machinery through which the territory could be placed under trusteeship. But the Court held by eight votes to six that the Charter did not impose a legal obligation upon the Union of South Africa to put the territory under trusteeship. Finally, the Court decided unanimously that the Union alone was not competent to modify the international status of the territory. Competence in this regard rests with the Union acting with the consent of the United Nations.

Reservations to the Genocide Convention. The Secretary-General reported to the Fifth Assembly that he had become concerned with the problem of the procedure to be followed with respect to reservations made by States when adhering to multilateral conventions concluded under the auspices of the United Nations. Of immediate concern was the question of reservations made by states as a condition of adherence to the Convention on the Prevention and Punishment of the Crime of Genocide. To clarify the situa-

[15] Chapter XII is devoted to the international trusteeship system.

tion, the Assembly on November 16, 1950, requested the Court to give its opinion on the following questions:

1. Can the reserving state be regarded as being a party to the Convention while still maintaining its reservation if the reservation is objected to by one or more of the parties to the Convention but not by others?

2. If so, what is the effect of the reservation as between the reserving state and (a) the parties which object to the reservation, and (b) those which accept it?

3. What would be the legal effect as regards the answer to the first question if an objection to a reservation is made (a) by a signatory which has not yet ratified, and (b) by a state entitled to sign or accede but which has not yet done so?

In its advisory opinion delivered on May 28, 1951, the Court first answered objections raised regarding its competence. It affirmed its competence by declaring: that it could decline to give an advisory opinion if there was doubt surrounding its competence; that the object of the advisory opinion was to guide the work of the United Nations; that the request of the Assembly for an opinion did not impair the right of the parties to seek an interpretation; and that both the Assembly and the Security Council had the authority under the Charter to request the opinion of the Court on any legal question.

By a vote of seven to five, the Court presented the following answers to the questions:

Question 1. A state which has made and maintained a reservation which has been objected to by one or more of the parties to the Convention but not by others, can be regarded as being a party to the Convention only if the reservation is compatible with the object and purpose of the Convention.

Question 2. (a) If a party to the Convention objects to a reservation which it considers to be incompatible with the object and purpose of the Convention, it can consider that the reserving state is not a party to the Convention. (b) But if a party accepts the reservations as being compatible, it can consider the reserving state a party to the Convention.

Question 3. (a) An objection to a reservation made by a signatory state which has not yet ratified the Convention can have the legal effect indicated in the answer to the first question only upon ratification. Until that moment it merely serves as a notice to the other state of the eventual attitude of the signatory state. (b) An objection to a reservation made by a state entitled to sign or accede which has not yet done so is without legal effect.

Effects of Awards of Compensation Made by the United Nations Administrative Tribunal. The Administrative Tribunal was created in 1949 by the General Assembly to hear complaints alleging nonobservance of contracts of employment of members of the Secretariat or of the terms of employment of the staff members. In 1953 the Secretary-General suspended certain nationals of the United States who were members of the Secretariat on grounds of subversion and refusal to testify before Congressional committees and various American tribunals.[16] They brought their cases before the Administrative Tribunal which in turn awarded damages amounting to $179,420.

At the eighth Assembly session in 1953, the Fifth Committee rejected the decision of the Administrative Tribunal. Its recommendation, subsequently approved by the Assembly, was to seek an advisory opinion from the Court on the following questions:

> 1. Has the Assembly the right on any grounds to refuse to give effect to an award compensation made by the Tribunal to a staff member of the United Nations whose contract of service has been terminated without his consent?
> 2. If so, what are the principal grounds upon which the Assembly could lawfully exercise such a right?

On July 13, 1954, the Court delivered its opinion by a majority of nine to three. After examining the powers of the General Assembly, the position of the Secretary-General and the Secretariat, and the Statute of the Tribunal, the Court declared that the Assembly did not have the right on any grounds to refuse to give effect to an award made by the Tribunal where the matters dealt with in the Tribunal's decision were within its competence. The negative finding on the first question made it unnecessary for the Court to rule on the second.

Voting Procedure on Questions Relating to Reports and Petitions Concerning the Territory of South-West Africa. Problems related to the supervision of the territory of South-West Africa were raised during the ninth session of the Assembly. Under the Covenant of the League of Nations, action taken by the League Council relating to the mandates system required a unanimous vote while under the Charter of the United Nations, such matters can be decided by a two-thirds majority in the Assembly. The Union of South Africa contended that in arriving at decisions relating to reports and petitions concerning the territory of South-West Africa by a two-thirds vote, the Assembly was exceeding the degree of supervision exercised by the League Council. The Court in its opinion of 1950 had stated that the degree of supervision exercised by the Assembly should not exceed that called for by the League mandates system and the procedure to be followed should correspond as far as possible to that applied by the League Council.

---

[16] For an examination of these cases brought before the Administrative Tribunal, see Chapter 11.

Unable to resolve these differences of opinion, the Assembly in November, 1954, decided to refer the matter to the Court and requested its opinion. In its unanimous decision of June 7, 1955, the Court held, in effect, that the two-thirds voting rule of the Assembly did not violate the Opinion of 1950. It would not be legally possible, said the Court, to arrive at decisions in the Assembly by means of 'a voting system entirely alien to that prescribed by the Charter.' An exact duplication of the League's procedure would be impossible and, therefore, there would be no reason to expect the Assembly to adopt a special unanimity rule in order to carry out responsibilities formerly belonging to the League.

Admissibility of Hearings by the Committee on South-West Africa. On December 3, 1955, the General Assembly, in connection with its deliberations on the matter of South-West Africa requested the Court's opinion on the following question: Was it consistent with the advisory opinion of the Court of July 11, 1950, for the Committee on South-West Africa, established by the Assembly in 1953, to grant oral hearings to petitioners on issues relating to the Territory of South-West Africa?

The opinion of the Court was delivered on June 1, 1956. By a vote of 10-5, it held that the Assembly could authorize a procedure for the granting of oral hearings by the Committee to petitioners who had already submitted written petitions. The Court argued that although oral hearings had not been granted to petitioners by the Permanent Mandates Commission during the lifetime of the League, the League Council had been competent to authorize the Commission to permit such hearings if it had wished to do so. There was nothing in the League Covenant or the United Nations Charter which would restrict the authority of the Assembly to less than that enjoyed by the League Council. The Court's Opinion of 1950 was not intended to restrict the Assembly solely to activities which had actually been applied by the League. At that time, it had held only that the degree of supervision should conform 'as far as possible' to the procedure followed by the League. Therefore, it would not be inconsistent with the 1950 Opinion for the Committee to grant oral hearings to petitioners if the Assembly was certain that such a procedure was essential for the maintenance of effective international supervision of the administration of the mandated territory.

Judgments of the Administrative Tribunal of the International Labor Organization Upon Complaints Made Against the United Nations Educational, Scientific and Cultural Organization. The Executive Board of UNESCO in November, 1955, challenged the decisions rendered by the Administrative Tribunal of ILO in favor of four UNESCO employees. The Board requested the Court to decide the following questions:

1. Was the Administrative Tribunal competent to hear the complaints against UNESCO introduced by four of its employees?

2. Should the answer to the first question be in the affirmative,

   a. had the Tribunal been competent to determine whether the power of the UNESCO Director-General not to renew fixed-term appointments had been exercised for the good of the service and the interest of the organization, and

   b. had the Tribunal been competent to pronounce on the attitude which the UNESCO Director-General, under the UNESCO constitution, should maintain in his relations with a member state, particularly as regarded the execution of the policy of the government authorities of that member state?

3. What was the validity of the decisions given by the Tribunal in the four cases in question?

By a vote of 9 to 4, the Court agreed on October 23, 1956, to comply with the request for an advisory opinion. The Court upheld the competence of the Tribunal to hear complaints (10 to 3) but refused to be seized with the second question (9 to 4) since the request for an advisory opinion under Article XII of the Statute of the Tribunal was not in the nature of an appeal on the merits of the judgments. With respect to the third question, the Court (10 to 3) stated that the decisions were valid inasmuch as it had upheld the competence of the Tribunal.

CONCLUSIONS

The Permanent Court of International Justice was perhaps the most successful feature of the League of Nations system. It enjoyed great prestige and probably has contributed more to the development of international law than any other body. Despite its relatively short lifetime, however, the present Court has provided every indication that it is a worthy successor to the first world tribunal. The competence of its judges, the standards of its justice, and the respect for its judgments and opinions provide every indication that the Court can have as distinguished a record as its predecessor.

Every member of the United Nations is automatically a party to the Court. Two nonmembers are also parties to the Court and, under certain circumstances, any nation in the world may place its case before it. The disputes brought before the Court have not been of great magnitude, yet they have been handled with the same efficiency and competence that was true of the old Court. The Assembly has called upon the Court for a number of important advisory opinions, some of which have contributed greatly to the functioning of the United Nations as a whole. The fact that there is a permanent Court, in continuous session, cannot help but contribute to the development of the peaceful settlement of disputes. The United States and two Latin American countries have been parties to disputes before the Court, which was not the case with the old Court. The number of states accepting compulsory jurisdiction has been low, yet several of the more important members of the Organization can be counted in this list. No party to a dispute before the Court has failed to abide by the judgment rendered.

Despite this evidence of capacity and respect, the Court functions today in a world society that is not yet ready to entrust it with disputes of major proportions. Much more use could have been made of its facilities in a number of instances that would not have materially prejudiced national objectives. It is unlikely that the Court at present can prevent war, certainly not a war involving the conflicting interests of the major powers. The Court cannot be expected to be presented with requests for advisory opinions on matters which concern the competing views of these same great powers. As long as the members of the United Nations are unable to resolve their basic differences, the Court will continue in a limited role, performing it with distinction but with little effect upon the course of international politics.

THE DEVELOPMENT OF INTERNATIONAL LAW

One of the functions of the United Nations is to encourage the development of international law and its eventual codification. The Charter in Article 13 specifically calls upon the Assembly 'to initiate studies and make recommendations for the purpose of . . . encouraging the progressive development of international law and its codification.' As we have seen earlier, an international organization, by its very nature, makes a contribution to the development of international law by its emphasis upon judicial settlement, the rules and procedures which govern its actions, the treatment of international problems through accepted customs and practices, and the occasional conclusion of international conventions. Little agreement has been reached on the codification of international law and this fact presents a great challenge to the members of a universal international organization such as the League or the United Nations.

The Hague Conferences codified some features of the laws of war and neutrality. Other portions of international law and the procedural rules governing states in their relations with each other were formulated in bilateral treaties prior to the League of Nations. With the establishment of the League came a renewed emphasis on codification. In 1924, the Council appointed a Committee of Experts for the Progressive Codification of International Law. Governments were asked by the Committee to present their views on a number of topics which might be appropriate for codification. As a result of this study, the League Assembly in 1927 decided to call a Codification Conference to examine questions of nationality, territorial waters, and responsibility of states for damage done in their territory to the person or property of foreigners. The Conference met in 1930 at The Hague and drafted a convention on nationality which was signed by thirty-one states. Much useful work was also done by various private associations as well as by inter-American conferences and institutes.[17]

The contribution of the League to the development and codification of international law, while it was valuable, nevertheless fell short of expectations owing to the reluctance of many states to ratify available conventions. The activities of the Permanent Court of International Justice were rewarding, however, and together with the experience gained from the practices and procedures developed by the League, plus the considerable number of treaties containing progressive elements of international law, the stage was set for the efforts of the United Nations to develop and codify international law. These efforts have been concentrated largely in the work of the International Law Commission.

THE INTERNATIONAL LAW COMMISSION

After considerable discussion by its Sixth (Legal) Committee, the Assembly on November 21, 1947, established the International Law Commission and provided it with a governing Statute. Article 15 of the Statute, in stating the functions of the Commission, distinguishes between 'development' and 'codification' of international law as follows:

> The expression 'progressive development of international law' is used for convenience as meaning the preparation of draft conventions on subjects which have not yet been regulated by international law or in regard to which the law has not yet been sufficiently developed in the practice of States. Similarly, the expression 'codification of international law' is used for convenience as meaning the more precise formulation and systematization of rules of international law in fields where there has already been extensive state practice, precedent and doctrine.

All recommendations of the Commission concerned with these two activities are sent to the General Assembly for action. The Assembly may refer

[17] Among the private associations should be mentioned the important work done by the Harvard Law School group led by Manley O. Hudson and the International Law Association. In the inter-American community, productive results have come from the efforts of the American Institute of International Law and the International Commission of Jurists at Rio de Janiero.

a proposal to the Commission for its study and suggestions or the Commission may initiate projects on its own.

The Commission consists of twenty-one members of recognized competence in international law who serve for three-year terms and may be re-elected. They serve in their private capacity, as do the judges on the Court, and are not responsible to their individual governments. No two members can be nationals of the same state. They are elected by the Assembly from a list of candidates nominated by the members of the United Nations, each of whom may not nominate more than four candidates. Two may be nationals of the nominating state and two, nationals of other states. The Commission sits at the headquarters of the United Nations in New York or in various European capitals and is assisted by the Secretary-General who makes staff and facilities available for its use.

The Commission has devoted most of its time to the problem of codification of certain aspects of international law. At its first session, in 1949, it compiled a list of items considered suitable for codification, which included: recognition of states and governments; succession of states and governments; jurisdictional immunities of states and their property; jurisdiction with regard to crimes committed outside national territory; the regime of the high seas; the regime of territorial waters; nationality, including statelessness; the treatment of aliens; the right of asylum; the law of treaties; diplomatic intercourse and immunities; consular intercourse and immunities; state responsibility; and arbitral procedure. In addition, the Assembly requested the Commission to submit proposals on the rights and duties of states and reservations to multilateral conventions.

The work of the Commission has been deliberate and by 1958 it had undertaken studies of about half of the items on the list. A Draft Declaration on the Rights and Duties of States was submitted in 1950 to the Assembly. Four basic rights of states were laid down, namely the right of independence, the exercise of jurisdiction over state territory and persons and things therein, equality in law, and the right of individual or collective self-defense against armed attack. Among the ten duties of states were those of nonintervention in the internal affairs of others, peaceful settlement of disputes, and the respect for treaty obligations.

Progress has been made on such matters as arbitral procedure, the law of treaties, the regime of the high seas and territorial waters, diplomatic intercourse and immunities, and reservations to multilateral conventions. Draft conventions have been prepared on the reduction and elimination of future statelessness.

On November 21, 1947, the General Assembly requested the Commission to formulate the principles of international law recognized in the Charter and in the judgment of the Nuremberg Tribunal established in 1945 to try war criminals of the European Axis Powers. The Commission was also asked to draft a code of offenses against the peace and security of mankind. After careful study, the Commission in 1950 agreed to the following seven principles of international law from the Nuremberg Trials that represented entirely new departures from previous state practice:

1. Any person who commits an act which constitutes a crime under international law is responsible therefor and liable to punishment.

2. The fact that internal law does not impose a penalty for an act which constitutes a crime under international law does not relieve the person who committed the act from responsibility under international law.

3. The fact that a person who committed an act which constitutes a crime under international law acted as Head of State or responsible Government official does not relieve him from responsibility under international law.

4. The fact that a person acted pursuant to order of his Government or of a superior does not relieve him of responsibility under international law, provided a moral choice was in fact possible to him.

5. Any person charged with a crime under international law has the right to a fair trial on the facts and law.

6. The crimes hereinafter set out are punishable as crimes under international law:

    a. Crimes against peace:

        (1) Planning, preparation, initiation or waging of a war of aggression or a war in violation of international treaties, agreements or assurances.

        (2) Participation in a common plan or conspiracy for the accomplishment of any of the acts mentioned under (1).

    b. War crimes:

        Violations of the laws or customs of war which include, but are not limited to, murder, ill-treatment or deportation to slave-labor camps or for any other purpose of civilian population of or in occupied territory, murder or ill-treatment of prisoners of war, of persons on the seas, killing of hostages, plunder of public or private property, wanton destruction of cities, towns, or villages, or devastation not justified by military necessity.

    c. Crimes against humanity:

        Murder, extermination, enslavement, deportation and other inhuman acts done against any civilian population, or persecutions on political, racial or religious grounds, when such acts are done or such persecutions are carried on in execution of or in connection with any crime against peace or any war crime.

7. Complicity in the commission of a crime against peace, a war crime, or a crime against humanity as set forth in Principle 6 is a crime under international law.

The Assembly has also requested the Commission to study other projects, such as the ways and means available to publicize customary international law, the definition of aggression, and the possible establishment of an international criminal court. The Assembly eventually established special committees to examine and report on the last two problems but no definite action has been taken on the committee reports by 1958.

The Commission has proceeded slowly, and at times too cautiously, with the tasks assigned to it. Yet the development and codification of international law is a gradual process, dependent entirely upon the willingness of national states to restrict their freedom of action. Studies by such bodies as the International Law Commission inevitably can be of value by encouraging the development of the rule of law.

11

CIVIL SERVANTS OF THE WORLD

THE League of Nations pioneered in practically all aspects of international organization. Undoubtedly one of the most novel innovations was the adoption, for the first time, of a truly international civil service. With the exception of a few international agencies with small staffs, such as the Universal Postal Union, traditional diplomacy served as the channel of contact between nations and managed to take care of the national interests of sovereign states, usually on a bilateral basis. The occasional international conferences and congresses which were held through the centuries were gatherings of diplomats and their staffs meeting on some specific problem or problems, as was the case with the Congress of Vienna in 1815 and the Hague Conferences at the turn of the twentieth century. When decisions had been made on the issues at stake, the conferees disbanded and returned to their countries.

At the conclusion of the First World War a new concept was introduced into international relations. The customary processes of diplomacy were unsuited to meet the tasks posed by a world in which the majority of nations associated themselves into universal organizations. The League of Nations and the International Labor Organization required permanent staffs to conduct the many activities assigned to these new entities by their governing charters. During the period between wars the League and the ILO developed a trained body of international civil servants recruited to work not as representatives of their own countries but as servants responsible only to the directions of these organizations whose interests they served. Gradually the activities of the League Secretariat expanded to cover executive, judicial, and political fields plus the nonpolitical work in social and humanitarian matters. By 1946 there had been established not just the idea but the structure of a civil service loyal to an international organization, immune from the control of both the servant's own state and the individual members of the organization.

340

The practice of the League not only has found expression in the constitutions and charters establishing the numerous international organizations formed since the end of World War II but has resulted in important innovations in matters of international administration. International civil servants today are employed by several different types of organizations scattered throughout the world. Foremost, of course, is the United Nations and its Secretariat with Headquarters in New York. There are also Secretariat personnel in Geneva, Bangkok, and Santiago, Chile, attached to the three regional commissions of ECOSOC, respectively the Economic Commission for Europe, the Economic Commission for Asia and the Far East, and the Economic Commission for Latin America. Others serve the International Court of Justice at The Hague, and in the United Nations Information Centers and regional offices of the Technical Assistance Board of the United Nations located in a number of different countries. Then there are the staffs for temporary commissions and agencies such as the United Nations Korean Reconstruction Agency, the United Nations Relief and Works Agency for Palestine Refugees in the Near East, the office of the United Nations High Commissioner for Refugees, and the United Nations Children's Fund. All told, there were in 1958 about 3,000 employees at the Headquarters in New York and another 2,000 working in different parts of the world. At no time did the total of civil servants employed by public international organizations between wars exceed 1,500 and the League never, at its maximum period, employed much more than 700.

The twelve specialized agencies of the United Nations, each with its charter, staff, budget, and headquarters, employ about the same total number of civil servants as does the United Nations itself. The largest is the Food and Agriculture Organization which has over 1,000 on its staff. The staffs work in a disciplined organizational structure with an administrative head similar to the United Nations Secretariat. All have compiled an enviable record of competence and achievement and represent the most successful forms of international organization yet constructed. The fact that their operational fields are primarily nonpolitical has made possible a large measure of their success. At the same time, these specialized agencies have contributed to the building of an atmosphere of co-operation which is one of the requisites for political agreement.

Regional organizations comprise a third group of international agencies that employ civil servants. The outstanding example of this category is the Organization of American States with headquarters in Washington, D.C., and regional branches in Latin America. Its membership is restricted to the nations of the Western Hemisphere and includes all of them except Canada. The North Atlantic Treaty Organization and the European Coal and Steel

Community are other examples. All have secretariats with duties and privileges similar to those of the officials of the United Nations and the specialized agencies.

In addition, there must be included in the total of international civil servants the technical assistance experts working for the Technical Assistance Administration of the United Nations Secretariat and for the specialized agencies participating in the Expanded Program of Technical Assistance. They are paid for their efforts by the organization for whom they work but a portion of their expenses is contributed by the country in which the project employing their skills is located. Such an expert, while serving as an advisor, demonstration leader, project director, or participant in the field, is contributing his particular training not only to assist the economic and social development of the recipient country but to advance the cause of international co-operation, the fundamental tenet of international organization.

Out of this welter of international organizational development which is rooted in the League experiment comes the shape and procedure of modern international administration. It is not an administration for which a comparable analogy can be found in the governments of national states. It is true that from a purely technical viewpoint, international administration resembles national administration as far as the processes of organization and office techniques and practices are concerned. Thus, it has been said that 'public administration is generic in character — applicable wherever organized activities are carried out in a continuing manner.' [1] However, international and national administration diverge in their relationship to the organs which dictate their policies. National administration is an inherent part of the executive branch of government, at all times under some form of control by the legislative branch of government. But an international secretariat has policy established for it not by a legislature but by a diplomatic body such as the General Assembly of the United Nations. While a secretariat is the only truly permanent element of an international organization, its directing head can never be compared to a chief executive such as a president or prime minister.

The individual international civil servant must perform duties with the same personal regard for efficiency, competence, and loyalty to his organization as the national administrator. But he is placed in a more difficult position than his national counterpart by virtue of his having to think and to act on occasion not only in ways contrary to his political convictions but in

[1] Stone, Donald C., *Administrative Aspects of World Organization: A Paper Presented at the Fourth Conference on Science, Philosophy, and Religion,* held at New York City, September 12, 1943 (Mimeographed), quoted in Ranshofen-Wertheimer, Egon F., *The International Secretariat,* Washington, D.C., 1945, p. 7.

a manner in conflict with his own national attachment, mores, and customs. This is a requirement that places a heavy burden on the international official and tests his capacity for the job to the utmost.

It is because of these peculiarities of international organization that international administration has had to improvise, to test by the trial and error method. The ground-breaking work of the League Secretariat under the direction of its Secretary-General for many years, Sir Eric Drummond, has provided invaluable training for many who serve in international organization today. Although international administration has progressed to high levels in the specialized agencies and regional organizations, it has been put to the greatest test in the Secretariat of the United Nations. It is there one can see, in broad outline, the problems, procedures, and practices of a dedicated international civil service, confronted by all aspects of international administration.

THE SECRETARY-GENERAL OF THE UNITED NATIONS

The Charter of the United Nations, in Article 97, states that the Secretariat 'shall comprise a Secretary-General and such staff as the Organization may require. The Secretary-General shall be appointed by the General Assembly upon the recommendation of the Security Council. He shall be the chief administrative officer of the Organization.' In this article the Charter follows the precedent of the League in creating a chief administrative officer. But later articles and the practice of the United Nations clearly have established the fact that the office of the present Secretary-General is one possessed of greater powers and responsiblities than that of the League.

During the years of the League, the Secretary-General came to play an increasingly important political role although, as Sir Eric Drummond has observed about his own position as League Secretary-General, 'It had to be done behind the scenes, but I do not think it was any less effective because of this. To take sides publicly in a political dispute would certainly have lessened my political influence.' [2] The Covenant imposed limitations upon his political activities. Unlike the present Secretary-General, he could not on his own initiative bring a dangerous situation to the attention of the League Council. But as the tensions among the Council members heightened, Sir Eric and his successor, Joseph Avenol of France, were forced to engage in diplomatic maneuvering. The political importance, therefore, of the Secretary-General under the League came to be very real, dependent

[2] Quoted in Schwebel, Stephen S., *The Secretary-General of the United Nations, His Political Powers and Practice*, Cambridge, 1952, p. 7. This is the standard work on the Secretary-General of the United Nations. Informative and interesting is the volume by former Secretary-General Trygve Lie, *In the Cause of Peace*, New York, 1954.

however upon the character of the individuals who held the post and the political cirucumstances of the day. Neither Sir Eric nor M. Avenol exhibited the aggressiveness of Albert Thomas, the first Director of the International Labor Organization. He was convinced that to the Director 'fell of necessity the task of leadership, the task of initiative, the task of taking all those measures which might be necessary to defend the Organization.' [3] His powers were not significantly greater than those of his League counterpart but he developed them to the fullest degree. Mr. Thomas, through his determination and his awareness of the need for exerting public as well as private leadership, lent credence to the view that a Secretary-General can be of great value in bringing political as well as administrative direction to an international organization composed of sovereign states with their multiplicity of interests and policies.

Appointment and Term of Office. The Charter describes the method of appointment but is silent on the term of office for the Secretary-General. As for appointment, practice now dictates that, due to the power of anyone of them to veto a nomination, the permanent members of the Security Council meet informally and decide among themselves on a candidate before that body engages in full debate on the matter. Only one candidate is recommended to the Assembly. The recommendation of the Council needs only a simple majority vote of approval in the Assembly. Although the Assembly could reject a candidate recommended by the Council, it cannot appoint a Secretary-General itself but must wait for another nomination from the Council.

In 1946 the General Assembly adopted a resolution which now governs the term of appointment. It provided that the first Secretary-General should be appointed for five years with the possibility of the appointment being open at the end of that period for an additional five-year term. However, both the Assembly and the Security Council were left free to modify the term in the future. The Assembly also stated that owing to the confidential nature of the office, no member of the United Nations should offer a retiring Secretary-General a government position immediately after retirement nor should the individual accept such a position if it were offered.

Unfortunately, the selection of a Secretary-General has not been kept out of political controversy. The first appointment of Mr. Trygve Lie, a distinguished Norwegian diplomat, cabinet officer, and internationalist, went smoothly enough. The Soviets urged the nomination of a European for the post and suggested the name of Stanoje Simitch of Yugoslavia. The United States backed Lester Pearson (Canada) while the British favored their own Sir Gladwyn Jebb. When it became obvious that the USSR would not

[3] Phelan, Edward J., *Yes, and Albert Thomas,* London, 1936, p. 253.

accept Pearson, the United States nominated Lie and there was quick agreement among the Big Five. The Assembly approved the nomination of Lie by a vote of 46 to 3, granting him a salary of $20,000 a year with allowances of an equal amount plus a residence.

Although considered by all concerned to be an admirable choice in 1946, Mr. Lie had become the center of acrimonious debate by the time his term of office expired in 1951. When he attempted to gain worldwide support for his peace program in 1950 which was designed to solve the impasse in the Organization caused by the Soviet boycott of the Security Council, he incurred the wrath of influential elements in the United States. In addition, Nationalist China was angered by Lie's attempt to espouse the cause of the Peiping regime. But with the outbreak of the Korean War, Lie urged that the United Nations act quickly to stop aggression. Suspicions in the United States lessened then but he immediately became anathema to the Soviets.

The question of recommending a candidate for the office of Secretary-General arose in the Council in September, 1950. The Soviet Union would not engage in preliminary discussions on the matter. Lie had the backing of the British, French, and American representatives but when his name came before the Council on October 12, nine voted for him, China abstained, and the Soviet representative cast a veto. The United States threatened to veto anyone else. The Council had to report to the Assembly that it was unable to recommend a candidate. With the scene shifting to the Assembly, the Soviet delegation then initiated a vituperative campaign against Mr. Lie while the United States backed him with equal vigor. Gradually a majority of the Assembly concluded that Mr. Lie had served well and should be retained. A fifteen-nation resolution proposing that his term of office be extended for three years was approved on November 1, 1950, 46-5 with eight abstentions. Mr. Vishinsky of the USSR then announced that it would not recognize Mr. Lie as Secretary-General after February 1, 1951, the date on which his first term was to end.

However, as the year 1951 wore on it became obvious that the usefulness of the Secretary-General was declining. Mr. Lie had again come under attack in the United States, this time in connection with United States nationals in the Secretariat who refused to testify before Congressional committees on the point of membership in the Communist Party. The Secretary-General himself was aware of the obstacles preventing his continuance as an effective administrator. By the fall of 1952, armistice negotiations were well underway in Korea and he believed the time propitious to request the appointment of a successor. It was not until March, 1953, that the Security Council made up its mind on a recommendation. After some preliminary skirmishes, a decision was reached on March 31. Another

Scandinavian was selected, this time a Swede, with an impeccable background as a statesman, economist, and professional civil servant. The Council accepted the name of Dag Hammarskjöld by 10 votes to 0, China abstaining. The Assembly quickly concurred by an overwhelming majority, 57 to 1 with one abstention and one not present. On September 26, 1957, the Assembly unanimously elected Mr. Hammarskjöld to a second five-year term.

Functions and Powers. Mr. Trygve Lie had the unenviable task of putting into effect the Charter provisions covering his duties and the responsibilities of the Secretariat. To him, therefore, belongs much of the credit for the development of the Secretaryship-General and the functions and powers attached to it. Dag Hammarskjöld inherited a functioning organization and though he has had to make some administrative changes, the way ahead had been paved by his predecessor.

The Preparatory Commission in 1945 grouped the chief functions of the Secretary-General under these six headings: general administration or management; technical matters; financial matters; the organization and administration of the Secretariat; representational duties; and political matters. Because the last named, or political, function is the most difficult and demands excessive time and energy, it is imperative that the Secretary-General delegate much of his administrative responsibilities to his staff. The reorganization undertaken by Hammarskjöld in 1954 and 1955 which is discussed later was prompted not only by budgetary reductions but also because of the need to free himself from administrative detail so that his executive-political functions could be exercised with clarity and dispatch.

The Charter, as we have seen, makes the Secretary-General the 'chief administrative officer of the Organization.' His administrative functions make him the channel of communication between the members and the organs of the United Nations. He must supervise the preparation of work for the different organs and execute decisions as directed by them. He is also responsible for co-ordinating the widespread activities of the United Nations. No other organ or official is in the same position as the Secretary-General as far as over-all integration is concerned. This is particularly true with respect to bringing the specialized agencies into relationship with the United Nations.

Article 98 of the Charter provides the framework for the Secretary-General's duties in connection with serving as the communicating link of the Organization and in respect to preparation of work and execution of decisions for the various organs. Except in the case of the Security Council, he calls special sessions on the request of the appropriate authority; makes routine notifications to members; processes credentials of delegates; keeps records of all meetings; provides and directs the staff for organs, commissions, and special bodies; publishes all documents, reports, and resolutions; registers and publishes treaties; and performs a number of routine duties called for in the Charter. The Secretary-General, in addition, has such discretionary and political responsibilities as drawing up the provisional agenda for the Assembly, the Security Council, and the Trusteeship Council and proposing items for inclusion on the agenda for each of these bodies. He is also required to make an annual report to the Assembly on the work of the Organization.

Technical functions involve the preparation of studies, reports, legal briefs, and surveys on almost every conceivable question within the range of the functions of the Organization. The Secretary-General or his deputy acting 'in that capacity in all meetings' of the organs, answers questions of detail and offers suggestions on technical matters.

Financial functions involve the preparation of the United Nations budget, the allocation of all funds, the collection of all contributions from the members, and the control over expenditures. The Secretary-General also maintains custody of all the funds. A twenty-two million dollar Working Capital Fund has been established to provide necessary resources for the United Nations when regular funds are low in the period when members are late in making their annual contributions. Fiscal officers of the Secretariat draw up the budget and the Secretary-General presents it to the Assembly as part of his annual financial report.

The Secretary-General is responsible for the organization and administration of the Secretariat. As the Preparatory Commission stated in its Report in 1945 'his choice of staff — more particularly of higher staff — and his leadership will largely determine the character and efficiency of the Secretariat as a whole. It is on him that will mainly fall the duty of creating and maintaining a team spirit in a body of officials recruited from many countries.' It is up to the Secretary-General to provide an example to his staff in subscribing to Article 100 of the Charter, which provides that 'in the performance of their duties the Secretary-General and the staff shall not seek or receive instructions from any government or from any other authority external to the Organization. They shall refrain from any action which might reflect on their position as international officials responsible only to the Organization.'

As the official spokesman for the United Nations, the Secretary-General performs representational functions. He represents the Organization in all its negotiations with the governments of members and nonmembers alike and with outside agencies. His press conferences, public addresses, and press releases speak authoritatively for the United Nations.

In his political functions the Secretary-General may exercise considerable influence on general policy as well as the position of individual members. In his relationship with the organs of the United Nations, there are several instances in which he may directly or indirectly bring influence to bear on decisions. Examples of this are his drawing up of provisional agenda for each of the principal organs and the placing of items on the agenda of the General Assembly and the Trusteeship Council. In addition, he may make oral or written statements to the Security Council, the General Assembly, the Trusteeship Council, and ECOSOC on any matter which has come before them. In the case of the Assembly, his statements need not be related to a question before it. He cannot make a statement to ECOSOC or the Trusteeship Council unless so invited by the appropriate presiding officer but such an invitation is not necessary with respect to the Assembly and the Security Council.

The Secretary-General has made extensive use of these formal powers and the effects have been considerable. The placing of items on the agenda of the Assembly, for example, enables him to bring matters to the attention of that body which are comparable in nature to those he can place before the Security Council in the interest of maintaining international peace and security. The addresses made by the Secretary-General to plenary sessions of the Assembly have not been numerous but they have contained subtle inferences, implied criticism, and, on occasion, support for certain measures of a controversial nature. Intervention in the work of the Assembly committees by the Secretary-General or his representatives has been frequent. Many of the resolutions coming before the Assmbly and other organs are drafted under the supervision of the Secretary-General.

Some resolutions provide the Secretary-General with *ad hoc* powers which may be political in nature. One example of this is to be found in that part of the 'Uniting For Peace' resolution adopted by the Assembly in 1950, which called for military contributions from members for service as United Nations units. The resolution established a Collective Measures Committee and directed it 'in consultation with the Secretary-General and with such member states as the Committee finds appropriate, to study and make a report to the Security Council and the General Assembly . . . on methods . . . which might be used to maintain and strengthen international peace and security.' The Secretary-General was also requested, with the approval of the Collective Measures Committee 'to appoint a panel of military experts who could be made available, on request, to member states wishing to obtain technical advice regarding the organization, training and equipment for prompt service as United Nations units of the elements referred to.'

An interesting illustration of the use of such *ad hoc* powers was the mission of the Secretary-General to Peiping in an effort to obtain the release of eleven American airmen and other detained military personnel of the United Nations Command. The United States brought the matter to the attention of the Assembly on December 4, 1954. On December 10 the Assembly adopted a resolution which condemned the detention of these prisoners as illegal and requested the Secretary-General 'in the name of the United Nations, to seek the release, in accordance with the Korean Armistice Agreement,' of all captured military personnel of the United Nations Command. Four meetings were held in January, 1955, between Mr. Hammarskjöld and Chou En-lai, Foreign Minister of Communist China. Formal communiqués issued at the time revealed little other than the cordial relationship established by the negotiations but contact was maintained between the Secretary-General and the Chinese after January. In May four American jet pilots were released and in August the eleven American airmen noted in the December 10, 1954, Assembly resolution were freed. Mr. Hammarskjöld deserves considerable credit for his efforts in this venture, although it is difficult to judge the exact nature of the influence he and the United Nations had on reversing the policy of the Peiping regime. The Communists had retained the airmen as pawns in the cold war in violation of the Korean Armistice Agreement and had nothing to lose in setting them free. Their release may well have been another propaganda move directed toward building support for Peiping's claim to the seat of China in the United Nations. However, the Secretary-General demonstrated another useful diplomatic aspect of his office.

The most celebrated example of granting *ad hoc* powers to the Secretary-General was in the Middle East crisis of 1956–57. At that time, it will be recalled, the Assembly authorized Mr. Hammarskjöld to draft the plans for the United Nations Emergency Force and once it was established, empowered him to direct its activities. Mr. Hammarskjöld was also instructed to conduct the negotiations leading to the removal of Franco-British troops from the Suez Canal area as well as the eventual withdrawal of Israeli forces from Egyptian territory. In addition, the Secretary-General was called upon to arrange for the clearing of the Suez Canal and supervise the force engaged in this operation. All of these activities required the greatest skill and patience.

The presentation of an annual report to the General Assembly on the work of the Organization must also be considered within the realm of political activities. The report is by no means a simple, factual summation of accomplishments and needs. Instead, it ranges over the entire course of the Organization's activities, at times bringing in the policies of individual members. Both commendation and criticism have been employed. Trygve Lie was noted for this type of report which, in its introduction, sought to influence the policies of the Assembly and expressed his personal convictions. Thus, in his third annual report, he stimulated discussion and invited Soviet criticism when he stated that 'The European Recovery Program . . . holds great promise for the restoration of Western Europe to economic and political stability, but it can have lasting results only if present political divisions are not permited to block coordinated action within Europe as a whole and an increase of trade between East and West Europe.' Mr. Hammarskjöld has been more temperate in his language, yet he has not failed to point out the problems confronting the Organization and the obligations of the members under the Charter.

The most significant Charter provision conferring political functions upon the Secretary-General is Article 99, which states that he 'may bring to the attention of the Security Council any matter which in his opinion may threaten the maintenance of international peace and security.' No such authority was ever vested in the Secretary-General under the League. Mr. Trygve Lie stated before the General Assembly on September 28, 1950, that he employed Article 99 'for the first time' before the Security Council on June 25, 1950, in regard to the aggression of North Korea. Although the matter was first brought to the attention of the Security Council by the United States, when the Council met the President called upon Mr. Lie before any others around the table stated their positions. After condemning the North Korean attack, the Secretary-General stated that 'the present situation is a serious one and is a threat to the international peace. The Security Council is, in my opinion, the competent organ to deal with it. I consider it the clear duty of the Security Council to take steps necessary to reestablish peace in that area.' This was a declaration clearly within the confines of Article 99.

Despite his observation that the Korean question was his first employment of Article 99, Mr. Lie had taken the initiative within the spirit of that article on other occasions. When the Iranian question was before the Security Council in 1946, that body had to decide whether it could and should remain seized of the matter when both parties had asked that it be taken off the agenda. At this point, the Secretary-General intervened by placing before the Council President a memorandum containing his legal views on the question. Another instance was the Greek question before the Security Council in 1946. Prior to a vote on a United States resolution which would establish a three-member commission to be nominated by the Secretary-General to investigate the Greek frontier situation, Mr. Lie made this statement:

> Just a few words to make clear my own position as Secretary-General and the rights of this office under the Charter. Should the proposal of the United States not be carried, I hope that the Council will understand that the Secretary-General must reserve his right to make such enquiries or investigations as he may think necessary in order to determine whether or not he should consider bringing any aspect of this matter to the attention of the Council under the provisions of the Charter.

Yet another aspect of the political functions of the Secretary-General should be noted. This is the largely unseen but important behind-the-scenes activity which involves his relations with individual governments. The office of the Secretary-General serves as a medium for endless consultations between members of the United Nations. In addition, the Secretary-General has taken the initiative on several occasions to attempt a settlement of serious and potentially dangerous situations. In the Palestine question, both Lie and Hammarskjöld have worked to implement the policies of the Assembly and the Security Council. Mr. Lie was influential in pushing the mediative efforts of Count Folke Bernadotte and Dr. Ralph Bunche. Mr. Hammarskjöld worked quietly throughout 1955 and especially in 1956 and 1957 to reduce border tensions between Israeli-Arab forces. In the tense circumstances surrounding the Berlin blockade in 1948, Mr. Lie was active in his attempts to overcome the impasse.

A good example of the mediative efforts of the Secretary-General came in 1950. What had started as a behind-the-scenes activity over a period of years came out in the open when Mr. Lie traveled widely to bring about a solution to some of the problems which were dividing the United Nations, in particular the question of Chinese representation in the United Nations. Following the Soviet boycott in January, 1950, Lie talked with government officials in Washington, Paris, London, and Moscow. The approach employed by him on Chinese representation was essentially a legal one. His general attitude can be seen from this statement made in the course of a speech delivered in March, 1950:

> I have been trying to help the member governments settle the question of who is to represent China in the United Nations. I am not doing this because the Soviet Union and its neighbors have refused to attend meetings at which China is represented by Nationalist delegates. I have never thought walking out of meetings and staying away from meetings was a good way to settle differences of opinion.
>
> It is a serious matter to have the Soviet Union staying away from United Nations meetings, but that is not the first consideration. The first consider-

ation is the people of China. There are 450,000,000 people in that country —
the greatest in the world and in the United Nations in terms of population
alone.

The 450,000,000 people of China are collectively original members of the
United Nations by the terms of the Charter itself. They have a right to be
represented by whatever government has the power 'to employ the resources
and direct the people of the state in fulfillment of the obligations of membership' in the United Nations. I repeat, whatever government is thus qualified,
regardless of its ideology.

Mr. Lie carried with him a legal memorandum on the Chinese question
and a twenty-year 'peace program' of ten points. In the memorandum he
sought to differentiate between representation in the United Nations and
the question of diplomatic recognition by the member states. He argued with
force that representation did not involve recognition, that China was a permanent member of the Security Council irrespective of the nature of her
government. In his view, it should be the task of the Security Council to
determine which of the two Chinese governments — Communist or Nationalist — actually represented the Chinese people and hence would be
entitled to membership. However, any success Mr. Lie was obtaining with
these arguments in foreign capitals was ended by the North Korean aggression in June of 1950.

Despite the interruption of his efforts by the Korean War and the stiffened
opposition to his position in the United States, Lie continued to argue his
case and to urge the consideration of his memorandum containing the 'peace
program.' Nothing came of his activities on behalf of Chinese recognition.
But the General Assembly did commend him 'for his initiative in preparing
his memorandum' and requested 'the appropriate organs of the United Nations to give consideration to those portions' of it with which they were
particularly concerned.

The Egyptian seizure of the Suez Canal in 1956 presented the Secretary-
General with another opportunity to employ his good offices to reach some
compromise among the nations most directly concerned. The direct high-
level negotiations between the foreign ministers of Egypt, France, and the
United Kingdom were instigated by Mr. Hammarskjöld. He was present
during these tense sessions and had much to do with the six-point resolution
later adopted by the Security Council as a basis for the adjustment of the
Canal problem.

In retrospect, it is clear that the political functions of the Secretary-General are significant. The extent to which they are utilized and the nature of
their employment depends in large measure upon the character of the person occupying the Secretaryship-General. Mr. Lie was a dynamic personality, convinced of his responsibilities, and determined to take the initiative

when the occasion warranted action. Mr. Hammarskjöld is more reserved, less inclined to the direct approach, more of the civil servant type of administrator. Yet he is aware of his political as well as his administrative duties. In a diplomatically veiled but unmistakable offer to resign following the Anglo-French vetoes in the Security Council during the first hours of the Middle East crisis in 1956, Mr. Hammarskjöld with rare candor revealed his devotion to the ideals of the Charter and the mandate of his office in the following prepared statement:

> The principles of the Charter are, by far, greater than the Organization in which they are embodied, and the aims which they are to safeguard are holier than the policies of any single nation or people. As a servant of the Organization, the Secretary-General has the duty to maintain his usefulness by avoiding public stands on conflicts between member nations unless and until such an action might help to resolve the conflict. However, the discretion and impartiality thus imposed on the Secretary-General by the character of his immediate task may not degenerate into a policy of expediency.
>
> He must also be a servant of the principles of the Charter, and its aims must ultimately determine what for him is right and wrong. For that he must stand. A Secretary-General cannot serve on any other assumption than that — within the necessary limits of human frailty and honest differences of opinion — all member nations honor their pledge to observe all Articles of the Charter. He should also be able to assume that those organs which are charged with the task of upholding the Charter will be in a position to fulfill their task.
>
> The bearing of what I have just said must be obvious to all without any elaboration from my side. Were the members to consider that another view of the duties of the Secretary-General than the one here stated, would better serve the interests of the Organization, it is their obvious right to act accordingly.

There followed a dramatic and unusual display of international unanimity as the members of the Security Council, one by one, rose to express their support of the unsmiling Secretary-General. Armed with what amounted to a complete vote of confidence, Mr. Hammarskjöld then proceeded to assume the many added responsibilities required of him by the nature of the Organization's involvement in the explosive affairs of the Middle East.

ORGANIZATION OF THE UNITED NATIONS SECRETARIAT

The organization of any administrative structure must follow certain accepted principles. In building the Secretariat, however, considerations other than sound administrative procedure were involved. Sovereign nations, each with its own view, approached the problem from different standpoints.

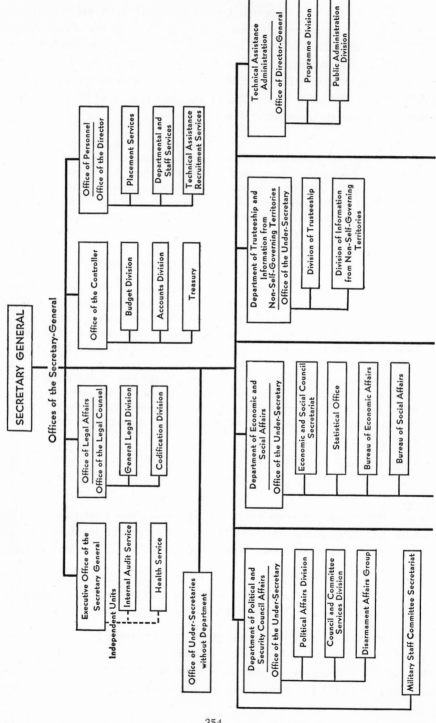

SECRETARY GENERAL

Offices of the Secretary-General

Executive Office of the Secretary General

Independent Units

Internal Audit Service

Health Service

Office of Legal Affairs
Office of the Legal Counsel

General Legal Division

Codification Division

Office of the Controller

Budget Division

Accounts Division

Treasury

Office of Personnel
Office of the Director

Placement Services

Departmental and Staff Services

Technical Assistance Recruitment Services

Office of Under-Secretaries without Department

Department of Political and Security Council Affairs
Office of the Under-Secretary

Political Affairs Division

Council and Committee Services Division

Disarmament Affairs Group

Military Staff Committee Secretariat

Department of Economic and Social Affairs
Office of the Under-Secretary

Economic and Social Council Secretariat

Statistical Office

Bureau of Economic Affairs

Bureau of Social Affairs

Department of Trusteeship and Information from Non-Self-Governing Territories
Office of the Under-Secretary

Division of Trusteeship

Division of Information from Non-Self-Governing Territories

Technical Assistance Administration
Office of Director-General

Programme Division

Public Administration Division

354

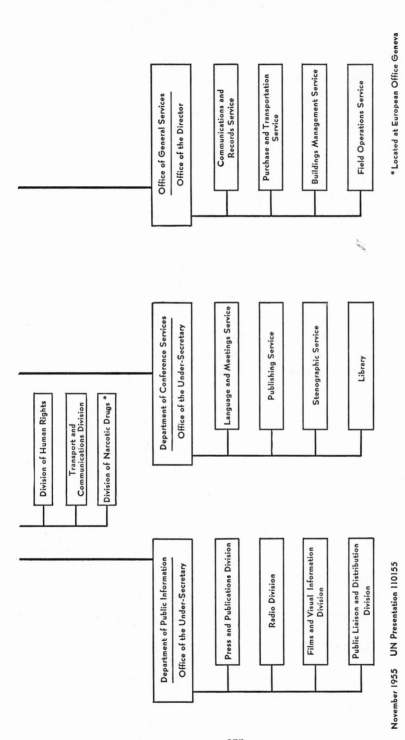

ADMINISTRATIVE STRUCTURE OF THE SECRETARIAT AT HEADQUARTERS

November 1955   UN Presentation 110155

* Located at European Office Geneva

In the discussions of the Preparatory Commission in 1945, two methods of organizing the Secretariat were finally considered. One would provide for a single, integrated organization, developed on a functional basis, to serve the requirements of all the organs of the United Nations. The other proposed separate units of the Secretariat to serve each organ, a so-called 'organically' constructed arrangement. The latter view was held by the minority in the Commission, advocated principally by the Soviets. As might be expected, what has resulted is a combination of both theories, a system which was recommended in essence by the Preparatory Commission and approved by the General Assembly in February, 1946.

As originally established, the Secretariat consisted of an Executive Office of the Secretary-General and eight departments, each under the direction of an Assistant Secretary-General. This arrangement appeared to be satisfactory for the first few years and made possible the functioning of the 'gentlemen's agreement,' arrived at by the permanent members of the Security Council. This was a political deal which apportioned the Assistant Secretaries-General among them. In January, 1946, meeting in London after selecting Trygve Lie for the top job, the permanent Council members decided that the USSR would be awarded the Assistant Secretaryship-General for Political and Security Council Affairs; the United States would have that for Administrative and Financial Services; and the post for Economic Affairs would be reserved for the British. The Assistant Secretaryships-General for Social Affairs and Trusteeship were given to the French and Chinese, respectively. The other positions — Legal Affairs, Conferences and General Services, and Public Information — went to Czechoslovakia, the Netherlands and Chile, respectively.[4]

It is highly doubtful whether such an arrangement was in keeping with the best interests of the Secretariat, or for that matter, with sound tenets of administrative organization. Mr. Lie, as Secretary-General, was presented with the distribution, by countries, of his chief assistants. Furthermore, each of the permanent members of the Council provided him with the name of the individual to serve in these jobs. The Secretary-General made it a practice in later years, when replacements in these posts were needed, to solicit suggestions from the Council members concerned.

Since 1951, the organization of the Secretariat has been under study and

---

[4] The reason the United States selected the post of Administrative and Financial Services has never been made clear. The Soviet Union received the most sensitive and important of the Assistant Secretaryships-General, that of Political and Security Council Affairs, which has proved to be quite unfortunate, particularly during the tense years of the Korean War. For example, some members of the Security Council and even the Secretary-General did not trust Constantin Zinchenko (who held the post) with confidential information. See Lie, op cit. p. 343.

certain changes were made in 1954 and 1955. In the course of the debates on the 1952 budget estimates during the sixth session of the Assembly in 1951, doubts were expressed concerning the adequacy of the existing administrative structure of the Secretariat. The Secretary-General was requested to make a preliminary study of the problem and report to the Assembly in 1952. This he did, making some preliminary suggestions, and the Assembly requested further study and a report in 1953. The 1953 report established the main outlines of the changes which went into effect in 1954 and 1955.

One principal change now in effect is the elimination of the Assistant Secretaries-General and their replacement with Under-Secretaries who are appointed by the Secretary-General for five-year terms.[5] Previously, the Assistant Secretaries-General, in addition to being heads of departments, served the Secretary-General in a representative capacity with individual member states and groups of states. Under them were officers known as Principal Directors who functioned as administrative officials charged with the conduct of operations of the various departments. This arrangement did not prove to be satisfactory and the present system now provides for only one echelon of officials heading departments, namely the Under-Secretaries. Their responsibilities, as was the case of the Principal Directors, is essentially administrative. Whatever political activities are required in the performance of their duties are delegated by the Secretary-General and exercised on his personal responsibility.

A second major change concerns the organization of the immediate staff of the Secretary-General. There is now an Executive office of the Secretary-General, an Office of Legal Affairs, an Office of the Controller, and an Office of Personnel. These offices operate under the immediate and personal direction of the Secretary-General. The separate Bureaus of Finance and Personnel, the Legal Department, and the Department of Administrative and Financial Services have been eliminated. This reorganization provides more direct control over personnel and financial matters. The position of the officials responsible for these matters, acting on the behalf of the Secretary-General, has been clarified and strengthened. The change from Legal Department to Legal Office reflects more clearly its role in providing legal advice to the Secretary-General and in acting for him in legal matters. What has been effected, therefore, is a concentration of administrative responsibility at the center with a simplification of procedures and an expected improvement in day-to-day administration.

[5] The Soviet Union opposed the abolition of the Assistant Secretaries-General and voted against the reorganization of the Secretariat on this score in 1953 and 1954. The Soviet delegate was joined by Czechoslovakia in claiming that this change violated the 'gentlemen's agreement' made in 1946.

In large part, the reorganization of the Executive Offices has brought about a reduction in the number of departments. The Department of Administrative and Financial Services disappeared in 1954 and the Legal Department was eliminated in 1955. Also in 1955, the Departments of Economic Affairs and Social Affairs were combined and the Department of Conference and General Services was divided into two units: the Department of Conference Services and an Office of General Services. In that year the Library was transferred from the Office of the Secretary-General to the Department of Conference Services and the Field Service was made a part of the Office of General Services.

As a result of these changes, there are four Offices of the Secretary-General, in addition to the Office of the Under-Secretaries Without Department, as follows:

Executive Office of the Secretary-General. This office is headed by an Executive Assistant to the Secretary-General (currently Andrew W. Cordier — USA) who aids the Secretary-General in the over-all co-ordination of the work of the departments and offices of the Secretariat, and with such matters as United Nations protocol, servicing the General Assembly, and implementing its resolutions. Assistance is also provided with respect to relations with the governments of members and nonmembers, the specialized agencies, and the various missions of the United Nations abroad.

Office of Legal Affairs. The Legal Counsel provides legal advice to the Secretary-General and acts in his behalf in legal matters. Legal advice and assistance is also offered to other departments of the Secretariat and the organs of the United Nations.

Office of the Controller. The Controller is responsible for the administration of fiscal and budgetary services, collecting the annual contributions of member states, and operation of the United Nations treasury.

Office of Personnel. The Director of Personnel supervises recruitment, staff relations, training, and general personnel policies.

The preceding four Offices of the Secretary-General had budgets totaling $2,117,050 in 1955.

Office of the Under-Secretaries Without Department. Beginning in 1955, two Under-Secretaries 'without portfolio' were appointed to advise the Secretary-General on special matters. The first selections were Ralph J. Bunche (USA) and Ilya S. Tchernychev (USSR). A budgetary allocation of $76,650 was made to this Office in 1955.

In addition to the Technical Assistance Administration, which will be discussed in Chapter 14, there are five substantive Departments and an Office of General Services, as follows:

Department of Political and Security Council Affairs provides services to the Security Council and its subsidiary organs, the Disarmament Commission, the First and Special Political Committees of the General Assembly, and other committees and subsidiary groups associated with political and security matters. It prepares working papers dealing with matters relating to the maintenance of international peace and security, makes surveys on international political events, conducts studies on the promotion of international political co-operation and disarmament, and advises on the pacific settlement of disputes. The Department is headed by an Under-Secretary and had a budget of $657,300 in 1955.

Department of Economic and Social Affairs offers substantive and technical services to the Second and Third Committees of the General Assembly, to the Economic and Social Council and its functional and regional commissions, and to other subsidiary groups. It conducts studies and issues publications on economic and social matters and maintains close relations with the specialized agencies. The Department also performs certain functions and undertakes activities under the international treaties and the resolutions and decisions of various organs of the United Nations in connection with such matters as narcotic drugs, child welfare, traffic in women and children, economic development, statistics, and aspects of technical assistance. An Under-Secretary, assisted by a Deputy Under-Secretary, directs the affairs of the Department. It had a budget of $3,687,000 to administer in 1955.

Department of Trusteeship and Information from Non-Self-Governing Territories is specially constructed to render service to the Trusteeship Council, the Fourth Committee of the General Assembly (trusteeship and non-self-governing territories), and the Committee on Information from Non-Self-Governing Territories. The Division of Trusteeship is primarily concerned with the functioning of the International Trusteeship System and makes studies and surveys as required, accepts and examines petitions, and examines the annual reports of the Administering Authorities. The Division of Information from Non-Self-Governing Territories studies social, economic, and educational conditions in these areas and summarizes and analyzes information transmitted about them. An Under-Secretary is in charge of the Department and administered a 1955 budget of $859,200.

Department of Public Information advises the Secretary-General on information policy, supervises and maintains facilities at the Headquarters of the United Nations for representatives of all information media, and maintains Information Centers all over the world to disseminate information about the Organization. It issues press releases and general information publications as well as having broadcasting facilities (United Nations Radio), and film and photographic services. The Department is headed by an Under-Secretary and also works with the specialized agencies in making available information about the activities of the United Nations as a whole. A total of $2,534,000 comprised the budget for this Department in 1955.

Department of Conference Services is directed by an Under-Secretary who makes arrangements and provides services for meetings of the General Assembly, the councils, committees, commissions, and special conferences held under the auspices of the United Nations. The Department also edits and publishes the journals and official records of conferences and meetings and now has charge of the library of the United Nations. It was allocated the largest budget of the Secretariat in 1955, a total of $6,238,800. The Library budget was separate and amounted to $489,000.

Office of General Services is headed by a Director who provides for the necessary purchases for the Organization, transportation and communications requirements, and buildings management services such as operations, safety, and security. It had a 1955 budgetary allocation of $2,976,150.

A European Office of the United Nations is maintained in the buildings of the League of Nations in Geneva. The Office is in charge of a Director representing the Secretary-General, and serves as a center for United Nations meetings in Europe. It provides office space and facilities for a number of specialized agencies on a reimbursement basis. The Geneva Office also serves as headquarters for the Economic Commission for Europe, the Geneva Information Center, the Drug Supervisory Body, the Permanent Central Opium Board, the Office of the High Commissioner for Refugees, and the Division of Narcotic Drugs of the Secretariat's Department of Economic and Social Affairs. The budget for 1955 was $5,406,300.

In addition, there are portions of the secretariats of the Technical Assistance Board, the United Nations Children's Fund, and the United Nations Korean Reconstruction Agency, as well as liaison officers for the Office of the United Nations High Commissioner for Refugees and for the United Nations Relief and Works Agency for Palestine Refugees in the Near East, with offices at Headquarters in New York.

In 1949, the General Assembly approved the request of Secretary-General Lie for the establishment of a United Nations Field Service as part of the United Nations Secretariat. It is now a part of the Office of General Services and had a 1955 budget of $484,000.

As presently constituted, the Field Service numbers no more than three hundred persons and provides the following services: provision of land transport for missions and such incidental air transport as may be required; maintenance of radio communications for missions; and security of United Nations premises and members of missions. Its personnel wear a special United

Nations uniform and are authorized to carry side arms on special occasions. Special training is provided in first-aid, police methods, shorthand, typewriting, and automotive repair with particular emphasis on jeep maintenance.

The Field Service does not act in any way as a military force or for the enforcement of Security Council decisions. Originally, Lie had requested the establishment of a United Nations Guard in 1948, to serve as truce observers, for protecting places neutralized during a truce and to supervise polling places during a plebiscite. Opposition in the General Assembly forced him to modify his earlier concepts.

THE STAFF OF THE UNITED NATIONS SECRETARIAT

As the highest administrative officer of the United Nations, the Secretary-General is given the authority by the Charter to appoint the staff of the Secretariat. The Charter, in Article 101, also establishes the principle that 'the paramount consideration in the employment of the staff and in the determination of the conditions of service shall be the necessity of securing the highest standards of efficiency, competence, and integrity.' Due regard must also be paid to 'recruiting the staff on as wide a geographical basis as possible.'

Staff Regulations and Personnel Policies. The duties of the staff of the Secretariat are specified in the Staff Regulations established by the General Assembly. These have been implemented by a set of staff rules issued under the authority of the Secretary-General. Included in the Regulations and rules are the various standard practices of civil service, such as job classification, appointments, promotions, probationary status, dismissal, leave, retirement, pensions, and various allowances. An International Civil Service Advisory Board, consisting of experts from the specialized agencies and the Secretariat, provides advice on personnel matters for the Secretary-General. In 1950, for example, it completed a report on recruitment methods and standards for the United Nations and the specialized agencies. Also assisting him on such matters are the Appointment and Promotion Board and the Personnel Selection and Review Board, both of them appointed by him from among senior officials in the Secretariat.

When accepting appointment in the Secretariat, staff members are required to take the following oath or declaration:

> I solemnly swear (undertake, affirm, promise) to exercise in all loyalty, discretion and conscience the functions entrusted to me as a member of the international civil service of the United Nations, to discharge those functions

and regulate my conduct with the interests of the United Nations only in view, and not to seek or accept instructions in regard to the performance of my duties from any government or other authority external to the Organization.

Clearly spelled out, therefore, is the fact that the members of the Secretariat are international civil servants, although they do not lose the rights of citizenship in their own countries. But while in the Secretariat, the staff is subject to the authority of the Secretary-General and to assignment by him to any of the activities or offices of the United Nations. They must conduct themselves at all times in a manner befitting their status as international civil servants. They must avoid any action or any kind of public pronouncement that may adversely reflect on their status 'or on the integrity, independence and impartiality which are required by that status.' Staff members may vote but cannot engage in any political activity inconsistent with their status.

The geographical distribution by countries of origin of the members of the staff follows roughly the percentages established for the scale of assessments levied upon the members of the Organization to finance its operations. That is, nationals of the United States comprise about 34 percent of the staff, the United Kingdom approximately 12 percent, France, 12 percent, and so on, with the exception of the Soviet Union, which has never had more than a handful of its citizens employed in the Secretariat. More than half the staff are on temporary appointment, with one-year renewable contracts. Permanent members receive a five-year contract, and normally must serve a two-year probationary period. The Secretary-General prescribes which staff members are eligible for permanent appointments. Job classification on any systematic basis has proved to be quite difficult although there have developed four series of levels, with base pay and provision for salary increment over a period of years to a maximum within the particular level.

Various allowances are granted the staff for their dependents, for rent, and for transportation to and from the location of their duties. Ample provisions are made for annual and sick leave. Home leave is permitted once every two years for those who are not nationals of the United States. Tax-exempt salaries, except for nationals of the United States, are an added inducement to employment. Educational allowances of $200 per year for each child are granted most members of the staff. A termination indemnity is available for many employees, subject to certain limitations with respect to the nature of termination of work, based upon the number of years served. A health service, primarily diagnostic, is also provided. In addition, a United Nations Joint Staff Pension Fund was established in 1948, into which Secretariat members and staff of the specialized agencies make regular contributions. These are added to by annual contributions from the employing bodies, to provide adequate pension allowances.

With over a decade of experience behind it, the Secretariat now functions much more smoothly than many had expected. The first few years witnessed a very rapid growth, resulting in a number of problems. At least 2,500 staff members were appointed during the first year alone. This was necessary because the various organs of the United Nations took up their responsibilities almost immediately on a broad scale of activity and the Secretariat had to be created to serve them. But there was not time to go through the careful processes of full international recruitment or to achieve the extent of geographical distribution which has now been attained. Further adjustments in some of the units of the Secretariat continue to be made in order to perfect the procedures and detail of this most complex of international civil service systems.

Privileges and Immunities. Prior to the establishment of the League of Nations, the immunities extended to international organization were not large. With the League came a body of extensive rules which has been expanded since the beginning of the United Nations and the specialized agencies. The privileges and immunities accorded to duly accredited representatives of member states of international organizations such as the United Nations and its Headquarters have already been discussed.[6] It is now essential to examine the status of members of the Secretariat.

Due to the nature of his work, the international civil servant needs some special protection. The Staff Regulations point out clearly that the immunities and privileges attached to the United Nations 'are conferred in the interests of the Organization.' The individual, thus, does not receive special treatment for himself or because respect should be due to the nation from which he comes. He needs the privileges and immunities only to perform his duties. They do not furnish an excuse 'to the staff members who enjoy them for non-performance of their private obligations or failure to observe law and police regulations.' Should there occur a situation where the question of privileges and immunities arises, the Secretary-General has the sole responsibility to decide whether they shall be waived or employed.

The basic document covering the privileges and immunities of the Secretariat is the Convention of Privileges and Immunities. A separate convention, almost identical in nature, is in effect for the specialized agencies. Applicable also is the Headquarters agreement between the United States and the United Nations. The principal features of the Convention applicable to the staff are summarized below:

[6] See above, pp. 108–10.

1. The Secretary-General and Under-Secretaries are 'accorded in respect of themselves, their spouses and minor children, the privileges and immunities, exemptions and facilities accorded to diplomatic envoys, in accordance with international law.'

2. Immunity from legal process in respect of words spoken or written by officials and all acts performed by them in their official capacity.

3. Exemption from taxation on the salaries and emoluments paid by the United Nations.

4. Immunity from service in national military forces.

5. Immunity for the official, spouses and dependent relatives from immigration restrictions and alien registration.

6. The same privileges are granted officials in respect to exchange facilities as are accorded to the officials of comparable ranks forming part of diplomatic missions to the government concerned.

7. Repatriation facilities in time of international crisis are accorded to officials, spouses and dependent relatives identical to those enjoyed by diplomatic envoys.

8. All officials have the right to import free of duty their furniture and effects 'at the time of first taking up their posts in the country in question.'

9. The right to have the United Nations *laissez-passer* accepted as a valid travel document is provided all officials of the United Nations. Applications for required visas are to be dealt with as 'speedily as possible,' together with 'facilities for speedy travel.'

The Secretary-General specifies the categories of officials to which these provisions of the Convention apply. A glance at the privileges and immunities quickly reveals their nature and intent. There is a similarity to the privileges and immunities enjoyed by diplomatic envoys but the protection is by no means as complete. The important immunity from legal process, for example, applies only to the staff member's official duties, unlike the diplomat who is accorded virtually full immunity for his acts, both private and official. The right to import duty-free furniture and effects is limited to the first entry of the official into the country where his duties call him. The important right of freedom of movement across frontiers is covered adequately under several provisions.

The failure of the United States to ratify either of the Conventions relating to privileges and immunities has caused difficulties and inconveniences. In 1945 the United States Congress passed the International Organizations Immunities Act which accords some but by no means all of the rights contained in the Conventions. For example, the exemption from the income tax is limited to members of the staff who are not citizens of the United States. Since salary scales have been drawn up on the basis of tax exemption, the national of the United States is placed in an inferior financial position to those citizens of the forty-three countries which have acceded to the Convention for the United Nations and hence do not collect such taxes. To eliminate this inequity, the General Assembly has established a special internal tax fund to refund taxes paid by United States citizens. Congressional legislation also does not specify immunity from military service for United States nationals nor are special exchange or repatriation facilities provided in time of international crisis.

Questions of Dismissal and Loyalty. Sound administrative organization and procedure must provide authority for the chief administrative officer to terminate the services of his subordinates for good cause. At the same time, there should be machinery adequate to protect the staff from unwarranted dismissals arising from prejudice or personal whim. The Staff Regulations of the Secretariat provide both of these requisites of a civil service system. They have been severely tested in practice.

The Secretary-General may terminate the appointment of a staff member on permanent or fixed-term appointment 'for serious misconduct' or 'if the services of the individual concerned prove unsatisfactory,' if his post is abolished or if his health incapacitates him for further service. All other members of the staff may be dismissed by the Secretary-General 'if, in his opinion, such action would be in the best interest of the United Nations.'

In 1953, further authority in this regard was granted the Secretary-General as a result of a series of unfortunate situations associated with the loyalty and integrity of staff members suspected of Communist subversive activities. Thus, the Secretary-General may dismiss a staff member holding a permanent or fixed-term appointment if his conduct indicates that he does not meet the highest standards of integrity required by the Charter, or

> If facts anterior to the appointment of the staff member and relevant to his suitability come to light which, if they had been known at the time of his appointment, should, under the standards established by the Charter, have precluded his appointment.

No termination can take place under these 1953 additions to the Staff Regulations until the matter has been considered by a special Advisory Board which has been constituted by the Secretary-General. In addition, the Secretary-General can dismiss a staff member under a permanent appointment 'if such action would be in the interest of the good administration of the Organization and in accordance with the standards of the Charter, provided that the action is not contested by the staff member concerned.' In this latter instance, the Secretary-General may pay to the dismissed staff member 'a termination indemnity payment not more than fifty per cent higher than that which would otherwise be payable under the Staff Regulations.'

Before examining the circumstances which instigated these new powers of the Secretary-General, other features of the protective machinery afforded the staff must be mentioned. A Staff Council elected annually by members of the Secretariat from all levels of the staff has been established 'to make proposals to the Secretary-General for improvements in the situation of staff members, both as regards their conditions of work and their general conditions of life.' A Joint Advisory Committee advises the Secretary-General regarding personnel policies and general questions of staff welfare. The Joint Disciplinary Committee and the Joint Appeals Board advise the Secretary-General in cases of appeal against administrative decisions or concerning proposed disciplinary action. Membership in these three 'joint' bodies is selected by both the Secretary-General and the Staff Council.

In addition, an Administrative Tribunal of seven members was established by the General Assembly in 1949. Its membership consists of independent experts appointed by the General Assembly to three-year terms. The Tribunal sits to hear and pass judgment on 'applications alleging nonobservance of contracts of employment of staff members' or their terms of appointment. It is open to any staff member of the Secretariat or employee of a specialized agency whose agency has requested this privilege for its staff when concluding a special agreement bringing it into relationship with the United Nations. The Tribunal normally hears cases only after they have been heard by the Joint Appeals Board.

Returning now to the circumstances which led up to the 1953 revisions of the Staff Regulations, the problem was one which concerned the Communist affiliations, past and present, of some United States nationals in the Secretariat. Although certain inconclusive reports on the matter had come to the attention of Mr. Lie earlier, the situation exploded in 1952–53. A number of United States nationals on permanent staff appointments refused to testify before a New York Federal Grand Jury and various Congressional committees on alleged subversion and espionage, claiming the protection of the Fifth Amendment of the United States Constitution which provided exemption from giving evidence in a criminal case, on grounds of possible self-incrimination. In this situation, the Secretary-General appointed an international Commission of Jurists to advise him on the correct course of action. While awaiting its advice, Mr. Lie dismissed temporary employees accused of disloyalty to the United States and placed on leave the contract-holders similarly suspected.

The Commission of Jurists late in 1952 advised the Secretary-General that staff members on permanent appointment could and should be dismissed under the provisions of the Staff Regulations which, in effect, provide that international civil servants 'must conduct themselves in a manner befitting their special status.' It advised that all members of the United Nations recognize the independence of the Secretary-General and his sole responsibility in the selection and retention of staff. The establishment of a special advisory panel was proposed by the Commission to advise the Secretary-General on such cases of suspected subversion. The Report of the Commission concluded with this statement:

> No organization dedicated to such high purposes as the United Nations can hope to serve those purposes unless it enjoys confidence and respect. Yet at the same time, no organization dedicated to law and order in world affairs can hope to survive if its own administrative actions are arbitrary and precipitate, based on mere suspicion and devoid of the due process to which all civilized peoples are dedicated. It should not be expected that the Secretary-General would arrive at serious decisions on evidence which has been denied him, or given him only through the press or by hearsay. The record shows that he has sought reliable information, day in and day out, and on the basis of available facts shaped his course as warranted within the framework of his legal responsibilities.

After first offering them the opportunity of reversing their policy on testifying (which they did not take), the Secretary-General on December 5, 1952, dismissed the contract-holders in the Secretariat on the grounds that their action constituted a fundamental breach of the obligations established in the Staff Regulations, making them unsuitable for continued employment. On January 16, 1953, Mr. Lie announced the appointment of an Advisory Panel which had been recommended by the Commission of Jurists and on February 4 he issued a lengthy report on his personnel policy explaining the circumstances leading up to the dismissals and justifying his course of action. He also announced the establishment of machinery by the government of the United States to screen and hear complaints against its nationals employed in the Secretariat. The Assembly, with some misgivings, expressed its confidence in the personnel policies of the Secretary-General by a vote of 41 to 13, with four abstentions.

Unhappily for the new Secretary-General, Mr. Hammarskjöld, the entire problem of handling cases of alleged subversion and refusal to testify was reopened in the fall of 1953. Twenty-one nationals of the United States had appealed their cases to the Administrative Tribunal which, in August, 1953, handed down its decision.[7] The dismissal of nine temporary employees was upheld. The case of one permanent employee was remanded to the Joint Appeal Board for review. In the remaining eleven cases — one temporary and ten permanent staff members — the Tribunal found that the

[7] See Cohen, Maxwell, 'The United Nations' Secretariat — Some Constitutional and Administrative Developments,' *American Journal of International Law*, Vol. 49, No. 3 (July 1955), pp. 295–319.

dismissals were technically defective, principally for procedural reasons. In seven cases, compensation was ordered in lieu of reinstatement, as requested by the applicants. Reinstatement was ordered in the remaining four cases. Under the Statute of the Tribunal, the Secretary-General is given the option of refusing reinstatement if he believes this to be the wisest course, in which instance the Tribunal decides on the amount of compensation. The Secretary-General refused reinstatement to the four who requested it, and the Tribunal awarded compensation for all eleven permanent contract employees totalling $179,420.

The action of the Tribunal aroused a storm of protest in the United States among those concerned with the subversive activities of United States nationals in the Secretariat. Later in the General Assembly, the United States sought to prevent the payment of the awards to the dismissed staff members. In a compromise move, the Assembly voted to refer the case to the International Court of Justice for an advisory opinion. In 1954, the Court declared that the Assembly did not have the right to reject the awards of the Tribunal when that body had acted within the provisions of its Statute.[8] In the meantime, the Secretary-General, believing that his authority should be strengthened in matters of discipline and dismissal, went before the Assembly with a request to make the necessary revisions and additions in the Staff Regulations designed to accomplish this purpose. These changes, agreed to by the Assembly in 1953, have already been commented upon earlier in this chapter. At the same time, the Assembly amended the Statute of the Administrative Tribunal so that where the Tribunal upheld the claim for an applicant, it would direct the payment of compensation instead of ordering that the decision of the Secretary-General be rescinded. The compensation now is no more than two years' net salary, with the possibility of a higher award in exceptional cases. These changes, in effect, provide the Secretary-General with wider latitude in dismissals if he is willing to grant awards for compensation in the amounts just noted.

Following the advisory opinion of the Court, the United States sought in 1954 at the ninth session of the Assembly to obtain extensive amendments to the Statute of the Administrative Tribunal. Among other things, an attempt was made to establish a Board of Review to examine a judgment of the Tribunal to which a member took exception. Instead of this, however, the Assembly voted to establish an eighteen-member committee to examine the question of some new review agency. A Special Indemnity

[8] See above, pp. 331–2, and *American Journal of International Law,* Vol. 49, No. 1 (January 1955), pp. 6–9.

Fund was also created, to be maintained at $250,000 and to come from staff assessment.

The Special Committee on Review of Administrative Tribunal Judgments heatedly debated the matter in 1955 and made one recommendation to the Tenth Assembly in its report. By a vote of 9 to 4 with 4 abstentions, the proposal was made that if a member of the Organization or of the Secretariat, or the Secretary-General himself believes that the Tribunal has committed an error of procedure, exceeded its jurisdiction or competence, or erred in a question of law relating to the Charter, a request in writing can be made within thirty days to a screening committee composed of the states which have served on the General Committee of the most recent regular session of the Assembly. If the committee decides that a judgment of the Tribunal is subject to question, an advisory opinion of the Court shall be requested.

From this protracted dispute has come some definite clarification of the position of the Secretary-General *vis-à-vis* the Secretariat and his authority has been increased accordingly. It has been established that a host country for an international organization can expect a certain mode of conduct from its nationals working for the organization with respect to their national loyalty. Similarly, the organization is bound to respect such an attitude on the part of the host state but must, at the same time, protect its employees, particularly those in high levels, against arbitrary action in cases of dismissal. Due process must be respected at all times in such matters. The advisory opinion of the court in the *Awards Case* determined that the General Assembly is not supreme in all matters referred to it by the Charter but instead is but one organ functioning within a constitutional framework which imposes limitations as defined by the judgments of the Court and by practices developing within the several organs of the United Nations itself.[9] It is unfortunate that the staff of the Secretariat had to be subjected to psychological and administrative strains resulting from the charges directed toward it of subversion and espionage. Some of the allegations were grossly exaggerated for political purposes in the United States, while others were verified. Nevertheless, the resulting constitutional developments, staff changes, and administrative reorganization already examined were long overdue. The streamlining undergone by the Secretariat, with budgetary savings and elimination of positions and personnel held to be unnecessary, has made that essential organ of the United Nations stronger, more efficient, and more productive.

[9] Cohen, op. cit. pp. 318–19.

INTERNATIONAL SECRETARIATS — SUMMARY
AND CONCLUSIONS

The examination of the United Nations Secretariat has revealed certain problems and principles of organization and procedure which, in general, are applicable to civil servants attached to all public international organizations. By their very nature, international secretariats the world over have much in common in that they serve groups of sovereign nations associating for some purpose, are multinational in composition and perform services for the members. These services range over a wide variety of activities: statistical, research, fiscal, arrangements for conferences and meetings, expert advice, and matters concerning internal administration. Differences in methodology and responsibility do arise between those organizations which are primarily functional and nonpolitical in character, such as the specialized agencies, and organizations which have been designed to perform political as well as nonpolitical duties. In this latter category would be, of course, the United Nations and the Organization of American States. A particular set of problems arises out of the political responsibilities of these two organizations, which places a heavy burden upon their highest civil servants. At the same time organizations such as the specialized agencies cannot escape being faced with questions which are essentially political, owing to the fact that their membership again comprises sovereign states.

International civil servants must develop a loyalty and attachment to the organization they serve. Although they are expected to retain allegiance to their own national states, these civil servants cannot permit such a natural attachment to interfere with their duty to the paricular organization which employs them. It is not easy to conduct oneself as an impartial arbiter, especially when matters of great significance may center around the policies of one's own country. Nevertheless, such a test must be faced and an international outlook developed which comprehends the needs and prejudices of many countries and nationalities.

Each international servant must be protected from interference in the conduct of his duties by states that are members of the organization in which he works. The Charter of the United Nations seeks to provide this independence of thought and action by providing in Article 100 that: 'Each member of the United Nations undertakes to respect the exclusively international character of the responsibilities of the Secretary-General and the staff and not to seek to influence them in the discharge of their responsibilities.' The heads of secretariats find themselves in a particularly vulnerable position with respect to pressures brought upon them for favorable action by important states. Conventions establishing certain privileges and immunities also are necessary to protect the freedom of action of all civil servants and provide their headquarters, archives, and property with a large measure of inviolability from interference by the host country.

The staff of an international secretariat should have as broad a geographical representation as possible. But efforts to recruit staff on such a basis must never prejudice the primary requirement of obtaining the most competent and skilled servants available. Security through an adequate merit system will attract the best qualified expert and keep him on the job. This presupposes adequate salary scales, job classification, allowances, opportunities for promotion, pensions, and job protection against arbitrary punishment and dismissal. The judgment of the International Court of Justice in the *Awards Case* has gone a long way in guaranteeing fair treatment for the staff of the United Nations Secretariat and those of the specialized agencies.

Finally, the responsibilities of international civil servants must be borne in mind by them without reservation. Their position as servants of the world, enjoying certain advantages of protection and immunity, cannot disguise their duty to conduct themselves at all times in a manner befitting their status. The cases of those nationals of the United States who would not testify on charges of espionage brought against them by the authorities of their state cannot help but raise doubts in the minds of many as to the integrity and loyalty of international civil servants. This may be an unfortunate commentary on the capacity of the public to recognize the situation for what it was, namely that only a handful of Americans who for reasons best known to themselves were unwilling to testify on charges akin to treason. But it is, nevertheless, the reaction which can be expected of a public unaccustomed to the nature of an international organization and rightfully indignant over earlier disclosures of the traitorous activities of some of its government employees, which were made possible by an incredible laxity in proper security regulations. It is essential, therefore, that the behavior of international civil servants be exemplary. The following excerpt from the 1953 Report on Standards of Conduct in International Civil Service issued by the International Civil Service Advisory Board should stand as an adequate guide:

> . . . an international outlook . . . flows from understanding of and loyalty to the objective and purposes of the international organization as set forth in its Charter or Constitution. The acceptance of the oath of office and of the basic obligation to serve wholeheartedly and completely the organizations' interests need to be worked out in many directions. It involves willingness to try to understand and be tolerant of different points of view, different cultural patterns, and different work habits. It also entails willingness to work

without prejudice or bias with persons of all nationalties, religions and cultures. It means a readiness to be continually conscious of how proposals, events and statements of opinion may appear to a very wide range of nationalities. . . . In fact, the highest type of loyal international civil servant is one who finds that whatever his personal views he can willingly conform to the observance of his international obligations and support the decisions of the international organization he serves . . . What is essential is not the absence of personal, political, or national views but rather restraint at all times . . . in the expression of such views.

ADDENDUM

RECENT EVENTS in the Middle East have resulted in the Secretary-General's being granted additional responsibilities. Early in June, 1958, the Security Council examined a Lebanese complaint 'of intervention by the United Arab Republic into the internal affairs of Lebanon.' The Secretary-General was then authorized to dispatch an Observation Group to go to Lebanon to ensure that there would be no 'illegal infiltration of personnel or arms or other material across the Lebanese borders.' On June 13, United Nations observers began reconnaissance in Beirut and later in frontier areas. Mr. Hammarskjöld was also present in Lebanon to inspect the activities of the Observation Group.

However, on July 15 the Security Council, meeting in emergency session on the call of the United States to consider the Lebanese situation, was faced with an additional complaint of UAR intervention, this time in the internal affairs of Jordan. Equally serious was the action of the United States in landing military units in Lebanon at the request of the Lebanese government. As the Council discussed the situation, the United Kingdom announced that British paratroopers had landed in Jordan at the urgent request of King Hussein. Before adjourning on July 22, the Council debated four resolutions, all of which were defeated. A Soviet proposal to have the Council call upon the United States and the United Kingdom 'to cease armed intervention in the domestic affairs of Lebanon and Jordan' received only one vote (USSR) while a Swedish resolution to suspend the Observation Group in Lebanon received only the support of the USSR. The Soviet Union vetoed two resolutions (raising its veto total to 85 out of 92): a United States proposal to expand the Observation Group and send a police force into Lebanon; a Japanese compromise plan to ensure Lebanese independence by having the Secretary-General take steps 'to fulfill the general purposes for which the observers had been sent to Lebanon.'

Following the failure of plans to hold a 'summit conference' of chiefs of state, the Security Council on August 7 voted unanimously to call a special emergency session of the General Assembly as provided in the 'Uniting for Peace' resolution. On August 21 the Assembly voted unanimously in favor of an Arab-sponsored resolution which called upon the members of the Arab League to observe the pledge of noninterference in one another's internal affairs contained in the League Pact. Further, the Secretary-General was requested to uphold 'the purposes and principles of the [UN] Charter in relation to Lebanon and Jordan . . . and thereby facilitate the early withdrawal of the foreign troops from the two countries.' Directed to report by September 30 to the Thirteenth Assembly, Mr. Hammarskjöld left for the Middle East on August 25.

IV

WELFARE AND TRUSTEESHIP

12

ECONOMIC AND SOCIAL ORGANIZATION

OF THE UNITED NATIONS

THE argument has long been advanced that order and peace require a certain degree of economic and social stability. The great Chinese leader Sun Yat-sen referred to 'the principle of livelihood.' The same concept is now often expressed by the term 'freedom from want.' This is an age when increased knowledge of natural phenomena and command over the sources of energy have placed greatly expanded productivity within the grasp of mankind and, at the same time, the nations of the modern world, through scientific discovery and technological progress, have gradually been increasing their interdependence. There is a strong belief that social discontent in one country may have a very marked effect upon other states, inasmuch as people who believe that they suffer from economic injustices or who endure a reduction in their standard of living or join a growing mass of unemployed, may become easy prey for those who would use them for their own purposes. Severe economic and social dislocation may encourage a government to risk war in an effort to divert attention away from misery to the honor and glory of aggressive pursuits.

While there is much to justify the conclusion that economic and social inequalities are in part responsible for the failure to preserve peace in the world and that economic and social factors are interwoven in the whole fabric of international relationships, great caution must be exercised in applying this reasoning. It is an oversimplification to state, as does a booklet of the United Nations, that 'It has long been recognized that to ensure peace, it is necessary to solve the world's economic and social problems.' [1] It is somewhat misleading to observe, as does the Constitution of the World Health Organization, that 'the health of all peoples is fundamental to the attainment of peace and security.' No one can deny that attention should

[1] *The Economic and Social Council*, Reference Pamphlet No. 2, United Nations, 1949, p. 1.

be directed to the alleviation of misery and poverty in the world. But it should never be inferred that once misery and poverty are eliminated or at least reduced, the world will live in peace and harmony.

Economic and social stability will not alone guarantee peace and security. Unstable economic and social conditions may very likely be the consequence of war and not its cause. In the final analysis, power, prestige, and national interests among the major powers will dictate the course of peace or war. History reveals how rarely have impoverished nations instigated major conflicts. It is not the Chinese or the Africans who, as reservoirs of misery and unrest, have perpetrated aggression in the past. Quite the reverse may be true. Certainly Germany in 1939 and France under Napoleon more than a century and a quarter earlier were as well-fed and as prosperous as any of their European neighbors. The peace failure of 1919–1939 cannot be attributed directly to economic factors since political and psychological considerations were much more significant. It is increasingly difficult to prevent the intrusion of political factors into fields which have traditionally been considered to be nonpolitical. It may well be that political tensions actually retard the effective functioning of agencies devoted solely to welfare purposes. Furthermore, when there is a relaxation of political conflict it is possible that greater efforts can be devoted to the accomplishment of social and economic objectives.

That hunger, poverty, economic dislocation, and disease can be alleviated by the combined efforts of states is a proved fact. The record of the League of Nations in the nonpolitical field has been obscured by political questions and the failure to answer them, yet it is a record, as we have seen already, in which the League can take considerable pride. The severe dislocations in the wake of the First World War necessitated strenuous League efforts to cope with such problems as refugees, inflation, plague, transport, and communications. The League's pioneering efforts in regard to these critical, emergency short-run problems lacked certain emphasis and scope but nevertheless solid contributions were made to the cause of human welfare. The important point here is that attempts to alleviate misery were made in an effort to meet specific emergencies and not as part of some broader plan which would contribute to the attainment of peace and security. In the same vein, the activities of the League which fell more in the category of long-range planning in social, technical, and economic matters, had the twin aspects of the contribution they would make to peace and security and the humanitarian ideal of a combined effort to improve the life of peoples everywhere, regardless of political considerations.

During World War II, the planning for a future world organization had these objectives under consideration when it was envisaged that a large share of the organization's activities would be devoted to work in the welfare field. In August, 1941, President Roosevelt and Prime Minister Churchill gave impetus to such planning by including in the Atlantic Charter the two following provisions for postwar social and economic aims:

> Fourth, they will endeavor, with due respect for their existing obligations, to further the enjoyment of all states, great and small, victor or vanquished, of access on equal terms, to the trade and to the raw materials of the world which are needed for their economic prosperity.
> Fifth, they desire to bring about the fullest collaboration between all nations in the economic field, with the object of securing for all improved labor standards, economic advancement, and social security.

By the time the San Francisco Conference convened in 1945, several of the specialized agencies had been formed and others were in the planning stage. There remained the formidable task of organizing the role which the United Nations was to play in the welfare field.

The framers at San Francisco immediately recognized the importance of economic and social stability. Consequently, in Article 1:3 of the Charter, one of the purposes of the United Nations is 'to achieve international cooperation in solving international problems of an economic, social, cultural, or humanitarian character. . . .' Later, in Article 55, the Charter gives full recognition to this purpose. The United Nations is dedicated to achieving conditions of stability and well-being by promoting:

> a. Higher standards of living, full employment, and conditions of economic and social progress and development;
> b. Solutions of international economic, social, health, and related problems; and international cultural and educational cooperation; and
> c. Universal respect for, and observance of, human rights and fundamental freedoms for all without distinction as to race, sex, language, or religion.

The objectives of the Charter are entrusted to a large network of agencies. Some of them, such as the specialized agencies, have been established by separate constitutions and functions within the broader confines of the United Nations system as supporting, affiliated bodies. Their nature and scope will be treated in the next chapter. Attention at this time will be directed to the structure and the methodology of those organs and bodies created by the Charter and directly controlled by the United Nations. These include the General Assembly, the Economic and Social Council, with various subordinate commissions and committees, and the Secretariat.

Structure

GENERAL ASSEMBLY

Exclusive final authority over economic and social matters rests with the General Assembly. It will be recalled that the League Covenant did not grant the League Assembly this singularly important position. Although the League Assembly came to assume primary authority, the framers of the Covenant placed responsibility for economic and social questions with both the Council and the Assembly and with various subsidiary bodies reporting to them.

A distinct departure from the structure of the League, although it was moving in that direction, was the establishment of the Economic and Social Council as one of the major organs of the United Nations. According to the Charter, ECOSOC functions 'under the authority of the General Assembly,' a fact which emphasizes the over-all responsibility of the Assembly. ECOSOC must obtain Assembly approval for much of its work, including such matters as concluding agreements with the specialized agencies, calling international conferences, submitting draft resolutions for consideration by member states, and the performance of services requested by members and specialized agencies.

The difficult task of exercising this authority over ECOSOC and its many subordinate bodies and of working with the specialized agencies is entrusted to three Assembly committees. Two of them, the Second Committee (Economic and Financial) and the Fifth Committee (Social, Humanitarian, and Cultural), are regular standing committees. The third is the nine member Advisory Committee on Administrative and Budgetary Questions.

Unlike the League, the Security Council has no direct responsibility in economic and social matters. If it is requested, however, the Security Council may furnish the Assembly and ECOSOC with information and assistance, as was done in drafting plans for the reconstruction of Korea.

THE ECONOMIC AND SOCIAL COUNCIL

As a principal organ of the United Nations, ECOSOC makes studies and reports on international economic, social, cultural, educational, health, and related matters. International conferences are called on matters which lie within its competence. In addition, ECOSOC makes recommendations on such matters to members of the United Nations and the specialized agencies. By no means the least of its activities is the act of co-ordinating 'the activities of the specialized agencies through consultation with and recommendations to such agencies and through recommendations to the General Assembly and to the Members of the United Nations.' These functions are essentially the methods by which the United Nations seeks to accomplish the objectives of the charter in the economic and social field. They will be examined below, following a description of the organization of ECOSOC and its subordinate bodies.

Membership. The General Assembly elects the eighteen members of ECOSOC from the ranks of the United Nations to serve three-year terms. There is no prohibition with regard to re-election. Each member is entitled to one representative who 'may be accompanied by such alternative representatives and technical advisers as he may require.' The permanent members of the Security Council have no privileged position but have served continuously as members of ECOSOC. Some attempt has been made to grant membership to different economic and cultural systems and allow geographical representation where possible. Any member of the United Nations may be invited to participate, without a vote, in its deliberations 'on any matter of particular concern to that member.' Arrangements are also made for representatives of the specialized agencies to participate in its deliberations on the same basis. Various nongovernmental organizations, which will be described later, consult with ECOSOC when matters of mutual concern are before it.

Voting, Officers, Conduct of Business. Each member of ECOSOC has one vote. Decisions are arrived at by a simple majority of the members present and voting. Sessions are held at least twice a year. Special sessions may be held if believed necessary by a majority of ECOSOC, the General Assembly, or the Security Council. With the approval of the Vice-presidents, the President of the Council may call a session and establish its date. Regular sessions are usually held in the Spring and again shortly before the annual session of the General Assembly. The second session normally reconvenes for a short time after the conclusion of an Assembly session to adopt a work schedule for the coming year. Sessions usually last from four to six weeks. Meetings generally are held in public but private sessions may occur if so voted.

Annually, at the start of its first session, the Council elects a President and a first and second Vice-President. These officers are eligible for re-election but may not hold office after the country they represent is no longer a member of ECOSOC. The Council has adopted its own rules of procedure and the President ensures their observance. He accords the right to speak, puts questions and announces decisions.

Items for the provisional agenda are submitted by members of the United Nations, by other principal organs, by the Secretary-General, by the specialized agencies, and by some of the nongovernmental agencies that have been accorded that right. The final agenda is very full, usually consisting of at least forty items and nearly as many sub-items. Social and Economic Committees of the Whole are usually established by ECOSOC at each session for preliminary discussion and recommendation on the many reports which are submitted. Following full Council debate which is frequently spirited, resolutions are adopted, usually numbering around one hundred per session, which are designed to further the objectives of the United Nations in the economic, social, and related fields. Much time is devoted to hearing reports from its subsidiary bodies and from the specialized agencies.

The Commissions. The Charter in Article 68 provides that ECOSOC 'shall set up commissions in economic and social fields and for the promotion of human rights, and such other commissions as may be required for the performance of its functions.' The Council was, therefore, required to establish at least three subsidiary commissions for the purpose of advising it in the performance of its broad responsibilities.

At the time of the San Francisco Conference, there was in existence a number of specialized agencies which were outside the United Nations but whose work would fall within the general scope of the Charter. These were to be co-ordinated with the United Nations through agreements made with ECOSOC. There still remained, however, certain special fields not covered by the specialized agencies, for which there should be established additional organs. The Preparatory Commission in 1945 recommended that additional specialized agencies should be created. Functional commissions, directly responsible to ECOSOC, were suggested by the Preparatory Commission to advise ECOSOC in still other fields of specialization. The recommendations of the Commission were followed and by 1948 ECOSOC had completed its organizational structure.

(1) FUNCTIONAL COMMISSIONS. At present, there are nine commissions in this category, which are: Transport and Communications, Fiscal, Statistical, Population, Social, Human Rights, Status of Women, Narcotic Drugs, and International Commodity Trade.[2] The Human Rights Commission has a Sub-Commission on Prevention of Discrimination and Protection of Minorities. Many of these bodies are direct continuations of the League technical committees.

The size of the commissions varies between fifteen and eighteen members serving three-year terms with no prohibition against additional terms. After considerable deliberation, ECOSOC in 1946 decided that states and not

[2] The Economic, Employment and Development Commission was abolished in 1951.

technical experts should comprise their membership.[3] The members of the commissions are elected by ECOSOC and each is entitled to one representative who is confirmed by the Council. With a view toward obtaining a balanced representation in the various fields, the Secretary-General consults with the states selected for membership prior to their nomination of representatives. Because of its more special nature, the Narcotics Commission was established on a somewhat different basis. It has fifteen members 'which are important producing or manufacturing countries or countries in which illicit traffic in narcotic drugs constitutes a serious social problem.'

These commissions fall into three categories according to the functions assigned them. The Statistical, Fiscal, and Population Commissions are concerned primarily with making studies and submitting technical data to ECOSOC. Although they engage in similar activities, the Transport and Communications, Social, Human Rights, and Status of Women Commissions make recommendations and advise on policy. The Narcotics Commission has supervisory as well as advisory powers, as can be seen from its terms of reference:

(a) assist the Council in exercising such powers of supervision over the application of international conventions and agreements dealing with narcotic drugs as may be assumed by or conferred on the Council;

(b) carry out such functions entrusted to the League of Nations Advisory Committee on Traffic in Opium and other Dangerous Drugs by the international conventions on narcotic drugs as the Council may find necessary to assume and continue;

(c) advise the Council on all matters pertaining to the control of narcotic drugs, and prepare such draft international conventions as may be necessary;

(d) consider what changes may be required in the existing machinery for the international control of narcotic drugs and submit proposals thereon to the Council.

The rules of procedure which govern the conduct of the functional commissions are quite similar to those of ECOSOC. Voting is by simple majority. Officers are selected annually and consist of chairmen, vice-chairmen and *rapporteurs*. Meeting annually are the Commissions on Status of Women, Narcotic Drugs, and Human Rights. The others meet every two years. The representatives are instructed by their governments and consequently, as

---

[3] The United States believed that the commissions should consist of experts serving in their individual capacities while the Soviet Union insisted that the membership should be composed of government representatives functioning under government instructions. See the comments on this point by Loveday, A., 'An Unfortunate Decision,' *International Organization*, Vol. 1, No. 2 (June 1947), pp. 280–90.

is the case with their colleagues on ECOSOC, do not enjoy the freedom of action that should govern impartial decisions on technical matters.

(2) REGIONAL ECONOMIC COMMISSIONS. As directed by the General Assembly, ECOSOC has created four regional economic commissions. In 1947 the Economic Commission for Europe was established and it includes all the European members of the United Nations plus the United States. In the same year, the Economic Commission for Asia and the Far East was created, consisting of the members of the United Nations in Asia and the Far East, plus Australia, France, the Netherlands, New Zealand, the USSR, the United Kingdom, and the United States. A commission was established for Latin America in 1948 with the membership open to United Nations members in North, Central, and South America and the Caribbean, plus France, Britain, and the Netherlands. All of them meet in annual session and operate procedurally in the same manner as the functional commissions. In 1958 the Economic Commission for Africa was created.

The Economic Commission for Europe, with the agreement of the country concerned, performs the following duties:

(a) initiates and participates in measures to facilitate concerted action for raising the level of European economic activity; maintaining and strengthening the economic relations of the European countries both among themselves and with other countries of the world; and dealing with European economic reconstruction.

(b) investigates and studies economic and technological problems and developments within member countries of the commission and within Europe generally;

(c) collects, evaluates and disseminates economic, technological and statistical information.

The Commission works through a number of subsidiary committees on Agricultural Problems, Coal, Electric Power, Industry and Materials, Inland Transport, Manpower, Steel, Timber, and Development of Trade.

The Economic Commission for Asia and the Far East has quite similar terms of reference. It, too, functions through subsidiary organs, such as the committees on Industry and Trade, Inland Transport, and various *ad hoc* and working groups. A Bureau of Flood Control, which is a part of the United Nations Secretariat, works under the direction of the Commission.

The Economic Commission for Latin America is assigned these tasks and performs them with the agreement of the countries concerned:

(a) initiates and participates in measures to facilitate concerted action for dealing with economic problems arising out of the war; raising the level of economic activity in Latin America; and maintaining and strengthening the

economic relations of the Latin American countries both among themselves
and with other countries of the world;

(b) investigates and studies economic and technological problems and
developments in Latin American territories.

Standing Committees. The Economic and Social Council has four standing committees, which vary in size and perform special functions for it.
The Technical Assistance Committee consists of all members of the Council and may sit when the Council is not in session. It is assisted by the
Technical Assistance Board which is an administrative body consisting
of representatives of the specialized agencies that participate in the expanded Technical Assistance Program of the United Nations. The Committee is a policy-making organ for ECOSOC on questions relating to technical assistance. It also reviews the working relationships between the
participating agencies and the effectiveness of the methods of co-ordination
in connection with their technical assistance programs.

The Committee on Negotiations with Inter-Governmental Agencies is
composed of eleven members, elected to indefinite terms by the Council
and is chaired by the Council President. It enters into negotiations with
intergovernmental agencies for the purpose of bringing them into relationship with the United Nations as specialized agencies. Agreements which
have been drafted are presented to ECOSOC for approval.

The Committee on Non-Governmental Organizations consists of seven
members of ECOSOC elected annually, in addition to the Council President. It 'considers the detailed information submitted by the Secretariat on
the nongovernmental organizations which apply for consultative status
and recommends to the Council what action should be taken.' This committee also screens requests from these organizations to have items placed
on ECOSOC's provisional agenda.

The Interim Committee on Program of Conferences has five members
serving indefinite terms who are appointed by the President of ECOSOC.
It consults with the Secretary-General 'in making adjustments in the calendar
of conferences of the subsidiary organs of the Council' and plans the draft
calendar of conferences for succeeding years.

Special Bodies. Several bodies, standing somewhere between the commissions and the specialized agencies in independence, report to ECOSOC.
The Permanent Central Opium Board exists virtually as it did under the
League. It is composed of eight persons acquainted with the problems involved who are appointed by ECOSOC for terms of five years in accordance
with the provisions of a treaty concluded in 1925. It is charged with the general supervision of the narcotics trade. Another League entity, the Drug
Supervisory Body, is composed of four recognized experts, two of whom

are appointed by the World Health Organization and one each by the Permanent Central Opium Board and the Narcotics Commission. It was established by a treaty in 1931 and conducts yearly examinations of government estimates of needs for narcotic drugs for scientific and medical purposes. A protocol signed in 1946 amended the treaties of 1925 and 1931 so that the United Nations could assume the duties previously performed by the League.

The United Nations Children's Fund (formerly known as United Nations International Children's Emergency Fund) was established in 1946 and closely resembles a specialized agency. Depending upon the contributions of individual governments and private donors, the Fund sought to replace the work of UNRRA in alleviating the plight of children and adolescents suffering from wartime dislocations. It has concentrated upon meeting emergency needs and aiding children in underdeveloped countries by conducting child health and welfare programs. Assistance from the Fund is normally in the form of equipment and supplies. An Executive Director administers the Fund in accordance with policies adopted by a twenty-six nation Executive Board and directives from ECOSOC and its Social Commission. The Executive Board is made up of the eighteen states which are members of ECOSOC's Social Commission and eight others, not necessarily members of the United Nations, who are appointed by ECOSOC on the basis of geographical distribution and representation of the major contributing and recipient countries.

The Administrative Committee on Co-ordination is composed of the heads of the specialized agencies which have been brought into relation with the United Nations and the Secretary-General who acts as chairman. It serves to provide the most effective implementation of the agreements concluded between the specialized agencies and the United Nations. Particular attention is devoted to avoiding a duplication of work by the agencies. Various interagency consultative bodies function within the framework of the Committee and are concerned with such matters as public information, and financial and administrative questions. Technical working groups endeavor to plan joint action in specific fields, such as migration, housing, and welfare activities for children and the rehabilitation of the physically handicapped.

The Technical Assistance Board, noted earlier, seeks to co-ordinate the various aspects of the United Nations Expanded Technical Assistance Program. It is composed of an Executive Chairman and representatives of the specialized agencies which participate in the Program. The Chairman is appointed by the Secretary-General in consultation with the participating agencies. It has its own secretariat and resident representatives in different countries or regions receiving assistance.

The Interim Coordinating Committee for International Commodity Arrangements was created by ECOSOC in 1947 at the request of the Preparatory Committee of the International Trade Organization, pending the establishment of that organization. It has attempted to facilitate intergovernmental consultation with respect to commodity problems. Certain of its duties were taken over by the Commission on International Commodity Trade formed by ECOSOC in 1954. Membership consists of a chairman nominated by the Interim Commission for the International Trade Organization and one member nominated by the Food and Agriculture Organization who is concerned particularly with agricultural primary commodities. Two additional members, one whose specialty lies in primary commodities of a nonagricultural type, and another experienced with the problems of underdeveloped countries whose economies are dependent upon the production and marketing of primary commodities, are nominated by the Secretary-General.

Ad Hoc Committees. Various special committees are established from time to time to render particular service for ECOSOC and its subsidiary organs. Examples of some of the matters covered by such committees are forced labor, slavery, prisoners of war, prevention of crime and treatment of offenders, restrictive business practices, and freedom of information. *Ad hoc* committees frequently remain in existence for a year or two until they complete the tasks assigned them by ECOSOC directive.

SECRETARIAT

The nature of the Secretariat's work was discussed in Chapter 11. It is only necessary to note at this time that the Economic and Social Council relies heavily upon the staff of the Secretariat not only for the performance of routine clerical duties, documentation, research, statistical data, and other information but for expert advice and assistance. About one quarter of the Secretariat's staff is engaged in work directly concerned with economic and social matters. The Secretary-General or the Under-Secretary for Economic and Social Affairs works closely with ECOSOC and its subsidiary commissions, committees, and other bodies. There is always at least one high official of the Secretariat present at all meetings of ECOSOC and its subsidiaries. The decisions arrived at by ECOSOC are frequently dependent upon data provided by the Secretariat. These decisions, in turn, invariably must rely upon the Secretary-General for their execution.

METHODS OF ACCOMPLISHING OBJECTIVES

As can be gathered from the foregoing survey, the Economic and Social Council, with its subsidiary units, is the heart and center of the work of the Organization in the general welfare field. Firmly placed in this position, ECOSOC has been given the responsibility for furthering the broad objectives of the Charter in social and economic affairs. This it does through the making of studies and reports 'with respect to international economic, social, cultural, educational, health, and related matters'; the discussion of these matters and recommendations concerning them; and finally and perhaps most important, the co-ordination of the activities of the specialized agencies.

Studies and Reports. The experience of the League showed that when it began its work in economic and social fields, there was a glaring shortage of information available on a worldwide basis. One of the great contributions made by the League was the compilation of statistical and other data which proved to be of inestimable value when any of its organs or members was confronted with questions which were related to such matters as population, migration, water resources, employment indices, and levels of industrial and agricultural productivity. By no means did all countries compile information on items such as these. Either they could not afford to do so or lacked the trained researchers required. Certainly many countries are not able to collect this type of information about other nations. Making available studies and reports to all states is a service which can be provided only by an international agency. The United Nations has continued the work begun by the League and, as a result of greater financial support, has expanded it to a remarkable degree.

Discussion and Recommendation. Many of the studies and reports which have been prepared are discussed at length before being acted on by ECOSOC. They are then quite frequently adopted by a resolution which contains a recommendation that the members of the United Nations heed the findings and subscribe to a particular course of action. Other recommendations are directed to the various organs and agencies of the Organization. In no case does a resolution have any binding effect on the member-states or on other organs of the United Nations. Too often, unfortunately, do the members pay only lip service to the large number of useful recommendations of ECOSOC.

Two additional methods of discussion and recommendation are the prerogatives of ECOSOC. One is the preparation of draft conventions which are submitted to individual members, and sometimes to nonmembers, for adherence. The Charter wisely made this provision in the belief that nations may be more receptive to signing an international agreement if they are offered the opportunity on an equal basis without the necessity of engaging in lengthy negotiations. The rough draft invariably originates in one of

ECOSOC's subsidiary organs. The initial suggestion for such a draft may come from such an organ, from ECOSOC, from the Secretariat, or from the General Assembly.

The other method is the calling of international conferences on items falling within its own competence. ECOSOC does this either on its own initiative or on instructions from the General Assembly. Certain rules which define its authority in the latter case were prescribed in 1949 for ECOSOC by the General Assembly. Care must be taken that the work to be done by the conference is not performed by some other organ or specialized agency. The terms of reference for the conference, the provisional agenda, the states to be invited, the date and place, the provisional rules of procedure, and the selection of an executive secretary are all matters taken care of by ECOSOC with the assistance of the Secretariat.

Co-ordination. One of the most difficult and important functions of ECOSOC is that of co-ordinating 'the activities of the specialized agencies through consultation with and recommendations to such agencies and through recommendations to the General Assembly and to the members of the United Nations' (Article 63:2). The specialized agencies, the nature of which will be discussed in the next chapter, are described in Article 57 of the Charter as those agencies which are established by intergovernmental agreement and which have wide international responsibilities, as defined in their basic instruments, in economic, social, cultural, educational, health, and related fields. These agencies are virtually autonomous international organizations. But to prevent duplication of effort and needless financial expenditures, ECOSOC has endeavored, under the guidance of the General Assembly, to co-ordinate their policies and activities with those of the United Nations. Within such a decentralized system, ECOSOC and the Assembly are limited in their co-ordinating efforts to consultation, negotiation, and recommendation.

(1) AGREEMENTS. The specialized agencies are brought into relationship with the United Nations through agreements negotiated by ECOSOC which are subject to approval by the Assembly. On February 16, 1946, ECOSOC appointed a standing Committee on Negotiations with the Specialized Agencies and it has been responsible for negotiating the agreements. The agreements concluded by ECOSOC fall into three categories: (1) those with the International Labor Organization (ILO), the Food and Agriculture Organization (FAO), the International Civil Aviation Organization (ICAO), the Intergovernmental Maritime Consultative Organization (IMCO), the United Nations Educational, Scientific and Cultural Organization (UNESCO), and the World Health Organization (WHO);

(2) those with the Universal Postal Union (UPU) and the International Telecommunication Union (ITU); (3) and those with the International Bank for Reconstruction and Development, the International Monetary Fund, and the International Finance Corporation (IFC).

The first and largest category includes the agencies which, in general, are broader in character and are largely new in origin: WHO, ILO, FAO, UNESCO, ICAO, and WMO. Using the agreement signed June 10, 1946, between the United Nations and the Food and Agriculture Organization as an example, the following points are typical of the agreements concluded in this category:

1. Reciprocal representation and participation, without vote in all meetings.

2. Reciprocal proposal of agenda items. However, the specialized agencies may propose only for ECOSOC, its commissions, and the Trusteeship Council.

3. Recommendations from the United Nations to the agencies, 'consultation with the United Nations upon request with respect to such recommendations,' and the obligation of the agencies to report the action taken 'to give effect to such recommendations.'

4. 'Subject to such arrangements as may be necessary for the safeguarding of confidential material,' provision is made for 'the fullest and promptest exchange of information and documents.'

5. Assistance as requested to the Security and Trusteeship Councils.

6. Information to the International Court of Justice and the right of the agencies to request advisory opinions from the Court on legal questions arising within the scope of their activities other than questions concerning the mutual relationships of the agencies and the United Nations.

7. Development of 'common personnel standards' with the recognition that the eventual development of a single unified civil service is desirable from the standpoint of effective administrative coordination . . .'

8. Maximum cooperation in statistical, administrative and technical services with a concerted attempt to avoid duplication of effort.

9. Recognition of the need for close budgetary and financial relationships with consultation concerning appropriate arrangements for the inclusion of the budgets of the agencies within the general budget of the United Nations.

10. Implementation of the agreements by mutual decision of the Secretary-General and the executive directors of the agencies.

11. Revision of the agreements through negotiation between the agencies and ECOSOC.

The second category of agreements which have been concluded with UPU and ITU follow the same pattern as those just described but are much more general. Both UPU and ITU have been in existence for many years and perform limited but highly specialized duties. Consequently they are not brought into such close relationship with the United Nations as the newer agencies which function in much broader fields closely associated with the objectives of the Charter in nonpolitical affairs. These agreements contain points 1–4 listed above but are much briefer and less detailed as to the assistance rendered to the United Nations, the personnel arrangements, and statistical, administrative, and technical services. The budgets must only be 'transmitted to the United Nations, and the General Assembly may make recommendations thereon. . . .' There must be six months' notice given on either side before the agreement may be revised.

The third category pertains only to the Bank, the Fund, and IFC, which also have unique functions requiring a special type of arrangement with the United Nations. This type of agreement permits the greatest autonomy enjoyed by any of the agencies and has been criticized for providing the least amount of co-ordination. Reciprocal representation is limited by the fact that representatives of the United Nations may only attend meetings of the Boards of Governors. Greater emphasis is placed on the need 'for the safeguarding of confidential information.' Only 'due consideration' need be given by the Bank, the Fund, and IFC to agenda items proposed by the United Nations instead of reciprocal proposals. Recommendations from the United Nations cannot be made 'without reasonable prior consultation with regard thereto.' Furthermore, the United Nations agrees that it is 'sound policy to refrain from making recommendations to the Bank with respect to particular loans or with respect to terms or conditions of financing by the Bank.' Limited exchange of information is provided and there is agreement on the need for the co-ordination of statistical, administrative, and technical services. Assistance is to be provided the Security and Trusteeship Councils and the Bank, the Fund, and IFC may request advisory opinions from the Court. But the appropriate authorities of the Bank, the Fund, and IFC 'enjoy full autonomy in deciding the form and content' of their budgets and need not transmit them to the United Nations.

(2) CO-ORDINATION PROCEDURES. The essential features of the various types of agreements just noted reveal that the specialized agencies need do little more than co-operate with the United Nations in some matters through certain procedures. The agencies submit their reports to ECOSOC and other appropriate organs. All except the Fund, the Bank, and IFC freely agree to consider the recommendations of the United Nations and report the action taken. Beyond this point, the burden of implementing co-ordination falls to the Assembly and ECOSOC.

The General Assembly has devoted a considerable amount of time to the problem and has established policies for the guidance of ECOSOC and the specialized agencies, and on November 20, 1947, adopted a series of major policy directives relating to co-ordination. Significant are the following items:

1. Co-ordination on the national level by the delegations of individual members of the United Nations.

2. Constant attention by ECOSOC to the relative priority of proposals and the consideration 'as a matter of urgency of the further steps which should be taken to develop effective coordination' between the United Nations and the specialized agencies.

3. Annual presentation by the specialized agencies to the session of the Economic and Social Council preceding the opening of the regular session of the General Assembly, of their 'reports on past activities and their programmes of operations for the subsequent fiscal year to enable the Council to promote the most efficient and practical use of the resources of the United Nations by recommendations concerning the definition of responsibility for specific projects and concerning priorities for action.'

4. Transmission by the specialized agencies of their budgets or budgetary estimates to the Secretary-General before 1 July of the preceding year, in order that the Secretary-General may incorporate these budgets or budgetary estimates as information annexes in his annual budget estimates for transmittal to the General Assembly, together with such summaries as he may deem appropriate and useful.

From 1947 on, the Assembly has continually urged efficient and economic performance by the specialized agencies and has directed ECOSOC and the Secretary-General to do all that is possible to avoid the initiation of projects which, although of some use, could be postponed or integrated with some other activity. The Secretary-General and ECOSOC have been urged particularly to ensure 'that no short-term activity becomes a continuing or permanent activity without a thorough examination of the size, efficiency and other relevant factors of the service concerned.' Individual members are constantly reminded that they should not request the inauguration of new activities unless deemed particularly urgent.

The Economic and Social Council has been aware of its responsibilities for the co-ordination of the activities of the specialized agencies. In 1946 the Secretary-General was requested by ECOSOC 'to establish a standing committee of administrative officers consisting of himself as chairman, and the corresponding officers of the specialized agencies brought into relationship with the United Nations, for the purpose of taking all appropriate steps, under the leadership of the Secretary-General, to insure the fullest and most effective implementation of the agreements entered into between the United Nations and the specialized agencies.' The request was complied with at once and the Administrative Committee on Coordination was created and eventually became a special body reporting to ECOSOC.[4] The Committee has had to undertake the major burdens of co-ordination, acting

[4] The original name was the Coordination Committee, later changed to the Secretary-General's Committee on Coordination. The present title was adopted in 1948.

on directives from ECOSOC and offering advice through periodic reports. Operating within the framework of the Committee have been such inter-agency consultative bodies as the Consultative Committees on Administrative Questions, Statistical Matters, and Public Information.

Largely on the advice of the Administrative Committee on Coordination, ECOSOC has established important policy directives on the following matters:

1. Submission of reports by the specialized agencies not later than May 1 of each year on their organization, the activities of the past year, the activities and work program of the current calendar year, with an indication of priorities for these programs, and the proposed activities and work programs for the following year.

2. Preparation by the Secretary-General in consultation with the specialized agencies, of reports 'on the action taken in pursuance of the agreements between the United Nations and the agencies.'

3. Preparation by the Secretary-General, after consultation with the Administrative Committee on Coordination of an annual *Catalogue of Economic and Social Projects* covering the programs undertaken by the United Nations and the specialized agencies.

4. Submission by the Secretary-General not later than June 1 of each year of a report to include information on the organization and allocation of personnel working on economic and social matters in the Secretariat, their work programs and those of ECOSOC's commissions.

5. Preparation by the Administrative Committee on Co-ordination of annual reports on the problem of overlapping or duplication in the activities of the United Nations and the specialized agencies and methods needed for the improvement of the annual reports of the agencies.

6. Establishment of work priorities by ECOSOC's commissions based on the importance of the various projects begun or contemplated.

7. Adoption of a standard form for reports from the commissions.

8. Establishment of criteria to provide the United Nations and the specialized agencies 'a common approach to the evaluation of priorities' for work projects, namely, urgency, feasibility, breadth or scope, adequacy of preparation and co-ordination, and value of potential results.

Important also has been the Technical Assistance Board which was established in 1950 to co-ordinate the activities of the various commissions and agencies participating in the United Nations technical assistance program.

(3) RELATIONS WITH OTHER INTERGOVERNMENTAL ORGANIZATIONS. As was seen in an earlier chapter, for many years there have existed intergovernmental organizations performing specialized, technical functions in economic, social, cultural, educational, health, and related fields. They have customarily been referred to in the literature on international organization as 'public international unions.' At the San Francisco Conference in 1945, it was recognized that only a certain number of these organizations could

qualify as specialized agencies within the meaning of Article 57 of the Charter, namely those having 'wide international responsibilities.' The Preparatory Commission in late 1945, when preparing recommendations for the various work programs of ECOSOC, again distinguished between specialized agencies and other intergovernmental organizations. The Commission suggested that the latter either be liquidated and their functions transferred to a specialized agency or to a United Nations committee or commission, or that some might be merged with other intergovernmental agencies. It was the firm belief of the Commission that 'more suitable organizational arrangements could be made for the exercise of the functions hitherto entrusted to many of them.' Certainly their number could be greatly reduced with a view toward bringing them into 'a more rational and unified organizational structure.'

At the request of ECOSOC, the Secretary-General in 1948 submitted a list of some seventy of these organizations having responsibilities similar to those of the United Nations and the specialized agencies. A resolution was approved which recommended that members and the specialized agencies submit their views regarding:

> 1. The possible termination, absorption or integration of any of these organizations into the United Nations or the specialized agencies;
> 2. Relationships which might be established between any of the listed organizations and the United Nations or the specialized agencies. . . .

The replies received by the Secretary-General indicated that the members of the United Nations were strongly in favor of the absorption of certain of these organizations. Close relationship was suggested for some of them, while it was believed that in the near future a large number could be dissolved. Periodic examinations of these organizations have been made by the Secretary-General and ECOSOC and an annual list of them has been issued for several years. Several have been integrated with specialized agencies and the Organization of American States has been able to bring a number of American regional organizations into its system of economic and social co-operation. But it is not an easy matter to absorb these organizations, many of whom have been in existence longer than the United Nations. New ones also are established from time to time with no intention of being a part of the United Nations system. Still others are of such a character that very little can be done to integrate their activities. There also remains the view expressed by Denmark that 'should the United Nations at some future date cease to exist in the same form as now, very regrettable interruptions of the continuous research work . . . might result, if a total incorporation in the organization of the United Nations takes place.'

(4) CONSULTATION WITH NONGOVERNMENTAL ORGANIZATIONS (NGO'S). A great number of private or nongovernmental associations have been established, as noted earlier, particularly toward the end of the nineteenth century, whose interests transcend national frontiers. Despite their variety of interests, most of these organizations have one thing in common: their desire for peace and their belief in the principles of international co-operation laid down in the Charter of the United Nations. The Charter recognized their existence in Article 71 and the need for ECOSOC to 'make suitable arrangements for consultation' with them. At its first session in 1946, ECOSOC established a temporary Committee on Arrangements for Consultation with Non-Governmental Organizations. Its Report was adopted by ECOSOC in June, 1946, and contained principles to govern the eligibility of NGO's for consultation. ECOSOC has devoted considerable attention to this problem and has made certain modifications in its procedures since 1946. It has established a standing Council Committee on NGO's which is responsible for most of the work with these organizations. Procedures have now been developed to permit certain NGO's consultative status by categories.

CATEGORY A.[5] Included are organizations which have a basic interest in most of ECOSOC's activities and are closely linked with the economic or social life of the areas which they represent.

1. These organizations may propose items for the provisional agenda of ECOSOC. Such items are first submitted to the Committee on NGO's for screening. The refusal by the Committee to propose an agenda item is final.

2. They may propose agenda items for ECOSOC's commissions, provided there is prior consultation with the Secretary-General. A two-thirds vote is required of a commission before such an item can be placed on its agenda.

3. Written statements by these organizations submitted to ECOSOC and its commissions for circulation are limited to 2000 words.

4. Authorized representatives may sit as observers at all public meetings. They may be invited by ECOSOC to consult with a standing committee appointed for that purpose, if ECOSOC so desires or if an organization so requests such consultation. If a Standing Committee so recommends, authorized representatives may appear before ECOSOC as a whole so that their views may be heard.

CATEGORY B. This includes about one hundred organizations which have a special competence but are concerned specifically with only a few of the fields of activity covered by ECOSOC.

[5] Category A includes the following NGO's as of December, 1957: International Chamber of Commerce, International Confederation of Free Trade Unions, International Co-operative Alliance, International Federation of Agricultural Producers, International Federation of Christian Trade Unions, International Organization of Employers, Inter-Parliamentary Union, World Federation of Trade Unions, and the World Federation of United Nations Associations.

1. No agenda items may be proposed, but written statements not to exceed 500 words may be submitted to ECOSOC. Statements of 2000 words may be addressed to the commissions.

2. Authorized representatives may sit as observers at public meetings of ECOSOC. Consultation with ECOSOC committees is possible if so desired by ECOSOC or specifically requested by the organizations.

REGISTER. A 'register' (formerly 'Category C,' which was abolished in 1950) has been established and is kept by the Secretary-General of all organizations not in full continuous consultative relationship but which might be consulted periodically as necessary by ECOSOC, its commissions, or the Secretariat. There are approximately 125 in this status. The register is concerned with organizations of a more specialized character for which forms of *ad hoc* consultation are more appropriate than a continuing consultative status.

Emphasis has been placed upon consultation between NGO's and ECOSOC's commissions. This has been done so that business coming from the organizations reaches ECOSOC only after careful preliminary consideration in a commission (or by a specialized agency) and after having been brought into proper relationship with other matters under consideration in the same field. Various NGO's have made frequent use of their right to appear before the Council Committee on NGO's and ECOSOC and its commissions. They have also managed to have proposals placed on ECOSOC's provisional agenda. Complaints have been lodged with ECOSOC against governments by some NGO's, particularly with respect to human rights. Written statements have been widely circulated and are usually directed to the Human Rights, Social, and Status of Women Commissions, and the regional commissions.

ECOSOC annually reviews the organizations in consultative status and, on the recommendation of its Committee on NGO's, adds new ones or drops others. In 1947, ECOSOC directed that NGO's with legally constituted branches in Spain whose policies 'are determined and controlled by the Franco Government' were to be excluded from relationship with the United Nations. The exclusion was lifted in 1951 on the grounds that the relationships of NGO's and ECOSOC are technical and largely nonpolitical in character. Communist dominated NGO's have caused considerable trouble, particularly the World Federation of Trade Unions and the Women's International Democratic Federation. The latter had its consultative status withdrawn in 1954 after a disagreeable debate in ECOSOC. The United States has been reluctant to have representatives of such organizations enter the United Nations Headquarters District, without restriction, to engage in propaganda attacks against the West. The withholding of visas by the

United States from representatives of these and other Communist-dominated organizations has led to repercussions within the United Nations. Some members believed that the representatives of all NGO's should be allowed to attend any of the meetings of United Nations organs without invitation. It was decided that they could attend meetings of the General Assembly, in addition to those of ECOSOC and its commissions, if ECOSOC so requests 'whenever economic and social matters are discussed which are within the competence of the Economic and Social Council and the organization concerned.' The United States, however, has continued to reserve its right of denying visas to those authorized representatives deemed inimical to its security.

CONCLUSIONS

The structure and machinery of ECOSOC is sprawling and complex. An examination of the multiplicity of its functions first reveals that it has some of the characteristics of a specialized agency. That is to say, ECOSOC has broad responsibilities through its commissions in various fields which resemble the activities of such bodies. The Commission on Human Rights and the regional commissions are good examples of this. Second, ECOSOC must co-ordinate the activities of the specialized agencies, certainly an important and continuing duty. Third, it functions as a group of diplomatic negotiators on important social and economic questions and in addition, offers advice and information on these matters. Finally, it serves as another forum for debating political and economic philosophies with its debaters fully cognizant of the propaganda value of their remarks.

Unquestionably, ECOSOC does serve as a useful research institute. The many studies and reports of its subsidiaries provide a valuable source of information unavailable elsewhere. That there is some duplication is undeniable. Lack of continuing direction is the basic cause which, of course, is related to the attempt to undertake too many projects. Most members of the United Nations are unable to resist the temptation of suggesting new studies, which are too often accepted as a result of individual pressures. Progress has been made in the co-ordination of the activities of the specialized agencies. The Technical Assistance Board and the Administrative Committee on Coordination have proved to be of value in the machinery of co-ordination. But a great deal more could be done. The crowded agenda permits ECOSOC to cast but a glance at the voluminous reports of the specialized agencies. If it were not for the assistance provided by the extremely overworked Secretariat, it is probable that even more of the essential details relating to co-ordination would be overlooked.

The extent of the economic and social responsibilities of ECOSOC poses one of its greatest difficulties. This was recognized in 1951 when ECOSOC and the General Assembly, in response to repeated requests, examined the organization and operation of ECOSOC and its commissions. Certain procedural reforms were adopted in an attempt to lighten the burdens. One commission (Economic, Employment, and Development) was abolished along with a few subcommissions. Meetings of commissions were reduced and the use of expert assistance from the Secretariat was encouraged. There was talk of reducing the work programs but individual objections proved to be too great an obstacle to a genuine overhaul. Moreover, even some of the reforms aimed at eliminating subcommissions and the frequency of commission meetings were revoked as early as 1952. An examination of ECOSOC's agenda still reveals about the same number of items. ECOSOC itself remains in a somewhat shapeless form, concerned with such essentially political questions as human rights in addition to those economic and social matters not performed by the regular specialized agencies. It is an entity, moreover, filled with politicians and diplomats not only within its own membership but also in its commissions and other subsidiaries.

The fact that government representatives who are not necessarily experts comprise the membership of ECOSOC and its subsidiaries has indirectly, at least, made some of its deliberations assume more of a political character than might have been expected of an organ assigned duties which lie within the field of general welfare. The East-West split has accentuated this situation and made it far more difficult for ECOSOC and its bodies to function as expected. Decisions arrived at are dictated by political considerations originating in the directives issued by governments to their representatives. Advice comes frequently in the form of compromise resolutions arrived at after debates resembling the sessions of the General Assembly and the Security Council in bitterness and propagandizing.

By its very nature, the General Assembly is unable to overcome these deficiencies exhibited by ECOSOC. Its committees working on economic and social questions are composed of delegates who rarely possess adequate training to cope with the problems confronting them. There is insufficient time to examine carefully the many reports and recommendations coming before it. Both in the committee discussions and in plenary sessions, the Assembly goes over the same ground which may already have been covered by a functional commission and several sessions of ECOSOC. Leadership is lacking, both from the Assembly and from ECOSOC. To a certain extent, it has had to be furnished by the Secretariat, a most unlikely source. The twelve hundred or so faithful members of the Secretariat assigned to economic and social questions have done their best to overcome some of the political differences and to serve the cause of economic and social co-operation.

In brief, it is obvious that ECOSOC simply has too many functions. It is entirely possible that the suggestion of Professor Loveday should be adopted.[6] This would divorce from ECOSOC its duties which make it resemble a board of a specialized agency and permit it to concentrate exclusively upon its responsibilities in the field of co-ordination. Should this reform come to pass, the economic and social activities now engaged in by ECOSOC would be located in a new and independent specialized agency. Within such a new entity, there would be a structural overhaul of commissions resulting in considerable integration and greater use of technical experts. Only with such a reform, believes Professor Loveday, can ECOSOC function efficiently and contribute toward developing a well-balanced, co-ordinated, and productive system of economic co-operation. Projects of importance that either get lost or are not submitted at all could have an adequate hearing and stand a reasonable chance of success. The independent structure of a specialized agency might prove to be the machinery needed for developing those economic and social programs which now on occasion languish within the sprawling shape of ECOSOC.

[6] Loveday, A., 'Suggestions for the Reform of the United Nations Economic and Social Machinery,' *International Organization*, Vol. 7, No. 3 (August 1953), pp. 325–41.

13

THE SPECIALIZED AGENCIES

THE Charter of the United Nations, in Article 57, establishes the principle that functional organizations or specialized agencies 'having wide international responsibilities, as defined in their basic instruments, in economic, social, cultural, educational, health, and related fields' should operate outside the framework of the United Nations itself. Close contact is maintained, however, between the individual agency and the United Nations through the conclusion of an agreement negotiated by the Economic and Social Council. A decentralized system, different from that of the League of Nations, was thereby set in motion by the Charter, in which the United Nations performs certain functions and the specialized agencies conduct others in the economic and social field. Over-all co-ordination of this system is given to the United Nations and is carried out, as has been seen in the preceding Chapter, by the Economic and Social Council.

The decision to confer certain functions on specialized agencies instead of granting full responsibility to the United Nations was made for several reasons. It was believed that it would not be possible or desirable for the United Nations to assume the full burden since such a plan would greatly increase the size and complexity of structure of the general organization. Many of the United Nations members would not look with much favor upon an organization possessed of the size and power that would result if all functional activities were made its responsibility. Since much of the work to be performed in the economic and social field is highly technical, the creation of smaller, specialized agencies staffed by skilled technicians was believed to be the wisest course of action. In addition, much of the work of the specialized agency is administrative, and this function had been performed by various international organizations with considerable success for some years. Although of necessity called upon to perform certain administrative functions, the United Nations is not an administrative body in the same sense that the specialized agencies are. There was little expectation, nor should there have been, that an agency such as the Universal Postal Union would cease to exist and turn over its functions to the United Nations. It is far better to permit such an agency to continue its independent role and bring it into harmonious contact with the United Nations in a joint effort to achieve the general objectives of the United Nations Charter. Similarly, with the establishment of newer specialized agencies, a more direct assault can be made upon economic and social problems in an atmosphere free to a degree from the political considerations surrounding the United Nations itself.

THE GENERAL NATURE OF THE SPECIALIZED AGENCY

All specialized agencies have certain definite characteristics in common. They owe their legal existence to treaties or agreements between the states which comprise their membership. All states are eligible for membership provided they agree to abide by the specified requirements of the constituent charters. Since membership is not confined to any geographical region, nor function and responsibility too narrowly limited, the specialized agencies can usually be clearly distinguished from public unions. All must enter into special agreements, freely negotiated with the United Nations. Each has its own constitution or charter which defines the duties and responsibilities of the agency, creates a structure of organization, and provides the officials necessary for the supervision and administration of the agency. All have their own budgets, independently arrived at, and based primarily upon contributions from their own members.

More specifically, each agency has the same general organizational structure: an assembly or conference, composed of all members, as a policy-making organ; an executive council, board or committee which has certain executive and supervisory duties; a director or secretary-general with functions similar to those of the Secretary-General of the United Nations. Each has its own secretariat, independently recruited, and its separate headquarters. These are in various parts of the world: Paris, Berne, Geneva, London, Rome, Washington, and Montreal. Most of them have regional offices and branches in other important centers throughout the world. The executive organs of all agencies are, in varying degree, responsible for the supervision of the duties of their secretariats. Each secretariat plays a significant role in assisting the councils and conferences by performing a myriad of essential duties: publication, research, information, budget preparation, document drafting, and conference preparation and direction, to mention some of the more noteworthy ones. However, when compared to a national bureaucracy the functions of the secretariats are greatly limited, lacking the power to direct, coerce, or arrest. The primary function is that of providing technical assistance.

None of the specialized agencies can do more than propose legislation to their members. Draft treaties are prepared which can become a portion of the domestic law of member-states only if the treaties are ratified. Limited sanctions are possessed by the International Monetary Fund and ILO but they either have proved to lack effectiveness or have not been employed. The Fund, for example, has the authority to fix the value of a member's currency. If the member, without the Fund's approval, changes this value, the violator can be prevented from borrowing from the Fund. When a member of ILO violates an international labor convention, complaints can be placed before the ILO Governing Body. A Commission on Enquiry can be convened to examine the charges and its findings made public. If this procedure is not successful, an economic boycott may be brought against the violator, a drastic step which has not been attempted in spite of a number of violations of ILO conventions.

Whenever agency programs overlap or concern themselves with the same general questions, there arises the inevitable and complex problem of co-ordination. The major aspects of co-ordination were examined in the preceding chapter where the responsibilities of the Administrative Committee on Co-ordination (ACC) and the Technical Assistance Board (TAB) were noted. While TAB is concerned exclusively with the expanded Technical Assistance Program, ACC is composed of the Directors-General of the specialized agencies under the Secretary-General of the United Nations and concentrates its attention on questions of over-all program co-ordination. The need for continuous effort in organizing and directing the work involved calls for considerable consultation and agreement between the agencies involved, the United Nations, regional organizations, the appropriate agencies of national governments, interested public unions, and nongovernmental organizations. For example, in dealing with the complex matter of development and conservation of the world's fisheries, an established unit of a specialized agency, such as the FAO Fisheries Division, is essential. To assist in this aspect of the work, UNESCO has established an Advisory Committee on Marine Science to unify the efforts of scientists working on various problems of the sea. FAO works in close co-operation not only with its seventy-odd member nations but also with the appropriate organs of the United Nations: the World Bank, the Organization for European Economic Cooperation, the United States International Cooperation Administration, the Colombo Plan, the International Council for Exploration of the Seas, and other organizations.

Joint agreements have been concluded and combined committees established between specialized agencies concerned with related aspects of a project. As an illustration, WHO and FAO have created a mixed advisory committee concerned primarily with the co-ordination of their efforts to promote improved nutrition. Similarly, ILO, UNESCO, and WHO appointed a committee of experts to study methods of defining and measuring the cost of living.

While the specialized agencies have many features in common, there are significant differences. To begin with, three of them — International Telecommunication Union (ITU), Universal Postal Union (UPU), and International Labor Organization — had been in existence for some years before the establishment of the United Nations. Two of them — ITU and UPU — antedated the League. After the outbreak of World War II, various conferences established seven additional agencies: Food and Agriculture Organization (FAO); International Civil Aviation Organization (ICAO); United Nations Educational, Scientific and Cultural Organization (UNESCO); World Health Organization (WHO); World Meteorological Organization (WMO); the International Bank for Reconstruction and Development; and the International Monetary Fund. Five of this group — ICAO, UNESCO, FAO, the Bank, and the Fund — resulted from joint action taken by various United Nations governments before the San Francisco Conference in 1945. The Economic and Social Council initially sponsored WHO, acting under the provisions of Articles 59 and 62 of the Charter. Some of these agencies are entirely new in scope and purpose, such as the Fund and the Bank. The other post-League agencies either grew out of former public unions or former League technical committees or have taken over the functions of certain more limited public unions.

Furthermore, some agencies, like FAO, WHO, and UNESCO, have staffs of several hundred persons, many of them located in different parts of the world. Others, such as UPU, ITU, and WMO, are much smaller with most of their staff located at agency headquarters. Four agencies — UPU, ITU, WMO, and ICAO — are primarily concerned with highly technical questions and possess some regulatory powers. In contrast, four other agencies — ILO, WHO, FAO, and UNESCO — have multipurpose functions of an educational, technical, research, advisory, and informational nature. The Fund, the Bank, and the International Finance Corporation (IFC), on the other hand, possess independent financial resources and occupy a unique position in this regard.

While the general pattern of structure, organization, and powers of the agencies is similar, there are some important differences. Admission of nonmembers of the United Nations is usually accomplished by a two-thirds vote of the Conference or Assembly. UNESCO, for example, requires that states not members of the United Nations may be admitted to membership, upon recommendation of the Executive Board, by a two-thirds vote of the General Conference. On the other hand, admission of such members to WHO is permitted by a simple majority vote of the Health Assembly. The composition of the various organs of the agencies consists, in general, of representatives of governments. In the case of the Executive Board of WHO, however, members are selected on the basis of 'their technical competence in the field of health.' The Constitution of UNESCO provides that in electing members of the Executive Board, the General Conference 'shall endeavor to include persons competent in the arts, the humanities, the sciences, education and the diffusion of ideas.' Ordinarily, each member has one vote in the policy-making body. But with respect to the Bank and the Fund, the number of votes cast by each member is approximately in proportion to its monetary contributions. A novel system of representation and voting holds true for ILO. Each member selects four delegates, two of whom represent the government; one, labor; and the other, the employers. Since each delegate casts one vote, it happens that on occasion the voting of an entire delegation is divided. At times the labor delegates vote in a bloc against those representing employers. Special provision is made for representation of the major powers, by virtue of their industrial, financial, or other special competence, on the executive bodies of the Bank, the Fund, ICAO, and ILO. The Board of Directors of IFC is composed of those Executive Directors of the Bank who represent at least one government which is also a member of IFC. Some agencies, especially WHO and ICAO, are granted limited quasi-legislative authority to approve certain technical regulations which become binding on their members unless rejected by individual member governments within a specified time limit. The executive councils of WHO, UPU, and ICAO have the right to settle disputes in certain well-defined administrative fields.

There are a number of wide divergencies between the agencies in the general field of administration. With respect to policy-making, some agencies, such as UPU and WHO, need relatively little leadership at the political level. But where problems are of an economic, agricultural, or social character, political leadership is frequently necessary. Leadership of this sort comes primarily from one or more of the major powers that are members of the agency. There is considerable variance in the practice of agencies regarding questions of personnel administration. Differences appear to be particularly evident with respect to recruitment and appointment, and several underlying philosophies are evident. There is the doctrine of ILO, for example, which holds that considerable influence should be exercised by representatives of the entire staff. Selection in FAO has been left primarily in the hands of department chiefs, subject to final approval of the Director-General. Somewhat different has been the practice of WHO, where personnel appointments, especially on the lower levels, are influenced by the Director of Administrative Management and Personnel. Unlike most other agencies, UNESCO and ILO have recruited many of the younger staff members from recently developed states for junior professional posts and trained them in the civil service methods which they might lack. Variations can also be noted in budgetary practices and in the conduct, composition, and procedure of the committees. Some agencies have strictly scientific committees which confine their work to the solution of a single problem, such as certain of the professional committees of WHO. Many agencies have various standing committees to deal with continuing problems. Most of them have advisory technical bodies such as the ILO Committee of Experts on Social Policy in Non-Metropolitan Areas. Occasionally, some agencies, such as WHO, appoint panels of experts from which small *ad hoc* committees may be selected as the occasion demands.

Nongovernmental or private international organizations (NGO's), work closely with most of the specialized agencies but the degree of relationship and co-operation varies. The Bank, IFC, and the Fund do not maintain official relationships with NGO's. Neither does the Universal Postal Union but UPU works with the International Air Transport Association in regard to air mail postal rates. The Convention establishing ITU provides for co-operation with NGO's having allied interests and although they are invited to participate in the Administrative Conferences of the Union and in the meetings of its International Consultative committees, they are not brought into direct relationship with the organization itself. ICAO, FAO, and WMO invite interested organizations to attend particular meetings. On the other hand, machinery has been established for bringing NGO's into direct relationship with WHO in particular, and also with ILO and UNESCO. Finally, there is a difference in the content of the agreements entered into by the specialized agencies and the United Nations. As noted in the preceding chapter, the agreements with the newer agencies — ICAO, IMCO, UNESCO, WHO, WMO, FAO — and with ILO, are the most detailed and bring these agencies into the closest relationships with the United Nations. The agreements with UPU and ITU contain fewer particulars, while those with the Bank, IFC, and the Fund are the broadest of all and call for the least amount of consultation and co-ordination with the United Nations.

The foregoing survey indicates that while the general outlines of the specialized agencies are similar, they vary in the organizational features and practices designed to fit their individual needs and functions. In one respect, it is comparatively simple to group the agencies together and claim for them a special role in international organization devoted to social progress and economic development. At the same time, each has its particular responsibility, unique problems, and definite procedures for obtaining objectives within each agency. The various organs may exert special or indirect influences, as do the members which contribute the largest share of the budget. A Director-General may possess a particular capacity for leadership in administration and thereby contribute materially to the efficiency and morale of his staff. In an agency whose field of activity is well-defined, common professional and scientific interests can break down national and cultural barriers and assist in uniting the entire international staff. A delegate or delegation to the annual or biennial conference can, through exercising constructive imagination and devotion to the fundamental aims of the agency, give the needed direction to planning programs of work. The presence or absence of these forces will, in large part, result in a successful or a mediocre performance.

In order to understand the full scope of a specialized agency, it will be useful to examine one of them in detail to learn the nature of its functions, structure, and organization, and to discover the range of its activities, the problems encountered in program-making and implementation, and various questions of administration which have an important bearing upon international organization in general. The World Health Organization has been selected as a case study because it is typical of the specialized agency with multipurpose functions and well-defined objectives. The other specialized agencies will be treated briefly at the end of this chapter; their activities will be examined in more detail in the following chapter within the general framework of economic and social co-operation under the United Nations.

WORLD HEALTH ORGANIZATION (WHO)

The Establishment of WHO. For many years it has been recognized that international action is the only feasible method of dealing with the many problems in the field of health. As a consequence, a number of international health organizations were created before the establishment of the United Nations: the International Office of Public Health, the Pan-American Sanitary Bureau, the Health Organization of the League of Nations, and the Health Division of UNRRA. Although each was able to make a contribution, none was able to satisfy the critical need. What was necessary was the building of a single worldwide health system within the broad framework of the United Nations. The United Nations Charter embodies this concept and the first international conference called by the United Nations met for the purpose of establishing such an organization. Sponsored directly by

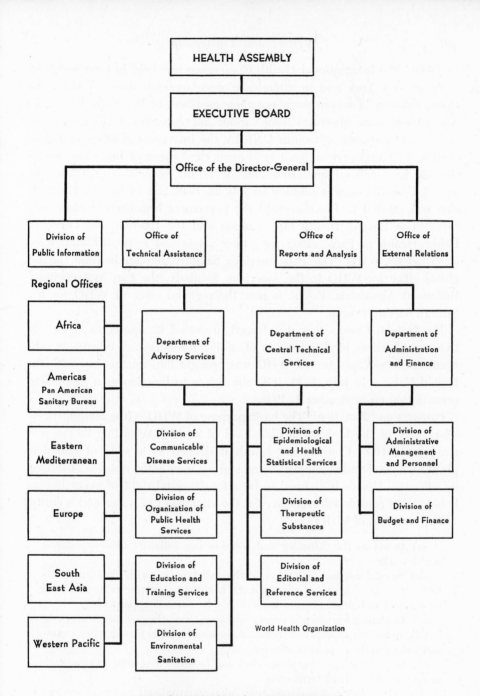

HEALTH ASSEMBLY

EXECUTIVE BOARD

Office of the Director-General

Division of Public Information

Office of Technical Assistance

Office of Reports and Analysis

Office of External Relations

Regional Offices

Africa

Americas
Pan American
Sanitary Bureau

Eastern Mediterranean

Europe

South East Asia

Western Pacific

Department of Advisory Services

Department of Central Technical Services

Department of Administration and Finance

Division of Communicable Disease Services

Division of Organization of Public Health Services

Division of Education and Training Services

Division of Environmental Sanitation

Division of Epidemiological and Health Statistical Services

Division of Therapeutic Substances

Division of Editorial and Reference Services

Division of Administrative Management and Personnel

Division of Budget and Finance

World Health Organization

ORGANIZATIONAL STRUCTURE
OF THE
WORLD HEALTH ORGANIZATION

ECOSOC, the International Health Conference was held in June and July, 1946, at New York and in attendance were representatives of sixty-four states, thirteen of whom were not then members of the United Nations. Also present were observers from various intergovernmental organizations and private associations such as UNRRA, the International Office of Public Health, the Pan-American Sanitary Bureau, the League of Red Cross Societies, the Rockefeller Foundation, and the World Federation of Trade Unions. A Constitution was adopted on July 22, 1946, and an Interim Commission was created to function until the permanent organization came into being. The League Health Organization and the International Office of Public Health in Paris, along with their assets and responsibilities, were absorbed by WHO. The Pan-American Sanitary Bureau became the regional office for WHO in the Americas. Similarly, the Pan Arab Sanitary Bureau at Alexandria, Egypt, is now the regional office of WHO for the Eastern Mediterranean.

The Interim Commission was forced to extend its operation for nearly two years because of the delay in obtaining the necessary twenty-six ratifications of the Constitution. WHO was brought into relationship with the United Nations in July, 1948. It finally began to function as a permanent organization on September 1, 1948.

Purposes and Functions. The basic purpose of WHO is 'the attainment by all peoples of the highest possible level of health.' According to the preamble of WHO's Constitution, health is defined as 'a state of complete physical, mental and social well-being and not merely the absence of disease or infirmity.' Health is claimed to be a fundamental right of every human being and is considered necessary for the attainment of peace and security.

The functions of WHO are:

(a) to act as the directing and coordinating authority on international health work;

(b) to establish and maintain effective collaboration with the United Nations, specialized agencies, governmental health administrations, professional groups and such other organizations as may be deemed appropriate;

(c) to assist governments, upon request, in strengthening health services;

(d) to furnish appropriate technical assistance and, in emergencies, necessary aid upon the request of governments;

(e) to provide . . . health services and facilities to special groups, such as the peoples of trust territories;

(f) to establish and maintain such administrative and technical services as may be required, including epidemiological and statistical services;

(g) to stimulate and advance work to eradicate epidemic, endemic and other diseases;

(h) to promote, in cooperation with other specialized agencies where necessary, the prevention of accidental injuries;

(i) to promote, in cooperation with other specialized agencies where necessary, the improvement of nutrition, housing, sanitation, recreation, economic or working conditions and other aspects of environmental hygiene;

(j) to promote cooperation among scientific and professional groups which contribute to the advancement of health;

(k) to propose conventions, agreements and regulations and make recommendations with respect to international health matters. . . . ;

(l) to promote maternal and child health and welfare and to foster the ability to live harmoniously in a changing total environment;

(m) to foster activities in the field of mental health, especially those affecting the harmony of human relations;

(n) to promote and conduct research in the field of health;

(o) to promote improved standards of teaching and training in health, medical, and related professions;

(p) to study and report on . . . administrative and social techniques affecting public health and medical care from preventive and curative points of view, including hospital services and social security;

(q) to provide information, counsel and assistance in the field of health;

(r) to establish and revise as necessary international nomenclatures of diseases, of causes of death, and of public health practices;

(s) to standardize diagnostic procedures as necessary;

(t) to develop, establish and promote international standards with respect to food, biological, pharmaceutical, and similar products.

Organization. Membership is open to all United Nations member-states willing to adhere to WHO's Constitution. Nonmembers of the United Nations may be voted into membership by a simple majority of the Assembly of WHO. Membership is not limited to sovereign states, since territories or groups of territories not responsible for the conduct of their international relations may be admitted as associate members by the Health Assembly upon application by the appropriate authority. In 1956, three newly independent states — Sudan, Morocco, and Tunisia, all previously associate members — were accorded full membership. Nigeria, the Gold Coast, and Sierra Leone were accepted as associate members, bringing total membership to eighty-eight.

The work of WHO is carried out by an Assembly, an Executive Board, and a Secretariat.

The Health Assembly includes all members of WHO, each represented by up to three delegates. It meets in annual session and every member has one vote. The basic function of the Assembly is the determination of policy for the Organization. It adopts a general plan of work and the annual program and budget based upon the proposals of the Director-General which have been reviewed by the Executive Board. It also reviews the work of WHO and instructs the Executive Board 'in regard to matters upon which action, study, investigation or report may be considered desirable.'

Conventions and agreements may be adopted by a two-thirds vote. The Assembly also has the authority to adopt regulations concerning:

(a) sanitary and quarantine requirements and other procedures designed to prevent the international spread of disease;

(b) nomenclatures with respect to diseases, causes of death and public health practices;

(c) standards with respect to diagnostic procedures for international use;

(d) standards with respect to the safety, purity and potency of biological, pharmaceutical, and similar products moving in international commerce;

(e) advertising and labeling of biological, pharmaceutical and similar products moving in international commerce.

An interesting and rather unusual feature of this authority is that such regulations come into force for all member-states, except those who specifically register a reservation or rejection within a specified period. This is a significant procedure, replacing the more traditional method whereby only states which ratify a convention are bound by it.

The Executive Board of Eighteen consists of persons technically qualified in the field of health. Members serve for three years and are designated by eighteen states selected for this purpose by the Assembly. Meeting twice a year, the Board acts as the executive organ of the Assembly and gives effect to its decisions and policies. On its own initiative, the Board submits advice or proposals to the Assembly. It may take emergency measures to deal with events requiring immediate action, such as epidemics and similar calamities. It also prepares the agenda for the meetings of the Assembly and submits to it a general program of work covering a specific period. In addition to reviewing the budget estimates, the Board examines the work of the Regional Offices of the Organization and appoints the Regional Directors who have been nominated by Regional Committees.

The Secretariat is headed by a Director-General appointed by the Health Assembly on the nomination of the Executive Board. He is the chief technical and administrative officer of WHO and serves as ex-officio secretary of the Assembly, of the Board, and of all conferences and committees of WHO. With respect to this last activity, the Director can exert considerable influence, since he has the authority to intervene in the discussion of any question before these bodies. Within limitations of the budget, he may establish committees of experts and study groups. He prepares the budget estimates upon the basis of estimates submitted by department heads and regional directors who are assisted in this task by regional committees. The budget for 1957 was $10,985,000. The Director-General is assisted by a staff of approximately seven hundred and fifty. Three offices and a division — Public Information, External Affairs, Technical Assistance, and Reports and

Analysis — serve in a staff relationship to the office of the Director-General. The Department of Advisory Services has subdivisions concerned with communicable disease, organization of public health, and professional education and training services. The Department of Central Technical Services has subdivisions devoted to health statistics, therapeutic services, environmental sanitation, epidemiological services, and editorial and reference services. A third department — Administration and Finance — directs its attention to questions of administrative management, personnel, and the budget and finance.

While a certain amount of its activity must necessarily be centered at its headquarters in Geneva, WHO has avoided a mistake of the League of Nations Health Organization by not becoming highly centralized in its organization. The emphasis on decentralization is seen by the establishment of six regional offices or organizations which function within WHO's structural framework. Each regional office has a Director who works with a Regional Committee. The Regional Office for Africa is located in Brazzaville, French Equatorial Africa; for the Americas, there is the Pan-American Sanitary Bureau in Washington, D.C.; Manila is headquarters for the Western Pacific; New Delhi, for South-East Asia; Geneva, for Europe; and Alexandria, Egypt, for the Eastern Mediterranean. A Tuberculosis Research Office is located in Copenhagen and an Epidemiological Intelligence Station is maintained in Singapore.

WHO at Work. As an established organization, WHO has not only combined the functions of earlier health agencies but also has expanded them a great deal. Its objectives are considerably broader than was true of the earlier bodies and its range of authority to achieve these goals approximates the added responsibilities. In addition, WHO has undertaken new activities necessitated by conditions unknown when the older organizations were established and made possible by discoveries which came during or after World War II. Greater emphasis has been placed upon advisory services to governments than was true during the years of the League. The various technical services have been developed more fully than before. WHO has been successful in combatting emergency epidemic conditions when they arose. In recent years WHO has worked very closely with the Technical Assistance Program of the United Nations. The work of WHO in both of these broad categories — advisory and technical — merits further study.

(1) ADVISORY SERVICES. The first Health Assembly in 1948 recognized that certain disease conditions required urgent attention and decided to concentrate its activities in combatting the most prevalent communicable diseases: malaria, tuberculosis, and treponematoses (yaws, syphilis, and bejel).

A malaria-control program in Greece was one of WHO's first projects. Several million people in that country contracted the disease annually, with deaths running into the thousands. With the assistance first of UNRRA and later of WHO, the Greek government began a nationwide anti-malarial campaign which involved spraying of thousands of homes and acres of malarial swamps with DDT. Within three years the death rate had dropped sharply and the control of malaria-carrying pests made possible an increase in olive and rice production because of the additional manpower available. Similar projects have been carried out in over twenty countries, with notable successes particularly in the Philippines, India, Vietnam, Lebanon, and the French Cameroons.

A co-ordinated program to combat tuberculosis on a worldwide scale has included such activities as tuberculin testing and the establishment of tuberculosis centers and BCG (vaccine) laboratories in Asia, Latin America, and Africa. In the BCG project in India, for example, in 1953 alone over ten million children and young adults were tested and over four million non-reactors to tuberculin were vaccinated by about 65 teams, each consisting of one doctor and six BCG technicians. Mass campaigns have demonstrated that with a carefully planned and systematically executed project, infectiousness can be completely suppressed and the incidence of treponemal disease reduced practically to the point of eradication. This has been true of yaws in Haiti and endemic syphilis in Yugoslavia. Techniques for mass treponematosis control have been developed that can be applied widely at a minimum cost by lay technicians. Demonstration, survey, and training projects to assist governments in developing programs for the control of venereal diseases have been completed in a number of countries. In Egypt and India, for example, extensive work has been done to provide health authorities with information on the extent and nature of the venereal disease problem, at the same time helping them to a wider appreciation of modern diagnostic and therapeutic procedures.

A network of influenza laboratories has been established with research facilities expanding gradually in more than a dozen countries. Assistance has been provided to control such other communicable diseases as trachoma, parasitic and virus diseases, and various childhood diseases. Veterinary health has not been neglected, with projects on animal diseases communicable to man, such as rabies and trichinosis. Since 1950, campaigns have been expanded against such pestilential diseases as smallpox, plague, cholera, yellow fever, and typhus.

The Health Assembly in 1948 also laid stress on problems of maternity and child welfare, nutrition, and environmental sanitation. Close co-operation is practiced in these crucial areas with other specialized agencies and with the United Nations, as is true of much of the work on communicable diseases. Consultative services on many aspects of maternal and child care have been provided to more than twenty countries. Teams of consultants specializing in the treatment of children with poliomyelitis have spent time in Chile and India, and joint WHO-UNICEF teams continue to work in South Korea and Malaya. Activity proceeds also on questions of mental health, psychiatric rehabilitation, and juvenile delinquency. In addition to its work with UNICEF in all fields relating to the health of mothers and children, WHO continues to co-operate with FAO on nutrition and food hygiene, with ICAO on the sanitation of airports, with ILO on occupational health, and with UNESCO on fundamental hygiene.

WHO assists a number of countries in building their own health services through the application of knowledge and techniques developed in one particular part of the world to other areas having similar problems. Services of this nature vary and are determined largely by the degree of development arrived at by the medical, health, and related services of the countries concerned. The general promotion of health is carried out by WHO's programs that seek to raise the technical level and the number of trained health and medical workers. Expert consultants are provided to advise training institutions and to organize demonstration centers which carry out certain health projects in many countries. Regional conferences and seminars on endemic health problems have been especially useful. Hundreds of fellowships have been granted by WHO to enable nurses, doctors, and other health personnel to study abroad. New techniques are thus learned which can be applied in the home countries. Thousands of annual subscriptions to medical and health periodicals, as well as books and teaching aids such as filmstrips, slide projectors, and anatomical charts, have been supplied by WHO.

(2) TECHNICAL SERVICES. Perhaps one of the best illustrations of a joint effort on the international level to meet problems common to all peoples is the technical or 'fact-finding' activity of WHO. Services of this nature, some of them begun by earlier health organizations, involve the computation of vital health statistics, the study and reporting of epidemics, biological standardization and quarantine regulations, and medical research and publication.

The absence of accurate and comprehensive vital statistics in many countries can be a serious detriment to the improvement of health on both national and international levels. A number of nations have been assisted by WHO to establish or improve their statistical systems. Particular care is taken to obtain the greatest measure of comparability between the statistical methods of all nations. The first Assembly of WHO, for example, adopted international regulations on health statistics and established certain criteria and principles to be followed everywhere.

With regard to epidemics, there are some that have their origin in specific parts of the world and, given favorable conditions, may spread rapidly over large areas. Diseases do not stop at political borders and therefore they represent a persistent menace. History has recorded numerous instances when plague, cholera, smallpox, and other such pestilential diseases have spread from a central place of origin to many adjacent regions. It is essential that countries be informed, as soon as possible, about such outbreaks so that the spread of infection can be restricted and infected ports and ships can be quarantined. The League of Nations began an epidemiological intelligence service which has been continued and expanded by WHO. The main Epidemiological Intelligence Station has been established in Singapore where direct epidemiological reports are received from a vast area extending from Dunedin, New Zealand, to Alexandria, Egypt. All countries receive these reports through weekly bulletins, by cable, and by daily radio broadcasts. A staff of epidemiologists at the headquarters of WHO in Geneva collects information from all parts of the world and distributes weekly and monthly summaries.

WHO has assisted dramatically in controlling epidemics that have broken out since 1945. The most outstanding and familiar example was the 1947 cholera epidemic in Egypt. Within eight weeks there were 20,000 cases, with a mortality rate of nearly 50 percent. Large quantities of vaccine were supplied along with information on advanced methods of cholera control. Widespread inoculations were carried out with WHO advice and assistance. When a typhus epidemic broke out in Afghanistan, WHO immediately dispatched trained personnel with drugs and equipment. Working with local health authorities, they soon controlled the disease. In the wake of earthquakes and floods in several countries have come outbreaks of disease and in each instance WHO has been able to provide advice, personnel, and medical supplies in the affected areas.

Equally important is the determination of standards for various drugs and biological products. This involves the comparison of existing standards in different countries and, frequently, the development of standards not yet in existence. This is an activity of great significance for all peoples, since, with the free flow of drugs across many national borders, it is essential that drugs and biological products be standardized in nomenclature, production standards, and directions for use. Much of this work has been done by expert committees appointed by WHO. Ordinarily, a group of the best qualified specialists will be called together to formulate the basic terms of a given problem and discuss the methods required to arrive at a solution. Experimentation and research is then conducted in various countries using comparative terms and procedures. Specialists and expert committees have reported on such problems as an international pharmacopoeia, standardization of biological products, and treatment of particular diseases. The study and control of habit-forming drugs is carried out in co-operation with the United Nations.

It is essential to minimize the spread of infectious diseases by establishing effective and uniform quarantine regulations between countries. Such an intricate activity is still another of the technical services performed by WHO. Each country has its own problems and customs. The task of obtaining uniform agreement by all countries is almost as complex as the original work of compiling adequate regulations for stemming the spread of disease. In spite of these difficulties, WHO has managed to compile a number of sanitary conventions which have become binding on all members not registering objections within a specified period.

Finally, WHO conducts specific research projects which contribute to the improvement of worldwide health problems. Examples of specific projects have been the intensive research done on such virus diseases as influenza and trachoma and on a number of parasitic diseases including filariasis and bilharziasis. Research is now underway on problems associated with the use of atomic energy. Studies are concerned with the protection of a population against radiation. The medical use of radioactive isotopes in the diagnosis and treatment of diseases is another aspect of the research and informational activities being carried on. A full program of information and publication is conducted, which includes *The Bulletin of the WHO, Chronicle of WHO, The WHO Technical Report Series, International Digest of Health,* and a *Monograph Series.*

WORK AT THE REGIONAL LEVEL. The six Regional Offices of WHO, integral parts of its structure, represent a noteworthy innovation. Their existence has prevented the development of a large central bureaucracy far removed from the pressing and immediate needs of the people. The Regional Committee, made up of members of WHO within the specific region, is an important link between the governments concerned and WHO itself, permitting a more concentrated emphasis on regional health problems. While the Offices recognize that they exist to further a master plan laid down by WHO, they nevertheless are aware that their needs and suggestions will receive thoughtful attention. The actual location of the Office in a region brings the role of WHO much closer to the people who are the subjects for specific health programs. The Regional Director is assisted by a staff and special experts familiar with local matters. For example, the attachment of a qualified ethnologist to a Regional Office can greatly increase that office's effectiveness. The following is a program outlined by an ethnologist working out of the Regional Office for Africa:

1. Collect, in an analytical and critical report, all the works already devoted to the population in question.

2. Complete, on the spot, the bibliographical data in order to have available a complete study of the culture in question, including those elements which may be the most difficult to understand in the first instance.

3. In carrying out this research, the ethnologist should in particular:

   a. Assess the material possibilities of the people in question so that the health measures contemplated shall not lay a greater burden on the people than they are able to bear;

   b. Study all the beliefs, attitudes, and practices having any relation to health, preventive medicine, and diseases;

   c. Make a list of the traditional remedies employed, and determine what particular relation may exist between these remedies and the peoples' religions;

   d. Study the taboos which are binding upon a whole people, or a tribe or a family, or one individual only, with regard to plants, animals or objects, even attitudes;

   e. Determine the attitude of the population to disease and medical care, the nature of the traditional social relations between sick persons and medical personnel, and between the latter and the various groups and subgroups. It is also desirable to get to know the members of the population group who act as medicine men or healers and the methods they use to combat epidemics or to prevent them.

4. Establish the method of carrying out the program on the basis of data collected in the above manner and in close liaison with health workers, from whom the ethnologist will obtain the necessary information about the requirements and details of the practical measures envisaged.

   a. This plan for carrying out the program will be accompanied by detailed explanations given to all members of the health team so that they may be instructed in the new problems with which they will be confronted.

5. During the carrying out of the program, the ethnologist will intervene to study the reactions of the population. If the cultural factors likely to arise while the program is in progress have been properly studied, the manner in which these cultural factors develop will then provide the ethnologist with indications which will enable him to make recommendations to the health technicians and thus to facilitate the approach to groups and individuals.

6. Any difficulties arising during the application of the program will be analysed jointly in order to find a solution.

Here can be seen the co-operative nature of a procedure employed in a Regional Office, justifying the belief that such offices would be in a better position to understand local problems and carry to native peoples the ideals of WHO and its methods of operation. The part which has been played by these offices in education and publicity and in the positive implementation of the specific programs evolved by the central organization have contributed in no small measure to the progress which has been made in meeting health problems.

RELATIONS WITH NONGOVERNMENTAL ORGANIZATIONS. The World Health Organization has worked consistently with certain important NGO's in the health field and the relationship has been rewarding. These organizations occasionally present ideas which have been worked out in detail and later have received official action. Their representatives have contributed to various meetings and conferences of WHO and some of them have been employed in a consultative status. NGO's have also assisted WHO by carrying out an educational program among their own members and with the general public. At times they have been able, through their national branches, to influence the attitudes of their governments toward principles and policies adopted by WHO.

Caution has been exercised by WHO to prevent NGO's from obtaining too much influence over its policies or otherwise prejudicially affecting its activities. Particular care has been taken to avoid too close a relationship with organizations which have narrow interests and are international only in name and not in spirit. Machinery was established soon after WHO came into being for bringing NGO's into relationship, extending to them the right to appoint representatives to participate, under defined conditions, in the meetings of the Health Assembly or in those of committees or conferences convened under its authority. The major criteria on which such relationship is based are as follows:

1. The organization shall be concerned with matters falling within the competence of WHO.
2. The aims and purposes of the organization shall be in conformity with the spirit, purposes, and principles of the contribution of WHO.
3. The organization shall be of recognized standing and shall represent a substantial proportion of the persons organized for the purpose of participating in the particular field of interest in which it operates.
4. The organization shall have authority to speak for its members through its authorized representatives.
5. The organization shall normally be international in its structure, with members who exercise voting rights in relation to its policies or action.

Nongovermental organizations which have been brought into official consultative relationship with WHO are:

1. Biometric Society
2. Council for the Coordination of International Congresses of Medical Sciences
3. Inter-American Association of Sanitary Engineering
4. International Association for the Prevention of Blindness

5. International Conference of Social Work
6. International Council of Nurses
7. International Dental Federation
8. International League Against Rheumatism
9. International Leprosy Association
10. International Pharmaceutical Federation
11. International Union Against Cancer
12. International Union Against Tuberculosis
13. International Union Against Venereal Diseases
14. International Union for Child Welfare
15. League of Red Cross Societies
16. World Federation for Mental Health
17. World Medical Association

Conclusions The activities of WHO represent a distinct contribution toward meeting the many and intricate problems in the field of health. Considering the limitless health needs of mankind, however, the progress made to date must be considered as only a beginning One cannot measure the time and effort required to accomplish the immediate objectives, let alone the ultimate goal of assisting every individual, regardless of his station in life, to arrive at the highest possible level of health. What is needed is the joint determination of all countries to make available the necessary resources in the struggle to assist less privileged human beings Just as essential is a willingness on the part of governments to support the work of WHO not only with generous financial contributions but also with a spirit of co-operation regardless of the nature of their political, economic, and social systems. In the final analysis WHO can only recommend a procedure or a plan of action. Nations are not legally required to carry out these suggestions But even though WHO is essentially a technical organization devoted to the betterment of the health of mankind, all nations do not feel a moral obligation to assist in this worthy goal and therefore do not give fullest support and co-operation.

Many local customs and taboos stand in the way of health progress. A simple example can best illustrate the seemingly insurmountable aspects of tradition. In a small township of Western Nigeria, a field mission from WHO dug several deep wells, lined them with concrete, and installed winches and steel cables to raise and lower water buckets. But the natives refused to use the wells. It was discovered that tribal customs are very specific about who has to do certain kinds of work. In this instance it was the man's job to dig the wells and the woman's to carry the water. Raising the water to the well-head, however, was something in between and the women flatly refused to do what they considered to be a man's job. As for the men, they refused to turn the handle of the winch to raise the water buckets. The result was that the women were sent a distance of two miles to bring water from a polluted, muddy stream. Even when the stream dried up, the well was not used. Instead, the women were sent to another stream, this time four miles away, where they had to fight the residents of another village who believed that stream to be their property. Patience, understanding, and considerable attention to sociological conditions *before* a project is begun are requisite elements in the work devoted to improvement of the world's health.

Although the annual budget is much larger than the combined resources of earlier organizations, WHO is in need of far greater financial support. In the vast tropical regions, for example, the exact loss of human life owing to the various helminthes (worms) which infest the intestines is not known. With attention directed to the outbreaks of the more spectacular tropical diseases, less emphasis has been placed on these other afflictions which are everyday occurrences. Inaptitude for work is easily explained on the part of millions of indigenous people who live under conditions favoring such infestation. It is extremely difficult for health services to change such a situation. Mass treatment has often been carried out but it can be effective only if it is repeated periodically and applied to millions of individuals. Where is the staff and the money to be found for such undertakings?

Medical progress must go hand in hand with other developments of a social, economic, and political order if it is to bear full fruit. The effort made to control trypanomiasis, for example, has certainly had social repercussions. It has saved hundreds of thousands of individuals from death by sleeping sickness because they were either detected as virus carriers or protected from the disease by the reduction of the virus reservoir. But these peoples' way of living has not been basically changed and in spite of success in the field of medicine, they are still exposed to all the risks of their total environment.

Thus, the progress made toward ending the great epidemics—an exclusively medical success—has not materially altered the way of life of the individual masses. The daily living conditions of these masses are the real cause of social diseases. Exclusively medical action—vaccination, elimination of virus reservoirs, individual treatment—is of a defensive order. The need is to push broad offensive methods. To the attempts to destroy the causal agents must be added increased efforts to achieve hygiene education, health education, transformation of living conditions, and a triumph over nature by economic and social progress. Wells and latrines in villages, better clothing, better housing, and better feeding are important factors for the improvement of health which do not come within the competence and resources of medicine alone. These facts are fully recognized by WHO and other specialized agencies. Their several joint projects and the expanded Technical Assistance Program of the United Nations represent a beginning toward an improvement of general health conditions. Much more is needed, however, and the burden of responsibility rests primarily with individual governments. What WHO, the other specialized agencies, and the United Nations will be able to do will be determined, not by international councils, but by governments and peoples the world over.

INTERNATIONAL LABOR ORGANIZATION (ILO)

The original constitution of ILO was adopted as Part XIII of the Treaty of Versailles and was included in the other peace treaties. On April 11, 1919, ILO was established as an autonomous institution associated with the League of Nations. Although the original members of the League were members of ILO as were all subsequent members, League membership was not a necessary prerequisite.[1] It functioned as one of the most successful of international agencies working at Geneva. The Second World War did not end its activities although the headquarters were moved to Montreal and the scope of its work was limited largely to aiding the cause of the United Nations. The Constitution was amended in 1945 and 1946 to strengthen the organization and make it possible to become associated with the United Nations as a specialized agency. The General Assembly approved the agreement which brought ILO into relationship with the United Nations on December 14, 1946.

Purposes and Functions. The General Conference of ILO meeting in its twenty-sixth session in Philadelphia adopted a Declaration Concerning Aims and Purposes on May 10, 1944. Later known as the Declaration of Philadelphia, it recognized in Article III the obligation of ILO to further programs to achieve:

(a) full employment and the raising of standards of living;

(b) the employment of workers in the occupations in which they can have the satisfaction of giving the fullest measure of their skill and attainments and make their greatest contribution to the common well-being;

(c) the provision, as a means to the attainment of this end and under adequate guarantees for all concerned, of facilities for training and the transfer of labour, including migration for employment and settlement;

(d) policies in regard to wages and earnings, hours, and other conditions of work calculated to ensure a just share of the fruits of progress to all, and a minimum living wage to all employed and in need of protection;

(e) the effective recognition of the right of collective bargaining, the

[1] The International Labor Organization was the only agency associated with the League that the United States joined.

cooperation of management and labour in the continuous improvement of productive efficiency, and the collaboration of workers and employers in the preparation and application of social and economic measures;

(f) the extension of social security measures to provide a basic income to all in need of such protection and comprehensive medical care;

(g) adequate protection for the life and health of workers in all occupations;

(h) provision for child welfare and maternity protection;

(i) the provision of adequate nutrition, housing and facilities for recreation and culture;

(j) the assurance of equality of educational and vocational opportunity.

Organization. Membership is open to any state. Members of the United Nations can automatically become members of ILO. Other states must receive a two-thirds vote of the General Conference, including two-thirds of the votes cast by the government delegates. ILO has three organs: the General Conference, the Governing Body, and the International Labor Office or Secretariat. The General Conference meets at least once a year and is composed of four representatives from each member-state. Two of them are government delegates and the other two represent employers and workers respectively. The latter two are appointed after consultation with national organizations representing the views of employers and workers. Each delegate may be assisted by two advisers for each item on the agenda of a session. Each delegate is allowed one vote. Most of the decisions of the Conference are in the form of conventions and recommendations requiring a two-thirds vote of the Conference. All members are required to submit the conventions adopted by the Conference to their appropriate national authorities for adherence. Members are also obligated to give effect in their national legislation to the views taken by recommendations and 'to report periodically on the position of their law and practice in relation to unratified conventions and recommendations.' Taken as a whole, the recommendations and conventions constitute an International Labor Code which reflects 'international standards of policy.' In the event of violations of a convention, complaint procedures are available through a Commission of Enquiry.

The Governing Body consists of thirty-two members, sixteen of whom represent governments; eight, the employers; and eight, the workers. Of the sixteen persons representing governments, eight are appointed by members selected for that purpose by the government delegates to the Conference, excluding the delegates of the eight members just mentioned. The employer and worker delegates elect the employer and worker members. All members serve three-year terms. The duties of the Governing Body include the appointment of the Director-General of the International Labor Office and the general supervision of that organ, the selection of agenda items for the

General Conference, and the supervision of the many subsidiary committees and commissions of ILO. It also considers proposals for ILO's budget which, for 1957, amounted to $7,617,708. Expenses are apportioned among the members.

The International Labor Office, headed by the Director-General, is the secretariat for ILO with headquarters in Geneva and branch offices in New York and several countries in Europe and Asia. In addition to assisting individual members with the framing of laws and regulations on the basis of the decisions of the Conference, the functions of the Office include:

> the collection and distribution of information on all subjects relating to the international adjustment of conditions of industrial life and labour, and particularly the examination of subjects which it is proposed to bring before the Conference with a view to the conclusion of international Conventions, and the conduct of such special investigations as may be ordered by the Conference or by the Governing Body. In addition to numerous technical publications which ILO issues from time to time is the very useful *Yearbook of Labour Statistics.*

FOOD AND AGRICULTURE ORGANIZATION (FAO) [2]

The first of the permanent United Nations specialized agencies to be launched was FAO. In May, 1943, at Hot Springs, Virginia, forty-four nations met in a United Nations Conference on food and agriculture. The Conference established an Interim Committee which eventually prepared a Constitution for FAO. The agency was formally initiated at Quebec in 1945 when the Constitution was signed. FAO was brought into relationship with the United Nations with the approval of an agreement between the two organizations by the General Assembly in December, 1946.

Purposes and Functions. The preamble to FAO's Constitution provides the purposes of the Organization in these words: 'The Nations accepting this Constitution, being determined to promote the common welfare by furthering separate and collective action on their part for the purposes of raising levels of nutrition and standards of living of the peoples under their respective jurisdictions, securing improvements in the efficiency of the production and distribution of all food and agricultural products, bettering the conditions of rural populations and thus contributing toward an expanding world economy. . . .'

The functions of FAO are contained in Article 1 of its Constitution as follows:

---

[2] The term 'agriculture' includes fisheries, marine products, forestry, and primary forestry products.

1. The Organization shall collect, analyze, interpret, and disseminate information relating to nutrition, food and agriculture;

2. The Organization shall promote and, where appropriate, shall recommend national and international action with respect to

   (a) scientific, technological, social, and economic research relating to nutrition, food and agriculture;

   (b) the improvement of education and administration relating to nutrition, food and agriculture, and the spread of public knowledge of nutritional and agricultural science and practice;

   (c) the conservation of natural resources and the adoption of improved methods of agricultural production;

   (d) the improvement of the processing, marketing, and distribution of food and agricultural products;

   (e) the adoption of policies for the provision of adequate agricultural credit, national and international;

   (f) the adoption of international policies with respect to agricultural commodity arrangements.

3. It shall also be the function of the Organization

   (a) to furnish such technical assistance as governments may request;

   (b) to organize, in cooperation with the governments concerned, such missions as may be needed to assist them to fulfill the obligations arising from their acceptance of the recommendations of the United Nations Conference on Food and Agriculture. . . .

Organization. Original members were those who signed the FAO Constitution in 1945. Additional members may be admitted by a two-thirds vote of the membership. There are three organs of FAO: the Conference, a Council, and a staff headed by a Director-General. Each member has a representative in the Conference, which meets at least once every two years. The Conference determines policy and reviews the work of the Organization. It makes recommendations by a two-thirds vote concerning questions relating to food and agriculture. These recommendations are submitted 'to member nations for consideration with a view to implementation by national action.' Conventions are adopted by a similar vote. Rules are established to guide 'proper consultation with governments and adequate technical preparation' prior to consideration by the Conference of proposed recommendations and conventions.

The council of FAO is composed of twenty-four members elected by the Conference which also appoints an independent Council Chairman. Sitting between sessions of the Conference, the Council has delegated to it by the Conference certain duties, including the constant review of the world food and agriculture situation. A Co-ordination Committee advises the Council on the co-ordination of technical work and the continuity of the activities of the Organization undertaken in accordance with the decisions of the Conference.

A Director-General, appointed by the Conference, has 'full power and authority to direct the work of the Organization.' He appoints the staff of approximately 1100 and it is responsible to him. Panels of experts on agriculture, economics and statistics, fisheries, forestry and forest products, nutrition, and rural welfare have been established by FAO. Regional commodity commissions also have been established, such as the International Rice Commission with headquarters in Bangkok, Thailand, and the Latin American Forestry and Forest Products Commission located in Rio de Janiero. National FAO Committees now exist in more than fifty member-countries and serve as contacts between FAO and governmental and non-governmental agencies. The annual budget is nearly $7 million with an additional $5 million available from technical assistance funds. The headquarters of FAO are in Rome, Italy, with regional offices in Washington, D.C., Rio de Janiero, Mexico City, Santiago, Cairo, and Bangkok.

THE UNITED NATIONS EDUCATIONAL, SCIENTIFIC, AND CULTURAL ORGANIZATION (UNESCO)

A conference held in London in November, 1945, launched UNESCO. After completing a Constitution, a preparatory commission was established to function until UNESCO came into being. The necessary instruments of acceptance by a sufficient number of signatories were deposited with the British government on November 4, 1946, and UNESCO was formally established. Its first regular conference was held in Paris from November 19 to December 10, 1946, and it approved the agreement which brought the Organization into relationship with the United Nations. The agreement came into force when adopted by the General Assembly on December 14, 1946.

Purposes and Functions. UNESCO firmly believes 'that since wars begin in the minds of men, it is in the minds of men that the defenses of peace must be constructed.' It has as its purpose the contribution to peace and security 'by promoting collaboration among the nations through education, science and culture in order to further universal respect for justice, for the rule of law and for the human rights and freedoms' of all peoples without distinction of race, sex, language, or religion.

To accomplish this purpose, UNESCO attempts to

(a) collaborate in the work of advancing the mutual knowledge and understanding of peoples, through all means of mass communication and to that end recommend such international agreements as may be necessary to promote the free flow of ideas by word and image;

(b) give fresh impetus to popular education and to the spread of culture,

by collaborating with members, at their request, in the development of educational activities;

by instituting collaboration among the nations to advance the ideal of equality of educational opportunity without regard to race, sex or any distinctions, economic or social;

by suggesting educational methods best suited to prepare the children of the world for the responsibilities of freedom;

(c) maintain, increase and diffuse knowledge;

by assuring conservation and protection of the world's inheritance of books, works of art and monuments of history and science, and recommending to the nations concerned the necessary international conventions;

by encouraging cooperation among the nations in all branches of intellectual activity, including the international exchange of persons active in the fields of education, science and culture and the exchange of publications, objects of artistic and scientific interest and other materials of information;

by initiating methods of international cooperation calculated to give the people in all countries access to the printed and published materials produced by any of them.

Organization. Membership in the United Nations carries with it the right to membership in UNESCO. Other nations that want to join must have a two-thirds vote of UNESCO's General Conference and approval by ECOSOC. The organs include a General Conference, an Executive Board, and a Secretariat.

The General Conference meets at last once every two years and is composed of all states that are members of UNESCO. Each member may have five delegates but a member has only one vote in the Conference. It determines policies and the main lines of work of the Organization. The Conference summons international conferences on all fields of learning. Recommendations are adopted by a simple majority vote, while international conventions require a two-thirds vote. The Conference also elects the members of the Executive Board and, on the recommendation of the Board, appoints the Director-General. Sessions are held in different countries as decided by the Conference. Observers from other international organizations and NGO's may be invited to attend sessions if recommended by the Board and approved by a two-thirds vote. Officers and committees are selected for each session.

The Executive Board consists of twenty-two members elected for four-year terms. The Conference endeavors to select persons competent in the arts, humanities, sciences, education, and 'the diffusion of ideas, and qualified by their experience and capacity to fulfill the executive and administrative duties of the Board.' Regard is paid to the diversity of cultures and a balanced geographical distribution. Except for the President of the Conference, not more than one national of any member-state can serve on the Board. Acting under the authority of the Conference, the Board executes the program adopted by the Conference and prepares its agenda and program of work.

The Secretariat is composed of the Director-General and staff of approximately eight hundred responsible to him. The Director-General as chief administrative officer participates without vote in all meetings of the Conference, the Board, and the various technical committees. He directs the day to day activities of UNESCO and assists in the furtherance of the several work projects underway. The annual budget is approximately $10 million. The headquarters of the Organization are in Paris.

Each member state is required to make 'such arrangements as suit its particular conditions for the purpose of associating its principal bodies interested in educational, scientific and cultural matters' with the work of UNESCO. Most members have done this through the establishment of national commissions broadly representative of the governments and of the educational, scientific, and cultural bodies concerned. These commissions or national co-operating bodies act in an advisory capacity to their respective delegations to the General Conference and to their governments in matters relating to UNESCO. They also serve as liaison agencies in all matters of interest to the Organization.

INTERNATIONAL CIVIL AVIATION ORGANIZATION (ICAO)

Fifty-two states were represented at the International Civil Aviation Conference which met in Chicago from November 1 to December 7, 1944. A Convention was adopted which called for the establishment of an International Civil Aviation Organization. An Interim Agreement created a provisional ICAO to function until the Organization could be formally set up. The necessary twenty-six states finally ratified the Convention and ICAO came into being on April 4, 1947. The following month, ICAO approved an agreement bringing the Organization into relationship with the United Nations. Two earlier agreements, the Paris Convention of 1919 which established the International Commission for Air Navigation, and the Pan-American Convention on Commercial Aviation of 1928, were superseded by the 1944 Convention as far as the contracting states are concerned.

Purposes and Functions. ICAO seeks to develop the principles and techniques of international air navigation and to encourage the planning and development of international air transport so as to:

(a) Insure the safe and orderly growth of international civil aviation throughout the world;

(b) Encourage the arts of aircraft design and operation for peaceful purposes;

(c) Encourage the development of airways, airports, and air navigation facilities for international civil aviation;

(d) Meet the needs of the peoples of the world for safe, regular, efficient and economical air transport;

(e) Prevent economic waste caused by unreasonable competition;

(f) Insure that the rights of contracting States are fully respected and that every contracting State has a fair opportunity to operate international airlines;

(g) Avoid discrimination between contracting States;

(h) Promote safety of flight in international air navigation;

(i) Promote generally the development of all aspects of international civil aeronautics.

Organization. Members of the United Nations, Allied states during World War II, or neutrals may become members by adhering to the Convention. Others must receive a four-fifths vote from the Assembly of ICAO and approval by the General Assembly of the United Nations. The Assembly and the Council are the two principal organs of ICAO. The Assembly is composed of all members of the Organization and is convened once every three years by the Council. All members are entitled to one vote. It examines and takes appropriate action on the reports of the Council and may 'decide on any matter referred to it' by that organ. All financial arrangements of the Organization are its responsibility. A President and other officers are elected at each meeting. Any matters within its sphere of action may be referred to the Council or subsidiary commissions or bodies.

In virtually continuous session, the Council is composed of twenty-one members elected by the Assembly who serve three-year terms. In selecting the members of the Council, the Assembly gives adequate representation to states of chief importance in air transport and states 'not otherwise included which make the largest contribution to the provision of facilities for international civil air navigation.' Attention is also paid to obtaining representation from all the major geographic areas of the world. The Council requests, collects, examines, and publishes information relating to the advancement of air navigation and the operation of international air services, 'including information about the costs of operation and particulars of subsidies paid to airlines from public funds.' It also adopts international air navigation standards and recommended practices. If requested by a member, the Council investigates any situation which may appear to 'present avoidable obstacles' to the development of international air navigation. The Council acts as an arbiter between two or more members of ICAO in any dispute which concerns the interpretation of the Convention and its annexes. It also functions as an arbitral board in any dispute arising among members that relates to international civil aviation.

Important subsidiary bodies are appointed by the Council and are responsible to it. The Air Navigation Commission of twelve members advises the Council on all matters relating to the advancement of air navigation. It assigns its technical work to the following divisions: Aerodromes, Air Routes and Ground Aids; Accident Investigation; Airworthiness; Communication; Aeronautical Maps and Charts; Meteorology; Operating Practices; Personnel Licensing; Rules of the Air and Air Traffic Control; and Search and Rescue. The Air Transport Committee studies such matters as air traffic, international ownership, and other related questions, and reports on them to the Council. There are also Legal and Financial Committees. A Secretary-General appointed by the Council is the chief administrative officer of the Organization in charge of the technical staff numbering nearly five hundred. The seat of ICAO is in Montreal, Canada, and the annual budget is slightly more than $3 million.

The Convention adopted in 1944 includes two important annexes—the International Air Services Transit Agreement and the International Air Transport Agreement—which are administered by ICAO. Members of ICAO who have not signed these Agreements cannot vote on any matters relating to them. Both the Air Navigation Commission and the Air Transport Committee advise the Council on pertinent aspects of these Agreements. The International Air Transport Agreement includes these 'five freedoms' which each contracting state grants to the other:

1. The privilege to fly across its territory without landing;
2. The privilege to land for non-traffic purposes;
3. The privilege to put down passengers, mail and cargo taken on in the territory of the State whose nationality the aircraft possesses;
4. The privilege to take on passengers, mail and cargo destined for the territory of the State whose nationality the aircraft possesses;
5. The privilege to take on passengers, mail and cargo destined for the territory of any other contracting State and the privilege to put down passengers, mail and cargo coming from any such territory.

INTERNATIONAL BANK FOR RECONSTRUCTION AND DEVELOPMENT (BANK)

The United Nations Monetary and Financial Conference met at Bretton Woods, New Hampshire, in July, 1944, and drafted the Articles of Agreement which established the Bank. On December 27, 1945, the Bank came into existence when twenty-nine governments had signed the Agreement.

The Bank was brought into relationship with the United Nations on November 15, 1947, when the General Assembly approved the contractural agreement.

Purposes and Functions. The purposes of the Bank are:

(a) To assist in the reconstruction and development of territories of members by facilitating the investment of capital for productive purposes, including the restoration of economies destroyed or disrupted by war, the reconversion of productive facilities to peacetime needs and the encouragement of the development of productive facilities and resources in less developed countries.

(b) To promote private foreign investment by means of guarantees or participations in loans and other investments made by private investors; and when private capital is not available on reasonable terms, to supplement private investment by providing, on suitable conditions, finance for productive purposes out of its own capital, funds raised by it and its other resources.

(c) To promote the long-range balanced growth of international trade and the maintenance of equilibrium in balances of payments by encouraging international investment for the development of the productive resources of members, thereby assisting in raising productivity, the standard of living and conditions of labor in their territories.

(d) To arrange the loans made or guaranteed by it in relation to international loans through other channels so that the more useful and urgent projects, large and small alike, will be dealt with first.

(e) To conduct its operations with due regard to the effect of international investment on business conditions in the territories of members, and in the immediate post-war years, to assist in bringing about a smooth transition from a wartime to a peace-time economy.

The authorized capital of the Bank is $10 billion which is divided into 100,000 shares having a par value of $100,000 each. The total subscribed capital of the Bank in 1958 was about $9.4 billion. The subscription of each member is divided into two parts. (1) Twenty percent represents the Bank's direct lending fund, 2 percent of which must be paid by members in gold or United States dollars almost immediately after joining. The remaining 18 percent is paid upon call in the currency of the members. (2) The balance is subject to call when the Bank is required to meet certain of its outstanding obligations. The Bank makes or participates in direct loans out of its own funds or from funds raised in the markets of members. It may also guarantee in whole or in part loans made by private investors through the usual investment channels. Loans may be made directly to member countries 'or any political sub-division thereof and any business, industrial, and agricultural enterprise in the territories of a member.' When the member in whose territories the project is located is not itself the borrower, the member or its central bank or some comparable agency acceptable to the Bank must guarantee the repayment of the principal and the payment of interest and other charges on the loan.

Before making a loan, the Bank must be satisfied that in the prevailing market conditions, the borrower would not be able to obtain the loan 'under conditions which in the opinion of the Bank are reasonable for the borrower.' The Bank also determines prior to lending funds that the borrower, or the guarantor if the borrower is not a member, is in a position to meet its obligations under the loan. Suitable compensation for the risk of the Bank is required. Interest has varied from 2 percent to 3½ percent. The Bank's commission for administrative expenses is one percent. Repayment of loans is on a flexible basis with provision for a relaxation of the conditions of payment 'if a member suffers from an acute exchange stringency.' Except in special circumstances, loans made or guaranteed must be for the purpose of specific projects of reconstruction or development.

Organization. Membership is open to states who were members of the International Monetary Fund before December 31, 1945. Others may be admitted by majority vote of the Board of Governors and must also belong to the Fund. If a member of the Bank ceases to be a member of the Fund, he loses his membership in the Bank unless the Board, by a three-fourths vote decides otherwise.

The Bank has a Board of Governors, Executive Directors, and a President. The Board consists of one governor and one alternate appointed by each member. They serve for five-year terms. All powers of the Bank are vested in the Board which meets annually to review the operations of the Bank and establish policy necessary for the conduct of its business. Each member has two hundred and fifty votes plus one additional vote for each share of stock held. Most decisions are arrived at by a majority vote.

The Board has delegated many of its powers to the sixteen Executive Directors who are responsible for the conduct of the general operations of the Bank. They normally meet once a month at the Bank's headquarters in Washington, D.C. Five of them are appointed by the five members having the largest number of shares and eleven are elected by the Governors of the other members. Each appointed director casts the number of votes belonging to the member appointing him while each elected director has the same number of votes as the countries that elected him. The votes of a director are cast as a unit.

A President is selected by the Executive Directors and he is chief of the operating staff of the Bank and is responsible for the organization, appointment, and dismissal of the officers and staff. He presides as Chairman of the Executive Directors and participates in the meetings of the Board without voting privileges in either body.

The Bank assists its members in the preparation and execution of loan projects and furnishes a wide variety of technical aid and assistance unrelated to immediate financial operations. Such assistance is designed to 'help member countries in assessing their own resources, in working out long-range programmes for raising productivity and standards of living, in setting up priorities for projects within these programmes, and in dealing with development problems in particular fields.' Aid in planning the development of member-states has come through the general survey mission which consists of a group of experts who study a country's resources and make recommendations designed to form the basis of a long-term development program. Special survey missions study a particular feature of a country's economy and recommend measures for its development. Staff members and other experts are provided to advise on certain problems of development.

International Finance Corporation (IFC). An affiliate of the Bank, IFC came into effect in July, 1956. It is a separate legal entity, however, and its funds are not a part of the Bank. The Corporation has an authorized capitalization of $100 million, of which $93 million had been subscribed by fifty-three nations in the spring of 1958. Membership is open only to those who are members of the Bank. With headquarters in Washington, D.C., IFC became a specialized agency in relationship with the United Nations in February, 1957.

The purpose of IFC is to encourage the growth of productive private enterprises, especially in the underdeveloped countries, thereby supplementing the activities of the Bank. To accomplish this goal, three undertakings are engaged in by the Corporation: 'the establishment, improvement and expansion of productive private enterprises . . . by making investments, without guarantee of repayment by the member government concerned'; serving as a broker between those seeking capital and those with capital to invest by investigating the soundness of the projects and thereby being able to provide expert information to potential investors; promoting in both capital exporting and capital importing countries conditions conducive to the flow of productive, private investment.

Four criteria govern the activities of the Corporation: the enterprise must be a sound investment; it must contribute to the general development of the country concerned; there must be a lack of private capital available on reasonable terms; the enterprise must be acceptable to the host country.

The Corporation is headed by a president and a Board of Directors, the latter composed of those Executive Directors of the Bank who represent at least one goverment which is also a member of the IFC.

INTERNATIONAL MONETARY FUND (FUND)

The Bretton Woods Conference in 1944 drew up the Articles of Agreement of the Fund. It came into existence in December, 1945, and was brought into relationship with the United Nations, along with the Bank, in November, 1947.

Purposes and Functions. Article I of the Articles of Agreement state the following purposes:

(i) To promote international monetary cooperation through a permanent institution which provides the machinery for consultation and collaboration on international monetary problems.

(ii) To facilitate the expansion and balanced growth of international trade, and to contribute thereby to the promotion and maintenance of high levels of employment and real income and to the development of the productive resources of all members as primary objectives of economic policy.

(iii) To promote exchange stability, to maintain orderly exchange arrangements among members, and to avoid competitive exchange depreciation.

(iv) To assist in the establishment of a multilateral system of payments in respect of current transactions between members and in the elimination of foreign exchange restrictions which hamper the growth of world trade.

(v) To give confidence to members by making the Fund's resources available to them under adequate safeguards, thus providing them with opportunity to correct maladjustments in their balance of payments without resorting to measures destructive of national or international prosperity.

(vi) In accordance with the above, to shorten the duration and lessen the degree of disequilibrium in the international balances of payments of members.

Each member of the Fund is assigned a quota which was set in the original Articles of Agreement or later established by a four-fifths vote and the consent of the member. Twenty-five percent is paid in gold and the remainder in the currency of the member. A change in the par value of a member's currency cannot be proposed unless it is necessary 'to correct a fundamental disequilibrium.' Any change requires prior consultation with the Fund, although if it does not exceed 10 percent 'the Fund shall raise no objection.' A majority vote of the Fund is necessary to permit a uniform proportionate change (i.e., change in the value of gold) in the par value of a member's currency, provided such a change 'is approved by every member which has ten percent or more of the total of the quotas.' The gold value of the Fund's assets is maintained irrespective of changes in the par or foreign exchange value of the currency of any member.

Subject to specific conditions a member is entitled to buy the currency of another member from the Fund in exchange for its own currency. A charge of three-fourths of one percent a year is made for such purchases on amounts not more than 25 percent in excess of the quota of a member. The charges increase gradually for larger amounts. If a member uses the resources of the Fund in a manner contrary to the purposes of the Agreement, it may be limited in or declared ineligible for the use of these resources. Purchases of currency from the Fund can be used only for purposes which are approved by the Fund. If the Fund discovers that there is a general scarcity of a particular currency, 'the Fund may so inform members and may issue a report setting forth the causes of the scarcity and containing recommendations designed to bring it to an end.' In addition, a member may not make net use of the Fund's resources 'to meet a large or sustained outflow of capital' and the Fund may request a member to prevent such use of the resources by exercising controls. Finally, members are expected to furnish the Fund with information of many sorts, including such items as official holdings at home and abroad of gold and foreign exchange, production of gold, national income, exchange controls, price indices, international investment position, international balance of payments, gold exports and imports, and total exports and imports of merchandise with particular respect to countries of destination and origin.

Organization. In addition to the original members, others may be admitted by the Board of Governors by a simple majority of the total voting power. Each member has two hundred and fifty votes plus one additional vote for each part of its quota equivalent to $100,000.00.

The Fund has a Board of Governors, Executive Directors, a Managing Director, and a staff. All powers of the Fund are vested in the Board, which consists of one governor and one alternate appointed by each member. The Board selects one of its members as chairman and holds an annual meeting. Each Governor casts as a unit all votes allotted to the member-state that he represents. Most decisions are arrived at by a simple majority vote. In voting on certain matters, such as the question of a waiver of conditions governing the use of the Fund's resources or declaring a member ineligible to use the resources, the voting power of each member is adjusted 'by the addition of one vote for each $400,000 of sales of its currency and by the subtraction of one vote for each $400,000 of its purchases of other currency.'

The sixteen Executive Directors meet in continuous session and are responsible for the conduct of the general operations of the Fund. They exercise a number of powers delegated to them by the Board but cannot perform such functions as revising quotas, admitting new members, and other special prerogatives of the Board. Five of the Directors are appointed by the five members having the largest quotas. The other Directors are elected by the Governors representing the remaining members of the Fund, as follows: two by Latin American countries and nine by members which are not Latin American. Each appointed Director casts as a unit all the votes allotted to the member that appointed him. An elected Director casts as a unit all the votes granted to those countries that elected him.

The Executive Directors select a Managing Director to be the chief of the operating staff. He acts as chairman of the Executive Directors and attends meetings of the Board but does not possess a vote in either body. He is responsible for the organization, and for the appointment and dismissal of the staff. Personnel are recruited on as wide a geographical basis as possible. The headquarters of the Fund are in Washington, D.C.

UNIVERSAL POSTAL UNION (UPU)

The first international Postal Congress held at Berne, Switzerland in 1874 established the General Postal Union. The name was changed in 1878 to Universal Postal Union. The Convention that founded the Union came into force in 1875 and has been revised at later Postal Congresses. In 1947, the Convention was amended to make it possible for the UPU to be brought into relationship with the United Nations. The General Assembly, in 1947, approved the agreement which made this prewar bureau a specialized agency of the United Nations.

Purposes and Functions. The countries which have adhered to the Postal Convention form a single postal territory 'for the reciprocal exchange of correspondence.' The essential purpose of UPU is 'to assure the organization and perfection of the various postal services and to promote development and international collaboration in this field.' The Convention governs the regular mail service. Special services form the subject of accessory agreements drawn up by the Congresses of the Union. These agreements cover such items as insured letters and boxes, parcel post, C.O.D., money orders, postal checks, collection orders, and subscriptions to newspapers and periodicals. The agreements are optional and apply to communications only between the countries which have signed them. The Union also performs research and information services, assists in arbitrating disputes between members, and functions 'as a clearing-house for the settlement of accounts of all kinds relative to the international postal service.'

Organization. Any sovereign country may, through diplomatic channels to the Swiss government, request the right to adhere to the Convention and thereby join the Union. At least two thirds of the members must approve a request for membership. The Union is composed of a Congress, the Executive and Liaison Committee, and a Bureau. The Universal Postal Congress meets not later than five years after the date of entry into force of the Acts of the preceding Congress, 'with a view to revising or completing those Acts, if necessary.' Each member is represented at a Congress by one delegate and all countries have but one vote apiece. Each Congress determines the meeting place of the next one, which is called into session by the country in which it is to be held after consultation with the Bureau of the Union. The Acts of the Congresses are ratified as soon as possible and are communicated to the government of the country where the Congress was held.

The continuity of the Union's work during the interval between Congresses is ensured by the Executive and Liaison Committee which is located at Berne. It is composed of twenty members elected by the Congress who in turn elect their own President and four Vice-Presidents and meet at least once a year upon convocation by the President. The functions of the Committee include: (1) the maintenance of close relations with members of the Union, 'with a view to improving the International Postal Service'; (2) the study of technical questions of interest to the postal service and the reporting of the results of studies to the members; (3) the establishment and maintenance of working relationships with the United Nations and its specialized agencies; (4) the control of the work of the Bureau of the Union. It also appoints the Director and other important personnel of the Bureau.

The International Bureau of the UPU, located at Berne, functions under the supervision of the Swiss postal authorities, serving as an 'organ of liaison, information and consultation for the countries of the Union.' It assembles, co-ordinates, publishes, and distributes information of all kinds concerning the international postal service. At the request of interested parties, the Bureau gives opinions on questions in dispute and offers interpretations of the Postal Convention. It undertakes the necessary preparations for congresses and conferences and serves postal administrations as a clearing house for the settlement of postal accounts, particularly those relating to transit payments and reply coupons. The Bureau also has the important duty, between meetings of the Congress, of receiving requests for modification of the Acts of the Congress and expediting any changes which are adopted. The annual budget is approximately $650,000.

INTERNATIONAL TELECOMMUNICATION UNION (ITU)

The predecessor to ITU, the International Telegraph Union, was established by the Paris Convention of 1865. In 1932, the International Telegraph Convention and the International Radiotelegraph Convention were merged to form the International Telecommunication Convention which was signed in Madrid. At that time ITU was created and replaced the International Telegraph Union. In 1947 a new Convention was drafted which reorganized ITU and established new permanent organs. This Convention came into force on January 1, 1949.

Purposes and Functions. The purposes of ITU are:

(a) to maintain and extend international cooperation for the improvement and rational use of telecommunication of all kinds;

(b) to promote the development of technical facilities and their most efficient operation with a view to improving the efficiency of telecommunication services, increasing their usefulness and making them, so far as possible, generally available to the public;

(c) to harmonize the actions of nations in the attainment of those common ends.

To accomplish these purposes, the ITU functions to:

(a) effect allocation of the radio frequency spectrum and registration of radio frequency assignments in order to avoid harmful interference between radio stations of different countries;

(b) foster collaboration among its members and associate members with a view to the establishment of rates at levels as low as possible consistent with an efficient service and taking into account the necessity for maintaining independent financial administration of telecommunication on a sound basis;

(c) promote the adoption of measures for ensuring the safety of life through the cooperation of telecommunication service;

(d) undertake studies, formulate recommendations, and collect and publish information on telecommunication matters for the benefit of all members and associate members.

Organization. A two-thirds vote of approval by the members is required for admission to ITU. A full member is entitled to one vote at any conference or in any organ of the Union on which it serves. Associate members are those areas, such as trust territories, which are not sovereign states. They possess all the rights and obligations of members but cannot serve on any organ of the Union and do not possess a vote. The organs of ITU are a Plenipotentiary Conference, Administrative Conferences, the Administrative Council, a Secretariat, and several important sub-bodies.

The Plenipotentiary Conference is the supreme organ of the Union at which all members are represented. It normally meets once every five years at a time and place fixed by the preceding Conference. Each Plenipotentiary Conference establishes the basis for the budget of ITU for the next five years, approves the accounts of the Union, elects the members of the Administrative Council, makes necessary revisions in the Convention and, in general, deals with such other telecommunications questions as may be necessary.

Two Administrative Conferences, at which all members are represented, generally meet at the same time and place as the Plenipotentiary Conference. These are the Administrative Telegraph and and Telephone Conference and the Administrative Radio Conference. Regional administrative conferences and special international administrative conferences, to deal with particular telecommunication questions, are held from time to time. The Administrative Conferences adopt special telegraph, telephone, and radio regulations which are binding on all members and associate members.

The Administrative Council is composed of eighteen members elected by the Plenipotentiary Conference. Due regard is taken for equitable geographical representation. It is responsible for taking all steps to facilitate the implementation of the Convention, the regulations adopted by the Administrative Conferences and decisions of the Plenipotentiary Conferences. The Council supervises the administrative functions of ITU between Plenipotentiary Conferences, approves the annual budget of approximately $1.5 million, and co-ordinates the work of the other organs of the Union. It meets at least once a year at the headquarters of ITU in Geneva and selects the Secretary-General and his immediate assistants.

Under the direction of the Secretary-General, the Secretariat of ITU performs research and publishing activities and circulates data both national and international regarding telecommunications throughout the world. Several other sub-bodies of ITU further its work. Chief among these is the International Frequency Registration Board of eleven persons chosen by the Administrative Radio Conference who serve 'not as representatives of their respective countries, or of a region, but as custodians of an international public trust.' The Board records all frequency assignments made by the different countries and furnishes advice to members of ITU 'with a view to the operation of the maximum practicable number of radio channels in those portions of the spectrum where harmful interference may occur.' Two technical advisory bodies, the Telephone and Telegraph Committee, and Radio Consultative Committee, are composed of national telecommunications and recognized private operating agencies which express a desire to have their experts participate in the work of these committees. Each Consultative Committee works through the medium of a Plenary Assembly, a Director, and a specialized Secretariat.

WORLD METEOROLOGICAL ORGANIZATION (WMO)

In 1878, the International Meteorological Organization (IMO) was established, composed of the directors of independent official meteorological services of various states and territories. It was decided in 1939 to transform IMO into an intergovernmental organization with members consisting of states that maintained independent meteorological services instead of just the directors of those agencies. It was not until 1947 that the Convention establishing WMO was drawn up and it came into force in 1950.

Purposes and Functions. Article 2 of the Convention states that the purposes of WMO are:

(a) To facilitate worldwide cooperation in the establishment of networks of stations for the making of meteorological observations or other geophysical observations related to meteorology and to promote the establishment and maintenance of meteorological centers charged with the provision of meteorological services;

(b) To promote the establishment and maintenance of systems for the rapid exchange of weather information;

(c) To promote standardization of meteorological observations and to ensure the uniform publication of observations and statistics;

(d) To further the application of meteorology to aviation, shipping, agriculture, and other human activities; and

(e) To encourage research and training in meteorology and to assist in coordinating the international aspects of such research and training.

Organization. All original signatories of the Convention and members of the United Nations are eligible for membership. States not in these categories may be admitted by a two-thirds vote of the members after adhering to the Convention. WMO consists of a World Meteorological Congress, an Executive Committee, Regional Associations and Technical Commissions created by the Congress, and a Secretariat headed by a Secretary-General.

All members are represented and entitled to one vote in the Congress which is the supreme policy-making body of the Organization. The delegates to the Congress, which meets at least once every four years, are the directors of the members' meteorological services. The Congress elects the President, Vice-Presidents, and members of the Executive Committee of WMO; adopts technical regulations covering meteorological practices and procedures; and takes action on the recommendations of the Executive Committee. All decisions are arrived at by a two-thirds vote except in the case of election of officers when a simple majority is sufficient.

The Executive Committee consists of the President and Vice-Presidents of WMO, the Presidents of Regional Associations, and an equal number of directors of the meteorological services of the members. Serving as an executive body, the Committee supervises the execution of the resolutions of the Congress, makes studies and recommendations, and provides members with technical information, counsel, and assistance in the field of meteorology. It meets at least once a year and is assisted by various consultative committees.

The Congress has established six Regional Associations which are composed of members whose networks lie in or extend into the respective regions. Each has its own officers and meets when necessary to promote the execution of the resolutions of the Congress, consider matters brought to their attention by the Executive Committee, and discuss and co-ordinate meteorological and associated activities in their regions. Eight Technical Commissions established by the Congress consist of experts who study and make recommendations to it in their respective fields. Their officers participate without vote in the meetings of the Congress and the Executive Committee.

The Secretariat is located at Geneva and, under the Secretary-General, functions in two divisions, one technical and the other administrative. It serves as the administrative, information, and research center and performs secretariat duties for the Congress and the Executive Committee. It also manages the finances and the annual budget, which is about $425,000.

INTER-GOVERNMENTAL MARITIME CONSULTATIVE ORGANIZATION (IMCO)

The Economic and Social Council of the United Nations initiated the United Nations Maritime Conference, which met in February–March, 1948, and drafted the Convention of IMCO. The Convention received the requisite number of signatories to bring IMCO into effect in March, 1958.

The functions and purposes of IMCO as stated in the Convention are:

(1) To provide machinery for cooperation among governments in the field of governmental regulation and practices relating to technical matters, including those concerning safety at sea;

(2) To encourage the removal of discriminatory action and of unnecessary restrictions by governments;

(3) To consider matters concerning shipping that might be referred to it by any organ or specialized agency of the United Nations;

(4) To provide for the exchange of information among governments on matters under consideration by the Organization.

The headquarters of IMCO are in London, and when in full operation the Organization will have an Assembly composed of all members, which will meet every two years; a sixteen-member Council; a Maritime Safety Committee of fourteen; and a Secretariat headed by a Secretary-General.

INTERNATIONAL REFUGEE ORGANIZATION (IRO)

The General Assembly of the United Nations adopted a constitution for IRO in 1946. The Organization began to function in August, 1948, and terminated its labors on January 31, 1952. It performed three useful tasks during its existence: the care and maintenance of refugees, their repatriation and resettlement, and their legal and political protection. IRO also maintained an International Tracing Service which attempted to learn the fate of the millions of persons who had been kidnaped by Nazi Germany or had disappeared for other reasons during the Second World War. Probably the most taxing responsibility of the Organization was to find permanent solutions for as many refugees as possible.

The controlling body of IRO was a General Council, composed of delegates from member-states which met at least twice annually and determined policy. An Executive Committee of nine met more frequently to give effect to the decisions of the General Council and take such emergency action as might be necessary. A Director-General was the chief administrative officer of IRO and served as the head of the Secretariat. The quasi-judicial five-member Review Board of Eligibility Appeals heard and determined individual appeals of eligibility decisions made by IRO officials in the field and advised the Director-General on eligibility matters which he referred to it. The headquarters of IRO was in Geneva and twenty-eight principal offices and a number of suboffices were maintained throughout Europe, the Western Hemisphere, the Middle and Far East.

In December, 1950, the General Assembly established the office of the United Nations High Commissioner for Refugees to continue the work of IRO. The Commissioner is responsible to the Assembly for his activities and reports to it through ECOSOC. His office is in Geneva and it is financed, for administrative purposes, by the United Nations. All other activities relating to relief are financed through voluntary contributions. The work of the Commissioner is entirely nonpolitical in character and is limited by policy directives from ECOSOC and the General Assembly. This represents a return to the League practice of more limited aid to refugees with an emphasis upon assisting governments in arriving at permanent solutions for the problems of refugees through voluntary repatriation or assimilation within new national communities. In 1953, the General Assembly decided that the Office of the High Commissioner should continue at least until December 31, 1958.

In January, 1957, Auguste Lindt, Switzerland's permanent observer at the United Nations was elected by the General Assembly to succeed the late Dr. G. J. Van Heuven Goedhart as High Commissioner.

INTERNATIONAL ATOMIC ENERGY AGENCY[3]

On December 4, 1954, following several weeks of deliberations, the General Assembly adopted a resolution which provided that an international technical conference of governments should be held under the auspices of the United Nations 'to explore the means of developing the peaceful uses of atomic energy.' This, of course, was an outgrowth of President Eisenhower's proposal in 1953 to the eighth session of the General Assembly. The resolution also encouraged the establishment of an International Atomic Energy Agency which would stimulate international co-operation in the development and practical application of atomic energy for the benefit of mankind.

The International Conference on the Peaceful Uses of Atomic Energy met in Geneva from August 8 to 20, 1955. All states that were members of the United Nations and the specialized agencies were invited to send delegates and observers. Seventy-three countries were representd by 1334 delegates who assembled for what Secretary-General Dag Hammarskjöld called 'a conference of master-builders of nuclear science and nuclear engineering . . . to discuss, exchange and share their knowledge with the aim of harnessing atomic energy to the purposes of peace and human welfare.' Messages of greeting came from the President of the United States and the Prime Ministers of France, the United Kingdom, and the USSR. Over 1100 papers were submitted, of which 450 were presented orally. The proceedings have been published in sixteen volumes of approximately 500 pages each in several languages.

The Conference consisted of an initial series of plenary sessions, a concluding plenary session, and three parallel series of section meetings dealing with technical and specialized matters. Public evening lectures were presented by a selected group of eminent scientists. The formidable task of organization was the responsibility of the United Nations Secretariat in New York and Geneva. Over seven hundred members of its staff were directly concerned. Documentation alone was a tremendous problem. About 16,000 pages of documents were printed and distributed. An Advisory Committee of seven members (Brazil, Canada, France, India, USSR, United Kingdom, United States) assisted the Secretary-General in general planning and drew up a topical agenda and rules of procedure for the Conference.

There was little doubt about the success of this vast undertaking. Sixty

[3] Although it is similar in many respects to a specialized agency, the International Atomic Energy Agency is not so classified officially. The relationship agreement places it under the auspices of the United Nations and requires it to report annually.

sessions were filled with detailed information from the entire field of atomic energy. There were descriptions of nuclear reactors and their operation and use as a source of nuclear power; the basic physics of the atom; and the chemical and metallurgical technology that forms the base for reactor technology. Fuel for nuclear reactors was described and emphasis was placed upon the need for more power in the expanding world. Many of the Conference sessions were devoted to radiation — to its use as a tool in many sciences, in industry, in medicine, in agriculture, and to efforts underway to protect people from the hazards produced by radiation. A number of countries maintained elaborate exhibits and conducted demonstrations on phases of nuclear reactions.

The Tenth Assembly in 1955 recommended that another conference be held within the next three years and continued the Advisory Committee to assist the Secretary-General with future planning. The Assembly also established a fifteen-member scientific committee to collect, evaluate, and disseminate information on the effects of atomic radiation.

On September 20, 1956, representatives of eighty-one nations gathered at United Nations Headquarters for the Conference on the statute of the International Atomic Energy Agency (IAEA). A draft statute prepared by the eight original states interested in creating such an Agency (Australia, Belgium, Canada, France, Portugal, the Union of South Africa, the United Kingdom, and the United States) had been available for the inspection of the Tenth Assembly which had subsequently requested the Secretary-General to study the relationship of the proposed Agency to the United Nations and assist those who had been working on the document. The Conference unanimously approved the Statute on October 23, 1956, and it came into force on July 29, 1957. By the time the Twelfth Assembly got underway, thirty-three states had deposited ratifications, including Canada, the USSR, the United Kingdom, and the United States — the four major atomic powers. The first session of the General Conference of IAEA opened in Vienna on October 1, 1957, and had before it recommendations on the initial program prepared by an eighteen-member Preparatory Commission. Sterling Cole of the United States was also appointed as the first Director-General.

According to the Statute, the objectives of the Agency are to 'seek to accelerate and enlarge the contribution of atomic energy to peace, health and prosperity throughout the world.' It will ensure, 'as far as it is able, that assistance provided by it or at its request or under its supervision or control is not used in such a way as to further any military purpose.' A Board of Governors of eight member-states, with headquarters in Vienna, is responsible for the day to day affairs of the Agency, and reports to the General Conference composed of all members. Functioning something like a bank, IAEA is to receive deposits of fissionable materials and nuclear equipment from members who already have such items in their possession and are able and willing to make them available to the so-called 'have-not' members.[4] The Agency is to specify the place and method of delivery and is responsible for storing and protecting materials deposited with it.

Any member or group of members desirous of conducting a research project involving atomic energy for peaceful purposes can request the assistance of the Agency in obtaining the necessary special fissionable materials, services, equipment, and facilities. Each project is considered by the Board of Governors which, prior to approval, determines the following: the usefulness of the project, its adequacy of equipment, funds and personnel to insure its execution; the existence of required health and safety standards; the equitable distribution of resources available to the Agency; and the special needs of underdeveloped areas of the world. The Agency also fosters the exchange of scientific and technical information and encourages the exchange and training of scientists and experts. Upon approval, the Agency may then arrange for supplying materials, services, equipment, and facilities.

Article XII of the Statute concerns the important matter of safeguards. After considerable discussion prior to and during the Conference, the Agency was granted the authority to:

1. Examine the design of specialized equipment and facilities, including nuclear reactors, making certain that it will not further any military purpose, that it complies with required health and safety standards, and that it will allow effective application of specified safeguards.

2. Require the maintenance and production of operating records to assist in ensuring accountability for source and special fissionable materials used or produced in the project.

3. Require that special fissionable materials recovered or produced as a by-product of the chemical processing be used for peaceful purposes.

4. Send inspection teams into recipient states to prevent diversion of borrowed materials for military purposes.

[4] In February 1956, President Eisenhower offered to make available to friendly nations for peaceful uses 20,000 kilograms of nuclear materials, an amount equal to that allocated for similar uses within the United States. He announced later that of this amount, 5000 kilograms (11,000 pounds) of nuclear fuel Uranium-235 would be made available to IAEA and that the United States 'will continue to make available to the International Atomic Energy Agency nuclear materials that will match in amount the sum of all quantities of such materials made similarly available by all other members of the International Agency, and on comparable terms, for the period between the establishment of the Agency and July 1, 1960.'

Should a recipient state fail to comply with any of the safeguard measures, the Agency has the power to suspend or terminate assistance and withdraw any materials and equipment it has made available.

The 1956 conference president, João Carlos Muniz, summed up the nature of IAEA in these words:

> In order to reach its goal, the Agency . . . will take advantage of the means that will be voluntarily placed at its disposal by the member states. Its aid can be extended either in the form of fissionable materials, source materials, special equipment or technical assistance.
>
> There is nothing compulsory in the relationship between the member states and the Agency, whose assistance will be based on agreements freely negotiated between governments and the Agency or between governments only.
>
> Projects will be carried out under a system of controls and safeguards, according to which fissionable materials cannot be diverted to non-peaceful purposes and will not endanger the health of populations or individuals.
>
> The Agency will not impose complete international control over nuclear fuels and, even less, controls over source materials produced by member states. The controls of the Agency will apply only within the limits of each project and the agreements voluntarily accepted by the nations concerned, and they are exclusively designed to guarantee the peaceful and safe utilization of the materials supplied by the Agency, or of their fissionable by-products.
>
> The International Atomic Energy Agency is meant to be, consequently, a free association of nations, intent upon helping one another, and determined to build a network of knowledge and technique which will bring to all peoples the benefits of atomic progress.

The establishment of IAEA represents one of the great experiments of the postwar world. Originally suggested in 1953 by the United States as a possible first step toward breaking the deadlock between East and West on nuclear control and inspection, the Agency, if it can function as expected may be a major effort in bridging the gulf between the 'haves' and the 'have-nots' in the world's peaceful development of atomic power. It will be some years before it can be determined whether or not President Eisenhower's hope that by acting together, nations might put atomic energy to peaceful uses 'in such a way as to help create economic and social conditions where many of the present reasons for tension and conflict would be eliminated' will be attainable. The statute is not the perfect instrument that it may become after more experience and additional scientific and technological information is acquired. Particularly novel is the system of safeguards and controls which will be administered by IAEA. Undoubtedly it will be put to the greatest test in the employment of inspection teams. The Agency is certainly no panacea for all the ills of the atomic world and must not be oversold before it has a chance to prove itself. Its successful operation will focus world attention and understanding on the benefits which atomic energy can bestow in enriching human life and may thereby dispel some of today's doubts and fears.

GENERAL SUMMARY

At this time, certain summary statements can be made with respect to the structural developments, procedures, and functions of the specialized agencies. The more detailed examination of the World Health Organization has revealed certain specific procedures and problem areas. It will be necessary to bear in mind this multiplicity and variety of questions when studying the more comprehensive aspects of economic and social co-operation in the next chapter.

A striking fact is the general continuity between the technical and welfare functions of the League of Nations and the specialized agencies. Three agencies — ILO, UPU, and ITU — were in operation before the establishment of the United Nations. Specific League activity in one form or another gave rise to all the others. In their present form, however, each of the agencies has been greatly expanded and provided with broader responsibilities and commensurate powers. In this respect, there has been a large amount of institutional experimentation and inventiveness. Each agency is now independent, with its own constitution, organs, officials, and budget. Where it is called for, there is much greater decentralization in organization than existed under the League. The development of regional units, perhaps best illustrated by WHO, is an example of this progressive innovation.

The wider use of the international expert and the efforts of joint working teams have been proved to be of value, particularly in connection with technical assistance programs. Increased emphasis has come to be placed upon long range programs instead of the more spectacular but less permanent effects of working upon isolated problems. With the exception of the more narrowly technical agencies, it is impossible to prevent some overlap within their broad fields of operation. WHO, ILO, and FAO are all concerned with questions of health, living standards, and welfare. UNESCO's main field of promise is education and understanding. It is impossible to separate or isolate these two broad categories or prevent one agency from working in more than one area. The co-ordinating function of ECOSOC has been of some assistance but the agencies themselves have sought to resolve certain jurisdictional differences themselves. Bipartite agreements, similar to those concluded between the individual agency and the United Nations, have been concluded by FAO, WHO, ILO, and UNESCO where functional overlapping is inevitable. Joint interagency committees work on matters requiring joint treatment. There also have been created specific interagency committees composed of experts working on specific problems of concern to the agencies involved. Consultation takes place on various aspects of administration, in the preparation of special reports, in the conduct of research, and the sharing of facilities.

All of the specialized agencies are restricted in the methods available for implementing their decisions. They cannot compel their members to do anything but must be content with making recommendations, offering assistance, and stimulating interest and action. In this regard they are typical of all forms of international organization where the membership unit is the sovereign state. The employment of sanctions by ILO and the Fund have proved to be ineffective. One significant feature is the power of WHO and ICAO to adopt technical regulations which are binding unless rejected within a given time limit.

Although each of the agencies has a much larger budget than any comparable League activity, all are still severely limited by inadequate financial support. The willingness of the United States, first to share in the building of the agencies and then to join them and provide much of the financial assistance as well as political direction, is a distinct departure from the past. The fact that the various agencies are so dependent upon the financial contributions of the United States places that country in a peculiar position of leadership, particularly since the Soviet Union until recently has been unwilling to participate in the programs of technical assistance or join many of the specialized agencies.

The wide functions and objectives of the specialized agencies represent a broad attempt to cope with the basic social and economic problems facing the world. It is just a beginning, however, and the success achieved by the agencies will depend primarily upon the political climate in which they must work.

14

ECONOMIC, SOCIAL, AND CULTURAL CO-OPERATION

SINCE 1945, the United Nations and the specialized agencies have worked unceasingly to fulfill the objectives of the Charter which calls for international co-operation in solving international problems of an economic, social, cultural, or humanitarian character, and the promotion and encouragement of respect for human rights and fundamental freedoms. These objectives are so broad and the work undertaken so ambitious that it is virtually impossible to describe the activities of the many agencies and commissions, relate their accomplishments, and evaluate their work in a brief space. The wide range of activities includes such matters as reconstruction in Korea, raising living standards in the Andes, narcotics control, discrimination in education and employment, stateless persons, currency stabilization, port development in Jordan, and postal and communications problems, to mention only a few. Frequently, the governments of the members of the Organization and other states of the world are influenced by recommendations made as a result of work that has been undertaken in their countries.

Only a brief examination of some of the more significant and typical activities undertaken by the United Nations and the specialized agencies in specific fields will be made in this chapter. What can be learned from this survey are the procedures utilized and the nature of the projects which have been completed or are underway.

ECONOMIC CO-OPERATION AND DEVELOPMENT

Whereas the specialized agencies deal with specific economic problems, the Assembly adopts general policies and the Economic and Social Council attempts to co-ordinate the broad programs of economic co-operation and development. Through the efforts of ECOSOC, regional economic commissions for Europe, Latin America, and Asia and the Far East have been established, conferences have been held to discuss basic economic problems, international trade has been promoted, as has a gradually expanding program of technical assistance.

The Regional Commissions. The first of the three regional commissions to be established was the Economic Commission for Europe (ECE) which came into being early in 1947. It was followed a short time later by the Economic Commission for Asia and the Far East (ECAFE) and then, in 1948, the Economic Commission for Latin America (ECLA) was created. ECE was concerned primarily with reconstruction in its first years and replaced several temporary advisory reconstruction agencies, but in recent years ECE has operated along lines similar to the other two and has concentrated upon economic development. All three are based on voluntary intergovernmental co-operation and engage in planning and advisory work for their regions. All function through committees and subsidiary bodies.

During its first eighteen months, ECE (headquarters: Geneva) studied and made recommendations on such problems as industrial development and trade, allocation of scarce supplies, improvement of transportation, and development of power resources. Much of this work, in terms of material assistance and general planning, was taken over during the next several years by the Economic Co-operation Administration (Marshall Plan) of the United States and the regional Organization for European Economic Co-operation (OEEC) established to work with the Marshall Plan in promoting Europe's recovery.[1] More recently, ECE has concentrated on trade and market development, and on technical questions involving the exchange of production experience and scientific and technical information.

The Committee on Agricultural Problems of ECE conducts market analyses, both short-term and long-term, as a means of promoting rational trade patterns in agricultural commodities and providing background for production planning. The Coal Committee has worked out an agreement for an international coal classification system and has made studies on the consumption of coal in homes and the relation of coal to other sources of energy. The Electric Power Committee is continuing a series of studies on a number of technical and economic factors in the production and consumption of power and has sponsored intergovernmental agreements in the field of electric power. The Housing Committee provides information on housing policy, trade in building materials, housing in less-industrialized countries, housing statistics, standardization and modular co-ordination. Equally useful tasks continue to be performed by committees on steel, timber, inland transport, and development of trade.

During its early years, the contribution of ECAFE to the economic development of Asia consisted primarily in collecting statistical data and in

[1] See pp. 571–3.

preparing studies. With headquarters in Bangkok, it has provided, for the first time, a forum where Asian and non-Asian countries can meet and exchange ideas and information on economic problems. Recently emphasis has been placed upon helping the countries of the region aid themselves by adopting sound fiscal, economic, and financial policies; recommending solutions for some of the more urgent technical problems in different economic fields; and supporting national and regional plans for training personnel to work in development programs. Activities of ECAFE have now extended into such matters as economic and industrial development, transport, flood control and water resources, power development, minerals, housing, and intraregional and international trade. Various committees and subsidiary groups work in each of these fields and on related matters. A mineral resources subcommittee, for example, is supervising the preparation of the first geological map of Asia and the Far East.

Regional and worldwide study tours have been organized to enable experts from the Asian region to see and discuss latest production methods and other techniques likely to be of use to their countries. An ECAFE working party on planning has reported the results of studies conducted on problems of economic growth, employment potentials in development plans, and international aspects of economic development. ECAFE also works closely with the technical assistance authorities of the United Nations. An example of a joint venture designed to increase the supply of trained personnel was the establishment in 1954 of a regional training center in Lahore, Pakistan, for railway operating and signalling officials of the Asian countries.

With headquarters at Santiago, Chile, ECLA first concerned itself with exploratory studies on the economic potentialities and development of Latin American countries. It is now concentrating on specific projects. For example, studies have been completed on a description of the iron and steel transforming industries in selected Latin American countries, in terms of the origin and use of raw materials, skilled labor, technological knowledge, existing equipment, relation of investment and production costs to production processes, output and size of the market. Similar work has been undertaken or is in the process of completion for the pulp and paper industry, and the chemical industries. International and inter-Latin American trade is constantly under review with the principal objective the expansion of the markets for Latin American goods by means of greater trade within the region.

In conjunction with FAO, UNESCO, and the technical assistance program of the United Nations, ECLA has been engaged in a unique project designed to co-ordinate the economic activities suitable to the individual countries of Central America in ways that will mutually benefit other countries in the region. This involves such questions as the development of specific industries, energy resources, transport facilities, and technical training. The Committee on Economic Co-operation in Central America meets regularly to review the work undertaken and plan for the continuation of the program.

International Trade. In addition to the projects undertaken by certain specialized agencies and the regional commissions, ECOSOC has been concerned with the general expansion of international trade.

A series of earlier conferences culminated in the adoption at Havana in the winter of 1947–48 of a Charter for a proposed International Trade Organization (ITO). The 106 articles of the Charter dealt with all aspects of commercial policy, including tariffs, subsidies, state trading, harmful restrictive business practices, and customs formalities. Standards and procedures limiting the negotiation of international commodity agreements were established and a system for the administration of the Charter's provisions was created. It was expected at the time that ITO would become a specialized agency of the United Nations.

But ITO never came into being, largely because it was abandoned by the United States for various reasons.[2] In Geneva just prior to the Havana Conference, negotiations between nineteen countries resulted not only in the conclusion of a large number of bilateral agreements but also in the adoption of a General Agreement on Tariffs and Trade (GATT). Consisting of commitments on 45,000 different tariff rates, GATT also included a commercial policy code similar to that laid down in the ITO Charter. Significantly, however, GATT was not a treaty and the signatories were not obligated to modify existing national statutes which were inconsistent with its terms. In addition, the principal features of the commercial policy code were based upon principles governing the reciprocal trade program of the United States. What has happened since 1947, therefore, has been the gradual development of GATT, through periodic meetings of its signatories, into a substitute for ITO. At these meetings, supplementary protocols were appended to the original Agreement, interpretations were developed or agreed upon, complaints voiced freely, and additional signatories obtained.

Five tariff negotiating conferences have been held between 1947 and 1957. Tariff rates applicable to about 60 percent of the world's trade have been concluded under the aegis of GATT. At the Conference in 1956, twenty-two nations concluded agreements on tariff reductions covering items amounting to $2.5 billion worth of trade. In addition, eleven regular

---

[2] In brief, its very comprehensive nature encouraged attacks from many quarters in the United States, chiefly from the protectionists, international investors, and those who opposed the application of measures to combat certain restrictive business practices.

sessions of GATT have taken place between 1948 and 1957. On these occasions, all parties to GATT have been able to discuss any trade problem which might be susceptible to collective action. A number of other accomplishments can be noted during this period, such as the settlement of trade disputes, the hearing of complaints, and the simplification of customs formalities.

As time went on, it became obvious that the rather loose organization of GATT was not adequate. There was no permanent secretariat or governing body. Steps to remedy this situation were taken in the spring of 1955 when representatives of thirty-four countries, meeting in Geneva, concluded the text of an agreement to establish an Organization for Trade Co-operation (OTC). Briefly, OTC, if and when the 1955 Agreement is duly ratified, will be an organization to administer GATT, 'facilitate intergovernmental consultations on trade matters, sponsor international trade agreements' and, in general, study and make recommendations on trade questions. OTC will not enter into force until it has been accepted by the countries responsible for at least 85 percent of GATT trade. Ratification by the United States is essential, since it is responsible for at least 20 percent of that trade. However, despite strong support by President Eisenhower, the Congress of the United States has refused to take any action. Protectionist forces have joined with those who consider both GATT and OTC an unconstitutional delegation of Congressional power.

Financing Development. The International Bank for Reconstruction and Development was established to fulfill certain tasks that could not be performed by private capital alone. Nearly eighteen months elapsed between the time the Bank was established and the actual granting of its first loan in May of 1947. Most of the early loans were for reconstruction projects in Europe. When the Economic Co-operation Administration of the United States began full operations in 1948, the Bank saw no need to concentrate its activities on European reconstruction and therefore began to use its funds to assist other parts of the world. After eleven years of operation, the Bank has made 189 loans totaling $3,480 million for postwar reconstruction or economic development in more than forty countries.

Prior to the granting of a loan, the Bank must make certain that the borrower cannot obtain the necessary capital through ordinary private-capital markets under reasonable conditions, that there is evidence that the borrower can repay the loan, and that the project contemplated is not only sound but productive. In the course of examining the request for a loan, the Bank is brought into close contact with the prospective borrower and has been able to offer sound advice. Bank engineers or consultants recruited with the help of the Bank for a particular job, have assisted in solving a variety of problems. Member governments frequently request the Bank for survey missions to help appraise their total economic resources and draft long-range programs to speed economic development. An Economic Development Institute of the Bank was opened in January of 1956 to offer six-month courses covering all aspects of the development process.

Specific loans have been made for a great variety of projects which have turned out to be far more successful than imagined at first. For example, a loan of $2.5 million to Peru has literally transformed the port of Callao. With improved management under a new Port authority and with modern equipment, Callao is at present one of the leading and most efficient ports of Latin America. Now that the congested conditions have been removed, annual savings from increased port efficiency are about equal to the amount of the original loan. Loans to Turkey for harbor improvement have increased foreign trade and accelerated essential coastwise traffic. In Pakistan, nearly 700,000 acres in the Thal desert are being irrigated and planted to wheat, cotton, and sugar, thanks to Bank-financed equipment. Although the loan was slightly over $3 million, it has been estimated that the value of the additional crops to be grown will reach about $20 million annually.

Despite the extent of lending operations of the Bank, there has been growing criticism, particularly from the less advanced countries, over the lack of financing for development. These countries have received technical advice, their needs have been surveyed, and they naturally wish to borrow the money to put the advice and planning to good use. They have complained that the policy of the Bank is far too conservative to meet their requirements, and that in any event it does not have funds adequate for the job to be done. As early as 1951, these countries persuaded the General Assembly to request from ECOSOC a plan 'for establishing, as soon as circumstances permit, a special fund for grants-in-aid and for low interest, long term loans to underdeveloped countries for the purpose of helping them, at their request, to accelerate their economic development and to finance non-self-liquidating projects which are basic to their economic development.'[3]

In 1952, ECOSOC requested the Bank to continue its study of the proposed International Finance Corporation and also decided to establish a committee to explore the idea of creating a special development fund. Nine experts were appointed by the Secretary-General and turned in a detailed report to ECOSOC in March, 1953. The plan envisaged a Special United Nations Fund for Economic Development (SUNFED). With an initial capital equivalent to $250 million in the form of voluntary contributions to

---

[3] Actually such an idea had been first proposed in 1949 in ECOSOC's Subcommission on Economic Development (an organ since abolished). It envisioned the establishment of an Economic Development Administration to make loans and grants-in-aid to underdeveloped countries.

be pledged by at least thirty members, SUNFED was planned as an international organization similar to a specialized agency, with the authority to make grants or loans at low interest rates. It was recommended that governments make long-term pledges, with regular and punctual payments, as income for the Fund. Aid would be given only to those who were contributing members. Control and management would be placed in a General Council or annual conference composed of all governments participating in the Fund. An Executive Board elected by the Council would exercise day-to-day control, together with a Director-General appointed by the Board after consultation with the Secretary-General of the United Nations. Close liaison should be maintained, the report emphasized, with the Bank and the International Monetary Fund.

In the discussion of SUNFED before ECOSOC and the General Assembly in 1953, the idea of obtaining funds by means of disarmament was introduced by the United States. Little enthusiasm was held for this suggestion by the underdeveloped countries, however, as they feared that the establishment of SUNFED would be tied to disarmament which might prevent the adoption of SUNFED indefinitely. All hope of establishing SUNFED in 1953 died when the United States observed that it was not ready to finance the plan at that time.

Continued opposition to SUNFED on the part of the United States and the United Kingdom has prevented its adoption. However, during the Twelfth Assembly in 1957, it was decided to establish a Special Projects Fund as an expansion of the technical assistance and development activities of the United Nations and the specialized agencies. The nature of the Fund will be discussed a bit later in this chapter when an examination is made of the entire United Nations technical assistance program.

The International Finance Corporation, as we have seen in the preceding chapter, came into being in 1956 when the required number of thirty nations completed action for membership and 75 percent of its $100 million capital was subscribed. During its first full year of operations, IFC made five investments totalling $5,980,000. These investments were for the expansion of electrical, engineering, copper mining, and aircraft repair enterprises in Latin America, and the development of a lumber business in Australia.

Monetary Policy. A healthy world economy necessitates a multilateral system of trade whereby buying and selling can occur in the best markets with a minimum of restriction and discrimination. Sound fiscal and monetary policies help provide currency convertibility which permits such a system to functon at its best. It was recognized even before the end of the war that it would be necessary to provide some future machinery for consultation and collaboration on international monetary problems. The International Monetary Fund was established for this purpose as well as to promote exchange stability, eliminate foreign exchange restrictions on current international transactions, and make available to its members short-term financial assistance so that they might correct temporary maladjustments in their balance of payments without employing restrictive measures.

Progress has been slow in working toward some of these objectives. The Fund has provided adequate machinery for consultation on foreign exchange problems and adjustments. Members of the Fund have received assistance in establishing or modifying central banking systems. Staff members of central banks and ministries of finance have been provided with special training programs. Technical co-operation has been extended by the Fund through the dispatch of staff missions for extended periods to countries which request them. But less progress has been made in the Fund's efforts to achieve a freer system of international payments. Some reduction in restrictions and discrimination has occurred but the movement toward convertibility has been slow. However, those countries which did relax restrictions on imports took advantage of their widened choice of import sources with attendant benefits to consumers. Twenty-four countries have purchased foreign exchange from the Fund to help meet foreign exchange problems and have pursued policies in keeping with the objectives of the Fund. These transactions have reached approximately $1,200 million.

The ultimate success of the Fund depends upon the willingness of its members to use it as a means of resolving problems relating to exchange rates and practices, and the balance of payments. Members must also be desirous of adopting sound financial policies designed to promote multilateral trade and currency convertibility. Mr. Ivar Rooth, the Managing Director of the Fund, has summed up the general situation as follows:

> The attainment of exchange convertibility and trade liberalization would, of course, be assisted if political tensions were eased. But the key to the effective functioning of the Fund is always the same — sound national policies in both deficit and surplus countries. If countries could get rid of inflation, if they were to follow proper fiscal, monetary and wage policies, and if trade policies were sufficiently liberalized, the objectives of the Fund could be achieved.

Also working on monetary policies is the Fiscal Commission of ECOSOC. It has been concerned with such matters as international tax problems, particularly the question of fiscal incentives to increase the international flow of private capital for the economic development of underdeveloped countries; a world tax service; taxation of agriculture; government finance and economic development; government financial reporting; public finance information services; and problems of municipal finance. The Fiscal Division of the United Nations Secretariat, under the supervision of the Commission, conducts most of the research on these items. Technical assistance also is provided to a number of underdeveloped countries, especially with respect to technical training and budget administration.

Statistical Services. The Statistical Commission of ECOSOC, working closely with the Statistical Office of the Secretariat, has functioned successfully to bring about a standardization of statistical methods. It has also been able to co-ordinate much of the statistical work of the United Nations and reduce appreciably the duplication which appears to be inevitable among those engaged in various surveys and research projects.

Among the specific matters included in the work program of the Commission are those relating to principles of statistics of external trade; development of national accounts; concepts and definitions of capital formation; construction of price and quantity indices in national accounting; definitions in basic industrial statistics; principles for vital statistics; and recommendations for migration statistics. The Statistical Office of the Secretariat also collects and publishes data in a number of fields. Some of the more important publications are: *Statistical Yearbook, Demographic Yearbook, Yearbook of International Trade Statistics, Monthly Bulletin of Statistics, Population and Vital Statistics Reports,* and *Statistics of National Income and Expenditure.*

Population and Migration. Activities in this field are conducted by the Population Commission of ECOSOC. It has become increasingly concerned with the relationship between economic and social policies and population in the less-developed countries. Work progresses on such questions as interrelationships of demographic, economic, and social factors; fertility and mortality rates in underdeveloped countries and their effects upon long-range planning of economic programs; population estimates and forecasts; and the demographic and social aspects of migration.

A World Population Conference was held at Rome in the summer of 1954 under the auspices of the United Nations. Over 450 experts in the field of population from seventy states and territories were joined by specialists in economics, sociology, anthropology, genetics, statistics, medicine, and public health. No international congress of this nature had been held since 1937. Clearly brought out at the Conference and in the work of the Commission is the fact that

. . . economic problems are the problems of people. Only when their precise terms are identified can solutions be formulated. A report on the technical assistance projects in the field of population reveals a growing realization by governments in underdeveloped countries of the benefits accruing from them.

The projects give tangible benefits in the form of essential information on which to decide the direction of action designed to raise levels of living. They indicate both the nature of population stresses and the spheres within which action is possible.[4]

Conclusions. Economic co-operation at the international level continues to be a most difficult and complex problem. Since it is impossible to divorce political considerations from economic policy, the existence of rivalries, fears, and competition, accentuated by the East-West split, inevitably poses handicaps and barriers which the United Nations has been unable to overcome. It is too much to expect that there will be greater success in co-operative ventures through the United Nations until there is a considerable lessening of political tensions. The major powers, especially the United States, prefer to emphasize a national and bilateral approach to development financing whereby at least indirect political gain can be had from offering economic assistance. Of the nearly $40 billion expended by the United States in economic aid since 1945, less than 15 percent has been channeled through the United Nations and the specialized agencies.

The expansion of world trade has been truly remarkable since 1946. Progress has been made toward the goal of freer and less discriminating trade with some relaxation of controls on imports and currency transfers. At the same time, the underdeveloped countries have not obtained the benefits of these developments to the same extent as the industrialized countries. One of the reasons is that a larger share of world output is now being produced in countries whose imports are small in relation to their output or income. Another factor is the lag in food consumption in relation to income, as well as the reduction in the raw material import content of manufacturing due to new economies which have accompanied the shift in the industrial countries from light to heavy industries. As a result, trade in primary products has not kept pace with total world trade. The problem of excessive price fluctuations has had a serious effect on many primary producers. ECOSOC established the Commission for International Commodity Trade in 1954 to advise on measures for the control of wide price fluctuations but it has been able to do little beyond keeping a close watch on general trends.

The United Nations Regional Commissions have sought to discourage exchange controls and import restrictions and thereby increase the free flow of trade within their regions. The Economic Commission for Europe, for example, recognizing that Europe economically and rationally is an indivisible entity, has done its best to encourage a relaxation of East-West trade

[4] 'Future Work in the Field of Population Will Concentrate on Less Developed Countries,' *United Nations Review,* Vol. 1, No. 11 (May 1955), p. 41.

restrictions. In general, there has been an improvement in freer trade within the various regions which can be traced to the efforts of the Commissions. There is yet no conclusive evidence, however, to indicate that a truly international trade organization such as the ill-fated ITO or OTC can command enough support to warrant its establishment.

The development financing of the Bank and the complementary activities of the Fund can be recorded as distinct achievements. The establishment of the International Finance Corporation will encourage the growth of productive private enterprise, particularly in the less developed countries. The continued demand for a broader development plan such as that envisaged by SUNFED, however, is ample testament to the great and continuing need for additional working capital to facilitate worthy development projects.

The other activities of the United Nations in the economic field can be evaluated primarily on the basis of their contribution toward developing plans and procedures for greater co-operation along international lines. The Regional Economic Commissions have offered valuable recommendations on industrial development, improved transport, expansion of power resources, the allocation of scarce supplies, fiscal policies, and general economic co-ordination. Valuable, too, have been the statistical services and various technical compendia issued by the functional commissions of ECOSOC. Certainly, the many tasks concerned with compiling data, conducting technical surveys, distributing information and publications unavailable elsewhere, make it possible for countries, especially the less developed ones, to obtain a clearer understanding of world economic problems and needs. But the implementation of procedures designed to bring about greater co-operation is a much more difficult undertaking. While a contribution to international understanding can lead to greater co-operation, it does not follow that such co-operation will take place until the basic adjustment of political differences has been achieved.

TECHNICAL ASSISTANCE FOR DEVELOPMENT

Technical assistance is basically advice, training, and demonstration. It involves the application of a body of knowledge developed in more advanced states to the needs and problems of underdeveloped countries. In the discussions of the General Assembly it has been referred to as a 'co-operative pooling of wits, wisdom and skills in economic development in which all countries are able to participate, that all may give as well as receive.'

Three basic reasons have been offered by the United Nations for the

development of an international program of technical assistance to complement the work of bilateral programs, such as those conducted by the United
States.[5] One reason is that

> . . . the exploitation and abuses often associated with development in the
> past have left a legacy of distrust, which in some cases hampers the intro-
> duction of new techniques into the less advanced countries. Their confidence
> and cooperation is likely to be given most freely to a program under inter-
> national auspices, in the direction of which the underdeveloped countries can
> take as full a part as the economically advanced countries.

Another reason concerns the nature of problems encountered.

> Epidemics and insect pests, such as locusts, do not respect national fron-
> tiers. Their control must be organized on an international basis. Some other
> problems are regional in character, transcending national lines as, for ex-
> ample, the technical control and use of rivers flowing through more than one
> country and the efficient organization of certain transportation systems.
>
> In other fields international standardization and uniformity are important,
> as, for example, in the facilities and regulations of international air transport
> and in the collection and classification of certain types of statistics.

Yet another reason takes note of the combined resources brought to bear
on problems of technical assistance.

> A sound international program of this character must combine and make
> use of the experience of many nations, with different social patterns and cul-
> tural traditions and at different stages of development, so as to facilitate
> progress in the less advanced countries and to help solve their technical and
> economic problems.

Development of Machinery. The idea of technical assistance was originally suggested in the Assembly during the fall of 1946 when modest advisory social welfare services were established. The following year ECOSOC
began studying the feasibility of such a program and advised its commissions and the Secretariat to furnish technical advice to members requesting
it. In 1948, ECOSOC repeated this request and included the specialized
agencies.

In the fall of 1948, the General Assembly took an additional interest in
the matter and requested that ECOSOC and the specialized agencies

> . . . give further and urgent consideration to the whole problem of the
> economic development of underdeveloped countries, in all its aspects, and

[5] The first two reasons are quoted from the report which laid the groundwork for the
program, published in 1949 under the title *Technical Assistance for Economic Development: Plan for an expanded cooperative program through the United Nations and the
specialized agencies.* The third reason is from the preamble of ECOSOC's resolution of
August 15, 1949, outlining its recommendations for the program.

that the Economic and Social Council include in its report to the next regular session of the General Assembly (a) a statement on measures already devised by the Economic and Social Council and the specialized agencies, and (b) proposals for other measures designed to promote economic development and to raise the standards of living of underdeveloped countries.

At the same time, the Assembly in Resolution 200 (III) provided for limited technical assistance for economic development through the use of experts and visiting missions, fellowships to train local experts abroad, seminars, local training programs, and 'exchange of current information concerning technical problems of economic development.' The modest sum of $288,000 was appropriated to implement the proposal. The Secretary-General was instructed to conduct these activities when requested by member states. Resolution 246 (III) established an International Center for Training in Public Administration and directed the Secretary-General to 'report detailed arrangements for such a center' to ECOSOC for consideration.

Encouraged by the fourth point in President Truman's inaugural address in 1949, which called for a 'bold new program' of technical assistance, ECOSOC in February, 1949, asked the Secretary-General, together with the heads of interested specialized agencies to prepare a 'comprehensive plan for an expanded cooperative program of technical assistance for economic development through the United Nations and its specialized agencies.' Also requested were recommendations as to financing and co-ordinating and executing the program. The report was completed in May and ECOSOC proceeded, in its ninth session, to develop a specific program which was contained in Resolution 222 (IX)A. This resolution, approved by the Assembly late in 1949, laid down the framework and governing principles for the Expanded Program of Technical Assistance for Economic Development of the Underdeveloped Countries. By Resolution 418V in 1950, the Assembly greatly expanded the advisory welfare services first authorized in 1946. This phase of technical assistance was thereby correlated with the earlier provisions for economic development adopted by the Assembly and ECOSOC in 1948 and 1949. Thus, by 1950, there had been authorized, in addition to the Expanded Program of Technical Assistance, the 1948 program for limited technical assistance for economic development (resolution 200 III), the 1948 program for public administration (resolution 246 III), and the program for advisory welfare services (resolution 418V).

The Expanded Program of Technical Assistance is, as its name implies, a greatly accelerated method of providing technical assistance to the less advanced countries. Its guiding principles include the following:

1. Technical assistance for the economic development of underdeveloped countries is given by the participating organizations only in agreement with the governments concerned and on the basis of requests made by them.

2. The kind of services rendered each country are decided by the government concerned.

3. The countries receiving assistance are expected to perform, in advance, as much of the work as possible in order to define the nature and scope of the problem involved.

4. The technical assistance furnished is not to be a means of foreign economic and political interference in the internal affairs of the country concerned and is only given to or through governments.

5. Experts are chosen not only for their technical competence but also for their sympathetic understanding of the cultural backgrounds and specific needs of the countries to be assisted.

6. Governments receiving assistance are expected to provide full details on the projects requested, give prompt consideration to the advice received, assume as much of the cost as possible, and give publicity to the program within their countries.

A Technical Assistance Board (TAB) has been established, composed of representatives of all specialized agencies participating in the Expanded Program. Its functions are to co-ordinate, integrate, and review the activities carried out by these organizations under the Expanded Program. In addition to its own Secretariat, it had in 1957 twenty-seven resident representatives covering forty-six recipient countries. There is also the Technical Assistance Committee (TAC), composed of all the members of ECOSOC, which makes a critical examination of activities undertaken and results achieved under the program and reports to ECOSOC concerning the information it receives from the TAB. Finally, there is the Technical Assistance Administration (TAA), set up within the Secretariat in 1950 by the Secretary-General, which is responsible for the operation and administration of all technical assistance programs authorized by the General Assembly, namely the advisory welfare services, the training in public administration, technical assistance for economic development, and the Expanded Program for Technical Assistance. These programs, it will be recalled, include the organization of technical assistance missions, the provision of expert advice, the award of fellowships and scholarships, and the organization of demonstration projects, seminars, and training institutes. The TAA is headed by a Director-General and is organized into five divisions.

Financing. Funds for technical assistance come from two sources. The three programs (public administration, advisory social service, economic development) other than the Expanded Program are supported directly by the United Nations budget. On the other hand, the Expanded Program is financed by voluntary contributions from the members of the United

Nations, as well as nonmembers. These contributions are placed in a special account. Since 1956, funds have not been automatically allocated to participating organizations in accordance with a formula fixed in advance. Previously, most of the funds for the Expanded Program had been divided on a fixed percentage. Distribution is now on the basis of requests for assistance submitted by governments in consultation with a TAB resident representative in the area. The allocation of funds to participating organizations is authorized by the TAC which also approves the annual program of activities. However, since the TAB resident representative assists the individual country in drafting its project, he has, and therefore so does TAB, a considerable influence in the distribution of available funds.

A total of $25.8 million was set aside for the Expanded Program in 1955. Contributions in the amount of $27.9 million were pledged by 71 governments, as compared with $25 million in 1954. At the sixth Pledging Conference in October, 1955, 61 countries pledged about $28 million toward the 1956 program. The figure was raised to nearly $30 million by additional pledges in 1956. Sixty-five nations pledged $30,295,000 for the 1957 program and about the same amount was promised for 1958 by seventy-five nations. To make certain that the program was placed on a sound financial footing, TAB decided to build up a reserve in the form of a working Capital and Reserve Fund. This has been done by depositing $3 million from the existing reserve and directing that $3 million be held back from the contributions for 1954, 1955, and 1956, to make a total reserve of $12 million. The Fund has proved to be a useful mechanism whereby TAB can make advances for projects pending the receipt of contributions, and emergency needs can also be financed more readily.

At its twenty-fourth session in July, 1957, ECOSOC adopted a resolution urging the General Assembly at its next session to establish a Special United Nations Fund for Economic Development (SUNFED) and to set up a preparatory committee to work out the necessary details. However, Britain, Canada, and the United States voted against the proposal and the stage was set for a spirited Assembly debate on the matter. What materialized from the Twelfth Assembly was a compromise resolution which combined elements of the ECOSOC resolution of July and a proposal of the United States to increase the financial resources of the expanded technical assistance program of the United Nations.

According to the Assembly resolution, a Special Projects Fund is to be established to assist underdeveloped countries in certain specific activities concerning their economic development and to extend the existing technical assistance program. The Fund is to be separate from present financial resources for technical assistance and will provide 'systematic and sustained assistance in the fields essential to the integrated technical, economic, and social development of the less developed countries.' The Assembly decided that in view of the resources probably available, 'which are not likely to exceed $100 million annually,' the operations of the Special Fund would be directed in the immediate future toward enlarging the scope of existing technical assistance programs 'so as to include special projects in certain basic fields' to be defined by a preparatory committee. Financial resources are to be derived principally from voluntary contributions and it is expected that the Fund might be established sometime in 1959.

Conclusions. In general, the outlines of the technical assistance program have been fairly well maintained. Efforts to improve financial management and administrative procedures continue and progress has been made on program planning on a country-by-country basis. Some individual projects have already been completed and others proceed slowly toward conclusion. Most of the recipient countries have proved to be willing workers in developing their own economies as well as those of their neighbors. The actual results on a worldwide basis will not be known for some years. Individual countries have already gained many positive benefits. What is more, governments have improved their administrative processes and learned how to help themselves by more efficient planning and saving.

However, despite the accelerated pace of technical assistance since 1950, the basic needs of the world's underdeveloped areas far exceed the financial resources available. Between 1950 and 1958 the number of contributing countries has gradually risen but the total amount pledged has not shown a substantial increase. In addition, short-term financing through a system of annual voluntary pledges has some particular shortcomings. Such a method makes it difficult for agencies to plan ahead adequately for their interrelated projects. Contributions are not always made on time, some coming in during the following year. Countries receiving assistance are faced with the problem of providing funds for local expenses without a guarantee that assistance will be forthcoming beyond the current year's operations. The uncertainty associated with this lack of continuity has been relieved somewhat by the existence of the Working Capital and Reserve Fund which can be used for making advances before the receipt of contributions. At the same time, there has arisen the problem of the inconvertibility of some of the funds contributed. More than forty of the contributions are in currencies which are expendable only within the contributing country and fifteen are in currencies with limited convertibility. This problem came before TAC and ECOSOC in 1956, where despite considerable discussion, it was decided to do nothing more than urge that contributions be made convertible to the largest extent possible.

In any conclusion on technical assistance, the words of one experienced participant should be remembered:

ExpandeD of Asse . pRoGRAm TecH

. . . The main problem facing such a programme as EPTA is not that of teaching modern skills to untrained individuals: it is that of adapting its methods and procedures to the varying needs of specific societies. Almost any stone-age individual can be taught almost any modern technique, but he and his dependents will profit little from his new skills unless the society of which he is a member moves as a whole into the technical world of the twentieth century. Such a move includes a radical transformation of the society's customs and value scales. It must be made voluntarily and consciously, and cannot be imposed from without. EPTA's ultimate success will largely depend on the ability of those responsible for it to grasp these facts and adapt their policy and procedures accordingly.[6]

REFUGEES AND RELIEF

The United Nations inherited the almost insoluble problem of caring for and resettling the many millions of persons uprooted from their homes by the Second World War. First to work in the field was the United Nations Relief and Rehabilitation Administration (UNRRA), followed by the International Refugee Organization (IRO), and the present High Commissioner for Refugees. In addition to the refugee problems caused by World War II, the United Nations has had to provide assistance to the refugees from the Arab-Israeli conflict and to the many who have suffered from the Korean War.

The Activities of UNRRA. UNRRA began its far-flung activities in 1943 with an agreement signed by forty-four nations. It was never a part of the United Nations but it functioned much like a specialized agency. It was largely financed by the United States and had its headquarters in Washington, D.C.

Work got underway in the spring of 1945 as the Allied armies advanced. The destitute in Central and Eastern Europe, and even in China, were provided with food, clothing, shelter, and medical care. Stringent health measures were adopted to prevent the spread of epidemics. Equipment and materials were given to liberated countries to be used as a start toward economic recovery. The most immediate problem which arose was the care of millions of persons discovered in Germany; some were refugees and others had been brought in as forced labor during the war. Within six months, over half of them were repatriated, largely with military assistance. However, many refused to return to their homelands, fearful of the Com-

---

[6] Blelloch, David, 'Bold New Programme: A Review of United Nations Technical Assistance,' *International Affairs*, Vol. 33, No. 1 (January 1957), p. 50. Mr. Blelloch was a Resident Representative in Colombia.

munist regimes which had been established at the close of the war. It became necessary for UNRRA to maintain huge assembly centers to care for these displaced persons and refugees until they could be resettled.

Unquestionably, UNRRA prevented a great amount of suffering and provided temporary help to countries and individuals alike. Over a million people were repatriated and nearly a million displaced persons were cared for. It was hampered in its efforts by the complexity of the tasks encountered, the inadequacy of a hastily recruited staff, and the incompetence and corruption of some local government officials. The widespread shortage of food in 1946 contributed to its troubles. Dissatisfaction with its progress mounted and its activities were ended in Europe in December of 1946 and in China the following spring. The problem of the refugee was turned over to a new agency, the International Refugee Organization.

The International Refugee Organization (IRO). The General Assembly was well aware of this question when it first met in February, 1946, and soon it instructed ECOSOC to study and make recommendations on the problem. ECOSOC suggested a nonpermanent specialized agency to be made responsible for all work with refugees. When the Assembly sought to establish the new agency in the fall of 1946, there developed an irreconcilable split over the meaning of the term 'refugees' and the treatment to be accorded them. The Western delegates maintained that any worthy individual should be assisted and his repatriation fostered according to his wishes. The Soviet countries claimed that the only refugee was the person who was a victim of the Axis Powers and that repatriation must be compulsory. No agreement on these points was ever reached and the Soviet bloc voted against the Constitution of IRO. A large group of states abstained from voting. Despite the decided handicap of this lack of support, IRO began its work in 1947.

The task faced by IRO was enormous. It had to identify refugees and displaced persons, classify them, and offer them material and legal assistance. Finally, repatriation had to be encouraged or resettlement arranged for in other countries. By the end of 1951 when IRO was dissolved, another million refugees and displaced persons had been repatriated or resettled in new homes. Only about 70,000 chose repatriation. The United States, Australia, and Canada accepted the majority of those resettled, taking in about 800,000. Western Europe could not absorb many although it did accept as many as possible. Latin American states were among the first to welcome newcomers. At one time IRO maintained a fleet of thirty-nine vessels to transport these people; it also chartered an average of forty-five trains a month, in addition to using busses and planes as means of transportation. The budget for the first year was $155 million, more than was available for the entire United Nations and specialized agencies combined. Much more could have been spent, however, as the need was endless. No less than 20,000 births occurred in the camps annually and new refugees continued to pour in.

An International Tracing Service was maintained for three years, which sought to determine the fate of millions of persons who had disappeared during the war. In addition to the care, maintenance, and transportation of refugees, IRO conducted vocational training and foreign language courses and offered apprenticeship opportunities in many trades. Every effort was made to prepare the refugee for a new life and orient him in the customs and habits of the country that opened its doors to him. The tireless efforts of IRO are indeed an outstanding contribution made by the United Nations, in the face of repeated obstacles to alleviate the sufferings of those unfortunate by-products of war, the refugees.

THE HIGH COMMISSIONER. When IRO went out of existence in 1951, there were still nearly a half-million persons needing assistance in addition to the continuing flow of new refugees. To replace IRO, the General Assembly created the Office of the United Nations High Commissioner for Refugees which began its work on January 1, 1951, some months before IRO was dissolved.

Under this new arrangement, there are virtually no funds available for caring and providing for the resettlement of refugees. Dependence is on voluntary contributions to a small United Nations Refugee Emergency Fund which is used to promote permanent solutions for existing refugees and provide emergency aid to the most needy cases. The task of the High Commissioner is, in brief, to encourage further repatriation and, whenever possible, to obtain from individual governments entry permits for the resettlement of refugees. The operational features of IRO are no longer applicable. Some headway has been made but at the present rate of repatriation and resettlement, there appears to be little hope that there will be a satisfactory solution to this problem of refugees in the near future.

Additional legal protection was given to the refugee by the adoption in 1951 of a Convention Relating to the Status of Refugees, drawn up by a special conference at Geneva attended by twenty-four states. The term 'refugee' was defined and certain persons were excluded from the provisions of the Convention. The juridical status of the refugee was determined and specific provisions were made relating to his gainful employment, his welfare, and nondiscrimination as to race, religion, or country of origin. In September, 1954, a United Nations Conference on the Status of Stateless Persons met in New York. Twenty-seven states were represented and a Convention Relating to the Status of Stateless Persons was concluded. This

Convention is similar to the one on refugees in that it specifically excludes certain groups, such as those who have committed a war crime or have been guilty of acts contrary to the purposes and principles of the United Nations. States that are parties to the Convention are obligated to grant to stateless persons who are lawfully in their territory the same treatment as nationals with respect to certain rights. These include freedom of religion, protection of artistic rights and industrial property, access to the courts of law, rationing of products in short supply, elementary education, labor legislation, and social security.

PALESTINIAN REFUGEES. The hostilities in Palestine have resulted in nearly one million Arabs becoming refugees. The problem of refugees became acute in July, 1948, and was first dealt with by the Arab governments. Largely through the efforts of the late Count Folke Bernadotte, the United Nations Mediator in Palestine, a temporary disaster relief program was begun. It was later replaced by the United Nations Relief for Palestine Refugees, an agency which worked closely with the Red Cross and the American Friends Service Committee in distributing supplies and providing some shelter and medical care.

In 1949 the United Nations Conciliation Commission for Palestine created an Economic Survey Mission to examine the entire situation and recommend measures to alleviate economic dislocations. Its main conclusion was that direct relief should be curtailed and a public works program instituted to improve the productivity of the areas in which the refugees were located and provide gainful employment to those able and willing to work. Late in 1949 the Assembly, acting on this recommendation, established the United Nations Relief and Works Agency for Palestine Refugees in the Near East (UNRWA). Its present mandate has been extended to June 30, 1960. A relief budget of about $25 million and a rehabilitation budget of $15 million for 1958 is financed by voluntary contributions from the individual members of the United Nations.

The program has not met with great success, in large part because of the lack of support by the Arab states. The refugees are not enthusiastic about resettling elsewhere and are determined to return to the areas from which they were dislodged. Some 20,000 to 25,000 new refugees are added to the relief lists annually. The development projects for rehabilitation have not progressed rapidly. The Arab countries where the refugees have been quartered have been hostile to UNRWA functioning within their territories. The fact is that UNRWA furnishes the basic necessities for a large part of the population of these countries, which is embarrassing to the host governments. There is an imperative need for parallel programs of economic development by these governments to supplement the projects of UNRWA, so that additional means of self-support for refugees can be provided. The burden of relief placed upon individual members of the United Nations cannot be borne indefinitely.

KOREAN RELIEF AND RECONSTRUCTION. The devastation resulting from the Korean War has been immense and the Republic of Korea cannot, by itself, begin to cope with the work of caring for the homeless and rebuilding the country. Once again the United Nations has attempted to fill the breach through the generosity of its members. Early in the war the Assembly established the United Nations Korean Reconstruction Agency (UNKRA) to assist the Korean authorities in relief and rehabilitation. Most of the assistance was channeled through the military command until the fighting front had been stabilized sufficiently to permit UNKRA to undertake its responsibilities.

Few people realize that, aside from Japan, Korean factories were producing more goods before the conflict than any other Asian country. There was a variety of products although most of the enterprises were relatively small. Most of the businesses have had to be rebuilt, and the people relocated and fed, clothed, educated, and provided with medical care. Such primary items as paper, fishing supplies, cement, textiles, farm equipment, and fertilizers were necessary to start economic recovery. UNKRA has concentrated on rebuilding the industries turning out these essential products and expanding vocational training. It has also sponsored such diverse projects as housing developments and exploration for mineral resources.

Progress has been made on the immense job of reconstruction but there have been delays resulting from a lack of funds. Generous assistance has come from the United States and sources other than the United Nations but hundreds of millions of dollars are still required to fulfill the needs of this war-devastated land.

Conclusions. The three primary relief agencies working through the United Nations — the office of the High Commissioner, UNRWA, and UNKRA — have sought first, to work on the problem of relief for those made homeless and destitute through war, and second, to pursue the difficult task of rehabilitation through resettlement or repatriation. There appears to be no immediate end to the need for providing for continuing millions of refugees. Nearly 150,000 Hungarians alone fled into Austria in the last two months of 1956 as a result of the Soviet depredations in their country. Emergency financial contributions relieved somewhat the desperate plight of Austria in caring for this added refugee burden.

The three agencies have continually had to struggle with inadequate financial support due to the failure of many members of the United Nations to contribute anything and a refusal of some to honor their commitments.

The High Commissioner's Office reported in 1956, for example, that contributions failed by $3.4 million to meet the target of $5,549,553. Shortly before his untimely death in 1956, Dr. Van Heuven Goedhart, the High Commissioner stated:

> not only were the United Nations failing to solve the humanitarian problem which it was within their power to solve, but . . . they were not keeping their part of the virtual agreement which they had entered into with the countries of residence of refugees under resolution 832(X). Under that resolution, the United Nations were to achieve certain results within a fixed limit of time. The counterpart of this was that the countries of residence had undertaken to make supporting contributions available and accept financial responsibility for any refugees within the scope of the program who still required assistance at the end of the stipulated period.

Political considerations continue to aggravate the refugee problem in the Middle East. Further economic development is necessary before much can be accomplished in the way of a solution. The representative of the United States observed before the General Assembly in 1955 that

> in the end what would benefit the refugees would benefit the Arab countries themselves. For example, the plan for the development of the Jordan Valley . . . would bring 125,000 acres of new land into cultivation in Jordan alone and would increase substantially the hydro-electric power available to Syria and Jordan. Carrying out that project would not only create new jobs for the refugees but would give impetus to new industries and create new sources of income in all the Arab countries.

Little can be done on such projects until political tensions have been reduced. The Israeli-Egyptian conflict of 1956, coupled with the Anglo-French-Arab crisis, have made further progress virtually impossible. The Agency has had to contend with continuing interference in its activities and a failure to accord it the rights and privileges due an organ of the United Nations. The New Zealand representative to the General Assembly brought these facts out clearly when he observed that

> it was disturbing to note that Israel refused transit rights to the Agency aircraft carrying Arab members of the Agency's staff, that the Arab Governments levied duties on relief supplies and that many persons were being given relief unnecessarily because the Agency had been unable to deal with the problem of fraudulent registration.

Rehabilitation and relief work in Korea, while an immense problem, has not been so dependent upon the United Nations for financial assistance as is true of the other refugee problems. The United States has spent and is continuing to spend hundreds of millions of dollars. Due to the industrial and commercial potentialities of the area, there is considerable hope for the success of these projects. UNKRA reached the peak of its activities in 1956 and some programs, such as those in the fields of power, irrigation, transport, and communication, have been concluded. Despite this cautious optimism, the *United Nations Economic Survey of Asia and the Far East, 1955* reported as follows:

> Given the limited resources of a divided Korea, the increasingly dense population of the Republic of Korea, the available foreign economic aid with certain probable inefficiencies in its use, and the fact that one-tenth of the labor force . . . is retained in the military services, the target date for economic stability at pre Korean-war standards must probably be set back. The plans drawn up thus far have for the most part anticipated recovery to that point in from three to five years. In view of the persistent trade deficit and inflation, however, a substantially longer period may be a more realistic estimate.

SOCIAL WELFARE

The broad category of social welfare encompasses the work of a large number of agencies and organs of the United Nations and the specialized agencies. A few of the tasks undertaken are the improvement of standards of living, rehabilitation of the physically handicapped, housing and town planning, child welfare, youth guidance, prevention of crime and the treatment of offenders, the reduction in the traffic in women and children, and social aspects of migration and refugees. Such matters are the concern of FAO, WHO, ILO, UNESCO, and several of the functional commissions serving ECOSOC. Much of the work has been assigned to the Expanded Technical Assistance Program of the United Nations. Probably the Social Commission of ECOSOC is most directly concerned with planning and advising on most of the aspects of social welfare. A welfare activity of great importance has been the work of the United Nations Children's Fund (UNICEF). An examination of both of these bodies — the Social Commission and UNICEF — will reveal the planning aspects of social welfare and specific undertakings and accomplishments in the special field of child welfare.

Social Commission. As a functional commission reporting to ECOSOC, the Social Commission advises on social questions of a general character and particularly on matters in the social field not covered by the specialized agencies. It recommends practical measures which may be needed, especially those necessary for the co-ordination of activities and any international agreements and conventions required for matters in the social field.

The Commission originated what is known as a program of 'social defense,' which is designed to prevent crime and improve the treatment

of offenders. This includes conferences and seminars, both local and regional, to study and discuss related problems. A recent seminar in Brazil,
for example, was attended by representatives from seventeen countries as
well as experts who presented papers and acted as discussion leaders. The
seminar dealt with the standard minimum rules for the treatment of
prisoners, the selection and training of correctional personnel, penal institutions, juvenile delinquency, and the trends of crime. Other studies suggested by the Commission have been undertaken on prison labor, parole
and after-care, and the practical results and financial aspects of probation.
The Commission also contributed to the Convention for the Suppression of
the Traffic in Persons and of the Exploitation of the Prostitution of Others,
which was adopted by the General Assembly in 1949.

UNICEF. The Second World War and the Korean War have caused suffering and misery for millions of children in Europe and Asia. Working with
the Social Commission, WHO, ILO, FAO, UNESCO, and the United Nations
High Commissioner for Refugees, UNICEF has brought material assistance
to over one million children and expectant or nursing mothers in more than
seventy countries. It is the only international agency that has continued to
provide relief inside as well as outside the Iron Curtain since the liquidation
of UNRRA. UNICEF is able to function primarily through the voluntary
contributions of states, with about half of its multimillion dollar annual
expenditures donated by the United States. The immensity of the program
can be seen from the fact that of the 900,000,000, children in the world, approximately two thirds or 600,000,000 are without adequate food, shelter,
clothing, sanitation, or minimum medical facilities.

The specialized agencies usually provide technical advice and skills,
whereas UNICEF makes available supplies unobtainable in the aided
countries. These include powdered milk, DDT, vaccines and penicillin to
control diseases, fish oil capsules for supplemental feeding, and medicines
and equipment for maternal and child welfare centers. The countries receiving assistance normally offer the labor, building materials, and other
resources available locally. UNICEF aid is not charity but serves to stimulate self-help to build stable and self-reliant nations. Aided governments
match every dollar spent by UNICEF by at least an equal amount. Often it
is much larger, going as high as ten dollars for every one dollar expended
by UNICEF. Orginally designed to offer emergency aid, UNICEF now
emphasizes long-range planning. During the first years, most of the work
was concentrated in Europe. At the present, efforts are directed at assisting
underdeveloped areas of Asia, Latin America, the Middle East, and Africa.

A large percentage of UNICEF expenditures has been devoted to mass
health campaigns against diseases attacking children, which can be con-

trolled relatively cheaply. Generous allocations have been made for the fight against the three major cripplers of children: tuberculosis, malaria, and yaws, the last named a disfiguring tropical disease. Modern insecticides and antibiotics can virtually eliminate malaria and yaws. Some of the other children's diseases which have been dealt with by UNICEF are diphtheria, whooping cough, trachoma, mycosis, dysentery, and leprosy. Diphtheria and whooping cough are still major causes of death among preschool children in the temperate zones. Trachoma, 'the disease of the dirty hands,' and its close relative, conjunctivitis, are especially prevalent in Pakistan, India, China, North Africa, and the eastern Mediterranean area. UNICEF not only ships medicines, penicillin, DDT, and equipment to combat these diseases but works to establish plants which can produce locally the drugs to treat these diseases. In 1955 alone, 14.5 million young people were vaccinated against tuberculosis.

Since malnutrition affects about half the world's children and expectant and nursing mothers, UNICEF has been active in improving diets to reduce food-deficiency diseases. Milk is the basis of the long-range nutrition programs. UNICEF also works to equip milk production plants which will become sources of supply for school feeding programs. In countries where there is no dairy industry, UNICEF has joined forces with FAO to push the production of locally grown high protein foods. UNICEF has shipped nearly one billion pounds of dried skim milk to malnourished children and approved aid for more than one hundred fifty milk processing plants. Assistance of this nature in 1957 was being given to more than sixty countries. At approximately 5,000 rural maternal and child welfare centers, mothers and children have access to basic health services which would be otherwise unavailable.

Conclusions. The few statistics which have been mentioned are an indication of solid accomplishment. But there are many more millions of young people who have not benefited materially to any great extent from UNICEF and other social welfare activities, to say nothing of the countless other millions of older people in need of assistance. There is, also, the problem of continuing the work already begun. A start has been made, primarily through projects falling within the scope of the technical assistance programs of the United Nations, to train and equip people to help themselves. But this is only a start, although, because of added funds and staff, more has been done than in the days of the League of Nations.

The Social Commission has offered some leadership in developing a number of projects but has had a habit already noted in other United Nations bodies, to attempt too much without establishing satisfactory criteria of needs and priorities. This is a natural tendency, since there is so much that needs to be done in so many fields. The inevitable problem of co-ordination arises here again owing primarily to the numerous agencies concerned.

NARCOTIC DRUG CONTROL

Some of the most concrete successes in international co-operation have occurred in the field of narcotic drugs. The process of building the machinery has been gradual and those responsible for its supervision have been willing to take a long-range view of the problem, undismayed by temporary setbacks.

The first efforts against narcotic drugs began in 1909 with the calling of an international conference on opium at Shanghai. In 1912, a Hague Opium Convention was adopted but it lacked administrative machinery for the implementation of its provisions. With the League of Nations came a rapid advance through the conclusion of a number of agreements and conventions and with the establishment of international machinery designed to meet the needs of narcotic drug control. One of the outstanding League agencies was the Permanent Central Opium Board which was given certain regulatory powers. Also useful was the Advisory Committee on the Traffic in Opium and other Dangerous Drugs which was appointed by the League Council and the Supervisory Body established by the Limitation Convention of 1931.[7]

The United Nations has assumed the responsibilities formerly belonging to the League and has continued the excellent work begun by that organization. The Commission on Narcotic Drugs is the direct successor to the League's Advisory Committee on Traffic on Opium and other Dangerous Drugs. It is the central supervisory body and assists ECOSOC in applying the nine conventions which form the basis of the international system. The Commission also considers the changes which may be required for the existing machinery and so advises ECOSOC. The Permanent Central Opium Board has been continued 'to watch the course of international trade in narcotic drugs.' Also continued is the Drug Supervisory Body to examine the estimate submitted annually by states specifying their legitimate needs for narcotic drugs. It has the authority to recommend a reduction in estimates furnished by governments. WHO is directly concerned with narcotic drugs, having been assigned the task of deciding whether a particular drug is habit-forming. The Social Commission is interested in certain social aspects of drug addiction.

As far as control is concerned, the United Nations can take no direct action

[7] See above, pp. 66–7, for the activities of the League of Nations in the control of narcotic drugs.

but it can promote collective control action and improvement in reporting methods by the individual governments that actually exercise control. On occasion, individual governments consult the United Nations and receive advice relative to the machinery for narcotics control. One principal method in control is obtaining information on the source of contraband opium. This has been done by having opium-producing countries submit samples of opium to a laboratory made available to United Nations chemists by the United States. Chemical tests made on opium seized in illicit traffic reveal the source of the opium on the basis of a comparison with the samples in the possession of the United Nations.

The discovery of new synthetic narcotic drugs has led to additional problems of regulation and control. On the basis of studies conducted by the Commission on Narcotic Drugs and other United Nations agencies, a new convention was adopted in 1948 designed to reinforce existing control measures. Its key feature is the obligation of each state party to its provisions to inform the Secretary-General of any drug used or capable of being used for medical or scientific purposes which is not covered by earlier conventions. The decision whether the drug in question is habit-forming is the responsibility of WHO. If WHO reports in the affirmative, the states that are parties to the convention are required to subject the drug to appropriate control. This is just a start, however, on the exceedingly complex problem of controlling the new synthetic drugs. In the case of the raw materials such as opium, cannabis, and coca leaf, which originally were the source of narcotics, it was possible to follow all the economic phases from agricultural production through manufacture to their final distribution for medicinal purposes. But the raw materials which form the basis of synthetic narcotic drugs may be by-products of coal tar and petroleum and the drugs themselves can be produced in various chemical compounds. Any system of control covering all phases of the manufacture of substances which are used industrially in countless ways and have many other useful applications would be impossible. The Commission and WHO have been working together on the problem of control but much remains to be done.

The most serious problem, however, continues to be the growing volume of illicit traffic. The development of drug addiction is closely associated with the question of limiting the production of raw materials used in the manufacture of narcotic drugs. Any excess of production beyond legitimate medical and scientific needs finds its way into the illicit traffic and that is the primary source of supply for addicts. The various United Nations agencies continue to seek broader and better perfected means of controlling production but it is a most complex problem, dependent upon the co-operation of all producers of narcotic raw materials. The failure of Communist China, the major producer, to assist fully in regulating production is a prime source of trouble. There is also an alarming increase in illicit cocaine, cannabis, and cannabis resin, the last named being one of the most widely consumed drugs. It is known in various parts of the world as hashish, marihuana, ganja, and bhang.

FOOD AND AGRICULTURE

Fiat Panis. Let there be bread — the motto of the Food and Agriculture Organization — is the symbolic expression of its duty to assist the millions of starving and undernourished people in the world. The teaching of efficient farming methods, good soil management practices, the full use of technological advances in agriculture, training in fish marketing, forestry development, research in food technology, are examples selected at random to illustrate the many different activities engaged in by FAO, all of which are directed toward the alleviation of suffering and the development of a higher standard of living for all peoples.

During the first year of its existence, FAO perfected its organizational structure and undertook an extensive survey of the food supplies of the world in relation to needs. Its report was published in 1946 and covered seventy countries representing about 90 percent of the world's population. A major conclusion resulting from the survey revealed the startling fact that food supplies would have to be increased over 100 percent in twenty-five years to take care of population growth and raise the diets of the poorly fed to a reasonable level. The key to this immense problem is, of course, the economic development of the areas where the majority of the undernourished live. But before FAO could embark on any long-range undertakings, the immediate postwar emergency of starving millions had to be met. An International Emergency Food Council was established to allocate scarce foodstuffs. FAO later took over this activity as well as the agricultural rehabilitation work of UNRRA. After 1948 most countries that had faced emergency shortages had overcome their immediate crises and FAO was able to concentrate on projects of a more lasting nature.

A major part of FAO's activity in recent years has been concentrated on technical assistance, some of which has been noted earlier in this chapter. At the same time, other programs and projects have been undertaken in agriculture and agricultural economics, fisheries, forestry, and nutrition. A few examples from each of these fields will illustrate the nature of FAO's work.

Agriculture. Co-operative programs in the breeding of rice are being carried on in Southeast Asia and in wheat and barley in the Middle East.

A Working Party on Fertilizers of the FAO International Rice Commission has recommended the collection and compilation of experimental data on fertilizer application and suggested methods for improving rice production. The Wheat and Barley Commission has developed plans for the establishment of more than eighty co-operative wheat and barley nurseries in the Middle East for the identification of disease-free stocks. Seeds for this project were provided by the seed distribution service of FAO. Anti-locust activities have been carried out extensively in Latin America, the Near East, and in North and East Africa. Attention has also been directed to the growing importance of agricultural surpluses, their effect on international markets, and methods of disposing of them so as best to encourage world economic development.

FAO has assisted in the control of animal diseases through the co-ordination of national programs and in the production of biologics. Progress in rinderpest (disease of bovine animals) control has reached a stage where most of the affected areas — Asia, the Far East, and Africa — have started eradication programs. Projects are well underway for artificial insemination and anti-sterility programs. Measures for the improvement of dairy production have been developed in co-operation with UNICEF.

Fisheries. FAO provides the secretariat for the general Fisheries Council of the Mediterranean and the Indo-Pacific Fisheries Council which are concerned with organizing consultation and co-operation between member-nations in their regions on fisheries, resources, techniques, and organization. The Indo-Pacific Fisheries Council in 1954, for example, considered a program dealing with inland, sea, and miscellaneous fisheries; food technology; fishing craft and gear; and fishery economics, including marketing and statistics.

Conducting training centers is a regular function of FAO. A Latin American center, for example, has provided fishery administrators, economists, technologists, biologists, and a general introduction to fishery science with special emphasis upon problems of the region. FAO sponsors an International Fishing Boat Congress which has studied such problems as boat types, safety at sea, hull shapes, sea behavior, engines, propellers, deck gear, and factory ships.

Forestry. An important feature of FAO's program is to help increase the world production of pulp and paper. Specialists sent out by FAO have made surveys to determine the possibility of increasing pulp and paper output from unconventional materials or in countries which do not have paper manufacturing industries. Some conclusions from these surveys have appeared in a published report, *Raw Materials for More Paper,* which explains recent technical advances in the manufacture of pulp and paper and the possibility and cost of making them from such unconventional materials as tropical woods, bagasse, and other agricultural residues. Another important related work has been issued on *World Pulp and Paper Resources and Prospects.*

FAO has helped to establish laboratories in forest products research in the Philippines, Austria, and Iran. Seminars, institutes, and congresses are sponsored by FAO on such subjects as improving sawing and machining practices, wood technology, wood chemistry, forest products research, and productivity in logging.

Nutrition. In this field FAO concentrates on such matters as food consumption and management, food technology, maternal and child nutrition, supplementary feeding, and education in nutrition and home economics. Regional nutrition officers have been stationed in the Near East, South America, and the Far East to assist members of FAO in creating and expanding nutrition services and in implementing the recommendations of regional conferences and committees.

FAO works in close conjunction with WHO and UNICEF to improve child nutrition, with special attention given to the development of the use of low-cost protein-rich foods. In connection with WHO, surveys are made of the incidence of protein malnutrition in certain countries. Emphasis has been placed on methods of processing cheap protein-rich foods in order to make these available and suitable for child feeding. An example of this is a project initiated in Indonesia by FAO and UNICEF for the manufacture of soybean milk. Extensive work on matters of nutrition has also been done through the participation of FAO, WHO, and UNICEF in the Expanded Program of Technical Assistance of the United Nations.

Conclusions. What can be said of FAO's contribution as an international organization to the intricate problem of developing the world's food and agriculture? On November 1, 1945, at the close of FAO's first conference session, Lester B. Pearson, Canadian Chairman of the session, observed: 'The first of the new, permanent United Nations agencies is now launched. There are few precedents for it to follow; it is something new in international history. . . .' After more than a decade of concern with all the earth's natural renewable resources and the nutritional needs of mankind, FAO can take pride in the fact that its activities have come to be taken for granted as a natural part of international co-operation. Particularly rewarding has been the regional approach to problems of mutual interest to countries in a particular area. The Near East Regional Desert Locust Control Project and the European Foot and Mouth Disease Commission are good examples. The many FAO projects within the technical assistance programs of the United Nations have increased in their effectiveness and are now being concentrated on solving major problems. The planning, development, and execution is now virtually handled by FAO together with the regular program in such a way that the total program is operated as an integrated whole.

Less heralded but a vitally important and fundamental activity best performed by an international agency is the collection and publication of worldwide information dealing with food and agriculture. FAO has now reached a point where hardly any significant contribution to the knowledge of world agriculture announced anywhere escapes its attention. The over-all surveys of FAO on agriculture, forestry, and fisheries, for example, are documents unavailable elsewhere. In this respect, FAO has assumed a particular responsibility for assisting in the diffusion of information on atomic energy in agriculture and related fields. It acts as a channel in informing and advising member-countries of progress in research and the application of such research to practical development.

World *per capita* agricultural production (excluding the USSR, Eastern Europe, and Communist China) which had decreased by 10 percent to 15 percent at the end of World War II, had regained its prewar level by 1956 in spite of an increase of about 25 percent in population. This general conclusion is encouraging but upon more careful analysis, there are specific problem areas remaining. Thus, agricultural production increased much more rapidly in advanced countries than in economically underdeveloped ones. *Per capita* production in Asia and Latin America, for example, was still below prewar levels, while surpluses had built up in the more advanced countries.

Much is being done by individual countries to influence the course of agricultural production along the lines of the general principles of the selective expansion of production and consumption repeatedly suggested by FAO. Relatively little progress has been made, however, in co-ordinating production policies between countries or in working towards a more complementary development of agriculture between countries. FAO has employed the device of holding regional conferences in dealing with such problems as agricultural surpluses and the development of complementary agricultural development policies. Some success has been achieved in outlining basic problems but much more co-operation from individual governments is necessary. To meet the pressing need of an increase in the productivity of agriculture in some areas, FAO continues to press its work programs in the fields of land and water utilization and conservation, plant and animal production and protection, and the expansion of agricultural institutions and services.

FAO has entered its second decade of work with a record of accomplishment, recognizing, nevertheless, that over large parts of the world the economic problem of providing people with the means to purchase the food they need is not yet solved. The most productive aspect of its work has been in the field of technical assistance. Political considerations still prevent a unified approach to world food problems, since a common global policy cannot emerge with the Soviet world unwilling to participate wholeheartedly in seeking to obtain FAO's objectives.

COMMUNICATIONS AND TRANSPORT

The need for international co-operation working toward technological improvements in communications and transport has long been recognized. Some of the most notable successes recorded in international organization have been in dealing with problems in this field. Today the following specialized agencies are the most vitally concerned: Universal Postal Union, International Telecommunication Union, International Civil Aviation Organization, World Meteorological Organization, and the International Maritime Consultative Organization. In 1946, ECOSOC created the Transport and Communications Commission to advise on measures for co-ordinating the activities of the specialized agencies concerned and to make recommendations on matters not covered specifically by them. Most of these agencies have participated in the technical assistance programs of the United Nations.

The Transport and Communications Commission. Considerable time has been devoted by the Commission to the problem of inland transport which encompasses transport by rail, water, motor, and pipeline. This is one of the fields not covered by the specialized agencies. At the instigation of the Commission a Convention on Road Traffic was concluded in 1949 and came into force in 1952. Work continues on the difficult problem of establishing a uniform system of road signs and signals. Other problems considered have been the question of uniform licensing of motor vehicle drivers, the integration of European railway systems, the transport of dangerous goods, and the removal of barriers to the international transport of goods. In addition, the Commission has concerned itself with facilitating the international movement of persons by suggesting means to simplify frontier regulations through easing passport formalities, reducing visa fees or even abolishing visas. Conventions have been drafted on customs formalities for the temporary importation of private vehicles and their equipment and for tourism or the personal effects of tourists traveling by any means of transport.

Another field of concentration recognized by the Commission has been that of maritime shipping. Until the Inter-governmental Maritime Consultative Organization became permanent in 1958, the Commission has had to serve in its place. Some progress has been made toward obtaining unification of maritime tonnage measurement. Efforts have been made, with less success, to reduce the pollution of sea water which is harmful to birds, plant life, fish, and beaches, and which also presents a fire hazard to ports. Remedies suggested have been separators on ships, facilities on barges or ashore for the discharge of polluted water, treatment of oil sludge by physical or chemical processes, and limiting the spread of oil discharged at sea.

Postal Services. The Universal Postal Union continues its useful but largely unpublicized activities begun three-quarters of a century ago. In addition to administering the regulations which govern the international exchange of mail between 95 countries, UPU has been assisting its members to meet current needs for faster postal services. Studies have been completed on such subjects as automatic postage stamp and postcard vending machines, the pneumatic post or delivery of mail through pneumatic tubes, transfer and mechanization at railway stations, mechanical accounting systems for various postal services, and the organization of postal delivery services. Besides distributing technical studies, UPU maintains a loan service through which members may borrow books, periodicals, films, and other reference material on postal services.

Extensive study has been devoted to improving and standardizing air postal services. UPU has worked closely with ICAO and the International Air Transport Association (airlines' association) and the latter two bodies have supplied much of the information on prices and air transport statistics. At Brussels in 1952 the thirteenth UPU Congress met and revised the Universal Postal Convention of 1947. Particular attention was given to airmail rates. Changes adopted included a maximum rate for the carriage of letters and postcards, newspapers, and periodicals.

Telecommunications. The International Telecommunication Union has been concerned chiefly with the rapid technical developments of radio transmission. A number of conferences have been held under its auspices which have considered such items as the drafting of basic definitions in connection with telegraphic transmission and distortion, the protection of voice-frequency telegraph channels, the establishment of standard rates for phototelegrams, protection of telegraph channels against disturbances, reform of telegraph statistics, telegraphy definitions and vocabulary, the operation and tariffs for intercontinental radio-telephone services, and many others.

The number of radio frequencies falls far short of the demand. There is also much competition in the field of high-frequency broadcasting. One of the important tasks of the Radio Consultative Committee of ITU is to make scientific studies designed to increase the number of frequencies available and to ensure their most economical use by the best possible techniques. The International Frequency Registration Board examines demands relating to the utilization of frequencies by individual radio stations. A new world-wide frequency allocation table extending up to 10,500,000 kilocycles has been established. A World Frequency Assignment List is maintained which is a comprehensive document containing all frequencies in the radio spectrum. Claims for frequencies are registered on the basis of this list. Records maintained by ITU are employed to negotiate settlement of disputes over alleged frequency interferences by states. Regulations that concern station identification signals, radar station frequencies and reservation distress frequencies for lifesaving, rescue, and urgent meteorological messages are kept up-to-date.

Meteorological Activities. The newest of the specialized agencies, the World Meteorological Organization concerned itself in its first years with the preparation and development of administrative measures. Technical regulations have now been completed and efforts have been turned to other technical and research problems.

An international cloud atlas has been adopted and considerable time has been spent on the preparation of world thunderstorm maps based on statistics collected from land stations in all parts of the globe. An Arid Zone Panel of Experts is collecting and distributing information on research work being carried out on the meteorological and hydrological problems of this zone. Studies are nearing completion on artificial inducement of precipitation, on the sources and utilization of wind energy, and on the icing of aircraft and other surfaces exposed in clouds. Other work is progressing on instruments and methods of observation, aerology and the publication of aerological data, climatology, and maritime, synoptic, and aeronautical meteorology.

In the field of agricultural meteorology, activities in progress include the collection and distribution of climatic information for agriculture and the improvement of systems of forecasts and warning especially designed for agricultural purposes. Advice on adverse weather conditions provides information on such questions as protection against frost damage, weather factors affecting plant diseases, and the preservation of stored and packed food in unfavorable weather. Surveys have been made concerning weather conditions affecting the breeding and migration of locusts and those influencing the successful use of combatant agents. WMO maintains close relations with FAO for these researchers and also with ICAO, UNESCO, and ITU for activities in connection with the technical assistance programs of the United Nations.

Aviation. Having completed its first decade of activity in 1955, the International Civil Aviation Organization can report steady progress in its objectives of developing the principles and techniques of international air navigation and fostering the planning and expansion of international air transport. Dozens of meetings and conferences have produced a substantial body of international agreement for civil aviation. So far, however, it has not been possible to reach accord on a multilateral convention on air routes and rates and bilateral agreements still govern most of international air transport.

The ICAO Convention has had added to it a total of fifteen annexes on such important matters as rules of the air, aeronautical charts, personnel licensing, operation of aircraft, aeronautical telecommunications, and aerodromes. The annex on aerodromes, for example, called for an integrated system of visual aids for approach and landing including a standard approach-landing system. A large number of regional plans have been put into effect which locate some 40,000 air navigation facilities and services around the globe. At no time does a pilot ever prepare for an international flight, 'no message ever passes between the air and the ground, and no aircraft proceeds on instruments across international boundaries to an assured arrival at its destination without experiencing the benefits of ICAO's work of the past decade.'[8]

Many states have had the benefit of a large number of technical studies published by ICAO. For example, fifty-two statistical digests have been issued, one of which includes data provided by forty-nine countries for one hundred and twelve airlines. Nontechnical publications have been distributed on many questions, among which are training manuals covering suitable curricula for qualifying students for different types of aeronautical employment. Circulars distributed by ICAO summarize available data on such items as aircraft communications, traffic control, and airport design. Another publication presents the scales which set the pattern of fees charged by governments and airport authorities for each aircraft landing.

The Council of ICAO has served successfully as an agency of mediation in a dispute between India and Pakistan. The dispute concerned the refusal of Pakistan to permit Indian aircraft engaged in commercial air services between India and Afghanistan to pass over Pakistani territory without landing. Working groups from the ICAO Council in 1953 assisted in the

[8] Warner, Edward, 'The Expanding Role of ICAO as Civil Aviation Grows,' *United Nations Review*, Vol. 2, No. 4 (October 1955), p. 42.

conclusion of negotiations which involved the opening of two corridors through which Indian aircraft could proceed unhampered on their way to Afghanistan and aviation gasoline for refueling purposes could be supplied to Afghanistan by Pakistan.

Working with ECOSOC and its appropriate commissions and with WHO, WMO, ITU, and UPU, ICAO has been an active participant in the United Nations Expanded Program of Technical Assistance. Training centers have been established in eleven countries. Experts and missions from ICAO have served as consultants to a number of governments requesting assistance on such problems as airport siting and management, air traffic control, aircraft and engine maintenance, the operation of navigational facilities, the drafting of laws and regulations, and air transport administration.

Conclusions. Since political considerations are not so evident in the more technical fields of international co-operation, the activities of the Postal and Telecommunication Unions have a long record of stability and achievement. Expediency and convenience are the apparent factors behind intergovernmental co-operation in this field. This has made possible the standardization of mail rates and the equitable allocation of wave lengths to assure absence of interference in transmittal of messages. Similarly, the World Meteorological Organization is concerned with technical and scientific problems, which recognize few political boundaries. Despite its short life, WMO has made an important contribution to various technical assistance programs.

In the field of aviation, there is a similar recognition of the need for identical air-safety rules. ICAO has been able to make considerable progress in standardizing rules of the air through the adoption of annexes to the ICAO Convention concerned with the problem. But accord has not been reached on such matters as air routes and rates. Politics has intervened in this problem and at present, bilateral agreements will have to suffice as the governing feature of international air transport until political interests are resolved sufficiently to permit the conclusion of a multilateral convention. In the technical assistance field, ICAO continues to make a positive contribution and works closely with other specialized agencies in a number of joint projects. The many technical studies published by ICAO, in addition to its growing informational and advisory services, make the agency increasingly useful in the field of transportation.

The Transportation and Communications Commission of ECOSOC has tried with some success, to co-ordinate the work of the agencies in the field, recommending interagency co-operation in certain matters and the eventual adoption of conventions and additional international facilities when needed. For the most part, the Commission works in specific areas falling outside the province of the established agencies.

LABOR AND LABOR STANDARDS

At the plenary session of the Paris Peace Conference on April 11, 1919, when the draft convention of the International Labor Organization was formally approved by the delegates of the Allied and Associated Powers, Sir Robert Borden of Canada said:

> It is possible that some of us would have framed the dispositions of the proposed Convention somewhat differently, but the main purpose and, after all, the great purpose, in respect of this Convention, as in respect of the League of Nations, is to secure the adhesion of the different states to an arrangement which will tend to the welfare of humanity in the future.

Few agencies of international co-operation have been more successful in tending to the welfare of humanity than has the International Labor Organization, one of the oldest independent agencies working during the lifetime of the League of Nations. Made a specialized agency of the United Nations in 1946, the ILO is the principal body devoted to the problems of labor. It has functioned closely with ECOSOC and its technical sub-units, and with FAO, UNESCO, and WHO.

Between world wars, the ILO pioneered in working toward the physical, moral, and intellectual well-being of the wage-earning class throughout the world. A vast number of conventions and recommendations were adopted through its efforts, including those dealing with the eight-hour day; the hours of work in commerce, offices, and mines; the hours of work in maritime occupations and in agriculture; a weekly rest-day for all workers; annual holidays with pay; the abolition of night work for women and children; and the protection of children, young people, and women in industry. It directed part of its attention to industrial hygiene and produced a remarkable study, *The Encyclopedia of Industrial Hygiene*, involving the studies of ninety-five collaborators from fifteen countries. Further, the ILO engaged in research for the prevention of industrial accidents, stressed the importance of factory inspection and adopted a significant recommendation in accident prevention in 1929. Draft conventions and recommendations concerning compensation for industrial accidents were prepared. International conferences were sponsored on labor statistics and special studies were issued in this field, looking toward the establishment of a minimum wage. The ILO not only compiled statistics on unemployment but examined national and international aspects of the problem and the question of social insurance.

After 1946, ILO continued the job it had begun under the blessing of the League of Nations. The annual General Conference and its Governing Body as well as commissions and committees working in specific fields have directed their efforts toward perfecting labor standards already established by earlier recommendations and conventions. Special problems and opportunities resulting from the War have been seized with determination.

All these activities were directed toward the building of what might be called an International Labor Code, dependent upon the ratification of conventions by member-states. Before World War II, about 65 conventions had been adopted with over 800 ratifications deposited by more than 50 countries. The General Conferences of ILO adopted fifty-six recommendations which establish general principles and guides without imposing any formal international obligations. The rate of ratification was steady throughout the prewar period and the conventions, according to the 1939 report of the Director, the late Mr. John G. Winant, had an indirect as well as a direct influence. He observed:

> Their influence sets up a standard which public opinion gradually tends to accept as normal, and one result of this is that they act as a check on any tendency to allow conditions of work to be depressed below that level in times of difficulty. This indirect influence is very hard to measure; but if the differences which exist in labour legislation now and twenty years ago are studied in relation to the conventions, there is little doubt that it is considerable.

Individual governments have proceeded to ratify the ILO conventions at a better pace than before the War although there is still present the tendency of the less advanced states to lag behind the countries in America and Europe which have already reached a comparatively high level in their labor standards. Conventions have been adopted on freedom of association and the right to organize and bargain collectively, social security, employment services, shipping, agricultural labor, to mention only some of the more noteworthy ones. The International Labor Code now totals well over one hundred conventions and about an equal number of recommendations. Ratifications have reached nearly 1,500 in number.

A particular postwar development has been the establishment of a group of industrial committees which study and make recommendations with regard to their particular industry. Each committee is composed of delegates — two each from labor, management, and government — from countries where the particular industry holds an important position in the economy. Committees already in existence are those related to the following industries: petroleum, iron and steel, inland transport, chemicals, textiles, mines, building and construction, and metal trades. The conclusions of these committees have been well-received by individual governments and industries. Frequently these committees deal with specific matters. For example, at the fourth session of the Chemical Industries Committee meeting early in 1955, it was recommended that there be adopted for international use five danger symbols pertaining to fire, explosion, poisoning, radioactivity, and corrosion.

Special committees of ILO meet frequently and perform a variety of tasks. For example, the ILO Asian Advisory Committee has considered and made recommendations on such questions as agrarian reforms in Asian countries and methods of increasing productivity with special reference to the improvement of workers' living standards and of mutual understanding and co-operation between workers and employers. The Permanent Agriculture Committee has studied such questions as vocational training and the employment of children and young people in agriculture. The Textiles Committee has considered the effect of international competition on the workers in the industry. A Committee on Freedom of Association conducts a preliminary examination of alleged violations of trade union rights prior to their submission to the Fact-Finding and Conciliation Commission on Freedom of Association.

No discussion of the ILO would be complete without some reference to its participation in the United Nations technical assistance programs. Much attention has been paid to developing a pattern of activity by which ILO can make the best contribution toward the economic and social development of the less advanced countries. ILO field offices in Latin America, the Middle East, and Asia engage in program planning and in supervising the work of experts in the field. Some projects assist in the task of development-planning by helping governments conduct manpower surveys and analyses of labor conditions and of handicraft problems. Other projects are concerned with production either by aiding in new development or by creating social and labor conditions which are essential prerequisites to economic progress. Those include the important missions which advise on improvement of working conditions in agriculture and industry and help to stimulate industrial welfare and hygiene.

Conclusions. The International Labor Organization has attempted to raise the working and living conditions of hundreds of millions of workers throughout the world through the establishment of labor standards, through study and research, and through technical assistance. Recognizing the great disparity between advanced and underdeveloped countries, ILO seeks primarily to encourage the adoption in the latter of the more progressive labor standards enjoyed in the former. In this respect, it has tried to remain within the limits of the reasonable and the possible, urging the raising of minimum levels instead of seeking to obtain the maximum.

The International Labor Code, representing over one hundred conventions and about an equal number of recommendations, provides a standard of behavior for member-countries with regard to such matters as child labor, forced labor, unemployment, freedom of association, migration for employment, maternity protection, social security, employment agencies, hours of work, holidays, protection of wages, night work for women, and many others. What uniformity there is in standards governing labor legislation in many countries outside the Soviet sphere has been, in large part, the result of the patient efforts of ILO. At the same time, it is extremely difficult to evaluate precisely the specific effects of ILO activity of this nature on the labor policies and legislation of most countries. For example, every piece of pertinent legislation in each country would have to be examined to determine the ILO influence exercised. Similarly, the contents of hundreds of labor agreements would have to be studied to discover the relationship between them and the recommendations of the ILO.

Despite the impressive compilation of conventions, the record of their individual ratification by member-countries has not been outstanding. Less than a quarter of the membership, past and present, has ratified more than one third of these documents and some have failed even to ratify a single one. The problem of adjusting national policies and beliefs to international standards remains as difficult in this area of international co-operation as in most others. Although few complaints of violations of ILO conventions have been registered, the occurrence of violations is not necessarily small. There are still far too many people suffering from insecurity and unemployment. Nevertheless, in spite of apathy and occasional national opposition, the world has taken the step to assume collectively through ILO the responsibility for working toward the alleviation of these conditions. The ILO approach is slow and piecemeal, permitting a careful and thorough development of ideas, special questionnaires, and reports. Despite the slowness of ratifications, there has been a good measure of agreement on many controversial subjects.

In recent years, much of the ILO's activity has been concentrated on technical assistance. Through funds of its own and those of the United Nations Expanded Technical Assistance Program, ILO has sent hundreds of experts to less developed countries to assist in raising productivity and working standards and to advise on other socio-economic problems. That this aid has been effective is seen from reports emanating from recipient countries and from the increasing number of requests for similar assistance.

EDUCATION, SCIENCE, AND CULTURE

Continuing the efforts begun during the years of the League by the International Committee for Intellectual Co-operation and the International

Institute of Intellectual Co-operation is the United Nations Educational, Scientific and Cultural Organization. It will be recalled that the purpose of UNESCO is to contribute to peace and security by promoting collaboration among the nations through education, science, and culture in order to further universal respect for justice, for the rule of law and for human rights and fundamental freedoms. To accomplish this, UNESCO was expected, by its Constitution, to advance 'the mutual knowledge and understanding of peoples, through all means of mass communication, to give fresh impetus to popular education and to the spread of culture, and to maintain, increase and diffuse knowledge.' Furthermore, in the preamble to its Constitution, UNESCO was created 'for the purpose of advancing . . . the objectives of international peace and the common welfare of mankind.'

However, as is so frequently the case, it is easier to write a constitution than to carry out its provisions. It took UNESCO several years and three Directors-General before a definite work pattern could be developed. Many of the early projects undertaken could well be justified on the basis of the Preamble of the Constitution, i.e., to benefit mankind, but it is doubtful whether they could meet the test of contributing to peace and security. A large number of educational and scientific groups, to say nothing of governments, had their own projects and ideas which they insisted fell within the scope of UNESCO and should be carried out. In addition, up to 1950, UNESCO was called upon to help rebuild education, science, and culture in countries devastated by war by gathering information on the nature and extent of needs and by co-ordinating the activities of voluntary agencies working in the field. UNESCO also has had to contend with widespread criticism of all sorts concerning its objectives, its operating methods, and the scope and nature of its projects. Despite these difficulties, progress has been made toward building understanding among peoples and in developing a program designed for this purpose. Concentration now is placed on these primary fields of activity: education, natural sciences, social sciences, cultural activities, exchange of persons, mass communication, and technical assistance. UNESCO also works closely with virtually all of the specialized agencies and, of course, with ECOSOC.

Education. UNESCO's program in education seeks the extension and improvement of education and the development of education for living in a world community.

More than half the population of the world is illiterate. For an international organization with limited resources to tackle this overwhelming problem might seem to be foolhardy. But there persists the belief that if the level of education can be raised, there is hope for better understanding, which, in turn, can contribute toward peace and security. UNESCO has tried to provide people with the minimum knowledge and skills which are deemed essential for the improvement of standards of living and which will permit the less fortunate to participate in the economic and social development of their country. Various techniques and activities are underway to foster these objectives. An Education Clearing House is maintained for the exchange of information and materials relating to the educational needs of members and the UNESCO program. International educational seminars bring together leaders from different countries to discuss problems of mutual interest. Fundamental education centers have been established at Patzcuaro, Mexico, for Latin America, and at Sirs-el-Layan, Egypt, for the Arab states, to train students, according to the Director-General of UNESCO,

> . . . under conditions resembling, as closely as possible, those under which they will be required to apply fundamental education . . . Closely connected with training is the production of the educational materials — books, films, filmstrips and the like. These materials are produced at the center in sample form for distribution and adaptation to the needs of the various countries of the region.

The hope is to establish a world network of these training centers. UNESCO works with WHO, FAO, and ILO in addition to the Mexican and Egyptian governments in operating the centers and developing their programs.

Activities designed to promote education for living in a world community are directed toward developing a healthy mental and social attitude among people, particularly the youth, toward international understanding. According to the Director-General, the program in this field is constructed to:

> 1. Make it clear that unless steps are taken to educate mankind for the world community, it will be impossible to create an international society conceived in the spirit of the Charter of the United Nations.
> 2. Make it clear that states, whatever their difference in creeds and ways of life, have both a duty to cooperate in international organizations and an interest in doing so.
> 3. Make clear that civilization results from the contributions of many nations and that all nations depend very much on each other.
> 4. Make clear the underlying reasons which account for the varying ways of life of different peoples both past and present, their traditions, their characteristics, their problems and the ways in which they have been resolved.
> 5. Make clear that throughout the ages, moral, intellectual and technical progress has gradually grown to constitute a common heritage for all mankind. Although the world is still divided by conflicting political interests and tensions, the inter-dependence of peoples becomes daily more evident on every side. A world international organization is necessary and it is now also possible.

6. Make clear that the engagements freely entered into by Member States of international organizations have force only in so far as they are actively and effectively supported by those peoples.

7. Arouse in the minds, particularly of young people, a sense of responsibility to this community and to peace.

8. Encourage the development of healthy social attitudes in children so as to lay the foundations of improved international understanding and co-operation.

One method to increase international understanding has been the effort to improve textbooks used in school systems. The eradication of misleading and false statements concerning other peoples often found in textbooks has been encouraged. Following a seminar in Brussels in 1950, a series of bilateral committees were created by professional groups to improve history textbooks through mutual consultation. International seminars have been conducted on the contribution of the teaching of modern languages toward education for living in a world community. Round table discussions were held on such topics as the cultural aspect of modern language teaching and language teaching as an aid to understanding foreign peoples and civilizations. Youth groups in sixty-five countries have been provided with study kits containing materials on some of the problems facing the United Nations and the specialized agencies.

Natural and Social Sciences. In the field of the natural sciences, UNESCO has attempted to assist the work of scientists, to encourage co-operation among them, and to promote the work of international scientific organizations.

Field Science Co-operation Offices have been established to help in the dissemination of scientific information. They are maintained in Montevideo for Latin America, Cairo for the Middle East, New Delhi for South Asia, and Jakarta for Southeast Asia with a branch at Manila. Each has several experts who get in touch with scientists within their area, attempt to bring them together, and familiarize them with the scientific research conducted in other countries. Lecture tours have been arranged for leading foreign scientists. Seminars are organized to consider problems of importance to the scientific life and economic development of the countries in the region. Similarly, several international scientific organizations have been established by UNESCO, such as the Union of International Engineering Associations, the Co-ordinating Council for International Medical Congresses, and the International Union for the Protection of Nature.

In the field of research, regional schemes participated in by groups of nations have been very successful. The best example is the European Organization for Nuclear Research, which has a research laboratory and provides co-operation among existing laboratories in theoretical studies of a nonmilitary character. UNESCO's General Conference in 1954 resolved that for the period of 1955–56, there should be fostered, through modest grants, meetings of atomic scientists working on the peaceful uses of atomic energy. UNESCO was also directed to carry out an information campaign about atomic energy in order that more people might learn of its benefits as well as its destructiveness. Another successful example of research sponsored by UNESCO has been the work of Advisory Committee on Arid Zone Research, which works to improve the living conditions of mankind in the world's arid and semiarid zones.

UNESCO has pursued similar programs with respect to the social sciences. International Political Science, Economic, and Sociological Associations have been formed as well as an International Committee of Comparative Law. In 1953, the UNESCO-sponsored International Social Science Council began working to combine the resources of all the social sciences for a joint study of the principal social problems confronting mankind. Social science field offices in the Western Hemisphere, Middle East, and South Asia have set up and developed national co-ordination and research bodies. The UNESCO Institute for Social Sciences in Cologne has been conducting a study of social integration and social participation throughout the Federal Republic of Germany, as well as the pattern of integration of foreign ethnic groups in the country.

Cultural Activities. In the broad cultural field, UNESCO is concerned with a large number of subjects. Pointing up this fact is the statement made in 1946 by Mr. Julian Huxley, the first Director-General:

> . . . we have to think about music and painting, about history and classical studies, about language and architecture, about theatre and ballet, about libraries and museums and art galleries and zoos, about the history of art and the world's different cultures, about creative writing, and about philosophy.

In practice, UNESCO has sought to focus its attention upon international cultural co-operation, the dissemination of culture, the protection of artists, writers, and scientists, and the preservation of the cultural heritage of mankind.

To further these activities, UNESCO has encouraged and strengthened such voluntary associations as the International Council for Philosophy and Humanistic Studies, the International Theater Institute, the International Music Council, the International Association of Plastic Arts, the International PEN Club, the International Association of Art Critics, the International Union of Architects, and the International Council of Museums. A greater exchange of ideas has come from the meetings and conferences held under the auspices of these associations. Traveling art exhibits have been sponsored as have translations of the great works of literature into the most widely used languages.

A Universal Copyright Convention has been drafted by UNESCO, designed to offer better legal protection for writers and artists. A draft International Convention for the Protection of Cultural Property in the Event of Armed Conflict has been circulated. An International Study Center for the Preservation and Restoration of Cultural Property has been established to assemble and disseminate information concerning the preservation and restoration of cultural properties and assist in the training of research workers and technicians. An agreement is now in force on the importation of educational, scientific, and cultural materials, and applies to five categories of materials: books, documents, and publications; works of art; visual and auditory materials; scientific instruments; and articles for the blind. The states that are parties to the agreement are obligated to give such items preferential treatment, such as a reduction or elimination of customs duties and other applicable charges. An ambitious convention which has been considered is the International Instrument for the Removal of Obstacles to the Movement of Persons Traveling for Educational, Scientific, or Cultural Purposes. Privileges to be accorded those eligible would include reduction of visa charges and tuition fees at universities; free entry into museums and public libraries; and reduction of costs in travel and housing. Because of its very broad scope, however, this draft has not met with much enthusiasm from a number of nations.

Exchange of Persons and the Development of Mass Communications. One of the best methods of promoting international understanding is facilitating contacts between peoples. UNESCO has been actively engaged in encouraging foreign study and travel. It awards its own fellowships for this purpose. Workers' Study Tours is a special project whereby different groups of European workers are provided grants to travel from their country to another in Europe to study social conditions and cultural activities. Under the Youth Travel Grant Scheme, travel costs have been paid for young people participating in international activities of an educational character. UNESCO also publishes an annual *Study Abroad — An International Handbook of Fellowships, Scholarships, and Educational Exchange* containing information on awards available in over fifty states.

In its work on mass communications, UNESCO seeks to increase the scope and quality of press, television, film, and radio services throughout the world. It has studied the barriers which obstruct the free flow of ideas and has initiated measures to break down such obstacles. An Agreement for Facilitating the International Circulation of Visual and Auditory Materials is now in force. UNESCO has also developed a system of coupons which permits people in soft-currency countries to purchase, with their own monies, books and educational materials from hard-currency countries. The film 'World Without End,' produced by UNESCO, presents the creative work undertaken by the United Nations and the specialized agencies in the social and economic fields.

Relief and Technical Assistance. As was noted earlier, UNESCO was almost immediately faced with the task of co-ordinating the efforts of rebuilding educational facilities in the war-devastated countries. A Temporary International Council for Educational Reconstruction was established to co-ordinate and plan relief campaigns. Some direct emergency grants were allocated from UNESCO funds for such essential visual and auditory aids as periodicals, movie projectors, radios, and museum and laboratory equipment.

Emergency assistance continues to be provided to the United Nations Relief and Works Agency for Palestine Refugees in the Near East and the Korean Reconstruction Agency. Working with these relief agencies, UNESCO has, for example, established primary and secondary schools in the Arab refugee camps. Vocational training has also been introduced in these camps. In Korea, an educational planning mission spent six months in 1953 surveying the educational needs of the country and then drafted a long-term plan for the rebuilding of the Korean educational system.

Under the United Nations Expanded Program of Technical Assistance, hundreds of UNESCO experts have been provided upon the request of governments; educational and scientific projects are underway in thirty-six countries. A large number of countries are receiving help in public school education, in fundamental education, and in technical education. In countries where the number of qualified teachers is not sufficient to meet school needs, special forms of assistance have been made available. In Pakistan, for example, school broadcasts were organized and middle schools in the Karachi region provided with radios. In Libya, trained teachers and textbooks have had to be dispatched from other countries. Also brought in were experts in child psychology, physical education, and in the production of textbooks.

Conclusions. In so vast an undertaking as UNESCO, it was inevitable that there would be criticism on a number of points from widely different sources. Disparaging attacks appear to fall into three categories: the UNESCO ideals, the structure of the Organization, and its program.

UNESCO has been charged, particularly in the United States, with being procommunist, atheistic, antireligious, and an advocate of world government. It has also been alleged that it seeks to impose Western ideas on the

Orient and fails to acknowledge the contributions made to civilization by Eastern countries. As far as structure is concerned, there have been claims that UNESCO's activities overlap those of other specialized agencies and that its governing authorities are not representative. Finally, the program has been held to be too big, with too many conferences and seminars accomplishing too little, and that of small appeal to the peoples of the world.

On most of these scores, UNESCO is not at fault.[9] It is by no means communistic, nor is there any positive evidence that it is antireligious or atheistic. On the matter of world government, there has been persistent confusion. UNESCO has sought to encourage understanding among all peoples, regardless of race, religious conviction, or geographical location. In so doing, it has pointed up the inherently dangerous aspects of violent nationalism and urged, in its place, greater loyalty and respect for all mankind. This does not mean, however, that UNESCO has attempted to undermine national loyalties or substitute allegiance to some world government, not yet in existence, for national allegiance to country, flag, and people. World citizenship in the political sense has not been advocated. As comprehended by UNESCO, world citizenship simply means international understanding, an interest in the problems of other peoples, and a recognition of the need for co-operative projects to assist those less well off.

Criticism appears justified, however, with respect to the failure of UNESCO to explain adequately its aims, purposes, and activities. A good example of this is the confusion over the meaning of world citizenship and UNESCO's relationship to world political government. It must be said, as well, that UNESCO still tries to do too much in too many diverse fields, with an apparent lack of understanding at times of what comprises a project or of what it can reasonably be expected to accomplish. The program involving the exchange of art treasures and visits of orchestras and dance groups is intrinsically valuable but it is difficult to believe that it contributes much toward relieving political tensions or builds concretely a greater sense of world understanding on the part of the peoples enjoying the performances.

Despite these shortcomings and some outright mistakes and failures,[10] UNESCO can be credited with far greater accomplishment than is gener-

[9] See, for example, *An Appraisal of the United Nations Educational, Scientific and Cultural Organization*, by the Delegation of the United States to the Second Extraordinary Session of the General Conference of UNESCO, Department of State Publication 5209, Washington, D.C., 1953.

[10] One notable mistake was the Haitian education experiment in the Marbial Valley. See Neal, Marian, 'United Nations Programs in Haiti,' *International Conciliation*, No. 468 (February 1951), pp. 102–11. For other critical views, see Niebuhr, Reinhold, 'The Theory and Practice of UNESCO,' *International Organization*, Vol. 4, No. 1 (February 1950), pp. 3–11.

ally recognized. It is important to revise history textbooks containing misleading and untruthful statements which only encourage nationalistic prejudices harmful to peace and understanding. It is also important to
encourage contacts between peoples at all levels. Above all, it is essential
that international understanding be promoted whenever there is an opportunity to accomplish something concrete toward building a more peaceful
world. These and other things have been done by UNESCO, not always as
adequately and efficiently as might be desired but nevertheless in a spirit
designed to benefit mankind, a worthwhile if somewhat elusive goal.

HUMAN RIGHTS AND FUNDAMENTAL FREEDOMS

Prior to the adoption of the Charter of the United Nations, the matter of
human rights had been almost exclusively the concern of the national state.
The individual state and not the international community was permitted to
determine the extent to which its citizens were to enjoy civil rights according to its own constitutional precepts. Not even the Covenant of the League
of Nations made reference to human rights although the Council of the
League was made a supervisory body for the minorities provisions of the
World War I peace treaties.

With the horrors perpetrated by Nazi and Fascist leaders in their minds,
the makers of the Charter were determined that the rights of the individual
be made an international concern. This was in keeping with the wishes of a
war-weary world which had been sickened by the Axis atrocities and was
aware that acts of inhumanity can develop into situations which might lead
to war. Consequently, seven specific references to human rights were written into the Charter giving the United Nations the mandate for 'promoting
and encouraging respect for human rights and for fundamental freedoms
for all without distinction as to race, sex, language, or religion.' [11] Although
both the Assembly and the Security Council may make recommendations,
no organ has the authority to intervene in the domestic affairs of states in
pursuit of the objectives established by the Charter in the field of human
rights.

The organ most directly concerned with the question of human rights is
the Economic and Social Council, which established a Commission on Human Rights in February, 1946. The terms of reference and membership of

[11] The seven references appear in the Preamble; among the purposes and principles of
the United Nations — Article 1:3; among the responsibilities of the Assembly — Article
13:2; among the objectives of economic and social co-operation — Article 55:c; among
the functions and powers of ECOSOC — Article 62:2; as a responsibility of one of
ECOSOC's commissions — Article 68; and among the objectives of the Trusteeship
System — Article 76:c.

the Commission were adopted the following June. The Commission is composed of eighteen members who are appointed by ECOSOC for three-year terms. Each member selects its own representative. As determined by its terms of reference, the Commission was directed to prepare recommendations and reports on the following items:

(1) an international bill of rights;
(2) international declarations or conventions on civil liberties; the status of women, freedom of information and similar matters;
(3) the protection of minorities;
(4) the prevention of discrimination on the basis of race, sex, language or religion;
(5) any other matter concerning human rights.

Some of these functions have been assigned to other bodies which have been created for the purpose, such as the Commission on the Status of Women, the Sub-Commission on Freedom of Information and of the Press, and the Sub-Commission on Prevention of Discrimination and Protection of Minorities. An *ad hoc* committee was established by ECOSOC to draft a convention on genocide. The Trusteeship Council has maintained a close scrutiny over the rights of non-self-governing peoples. Special conferences and meetings have been devoted to other specific aspects of the question.

The Declaration of Human Rights. The first task undertaken by the Commission on Human Rights was the preparation of an international bill of human rights. It became apparent, at the outset, that there existed a wide difference of opinion between governments on just how far they would go toward permitting themselves to be bound by such an international document. The decision was made to proceed by various stages: first, the adoption of a general declaration of human rights, then a definitive covenant or treaty binding on the signatories, and finally, some implementing machinery.

The drafting of the Declaration proved to be a most difficult undertaking. It was essential to reach the fullest accord possible on such an important matter so that it would have the greatest support from the members. Yet the drafters had to contend with wide variations in cultural, legal, and philosophic views. The Anglo-Saxon world is in general agreement on certain particular principles and values which have concrete meaning in the law. But what may appear to be an obvious fact to the Anglo-Saxon may be unclear to others. Hindu and Islamic philosophy, and the ethics of China do not necessarily correspond to the views of the Western world.[12] It is also impossible to resolve the divergencies between the Soviet and non-

[12] For examples of these conflicting views, see the symposium edited by UNESCO entitled *Human Rights: Comments and Interpretations*, New York, 1949.

Soviet worlds. It is easy to see that disagreement would be prevalent on such issues as the relationship of the individual to the state and the type of rights to be protected, namely whether they should be individual or economic and social rights. It was also difficult to obtain a consensus on the origin and nature of human rights.

For more than eighteen months the Commission, and finally ECOSOC and the General Assembly, worked painstakingly on the Declaration, which was adopted in December, 1948. The vote was 48 to 0 with eight abstentions (the Soviet bloc, Saudi Arabia, and the Union of South Africa).[13] General agreement was reached on most of the basic issues. Human and not state rights are emphasized, with freedom from arbitrary government action a central theme. Both individual and economic-social rights are included with the emphasis on the former. The philosophy of natural rights is adopted in Article 1 of the Declaration which states that 'all human beings are born free and equal in dignity and rights. They are endowed with reason and conscience and should act toward one another in a spirit of brotherhood.' Care was taken to avoid the use of terms and words which did not have the same meaning in all languages. The preamble and the thirty articles which make up the Declaration represent a remarkable effort to arrive at unanimity on so complex and fundamental a matter as that of human rights.

Briefly, the civil and political rights laid down by the Declaration are:

> The right to life, liberty and security of person; the right to freedom of thought, speech, and communication of information and ideas; freedom of assembly and religion; the right to government through free elections; the right of free movement within the state and free exit from it; the right of asylum in another state; the right to a nationality; freedom from arbitrary arrest and interference with the privacy of home and family; and the prohibition of slavery and torture.

Included are the following in the list of economic and social rights:

> The right to work, to protection against unemployment, and to join trade unions; the right to a standard of living adequate for health and well-being; the right to education; and the right to rest and leisure.

Each of these rights are to be protected without distinction as to race, sex, color, language, religion, political or other opinion, property or other status, birth, or national or social origin.

All member states were urged by the General Assembly to give the Declaration the widest circulation and publicity possible. All specialized agen-

[13] The Soviet bloc was disappointed that there was not included, among other things, a denunciation of fascism and aggression and a broader treatment of economic and social rights. The Union of South Africa held that the Declaration exceeded the expectations of the Charter and was unrealistic. Saudi Arabia believed that it reflected too much of a Western pattern of culture.

cies and NGO's were asked to participate in the task of disseminating the text and meaning of the Declaration to their members. The Secretariat has translated it into many languages and distributed informational and teaching aids in great numbers. December 10 is celebrated as Human Rights Day in commemoration of the Declaration's adoption. The Declaration serves as a moral standard for the International Court of Justice and a large number of national courts. Although only a recommendation with no binding authority and open to question in the United States and elsewhere, the Declaration stands as an ideal for oppressed peoples everywhere.

The Covenants on Human Rights. Far more difficulty has arisen over the adoption of a covenant or treaty on human rights. The General Assembly decided in 1950 to include both civil and political rights as well as economic, social, and cultural rights in one covenant. But in 1951, at the urging of the United States, the Assembly voted to request the Commission on Human Rights to draft two covenants — one containing civil and political rights, the other containing economic, social, and cultural rights — and present them to the seventh session of the Assembly in 1952 for simultaneous consideration. However, covenants were not presented until 1953 and they met with considerable opposition, which continues to prevent their adoption.

The covenant on civil and political rights is the less controversial of the two. Taken together, they repeat substantially the rights proclaimed in the Declaration although some of the economic and social rights are more qualified. Examples of the rights included in both covenants include the right to work, under good conditions and at fair wages, and to join trade unions; the right of mothers and children to special care; the right to education; the right to life, to freedom from torture, to freedom from slavery, to liberty and security of the person, to fair and equal treatment and recognition before courts; the right to privacy, to freedom of thought, conscience, and religion, and to freedom of association. The family is stated to be the fundamental group unit of society. Virtually every aspect of the individual's life in society is covered.

Criticism comes from various sources and is persistent and frequently bitter. Several states regret the 1951 decision to separate human rights into two covenants. They argue that all such rights are of equal importance and are mutually interdependent. Since certain economic, social, and cultural rights are necessary for the fulfillment of civil and political rights, it is believed that any distinction is merely artificial. Thus, the Yugoslav delegate observed in the 1954 Assembly that 'the rights dealt with by the two covenants formed a mutually interdependent whole, and . . . no definite line of demarcation could be drawn between the two sets of rights, despite their unequal development in different parts of the world.' Other states were equally insistent that the nature of the two categories of rights made it necessary to treat them separately. It is argued that the covenant on economic, social, and cultural rights expresses aspirations to be achieved progressively over a period of time, while civil and political rights should be guaranteed immediately by a state on becoming a party to that covenant.

Sharp disagreement still remains over certain of the articles in both covenants. Most controversial are those dealing with the right of peoples and nations to self-determination and the federal-state clause. The colonial powers are particularly opposed to the provision in both covenants on self-determination. Such articles, declared the delegate of the United Kingdom in 1954, were totally 'unacceptable to her delegation which held that provisions that were not concerned with an individual right had no place in the covenants.' Others took issue with this view, and tried to refute the argument that self-determination was a collective instead of an individual right. The Egyptian delegate declared that 'in the final analysis, it was the individual who exercised the right, even though the result affected his community.' Equally disputed has been the federal-state clause found in both covenants which declares that the provisions of the covenants must be applied throughout federal states 'without any limitations or exceptions.' Australian and Canadian delegates have consistently opposed this clause, arguing that it would destroy the federal character of their governments. Others argue that it would be unfair to expect unitary states to apply the covenants throughout their countries if federal states were not required to do the same.

The United States has come out with the most unequivocal opposition to the covenants. As early as 1953, a representative announced that the United States would not sign either of them because the treaty method was not held to be the best manner in which to advance human rights at the present time. American opposition is directed primarily against the covenant on economic, social, and cultural rights although certain aspects of the other covenant remain unacceptable. The Soviet bloc stands just as adamant for detailed and lengthy economic and social rights which the Anglo-Saxon countries maintain are adequately covered in their own domestic law.[14]

Implementing Machinery for Human Rights. One of the reasons for preparing two separate covenants was the view that different measures for implementation would be necessary for the two categories of rights. Only the covenant on civil and political rights contains enforcement machinery. A Human Rights Committee is proposed, consisting of nine members

[14] On this and other criticisms, see Neal, Marian, 'The United Nations and Human Rights,' *International Conciliation*, No. 489 (March 1953).

elected by the International Court of Justice. It would hear and mediate disputes arising over violations of the rights contained in the covenant. If a state party to the covenant is of the opinion that another state party is not respecting a provision of the covenant, it would first call the matter to the attention of that state. Should the matter not be settled amicably within six months, either state would then have the right to place it before the Human Rights Committee. The facts would then be ascertained by the Committee which would make available its good offices for a solution. If no friendly solution is reached, the Committee would then compile a report on the facts and publish its opinion on whether there had been a violation of the obligations contained in the covenant. Either state could then submit the case to the International Court of Justice. Some states, particularly among the Soviet bloc, are opposed to this procedure, believing that it would interfere in the internal affairs of member-states in violation of the Charter.

An additional means of implementation proposed is a system of reporting on legislative or other measures, including judicial remedies, adopted by individual states which give support to the rights in both covenants. Complaints also have been lodged against the reporting system, particularly with respect to civil and political rights. It is argued that these rights should be guaranteed immediately and it was therefore pointless to request states to report on gradual progress. Domestic legislation should conform to the covenant before a state could effectively become a party. There are those who also maintain that the reporting system would interfere with the domestic affairs of states.

Self-determination. The question of self-determination is a continuing concern of the General Assembly and has been considered apart from the covenants on human rights. In 1952, the Assembly requested the Commission on Human Rights to prepare 'recommendations concerning international respect for the right of peoples to self-determination, and particularly recommendations relating to the steps which might be taken . . . by the various organs of the United Nations and the specialized agencies to develop international respect for the right of peoples to self-determination.'

Two proposals were presented to ECOSOC in 1954 by the Commission which reflected the views of members which are nonadministering countries. One dealt with the right of peoples and nations to permanent sovereignty over their natural wealth and resources and proposed that a commission be created to make recommendations for strengthening such sovereignty. The second suggested the establishment of still another commission to study any situation arising from a denial of self-determination if reported by any ten members of the United Nations. However, because of their controversial nature, ECOSOC returned them to the Commission for reconsideration.

In the spring of 1955 the Commission readopted the proposals in their original form. ECOSOC added a third to the list in July which was sponsored by the United States and other countries administering non-self-governing peoples. It calls for the creation of an *ad hoc* commission to be appointed by the Secretary-General to examine the concept of peoples and nations, the essential attributes and applicability of the principle of equal rights and duties of states under international law, the relationship between the principle of self-determination and other Charter principles, and the economic, social, and cultural conditions which facilitate the application of the principle. None of these proposals, however, had received favorable action by 1958.

Freedom of Information and the Press. In 1944, the American Society of Newspaper Editors, the most representative editorial body in the United States, adopted a resolution which urged

> . . . international agrements permitting direct communication between each and every nation of the world wherever feasible; eliminating conventions and customs which prevent utilization of any advance in the science of communications; removing all restrictions imposed for the commercial or political advantage of any nation or groups of nations, giving to the press correspondents of all nations equitable access to the available communications facilities, and making dominant in all communication matters the principle of fostering an unrestricted flow of news and information to all parts of the world.

The General Assembly gave full recognition to these views in 1946 when it stated in a resolution that 'freedom of information is a fundamental human right and is the touchstone of all the freedoms to which the United Nations is consecrated. . . . Understanding and cooperation among nations are impossible without an alert and sound world opinion which, in turn, is wholly dependent upon freedom of information.' To implement this resolution, ECOSOC established a Sub-Commission on Freedom of Information and of the Press (of the Commission on Human Rights). This Sub-Commission was given two functions to perform: to examine what rights, obligations, and practices should be included in the concept of freedom of information; and to draft an annotated agenda and make other preparations for a United Nations Conference on Freedom of Information.

The Conference met in Geneva in the spring of 1948 and was attended by delegates representing fifty-four governments, not all of whom were members of the United Nations. After discussing for nearly a month the entire question of freedom of information, the Conference adopted a series of resolutions and three draft conventions. Sponsored by the United States was the Draft Convention on the Gathering and International Transmission of News. The United Kingdom submitted the Draft Convention on Freedom of Information, while France sponsored the Draft Convention on the Institution of an International Right of Correction (which would permit a state, believing a news report circulated about it in another state to be false and injurious, to submit a corrected version and obligate the injuring state to publish it).

When the Assembly first considered these conventions in 1949, at the suggestion of France two of them were amalgamated and given the title of 'Convention on the International Transmission of News and the Right of Correction.' The Convention was subsequently approved by the Assembly by a vote of 33 to 6 (Soviet bloc) with 13 abstentions. However, in 1952, the combined convention was split into two parts and the provisions on the right of correction were opened for signature as a separate treaty. The Convention on International Transmission of News will not be opened for signature until the one on Freedom of Information is approved.

In the discussions of the Sub-Commission and other United Nations bodies, divergent views have blocked any agreement on the remaining convention.[15] The Anglo-Saxon concept of a free press is totally foreign not only to the Soviet bloc but to many other members of the United Nations. The Soviets take the most extreme position, demanding freedom of information only to the extent that it advances communist doctrines and objectives. Others go part of the way in condemning Western news gathering practices, believing that definite abuses exist in the United States in particular, and, as a result, urge that restraints be placed upon the freedom of journalists, broadcasters, and film producers. They are not at all adverse to adopting a convention with definite censorship provisions in order to limit what in their view are abuses of freedom of information. Given this situation, it is doubtful whether there will ever be a convention on freedom of information that will win the acceptance of a majority of the United Nations. If there is a majority, it will not be one favorable to the Anglo-Saxon position.

Other Problems of Human Rights. In 1948, an *ad hoc* committee established by ECOSOC completed its labors on a draft International Convention on the Prevention and Punishment of the Crime of Genocide which was adopted by the Assembly. Coming as a direct result of Nazi atrocities, the Convention seeks to make genocide, or the destruction of groups of human

---

[15] The Subcommission was dissolved in 1952, largely because of the impasse arrived at over the widely divergent views on the meaning of freedom of information.

beings, an international crime. Article II of the Convention defines genocide as any of the following acts committed with the intent to destroy, in whole or in part, a national, ethnical, racial, or religious group:

(a) Killing members of the group;
(b) Causing serious bodily or mental harm to members of the group;
(c) Deliberately inflicting on the group conditions of life calculated to bring about its physical destruction in whole or in part;
(d) Imposing measures intended to prevent births within the group;
(e) Forcibly transferring children of the group to another group.

Punishable acts are genocide, conspiracy to commit genocide, direct and public incitement to commit or attempt to commit genocide, and complicity in genocide. Persons committing any of these acts 'shall be punished, whether they are constitutionally responsible rulers, public officials or private individuals.'

The Genocide Convention went into effect in 1951 after it had been ratified by twenty nations. However, the United States has definite reservations and has not ratified it.[16]

Since 1947, a subsidiary agency of the Commission on Human Rights has been working on problems of discrimination and minorities. This is the Subcommission on Prevention of Discrimination and Protection of Minorities, which has conducted studies and prepared reports on such matters as the abolition of discriminatory measures with particular reference to racial discrimination and discrimination practiced against persons born out of wedlock. It has recommended that the Secretary-General arrange 'for as complete as possible a collection of provisions for the protection of minorities to be made available, and kept up to date, for use in the drafting of clauses to be included in international and national instruments which deal with the protection of minority rights.' A useful document has been circulated which sets forth the main types and causes of discrimination. Studies on discrimination in education and employment are continuing. But the efforts of the Subcommission have received relatively little support, especially those in connection with minorities. Divergent views and national interests have prevented much progress.

[16] The Genocide Convention was sent to the United States Senate in June of 1949 and hearings were held by the Foreign Relations Committee from January 23 to February 9, 1950. Indifference and opposition prevented favorable action for the next eight years. In April 1953, for example, Secretary of State Dulles said that there would be no pressure by the Administration for Senate acceptance 'at this time.'

Basic opposition centers on the unwillingness of the United States to extradite or try offenders against rules contained in the Convention which are not clearly illegal under federal law. The British have maintained this same general position. The arguments pro and con can be found in *Hearings before a Subcommittee on Foreign Relations, the International Convention on the Prevention and Punishment of the Crime of Genocide,* United States Senate, 81st Congress, 2nd Session, Washington, D.C., 1950.

The Commission on the Status of Women has been able to report definite signs of progress in its efforts to obtain greater equality for women. There are still many women in the world who simply do not know what rights they have or how to exercise the rights they do know about. In 1952, the General Assembly adopted the Convention on the Political Rights of Women, which had been prepared by the Commission. In 1956, work was completed on the Draft Convention on the Nationality of Married Women. The object of the Commission in drafting the Convention was to insure against a woman automatically losing her nationality through marriage to an alien, or automatically acquiring the nationality of the husband. Other activities of the Commission include recommendations of equal pay for equal work, the end of discrimination in employment in governmental services, equality between parents in the exercise of rights and duties with respect to their children, and the right of a married woman to an independent domicile. The Commission has worked closely with UNESCO, ILO, WHO, and many NGO's. As an example, the Commission has suggested that women in underdeveloped countries be given increased educational opportunities through the technical assistance programs of the United Nations and UNESCO.

Other useful activities related to human rights and fundamental freedoms include the studies conducted by an *ad hoc* Committee on Forced Labor and an *ad hoc* Committee of Experts on Slavery.

Conclusions. As each year goes by, there appears to be less chance of reaching agreement on the covenants on human rights. Any conclusive reconciliation between the divergent economic and social systems, legal traditions, political systems, and religious faiths of the members of the United Nations becomes more remote as succeeding futile attempts are made to draft compromise covenants. It is obvious, as a United States representative to the General Assembly stated in 1952, that 'Something far more basic than the writing of legal language must take place before we can go forward profitably with the drafting of treaties. There must be a drawing together of the minds — of the minds that now are widely divergent in their thinking.' What is surprising, in the face of all this disagreement, is that the United Nations ever managed to adopt the Universal Declaration of Human Rights.

Not only are there these fundamental legal, philosophical, economic, political, religious, and social variances of opinion, but there has been the introduction of subject matter into various articles of the draft covenants for purely political and propaganda advantages. Instead of seeking to obtain a common meeting ground, members of the United Nations try to embarrass each other by insisting upon the inclusion of highly controversial articles. The Soviet bloc stands adamant against the majority who would make provision for machinery to implement the covenants. There is even a serious conflict between those states who possess a unitary form of government and the smaller number of federal states. Each draft covenant is now so long and detailed that it is not difficult for every United Nations member to discover an objectionable word or phrase.

Little more in the way of agreement can be expected from other activities to foster human rights. With respect to the problem of self-determination, the members who do not administer dependent territories are just as adamant in their stand as the administering members. Should the nonadministering members manage to maneuver their proposals to a formal vote, they could probably obtain the required majority, but the major powers would probably ignore whatever machinery might be established. The Genocide Convention is in force but remains a source of contention in most countries. Hopes are dim for some fundamental agreement on such other questions as freedom of information, discrimination, and minorities.

There is a growing body of opinion which holds that a treaty is not suited to the field of human rights in view of the widely differing systems of law, religions, cultural traditions, social practices, and economic standards which prevail among the members of the United Nations. Although the recommendations reported out by the Commission on the Status of Women have received wider support in the General Assembly than is true of other work in the field of human rights, the reluctance to use the treaty form to guarantee women's rights can be seen by the attitude of the United States. Despite the fact that the United States voted for the Convention on the Political Rights for Women, Secretary of State Dulles testified before the Senate of the United States in 1953 as follows:

> This Administration does not intend to sign the Convention on Political Rights for Women. This is not because we do not believe in the equal political status of men and women or because we shall not seek to promote that equality. Rather it is because we do not believe this goal can be achieved by treaty coercion or that it constitutes a proper field for exercise of the treaty-making power. We do not see any clear or necessary relation between the interest and welfare of the United States and the eligibility of women to political office in other nations.

There are those who claim that the United Nations has moved too fast, that there should have been an attempt made to arrive at minimal agreement and then continue to push from there to eventual maximal goals. Such a point of view implies that by introducing too much into the various covenants, they are certain to be rejected, thereby weakening the force of the

Universal Declaration of Human Rights and indirectly, at least, bringing forth additional criticism of the entire United Nations. While there is much to be said for this attitude, it is doubtful whether a series of watered down covenants would be worthy of the United Nations and its objectives. It is also questionable whether, in view of the past acrimonious record, there could be much agreement on what should be included in a document seeking to define minimum standards. It has been said that half a right is no better than no right at all.

Although it is difficult, if not impossible at the present time, to devise legally enforceable standards for human rights, the attempt to do so has not been entirely a failure. If nothing else, the problem areas and the dangers have been focused upon clearly and for all the world to see. Limitless ideas and suggestions have been circulated and the sharing of experiences has been rewarding for some of the less developed and newer nations. The fact that debate will continue is important since inequalities and the absence of adequate protection and guarantees in certain parts of the world will consume the attention of the many members who are determined to broaden the human rights of mankind, irrespective of the obstacles. As an organization dedicated not only to the preservation of peace but also to the bettering of the welfare of mankind, the United Nations must continue to push forward, by advice and by example, by encouragement and by persuasion, toward the universal goal of freedom and justice.

WEIGHING THE RECORD

The foregoing description and analysis of the activities of the United Nations and the specialized agencies has touched only the highlights of the economic and social activities of these organizations. The evaluation so far has been confined essentially to the more immediate objectives of each organization in these general fields. There can be no doubt that in terms of the relatively small amount of money expended, the contribution made toward improving the lot of millions of people throughout the world has been significant. The annual expenditure of less than $30 million, for example, on the entire Expanded Program of Technical Assistance is a pittance when compared to the domestic programs in comparable fields in many countries. Yet there are nearly forty states which could or would spend virtually nothing on self-improvement were it not for these and other funds spent through the United Nations and its specialized agencies. The story told in the preceding pages has demonstrated how even a small financial outlay can teach less fortunate peoples the rudimentary elements of hygiene, food production, soil conservation, and the many other fundamental aspects of ordinary social and economic life which are taken for granted in most of the more advanced countries.

It can be concluded, then, that the money and effort spent has been worthwhile in terms of the immediate objectives of the technical assistance and other economic and social programs of the United Nations. This does not mean that some projects have not failed or have not been worth the effort, nor does it mean that the agencies involved have functioned as efficiently as desired when compared to their counterparts on the domestic scene. It does mean, however, that a start has been made, building upon the modest, pioneering efforts of the League. Attention should now be directed toward evaluating this effort in terms of its contribution to international understanding and co-operation, and in terms of its contribution to the building of a more peaceful world.

It is extremely difficult to prove that the economic and social activities of the United Nations system have contributed, in a tangible fashion, to an atmosphere of co-operation in the world. It is probably true that the individuals who work for international agencies in these fields, coming from different countries and working in foreign areas, have come to know and understand each other's national problems and the way of life in the lands where they may be stationed. More concretely, governments have learned to work with international agencies on a give and take basis, recognizing the basic truth that these agencies are devoted to assisting them in the solution of some of their more important problems. A spirit of co-operation inevitably will arise among those who labor on joint projects, and governments themselves learn to co-operate with each other through the medium of the international agency. By directing attention to fields of common interest, the agencies may condition certain responsible individuals to a system of international intercourse based upon positive, constructive collaboration. Beyond this, however, the measure of co-operation which is developed is highly debatable. International agencies themselves do not touch directly upon the lives of many individuals and ordinarily are concerned with matters which do not arouse interest to any degree comparable to that of the activity engaged in by national governments. Loyalty to national institutions is very real, associated as it is with national myths, symbols, and beliefs. People are interested in the practical aspects of life, such as a better standard of living, improved educational and sanitary facilities, and agricultural development, but projects such as these cannot compare in emotional impact with national symbols. By and large, then, much of the contact fostered by these agencies is intergovernmental and, while it is important as far as it goes, such contact represents only a small beginning toward a goal of universal contact and understanding among all peoples.

In another sense, however, it is argued that international agencies can contribute indirectly toward greater understanding by assisting in the development of wider means of communication among peoples. By expanding educational facilities as well as improving standards of living, these more productive and educated peoples will be provided with horizons much broader than the immediate need for keeping body and soul together. They will be better prepared to participate in the daily life of their countries, to understand the problems not only of their own countries but of their neighbors. It is possible that such a development can take place. But only a very modest start has been made toward alleviating the conditions which make for misery and poverty. When more progress has been made, it will be easier to assess the inherent possibilities of this approach to world understanding and co-operation. In any event, the development of new habits and the abandonment of ancient customs and traditions is a slow and tedious process.

It is equally difficult to prove that the functional activities of international organization, that is, the work in social and economic fields, has contributed to the building of a more peaceful world. The problem is, of course, intimately related to the question of building international co-operation. A strong case has been advanced by David Mitrany and others supporting the functionalist approach to international relations. Briefly stated, there is the belief that war can be traced to a large number of causes deeply rooted in social and economic maladjustments. Misery, poverty, and injustice create fear, hatred, and suspicion, which are the breeding places of war. The most appropriate way to eliminate these causes is to encourage the development of functional organizations that presumably serve the highest common measure of interests among peoples. Such interests are not represented alone by national sovereignty and political authority. They can be stated only in terms of individual well-being, social security, and human welfare. Therefore, it follows that only organizations effectively serving such ends can satisfy these needs. Fundamental to this approach is the assumption that technical or welfare activities are separate from the realm of politics, that technical matters are nonpolitical and noncontroversial. In accepting this thesis, it is held that such nonpolitical activity can be made the foundation for international organization because nations will not protest against the granting of noncontroversial authority to institutions that will work to satisfy the basic needs and demands of all peoples.

The inherent weakness in the functionalist approach is the assumption that it is possible to prevent the intrusion of political influences into the realm of technical and welfare activities. There is no clear dividing line. It can be said that only with respect to certain specific technical functions, such as postal rates, that political considerations remain unimportant. Until political tensions subside and until fundamental political agreement is reached, there is little possibility that greater economic and social co-operation will take place. More and more have the specialized agencies and ECOSOC been drawn into the political arena of the East-West conflict. The majority of members of the United Nations and the specialized agencies are committed to the political objective of restraining the spread of communist influence. Supposedly nonpolitical policies are pursued in functional activities to obtain this political objective. It appears that economic and social co-operation will not increase to any degree until the political climate of international relations is ready for it. When global rivalry exists to the extent that is does today, there is virtually no activity which can be labeled noncontroversial and nonpolitical. The basic task of functionalism should be the building of closer economic and social ties between the United States and the Soviet Union. But functionalism can never do this until there has been some acceptance of a political status quo between these two great poles of power.

Given a different political climate, the functional approach may have a greater opportunity of demonstrating its validity. The absence of political agreement, however, should not obscure the progress which has been made to improve economic and social conditions nor should it blur the need to expand these functional activities. The various technical assistance and development programs, underway or completed, have already proved their worth by contributing to the building of a more productive life for a large number of the world's inhabitants.

15

◇━☀━◇

THE TRUSTEESHIP SYSTEM AND

NON-SELF-GOVERNING TERRITORIES

APPROXIMATELY two hundred and twenty million people in the world have not yet attained a full measure of self-government. They reside today in some sixty colonial and ten trust territories. The Charter, like the League Covenant, recognizes that misery and instability in such areas offer opportunities for international tension and rivalry which are a direct challenge to peace and security. The members of the United Nations, therefore, have assumed a certain measure of responsibility for the well-being of these people.

No less than three chapters of the Charter are devoted to the problem of dependent areas. Chapter XI contains the declaration of the purposes and principles regarding the administration of non-self-governing territories. Chapters XII and XIII are concerned with the objectives of the Trusteeship System and the functions and powers of the Trusteeship Council of the United Nations. There is a fundamental distinction, however, between Chapter XI and Chapters XII and XIII, not in basic objectives and principles, but in types of territories concerned. In Chapter XI, non-self-governing areas are discussed in general, while the other two chapters are devoted specifically to territories falling within the Trusteeship System of the United Nations. Within the colonial system the right of sovereignty is possessed by colonial powers over non-self-governing territories. On the other hand, the Trusteeship System established by the Charter grants certain powers and jurisdiction to administering states which do not possess sovereign rights over the territories assigned them. There is the hope expressed in the Charter that colonial powers eventually will voluntarily place their colonies under the Trusteeship System. In the meantime, these nations are provided a 'colonial charter' in Chapter XI which is to serve as a guide for their administration of the colonial territories owing allegiance to them.

507

THE TRUSTEESHIP SYSTEM

The Mandates System of the League of Nations was the first experiment in international organization designed to improve the well-being of dependent peoples. It will be recalled that Article 22 of the Covenant stated that the best method of giving practical effect to this principle of aiding underdeveloped areas was to entrust their tutelage 'to advanced nations who, by reason of their resources, their experience, or their geographical position, can best undertake this responsibility. . . .' This tutelage was exercised by certain states as Mandatories in behalf of the League.

The experience of the League proved the wisdom of establishing the Mandates System and the need for its continuance in some form under the United Nations. The Trusteeship System is the successor to the League experiment but it would be a mistake to consider it as simply a prolongation of the Mandates System. While the principles are essentially the same, the organization, functions, and powers of the United Nations system are quite different. Basically, the scope of the Trusteeship System is wider and the opportunities provided are undoubtedly greater than was the case with its predecessor.

Article 76 of the Charter lays down the objectives of the Trusteeship System. Certainly they are much broader than those contained in the Covenant for the Mandates System. They included the following basic principles:

(a) The furtherance of international peace and security;

(b) The promotion of the political, economic, social, and educational advancement of the inhabitants of the trust territories, and their progressive development towards self-government or independence, as may be appropriate to the particular circumstances of each territory and its peoples and the freely expressed wishes of the peoples concerned;

(c) The encouragement of respect for human rights and for fundamental freedoms for all without distinction as to race, sex, language, or religion, and the recognition of the interdependence of the peoples of the world;

(d) The ensuring of equal treatment in social, economic, and commercial matters for all members of the United Nations and their nationals, and the equal treatment for the latter in the administration of justice.

The Trusteeship System applies to three types of territories. These include former League Mandates, territories detached from enemy states as a result of the Second World War, and 'territories voluntarily placed under the system by States responsible for their administration.' The first category is obvious; the second refers to former Italian and Japanese colonies. The third category was made very broad in the hope that a colonial power might, for reasons of economy and convenience, give up a dependent territory within its domain and at the same time be assured that some competing nation would not annex the area for hostile purposes. No state, however, has availed itself of this opportunity.

Article 79 of the Charter provides in somewhat unclear terms the method through which dependent territories are to be brought into the Trusteeship System. An agreement is to be concluded between the appropriate organ of the United Nations (the General Assembly or, in the case of strategic areas, the Security Council) and 'the states directly concerned.' A great deal of discussion has centered around the phrase 'the states directly concerned.' It was clear that if a state volunteered to place one of its nonself-governing territories under trusteeship, it would be considered as a state 'directly concerned.' Similarly, a state occupying a territory detached from an enemy state as a result of World War II would also be 'directly concerned.' But with respect to former mandated territories, were all members of the League 'directly concerned' or just the League Council, or only the mandatory powers? For territories detached after World War II, were not the 'states directly concerned' possibly all the victorious states? The British and French believed that geographical propinquity was a factor of importance. The Soviet Union, on the other hand, stoutly maintained that the permanent members of the Trusteeship Council (the Big Five) should also be considered as 'states directly concerned.'

This complex issue was partially resolved in 1946 when all but the Soviet bloc agreed to an interpretation of the United States that the 'states directly concerned' need not be specifically defined. As a result, the 'states directly concerned' are those which were either former mandatory powers or administrators of the areas to come under trusteeship. Agreements have been concluded in these instances, despite Soviet objections, between such states and the General Assembly in ten instances (reduced to nine in 1957 when British Togoland became the independent state of Ghana) and with the Security Council in the one case of a strategic area. The terms of the agreement provide for an 'Administering Authority' which in every case has been a single state exercising responsibility for the territory.[1] The term 'Administering Authority' can mean also a group of states or the United Nations itself. The boundaries of the area are defined and the rights and obligations of the Administering Authority are enumerated. Particular emphasis is placed upon the duty of the Administering Authority to further the general objectives of the Trusteeship System, which have been noted

[1] A special arrangement has been worked out for the trust territory of Nauru. Australia exercises full powers of legislation, administration, and jurisdiction on behalf of New Zealand and the United Kingdom who, together with Australia, jointly constitute the Administering Authority.

previously, as well as to provide for any specific requirements peculiar to the territory concerned.

The Charter takes particular account of areas that may be of strategic importance and grants them special treatment. In the trusteeship agreement, any part or the whole of the trust territory to which the agreement applies can be designated a 'strategic area.' The functions of the United Nations relating to strategic areas, including approval of the terms of trusteeship agreements, are exercised by the Security Council, and not, as in the case of all nonstrategic territories, by the General Assembly. These provisions were insisted upon at San Francisco by the United States in order to permit the continuance of control over areas believed to be of military importance. The permanent members of the Security Council are thus granted significant authority over strategic areas since any one of them, through the use of the veto, can prevent the adoption, alteration, or termination of agreements to which there may be objections. All the basic objectives of the trusteeship system apply to areas designated as strategic. However, the only trusteeship agreement covering a strategic area (the Pacific Islands entrusted to the United States) recognizes that the provisions for human rights, fundamental freedoms, and the equal treatment of other members of the United Nations are 'subject to the requirements of security.'

Administering Authorities of strategic areas and the Security Council are expected to avail themselves of the assistance of the Trusteeship Council in performing those functions of the United Nations under the trusteeship system that relate to political, economic, social, and educational matters. The functions and powers of the Council, however, are restricted by the needs of security and the measure of supervision exercised is not as great as is the case with nonstrategic territories.

In total contrast to the League Mandates System, the Administering Authorities of both strategic and nonstrategic territories are expected to satisfy the requirements of collective security by utilizing the peoples and the resources of these areas for military purposes. No limits are placed upon the building of fortifications and air, military, and naval bases. The native inhabitants cannot be conscripted into armed forces but volunteer units may be created and used to meet local needs or to fulfill any military obligations which the Administering Authority has assumed. Under the Covenant the mandatory states were specifically forbidden to establish fortifications or use native inhabitants for military purposes other than for police and defense in the mandates.

THE TRUSTEESHIP COUNCIL

Although it is one of the six principal organs of the United Nations, the Trusteeship Council, like the Economic and Social Council, is a subordinate body. Article 85 of the Charter states that the 'functions of the United Nations with regard to trusteeship agreements for all areas not designated as strategic, including the approval of the terms of the trusteeship agreements and of their alteration or amendment, shall be exercised by the General Assembly.' Operating under the authority of the General Assembly, the Trusteeship Council assists the Assembly in carrying out these functions. Unlike ECOSOC, however, which has gradually assumed more initiative in its relationship with the Assembly, the Trusteeship Council has remained essentially in a subordinate position.

Organization and Procedure. The membership of the Council is broken down into three categories. Automatic representation, first, is given to all member states of the United Nations that administer trust territories. Membership is also automatic for all permanent members of the Security Council who do not serve as Administering Authorities. Finally, the number of administering states is balanced by an equal number of nonadministering states who are elected by the General Assembly for terms of three years. There were, in 1958, seven members who were administering states, two members who were permanent members of the Security Council but not administering states, and five elected nonadministering states, making a total of fourteen.

It has become customary to award two of the elected seats to Latin America and one each to Asia and the Arab League. An awkward situation arose in 1950 when Italy, a nonmember of the United Nations at the time, was made the Administering Authority for Somaliland. The rules of procedure for the Trusteeship Council were amended to permit Italy to participate without vote in the Council deliberations on Somaliland. Italy was allowed to join the Council when it discussed general questions affecting the operation of the trusteeship system. The Advisory Council, which was established to aid and assist Italy in the discharge of trusteeship responsibilities, also was granted the right to engage in the Council's deliberations on Somaliland.

Each member of the Trusteeship Council designates 'one specially qualified person' to be its representative. The fact that government delegates serve as representatives has been regarded by some as a step backward from the composition of the League's Mandates Commission which consisted of independent experts. However, most of the representatives on the Council have been selected with care and possess experience in matters of colonial administration. It should also be remembered that most of the members of the Mandates Commission were nationals of states possessing colonies, while about half of the representatives on the Trusteeship Council come from noncolonial countries.

Each representative on the Council has one vote and none, despite the presence of the permanent members of the Security Council, has a veto. Decisions are arrived at by majority vote, normally in open sessions, which occur usually in January and June of each year. The Charter authorizes the Council to adopt its own rules of procedure which govern the conduct of its meetings and bear a likeness to those of other principal organs. A president and vice-president are elected at each June session.

The Trusteeship Council functions through two standing committees and such *ad hoc* committees as are necessary. The Standing Committee on Administrative Unions was established in 1950 and consists of four members elected by the Council for the purpose of examining the operation of these bodies.[2] It reports to the Council at each session on any union in which a trust territory under review participates. There is also the Standing Committee on Petitions created in 1952 and consisting of three administering and three nonadministering members of the Council appointed at the end of each session to serve until the close of the next session. Its duty is to screen certain petitions from trust territories which involve general problems and communications to the Council. In consultation with the Administering Authorities, the Committee also conducts a preliminary examination of all petitions and recommends the action to be taken by the Council.

Whenever appropriate, the Council avails itself of the assistance of the Economic and Social Council and the specialized agencies. In practically all aspects of its work, the Council is aided by experts in the Secretariat who conduct extensive research and analysis on problems relating to trusteeship and furnish trained personnel for the preparation of reports and visits to trust areas. Representatives from ECOSOC and certain specialized agencies, expecially FAO, UNESCO, and ILO, are in regular attendance at the meetings of the Council.

Functions and Powers. Although it is not mentioned in the Charter, the Trusteeship Council with the guidance of the General Assembly, has as its basic general purpose supervision over the administration of trust territories. As a result of Charter provisions and through the implementation of directives from the Assembly, the Council conducts its supervisory work on the basis of reports submitted by administering authorities, petitions from the trust territories, and visits to the areas themselves.

Reports must be submitted annually by each Administering Authority

[2] For additional information on the problem of administrative unions, see below, pp. 520–22.

and are based on an exhaustive questionnaire prepared by the Trusteeship Council. Originally prepared in 1947 and revised in 1952, the questionnaire is an extraordinary document which permits the Council to obtain information on a number of matters that might be passed over by an ordinary report. The questionnaire includes a series of definitions which serve to clarify specific points and terms. Its main portion consists of eleven parts which contain 190 questions. These are listed under the following headings:

I. Introductory descriptive section (questions 1–4).

II. Status of the territory and its inhabitants (questions 5–7).

III. International and regional relations (questions 8–11).

IV. International peace and security and the maintenance of law and order (questions 12–13).

V. Political advancement (questions 14–28). Items covered include general political structure; territorial government; local government; civil service; suffrage; political organizations; the judiciary and legal system.

VI. Economic advancement (questions 29–78). Items are grouped under four sections which are: finance of the territory; money and banking; economy of the territory; economic resources, activities, and services.

VII. Social advancement (questions 79–149). Included are such items as general social conditions, human rights and fundamental freedoms, labor, status of women, social security and welfare services, standards of living, all aspects of public health, narcotic drugs, alcohol and spirits, prostitution, penal organization, and housing and town and country planning.

VIII. Educational advancement (questions 150–186). This part includes questions on types of schools and institutions of higher learning; teachers, adult and community education, and culture and research.

IX. Publications (questions 187–188).

X. Resolutions and recommendations of the General Assembly and Trusteeship Council (question 189).

XI. Summary and conclusions (question 190).

The rules of procedure for the Trusteeship Council are quite specific and detailed on the method of presenting and acting upon the annual reports. Administering Authorities are permitted to have special representatives present during the examination of the annual reports in the Council. It is customary to have such a representative present an oral statement prior to a discussion of the report. Written questions are then directed to the representative and he returns written answers. Oral questioning of the representative follows, usually based upon the original oral statement and the written questions and answers. The Council next engages in general debate at which time views are exchanged and recommendations offered. Eventually the Council adopts its own reports on each of the trust territories and submits them to the General Assembly or, in the case of strategic areas, to the Security Council. These final reports, which contain conclusions and recommendations and the individual views of Council members, are discussed by the Assembly and the Security Council and form the basis for recommendations by those bodies to the Administering Authorities.

Petitions. Supplementing the information provided from the reports is the right of petition, an ancient device designed to permit the hearing of grievances. Under the League, all petitions had to be presented through the mandatory power in writing. The rules of procedure adopted by the Trusteeship Council have broadened considerably the methodology governing petitions. The Council accepts and examines petitions if they involve 'the affairs of one or more Trust Territories or the operation of the International Trusteeship System as laid down in the Charter.' Most petitions originate with inhabitants of the trust territory but may also come from other interested parties. They may be oral or in writing. If written, petitions can be in the form of telegram, letter, memorandum, or other document. They are usually addressed to the Secretary-General or to him through the Administering Authority, although they may also be presented to members of official missions visiting a trust territory.

The contents of the petitions vary from such broad matters as education or the status of women to specific complaints or questions from individuals or organizations. For example, numerous petitions have come from Somaliland containing complaints about inadequate medical and educational facilities for Somalis, the shortage of housing and the high cost of rents, the low standard of living and poverty of the Somali people, and the backwardness of indigenous agriculture. The Central Committee of the Somali Youth League has expressed its opposition to the Italian administration, which it claimed was not implementing the Trusteeship Agreement. Petitions have been received from Ruanda-Urundi, administered by Belgium, pointing out that there was discrimination against Africans in judicial matters and in admittance to hotels and restaurants. By contrast, the *Union des colons du Ruanda-Urundi* has claimed that there was discrimination against Europeans in social and labor legislation and in electoral matters. The only truly limiting prohibition on the contents of these petitions is that they cannot be directed against the judgments of competent courts of the Administering Authority. Also petitions must not present a dispute to the Trusteeship Council with which the courts have competence to deal.

All written petitions received by the Secretary-General that contain requests, complaints, and grievances are transmitted promptly to the Trusteeship Council. Written petitions are normally placed on the agenda of a regular session of the Council provided that they have been received by the Administering Authority either directly or through the Secretary-General at least two months before the date of the next following regular session. The Administering Authority concerned attaches whatever observations or recommendations are believed pertinent to the petitions and forwards them to the Council. The Standing Committee on Petitions conducts a preliminary examination and screening of petitions directed to the Council, at which time the appropriate Administering Authority may explain its position. All recommendations from the Committee are then forwarded to the full Council for discussion and action.

The action taken by the Trusteeship Council on a petition is in the form of a resolution. Such a resolution may establish a general principle, refuse to take any action, direct the Secretary-General to undertake a specific administrative step, or encourage the Administering Authority to rectify a situation or pursue a certain policy. In more extreme cases, the Council may decide to dispatch a visiting mission to investigate and report upon an urgent problem. Annual reports submitted by the Council to the General Assembly contain information on action taken on petitions and the Assembly itself may conduct an examination of a problem raised by a petition and its treatment by the Council.

Visiting Missions. The authority of the Trusteeship Council to send visiting missions to trust territories is a power which was not enjoyed by the League Mandates Commission. The Council now sends annual missions, usually composed of four of its members, to groups of territories selected so that each territory will be visited at least once every three years. Special missions are sent should the occasion warrant an immediate on-the-spot investigation. The Council establishes the terms of reference for each visiting mission and they may include special assignments in addition to their normal duties. Each mission may be assisted by experts from the Secretariat and by representatives of the local administration. While engaged in a visit, a mission and its individual members act only on the basis of the instructions from the Council and are responsible exclusively to it.

The first regular mission was sent to East Africa in 1948 and visited the trust territories of Ruanda-Urundi (under Belgian trusteeship) and Tanganyika (under British trusteeship). The Trusteeship Council's directive reveals the nature and duties of the mission:

> To observe the developing political, economic, social and educational conditions in the trust territories of Ruanda-Urundi and Tanganyika, their progress toward self-government or independence, and the efforts of their respective Administering Authorities to achieve this and other basic objectives of the International Trusteeship System;
> To give attention, as may be appropriate in the light of the discussions in the Trusteeship Council and resolutions adopted by the Council, to issues raised in and in connection with the annual reports on the administration of Ruanda-Urundi and Tanganyika and in petitions received by the Trusteeship Council relating to those Trust Territories; and
> To transmit to the Trusteeship Council, no later than 31 October 1948,

in accordance with Rule 99 of the Rules of Procedure of the Trusteeship Council, a report on the findings of the Mission and with such observation and conclusions as the Mission may wish to make.

The mission spent three weeks in Ruanda-Urundi and over five weeks in Tanganyika, during which time it traveled widely interviewing local officials, native leaders, and their peoples. Public meetings were held occasionally and visits were made to schools, churches, hospitals, and agricultural areas. A comprehensive report was submitted to the Council, as is done by each mission. Included in the report on Tanganyika, for example, were observations and conclusions on such items as political advancement, interterritorial organization, agriculture, European colonization, mines, labor, medical health services, and educational advancement. Reports such as these are designed to assist the Council advising the administering authorities and provide information which form the basis of subsequent resolutions and directives. Frequently the Council, as was the case with the first mission to East Africa, recommends that the Administering Authorities concerned give attention specifically to the observations and conclusions of the visiting mission.

THE TRUSTEESHIP SYSTEM IN OPERATION

Establishment of Trust Territories. Before the Trusteeship Council could be created and begin its important duties, it was necessary to conclude trusteeship agreements between the administering states and the General Assembly. The Preparatory Commission had recommended that the Assembly call upon those members of the United Nations that were administering territories under mandate to place them under the trusteeship system. Without waiting for the recommendation of the Commission to be considered by the Assembly, some former mandatories in January, 1946, signified their intention of negotiating agreements and the Assembly in February of that year urged that all such states submit agreements for the approval of the Assembly in the second part of its first session to be held in the fall of 1946.

There were sixteen territories under mandate during the lifetime of the League. The Class 'A' mandates — Syria, Lebanon, Palestine, Iraq, Transjordan — had either become independent by the end of 1946 or expected to receive such a status in the near future and hence were never considered as territories eligible for trusteeship. This left six Class 'B' and five Class 'C' mandates whose future had to be determined. By the time the Assembly reconvened in October, 1946, eight agreements were submitted by Britain, France, and Belgium covering all the former 'B' and 'C' territories except the previously Japanese-administered islands in the Pacific (Marshalls, Carolines, and Marianas), Nauru, and South-West Africa. These were approved by the General Assembly in December, 1946. The Pacific mandated territories were submitted by the United States to the Security Council in February, 1947, as strategic areas and an agreement was approved by that organ in April of that year. The agreement for Nauru was delayed because of protracted deliberations between Britain, New Zealand, and Australia but was finally adopted in November, 1947, by the Assembly.

South-West Africa has presented a continuing problem which has not yet been solved. The territory was a Class 'C' mandate administered by the Union of South Africa and the Union has steadfastly refused to place it under the trusteeship system. In 1946 the Assembly was told by the Union's representative, Mr. Forsyth, that the peoples of South-West Africa desired incorporation with his state. However, the Assembly refused to accede to this view, stating that it considered the inhabitants of the territory not politically mature enough to reach such a conclusion. Instead, the Assembly encouraged the Union, as it has done subsequently each year, to place the area under trusteeship. In 1947 the Union agreed not to proceed with the incorporation of the area but to maintain the *status quo* and continue to administer the territory in the spirit of the mandate. Annual reports were to be transmitted to the United Nations on its administration of the former mandate.

Reports were received by the Trusteeship Council in 1947 and 1948 but since that time the Union has refused to submit any information to the United Nations. As we have seen earlier, the problem has twice been before the International Court of Justice. In 1953 the Assembly established a seven-member Committee on South-West Africa to work 'until such time as an agreement is reached between the United Nations and the Union of South Africa.' The Committee was to function as far as possible within the scope of the former Mandates Commission in examining reports and petitions from the Union and the territory. Although the Union has not submitted any information, the Committee does present its own annual report to the Assembly based upon information supplied by the Secretariat, publications in the Union of South Africa, petitions, and statements from qualified observers.[3] A report was unanimously adopted by the Committee on June 8, 1955, and forwarded to the Assembly. It concluded that 'after

[3] The Committee adopted procedures for the Assembly's examination of reports and petitions relating to the mandated territory. It recommended that decisions in the Assembly on these matters be taken by a two-thirds vote, despite the unanimity rule which governed the League's Council on questions of this nature. The Union objected to this voting procedure and the question was placed before the Court which, in June 1955, unanimously upheld the view of the Committee. For more details on the decision of the Court see Chapter 10.

nearly four decades of administration under the Mandates System, the native inhabitants are still not participating in the political development of the territory. Their participation in the economic development is restricted to that of laborers and the social and educational services for their benefit are far from satisfactory. . . . After examining for the second successive year conditions in the territory, the Committee has found no significant improvement in the moral and material welfare of the native inhabitants.'

The Twelfth Assembly in 1957 decided to adopt a new approach and established a Good Offices Committee to discuss with South Africa 'a basis for an agreement which would continue to accord to the territory of Southwest Africa an international status.'

Somaliland became a trust territory in 1950 and represents a successful undertaking by the United Nations. In November, 1949, the General Assembly decided that the former Italian colony of Somaliland, which had been placed temporarily under British military administration as a result of the Second World War, should become sovereign in 1960 following a period of preparation for independence. The territory was to be placed under the Trusteeship System with Italy as the Administering Authority, assisted by an advisory council composed of representatives of Colombia, Egypt, and the Philippines. This agreement is unique in that it is the only one to set a time limit on the trusteeship arrangement and to call for a special body to advise the Administering Authority. It is also much more detailed than the others, with particular emphasis placed upon the social and political advancement of the native peoples.

Territories Under the Trusteeship System (1958)

Trust Territories	Square Miles	Population	Administering Authority
Tanganyika	360,000	7,400,000	United Kingdom
Ruanda-Urundi	20,500	3,960,000	Belgium
Cameroons	166,489	3,000,000	France
Somaliland	194,000	1,266,000	Italy
Cameroons	34,136	1,160,000	United Kingdom
New Guinea	93,000	1,000,000	Australia
Togoland	21,893	999,000	France
Pacific Islands	687	55,000	United States
Western Samoa	1,133	85,000	New Zealand
Nauru	9	3,432	Australia

A Typical Council Session. A good illustration of the matters considered by the Trusteeship Council is provided by its eighteenth session in 1956. Meeting continuously for more than two months, the Council devoted a good share of its time to reviewing conditions in the four trust territories in the Pacific — New Guinea, Nauru, Western Samoa, and the Pacific Islands Trust Territory — and three territories in Africa — British and French Togoland and Somaliland. In addition, hundreds of petitions had to be examined, reports from committees were studied, and action was taken on matters involving recommendations from the General Assembly. Also an annual report was adopted for transmission to the eleventh Assembly.

The types of problems confronting the Council can be seen from its examination of the annual report submitted on Somaliland by Italy, the Administering Authority. Two items were of particular concern. One was the question of the frontier between the territory and Ethiopia and the other was the serious economic condition of the area. The frontier problem actually dates back to the situation prior to World War II. An Anglo-Ethiopian protocol in 1948 established a temporary administrative border between the two countries. Bilateral negotiations have continued since that time in a friendly atmosphere, but with no conclusive results. The Council has had the problem before it during this period and was forced, once again, in 1956, to re-examine the situation. No direct action was taken although the Council repeated its desire for an early settlement of the matter.

With respect to the economic situation in Somaliland, the Council was informed that an economic survey mission from the International Bank had recently conducted a study in the area. No immediate recommendations were made, since the Council did not have the report nor the Italian reactions to it. A general consideration of the issue was made, however, following which the Council decided that its President, in consultation with Council members, should decide when to hold a special session to discuss the Bank's survey.

The Council also noted with satisfaction the progress made by the Administering Authority and the Somali people toward the goal of self-government. A legislative assembly was recently established and the first government of Somaliland came into being with a Prime Minister and Cabinet responsible for the internal administration of the territory. The Council found it necessary, however, to make a number of recommendations in political, social, and educational fields.

Political Advancement. Both the Trusteeship Council and the General Assembly have devoted most of their attention to the political advancement of the trust territories. All of the territories concerned have their own problems, which must be dealt with in turn; but there has been an increasing emphasis on the need for additional efforts directed toward training the native inhabitants for eventual self-government. The Assembly has acted more consistently and with more determination in this regard than has the

Council, largely because the latter's role is primarily that of a supervisory organ. But the Council has encouraged the adoption of measures that will assist the peoples of the trust territories to become prepared socially and economically for eventual control over their own affairs. Anti-colonial sentiment is reflected in the Assembly, where a majority of the members have had little or no sympathy with the position taken by colonial powers. The Afro-Asian bloc, for example, is composed of a number of states that were dependencies in years past, and it is growing increasingly restive over the slowness of the progress made within the trusteeship system toward self-government.

It is inevitable that serious and complex problems would arise in connection with the general question of political advancement. One of the most persistent has been the matter of integrating a trust territory closely with the neighboring territories of Administering Authorities or with the Administering Authorities themselves, presumably for the purpose of achieving greater administrative and economic efficiency. Such arrangements are customarily referred to as administrative unions. Seven of the trust territories have been involved: French and British Cameroons and Togoland, Tanganyika, New Guinea and Ruanda-Urundi. Administrative, fiscal, and customs unions with neighboring territories of the Administering Authorities are permitted for the territories by the trusteeship agreements. With the exception of Tanganyika, the Pacific Islands, and Western Samoa, the territories may be administered as integral parts of the Administering Authority. Although the Administering Authorities must not employ the device of the administrative union to forestall future self-government, the Assembly has been acutely aware of this possibility. It can be argued that if no union is allowed where cultural and geographical boundaries transcend the political, there will be an artificial separation which leads to inefficiency and duplication in administrative matters. Thus, for example, if the British are not permitted to integrate the trust territory of Tanganyika with the adjacent colonial possessions of Kenya and Uganda, overlapping and wasteful administrative services will be necessary. On the other hand, if close integration is granted to these areas, there is the strong possibility that Tanganyika will be absorbed within the British colonial system and this could prevent the full development of self-government.

In 1948, the entire problem was raised in the Fourth Committee of the Assembly and it was generally agreed that an administrative union must operate in the interests of the inhabitants of the territory concerned and must not prejudice the political identity of a territory nor assume the proportions of a political union. The Assembly itself in the same year endorsed this view and similar opinions of the Trusteeship Council and recommended that the Council should

(a) Investigate these questions in all their aspects with special reference to such unions already constituted or proposed and in the light of the terms of the Trusteeship Agreements and of the assurances given by the Administering Authorities in this connection;

(b) In the light of this investigation, recommend such safeguards as the Council may deem necessary to preserve the distinct political status of the Trust Territories and to enable the Council effectively to exercise supervisory functions over such Territories;

(c) Request, whenever appropriate, an advisory opinion of the International Court of Justice as to whether such unions are within the scope of and compatible with the stipulations of the Charter and the terms of the Trusteeship Agreements as approved by the General Assembly.

The Trusteeship Council in 1950 established a Standing Committee on Administrative Unions in order that constant attention might be devoted to the problem. At the same time, the Council adopted the following safeguards believed necessary to avoid the possibility of an administrative union interfering with the attainment of the objectives of the trusteeship system:

(a) That the Administering Authorities furnish clear and precise separate financial, statistical, and other data relating to Trust Territories participating in administrative unions;

(b) That the Administering Authority facilitate the access of visiting missions to such information on an administrative union as may be necessary to enable the mission to report fully on the Trust Territory concerned;

(c) That the Administering Authorities continue to maintain the boundaries, separate status, and identity of Trust Territories participating in administrative unions;

(d) That the Administering Authorities ensure, with regard to Trust Territories participating in administrative unions, that expenditures on the administration, welfare, and development of any such Trust Territory for a given year be not less than the total amount of public revenue derived from the Territory in that year.

In 1953, the Council authorized the Standing Committee to study unions not only with regard to these safeguards but 'in the interests of the inhabitants of the Territory' and with special regard for the provisions of the Charter and the trusteeship agreements.

The General Assembly has continued to recommend careful supervision of administrative unions by the Trusteeship Council in the light of the resolutions already noted. The increased attention paid to the general problem has resulted in the accumulation of a large amount of information on the operation of specific unions and thereby has forced the Administering Authorities concerned to proceed more cautiously in expanding the functions of unions under their control. The entire issue remains a complex one although no union has yet become so prejudicial to the interests of the territories that the Council or Assembly has recommended its abolition. Certainly, the advances made in the British Cameroons may very well be attributed to its close integration with Nigeria.

A problem which in many respects defies solution is the degree to which native institutions should be continued or replaced by modern administration. It is here that the question of political advancement in particular cannot be divorced from social and economic forces, which shape the destiny of most trust territories. The Administering Authorities are reminded repeatedly by both the Trusteeship Council and the Assembly of their obligations to develop self-government and of the slow rate of progress made. Yet the complexities of the task are tremendous. The British system of indirect control whereby the governing authorities operate through the existing tribal system has the merit of permitting the least disruption to native institutions. But it has been criticized as being undemocratic and perpetuating a situation not conducive to the development of a broader political understanding. One alternative suggested in the deliberations of the Council is to train a select group of natives abroad and return them to govern their fellows under the supervision of the Administering Authority. This may be an improvement over indirect control but it does not necessarily speed up the process of native political development. A great deal can be done through expanding educational facilities but this is a slow and frequently a most difficult process due to the problem of where to draw the line on maintaining native customs and institutions.

New Guinea presents a good example of the problems of developing self-government in a backward trust territory. This territory, which is administered by Australia, comprises the northeastern part of the island of New Guinea, the Bismarck Archipelago, and the northern parts of the Solomon Group. It has a land area of 93,000 square miles and includes over six hundred islands. Lying less than eight degrees from the Equator, it is always hot and one of the wettest areas in the world. Approximately one million people inhabit this region, frequently living in Stone Age conditions of primitive savagery. There are so many different tribes that it is rare to find more than five thousand people who speak the same language or dialect. It has been estimated that there are at least fifty different Melanesian languages spoken. Some areas have only recently come under any form of administration; a number of others have been under nominal control for a while. Highlands of more than 15,000 feet, immense river valleys, impenetrable jungle forests, mangrove swamps, and volcanic islands present a topographical variety difficult to imagine.

In the face of this almost insurmountable problem, Australia is continually prodded by the anti-colonial bloc to provide wider indigenous participation in territorial administration. Indian representatives in the Council and the Assembly have taken the lead here, as they have with other trust territories, in complaining about the slowness of native political advancement. But as the Administering Authorities emphasize, guidance and experience is necessary before native populations can participate fully in territorial political life. Australia has attempted to establish a series of statutory Village Councils to replace gradually the existing tribal structure as a starting point toward greater comprehension of political institutions. But it is necessary at the same time to weld the many tribal groups into a single people speaking a common language. The widespread use of Melanesian 'pidgin' English has helped to bring these native groups together as one people. It would be preferable to have the inhabitants speak English and this is recognized by Australia. But it is not a simple task, as some on the Trusteeship Council appear to believe, to eradicate 'pidgin.' If this were done at once, it would mean ending daily radio broadcasts and the publication of newspapers in this language, thereby eliminating two methods widely used for educational purposes.

New Guinea is an extreme example of the difficulties encountered by Administering Authorities, although there are similar problems in most of the other trust territories. The vigilance of the Trusteeship Council and its concern for progress in things political, while at times short-sighted and impatient, nevertheless serves as a useful reminder to all Administering Authorities of their obligations under the trusteeship system. Advances in training native personnel for local administrative and judicial positions, wider political representation, increased use of the ballot and other democratic processes, can be attributed, indirectly at least, to the recommendations and advice of the Council.

One final problem should be noted, that of native nationalism. The question of the Ewe tribe is a case in point and one of the most vexing yet to come before the Trusteeship Council. The Ewe people of West Africa, about one million strong and the largest ethnic tribe in the area, are located not only in what is now Ghana (formerly Gold Coast and British Togoland) but also in French Togoland to the east. In 1947 the Council received a petition from the All-Ewe Conference which requested that these peoples be united under a single administration. The French and British governments later established a Consultative Commission elected by the Ewes and adopted other similar measures but these have not proved to be satisfactory.

The unification problem, as it is called, has consumed endless hours of debate and discussion in the Council and also in the Assembly. To further complicate the problem there have been conflicting views expressed by indigenous spokesmen concerning the future of the two Togolands. No single plan of unification appeared to be acceptable to all Togolese. The impending decision on independence for the Gold Coast was an added factor to be considered, since British Togoland had been administered as an integral part of the Gold Coast through an administrative union. In 1954 the Assembly decided that the wishes of the people of British Togoland should be ascertained as to their future 'without prejudice to the eventual solution they may choose, whether it be independence, unification of an independent Togoland under British administration with an independent Togoland under French administration, unification with an independent Gold Coast, or some other self-governing or independent status.' A special mission visited the territory in 1955 to ascertain the wishes of the people and reported that a plebiscite should be held which would permit the Togolese under British Administration to decide their political future.

As directed by the Tenth Assembly, the first plebiscite ever to be held in a Trust Territory was conducted on May 9, 1956, under United Nations supervision. Asked to choose between union with an independent Gold Coast or separation from the Gold Coast and continuance under trusteeship pending the ultimate determination of their political future, fifty-eight percent of the inhabitants voted in favor of union with an independent Gold Coast. The following August, the Gold Coast Legislative Assembly passed by a 'reasonable majority' a motion requesting that the British Government grant the colony independence within the Commonwealth. Shortly thereafter the request was granted by the British Parliament and the new state of Ghana came into being on March 6, 1957. The name is derived from a Negro empire which existed near Timbuktu in the Western Sudan during the early Middle Ages.

The Trusteeship Council was requested by the British to hasten the termination of the Trust Territory and provide for its union with the Gold Coast when that land became independent. By a vote of 13-0-1, the Council recommended this action to the Eleventh Assembly which on December 13, 1956, unanimously voted to end the trusteeship agreement as of March 6, 1957.

The matter of French Togoland had not been fully resolved by 1958. The Territorial Assembly of the area in 1955 requested France to proceed with a definition 'of the status of French Togoland with the French community' and thereafter 'to put an end to the Trusteeship system.' The French Parliament in June, 1956, adopted an enabling act which provided new regulations for the colonial possessions of France and in Article 8 empowered the government to grant universal suffrage to Togoland and 'to promulgate by decree, after consultation with the Territorial Assembly, a statute for Togoland in conformity with the objectives laid down by the Trusteeship Agreement.' In addition, there was to be a referendum 'in which the inhabitants would have an opportunity of choosing between that statute and the continuance of the Trusteeship System.'

The Trusteeship Council was then presented with the outline of the statute and with a French request for the presence of United Nations observers at the referendum to be held in October. The debate which ensued in the Council was particularly acrimonious and the French request was denied. Opposition came from all the nonadministering members who pointed out that France, in contrast to Britain, did not provide the United Nations with an opportunity to frame the questions and shape the arrangements for the referendum. Some opponents also argued that France had not presented a full explanation of what was planned in lieu of trusteeship and that the referendum did not include independence as one of the choices offered. The French delegate then stated that his country would refuse 'to share the responsibility which the Council has just assumed in delaying the accession of Togoland to self-government. The referendum will therefore take place at the established time and under the conditions envisaged, but in the absence of United Nations observers' and his government 'explicity reserves its right to determine, as a result of this consultation, its future behavior.'

The Territorial Assembly later studied the statute, suggesting a number of amendments which were subsequently agreed to by France, and it became the governing law on August 30. The 'Autonomous Republic of Togoland' was thereby created, with a prime minister whose government is responsible for most internal affairs, leaving to France the regulation of defense matters and foreign affairs. The referendum was held in October, after the establishment of universal suffrage, and 313,458 votes out of 335,778 were cast in favor of the new statute and the end of trusteeship. The General Assembly voted early in 1957 to send a six-member commission to the area to examine conditions resulting from the new statute and postponed a decision on whether or not to terminate the trust arrangement.

The Commission reported to the Trusteeship Council in August that although Togoland 'possesses a large measure of internal autonomy or self-government,' certain revisions in the governing statute should be undertaken which would give Togoland full responsibility for modification of the provisions for the internal organization of the country. Also suggested was the holding of new elections for the Territorial Assembly in order that 'the support of the entire population might be thrown behind the new political institutions created by the statute.' Acting on these and other recommendations of the Commission and the Council, the Twelfth Assembly decided to send a commissioner representing the United Nations to supervise new elections to the Togoland Assembly scheduled for 1958 and encouraged that body and the Togoland government, in consultation with France, to formulate plans for early complete self-rule and the end of the trusteeship agreement.

Economic Advancement. The need for progressive economic development is evident in all trust territories. Each one suffers from the same general malady — a low native level of subsistence dependent primarily upon agricultural and extractive enterprises which are impeded by topographical difficulties, climatic conditions, indigenous customs, and the remnants of colonial exploitation. These and related problems present themselves annually in the reports of the Administering Authorities to the Trusteeship Council where it is difficult at times to do more than study the reports and make a few recommendations.

Possibly the economic situation is best in western Africa territories — Togoland and the Cameroons. French Cameroons, for example, is undergoing active development economically and fortunately possesses numerous and diverse resources. The chief port of Douala has grown rapidly and now has a population of about 100,000. Cocoa is the territory's principal source of wealth and it is cultivated primarily by the native inhabitants. European investments on a large scale in recent years attest to the economic vigor of the area. The British Cameroons is also dependent upon agriculture and can be compared favorably with its French counterpart. Plantation lands leased to the Cameroons Development Corporation are the dominant economic factor of the whole territory. French Togoland, however, is somewhat less well off. Although agriculture is the basis of the economy, poor irrigation and soil make agricultural development difficult. The area exports products similar to those of the former trust territory of British Togoland but it has never had the advantage of a close tie-up with (an adjacent) colony similar to the advanced Gold Coast.

In eastern Africa — Somaliland, Tanganyika, and Ruanda-Urundi — the general economic situation is much worse. Somaliland has a sparse nomadic population and few natural resources; it is one of the poorest countries in the world. The principal crops are bananas and sugar cane but the restricted market for these exports is a severe handicap. Subject to erosion and drought, the territory badly needs an adequate irrigation system and the development of other enterprises. Tanganyika also suffers from erosion due to poor agricultural and stock-raising methods and to recurring drought.

The ravages of the tsetse fly also plague the territory. Ruanda-Urundi is overcrowded and wholly rural. Cattle-raising is the primary activity, but the majority of the native inhabitants regard cows as mystical animals and would rather starve then give up any of them. This obsession creates a serious economic problem and complicates the developement of new lands, which is essential to the needs of the territory.

The economic situation in the Pacific, reflecting most of the problems noted in Africa, remains fairly constant and in most respects does not offer a base for future expansion. New Guinea, as has already been seen, is the worst off and there is relatively little hope for the immediate future. The small island of Nauru depends upon its phosphate beds which constitute about four fifths of the entire area. This asset is gradually diminishing and it is expected that the beds will be exhausted in approximately forty years. The Trust Territory of the Pacific covers an ocean area as large as the continental United States and is concentrated in three main island groups — the Marshalls, Marianas, and Carolines — comprising over 2100 different islands. The traditional Micronesian customs present certain features inhibiting to economic development. The main cash crops are copra and phosphate, and the latter is diminishing rapidly. A certain degree of agricultural expansion can be expected but the future holds little else in store for this oddly-constructed trust territory, the only one labeled 'strategic.' Western Samoa has its own peculiar problems but has enjoyed more progress as will be shown later.

This brief survey of economic conditions throughout the various trust territories indicates the magnitude of the problem faced by the Trusteeship Council in fostering the economic objectives of the Trusteeship System. The Council has learned much from its visiting missions and has been able to offer suggestions on certain local problems. Stress has been placed upon the need for comprehensive economic planning and the various programs of this nature underway in Somaliland, French Cameroons, and Tanganyika have been encouraged. Wherever possible the Council has recommended an increase in native participation in the administrative features of a territory's economy, the board of directors of the British Cameroons Development Corporation being one example. The Council repeatedly recommends the assistance of the specialized agencies of the United Nations, particularly of FAO. This agency has been helpful in awakening interest in various agricultural reforms and development projects: soil conservation, land reclamation programs, and the like. In this connection, the Council in 1951, acting in accordance with a 1950 resolution of the Assembly, established a Committee on Rural Economic Development. It has conducted studies and made recommendations on the prevail-

ing laws, practices, and policies in the trust territories relating to land. The
Committee has been assisted generously in its work by FAO and ILO. The
conclusions of this Committee have been particularly useful in helping the
Council to arrive at suggestions for the Administering Authorities on these
matters.

Practically every visiting mission reports on the need for additional roads,
other means of communication, transport facilities, and the development of
light industries. Diversification of agriculture is a recurring suggestion.
The various Administering Authorities are well aware of these needs but
constantly point out the lack of funds available to finance these necessary
projects. As is the case with political advancement, progress is slow, not
because of a lack of interest on the part of the Trusteeship Council or
the Administering Authorities but primarily as a result of the magnitude
of the problem which is further complicated by the absence of adequate
financial resources.

Advancement in Social Welfare. Social conditions in the trust territories
are, of course, intimately associated with the rate of economic and political
progress. It does not take much imagination to visualize the many social
problems that confront the Administering Authorities in the jungles of
Africa or the lush Pacific Islands. Indigenous customs relating to labor, status
of women, marriage, education, and health all present to an Administering Authority a particular challenge. It is sometimes difficult for the nonadministering members of the Trusteeship Council and the anti-colonial
members of the Assembly to appreciate the difficulties involved in the
process of changing ancient ways of life and stamping out barbarian practices
imbedded in native cultures.

The Council has made progress toward solving such important social
matters as migrant labor and penal sanctions for breach of labor contracts
by native inhabitants. Experts from ILO have assisted in these efforts and
also have contributed valuable cost-of-living studies. Analyses of labor
standards, discriminatory practices, and methods of vocational training have
proved to be of use for the Administering Authorities in most trust territories. Wage increases have been provided, for example, in the British
Cameroons and Western Samoa, as the result of Council recommendations.
A more enlightened industrial-labor policy has come to Ruanda-Urundi,
together with improvements in urban housing. This has also been true in
Tanganyika although it has not been possible to abolish racial discrimination despite consistent efforts of the Council. The French have been con-
gratulated for their application of an improved labor code for the Cameroons
and Togoland. It condemns and prohibits forced labor, grants the right to

form labor unions and bargain collectively, and abolishes the distinction between laborers of metropolitan origin and indigenous laborers.

In most trust territories it has been traditional to relegate woman to an inferior status in society. Wives and mothers have always lived a life of toil in the home and in the fields and taboos have prevented them from assuming more than a secondary role in the community. Some progress has been made in this respect, particularly in education which can bring about far-reaching changes in the depressed status of women generally and specific improvements in Pacific and African society. But such institutions as child marriage and the bride-price system persist, particularly in the Cameroons. In some areas it has been traditional for native chiefs to take as wives all the first-born daughters and all female twins of certain families within their tribes. These young girls are chosen at an early age by the senior wives and enter a chief's compound to be trained in cooking, farm work, and etiquette. In other areas the payment for a bride has been a tribal custom symbolizing the marriage bond and guaranteeing conjugal stability. The practice has got out of hand in the Cameroons and has deteriorated into a means of bargaining and speculation and the rates for brides have become exorbitant. Some cannot afford wives while others who are better situated can afford several and use them to work in the fields or sell them off to others at a profit. The Council has tried to prohibit these uncivilized marriage practices but the Administering Authorities prefer to pursue a policy of gradual change in customs through an expansion of educational facilities.

Health matters and medical services come under repeated scrutiny by the Council and steady progress can be noted. The need is limitless, however, and the financial means available are simply not up to the task at hand. Once again the problem of native customs must be overcome. Traditional 'medicine-men' still practice their sorcery and magical formulae. Native diseases such as tuberculosis, leprosy, and filariasis persist. Constant attention is being devoted to these questions with added assistance coming from the World Health Organization. Annual reports to the Council and observations from visiting missions provide evidence that public health services are expanding, hospitals and clinics are increasing, and efforts are being made to train natives in nursing and other technical aspects of the medical profession. The Pacific Islands Trust Territory has enjoyed the largest single increase in medical facilities owing in large part to the opportunities afforded by the presence of military personnel and their medical services. Personal hygiene has long been a matter of importance in both rural and urban areas in all trust territories and has become an integral part of the educational programs among indigenous people.

Both the Assembly and the Trusteeship Council have placed great emphasis upon the expansion of educational facilities. In 1948 and 1949 the Assembly adopted resolutions encouraging the development of educational institutions and instructed the Trusteeship Council to include in its annual reports to the Assembly a special section on the manner in which Administering Authorities had complied with the recommendations of the United Nations for educational advancement in their territories. Since that time the Council has been able to report a steady improvement in the building of schools and libraries, the establishment of adult education centers, and the training of native teachers. Administering Authorities have been encouraged to avail themselves of United Nations educational technical assistance resources in co-operation with UNESCO. These resources include scholarships, fellowships, and internships in public and private institutions abroad.

The United States has had a particularly difficult task with education in its Pacific trust territory. Most school buildings were destroyed during World War II and the few books and teaching materials left by the Japanese were unsuitable for the Micronesian inhabitants. In 1953 the expenditures in education amounted to $435,440 compared to $338,000 in 1948. By 1958 there were more than 150 elementary schools and six intermediate schools, in which the emphasis has been placed on the development of an agricultural and vocational program. Similar progress can be noted for Western Samoa, British and French Cameroons, and Tanganyika. Educational facilities, however, continue to be a problem in all trust territories and the Council never fails to urge additional efforts and expenditures on the part of each Administering Authority. The Council has been critical of the failure of some authorities to educate the native inhabitants on the meaning and purposes of the United Nations and the Trusteeship System. Wherever it appears appropriate, the Council has recommended that United Nations information centers be established and that some lectures and discussion groups in schools be devoted to the aims and objectives of the Charter.

Western Samoa: An Example of Progress under Trusteeship. Living primarily on two islands approximately 1440 nautical miles northeast of the tip of New Zealand, the 85,000 people of Western Samoa are gradually progressing toward self-government. The area was first occupied by New Zealand in 1914 and military control lasted until 1920 when the League of Nations granted New Zealand a mandate over the islands. The mandate continued until the territory was placed under United Nations trusteeship in 1946 with New Zealand as the Administering Authority.

Samoans are of Polynesian extraction with a traditional socio-political system based on large family groups formed by kinship and adoption. The head of a group is called the *matai* and is chosen by the family. Most Samoans are villagers who fish and raise food crops: cocoa, copra, bananas, and some cattle. Conditions have generally been prosperous but the rate of population growth is one of the world's highest and poses a serious problem for future economic development.

The primary concern of both Samoans and New Zealand has been the progress of the territory toward self-government. At its first session, the Trusteeship Council authorized the sending of a visiting mission to the territory to investigate a petition from leaders and representatives of Western Samoa requesting self-government. The mission reported that the political organization and social structure of the area was sufficiently advanced 'to serve as the basis for progressive self-government' but the people were not ready to assume full governmental responsibility without assistance. Reforms calling for greater representation and participation in government by the Samoans, in addition to rather extensive administrative changes, were recommended, and the Trusteeship Council approved the suggestions. The government of New Zealand responded immediately and by 1948 had put into effect most of the recommendations. The people of the territory were given the same guarantees as New Zealand citizens with regard to the protection of their persons and property. However, as pointed out by the Trusteeship Council in 1949, there still remained a differentiation in some legal and social rights between 'Samoans' and 'Europeans.' The Council encouraged New Zealand to plan to introduce universal suffrage and other reforms that would lessen the differences.

A visiting mission in 1950 re-examined the political advancement of Western Samoa and was able to report continuing progress. It discovered an urgent desire among some native leaders and their representatives for self-government and a dissatisfaction with the part they were playing in the affairs of the territory. The mission was impressed with the political sense of the Samoan leaders and the progress made since 1947 in governmental matters but was convinced that the people were not yet ready for self-government. Samoans could manage their own affairs in their own traditional ways but a serious problem existed in adapting these ways to the complexities of a modern political system. The element of democracy implicit, but by no means dominant, in the Samoan social structure needed development along with more political education and participation in the policy-making and administrative levels of the executive branch of government.

In 1951 the Trusteeship Council recommended that an executive council be established in order to bring representatives of the native inhabitants into closer touch with problems of an executive and administrative nature.

This was done in 1953 by the Administering Authority, which also announced that in 1954 a constitutional convention would be called to consider a plan for a future self-governing state of Western Samoa. At the time of that announcement a Statement of Policy was issued by New Zealand placing before the Samoans varied suggestions as to the manner in which they might proceed in solving their social and economic problems and in drawing up their constitution.

The convention sat from November 10 to December 23, 1954, at the Samoan village of Mulinu'u and was attended by over one hundred representatives selected from native districts, assemblies, and governments. Among the conclusions reached were the following: the territory was not yet ready for self-government and New Zealand should continue for the time being to have responsibility in foreign affairs, defense, and general administration; a new, single legislature to replace the existing Assembly and Fono of Faipule (a broadly representative advisory group made up of one member from each of the forty-one traditional districts in the islands) should be created; a parliamentary system of government, with a premier and cabinet, should be established; only Samoan *matai* should have the right to vote or be nominated as candidates for election. These ideas were endorsed by the Trusteeship Council in 1955 and it warmly commended the Administering Authority for its continuing interest and encouragement of the political development of the territory, as well as for its patient and enlightened policy on economic and social matters.

At the present time Samoa is prosperous. An important facet of the economy is the New Zealand Reparation Estates, which is a New Zealand government organization operating former German lands that were taken as reparations payments after the First World War. The estates produce large quantities of cocoa, copra, timber, and beef. They serve as a center for agricultural experiment work and the profits are used for the welfare of the territory. New Zealand has already announced that ways and means are now being studied to discover the most satisfactory method of turning over the estates to the Samoan people. The main problem concerns the traditional Samoan custom which requires ownership in small parcels. Breaking up the estates in such fashion would not be sound economically for Samoa, and some compromise must be worked out before the transfer of ownership can be accomplished.

The Administering Authority has also encouraged the Samoans to increase their production, establish secondary industries, and learn the advantages of crop diversification. Co-operative societies have been established in recent years and others are contemplated. Medical facilities and services have been enlarged and an increasing number of native personnel is being employed in medical work. An extensive school building program has been underway since 1950. Studies are now being made for a ten-year program under which there will be compulsory education for all children between the ages of seven and thirteen. Adult education is a going concern and information on local and world news, health, commerce, and agriculture is available through a weekly newspaper and a local radio station.

New Zealand has done much to make the ideals inherent in the trusteeship system a living reality. Although Western Samoa remains a backward and underdeveloped area with many problems associated with such a status, the Administering Authority has done its best to prepare the native peoples in its charge for eventual self-government without hastening unduly the actual transfer of responsibility. The Trusteeship Council recognizes the needs that must be met and has offered many helpful suggestions as well as frequent expressions of satisfaction with the progress made by the territory within the trusteeship system.

Conclusions and Evaluations. A comparison between the League mandates system and trusteeship under the United Nations reveals that the latter is far more ambitious than the former, is equipped with broader powers and objectives and devotes more time to the special problems involved. It should be noted, however, that from the end of World War II to the present there has been a much stronger sentiment against colonialism than there was following World War I. This sentiment has become worldwide in scope, resulting in demands that action be taken within the framework of the United Nations to hasten the accomplishment of the Charter objectives pertaining to trusteeship. It is here that the trusteeship system enjoys greater support than its predecessor, but it suffers from demands that are too frequently the product of political machinations and emotional objectives blind to the realities of the situation.

That there have been accomplishments under the present system can be proved objectively. The device of the free and virtually unrestricted petition has been a great boon to the native inhabitants of the trust territories. The fact that the Trusteeship Council has studied them and even dispatched special visiting missions to investigate the truth of their contents attests to the workability of the petition process. The visiting missions, in turn, both periodic and special, have gone about their tasks with purpose and determination and have been able to supply the Council with much useful information. The Council and the Assembly, within the limits of their competence, have continually prodded the several Administering Authorities to undertake measures that might otherwise have been delayed or postponed indefinitely. The careful scrutiny of annual reports has put the Authorities on their mettle to defend policies and justify acts of commission or omission, which would never be the case if there were no organ such as the Trusteeship Council. Studies of specific issues, such as labor conditions, educational progress, the question of administrative unions, and rural economic development have been penetrating and useful, and have produced effective results in several territories. Health conditions have been improved remarkably in certain areas and the Council can share in the credit. Political advancement has been slow, regrettably so in some instances, yet the Council has done much to keep the Administering Authorities alerted to the responsibilities and the objectives of the Charter in this field.

However, there is a dark side to the picture which needs illumination. One fundamental conclusion is inescapable. Progress is possible to a remarkable degree only where an Administering Authority is willing to cooperate. The most noteworthy examples have been Western Samoa and the enlightened role played by New Zealand as the Administering Authority, and the former British Togoland. At the other extreme is the situation in South-West Africa and the refusal of the Union of South Africa to respond to the logical recommendation of the United Nations that the area be made a trust territory. This points up a basic weakness in the position of the Council, namely that it has no authority to go beyond the use of advice, recommendations, and persuasion. This is a weakness primarily in that the objectives of the Charter, if they are accepted as just and reasonable, cannot be accomplished to the degree desired unless the Trusteeship Council is equipped with more than supervisory powers. It is futile to speculate beyond this point, however, because the colonial powers who, for the most part are Administering Authorities, are powerful enough to prevent the transformation of the Trusteeship Council into a true administrative body with sufficient powers to carry out its directives.

The Trusteeship Council is essentially a political body; it has acted as such and as a result its effectiveness has been reduced. The Soviet Union never ceases to find fault with all Administering Authorities, regardless of the issues involved. Consequently the administering powers have had to defend themselves and tend to support each other regardless of the soundness of their position on a particular matter. The resulting East-West conflict impairs the usefulness of the Council and wastes valuable time. At the same time, the Afro-Asian bloc in the Assembly is frequently joined by a host of small states who are bitterly anti-colonial; all of them together can bring to bear voting influence far in excess of what their experience, position, and resources would appear to justify. Pressure of this kind results in Assembly decisions that are as unwise as they are untimely, such as the recommendation that the Administering Authorities estimate the period at which they believe the territories in their trust will be ready for self-government. Action such as this presents a false picture of the situation, encourages uncalled for optimism on the part of the general public, and provides comfort to nationalistic movements in the territories, all of which impedes progress and makes the task of the Administering Authority that much more difficult.

Too much emphasis has been placed upon the need for self-government or independence, or both, in the Council and in the Assembly. It may very well be that some of these territories should never be completely independent but joined instead to neighboring areas or colonies and provided, in due time, with a large measure of autonomy. It is difficult indeed to visualize the day when New Guinea, or most of the islands in the Pacific Trust Territory, could be independent. Yet the growing sense of nationalism in many of the trust areas is a force which cannot be ignored even though it is not, of itself, sufficient for the viability of a state.

The policies of Administering Authorities should never escape close surveillance and helpful advice. But the absence of specialists on colonial affairs on the Council sometimes leads to certain unjustified conclusions based upon ignorance and sentiment and, unfortunately, on information often incomplete or out of date. The older colonial powers, such as the French, British, and Belgians, have had wide experience in governing colonial peoples but they fear the extension of the Trusteeship Council's authority to other colonial areas and, consequently, are prone to adopt a cautious and defensive policy on the Council. New Zealand, the United States, and Australia have proved to be more conciliatory and co-operative than the older colonial states but they have had occasion to take offense at attempts to equate their performance as Administering Authorities with that of the traditional colonial exploiters. Anti-colonial charges of failure to expend enough funds to meet the needs of the territories appear harsh when one considers the difficult financial situation of all Administering Authorities except the United States. It is not reasonable to expect nations to invest large sums in territories whose future status is in doubt.

After more than ten years of experience, the trusteeship system suffers, as does the United Nations itself, from having too much expected of it. Its accomplishments, while modest, are real, and if some of the inhabitants in the discouraging areas under its surveillance have realized benefits from the efforts of the Council and the Assembly, due credit should be given.

NON-SELF-GOVERNING TERRITORIES

The issue of colonialism has become more and more explosive since the end of World War II. The war itself shook centuries-old colonial systems to their foundations. The Japanese surrender in 1945 signalled the beginning, not the end, of the really vital struggle — the struggle for freedom from foreign domination for over half the peoples of the world.

The efforts to destroy the structure of colonialism have met with a large measure of success. There were about 200 million people still in colonial status at the end of 1957 but this figure represents a considerable reduction from the 600 million in this condition when the San Francisco Conference first met in the spring of 1945. Since that time self-government has come to Burma, Ceylon, the Gold Coast, India, Indonesia, Israel, Jordan, Libya, Morocco, Pakistan, the Philippines, the Sudan, and Tunisia. Other territories have been granted varying degrees of autonomy and self-rule. The Netherlands, for example, reported in 1955 that as a result of a new constitution, its former colonies in the Caribbean — Surinam and the Netherlands Antilles — had become equal partners with the Netherlands government itself. This condition resulted from a Round Table Conference held in The Hague late in 1954 which established the new legal order.

Added momentum was given to the drive for independence by the conference of Afro-Asian nations held at Bandung, Indonesia, in the spring of 1955. The colonial issue exploded with violence at the Tenth Assembly in the fall of 1955, reaching its climax on the issue of French Algeria. In 1954 a group of African and Asian nations attempted to bring up the Algerian question in the General Assembly, as a result of rioting and violence in that territory. They were not able to gain the approval of the General Committee in their bid to place the matter on the agenda for the ninth session of the Assembly and did not press the issue further. But as the Assembly opened its tenth session, the same bloc of nations moved again to include the Algerian question on the agenda. This time they waged a bitter fight, arguing that France had been given a full year to deal with the Algerian problem and had only made it worse. Now, it was claimed, it was a threat to the peace and no longer a purely French internal matter. For a time it appeared that the arguments had been in vain. The General Committee voted eight to five against the resolution to include Algeria on the agenda. It was taken for granted that the Assembly would back up the Steering Committee when the matter came to a vote in full plenary session. Never had the Assembly rejected the recommendation of its General Committee on a major issue. But the Assembly voted 28 to 27 to put Algeria on the agenda. The Arab and Asian nations, joined by the Soviet Union, its satellites and a sprinkling of nations had managed to defeat the Western powers. After the voting, French Foreign Minister Antoine Pinay said to the Assembly:

Twice I have warned the Assembly of the consequences of a violation of the Charter. . . . Any government will consider as null and void any recommendation which the Assembly might make in this connection. I must add — and I say this in all seriousness and sincerity — that I do not know what will be the consequence tomorrow of this vote on relations between France and the United Nations.

M. Pinay and the entire French delegation thereupon walked out of the Assembly chambers. The following day the French government ordered its delegation to the United Nations to return to France. Later in the session, however, the item was removed from the agenda and the French delegation returned to the Assembly.

During 1956, the situation in Algeria gradually worsened and the National Liberation Front (Algerian) firmly rejected any French proposal designed only to grant autonomy for the area, demanding instead a French recognition of the principle of Algeria's independence and the establishment of an Algerian provisional government for negotiation. A virtual state of civil war has been the result and has led to a request by members of the Afro-Asian bloc that the Security Council consider the matter immediately. However, on June 26, the Council, by a vote of 7-2-2, decided against placing the question on its agenda. Undaunted, the same members had the item placed on the agenda of the Assembly. Just prior to its consideration by the Political Committee, French Foreign Minister Pineau reiterated the long-standing position that Algeria is not a subject for a United Nations debate, declaring that 'it is a French national question' and 'the United Nations can do nothing about it.'

As a result of the positive leadership of the United States, however, efforts made by the Afro-Asian and Soviet blocs to recommend that France grant self-determination to Algeria were defeated. Instead, the Assembly in a compromise move, unanimously expressed the hope that 'in the spirit of cooperation, a peaceful, democratic and just solution will be found' for the problem in conformity with the Charter. No specific action was called for in the proposal. In actual fact, France was given the opportunity to prove that something positive would be forthcoming to resolve the Algerian impasse. French Foreign Minister Pineau recognized this and observed that 'the approval we have received at the United Nations, notably on the part of the United States, was largely due to the fact that we proposed a constructive solution to the Algerian problem.' The 'constructive solution' was still largely on paper but it called for a cease-fire, elections in peaceful areas, and then negotiation with the elected Algerians.

In 1957, the Twelfth Assembly unanimously repeated the hope for a solution and called upon the parties concerned to engage in informal discussions to this end.

Declaration regarding Non-Self-Governing Territories. During the discussions on the establishment of the Trusteeship System at the San Francisco Conference, it was soon evident that the Charter would be so written that it would go beyond the provision for trust territories. Australian and British proposals gave concrete evidence of this development. A British draft based on the Covenant's statement on colonial peoples outlined principles relating to all non-self-governing areas. The Australian proposal about these areas was much more detailed and provided that it should be 'the duty of the states responsible for their administration to furnish annual reports to the United Nations upon the economic, social, and political development of the territories.' It remained for the United States delegation to present a working paper based on these proposals, which resulted in the agreement at the Conference to separate trusteeship arrangements from any statement or declaration of principles applying to the administration of all non-self-governing peoples. Provisions for trusteeship, therefore, were placed in Chapters XII and XIII while Chapter XI, embodying two articles (73 and 74) is devoted to the Declaration Regarding Non-Self-Governing Territories.

For the first time in history, states which administer non-self-governing territories have agreed to be bound by a set of principles which apply to all such areas. Article 73 of Chapter XI contains the heart of the declarations and first establishes a general obligation for all administering states:

> Members of the United Nations which have or assume responsibilities for the administration of territories whose peoples have not yet attained a full measure of self-government recognize the principle that the interests of the inhabitants of these territories are paramount, and accept as a sacred trust the obligation to promote to the utmost, within the system of international peace and security established by the present Charter, the well-being of the inhabitants of these territories. . . .

To this end, the nations which administer these territories agree:

> a. to ensure, with due respect for the culture of the peoples concerned, their political, economic, social, and educational advancement, their just treatment, and their protection against abuses;
> b. to develop self-government, to take due account of the political aspirations of the peoples, and to assist them in the progressive development of their free political institutions, according to the particular circumstances of each territory and its peoples and their varying stages of advancement;
> c. to further international peace and security;
> d. to promote constructive measures of development, to encourage research, and to cooperate with one another and, when and where appropriate, with specialized international bodies with a view to the practical achieve-

ment of the social, economic and scientific purposes set forth in this Article; and

    e. to transmit regularly to the Secretary-General for information purposes, subject to such limitation as security and constitutional considerations may require, statistical and other information of a technical nature relating to economic, social and educational conditions in the territories for which they are respectively responsible other than those territories to which Chapters XII and XIII apply.

In addition to the obligations contained in this article, which relate specifically to the interests of the inhabitants of colonial territories and the promotion of their well-being, Article 74 commits the members of the United Nations to

    . . . agree that their policy in respect of the territories to which this Chapter applies no less than in respect of their metropolitan areas, must be based on the general principle of good-neighborliness, due account being taken of the interests and well-being of the rest of the world, in social, economic, and commercial matters.

In other words, this is a guiding principle of policy which is to serve as a reminder to administering nations that other countries have interests in colonial territories. If these interests are affected by arbitrary policies in relation to such matters as immigration, trade, and commerce, such non-administering countries might well have grounds for complaint. The expression of policy is very similar to the requirement of the equal treatment provision contained in Chapter XII on trusteeship.

What Is a Non-Self-Governing Territory? The Charter is silent on the exact meaning of the term 'non-self-governing' although it has been generally agreed that the areas concerned would be colonies. What are the criteria to be applied in making the determination? At what point does a territory arrive at a condition of self-government which would make the provisions of Chapter XI inapplicable?

It appears that regardless of what the criteria are, the administering state is the sole judge of whether a particular territory is to be regarded as non-self-governing, thus requiring a report on its status to the Secretary-General. However, once a member has so reported a territory, a question has been raised whether a member can solely on his own authority determine at a later date that there is no longer a need to report on the territory concerned. In 1948, the Assembly adopted a resolution in response to India's request, which contained these provisions:

    . . . having regard to the provisions of Chapter XI of the Charter, it is essential that the United Nations be informed of any change in the constitutional position and status of any such Territory as a result of which the re-

sponsible Government concerned thinks it unnecessary to transmit information in respect of that territory . . . ;

Requests the Members concerned to communicate to the Secretary-General,
within a maximum period of six months, such information as may be appropriate pursuant to the preceding paragraph, including the constitution, legislative act or executive order providing for the government of the territory and
the constitutional relationship of the territory to the Government of the
metropolitan country.

The major administering states — Belgium, France, and the United Kingdom — were opposed to the resolution, claiming that the United Nations
had no authority to exercise any control over the administration of non-self-
governing territories or the political and constitutional relationships involved. This is a valid position but the increasing efforts of the anti-colonial
bloc have led to some alteration of this viewpoint. In 1951, for example,
the representative of Cuba was supported by several others when he stated
during a protracted discussion of the matter in the Fourth (Trusteeship)
Committee of the Assembly that the full and final responsibility of deciding
whether a territory might be removed from the non-self-governing list
rested with the United Nations. In 1954, the Assembly adopted a resolution
which stated that 'communications relating to the cessation of the transmission of information . . . should be examined . . . with particular emphasis on the manner in which the right of self-determination has been
attained and freely exercised. . . .' The resolution went on to observe that
in order

> . . . to evaluate as fully as possible the opinion of the population as to the
> status or change in status which they desire, a mission, if the General As-
> sembly deems it desirable, should, in agreement with the Administering
> member, visit the non-self-governing territory before or during the time when
> the population is called upon to decide on its future status or change in status.

While it is an almost impossible task, the General Assembly has attempted to compile a list of criteria for establishing the existence of a 'full
measure of self-government.'[4] This effort began in 1949 when the Assembly
decided that it was within its responsibility 'to express an opinion on the
principles which have guided or which in the future guide the members
concerned in enumerating the territories for which the obligation exists to
transmit information. . . .' Subsequent recommendations by the *Ad Hoc*

---

[4] The extreme difficulty involved in developing a list of criteria was recognized in the
1953 report of the Assembly *Ad Hoc* Committee which had been assigned this task. The
report stated: 'From the beginning, it was agreed that no list of factors can serve as
more than a guide in determining whether any particular territory has attained a full
measure of self-government. Moreover . . . each concrete case should be considered
and decided in the light of the particular circumstances of that case.' The Committee
was unable to discover a satisfactory definition of 'the concept of a full measure of self-
government.'

Committee on Factors resulted in the decision of the Assembly in 1953 to approve a list of factors 'indicative of the attainment of independence or of other separate systems of self-government.' Among the more important noted are:

1. Degree or extent to which the territory exercises the power to enter freely into direct relations of every kind with other governments and with international institutions and to negotiate, sign and ratify international instruments freely.

2. Complete freedom of the people of the territory to choose the form of government which they desire.

3. Freedom from control or interference by the government of another state in respect of the internal government (legislative, executive, judiciary) and administration of the territory.

4. Complete autonomy in respect of economic, social, and cultural affairs.

5. Political advancement of the population sufficient to enable them to decide upon the future destiny of the territory with due knowledge.

6. The opinion of the population of the territory, freely expressed by informed and democratic processes, as to the status or change of status which they desire.

7. Degree to which the sovereignty of the territory is limited by its own free will when that territory has attained a separate system of government.

The *Ad Hoc* Committee on Factors included in its report the statement that 'among the features guaranteeing the principle of self-determination of peoples in relation to Chapter XI of the Charter might be found the following':

A. The political advancement of the population sufficient to enable them to decide the future destiny of the territory by means of democratic processes.

B. The functioning of a representative system of government, with periodic elections in which the peoples fully participate, or other democratic processes by which the peoples can exercise their free will.

C. The enjoyment of individual rights, including:
    (a) Freedom of the individual and his ability to participate and to have a voice in his government,
    (b) Guarantee of basic rights, e.g., freedom of speech, press, assembly, religion and the right to a fair trial,
    (c) Universal adult suffrage, based on adequate educational opportunities,
    (d) Freedom of the individual to join political parties and of all the parties to participate freely in the political life of the territory.

D. The absence of any pressure or coercion on the population so that they may be in a position freely to express their views as to the national or international status which they may desire (attainment of independence, attainment of other systems of self-government in continuing association, or free association as an integral part of the metropolitan or other country).

E. Assurance that the views of the population will be respected.

F. Freedom of the peoples of Non-Self-Governing Territories, which have freely limited their sovereignty in favour of the metropolitan or other country, to change their status by democratic processes.

The Committee on Information from Non-Self-Governing Territories. Nowhere in the Charter is provision made for any machinery or any organ to deal with non-self-governing territories. In Chapter XI, administering states are required to transmit regularly to the Secretary-General information 'of a technical nature relating to economic, social and educational conditions in the territories for which they are respectively responsible. . . .'[5] But there is no mention of the use to be made of such information or of the functions, if any, to be performed by any organs other than the Secretariat with respect to it.

However, acting under the broad authority contained in Article 10 of the Charter, which permits it to discuss any questions or any matters within the scope of the Charter, the Assembly has proceeded to construct machinery for the purpose of extending its authority over the matters related to non-self-governing territories. In 1946 the Fourth (Trusteeship) Committee of the Assembly devoted considerable time to the problem and has been increasing its attention at each succeeding session. In the same year the Assembly established a sixteen member *ad hoc* committee (equally divided between administering and nonadministering states), now known as the Committee on Information from Non-Self-Governing Territories, to work on the question of non-self-governing territories.[6] Its terms of reference laid down in 1949 were

. . . to examine . . . the summaries and analyses of information transmitted under Article 73e on the economic, social and educational conditions in the Non-Self-Governing Territories, including any papers prepared by the specialized agencies and any reports or information on measures taken in pursuance of the resolutions adopted by the General Assembly concerning economic, social and educational conditions in the Non-Self-Governing Territories; . . . to submit to the . . . General Assembly . . . reports containing such procedural recommendations as it may deem fit and such substantive recommendations as it may deem desirable relating to functional fields but not with respect to individual Territories. . . .

The Committee is precluded from discussing the political progress of the territories and hence, concentrates upon economic, social, and educational conditions. It has been customary to devote a year to the study and reporting of each of these categories. A standard form for transmitting informa-

[5] The word 'regularly,' used in Article 73:e, has been interpreted to mean the annual transmission of reports.

[6] The original committee continued on a year-to-year basis until 1949 when its term was extended to 1952. It was given another three-year extension to expire in 1955 but was renewed again.

tion was adopted in 1947 and revised in 1951 to serve as a guide for the administering states. It is divided into four parts: general information; economic conditions; social conditions; and educational conditions. Included in the general category is a section on government and a description of the territorial and local governments and any 'significant events or projected developments . . . as would increase the participation of the local inhabitants in the government of the Territory.' The reporting of such political matters is purely optional and has been opposed by most of the administering states with the result that only a few of them, including the United States, transmit any information in this category.

The information contained in the annual reports is analyzed by the Secretariat and turned over to the Committee together with such additional information as that organ may possess. In its own report to the Assembly, the Committee has made use of the opportunity to recommend action upon a large number of matters in the three fields within its competence. The Assembly, in turn, has proceeded to adopt an increasing number of resolutions urging the adoption of measures by the administering states to facilitate progress in these fields. Particular emphasis has been placed upon advancement in educational facilities. Attention has also been directed to such questions as the indigenous standard of living, purchasing power of natives, the prevailing system of taxation in the territories, the status of agriculture and the methods used to increase production, and diversification in the economy of the territories. The specialized agencies have also been encouraged to work closely in assisting the non-self-governing peoples to improve their general status.

Conclusions. A Trusteeship System in Disguise? Clearly the provisions of Chapter XI are pioneering in that the colonial powers are obligated to abide by its objectives. Never before has the colonial system been subjected to the public scrutiny that has developed as a result of Chapter XI. Such a development has not met with general favor among the colonial authorities who have had to contend with a growing demand on the part of the anti-colonial bloc for an extension of United Nations supervision over the non-self-governing territories.

There is little doubt that the colonial system is on the defensive and the machinery so far in operation with respect to colonial territories represents an attempt to institute procedures of supervision and inspection similar to those of the trusteeship system. The discussions in the Fourth Committee and in the Assembly itself reveal the insistence of the nonadministering members to consider political as well as nonpolitical matters in the territories. In 1952, for example, the Assembly recommended that administering states voluntarily include in their annual reports 'details regarding the extent to which the right of peoples and nations to self-determination is exercised by the peoples of those Territories, and in particular regarding their political progress and the measures taken . . . to satisfy their political aspirations and to promote the progressive development of their free political institutions.' The Assembly also voted to place this resolution on the agenda of the Committee of Information in 1953. This move prompted Belgium, long an opponent of the Committee on the grounds that its authority goes beyond the provisions of the Charter, to announce that it would not longer participate in its work. The letter announcing this decision states the Belgian attitude, concurred in at least by Britain and France, toward the developing role of the United Nations in colonial matters as follows:

> On many occasions the Belgian delegation has pointed out the fundamental differences which the authors of the Charter intended to establish between the obligations under Chapter XI regarding Non-Self-Governing Territories and those under Chapters XII and XIII, which set up an International Trusteeship System for the administration and supervision of such territories as might be placed thereunder by subsequent individual agreements. It has hitherto shown its readiness to apply the provisions of Chapter XI in the most liberal spirit, substantially exceeding the requirements of a strict interpretation of the texts. It does not, however, intend to yield to the tendency of members of the United Nations which are, more or less openly, desirous of progressively assimilating the system of Non-Self-Governing Territories to the International Trusteeship System — nor has it any intention of permitting discriminatory attempts on Belgian sovereignty which are in no way authorized under this Charter.

The increasing tendency on the part of many members within the Assembly to regard that organ as competent to determine when an administering state should cease to submit information on a territory is but another aspect of the trend toward fuller supervision of the colonial system. In 1946 eight states reported information on seventy-four territories. Each year the administering states have reported on fewer territories and this has led to demands for closer scrutiny of just what constitutes a change in status for a territory. The Assembly was unwilling for several years to accept the claim of the Netherlands that Surinam and the Netherlands Antilles had been granted full self-government. When the Assembly in 1954 recommended the dispatch of a special mission to evaluate 'the opinion of the population as to the status or change in status which they desire,' it was simply perfecting its machinery of supervision and coming closer to the trusteeship system. To be sure, the agreement of the administering member would be necessary prior to the dispatch of such a mission but the pressure upon administering states to permit such visits would be very great.

The colonial system in many respects has been an evil thing but it has not been a wholly vicious institution of cruelty and exploitation by all colonial powers in each of their dependencies. Certain positive benefits have come to native peoples from their contacts with colonial overlords. At the same time, the administering states today should not place obstacles in the way of political, economic, and social progress in their remaining colonial territories. Neither should the impatience naturally centered in former colonial peoples result in a too hasty demise of the system of dependencies. Zafrulla Khan of Pakistan has stated before the Assembly that 'the fewer the number of what may even mistakenly be regarded as colonial prizes the smaller will be the temptation to make bids for winning them.' This is undoubtedly true and it is up to the colonial powers to respect their obligations under Chapter XI and eventually abandon a system that involves the domination of one people by another. Constructive criticism and helpful reminders of duties and obligations under the Charter can serve to hasten the end of colonialism. This should be the role of the Assembly. Unless the Charter is amended, the Assembly can do little more than this. Administering states are extremely sensitive to the criticism, much of it unreasonable and unwarranted, which has been directed at them in the Assembly. Such attacks will never lead them away from colonialism but will encourage an attitude of defiance and a policy of non-co-operation with the United Nations which would benefit none, least of all the peoples of the non-self-governing territories.

V

THE FUTURE

16

REGIONALISM

THE regional approach to the problem of world peace has a number of adherents who believe that a universal organization is too ambitious and cannot command the allegiance necessary to fulfill its objectives in a world still divided by national sovereignty. Some scholars and statesmen contend that an international organization built upon the narrower confines of a particular region delimited geographically, economically, or politically has a greater opportunity of securing peace and order in the particular area concerned than a global agency. Its underlying principle is not uniformity but some form of union which divergent peoples and social systems can recognize as concrete and to which they could attach their loyalty. Advantage can be taken of existing loyalties and there is no necessity for the development of allegiance to some new and broader institution. It may even be possible to utilize some existing machinery and expand it as the needs arise.

There is no general agreement upon an exact definition of the term 'regionalism' for international organization. Physical proximity of states is considered by some to be the essential element for a regional organization since it may be easier to develop a sense of community in a compact geographical area. At the same time, it is often difficult to determine any exact geographic confines of a region. Its delineation may depend upon the nature of the problem confronting the members. The North Atlantic Treaty Organization (NATO), with a membership representing at best only a very rough geographic area, seeks a joint military defense against possible aggression from communist sources. Although the nations of the Organization of American States (OAS) are all located within the Western Hemisphere, certain areas of South America remain closer geographically and culturally to Western Europe than to North America. Indeed, Canada, an important nation in the Americas, is not now and shows no inclination to become a member of OAS. However, the fact that all members of OAS are contained

within the Western Hemisphere and can call themselves Americans —
North, Central, or South — is an indication that cultural, social, and linguistic handicaps can be overcome by common objectives in a geographic
region of great extremes and divergencies. Neighboring states with common
backgrounds and objectives are most ideally suited as partners in a regional
arrangement since similar ideological and governmental institutions contribute tangibly to the successful regional structure.

Security and defense are primary objectives of many regional arrangements. Skeptical of the effectiveness of a world system and even distrustful
of its aims, nations appear willing on occasion to depend upon a more limited organization for joint protection against aggression. There is the hope
that punishment for aggression will be more certain on the part of such a
group. It appears simpler to prepare against all major avenues of attack
within the region and to secure firm collective measures designed to provide
effective economic and military sanctions whenever necessary. Defensive,
not offensive, measures characterize the regional agreement. Neither the
territory nor the rights of any member can be involved without the consent
of the entire membership.

The regionalist presents his case, confident that he is more the realist,
the practical politician viewing the world as it is and not susceptible to
visionary schemes. He argues that a smaller organization, restricted in a
geographical sense to states and peoples living in close proximity to each
other, can provide the machinery necessary for meeting common problems
more effectively than the global agency. States located at great distances
from each other cannot appreciate mutual problems so easily nor can they
act rapidly to counter some aggression occurring far from their own territory. If some security threat develops between neighbors, as is often the
case, states in the general area are most immediately concerned and are
most apt to be the ones to apply security measures. Certainly, it is argued,
there would be less delay and unwillingness to act decisively than in a universal organization. Community interest based upon centuries of familiarity
and tradition in a given area tends to sharpen the allegiance which is so
essential to the success of any organization. The regionalist, therefore, contends that within his type of organization, it is far easier for people to accept
the principle that an attack against one member must be considered an
attack upon all within the region. The League of Nations thus failed to
develop an effective response to a call for sanctions because the task set
was worldwide and not limited to regions where the need for acting swiftly
and adequately might have been understood more readily.

Various social, linguistic, religious, and cultural ties cannot exist so concretely in a world organization, according to regionalist theory. Many prob-

lems are essentially local and can best be studied and shared by those in the area who are obviously better equipped by knowledge and experience. The regionalist optimistically contends that the tendency to work out problems locally could contribute toward a lessening of nationalist pressures. This, in turn, would have a tendency to isolate danger spots and would eventually permit federations of regional groups to evolve into a world security system.

The universalist is equally certain of his ground. He contends that it is virtually impossible to determine regions suitable for any comprehensive system. How is one to determine who can qualify for membership in a regional system and who will be forbidden? He points to the fact that some nations located many hundreds or thousands of miles apart may have far more in common than those situated close together by geographical accident. When such regions do exist, disintegrating forces appear at once to destroy what should be a compact unit. In the Balkan area, for example, there are the most compelling economic and material arguments in favor of a union, while at the same time, racial, nationalistic, and political factors are so devisive that such a necessary grouping appears impossible. In any event, the vital problems of peace and security are worldwide and must be handled by a universal system. Sanctions, particularly economic, must be universal to have positive effect. Any conflict, no matter how local in origin, may have ramifications far exceeding those of a particular region.

One of the most serious charges against regionalism is that it encourages nations to limit their obligations and thereby leads to an encouragement of isolationism and neutrality regardless of international responsibilities. For those who disparage a balance of power system, regional systems take on the character of old-fashioned alliances which can lead only to intercontinental disputes and global wars. Regionalism thus becomes merely an excuse for containing traditional enemies, with major nations surrounding themselves with unwilling weaker states in clusters of military alliances deeply involved in the ancient game of power politics. Smaller states have no universal organization to which they can turn for protection from possible arbitrary intervention in their internal affairs by the predominant nation in their region. Needing peace and stability, which are denied them in their region, their only recourse is to solicit aid from some other regional system, in which case a local problem might be expanded into a serious worldwide dispute.

The universalist points out the grave dangers of overemphasizing religious and racial ties and establishing regional organizations on the basis of these factors. Should there be a strict Mohammedan association or even federation, it would be absurd to expect Mohammedans of Morocco to have closer economic ties with Mohammedans of India or Iran than with Spanish Catholics located a short distance across the Strait of Gibraltar.

It is unfortunate that frequently the arguments for and against regionalism become vehement and heated. There is much to be said for both sides and there is no need to abandon one completely for the sake of the other. It is quite true that the problem of peace and security is universal and is not restricted to a particular geographical area. A dispute that at first appears to be purely local in character may suddenly explode and be of concern to the peace of the world. Similarly, many problems of health, trade, and intellectual co-operation cannot be the concern solely of any specific region. From the standpoint of a common legal order, the law must apply to all states regardless of their association in regional groups. If for no other reason, a universal system is necessary to arbitrate, if not contain, disputes between regions.

Nevertheless, regionalism is useful as the demonstration of a desire to share the responsibility for meeting problems of peace and security by a group of states. No matter how local the organization, it is a step toward a stable and regulated world order. Many problems are sufficiently restricted in character that a regional association can best adjust them. Such local groups can relieve the universal system of many less significant details and thereby assist in the work of building an orderly world. Certainly regionalism, as a process of consolidation, integrates various units within itself and may be able to supplement a universal system in various ways. Above all else, the spirit of community interest which is so frequently the motivating element behind a regional system should be preserved. Both forms of international organization, each functioning in its proper sphere, should operate to lessen international tension.

REGIONALISM UNDER THE UNITED NATIONS CHARTER

The controversy between regionalists and universalists was fully aired at the San Francisco Conference of 1945. On several occasions it was feared that the sessions of the entire Conference would be endangered by the intransigence of both sides. The Covenant of the League of Nations, in Article 21, had made a provision for regionalism by stating that 'Nothing in this Covenant shall be deemed to affect the validity of international engagements such as treaties of arbitration or regional understandings like the Monroe Doctrine for securing the maintenance of peace.' Latin America, encouraged by the United States, was determined to secure at least as much recognition for the Pan-American movement as was provided in the League Covenant, particularly in view of the fact that a few weeks before San

Francisco there had been a revitalizing of the inter-American system at a conference in Mexico City.

Soviet Russia was anxious to secure the means within the Charter by which Soviet interests in Central and Eastern Europe could be isolated and protected. Also, the agreement creating the League of Arab States had been signed just prior to the San Francisco Conference. Then there were a number of bilateral treaties directed against possible future German and Japanese aggression which had been drawn up during the War. The sum total of such a rebirth of regionalist thinking was largely the product of a thinly disguised disappointment with the worldwide collective security of the League of Nations and a determination to provide some protection against the possibility of a similar breakdown of a future global system. It became obvious as soon as the Conference in San Francisco got under way that there had to be a formula devised whereby there could be some legal compatibility between regional and global organization while granting the latter final authority to determine the application of enforcement measures.

A compromise was finally worked out and embodied primarily in Articles 52 and 53 of the Charter. Nowhere is there a definition of regionalism but Article 52 provides some general rules by stating that 'Nothing in the present Charter precludes the existence of regional arrangements or agencies for dealing with such matters relating to the maintenance of international peace and security as are appropriate for regional action, provided that such arrangements or agencies and their activities are consistent with the Purposes and Principles of the United Nations.' Regional groups are encouraged to arrive at 'pacific settlement of disputes . . . before referring them to the Security Council,' and (Art. 53) 'the Security Council shall, where appropriate, utilize such regional arrangements or agencies for enforcement action under its authority.' Further encouragement to local action is found in an earlier Charter provision (Art. 51) which affirms that 'Nothing in the present Charter shall impair the inherent right of individual or collective self-defense if an armed attack occurs against a Member of the United Nations, until the Security Council has taken the measures necessary to maintain international peace and security.'

Certain safeguards are contained in these and other articles in an effort to prevent regional arrangements from challenging the basic Charter principle of universal collective security. It was foreseen that local agreements might degenerate into simple aggressive alliances incompatible with the aims and policies of the contemplated world organization. Thus, enforcement measures by regional organizations cannot be undertaken without the approval of the Security Council, except in certain limited cases. Any action under regional agreements must conform to the aims and policies of the

Charter. Should there be any conflict in the obligations under the Charter and those in any other compact, those of the Charter prevail. Any action in the nature of self-defense must be reported at once to the Security Council and does not in any way limit the Security Council's freedom of action to undertake whatever measures it believes necessary. Every regional agreement must be registered with the Secretariat of the United Nations and published by it. To the Security Council is reserved the right to investigate any dispute, no matter what regional arangements exist and regardless of how local in character a dispute appears to be. Finally, Article 54 of the Charter requires that 'The Security Council shall at all times be kept fully informed of activities undertaken or in contemplation under regional arrangement, or by regional agencies for the maintenance of international peace and security.' The framers of the Charter realistically faced the problem and made universalism and regionalism as compatible as possible in these provisions.

THE ORGANIZATION OF AMERICAN STATES (OAS)

While the formal structure of the Organization of American States dates from 1948, its origins can be traced back to 1826 when Simon Bolívar sought the establishment of a Latin American League of Nations at a conference in Panama. The voluntary movement for harmony and co-operation among the peoples in the Western Hemisphere has been the product of a community of interest based upon a sense of geographical propinquity, similar historical backgrounds in the breakup of colonialism by revolution, and a spirit of dissociation from old-world struggles. Pan-Americanism was spurred primarily by Latin Americans with varying degrees of success until 1889 when, on the initiative of United States Secretary of State James Blaine, the first true Conference of American States convened in Washington, D.C. The most noteworthy achievement of the Conference was the creation of a permanent agency designed to encourage friendship and co-operation within the Western Hemisphere, the Bureau of American Republics. Its name was changed in 1910 to the Pan-American Union and it has been the unifying factor in developing the best example of an effective regional system now in existence.

Foundation and Purposes. Pan-Americanism concerned itself primarily with nonpolitical fields until World War II. The spread of the War in Europe and the attack on Pearl Harbor soon proved that a threat to the security of the Americas could not be met by the loose-knit system of *ad hoc* conferences, resolutions, and good intentions. The war years saw the United States take the lead in creating the Inter-American Financial and Economic Advisory Committee, the Inter-American Defense Board, the Inter-American Emergency Advisory Committee for Political Defense and similar agencies in other specialized fields. The spirit of collaboration engendered by the War and the vital need for effective security arrangements made inevitable a thorough overhaul of the entire Inter-American system. As a result, at the Mexico City Conference on Problems of War and Peace early in 1945, the American states charged the Governing Board of the Pan-American Union with the preparation of 'a draft charter for the improvement and strengthening of the Pan-American system.' It was also decided that 'for the purpose of meeting threats or acts of aggression against any American Republic following the establishment of peace,' the American states should 'consider the conclusion . . . of a treaty.'

The Inter-American Treaty of Reciprocal Assistance of 1947 was the first result of the decisions made in 1945 in Mexico City. Commonly referred to as the Rio Pact, it provides for a system of collective security whereby an act of aggression committed within the Western Hemisphere will be acted upon jointly by all the American Republics. The Ninth International Conference of American States meeting at Bogotá, Colombia, in 1948, completed the long-needed revision of the Inter-American system by drawing up for the first time a formal charter defining the objectives and organization of what is now the Organization of American States. The Charter and the Rio Pact are closely linked for security purposes, as will be seen later.

The Charter of OAS carefully notes in Article 1 that 'within the United Nations, the Organization of American States is a regional agency.' A five-fold list of essential purposes of OAS is proclaimed as follows: 'to strengthen the peace and security of the hemisphere; to prevent possible causes of difficulties and to ensure the pacific settlement of disputes that may arise among the Member States; to provide for common action on the part of those States in the event of aggression; to seek the solution of political, juridical and economic problems that may arise among them; and, to promote, by cooperative action, their economic, social and cultural development.' The principles inherent in the development of the Pan-American movement — territorial integrity, nonintervention, law instead of force, equality — are mentioned frequently.

Organization. Geography limits membership to American states willing to ratify the Charter. No restrictions are placed upon the admittance of Canada to OAS but this member of the British Commonwealth has preferred to remain outside the Inter-American system while supporting its aims and principles. Membership in OAS, as is true of the United Nations, is based upon equal and sovereign representation and in no way limits the full freedom of action of any nation. Policy decisions are the result of the

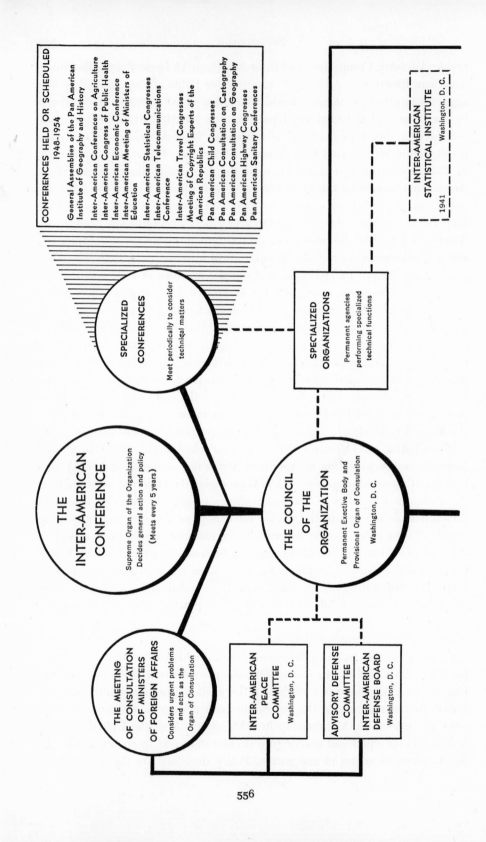

CONFERENCES HELD OR SCHEDULED
1948-1954

General Assemblies of the Pan American
Institute of Geography and History

Inter-American Conferences on Agriculture
Inter-American Congress of Public Health
Inter-American Economic Conference
Inter-American Meeting of Ministers of
Education

Inter-American Statistical Congresses
Inter-American Telecommunications
Conference

Inter-American Travel Congresses
Meeting of Copyright Experts of the
American Republics

Pan American Child Congresses
Pan American Consultation on Cartography
Pan American Consultation on Geography
Pan American Highway Congresses
Pan American Sanitary Conferences

**INTER-AMERICAN
STATISTICAL INSTITUTE**

1941   Washington, D. C.

**SPECIALIZED
CONFERENCES**

Meet periodically to consider
technical matters

**SPECIALIZED
ORGANIZATIONS**

Permanent agencies
performing specialized
technical functions

**THE
INTER-AMERICAN
CONFERENCE**

Supreme Organ of the Organization
Decides general action and policy
(Meets every 5 years)

**THE COUNCIL
OF THE
ORGANIZATION**

Permanent Exective Body and
Provisional Organ of Consulation
Washington, D. C.

**THE MEETING
OF CONSULTATION
OF MINISTERS
OF FOREIGN AFFAIRS**

Considers urgent problems
and acts as the
Organ of Consultation

**INTER-AMERICAN
PEACE
COMMITTEE**

Washington, D. C.

**ADVISORY DEFENSE
COMMITTEE**
**INTER-AMERICAN
DEFENSE BOARD**

Washington, D. C.

556

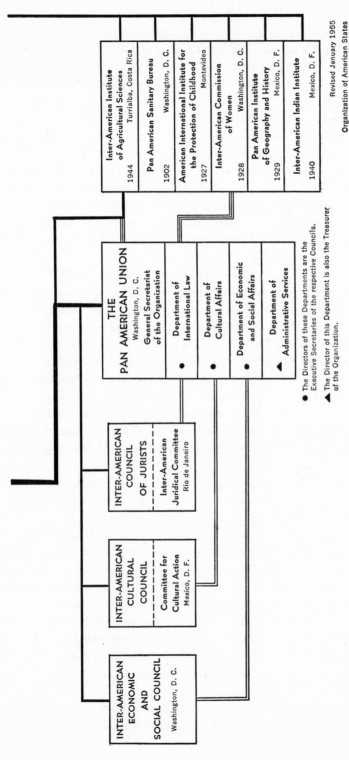

ORGANIZATION OF AMERICAN STATES

INTER-AMERICAN ECONOMIC AND SOCIAL COUNCIL
Washington, D. C.

INTER-AMERICAN CULTURAL COUNCIL
Committee for Cultural Action
Mexico, D. F.

INTER-AMERICAN COUNCIL OF JURISTS
Inter-American Juridical Committee
Rio de Janeiro

THE PAN AMERICAN UNION
Washington, D. C.
General Secretariat of the Organization

- Department of International Law
- Department of Cultural Affairs
- Department of Economic and Social Affairs
▲ Department of Administrative Services

● The Directors of these Departments are the Executive Secretaries of the respective Councils.

▲ The Director of this Department is also the Treasurer of the Organization.

Inter-American Institute of Agricultural Sciences   1944   Turrialba, Costa Rica

Pan American Sanitary Bureau   1902   Washington, D. C.

American International Institute for the Protection of Childhood   1927   Montevideo

Inter-American Commission of Women   1928   Washington, D. C.

Pan American Institute of Geography and History   1929   Mexico, D. F.

Inter-American Indian Institute   1940   Mexico, D. F.

Revised January 1955
Organization of American States

557

voluntary co-operation characteristic of all functioning international bodies.

The organs of OAS are listed by the Charter as follows:

1. The Inter-American Conference
2. The Meeting of Consultation of Ministers of Foreign Affairs
3. The Council
4. The Pan-American Union
5. The Specialized Conferences
6. The Specialized Organizations.

Meeting every five years is the Inter-American Conference, the supreme organ of OAS. Each member is represented and is entitled to one vote. All major policy decisions are determined by the Conference which also 'has the authority to consider any matter relating to friendly relations among the American States.' A special Conference may be called at the request of a two-thirds vote of the members.

To the Meeting of Consultation of Ministers of Foreign Affairs is assigned the task of considering 'problems of an urgent nature and of common interest to the American States.' It is the agency designed to activate security measures for the protection of the Americas. Any member may request that a Meeting of Consultation be held. Such a request is directed to the Council which decides by majority vote whether such a meeting should be called. The Meeting of Consultation is advised on military matters by an Advisory Defense Committee composed of high military representatives of each Foreign Minister. The Committee is not in permanent session, meeting only when assigned a technical study by the Conference or Meeting of Consultation or in the event that 'matters relating to defense against aggression' arise.

The central, co-ordinating agency of OAS is the Council, composed of one representative from each member state particularly selected for the purpose. Its present headquarters are in Washington, D.C., where it meets twice a month except for the months of July, August, and September. The Council can act provisionally, in an attempt to settle or at least contain a dispute, until a Meeting of Consultation convenes. However, it is not comparable to the Security Council of the United Nations. Its restricted responsibilities and broader, equal membership alone place it in an entirely different position. Assisting the Council in its various technical ventures within the inter-American system are three subsidiary organs: the Inter-American Economic and Social Council, the Inter-American Council of Jurists, and the Inter-American Cultural Council. They are composed of representatives of all members of the Organization.

The Inter-American Economic and Social Council meets permanently at the Pan-American Union in Washington, D.C. It has for its principal purpose the promotion of the economic and social welfare of the American nations 'through effective cooperation for the better utilization of their natural resources, the development of their agriculture and industry and the raising of the standards of living of their peoples.' Acting as the co-ordinating agency for all official inter-American activities of an economic and social nature, it undertakes studies on its own initiative or at the request of any member, assembles and prepares reports on economic and social matters, and suggests and plans for the holding of specialized conferences.

The other two technical councils (Jurists, Cultural) ordinarily meet every two years and in the interval, permanent committees carry out preparatory work. The Inter-American Juridical Committee, originally created in 1939, as the Inter-American Neutrality Committee, now serves as the Permanent Committee of the Council of Jurists with headquarters in Rio de Janiero. The Committee is composed of jurists from the nine countries selected by the Inter-American Conference. The Inter-American Council of Jurists serves as an advisory body on juridical matters, promotes the development and codification of international law, and studies the possibility of attaining 'uniformity in the legislation of the various American countries, insofar as it may appear desirable.'

The Committee for Cultural Action serves as the Permanent Committee of the Inter-American Cultural Council, with headquarters in Mexico City. The Council promotes co-operation among the American nations 'in the fields of education, science and culture by means of the exchange of materials for research and study as well as the exchange of teachers, students, and specialists and seeks to protect, preserve and increase the cultural heritage of the continent.'

The secretariat of OAS is the Pan-American Union, headed by a Secretary-General elected for a ten-year term by the Council. Until 1948, the Union had been the only co-ordinating agency for the many facets of inter-American co-operation. Its functions have now been greatly expanded under the Charter of OAS, and its primary mission is to promote, through its technical and information divisions and under the direction of the Council, economic, social, juridical, and cultural relations among the members of the organization. The various divisions functioning at the headquarters of the Union are grouped into the following four departments: International Law, Economic and Social Affairs, Cultural Affairs, and Administrative Services. The directors of the first three departments are also the executive secretaries of the three technical councils just described.

For years one of the characteristics of inter-American co-operation has been the holding of technical conferences under the sponsorship of one or more countries or specialized organizations in the Western Hemisphere.

These conferences often duplicated one another and there was a singular lack of integration among them. The Charter attempts to regularize these activities and permit all American states to participate in their programs under the leadership of OAS. Conferences are now called by some body of the Organization or one of the autonomous agencies brought into relationship with OAS as a 'specialized organization.' The relations between these organizations and OAS itself are determined in agreements concluded with them by the OAS Council and are similar to the arrangements between the United Nations and the specialized agencies which have been studied earlier.

Collective Action. The Charter of OAS provides a positive organizational basis for collective action against aggression. Together with the Rio Pact of 1947 and the American Treaty of Pacific Settlement completed at Bogotá in 1948, the Charter offers a means whereby the application of force as a final resort to counter aggression stands alongside exhaustive measures for pacific settlement of conflicts. The most significant security statement in the Charter is the principle of 'all for one and one for all' contained in Article 24 as follows:

> Every act of aggression by a state against the territorial integrity or the inviolability of the territory or against the sovereignty or political independence of an American State shall be considered an act of aggression against the other American States.

Article 25 clearly calls for collective action in these words:

> If the inviolability or the integrity of the territory or the sovereignty or political independence of an American State should be affected by an armed attack or by an act of aggression that is not an armed attack, or by an extra-continental conflict, or by a conflict between two or more American States, or by any other fact or situation that might endanger the peace of America, the American States, in furtherance of the principles of continental solidarity or collective self-defense, shall apply the measures and procedures established in the special treaties on the subject.

The 'special' treaty for security purposes mentioned in Article 25 is, of course, the Rio Pact, which is thereby closely linked with the Charter.

In the event of a conflict between two or more American States, the Charter again is co-ordinated with the Rio Pact, which provides that the Meeting of Consultation of Foreign Ministers 'call upon the contending States to suspend hostilities and restore matters to the *status quo ante bellum.*' The Foreign Ministers may take any 'other necessary measures to reestablish and maintain inter-American peace and security and for the solution of the conflict by peaceful means.' Regardless of whether the aggression has been committed by an American state, the Meeting of Consultation, through Article 8 of the Rio Pact, is provided with a list of measures, any of which it or an individual state may adopt in opposition to an aggressor.

Inherent in every reference to any threat to security is dependence upon peaceful settlement. This applies particularly to intracontinental situations. The Charter requires that 'all international disputes that may arise between American States' must be submitted to the following peaceful procedures: 'direct negotiation, good offices, mediation, investigation and conciliation, judicial settlement, arbitration, and those which the parties to the dispute may especially agree upon at any time.' These provisions are reinforced by the American Treaty on Pacific Settlement concluded at Bogotá in 1948 which incorporates a more rigid system of pacific settlement including compulsory judicial or arbitral settlement.[1]

The combined effects of these provisions have greatly increased the opportunities for solving intra-American disputes. Several controversies have actually been negotiated satisfactorily: Costa Rica v. Nicaragua (1948); Haiti v. the Dominican Republic (1949); the 'Caribbean Conspiracies' involving Haiti, the Dominican Republic, Cuba and Guatemala (1950); and Costa Rica v. Nicaragua (1954-55). In each case, there was the charge by one government that a rival state had encouraged revolutionary activities. The Council of OAS received the complaints in each instance, appointed investigatory committees and on the basis of their reports, handed down its conclusions and recommendations which were accepted by all parties concerned. The Security Council of the United Nations was informed in each instance by the Council and kept abreast of all developments but at no time was it necessary for it to become involved. While these disputes were of a relatively minor nature, the machinery for pacific settlement of OAS functioned smoothly and gives promise for the future.

There has been one Meeting of Consultation of the Ministers of Foreign Affairs since 1948. It was held in Washington, D.C., in the spring of 1951, at the request of the United States, for a discussion of the 'aggressive policy of international Communism . . .' A total of twenty-seven resolutions were approved, concerned primarily with measures designed to increase the internal security of American Republics, military and economic collaboration, and support of the United Nations. All members were present and all but one were represented by their Foreign Ministers.

At the Tenth Inter-American Conference meeting at Caracas, Venezuela, in March, 1954, the United States raised the question of communism in Guatemala. The Conference condemned communist intervention in the

---

[1] This treaty, however, is not operative since it has not received the required minimum number of ratifications.

Americas and expressed 'the determination of the American States to take the necessary measures to protect their political independence against the intervention of international communism, acting in the interests of an alien despotism.' It also recommended that each of the American governments give special attention to the following steps 'for the purpose of counteracting the subversive activities of the international communist movement' within their respective jurisdictions:

> 1. Measures to require disclosure of the identity, activities, and sources of funds, of those who are spreading propaganda of the international communist movement or who travel in the interests of that movement, and of those who act as its agents or in its behalf;
> 2. The exchange of information among governments to assist in fulfilling the purpose of the resolutions adopted by the Inter-American Conferences and Meetings of Ministers of Foreign Affairs regarding international communism.

On June 28, 1954, the representative of the United States on the Council of OAS requested that a meeting of the Organ of Consultation be convened on July 7, 1954, to investigate an insurrection which had broken out in Guatemala. The Council agreed to this request but the meeting was postponed indefinitely due to the subsequent ousting of the pro-communist Guatemalan government and the establishment of a new provisional government by Castillo Armas on July 1. As was seen earlier, the matter had previously come to the Security Council.[2]

The Guatemalan case is a good example of the complexity of interaction between regional and universal international organizations. The vital issue concerns the right of United Nations members to demand action by that organization in a case of aggression when there is the alternative of referring the question to a regional body. Mr. Lodge of the United States believed that OAS should have precedence and based his argument on Article 33 and Chapter VIII of the Charter. It is possible that the United States preferred inaction by the United Nations and was actually not greatly concerned with the legal aspects of the authority of OAS, since its objective in Guatemala was the overthrow of the existing government. Guatemala, on the other hand, probably feared the great influence of the United States in OAS and therefore insisted upon the primacy of the United Nations. This was the view of the Soviet Union and was so stated on several occasions. Consequently, both of these nations based their position upon Articles 24, 34, 35, and 39 of the Charter.

These opposite views were not resolved in the Council deliberations but there may very well have been established the precedent whereby some

---

[2] See above, Chapter 7.

other regional system could justify preventing action by the United Nations until events had progressed to the satisfaction of the major partner in that system.[3] Mr. Lodge made very clear the position of the United States which held that unless the jurisdiction of OAS was certified, 'then the United Nations will have destroyed itself in 1954 and it would have been destroyed stillborn in 1945' had not the impasse at San Francisco over regionalism been resolved in favor of such systems by the inclusion of Articles 51 and 52 in the Charter. The challenge to the primacy of the United Nations was unmistakable in spite of the inconclusive ending of the matter.

THE LEAGUE OF ARAB STATES

Plans and hopes for some positive form of union among the troubled remnants of the Ottoman Empire have been continually advanced since World War I. The British had long championed such an association. But progress toward it did not come until the Second World War. The first Arab move was taken by Iraq, whose Prime Minister suggested a union among the Arab-Asian countries exclusive of the countries of the Arabian peninsula and Egypt. This proposal failed because of Egyptian opposition, but the initiative was then taken by Egypt and after nearly two years of preparation an Arab Conference met in Alexandria. It was presided over by Nahas Pasha, Prime Minister of Egypt, and attended by delegates from Iraq, Lebanon, Transjordan (now Jordan), Saudi Arabia, Syria, and Yemen. While there existed much suspicion and distrust among the participants, British pressure finally succeeded in bringing about an agreement for some type of Arab association. The Conference adopted the Protocol of Alexandria which laid the basis for the Arab League. A pact establishing the League was signed on March 22, 1945, in Cairo, with the seven signatories of the Alexandria Protocol as members. By 1958 the membership had grown to nine with the addition of Libya and the Sudan.

Purposes and Organization. The goal of the League, according to the Pact, 'is to draw closer the relations between member States and co-ordinate their political activities with the aim of realizing a close collaboration between them, to safeguard their independence and sovereignty,' and to consider in a general way the affairs and interests of the Arab countries. Close co-operation is envisaged in economic, financial, social, and cultural matters, as well as in the development of communications. The League is clearly a loose-knit organization of sovereign states, with the emphasis placed on voluntary co-operation and consultation. Any independent Arab state is eligible for membership.

[3] Houston, John A., *Latin America in the United Nations*, New York, 1956, p. 112.

The primary organ is the Majlis or Council, composed of a representative from each member and meeting twice a year. Unanimous decisions of the Council are binding on all members while those reached by a majority vote 'shall bind only those that accept them.' In case of aggression or a threat of aggression against a member of the League, 'the attacked or threatened with attack may request an immediate meeting of the Council,' at which time that body is to determine the measures necessary to repel aggression. Decision on such measures must be reached by a unanimous vote. In addition to these relatively weak provisions for collective security, the Council has certain mediative powers. Decisions relating to mediation or arbitration are reached by a majority vote. The character of sanctions which might be applied is not spelled out except for expulsion from the League for failure to abide by its decisions.

Seven permanent committees operate under the authority of the Council to assist in the preparation of various political, economic, cultural, social, and health matters. Each member is represented on the committees by permanent delegates who meet at least once a year. The headquarters of the League is in Cairo where the League Secretariat is located. It consists of a Secretary-General, three Assistant Secretaries, and a permanent staff of about seventy-five members. Work is apportioned among the following departments: Political, Economic, Legal, Cultural, Press and Publicity, Administrative and Financial, Social, and Palestine Affairs. Attached to the Secretariat is an Institute of Arab Studies, an Institute of Arab Manuscripts, a Refugee Boycott Office, and Anti-Narcotics Office. Only on rare occasions are the resolutions, recommendations, and minutes of the Council and the committees made public.

In an attempt to strengthen Arab security and prevent some of the mistakes committed in the Arab-Israeli War of 1948–49, a Treaty of Joint Defense and Economic Co-operation was concluded on June 17, 1950. Patterned after the North Atlantic Treaty, this instrument has established an automatic collective security system which declares that 'an act of armed aggression made against any of the contracting states is to be considered as an act against them all.' Each member is obligated to come to the assistance of the attacked state and adopt all available measures, including armed force, to repel the aggression. The Treaty also has established a Joint Defense Council, composed of Foreign and Defense Ministers, a military organization functioning under a Commander-in-Chief, a Permanent Military Commission representing the general staffs of the members' armed forces, and an Economic Council consisting of the ministers of economic affairs of the members. Significantly, Article 10 of the Treaty provides that the contracting states conclude no international agreements which may be contradictory to its provisions nor may they act in their international relations in a way contrary to its aims.

Activities of the League. With a relatively insecure organization and only partial representation of the Arab world, the League has had to face a series of political crises. Factionalism has been prevalent, particularly between Egypt and Jordan in the earlier years and more recently between Egypt and Iraq. Egypt has attempted to employ the League to obtain the advancement of national objectives and prevent the expansion of Jordanian authority. Disagreement among the members destroyed what might have been a strong, common military venture against Israel in 1948. Joint efforts to gain independence for colonial areas in the Middle East have been largely successful and there is a close bond between the members in opposing the new state of Israel. Beyond this, however, factionalism weakens the political objectives of the League. In November, 1955, for example, Iraq signed the British-sponsored Baghdad Pact which was designed to establish a northern zone of defense in the Middle East against communism.[4] The other members of the League bitterly oppose the Pact, however, and have denounced Iraq. Jordan, under British pressure, first appeared to be ready to join but after three government upheavals in less than a month, the Jordanese, in January, 1956, turned against their British supporters. Serious rioting was stirred up by violent anti-Israeli elements who identified the Pact with the West and the West with Israel.

More success has been recorded by the League in the welfare field. While specific achievements are few in economic matters, a groundwork has been established for future co-operation. Lebanon has been the most active member in working toward closer economic ties in the Arab world. A start has been made toward the lowering of trade and tariff barriers, and Postal and Telecommunication Unions have been established. Some steps toward social and legal advancement have been taken on such questions as social welfare in rural areas, agreements on extradition, execution of judgments and other features of inter-Arab private law.

Most successful has been the work in the cultural field. Highly conscious of a rich common heritage, the members of the League adopted a Cultural Treaty in 1945 outlining the aims of inter-Arab cultural co-operation. One goal is the standardization of educational systems through such measures as teacher exchange and uniform educational syllabi and certificates. Another is the enrichment of Arab culture through translations of foreign works and the establishment of scientific and literary research institutes. A number of conferences have been held to implement these and other objectives of cultural co-operation.

[4] For more details on the Baghdad Pact, see below, pp. 567–8.

In many respects, however, the League has fallen short of its expectations and has not greatly increased the unity of the Arab world. The League has been responsible for developing a strong Arab bloc in the United Nations with more influence for the Arab countries than would otherwise have been the case. It does represent a symbol to the Arab peoples of the first nonwestern international organization of the Middle East. But beyond this and some nonpolitical accomplishments, it has little to show for over a decade of activity. Above all, it never has expressed, and still does not express, the political realities of the Arab world.

In a very real sense, the dream of Arab unity may well come not from the Arab League but from Gamal Abdel Nasser and the United Arab Republic. This new political entity came into being in February, 1958 and represented a merger of Egypt and Syria into one government with Nasser as President. Yemen later joined the UAR on a federated basis which permitted the ruling monarch of that small country, Imam Ahmed, to retain his throne and a considerable measure of autonomy. Egypt and Syria were to have a single parliament in Cairo, joint armed forces, and, eventually, a unified economy.

The principal unifying force in the Arab world has been hostility toward Israel. Otherwise, the occasionally arbitrary borders of some states and age-old rivalries and territorial ambitions tend to disrupt Arab unity. In this situation, two main nuclei of power have been developing in the Middle East since the British and French withdrawal after World War II created a power vacuum. Cairo has been the locus of one. Colonel Nasser made no secret of the fact that he has harbored pan-Arabic aspirations as soon as he came to power in Egypt in 1954. Republican Syria, at odds with the neighboring kingdoms of Jordan and Iraq, has gravitated toward the Egyptian orbit.

The other power grouping has been a shifting alignment of Middle East states that feared Nassar's ambitions. The main participants in the counter-bloc have been Iraq, Jordan and Saudi Arabia. All three monarchies are linked by family ties, and the rulers of Iraq and Jordan have a common Hashemite ancestry. They represent the Arab pashas as opposed to the more popular appeal of Nasser's revolutionary movement.

As a reflection of this situation, shortly after the consummation of the UAR, Iraq and Jordan announced a new union to be called the Arab Federation. The kings of both countries were to retain their thrones and sovereignty in their own nations. Faisal of Iraq was to serve as chief of the federal state but the Cabinet was expected to split equally between Iraqis and Jordanians and would hold its sessions half the year in Iraq and the other half in Jordan.

It is obvious that many questions concerning these political developments remained unanswered. There was the problem, for example, as to how Yemen's absolute monarchy could be brought into a republic headed by Nasser. With respect to the Iraq-Jordan merger, the main questions center on the Baghdad Pact. The federation agreement provided that neither country was committed by treaties signed by the other prior to federation. Thus the Iraq-Jordan union did not bring Jordan into the Baghdad Pact but presumably left Iraq free to remain a member. But it was not at all clear how one half of a country that was supposed to have a unified economy, army, and foreign policy could stay committed to a treaty while the other half was not.

Furthermore, there was the question of which way Saudi Arabia would turn, particularly with the eclipse of King Saud and the emergence of Crown Prince Faisal in March, 1958. Finally, despite personal differences between individual leaders, there was always the possibility that the Arab Federation might ultimately merge with the United Arab Republic.

THE BAGHDAD PACT COUNTRIES

In 1955, Iran, Iraq, Pakistan, Turkey, and the United Kingdom joined in signing the Baghdad Pact designed to promote a northern zone of defense against the spread of communism into the Middle East. Meeting together for the first time in November, 1955, representatives of these countries formed a political, military, and economic organization, known as the Council of the Baghdad Pact, with permanent deputies and a secretariat in Baghdad. The policy-making body is the Ministerial Council, to which are attached ten permanent military, economic, political, social, and technical committees. There is no joint military command but the permanent military committee consists of the chiefs-of-staff of the member countries. Emphasis is placed on the fact that the organization is purely defensive in nature and that its functions are to be primarily ideological and economic.

Agreement has been reached on a plan for a combined effort to combat subversion in member countries in which the information and resources of the members will be pooled in a special security agency. Co-operative programs have been considered for the joint mobilization of military forces in case an emergency should arise.

The West hoped that the Pact would serve not only as an anti-communist bulwark but also might draw other Arab states besides Iraq into its orbit. However, as a barrier to Soviet penetration, the Pact has proved ineffective and even less successful as a power magnet for the other Arab states. Communist influence in Syria and Egypt had become a fact by 1958. The building of the United Arab Republic and the Arab Federation indicated clearly that the Arab world was in the process of working out other alignments directed at unity and were ignoring the possibility of joining the Baghdad Pact. Furthermore, many Arabs claim the Pact was set up to keep the Arabs disunited and thereby at the mercy of the British.

THE UNIFICATION OF WESTERN EUROPE

The hope for some type of integrated Europe has been expressed for centuries. Some advocates stressed political unification, as did Aristide Briand, the French Foreign Minister, when he suggested a plan for a European federal union in 1930. During the Second World War, much attention was focused upon a number of proposals for international organization. Among the numerous expressions of support for Western European union were those of Winston Churchill and Field Marshall Jan Smuts. The creation of the United Nations in 1945 overshadowed prospects of European regionalism until serious postwar problems lent encouragement to those who believed that at least partial solutions could be obtained by various types of integration. The emerging forms of European postwar regionalism have followed broad economic, military, and political lines.

Economic Union. Three specific experiments have been undertaken in the field of economic co-operation. These are Benelux, the Organization for European Economic Co-operation, the European Coal and Steel Community. In 1958, a fourth began to function, namely, the Common Market or European Economic Community.

Belgium, the Netherlands and Luxembourg gave the first real substance to earlier theoretical plans for economic co-operation when they signed a customs convention on September 5, 1944. Known as 'Benelux' and designed to create a common tariff, the original agreement envisaged full economic union between the three countries. Considerable interest has been focused on this experiment, since many have taken the position that if the Benelux idea failed, there would be little hope for economic integration on a larger scale in Europe. While there is something to be said for this point of view, it should be remembered that the problems facing the Benelux countries have been somewhat unusual. Furthermore, Benelux is an illustration of only one possible form of economic unification while the Coal and Steel Community, less comprehensive in nature, is another type of integration, and the problems encountered in one are not necessarily found in the other.

The 1944 convention entered into effect on January 1, 1948. The target date of January 1, 1950, for the beginning of economic union has been postponed repeatedly since the obstacles encountered have been far greater than originally expected. Difficulties have been encountered, for example, with the balance of payments problem. It was believed that the Belgian and Dutch economies would be in virtually the same condition when the convention entered into force as when it was first negotiated. However, the Nazi occupation of the Netherlands lasted about eight months longer than that of Belgium, giving the latter a head start toward recovery which the Netherlands has had to make up. While Belgium was able to permit more freedom in her economy, the much poorer Dutch have been forced to engage in an austerity program involving such policies as soft currency, low wages and prices, and government subsidies, all of which were directly opposite to those adopted in Belgium. In addition, instead of their economies being complementary — an essential condition favoring economic union — Belgian and Dutch economic development has tended to be more and more competitive.

In spite of these and other difficulties, sincere efforts have been made to consummate economic union; progress has been made in developing an effective tariff union; and the organization provided for by the 1944 convention, modified by later decisions, has come into being. It includes (1) the Conference of Cabinet Ministers; (2) the Council for Economic Union; (3) the Administrative Council on Customs duties; (4) the Administrative Council, which 'has the function of insuring the coordination of measures in respect to relationships established with third countries'; and (5) the General Secretariat, with headquarters in Brussels. The continuing difficulties associated with forging an economic union have led to the belief that these obstacles can be overcome only within a wider framework of economic union embracing the countries participating in the European Coal and Steel Community. This is especially true with regard to the problem of the free convertibility of the several Benelux currencies. That may well depend upon greater economic integration with at least France and Western Germany. Progress toward this goal will be studied later in this chapter in the section devoted to the Coal and Steel Community.

The Marshall Plan, through which the United States assisted in speeding the economic recovery of Europe, was the direct cause of a much broader attempt to bring about a measure of European economic co-operation. When first stating his proposal at Harvard University on June 5, 1947, Secretary of State George C. Marshall emphasized that there must be a joint European effort to hasten economic recovery. Before the United States could offer assistance, 'there must be some agreement among the countries of Europe as to the requirements of the situation and the part these countries themselves will take.' This was necessary, he declared, 'in order to give proper effect to whatever action might be undertaken' by the United States.

No European nation should be excluded from this offer, he said, which meant that the Soviet world could participate.

Shortly thereafter, the British and French Foreign Ministers were joined by Mr. Molotov in Paris to discuss the possibility of creating a joint program. Molotov stayed but a few days, however, indicating his opposition to any scheme which contemplated a unified effort. Soon the Soviet press attacked the idea as 'President Truman's plan for political pressure with dollars . . . , a program of interference in the internal affairs of other states.' France and Britain went ahead, nevertheless, and on July 12, 1947, sixteen nations met in Paris to plan for the drafting of a report for submission to the United States. Before adjourning, the conference formed a sixteen-member Committee of European Economic Co-operation (CEEC) to proceed with the drafting.

By September 22, 1947, the Report of CEEC was completed. It presented a recovery program for the participating countries, including Western Germany, aimed at achieving a condition of European self-support by 1951. Among other things, the Report analyzed the maladjustments resulting from the War and examined the extent to which these countries could help themselves and each other in a combined effort to arrive at a lasting solution for Europe's economic problems. The recovery program outlined was based on these major points: a strong production effort by each country; creation of internal financial stability; maximum co-operation between the participants; and assistance from the United States in the form of food, fuel, raw materials, capital, and equipment, totaling $19 billion over a four-year period. The Report was a truly remarkable document in many respects, chief of which was the ability of sixteen nations (Austria, Belgium, Britain, Denmark, France, Greece, Iceland, Ireland, Italy, Luxembourg, the Netherlands, Norway, Portugal, Sweden, Switzerland, and Turkey) of diverse customs and histories to meet and, in the space of approximately two months, produce such a plan.[5] All agreed to co-operate on tariff reduction, to remove barriers to the free flow of trade, and to reduce obstacles to the movement of peoples.

Following a careful analysis of the CEEC Report in the United States, in April, 1948, Congress adopted the Foreign Assistance Act of 1948 which made available for the first year $4,300,000,000 in grants and another billion in loans for European recovery. The President recommended that the program should be supported, over a four-year period, by a total allocation of $17 billion.

---

[5] In addition to the Soviet Union, the following countries were invited to participate but declined: Albania, Bulgaria, Czechoslovakia, Finland, Hungary, Poland, Rumania, and Yugoslavia.

Soon after the adoption of the Foreign Assistance Act of 1948, the CEEC countries signed a Convention for European Economic Co-operation on April 16, 1948, which established the machinery necessary to implement the aims of the CEEC Report. This was the Organization for European Economic Co-operation (OEEC). The Convention consisted of two parts: the first, devoted to the principles of individual action and co-operation agreed upon by the contracting states; and the second, containing the Charter of the OEEC. The aim of the OEEC was declared to be:

> The achievement of a sound European economy through the economic co-operation of its members. An immediate task of the Organization will be to ensure the success of the European Recovery Program, in accordance with the undertakings contained in Part I of the present Convention.

The members agreed 'to work in close cooperation in their economic relations with one another' with the object of strengthening 'their economic links by all methods which they may determine will . . . achieve as soon as possible and maintain a satisfactory level of economic activity without extraordinary assistance.' Thus, the OEEC was established not only to assist in the administration of the Marshall Plan but to continue efforts toward achieving a sound European economy. In 1949, the semi-permanent aspects of the OEEC were emphasized in a statement from its Council 'that in the spirit of the Convention the work of cooperation which has been undertaken must continue after the cessation of American aid, in order to secure a sound European economy.'

To carry out its immediate and long-range tasks, the OEEC has functioned through several organs. The central governing body is the Council 'from which all decisions derive.' It is composed of the original members plus the German Federal Republic and meets to decide policy several times a year at the headquarters of the OEEC in Paris. Many of the meetings are attended by representatives at the ministerial level. The Council has an Executive Committee of seven which is selected annually to execute its orders. A Secretariat of some six hundred employees, headed by a Secretary-General, assists the Executive and other committees as well as the Council with the routine of the Organization and performs various research and statistical functions. Finally, there is a series of technical committees composed of representatives of members most immediately concerned with their activities. They are classified as 'horizontal' or 'vertical.' The horizontal committees deal with more general matters such as trade, payments, and manpower; the vertical committees work upon specific aspects of economic activity such as coal, iron, steel, and agriculture. They all function under the Council and submit recommendations to it. Special bodies, such as the

European Productivity Agency, have been created from time to time to perform various technical functions. Close contact is maintained with various United Nations bodies, in particular with the regional Economic Commission for Europe.

After accomplishing the initial task of obtaining a measure of economic recovery by planning the distribution of assistance from the United States, the OEEC has concentrated upon the long-term objectives of increasing European economic co-operation and integration and developing intra-European trade. In 1954, for example, it recommended to France that it abolish the compensatory taxes on imports which had been introduced along with certain measures of trade liberalization. France stated in 1955 that it had reduced the compensatory taxes as recommended and would follow in principle a suggested percentage of trade liberalization. In 1956, the Council announced that all steps had been taken in a number of member countries to abolish artificial aids, such as hidden subsidies for exports.

As a co-operative instrument, OEEC has had considerable influence in shaping the economies of its various members and has brought about a surprising degree of mutual effort. Some progress has been made in planning for economic integration in co-operation with other European agencies.[6] One of its most successful experiments was the establishment of the European Payments Union (EPU) in July, 1950. It became obvious soon after the war that unless a system of providing convertibility of European currency was devised, the accomplishment of increased intra-European trade would be impossible even with a reduction of trade barriers. The Marshall Plan had as its basic objective the reconstruction of the European economy in such a fashion that it would become independent of abnormal assistance from the United States. But as the program got underway, just the reverse took place. For example, France applied for dollar aid from the United States to finance imports of American farm equipment at a time when supplies of that machinery were available in Britain but could not be obtained there because France's means of making payments to the British had been exhausted. The EPU was established to remedy this situation and promote the flow of intra-European trade. This is done by creating a more or less automatic system by which each OEEC country is able to settle its current payments with the other members. The multilateral character of this arrangement makes it possible for any member country to use a surplus of currency which has been built up with another member to finance its deficit with a third. This means that each country may ignore its

[6] Most notable have been the efforts to achieve a common market and a pooling of all atomic research and development. Leadership in this area has come particularly from the European Coal and Steel Communities. See below, pp. 574–8.

balance of payments difficulties with each individual member and concentrate on its balance with the group as a whole. Trade has thereby been encouraged by permitting two members whose accounts are not in balance to disregard this situation and trade with each other by drawing upon surpluses with other members.

Great strides have been made through this arrangement toward making the currencies of the OEEC countries inter-convertible. In 1956 the OEEC Council decided to extend the life of EPU for at least one more year and carefully examined what system should be adopted for intra-European payments after one or more European currencies had been made convertible. It was finally agreed to establish a European monetary fund to replace the EPU system after some of the major currencies had been made convertible. A European Monetary Agreement was drawn up to make short-term credits available to members individually to assist them in overcoming temporary difficulties in their balance of payments should trade liberalization become threatened. The Agreement will enter into force when so desired by the EPU members, after those representing more than 50 percent of the present EPU quotas indicate their willingness to make their currencies convertible.

A Managing Board of seven members elected annually by the Council of OEEC supervises the work of the Union. However, the Council of OEEC determines policy decisions. Financial transactions are handled by the Bank for International Settlements at Basle, Switzerland, under the direction of the Managing Board.

More challenging has been the creation of a European Coal and Steel Community in the spring of 1952, composed of Belgium, France, Italy, Luxembourg, the Netherlands and Western Germany. Its establishment was the direct result of a plan announced by French Foreign Minister Robert Schuman, on May 9, 1950. On that day he stated to the press that France wished to contribute to European stability and peace by encouraging the development of an organization which would make another war between France and Germany not only unthinkable but impossible. This could be brought about by creating a system that would place German and French coal and steel production under a single high authority open to all European countries. Schuman envisaged such a system as the first step toward a federation of Europe.

The fundamental reason for suggesting this revolutionary proposal was the French fear of German economic resurgence, which might later be associated with a rebirth of German militarism. French efforts before 1950 to prevent an expansion of German industrial might had been unsuccessful. A pooling of French and German coal and steel resources would permit France to exercise an indirect control over German heavy industry, which was the source of strength for any armament program. In addition, there were economic arguments in favor of establishing a unified market in coal and steel which might result in increased production and lower prices. Italy and the Benelux countries would be interested in any plan that might reduce friction between France and Germany. Finally, the United States would welcome a means by which a closer integration of the European economy might be achieved, an objective inherent in the Marshall Plan and repeatedly urged by American officials.

Negotiations began in June, 1950, between Belgium, France, Germany, Italy, Luxembourg, and the Netherlands and were consummated in April, 1951, with the signing of a Treaty establishing the European Coal and Steel Community (ECSC). This document is extremely complicated with provisions scattered throughout its hundred articles for the rights and duties of the members and the functions of its organs. It is divided into four parts: the first containing general objectives, the second dealing with the organs, the third establishing economic and social principles, and the fourth concerning general provisions and definitions.

The basic objective of the Community 'is to contribute to economic expansion, the development of employment and the improvement of the standard of living in the participating countries through the institution, in harmony with the general economy of the member States, . . . of a common market.' It is to 'progressively establish conditions which will in themselves assure the most rational distribution of production at the highest possible level of productivity.' The institutions of the Community have the following tasks (Article 3):

1. See that the single market is regularly supplied, taking account of the needs of third countries;

2. Assure to all consumers in comparable positions within the single market equal access to the sources of production;

3. Seek the establishment of the lowest prices which are possible without requiring any corresponding rise either in the prices charged by the same enterprises in other transactions or of the price-level as a whole in another period, while at the same time permitting necessary amortization and providing normal possibilities of remuneration for capital invested.

4. See that conditions are maintained which will encourage enterprises to expand and improve their ability to produce and to promote a policy of rational development of natural resources, avoiding inconsiderate exhaustion of such resources;

5. Promote the improvement of the living and working conditions of the labor force in each of the industries under its jurisdiction so as to make possible the equalization of such conditions in an upward direction;

6. Further the development of international trade and see that equitable limits are observed in prices charged on external markets;

7. Promote the regular expansion and the modernization of production as well as the improvement of its quality under conditions which preclude any protection against competing industries which is not justified by illegitimate action on the part of such industries or in their favor.

The Community is to accomplish these tasks and objectives with a limited amount of direct intervention and with as little administrative machinery as possible. It does not own any coal mines or steel mills but it has broad authority to advance free competition. To this end, the Community functions as follows (Article 5):

1. To enlighten and facilitate the action of the interested parties by collecting information, organizing consultations and defining general objectives;
2. To place financial means at the disposal of enterprises for their investment and participate in the expenses of readaptation;
3. To assure the establishment, the maintenance and the observance of normal conditions of competition and take direct action with respect to production and the operation of the market only when circumstances make it absolutely necessary;
4. To publish the justifications for its action and take the necessary measures to ensure the observance of the rules set forth in the present Treaty.

The members of the Community themselves assume specific obligations. The following practices are listed in Article 4 as 'incompatible with the single market for coal and steel, and are, therefore, abolished and prohibited within the Community':

1. Import and export duties, or charges with an equivalent effect, and quantitative restrictions on the movement of coal and steel;
2. Measures or practices discriminating among producers, among buyers, or among consumers, specifically as concerns prices, delivery terms, and transportation rates as well as measures or practices which hamper the buyer in the free choice of his supplies;
3. Subsidies or state assistance, or special charges imposed by the state, in any form whatsoever;
4. Restrictive practices tending towards the division of markets or the exploitation of the consumer.

Other articles reinforce these obligations. At the same time, the Treaty emphasizes that the Community is in no fashion to alter or interfere with the existing form of ownership of the coal and steel industries, whether they are privately owned or function under some form of nationalization.

The Community is governed by four principal institutions: a High Authority; a Common Assembly; a Council of Ministers; and a Court of Justice. The High Authority is composed of nine persons chosen for their general competence for six-year terms. Eight are designated by the governments of the members and they, in turn, elect the ninth. All must be nationals of member-states and not more than two can be of the same nationality. A President and Vice-President are selected by a similar procedure. This body is the principal executive organ of the Community; it also has some legislative and judicial authority. Its main responsibility is to assure the fulfillment of the purposes of the Community. Acting by majority vote, it issues decisions which are binding, as well as recommendations and opinions.

A Consultative Committee is attached to the High Authority as an advisory group. It consists of not less than thirty and not more than fifty-one members and includes producers, workers, and consumers in equal numbers. Its membership is appointed by the Council of Ministers (described below). The High Authority can consult the Committee on any matter but must do so in respect to decisions or recommendations upon such questions as production, marketing, pricing, and employment.

The Assembly is 'composed of representatives of the peoples of the member States of the Community' and exercises 'supervisory powers.' Delegates to the Assembly are designated annually by the parliaments of each of the members, France, Germany, and Italy each have thirty-six seats; Belgium and the Netherlands, fourteen each; and Luxembourg, six. The Assembly meets annually to pass upon the general report of the High Authority. If a motion of censure on the report is adopted by a two-thirds vote, the High Authority must resign in a body. The work of the Assembly is essentially supervisory; that is, it reviews the activities of the High Authority, and does not act as a legislative body.

The Council of Ministers is composed of one minister from each of the members and has, as its basic function, the duty of 'harmonizing the acts of the High Authority with that of the governments, which are responsible for the general economic policy of their countries.' The High Authority must obtain the permission of the Council before it can make a number of important decisions, such as those concerning the fixing of prices and the granting of loans. A complicated voting procedure results in the requirement of a unanimous vote of the Council for approval of much of the work of the High Authority. The Council, therefore, is the basic compromise between complete independence for the Community and the retention of national sovereignty by its members.

The Court is 'composed of seven judges, appointed for six years by agreement among the governments of the member States from among persons of recognized independence and competence.' Its purpose is 'to ensure the rule of law in the interpretation and application of the present Treaty and of its implementing decisions.' This gives it the authority to nullify the decisions and recommendations of the High Authority in a manner similar to the declaration of unconstitutionality of laws by courts in the United States. Complaints on certain specified grounds may also be heard from member governments, enterprises, and individuals.

The High Authority, the Assembly, and the Council each have their own secretariats, numbering approximately 600, 70, and 60 employees respectively. Administrative divisions to handle specialized matters have been established in all three secretariats. The Secretariat of the High Authority, for example, has the following ten divisions: Economic Affairs, Agreements and Concentrations, Finances, Investments, Market, Production, Transport, Labor Problems, Statistics, and Personnel and Administration.

The Treaty of the Community entered into force on July 25, 1952, and the High Authority began operations the following month. Although it is still too early to forecast what the future holds for the Community, certain of its activities up to 1958 can be noted and evaluated. By the spring of 1953, a common market for coal, iron ore, scrap iron, and steel had been established and tariffs, licenses, and other trade restrictions removed. In August, 1954, restrictions on trade of special steel were removed and the common market for all products coming within the jurisdiction of the Community had come into being. Although it is difficult to assess the influence of the Community, the total steel output of the Community by 1958 was larger than the joint production of all six countries had been at any time previous to its establishment. Trade within the Community has increased remarkably. Discriminatory practices and double-pricing have been eliminated with respect to freight rates. In 1957 a system of direct, tapering freight rates came into operation, calculated to save over two million dollars annually on transport costs within the Community.

There has been no appreciable decrease in prices but the existence of the Community has produced a certain stablizing effect. Marginal enterprises have been consolidated or shutdown. Housing projects are underway through loans advanced by the High Authority.

The various organs of the Community have all been in operation and have managed to overcome a number of organizational difficulties. In general, the High Authority has exercised great restraint in employing its broad powers, but it has not failed to use them when believed necessary. For example, it has had to direct Italy to suspend duties on pig iron and end discrimination against imports of raw materials and finished goods from other ECSC countries for the Italian shipbuilding industry. Luxembourg was ordered to abandon license requirements on coal imports because they were impeding trade in the single market. Steelmakers in France agreed to stop granting a rebate on the published list of steel to all their French customers. A Dutch firm was fined for an offense against the rule of non-discrimination in prices.

Similarly, the Court of Justice has had its share of activity. As an instance, it rejected appeals brought by the Belgian coal federation (FEDECHAR) and three Belgian coal companies against the High Authority's revision in May, 1955 of the transitional compensation plan for Belgian coal. The revision had lowered the compensation paid to specific companies possessing natural advantages and eliminated compensations for and later freed prices on certain types of coal.

Although it maintained a discreet aloofness at the start, the United Kingdom has shown increasing interest in the activities of the Community and in December, 1954, signed an agreement which established a Standing Council of Association with the Community. Composed of four British and four High Authority representatives, this arrangement is an attempt to 'provide a means for the continuous exchange of information and for consultation in regard to matters of common interest concerning coal and steel and, where appropriate, in regard to the coordination of these matters.' [7]

To accomplish its aims in the fullest sense, it is necessary to obtain a greater measure of economic integration among the ECSC countries and a certain amount of progress already has been made in this direction. Meeting in Messina, Italy, in June, 1955 the six members were presented with a memorandum prepared by the Benelux countries which called for a pool of transport, electric power, and atomic energy for peaceful purposes. It also contained suggestions for broadening the common market to include products other than coal and steel, and for the progressive abolition of customs duties. An intergovernmental committee was later established to explore these ideas. Working through various technical subcommittees and with the close co-operation of OEEC and the Council of Europe, the committee was able by 1957 to report the drafts of two treaties for submission to the several governments. One concerned the establishment of the Common Market or, to use its official title, the European Economic Community (EEC). The other called for the creation of the European Atomic Energy Agency or, as it is more commonly known, 'Euratom.' Both came in effect on January 1, 1958 following approval by the parliaments of the six countries concerned.

The basic objective of EEC is the establishment of an area comprising 160,000,000 people within which goods, services, capital, and people can circulate with increasing freedom. Fundamental to this goal is the creation

[7] Article 6 of the agreement for the Standing Council of Association.

of a customs union among the six participants which involves a gradual elimination of customs duties between the members and the adoption of a common external tariff. The accomplishment of the customs union is to take twelve years in three four-year stages. The period may be extended to fifteen years if a prolongation is deemed desirable, but no longer than that. Export duties are to be eliminated by the end of the first stage. No new import duties can be instituted from the beginning nor can any of them be increased. As far as the reduction of import duties is concerned, there is the following timetable: a 25 percent reduction of the duty on each product by the end of the first stage; by the end of the second stage the reduction is to reach 50 percent, and will then be completed by the end of the twelve (or fifteen) year period. Import quotas are also to be eliminated gradually.

Other features of the Common Market plan which should be noted include the following: progressive harmonization of social and tax legislation; eventual establishment of a common agricultural policy; progressive elimination of 'restrictions on the movement of capital belonging to persons resident in the Member States and also any discriminatory treatment based on nationality or place of residence of the parties or on the place in which such capital is invested'; a limited common transport policy involving particularly an elimination of forms of discrimination; and the gradual achievement of the free movement of workers. However, on most of these items, specific details and requirements are often lacking. The decisions which will be needed for implementation ordinarily require a unanimous vote in the Council of EEC (discussed below). The flexibility and vagueness of many provisions reflect positive economic differences among the several members of EEC and a failure to reach agreement on a number of items. This is particularly true, for example, with respect to the problem of the co-ordination of economic policies among the members. The EEC treaty states in Article 103 that members 'shall consider their policy relating to economic trends as a matter of common interest. They shall consult with each other and with the Commission on measures to be taken in response to current circumstances.' Measures such as these require the unanimous consent of the Council. In other words, EEC does not have the authority to impose any common economic policy on the members.

The Common Market has four major institutions: the Council, the Commission, the Assembly, and the Court of Justice. There are also several subsidiary and advisory bodies and secretariats for the major institutions.

The Council is composed of one member from each government, is responsible for obtaining co-ordination of general economic policies, and has supreme authority with respect to problems of major importance. On most important decisions, a unanimous vote is required. Some matters call for a qualified majority where a system of weighted voting prevails which, in effect, frequently enables the major powers to enjoy a special voting privilege. The Council chairmanship is rotated among the six members.

The permanent organ of EEC is the Commission, composed of nine nationals of member states who are independent of governments and serve the Community. They have four-year terms and are selected for their general competence by agreement among the several governments. Voting is by a simple majority. The Commission has the task of supervising the application of the treaty governing the Community and administering measures called for by the various Community organs. In some instances it can make independent decisions, but actions of this nature are subject to the veto of the Council. Furthermore, a two-thirds vote of censure by the Assembly results in an immediate, total resignation of the Commission.

The Assembly has 142 members appointed by the parliaments of the members according to a quota granted each state (France, Germany, and Italy have 36 each, Belgium and the Netherlands 14 each, and Luxembourg 6). The Assembly is not a legislative body but is essentially a supervisory body, exercising parliamentary control over the executive and able to adopt a vote of censure at any time. A novel feature is the fact that the Assembly for EEC is the same as that for ECSC and Euratom. When acting as the Assembly for EEC, however, it has greater authority than for ECSC since in the latter instance, censure can be voted only when the High Authority submits its annual report, that is, but once a year.

Similarly, the Court of Justice of EEC serves both ECSC and Euratom. It is to 'ensure observance of law and justice in the interpretation' of the EEC treaty and review the legality of the decisions of the Council and Commission with the power of annulment. Appeals may be brought to the Court by member states against each other and by the Commission against members. Also to be heard are appeals against the Council or Commission and disputes involving the newly-created European Investment Bank (discussed below).

An Economic and Social Committee advises the Council and the Commission and there are additional special committees for advisory purposes. A European Investment Bank has been created to finance 'projects of common interest to several member states, . . . projects for developing less developed regions' and 'projects for modernizing or converting enterprises or for creating new activities which are called for by the progressive establishment of the common market where such projects by their size or nature cannot be entirely financed by the various means available in each of the member states' (Art. 130). A European Social Fund is to further 'within the Community employment facilities and the geographical and occupational mobility of workers' (Art. 123). The financing of social and economic projects in colonial areas is to be assisted by the creation of a Development Fund for the Overseas Countries and Territories.

Unquestionably the establishment of EEC is one of the most challenging developments of post-war Europe. Should the objectives sought be fully realized, the common market which would result would make another Franco-German war quite unlikely and in time might even lead to the adoption of a common budget by the six countries. This would be, of course, exactly the type of development originally envisaged by the Marshall Plan. However, many questions have been left for later decision. There will have to be a continuing process of adjustment, reassessment, and readjustment. As certainly as the common market will mean competitive advantage for some enterprises, it will mean competitive disadvantages for others. Above all, the ever-changing economic and political picture will determine the course of events. A domestic crisis could lead to the demand for release from obligations, and a major depression might easily result in the total collapse of the Community itself. It is obvious that it is impossible to predict in detail what might take place in the future.

The European Atomic Energy Community, or Euratom, entails the creation of a common market among the six EEC nations for nuclear raw materials and equipment, the establishment of a technical pool, and the coordination of research. Actual reactor construction, however, is to be left to individual members. Rules are provided by the Euratom treaty to govern a precise safety and control system. Special fissionable materials, for example, are to remain the property of Euratom, much as they are assigned, in the United States, to the Atomic Energy Commission.

The essential purpose of this new organization is to stimulate atomic power development, an objective which has been made more urgent since the Suez crisis emphasized Western Europe's dependence on Middle Eastern oil. Institutions similar to those of EEC are now in operation to further this goal. The Council of Ministers provides co-ordination between national and Community action and is, in effect, the policy-making organ. A five-member Commission executes the provisions of the treaty and the directives of the Council. As has been noted earlier, a common Assembly and Court serve ECSC, EEC, and Euratom.

Military Union. The widespread fear of Soviet aggression has caused the nations of Western Europe to go beyond the structure of the United Nations in an effort to strengthen their military defenses. Several attempts have been made to obtain unified military organizations for the defense of Western Europe. These include the Brussels Treaty Organization, the

North Atlantic Treaty Organization, the European Defense Community, and the Western European Union.

The first move was the consummation of the Brussels Pact in March, 1948, providing for military and other assistance in the event of an armed attack, regardless of its source. It was signed by the United Kingdom, France, and the Benelux countries and became known as the Brussels Treaty Organization (BTO). The principal institution was the permanent Consultative Council, consisting of the foreign ministers of the five signatories.[8] The Council established a joint military organization under the command of Field Marshall Montgomery but no real military unification was achieved. Social and Cultural Committees were established which laid the groundwork for the conclusion of multilateral conventions on social security, public health, the regulation of wages, and the living conditions of frontier workers (those who live on one side of a national border and work on another).

But it became apparent at once that the problem of providing equipment and supplies was beyond the capacity of BTO members. Canada and the United States, both of whom had indicated great interest in these military developments, were invited to meet with the Consultative Council as observers in the hope that they might be willing to offer some solution to its problem. Discussions began between the United States and the Consultative Council in the fall of 1948 and culminated in the signing of the North Atlantic Treaty in the spring of 1949.

While the North Atlantic Treaty is primarily an alliance for defense of indefinite duration, its ramifications and subsequent developments have resulted in the building of a complicated regional organization. Heated debate has raged in and out of the United Nations concerning the legality of the Treaty as a regional arrangement within the framework of the Charter. Once again the absence of a satisfactory definition of regionalism, not only in the Charter but among specialists in the field, tends to confuse the issue. There is nothing in the Charter to prevent a regional arrangement from providing for collective self-defense against aggression either on the part of one of its own members or from some outside source. However, the framers of the Charter did not expect that regional groupings would develop among members of the United Nations to be directed against a United Nations member rather than against former enemies of World War II. One of the basic reasons for negotiating the Treaty and the other regional defense agreements was the fear that the Soviet veto would prevent the Security Council from taking any action. Nevertheless, the North

---

[8] The Brussels Treaty Organization was supplanted in October 1954 by the Western European Union. See below, pp. 587–8.

Atlantic Treaty remains in force and through its provisions has come a regional security organization with a multinational army.

Any nation in Europe can become a signatory by establishing its capacity to advance the principles of the Treaty and contribute to the security of the North Atlantic Community. The signatories aim 'to unite their efforts for collective defense and for the preservation of peace and security,' agreeing 'to refrain in their international relations from the threat or use of force in any manner inconsistent with the purposes of the United Nations.' There is to be immediate consultation whenever 'the territorial integrity, political independence or security of any of the Parties is threatened.' The familiar principle basic to the Inter-American system is repeated in Article 5 of the treaty where the signatories 'agree that an armed attack against one or more of them . . . shall be considered an attack against them all.' A firm commitment to aid the victim of an armed attack is weakened, however, by the provision that should such an attack occur, each signatory is to assist the nation or nations attacked with 'such action as it deems necessary.' This permits each party to the treaty to decide the type and method of assistance it will provide 'in the event of an armed attack.' National sovereignty and individual freedom of action are not infringed upon.

Article 9 of the North Atlantic Treaty provided the framework for establishing a permanent regional organization. It called for the creation of a Council, with each party represented, 'to consider matters concerning the implementation' of the treaty. From this has come the North Atlantic Treaty Organization (NATO). The principal organ is the Council of Ministers, on which sit Foreign, Finance, or Defense Ministers, or all three, depending upon the problems to be discussed. It meets several times a year and sets general lines of policy for the North Atlantic community. In continuous session and the focal point of NATO is a second organ, the Permanent Council, composed of representatives empowered to speak in the name of their respective governments and acting between sessions of the Council of Ministers. Attached to the Permanent Council is a Secretary-General and an international staff engaged in the activities of a secretariat, with headquarters in Paris.

The military committee of the Permanent Council, on which all fifteen governments are represented by responsible military leaders, plans for military build-up.[9] The Supreme Allied Commander in Europe (SACUER) reports to what is known as the Standing Group of the military committee,

[9] There were twelve original members of NATO: Belgium, Canada, Denmark, France, Ireland, Italy, Luxembourg, the Netherlands, Norway, Portugal, the United Kingdom, and the United States. In 1952, Greece and Turkey were admitted and, in 1955, the Federal German Republic became the fifteenth member.

staffed by British, French, and United States officers with permanent head-quarters in Washington. Supreme Headquarters of the Atlantic Powers in Europe or SHAPE contains the European military forces of NATO under the command of SACEUR.

Remarkable progress has been made in the years since the North Atlantic Treaty was signed. In the words of its first Secretary-General, Lord Ismay, NATO has become 'a revolutionary and constructive experiment in inter-national relations.' Back in 1949 the European countries now members of the Organization were virtually defenseless. Although they had armies, they lacked trained men and equipment. There was little unity among them except for the Brussels Treaty Organization and there was no over-all plan for defending the North Atlantic area. Furthermore, many of them lacked the morale and the will to fight, essential ingredients of any military es-tablishment.

By 1958 the picture had changed completely. Defense budgets had more than doubled. Through the Mutual Security Program, the United States has made available billions of dollars of credit and military equip-ment. A firm esprit de corps has been created under the able leadership in SHAPE, beginning with General Eisenhower and continuing under his successors. Inspiration has also come from Lord Montgomery and Lord Ismay who have contributed greatly to the development of NATO. Supreme Commands have been established in the Atlantic, Mediterranean, and European areas. Military production in each of the participating countries has expanded to the extent that much of the equipment for the armies is produced in Europe. Tank, gun, and plane production, while inadequate for wartime purposes, is approaching the requirements of SHAPE. The basic objective of developing the strength to withstand a limited attack directed at Western Europe from the East has been accomplished, according to statements made by General Gruenther in 1956. Much of the fear and apathy extant in 1949 has been replaced by a measure of confidence. Part of this has come from the support provided by the United States. The morale of the average European has been given a decided lift by the fact that the United States has made clear to all its intention of supporting Europe in any struggle for freedom.

Another aspect of the NATO experiment has been the impetus given to economic co-operation between the member-states. Article 2 of the North Atlantic Treaty actually calls for this when it directs the signatories to 'eliminate conflict in their international economic policies' and encourage economic collaboration. The NATO Council has been fully aware of eco-nomic problems and has given close attention to a unified effort. Consideration must still be given to the economic aspects of rearmament and the problem of increasing production of military items without disturbing the processes of recovery and stability. Economic and financial aspects of security are reviewed and studied repeatedly by such NATO bodies as the Defense Production Committee, the Planning Board for Ocean Shipping, the Civilian and Military Budget Committees, to name a few. The most careful attention has been given to the pooling of resources whereby unnecessary duplication can be eliminated and the proper utilization made of materials and factories of all countries. For example, the United States remodeled an aircraft plant near Amsterdam so that jet planes for NATO air forces could be assembled. Original plane and engine designs were made by the British. Rolls Royce engines are built in Belgium and the body aluminum comes from Canada.

Politically, the members of NATO have been brought closer together through common needs and aspirations. It is inevitable that in the meetings of the NATO Council, attended by the highest officials at the ministerial level, there is a discussion of the political aspects of security. The best example of this was the decision to bring the German Federal Republic into NATO. This act, undertaken with trepidation by some members as it was certain to antagonize the USSR, signalled a high point in NATO political cooperation. When Germany took its seat in the NATO Council in 1955, it marked an historic military and diplomatic realignment that may lead Western Europe away from its political and military animosities of the past century. In 1957, a German, General Hans Speidel, was given command of NATO's Central European land forces. The European balance of power can be profoundly affected in the years to come by this NATO maneuver in the cold war.

Though considerable progress has been made toward a stronger Europe militarily, economically, and politically, NATO has not been without its problems. The principal weakness still is the lack of armed strength, a problem which faced General Eisenhower and which continues to confront the NATO planners. New armies cannot be created overnight. The very complexity of modern warfare imposes severe limitations upon rapid mobilization. The military burden on European countries is very great. Increased defense budgets, higher taxes, longer conscription periods, and other measures are voted reluctantly, and understandably so, by European parliaments. Major political questions, such as German reunification, disarmament, the Suez Canal, and the problems of the Middle East and Asia produce constant tensions and inevitably strain the unity of the Atlantic partners. Western Europeans, living in the shadow of Soviet power and fully cognizant of the frightful destruction which would be theirs in the event of an atomic war, are prone to a feeling of 'neutralism,' anxious to be a buffer but not a battleground in the conflict between East and West.

The NATO problem is one which can be met by moving steadily forward with the job of building defensive strength but never so rapidly that the foundations upon which a sound defense system can be based are destroyed. Political, economic, and military factors must be kept in balance. Conscription must not waste manpower and the civilian sacrifices must not be such that added political and economic strains will result. Although the need is urgent, a too-rapid build up of strength can be self-defeating and result in weakening, not strengthening, the NATO community.

An additional and novel feature of Western European security arrangements was contemplated by the signing of the European Defense Community agreement in May, 1952, by the Foreign Ministers of France, Italy, Germany, and the Benelux countries. This revolutionary scheme for a military and political unification of Western Europe was, however, defeated in the French National Assembly in August, 1954, and never had the opportunity to prove itself. Despite its unhappy demise, the inherent concept of the plan originally proposed by the French Premier René Pleven in 1950, is worthy of brief comment.

The essential purpose of the plan was to make it possible for Germany to rearm and provide German military units for a European Army in which they would be merged with similar contributions from other countries. It would have complemented the European Coal and Steel Community as a means of recognizing Germany as an integral part of the European community without arousing fears of a revived German militarism. Under the agreement, military contingents, funds, armaments, and supplies would have been administered by instrumentalities similar to those of the European Coal and Steel Community. The executive arm was to be a Commissariat which resembled the High Authority, and a Council of Ministers was to function with authority much like that of the Council of the Coal and Steel Community. The Assembly and the Court of the Coal and Steel Community would have served the Defense Community as additional organs. The military forces were to have a common uniform and budget, and a Supreme Commander, all serving under SHAPE as a unit together with the military contingents contributed individually by other NATO members.

The rejection of the European Defense Community by the French parliament led to a period of intensive diplomatic negotiation designed to salvage as much as possible from the wreckage of the European Army idea. A nine-power conference began in London on September 28, 1954, attended by Canada, the United Kingdom, the United States, and the signatories of the European Defense Community Treaty. On October 3 a series of agreements were concluded which necessitated further negotiation before final signatures could be obtained. All arrangements were completed on October 23 in Paris and the agreements decided upon included the following:

1. The powers of the Supreme Commander, Europe, (Saceur) of NATO, were to be strengthened by the placement, under his authority, of all forces of NATO countries stationed in Europe (except those which NATO decided should be left under national command). These forces would be deployed under NATO strategy and their location and redeployment would be subject to Saceur's approval.

2. Western Germany was to be granted sovereignty and invited to join NATO.

3. The Brussels Treaty of 1948 was to be completely overhauled.

To make it a 'more effective focus for European integration,' the Brussels Treaty Organization was expanded into the Western European Union (WEU) and Italy and Germany were admitted to membership. This organization is by no means the type of supranational institution which had been planned for the European Defense Community. The British would never have joined it if it had been more than the old Brussels Treaty Organization with somewhat different functions.

The Consultative Council of the old Brussels Treaty Organization became the key organ of the Western European Union with definite powers of decision instead of consultation. Under it there is to be supervision of German rearmament whereby Germany is permitted military contingents similar to those which would have been made to the Defense Community: twelve divisions, a tactical air force of about 1100 aircraft, and a small navy for coastal defense. An Assembly was also established, composed of representatives of the members to the Consultative Assembly of the Council of Europe.[10]

The strength and armaments of the members of the Union are fixed by agreements within the Union. A special control agency is to regulate the armaments of the members in order that certain agreed armaments may not be manufactured and a level of stocks of certain weapons held by each member on the continent may be maintained. The agency also is to control production and imports to guarantee this level. A system of inspection was provided for the agency whereby it could examine and collate statistical and budgetary data and conduct spot checks. Should violations occur, the agency is to report to the Council of the Union, where measures to deal with such situations are to be decided upon by a majority vote. Agreement could not be reached on a French plan for an arms procurement agency and arms

[10] For a discussion of the Council of Europe, see below, pp. 589–91.

pool; therefore the matter was turned over to a working party for study and report.

On May 6, 1955, the Western European Union formally came into existence. Louis Goffin (Belgium) was made Secretary-General, and Admiral Ferrari (Italy) was appointed director of the Agency for the Control of Armaments. A Standing Armaments Committee was established, on the recommendation of the working group studying the French plan for an arms procurement agency and arms pool, with the duty of 'the development of the closest possible cooperation between member countries of Western European Union in the field of armaments, in order to seek the most practical means of using the resources available to these countries for equipping and supplying their forces and of sharing tasks in the best interest of all.' The seat of the Standing Committee was located in Paris so that close liaison could be maintained with NATO.

The Western European Union, as presently constituted, is essentially a means by which a defensive alignment of European nations can regulate the production of its own armaments. It is also the mechanism, replacing the European Defense Community, whereby limited German rearmament is now possible within the structure of NATO. It may offer the means for a more certain control over a rearmed Germany. In another sense, WEU is a symbol of a new and closer relationship between Britain and the countries of Europe. As a group of NATO countries, it may go further than NATO itself in co-ordinating production and in submitting armament stocks to impartial checking and the size of continental forces to unanimous decision. If these items are accomplished, it will be a definite sign of the increased mutual confidence among the nations concerned. But WEU can never be disentangled from NATO, since it has no separate command structure and the procedure for changing the limits on forces is inseparable from the process by which NATO decides on force goals. The economic, cultural, and social collaboration called for in the Brussels Treaty will be exercised largely by other organizations, such as NATO, OEEC, and the Council of Europe. Much of WEU's success will depend upon the support given it, not only by its members, but by the United States. That country has not yet committed itself, as it had with the Defense Community, to provide capital and equipment. It remains yet another link, however, in the growing series of interlocking organizations endeavoring to bring closer a united Europe.

Political Union. Soon after the end of the War, Europeans of widely differing political backgrounds began to think in terms of some form of a United States of Europe. It was not long before a number of private organizations were created to further this objective. An International Committee for the Co-ordination of the Movements for a United Europe was established in December, 1947, to combine the efforts of these various groups and eliminate duplication of effort. A Congress was held under its auspices in May, 1948, at The Hague, at which more than eight hundred Europeans called for the establishment of a European Assembly representing national parliaments and other measures designed to unite Western Europe. Later in the year the Committee was replaced by a permanent federation of groups called the 'European Movement' which met in Brussels. The Proposals for a European Assembly were forwarded to the Consultative Council of BTO for consideration. That organization established a study group to work on the matter, and by early 1949 a plan had been formulated. In March, representatives of the BTO members were joined in London by the ambassadors of Denmark, Italy, Norway, Sweden, and the High Commissioner for Ireland in forming the Preparatory Conference for the Creation of a Council of Europe. A Statute was completed in May and signed by the foreign ministers of the ten countries. It came into effect in August, 1949, and the Council of Europe began to function from its headquarters in Strasbourg.

It should be noted at once that the Council of Europe is little more than an experiment, a halting step forward in the direction of a United States of Europe. It is not a government nor does it comprise a regional system of security. As a matter of record, according to its Statute, 'matters relating to national defense do not fall within the scope of the Council of Europe.' The objective of this ambitious organization is to obtain 'greater unity between members for the purpose of safeguarding and realizing the ideals and principles which are their common heritage and facilitating their economic and social progress.' The Statute, in essence a treaty of forty-two articles, would have the Council of Europe develop its aims by a 'discussion of questions of common concern and by agreements and common action in economic, social, cultural, scientific, legal and administrative matters and in the maintenance and further realization of human rights and fundamental freedoms.'

Any European state may become a member if invited by a two-thirds vote of the Committee of Ministers. Associate members may be added with their representation limited to the Consultative Assembly. The original ten members — Belgium, Britain, Denmark, France, Ireland, Italy, Luxembourg, the Netherlands, Norway, and Sweden — were augmented by the addition of Greece, Iceland, and Turkey in 1949 and Germany in 1951.

The Council of Europe consists of a Committee of Ministers, a Consultative Assembly, and a Secretariat. The Committee of Ministers represents the governmental element in the Organization and is composed of the Foreign Ministers of all the full members. Each is entitled to one vote and, with minor exceptions, a unanimous vote is required on all items considered on its own initiative or by a recommendation of the Consultative Assembly. The Committee has the power to consider any action necessary to advance the aims of the Council of Europe. It decides 'with binding effect all matters relating to the internal organization and arrangements of the Council,' except for minor internal organization of the Consultative Assembly. Although it is the key organ of the Council of Europe, the Committee can only recommend action or make requests of the member-states. The presidency rotates among the member-states and the Committee meets just prior to the sessions of the Consultative Assembly in Strasbourg.

The Consultative Assembly is the self-styled 'deliberative organ' of the Council of Europe. Representation is based upon population and varies from eighteen seats each for France, Italy, and the United Kingdom to three for Luxembourg. Each member government determines its own method of selecting delegates. Most of them are elected by parliaments but some are appointed by cabinets. All delegates speak and vote as individuals and do not represent their countries in the Assembly. Ordinary sessions are held annually and are not to exceed one month in duration unless directed by the Committee of Ministers. The Assembly adopts its own rules of procedure and annually elects a President. Six General Committees facilitate the work of the Assembly and bear a resemblance to those of the United Nations. They are: General Affairs (Political), Rules of Procedure and Privileges, Economic Questions, Social Questions, Cultural and Scientific Questions, and Legal and Administrative Questions. A Standing Committee, composed of the President, six Vice-Presidents, the six Chairmen of the General Committees *ex officio,* and fifteen other representatives, meet quarterly between regular Assembly sessions to co-ordinate the work of that body. A Joint Committee of twelve, five from the Committee of Ministers and seven from the Assembly, functions to maintain close contact between the two organs.

The deliberations of the Consultative Assembly are not unlimited. It can only discuss matters referred to it or placed on its agenda by the Committee of Ministers. Decisions reached by the Assembly are in the form of recommendations to member-states but are subject to the approval of the Committee.

A Secretary-General and a Deputy Secretary-General, appointed by the Assembly, head the Secretariat which serves both organs of the Council of Europe. The staff of about two hundred is appointed by the Secretary-General and serves the Organization 'uninfluenced by any national considerations.' The work of the Secretariat is under the supervision of the Committee of Ministers. Contributions to the Secretariat's budget are made by each member-state on the basis of population.

While its goals are high-minded and deserving, the Council of Europe is little more than a hybrid between a very loose-knit international parliament with purely advisory powers and a dignified international forum devoted to debating crucial issues of primary concern to Western Europe. There has been a considerable amount of friction between the two primary organs, frequently because of the subservient position of the Consultative Assembly and the fact that the Committee of Ministers has been reluctant to endorse the more far-reaching recommendations and resolutions of the Assembly. Another difficulty is concerned with determining the best methods of bringing about a more closely integrated European community. The British are extremely reluctant to endorse anything approaching a true federated or supranational European state. France is unwilling to proceed with anything that would fail to obtain British support, always fearing the potential strength of Germany.

While little progress toward a new political authority has resulted from the deliberations in the Council of Europe, it has come to serve as a bridge or link between the various European agencies for economic and military co-operation. In this connection, the Consultative Assembly has made repeated overtures for a merger of OEEC with the Council of Europe. Close studies have been made of the relationship of the nonmilitary activities of NATO and the Council of Europe. Full debates each year are conducted upon all aspects of Europe's problems, always with a view toward achieving a greater degree of integration. The most recent efforts of the Consultative Assembly in this respect have been directed at the new Western European Union. In 1956 emphasis was placed on the need for the closest working arrangements between the Assembly of WEU and the Consultative Assembly of the Council of Europe. Under consideration is a plan to have a single secretariat for both Assemblies. Suggestions have been made for joint annual sessions of the Consultative Assembly, the WEU Assembly, and the Common Assembly of the Coal and Steel Community. Thus, instead of the earlier hopes that the Council of Europe, either itself or from its deliberations, would achieve a unified political authority for Europe, there has been a slower, more deliberate emphasis upon the development of functional organizations such as the OEEC and the Coal and Steel Community and their integration within the framework provided at Strasbourg. It should be noted that the Council of Europe has initiated a number of social and cultural measures and projects, among them a European Convention on Human Rights, and it works unceasingly to bring about greater co-operation in these and related fields.

The most positive action directed toward the establishment of a politically integrated Europe has come, interestingly enough, from the Coal and Steel

Community. The members of the Coal and Steel Community Common Assembly were invited by the Council of Ministers of the Organization in
September, 1952, 'to draft a treaty constituting a European Political Authority.' The inspiration for such a directive actually came from Article 38 of
the treaty which had drawn up the ill-fated European Defense Community.
It had provided that an Assembly, to complement the Defense Community,
should be created, to be 'elected on a democratic basis in such a way as to
be able to form part of a subsequent federal or con-federal system based
upon the principle of separation of powers and, in particular, on a bicameral system of representation.' Doubts were already expressed in 1952 as
to the feasibility of the Defense Community and the Foreign Ministers, supported by a resolution from the Council of Europe, decided to proceed with
the drafting of the European political authority.

The Common Assembly of the Coal and Steel Community accepted the
invitation, and working through various committees constituted for the
purpose, completed a draft which was adopted unanimously in March,
1953. The Foreign Ministers examined the draft briefly in May and again
in the fall without arriving at any decision. Negotiations were broken off
by the time EDC was killed by the French National Assembly in August,
1954. An entirely new start will have to be made, since EDC was a part of
the foundation for the contemplated political authority.

What the draft sought to do was bring together, insofar as possible, both
the European Coal and Steel Community and the European Defense Community under one sweeping political constitution without greatly disturbing
the treaties governing these two institutions. Thus, a bicameral Parliament
would replace the Coal-Steel and EDC Assemblies.[11] A council of National
Ministers would take the place of the Council of Ministers in the two Communities. The Court of the Coal and Steel Community, which was to serve
as well for EDC, would have become the Court of Justice for the new authority. A European Executive Council was charged with the 'general administration of the Community,' headed by a President elected by the Senate. He, in turn, would select the members of the Council. The Executive
Council eventually was to replace the EDC Board of Commissioners but
the High Authority of the Coal and Steel Community would have been retained 'as an administrative body having the character of a board.'

Despite the many years of effort, the establishment of a United States of
Europe appears to be impossible for some time to come.[12] Sentiment among

---

[11] The Upper House or Senate would have permitted representation from each State
and the Lower House or People's Chamber was to represent 'the peoples united in the
Community.'

[12] In 1956, for example, the Council of Europe's Committee on Cultural and Scientific
Questions reported that the Council 'had not yet made the impact upon European public
opinion which had been hoped for and expected at its inception.'

the peoples of Europe has not yet reached the stage where there can be a submerging of national interests and sovereign rights within a common political framework. Functional progress has been made, however, through the establishment of OEEC, ECSC, EEC, WEU, NATO, Benelux, and Euratom, with a degree of co-operation and understanding that would have been impossible before the war. The Council of Europe does its best to foster integration among this network of organizations and bring about a European, instead of a national, attitude of mind.

Nevertheless, despite the common organs in effect for ECSC, EEC, and Euratom, all of these new organizations function with virtually no connecting link or positive co-ordination. No amalgamation of institutions appears likely at this writing. Even with the common Assembly for EEC, ECSC, and Euratom, there has arisen "the unprecedented situation of three international executive bodies with different statutes, operating in the same area together with six national governments, all three bodies responsible to a single parliamentary Assembly appointed by the six national parliaments.' [13]

THE CARIBBEAN COMMISSION

A six-member Anglo-American Caribbean Commission was established in March, 1942, to further the economic and social development of the islands in the Caribbean. During the difficult days of submarine warfare in the region, the United States and Britain were forced to concentrate on measures to alleviate the serious food shortage in the area. A number of projects were undertaken, the most significant being the Emergency Land-Water Highway whereby food could be safely shipped from the United States. To eliminate an 800-mile voyage exposed to submarines, a shuttle cargo service was created from Florida and the Gulf ports to Havana, Cuba; across Cuba by railroad; small-boat service to Haiti; across Haiti to the Dominican Republic by truck; and final shipment by small boat to Puerto Rico.

When the submarine danger ended late in 1943, the Commission returned to its original purpose of advising the two governments on matters relating to labor, social welfare, housing, finance, education, and agriculture within the region. Two auxiliary bodies were established to assist the Commission in carrying out its functions. One was the Caribbean Research Council, created in 1943 to advise on scientific, technological, social, and economic research in the region and composed of representatives of Britain, the Netherlands, and the United States. The other, established in 1944, was the West Indian Conference, designed to serve as a forum for the discussion

[13] Hurtig, Serge, 'The European Common Market,' *International Conciliation* (March, 1958), p. 338.

of matters of social and economic interest to the Caribbean countries, each of whom was to send two delegates.

In 1946 the Commission adopted its present name and added France and the Netherlands to formal membership. Each member is represented by four commissioners. It is still only an advisory and consultative body, with all decisions being made by unanimous vote, yet important recommendations have been made to the national and territorial governments concerned. Progress has been made in social welfare, exchange of trade data, industrial expansion, and tourist development. A number of conferences on special topics are sponsored annually, such as those held in 1956 on cacao cultivation, trade promotion, education, and small-scale farming. Close contact is maintained with such United Nations specialized agencies as FAO, UNESCO, WHO, and ILO.

A small Secretariat has been established for the Commission and is located at Trinidad.

ORGANIZATION OF CENTRAL AMERICAN STATES

The foreign ministers of Costa Rica, El Salvador, Guatemala, Honduras, and Nicaragua met in San Salvador in October, 1951, and drafted the Charter of San Salvador to 'promote by group action the strengthening of the bonds of fraternity among the five Central American states and to serve as an instrument for the study and solution of their common problems.'

The principal organs are the Meeting of Presidents which convenes irregularly as the Supreme Organ; the Meeting of Foreign Ministers which occurs biennially except when called into special session by any three of the members; the Meeting of Ministers of other governmental departments which considers special problems; and a Secretariat located at San Salvador.

The first formal meeting of the Organization did not take place until August 13, 1955, because of the withdrawal until 1954 of Guatemala in protest against the anti-communist attitude of the other members and the tension between Nicaragua and Costa Rica. In 1955 a Council of Culture and Education was established within the Organization as a specialized agency; the Secretariat was directed to make a study of a Central American customs union; and a Commission of Jurists was established to work on a codification of Central American legislation.

REGIONALISM IN THE PACIFIC

Several economic and military agencies have been established in the Pacific region since the end of World War II. Even before the war, New

Zealand and Australia had given serious consideration to some form of regional security arrangement. After a Pacific War Council had been established in Washington in 1944 to concentrate upon the Allied war effort in the Pacific, Australia and New Zealand concluded the Canberra Agreement (ANZAC Pact) calling for a regional zone of defense. The Agreement anticipated the formation of a South Seas Commission to be devoted to the interests of native peoples.

South Pacific Commission. The South Pacific Conference meeting in February, 1947, established the South Pacific Commission, composed of six governments with colonies in the area, namely Australia, Britain, France, the Netherlands, New Zealand, and the United States. It has taken the Caribbean Commission for its model and is an advisory agency concentrating upon the nonpolitical problems of the region. Each member is represented by two commissioners and a Secretariat is located at Nouméa, New Caledonia. There is also a Research Council and a South Pacific Conference.

The Commission's purpose is 'to encourage and strengthen international cooperation in promoting the economic and social welfare and advancement of the peoples of the non-self-governing territories in the South Pacific region.' Health education has been considered an activity of high priority, as have nutrition and economic development. In the last-named field, for example, the Commission dealt with the following matters in 1957: soils and land use; subsistence economies; the coconut and rice industries; fisheries; and plant collection and introduction. Close contact is maintained with several specialized agencies of the United Nations.

The Colombo Plan was initially conceived as an organization of British Commonwealth countries to focus attention on the problems of economic development for South and Southeast Asia. The use of the word 'plan' is somewhat misleading, in that the arrangement which has materialized is an intergovernmental committee, consultative in nature, composed of nations constructively interested in the economic development of the countries in the area. Formative meetings occurred in 1950 and 1951 at Colombo (Ceylon), Canberra, and London. Since 1952 there have been annual meetings to review progress in economic development and to assess prospects for the future. The plan is known more formally as the Consultative Committee for Economic Development in South and Southeast Asia. No longer is the Committee restricted to Commonwealth nations but now includes seventeen countries, among them such noncommonwealth states as Cambodia, Indonesia, Japan, Laos, the Philippines, Thailand, the United States, and Vietnam. The area covered stretches from Pakistan to the Philippines, within which reside 720 million people or about 29 percent of the world's population.

During the early meetings, the countries of the area formulated development programs which were to begin in 1951 and reach completion by the end of 1957. These economic programs — each of which is a development plan for an individual country — are known collectively as the Colombo Plan. The present annual meetings are devoted to review and discussion of mutual problems and reporting of progress on individual projects. Whatever financial or technical assistance is made is on a bilateral basis between countries participating in the development programs. Nothing is contributed to the Consultative Committee and then distributed to various recipients, as has been the case with OEEC in Europe. No obligations are incurred by any participant by virtue of his membership on the Committee. There is no executive or permanent secretariat for preparing or executing the various plans. There is a bureau located at Colombo which facilitates the exchange of experts needed for the different projects.

The Colombo Plan has made possible the planning for and financing of economic development on a co-operative basis between the Asian countries themselves and between them and the Western nations. This has, in turn, contributed a great deal to the strengthening of the individual countries of the region.

Security Arrangements. In addition to defense treaties signed by the United States with Japan and the Philippines, two regional security arrangements have come into being. These are the ANZUS Pacific Security Pact and the Southeast Asia Treaty Organization (SEATO).

The signatories of the ANZUS Pact, which came into force in 1952, are Australia, New Zealand and the United States. ANZUS had its origin in a speech to the Australian Parliament in 1950 when the Australian Minister of External Affairs, Mr. Percy G. Spender, urged a military alliance to resist communism. In effect, the Pact creates a military zone of defense against possible Japanese or communist attack. A Pacific Defense Council, composed of the foreign ministers of the three members, meets annually in the territories of the parties. Special meetings of deputies occur from time to time between annual meetings and are held in Washington, D.C., where the Secretariat is located. The staff for the Secretariat is drawn from the Department of State and the Australian and New Zealand embassies in Washington. A Military Committee composed of high military officers with Pacific Commands meets irregularly in the capitals of the three members and advises the Council.

In Manila on September 8, 1954, representatives of Australia, France, New Zealand, Pakistan, the Philippines, Thailand, the United Kingdom, and the United States signed the Southeast Asia Collective Defense Treaty. At the same time they concluded the Pacific Charter, a declaration which set forth the following aims of the signatories in Southeast Asia and the Southwest Pacific: to uphold the principle of equal rights and self-determination of peoples; to co-operate in economic, social, and cultural fields for the promotion of higher living standards, economic progress, and social well-being; and to prevent a subversion of freedom or destruction of sovereign rights or territorial integrity.

The Defense Treaty calls for consultation only in the event of a threat to the inviolability or integrity of any signatory that is not an armed attack. Should there be aggression or an armed attack, the parties are pledged solely 'to meet the common danger in accordance with (their) constitutional processes.' These unique security provisions are further weakened by a provision which limits the obligations of the United States to consultation unless there is 'communist agression.' Whatever measures are undertaken must be reported immediately to the Security Council of the United Nations. The region encompassed by SEATO covers the general area of Southeast Asia, the Southwest Pacific, and 'the entire territories of the Asian Parties.' Specifically excluded are South Korea and Formosa, although Cambodia, Laos, and the free territory under the jurisdiction of Vietnam are included.

All members of SEATO are represented on the Council which provides for 'consultation with regard to military and any other planning as the situation obtaining in the treaty area may from time to time require.' The Council is organized to meet from time to time and a Secretariat is in the process of being established. Committees are assigned special military and technical duties.

The major consideration of SEATO, in addition to matters of organization and military collaboration, has been the discussion of measures to combat communist infiltration and subversion in Southeast Asia. It is significant, however, that India, Burma, Ceylon, and Indonesia have been unwilling to join in the very limited SEATO obligations. Although they were invited to the Manila Conference in 1954, they declined in the belief that their policy of avoiding commitments to either East or West in the cold war would prevent their becoming parties to the alliance. Their absence considerably weakens the scope and the effectiveness of the agreement. Moreover, India is openly hostile to the idea of such an alliance, since it was inspired by 'western imperialist nations' and thus can only heighten the tensions between the communist and noncommunist worlds. Preferable to SEATO, in this view, is a neutralist position in South Asia which would allow the Asian peoples to work out their own problems with only technical and financial assistance from the West.

SOVIET REGIONALISM

Since World War II, the USSR has attempted to integrate the economies and the foreign policies of its seven satellite nations — Albania, Bulgaria, Czechoslovakia, the German Democratic Republic, Hungary, Poland, and Rumania. The old Third Communist International or Comintern used prior to the war as a means of co-ordinating and directing the activities of communist parties throughout the world was eliminated in 1943. After the announcement of the Marshall Plan in 1947, the Kremlin established the Communist Information Bureau (Cominform) to supervise the execution of Soviet-determined policies in the satellites. Originally located in Belgrade, it was moved to Bucharest following the defection of Tito's Yugoslavia in 1948. Not much is known of its organization or the extent of its activities but it is certain that it is not a co-operative venture similar to the regional institutions established elsewhere in the world.

In 1949 the USSR established a Council for Mutual Economic Assistance to carry out what was known as the Molotov Plan of economic integration of Eastern Europe. Emphasis is placed upon the development of trade within the communist area of Eastern Europe, industrial expansion, and the production of goods essential to the Soviet economy.

In the military sphere, the Soviet Union first concluded bilateral mutual defense pacts with the satellites whereby each would come to the assistance of the other if attacked. Similar arrangements were completed between most of the satellites themselves, again primarily on a bilateral basis. This system of security was capped in May, 1955, with the conclusion of a Collective Security Pact signed by the Soviet Union and the seven satellites in Warsaw. Intended to counter the threat of German rearmament, the Warsaw Pact is to run for twenty years. Under its terms, the parties agree to the following provisions:

1. to settle international disputes peaceably and refrain from acts or threats of violence;
2. to cooperate 'in all international actions' to further peace, including participation in plans for disarmament;
3. to consult on all significant international problems, especially should there be a threat of armed attack to one or more parties;
4. to provide immediate assistance in case of armed aggression in Europe against any of the parties, such assistance to end when the Security Council of the United Nations had adopted measures designed to bring about peace.
5. to establish a joint command of their armed forces and strengthen their defenses;
6. to create a political committee for consultative purposes;
7. to abstain from joining agreements contrary to the Pact;

8. to advance economic and cultural links betwen the parties without interference in the internal affairs of any party;

9. to encourage the adherence of other states to the Pact, regardless of
their political or social systems.

In practice, the Warsaw Collective Security Pact does nothing more than superimpose a formal structure on top of existing political, military, and economic arrangements. Decisions are arrived at in the Kremlin and executed through this instrumentality. There is a certain propaganda value attached to its adoption in that it is supposed to be a counterpart of NATO and WEU, but open to any nation willing to subscribe to its terms.

ADDENDUM

THE OVERTHROW of the pro-Western government of Iraq on July 14, 1958, took place after this manuscript had gone to press. In the wake of this unexpected development has come a realignment of forces in the Middle East. During its first moments in power, the Iraqi revolutionary regime entered a mutual defense alliance with Nasser's U.A.R. and withdrew from the short-lived Arab Federation between Iraq and Jordan.

Still open by September, 1958, was the question of Iraq's role in the Baghdad Pact, since Iraq had not indicated whether or not it would continue as an active member. However, Iraq did not attend the July, 1958, meeting of the Baghdad Pact Council in London. At that time, Secretary of State Dulles announced that the United States, which never had been a member of the Pact, would associate itself much more closely with the Pact members and would co-operate with them fully to ensure their security and defense.

In the meantime, interest in the future role of the Arab League was revived by the general developments in the Middle East. The union of Egypt and Syria in the U.A.R. reduced the League's membership to eight, but Tunisia and Morocco indicated their intention of joining at an early date.

17

◇⚚◇

REFLECTIONS AND CONCLUSIONS

THE need for a deterrent to war is a generally accepted fact. For more than thirty-five years the task of preserving peace has been undertaken by international organization. In itself, the League of Nations was not able to prevent World War II because of the climate of world politics in which it was forced to operate. But the League did continue and greatly improved upon earlier efforts directed toward developing international economic and social co-operation.

The achievement of peace and prosperity is now the vital concern of the United Nations and, to a lesser degree, of certain regional organizations. One can ask to what extent today is international organization carrying out its grave responsibilities? To answer this fundamental question first requires a review and an assessment of the United Nations, the principles which determine its functions, the pressures which tend to govern its activities, and the criterion of its performance. The claim that the United Nations Charter must be revised in order to permit the Organization to function as expected needs to be analysed in connection with the changes that have taken place. The role and nature of regional systems should be discussed in this latter connection. Finally, we must take a careful look at the suggestions for world government and the minimum requirements necessary for its attainment.

PEACE AND SECURITY: THE UNITED NATIONS

At the outset, it is necessary to review a few fundamentals, destroy some illusions, and restate some realities. The United Nations is a human contrivance, subject not only to the whims of personal frailty but also to the national interests of eighty-one different sovereign states. Success or failure depends not only upon the procedures and techniques developed but primarily upon the willingness of the members to respect their solemn obligations. To think that the United Nations can legislate or resolve away power

600

politics is ridiculous. Politics is latent or active in any organization and certainly in a body such as the United Nations which, in a way, mirrors perfectly the power relationship and the pull and haul of competitive struggle always extant in international as well as national society. It serves no useful purpose to castigate those who 'play politics' in the United Nations, claiming that such an organization with its high principles should be above that sort of activity. The sooner the friends of international organization recognize that this maneuvering and even double-dealing is part of the United Nations game, the easier it will be for them to realize the limitations of such an organization and the possibilities for accomplishment that do remain. The United Nations must never be oversold with the consequent evil of expecting too much from the restricted possibilities inherent in its make-up.

In this same vein, the framers of the Charter never believed that all disputes should be referred to the Organization for immediate treatment. What was laid down in that document was a code of international conduct which was expected to govern all members of the United Nations in their international contacts. In Article 2:3, all members are to 'settle their international disputes by peaceful means in such a manner that international peace and security, and justice, are not endangered.' This process does not necessarily begin with some organ of the United Nations. Should a dispute arise, the parties are required to, 'first of all, seek a solution by negotiation, enquiry, mediation, conciliation, arbitration, judicial settlement, resort to regional agencies or arrangements, or other peaceful means of their own choice.' Too often, well-meaning persons charge that the United Nations is being by-passed when members are attempting a solution outside its confines. It is far more important that states obey the code of international conduct and attempt to resolve their differences between themselves through the customary methods of diplomacy. As long as they remain in contact with each other, with an outside chance for continued discussion, they should be left alone and not have the glare of international publicity focused on their efforts to reach a peaceful settlement. Only if the parties have exhausted all the means referred to in Article 33 should the matter be brought before the United Nations, either by one of the parties or through the intervention of the Security Council or the General Assembly.

What is the role of the United Nations in handling the complex problems bearing on peace and security? By its very existence it offers a number of opportunities whereby states, by their contact with one another, may find agreement on disputed issues. The small- and medium-sized nations gain by having a forum in which to express their views. They can obtain information not always available elsewhere, and, in general, exert a constant public and private pressure on the major powers. Restraints may be imposed indirectly which could lead to a modification in the positions taken by the leaders of East and West. The regular channels of diplomacy are augmented by the personal relationships developed within the Organization. Though the members of the Eastern and Western blocs are far apart in their policies and in their views on world questions, they still remain physically within the framework established by the Charter, under one roof so to speak. Within the Organization they cannot escape each other's presence, whereas outside its confines the two political worlds could easily become isolated with little opportunity for contact. In the absence of an international organization, it might be difficult if not virtually impossible to establish diplomatic communication. While these are intangible examples of the usefulness of international organization, they are nevertheless real and can be of value in this world of bipolarized power.

International organization also offers numerous opportunities for peaceful settlement through the availability of its procedures and its machinery. The United Nations has demonstrated a certain flexibility in this regard. The processes of mediation in various forms are always available; fact-finding panels can be established and the processes of inquiry and conciliation stand ready to be employed in many varieties of disputes. Recourse to the Court as an impartial tribunal for the settlement of conflicts and the rendering of opinions reinforces the entire system of peaceful negotiation.

Moreover, the role of the Secretary-General has become increasingly important as an arbiter of conflicting claims and in the delicate contacts which can be kept alive on his initiative or even merely by his presence. By quiet, behind-the-scenes persistence the Secretary-General can utilize the resources of his staff to combine with his own skill in bringing seemingly irreconcilable views closer to a position of compromise. It is true that his executive power is limited to the international civil servants who work in the Secretariat, plus whatever observation teams, truce supervisors, or military contingents the member states place at his disposal for specified purposes. But Mr. Hammarskjöld, largely because of his diplomatic skill, has been given unique duties to perform in the name of the United Nations. The Assembly created the United Nations Emergency Force in 1956 and then placed in his hands the tremendously difficult responsibility of bringing it into being and supervising its activities in accordance with certain rather ill-defined directives. The Secretary-General was also authorized to negotiate with Egypt over the question of clearing the Suez Canal and then given the task of assembling and directing the actual clearance operations. A major part of any success that can be recorded in favor of the Organization in the Middle East crisis should be credited primarily to the Secretary-

General and the other trusted subordinates working with him ceaselessly to bring some measure of reality to the objectives of the Charter. Thus, the world at large has learned that the Secretary-General of the United Nations, particularly if he possesses the qualities of Mr. Hammarskjöld, can provide extremely important services. Because of his office, he can conciliate where no national representative would be effective, always able to provide a neutral meeting ground for foreign ministers of opposing views. In dangerous situations, he may avert the imminent danger of war by carrying with him, and carefully exploiting, the authority and the prestige of the United Nations, whose constant servant he remains.

Although the United Nations can claim successes in some disputes and situations brought before it, notably in the Indonesian and Iranian cases, there still continues to be a number of instances in which little progress has been made. The condemnation of the Soviet Union by the General Assembly for its conduct in Hungary has focused world attention on Soviet motives and actions but it has not put an end to the continuation of inexcusable atrocities. The end of racial discrimination in South Africa has not been brought about, nor has the universal abolition of forced labor, or the reunification of Korea in freedom. India continues to defy the Security Council in the problem of Kashmir. Virtually nothing has been accomplished in the tedious efforts to arrive at some compromise on disarmament. As the Twelfth Assembly drew to a close in December, 1957, with many major world problems presented to that body still left unsolved or hanging in the balance, the United Nations found itself increasingly on the defensive.

Since the Assembly has become the focal point of the Organization, does this important body remain the 'only hope for peace,' as some have claimed? Although each of its eighty-one members has an equal vote, states comprising but about 10 percent of the world's population are able to claim a two-thirds majority in the Assembly. This has come about from the increased membership which now includes a large proportion of small nations. It means that numerically speaking slightly less than half the population of the world is represented by four delegates and the other half by seventy-seven delegates. The vote of 400 million Indians or 170 million Americans is equated to the vote of 1.125 million Libyans or 145,000 Icelanders. The vote of any country in Western Europe, the cradle of Western civilization, can be matched by that of Yemen, the so-called 'Tibet of the Red Sea,' a land of armed men ruled by the Imam who permits no government in the Western sense, where justice is his personal business and the treasury belongs to him as a sort of privy purse out of which he pays the nation's expenses. Two members of the Organization — the Ukrainian SSR and Byelorussian SSR — are not even sovereign states but are part of the USSR.

Four militarily and economically weak nations — South Africa, Egypt, India, and Israel — have continually defied the United Nations. In the light of this, some agree with Senator William Knowland, former minority leader of the United States Senate, who charged in 1957 that one of the major defects of the Organization was the 'unwillingness of many of the . . . members to share equitably the monetary costs and other obligations . . . while insisting on a full and equal voice in the making of decisions.'

There is an increasing tendency to claim, as did Senator Knowland, that there 'is a growing double standard of international morality,' brought about by the strength of bloc voting and the large numbers of small, weak states unfriendly to the West and anxious to foster a neutralist position. Evidence of this is cited by the desire of the Afro-Asian bloc to vote sanctions against Israel in the Middle East crisis but not against the Soviet Union for its suppression of the Hungarian revolt. Similarly, there has been the strong stand taken against the Anglo-French-Israeli invasion of Egypt but no effort made to punish Egypt for continuing violations of the Armistice Agreement for Palestine, or its defiance of the Security Council with respect to freedom of Israeli shipping in the Suez Canal and through the straits of Tiran. Thus, Egypt and the USSR are condemned, to be sure, but no specific action is taken, while democratic nations of the West, if they violate the Charter, are moved against swiftly and with determination. Such an obviously unjust situation, it is held, only reflects upon the incapacity of the Assembly, and hence, the United Nations, to act as an impartial arbiter and a symbol of justice for all.

Such an attitude is indeed difficult to refute since it has its foundation in a sense of fair play. A dangerous corollary of this view is the argument that since the United Nations did nothing to punish the Russians or the Egyptians, it should not punish the British, the French, or the Israeli. It is at this point that one must again adopt a realistic understanding of the United Nations. Whether or not there is a double standard of justice is actually not the question. The same standard is applied by the majority in the United Nations to each of these disputes and all parties are expected to follow the same code of international conduct. It is the means of implementing decisions in relationship to violations of the code that is the vital problem. Implementation is dependent upon the support of both poles of power. When the Soviet Union and the United States agreed on implementing the decisions of the Assembly in the Middle East crisis, no great obstacles had to be overcome. But when the Soviet Union was itself an accomplice to violations of the Charter, as it was in Hungary, the Organization could do no more than condemn and hope that the violator of the code would cease such actions. In this more realistic sense, the role of the United

Nations might be said to be that of facilitating the art of accomplishing the possible. It cannot act against either the United States or the Soviet Union, or any partner of either of these powers unless, as was the case in the Middle East in 1956, one of them — the United States — temporarily abandons its partners in an attempt to uphold the code of the Charter.

Certainly, therefore, the Assembly, or, for that matter, the Security Council, is not the 'highest tribunal in the world' even in the loosest sense of that term. There is no pretense that it is a judicial body or that it can dispense justice impartially. No one pretends he is influenced by the evidence or the torrents of oratory or the printing of millions of words. Split into a number of blocs, the members tend to vote together according to their own frame of reference, and in accordance with instructions from the home government.

What of collective security, the supposed means of restraining aggression and ending breaches of the peace? It is necessary to take a hard look again at enforcement action since the United Nations is anchored to this method of providing peace and security for its members. The original intention of collective security was that the great majority of peace-loving states, by the employment of sanctions in varying forms, would be able to restrict aggression. But the present concentration of military power makes it impossible to coerce either the United States or the USSR. A threat against either would be ineffective because each is capable, on its own, of resisting the combination of power which might be drawn up by the middle- and small-sized nations. Neither of these states would have to stand alone, however, as each has a constellation of supporting nations which, no matter how reluctant they might be, would be drawn into the conflict.

The claim is still made that the United Nations stopped the North Koreans from overrunning South Korea. Nothing could be more misleading since the United States was able to obtain United Nations blessing for military action on that ocasion because the Soviet delegate had absented himself from the Security Council and could not interpose his veto in time. What followed was an improvisation of forces nominally under United Nations command but actually responsible to the military and civilian policy-makers in the United States who found it convenient to employ the United Nations as a shield for its Korean policy. The improvisation technique may prove useful at some future time given comparable circumstances, which, however, is highly improbable.

The ability of the General Assembly to direct military sanctions has yet to be tested. The development and use of UNEF cannot be construed as enforcement action since it does not possess the mandate to compel compliance with Assembly recommendations. It was not ordered to evict Israel from Egyptian territory nor to enforce the clearance of the Suez Canal. It was Egypt and not the United Nations or UNEF which first held up the clearing of Canal obstructions (placed there primarily by Egyptian action) until the Anglo-French forces were evacuated, and then slowed clearance operations in an effort to pressure the Israeli into leaving the Gaza and Gulf of Aqaba areas. However, the United Nations proved to be a most useful institution in this unfortunate affair since it was the only convenient mechanism available to provide military units, impartially led, to replace the forces of the invaders.

The experience of the League and the United Nations with collective security indicates that as a method of organizing peace, it is absolutely essential to have a firm set of rules fully understood by all concerned and universally applicable, supported by adequate means, including force, to guarantee that these rules are observed. All this assumes a high degree of rational and moral conduct on the part of the members of the security organization. Indeed, it comes quite close to saying that the functioning of such an organization must be motivated by considerations other than those of power politics. It can be said in this connection, that collective security depends on conditions which, if they are present, makes the need for a security organization unnecessary. Both the League and the United Nations have assumed the existence of conditions which were not present and the consequent difficulty of making these organizations function as intended has been apparent to all. The fact remains that at present the maintenance of peace is essentially a problem of power relationships inherently inimical to the requirements for the effective operation of collective security.

It should be clearly understood by this time that what is necessary for the functioning of such a security system is an ideal situation 'characterized by the peaceful existence of free peoples under the rule of a universal legal order having its basis in the natural community of interests and ultimately depending for its observance on generally acepted standards of reasonableness and good will.' [1] Collective security does have a rewarding element in that it encourages the belief that war anywhere must be considered to be a threat to peace and order everywhere. But to state that the United Nations is 'the only hope for peace' misses the main point. Rather, the only hope for peace depends upon the will of the great powers, more specifically, the United States and the Soviet Union, who will determine whether there shall be war or peace.

The United Nations as an institution dedicated to bringing peace and security to mankind can become more than an ideal when trust is placed in its capacity to complement and even foster the traditional processes of

[1] Schiffer, Walter, *The Legal Community of Mankind*, New York, 1954, p. 298.

diplomacy. An emphasis upon its procedures for collective enforcement, at the present at least, is futile. There can be enforcement only when there is superior authority with physical force greater by far than that of any potential aggressor. There must also be a body of law that clearly states what is illegal and provides the penalties for its defiance. In the absence of such prerequisites and in the present situation where nations have the opportunity to block measures inimical to their national interests, it is readily apparent that little reliance can be placed on the enforcement machinery of the Charter.

ECONOMIC AND SOCIAL CO-OPERATION: THE UNITED NATIONS SYSTEM

Justification for the United Nations must rest on its capacity to provide peace and security, and defense of it in terms of its success in nonpolitical matters is begging the question. Yet it is important to review briefly the work of the Organization in economic and social fields because here is offered the hope of solving many problems which may underlie areas of tension. The work of the specialized agencies also merits consideration, for it is with them that the greatest success can be recorded.

It must be emphasized again that the activities of the United Nations in economic and social matters by no means have escaped the political considerations noted in its other efforts. It must also be clearly borne in mind that the United Nations has no authority to compel its members to undertake action in the welfare field. Action cannot be initiated beyond making recommendations, reports, preparing multilateral conventions, and convening international conferences. Progress toward promoting the social and economic advancement of all peoples is achieved slowly, on an evolutionary basis, governed primarily by the political atmosphere surrounding the United Nations and the national policies of its members. Responsibilities have arisen out of the activities of the Organization in political and military matters. The Palestine situation created a serious refugee problem which had to be faced. The Korean War has, in like fashion, presented additional problems of rehabilitation and reconstruction which have provided the United Nations with grave additional duties.

The General Assembly and the Economic and Social Council have been given the responsibility of achieving 'international cooperation in solving international problems of an economic, social, cultural or humanitarian character.' The direction given by the Assembly has been marred frequently by political considerations and the inability of that organ to offer the unified leadership necessary for programs of economic development has resulted in halfway measures and compromise recommendations. Much of the postwar accomplishment in such basic matters as trade development, foreign exchange, and employment has come from regional institutions. In spite of the handicaps which result from the division in its membership and the unwieldy, transient nature of its meetings, the Assembly has, nevertheless, by the persistence of smaller nations managed to develop a certain continuity of purpose which has resulted in the establishment of technical assistance programs of significance and may eventually launch a worthwhile, lasting method for economic development. Measures for social and humanitarian betterment have lagged behind expectations, yet there are a number of conventions which have been concluded that owe their inspiration to Assembly recommendations.

see p. 446

The Economic and Social Council has undertaken a great variety of projects and has made some definite contributions, particularly through its regional economic commissions. It has managed to bring about a degree of co-ordination for the various activities of the United Nations and the specialized agencies. But its structure is sprawling and complex with a proliferation of projects which at times have no basis in reality. Too many members of the United Nations cannot resist the temptation of suggesting new studies. There has been talk of reducing work programs but no genuine overhaul has been accomplished. The commissions frequently become microcosms of the Assembly where debate and decisions are dictated by political considerations originating in the directives issued by governments to their representatives. The fact that ECOSOC simply has too much to do prevents it from doing the necessary tasks in an efficient and productive manner.

Most of the specialized agencies have done excellent work, some of it absolutely vital, while a few have proved to be less praiseworthy. The work of the World Health Organization on such problems as malaria, tuberculosis, venereal diseases, and the promotion of maternal and child welfare has been outstanding. Its contributions to the welfare of mankind cannot be measured accurately enough to portray the over-all usefulness of the agency, but it can be said that the work of WHO has been an unmitigated blessing. The activities of the Food and Agriculture Organization approach the efforts of WHO in competence and recorded achievements. The preparation of a large number of conventions concerning labor standards, many of which pertain to women, children, and maritime workers, are a credit to the continuing efforts of the International Labor Organization. The development of a system of industrial committees and the measures to improve the conditions of laborers in non-self-governing territories have also been valuable. The technical competence of the Universal Postal

Union, the International Civil Aviation Organization, the World Meteor-ological Organization, and the International Telecommunications Union are unquestioned.

Economic development through the World Bank has not been an un-qualified success although its loans have supplied many countries with funds to initiate worthwhile projects. Critics point to the fact that the Bank is dominated by the United States, which prevents a less conservative inter-pretation of the limitations prescribed by its Charter. Complaints are di-rected at the difficulty of obtaining loans and what is believed to be undue interference with sovereign rights through loan-supervision policies. But its very nature dictates that the Bank develop conservative criteria for making capital grants in terms of the soundness and the priority of the projects. There have been suggestions that the Bank could function more success-fully if policies could be determined on the basis of a 'one country, one vote' system instead of the present method of weighted voting. A reform of this nature might have just the opposite result, however, since it suggests the possibility of difficulties and disagreements surrounding the granting of loans on a political rather than economic basis. The International Finance Corporation may relieve the Bank of some of the criticism, since the new institution is able to approve loans which the Bank is now unwilling or forbidden to undertake.

The need to provide some machinery for consultation and collaboration on international monetary problems was recognized before the end of World War II. The International Monetary Fund was established to do this as well as to promote exchange stability, eliminate foreign exchange restrictions on current international transactions, and make available to its members short-term financial assistance to correct temporary maladjustments in bal-ance of payments without resort to restrictive monetary and trade measures. Progress toward these objectives has been slow and not much success has been achieved in arriving at a freer system of international payments. Some reduction in discrimination has occurred but the movement toward con-vertibility has not been rapid. Criticism of the Fund centers around what is claimed to be too restrictive a lending policy and the absence of auto-matic access to its resources by members through some established formula. But the United States, which has contributed most of the funds, is opposed to standards believed unsound from the standpoint of its own fiscal policies. The ultimate success of the Fund will depend upon the willingness of its members to employ it as a means of resolving problems of exchange rates and practices. The adoption of trade and financial policies designed to en-courage multilateral trade and currency convertibility is also necessary.

Despite the problems of duplication and co-ordination, the technical assistance programs of the United Nations, particularly those which employ the services of the specialized agencies, have enjoyed a measure of success. There has been relatively little political controversy and the methods of administration have been reasonably good. The sharing of technical knowledge and experience through international instrumentalities can have rewarding results. It is possible to utilize experts from all countries on a selective basis and employ those most appropriately fitted for tasks peculiar to underdeveloped countries. At the same time, it is already evident that there is a shortage of trained specialists and that can limit the effectiveness of a number of projects. As compared with the United States Point Four Program of technical assistance, those of the United Nations suffer from a lack of integration with loan programs of the Organization. Efforts are under-way to relieve this problem through greater liaison between lending and technical assistance agencies.

UNESCO has been the most controversial of the specialized agencies. Most of its objectives are praiseworthy but their implementation leaves much to be desired at times. The attempt to encourage understanding among all peoples, regardless of race, creed, color, or geographical location should occasion no argument. It is also important to promote contacts between people at all levels. The vicious claim that UNESCO is engaged as a partner with the United Nations in a monstrous scheme to foist some communist type of world government on the United States is ridiculous.[2] There is plenty of room to criticize UNESCO on other grounds. It is also possible to give UNESCO credit for its educational projects which form part of a long-range program of reducing illiteracy in the underdeveloped countries.

UNESCO has failed to explain its aims, purposes, and activities in adequate terms. Its national commissions throughout the world have been too frequently composed of well-meaning but uninformed private citizens who have overstated its case and made illusory claims. Knowledge and understanding can contribute toward the building of a gradually developing world community but will not necessarily allay the immediate fears and suspicions which endanger peace.

A great deal of UNESCO's activity is supposed to reduce the tensions which provoke international conflict but too much is attempted in too many diverse fields on a short-range basis. It is highly desirable to eliminate distortions and falsehoods from school history books and to encourage the introduction of communications media to explain cultures and habits. However the goals desired cannot be reached except through a patient and persistent effort that will take a considerable amount of time. UNESCO

[2] For a good example of the extremist position, see Watts, V. Orval, *The United Nations: Planned Tyranny*, New York, 1955.

will not remake the world and is no substitute for the traditional processes of diplomacy and the employment of the machinery available for peaceful settlement. It can serve to stimulate thinking on world problems, reduce illiteracy, strive for minimal standards of justice, and develop tolerance for competing cultures. Continuous action along these lines will justify the relatively small national expenditures on its behalf.

IS REVISION OF THE CHARTER NECESSARY?

One reaction to the shortcomings of the United Nations has been the demand for a revision of its Charter. Many people who have watched the Organization muddle along on serious problems are convinced that the only way out of the apparent impasse is to adopt amendments that would, in their view, strengthen the Charter provisions and bring them into line with existing conditions in the world. It is argued that the development of nuclear weapons and the intercontinental missile have raised new problems which alter the traditional concepts of peace and security upon which the United Nations was built. Most of the thinking along these lines involves the reconstitution of the United Nations into some form of world government.

Other suggestions for revision include those that would limit its present authority in economic and social questions and in the field of collective security or drastically change the nature of the Organization by eliminating certain of its members and joining the remainder into a huge military alliance. Then there are proposals which seek to improve the functioning of the Charter on certain matters by expanding mechanisms for the maintenance of peace and overhauling some of the existing machinery. More specifically, this last category includes items such as the veto in the Security Council and its relationship to questions of peace and security and the problem of domestic jurisdiction.

Impetus for revision came from Article 109 of the Charter which stated that the question of a review conference was to be placed on the agenda of the tenth session of the Assembly in 1955 if no such conference had been held prior to that time. Confidence was expressed generally that the Assembly would vote to review the Charter and that a conference would be called for that purpose in 1956. Study groups in several countries, notably in the United States, devoted their energies to matters believed worthy of review and transmitted their conclusions to appropriate government agencies.

But the General Assembly in 1955 voted to postpone a decision on whether to call a review conference and, instead, appointed a committee to study the matter and to recommend a time and place for such a conference. This committee was instructed not to report until 1957.[3] The basic reason for the postponement was that not even the most unimportant amendment can be made without the approval of the permanent members of the Security Council. Since the Soviet Union is still opposed to any restriction on the use of the veto or any other change in the Charter, the delegates in the Assembly believed that no useful purpose could be served by holding the conference in 1956. Moreover, the neutralist bloc of Arab and Asian members has become increasingly insistent that no stand be taken on an issue unless it is acceptable to the Soviet and Western blocs and to themselves.

There has been general resentment against the use of the veto on questions of peace and security and this has led to demands for its abolition or limitation. It is useless to speculate on any alterations in the voting procedure with respect to enforcement measures. None of the permanent members, particularly the United States and the Soviet Union, would ever agree to a situation whereby the United Nations could undertake sanctions without their consent. Any amendment of the Charter which would permit this would immediately be killed in the Security Council, a fact which should be obvious.

It would, however, be logical to expect the veto to be limited when the Security Council is seeking to bring about the peaceful settlement of a dispute. The Council is by far the most suitable organ to initiate the machinery of pacific settlement, since it is a small, compact group, usually representing the most important areas of the world, and is in continuous session. The Secretary-General can perform useful mediative functions and so can the General Assembly, but both operate under more handicaps than would a Security Council free to work on 'all questions involving peaceful settlement of international disputes and situations.' If decisions on matters of substance could be reached by a simple majority vote, the Council would be able to establish subsidiary organs of conciliation, fact-finding commissions, and so forth. Furthermore, it could grant them flexible terms of reference and direct their activities through each stage of their efforts to arrive at general or specific recommendations for settlement.

Although it is not essential, it might be wise, in addition, to modify Article 37 of the Charter, which permits the Security Council to make recommendations on cases where it decides that 'the continuance of the dispute is, in fact, likely to endanger the maintenance of international peace and security.' A state that is a party to a dispute does not want to have its activities labeled a danger to international peace. It would be more politic

---

[3] The Committee, at its first and only meeting, decided that it would be better to delay a review conference recommendation until 1959.

and undoubtedly more helpful toward reaching a settlement if a less positive phrase could be devised which would remove the stigma of suspicion and make consideration more routine. Certainly a dispute placed on the agenda of the Security Council is already serious or recourse to the Council would not have been made.

The question of domestic jurisdiction is as contentious as the problem of enforcement action and involves not only the problem of a veto in the Security Council but the difficulty of getting action in the bloc-ridden General Assembly. The United Nations is an association of sovereign states, each of which is determined to protect its own interests when they are challenged. Article 2:7 protects sovereign rights by forbidding the intervention of the United Nations 'in matters which are essentially within the domestic jurisdiction of any state.' But where to draw the line is a most difficult decision. In practice the Organization has tended to disregard the protection offered by Article 2:7 in doubtful cases, with results that have ranged from loud complaints to protest walkouts.

It is highly unlikely that there can be a satisfactory revision of the domestic jurisdiction provisions of the Charter. No codification is possible on all the subtleties of interpretation, despite the insistence of the anti-colonial powers that an attempt should be made to do so. The great powers are especially sensitive on this point and would never support an amendment that would injure their sovereign position. There are even suggestions that Article 2:7 be tightened to make certain that there may never be even the slightest interference in domestic affairs. The supporters of the Bricker amendment reflect this point of view in the United States. The United Nations will be exposed, therefore, to continuing efforts to reach some modification of the Charter on this issue and the colonial powers can expect repeated efforts to pry them loose from their defense of the status quo.

No amendment of the Charter had been made by 1958 and there is little likelihood that there will be formal modifications of any nature in the foreseeable future. Yet the United Nations is not the same organization it was in 1945. The application (or nonapplication) of the Charter has led to a number of changes in procedure and *de facto* modification which have revised varying degrees of support.

Over twenty articles of the Charter have been modified, become obsolete, or remained dormant.[4] All of these articles are minor in nature with the exception of the military features of enforcement (Articles 43–50). The practice in the Security Council of not counting an abstention from voting

[4] See Robinson, Jacob, 'The General Review Conference,' *International Organization*, Vol. 8, No. 3 (August 1954), pp. 324–6.

on a substantive question as the equivalent of a veto is a good example
of Charter modification by custom and usage. The most significant change,
however, has been the ascendancy of the General Assembly and its sharing of security functions formerly held to be the exclusive domain of the
Security Council. The 'Uniting for Peace' resolution is the clearest indication of the changed relationship between the two organs. Other significant
developments have been the creation of the Little Assembly, the action
against aggression in Korea, suggestions for the control of nuclear weapons
and the peaceful uses of atomic energy, the establishment of UNEF, and the
creation of regional defense pacts within the meaning of the Charter.

Most of these changes were initiated by the United States, which is an
indication of its influence during the life of the United Nations. Up to 1958,
the United States had never lost a vote in the Assembly on any vital issue,
and had been defeated in the Security Council only by the veto. Although
the influence and prestige of the United States will always continue to
remain strong, its ability to obtain in the future the overwhelming majorities
that it has had in the past appears to be less certain. When they join together,
as they have on many colonial issues and in the Middle East crisis, the
Soviet and Afro-Asian blocs possess nearly half the membership in the
Assembly and can easily block a two-thirds majority.

With this in mind, the wisdom of holding a review conference on the
Charter in the near future may be questioned. If the purpose of such a conference is merely to eliminate certain extinct articles or bring others in
line with common usage, a sort of 'punctuation' conference, so to speak, little
harm could ensue. Also, if a conference devoted its energies to reviewing
and evaluating the work of the Organization since its inception, eliminating
weak spots and noting where improvements could be made without formal
Charter amendment, it might, as a State Department official once stated,

> . . . bring greater understanding to our people and to the peoples of the
> world as to how essential the United Nations is . . . , of the extent to which
> the potentialities of the Charter are being realized. It can help measurably to
> refurbish the faith we have in the present Charter without raising false hopes
> and expectations.

But any attempt at a wholesale revision or a 'showdown' conference to drive
the Soviet Union out of the Organization might not only raise false hopes
but result in accentuating existing bitterness and weakening even further
whatever unity exists within the Organization. Structural changes involving
more machinery, new procedures, and more law will not eliminate the serious disturbances which exist in the world today. Defects in the Charter are
not the cause of basic differences separating peoples. What is essential is
more support for the law already laid down and the organs now in opera-

tion. As former Ambassador Ernest A. Gross stated: 'We do not face a band of cattle rustlers. Something close to one-quarter of the human race, led by despots, defies the Charter. This is not to say they will always stay that way; but it does say that a mere reformulation of the obligation will not change the nature either of the revolt or the threat.'

SUPRA-NATIONAL GOVERNMENT

There is a body of thought that is convinced that an association of sovereign states is not capable of preventing war and organizing peace. It believes that 'wars between groups of men forming social units always take place when these units — tribes, dynasties, churches, cities, nations — exercise unrestricted sovereign power.'[5] The answer suggested is to remove the sovereign power from states and place it in a higher authority or world government. Those who condemn the existence of unrestricted national sovereignty are by no means in agreement on the details of the higher authority or the steps necessary to bring it into being. They do share a common set of principles, drawing illustrations from history and expressing views similar to those philosophers of the past who have contributed to the literature on international organization.

In recent years the world government movement has concentrated upon the development of some form of federation by which national states would be joined together through a common government and body of law applicable both to the units of the federation and their peoples. A constitution for the world government would grant certain powers to the new central authority and leave others to the member-states. All plans for federation would require the individual national states to give up the right to possess military forces beyond the needs of local police establishments. The backers of this idea frequently cite the development of federalism in the United States as justification of the theory. This central idea represents the frontal attack upon the sovereign state since '. . . it seems clear that war as an institution could only persist in a world of sovereign states, each claiming the right to decide its own affairs as it sees fit. . . . and refusing to recognize any authority as superior to its own. It follows to a certain extent that sovereignty is a cause of all wars, and that the most straightforward and only permanent way to abolish war is to abolish sovereignty.'[6]

In the United States, it is argued, where each of the 48 states has given up its sovereign rights, one state does not need to 'defend' itself against

[5] Reves, Emery, *The Anatomy of Peace*, New York, 1946, p. 38.
[6] Curry, W. B., 'The Paradox of Sovereignty,' *New Republic*, Vol. 102 (February 5, 1950), p. 176.

another state except possibly in the federal courts. Defense and foreign affairs are the concern of the federal government which also settles disputes among the states. Why not construct a similar world federal system, suggest the federalists, in which each state would be freed from the need to defend itself and could spend the huge savings on needed public works and social services? The 'freedom' enjoyed by the present sovereign state is purely artificial since people are compelled to forego things they desire so that they can spend their resources on armaments which they do not really want. This 'freedom' actually prevents the free exchange of ideas and trade and impedes travel. It results in periodic world wars in which people lose not only what little true freedom they possess but also their very lives. Hence the great 'paradox of sovereignty' and the absurdity of its retention.

There have been a number of organizations in the United States working toward some form of federal union, chief of which are the Atlantic Union Committee and the United World Federalists.[7] The former has for its goal a regional federation of democracies within the United Nations composed of the seven countries which sponsored the North Atlantic Treaty (Belgium, Canada, France, Luxembourg, the Netherlands, the United Kingdom, and the United States). On July 26, 1949, shortly after the ratification of that Treaty, an Atlantic Union Resolution was introduced simultaneously in both houses of the United States Congress. It requested the President of the United States to:

> . . . invite the democracies which sponsored the North Atlantic Treaty to name delegates, representing their principal political parties, to meet this year with delegates of the United States in a Federal Convention to explore how far their peoples, and the peoples of such other democracies as the convention may invite to send delegates, can apply among them, within the framework of the United Nations, the principles of free federal union.

The Atlantic Union Committee has offered no blueprint for a federal structure of Atlantic democracies and has no draft for an Atlantic Constitution. It believes instead that this is the task for a federal convention of democracies. There is envisioned a common defense force and a common foreign policy as the initial step toward later unification of other functions. Atlantic Unionists are firmly convinced that such an organization would strengthen the United Nations since the establishment of a common foreign policy for the democracies would turn a portion of present international disputes into domestic problems. Controversies over issues would be resolved within the Union, thereby reducing the number of possible

[7] Others include Clarence Streit's Federal Union, the Citizens Committee for United Nations Reform, the American Committee for a United Europe, World Republic, Foundation for World Government, and the Committee To Frame a World Constitution. Similar arrangements are in existence in Britain and other countries of Western Europe.

issues for and parties to international conflict, and disruption of United Nations procedures.

Founded in 1947, the United World Federalists (UWF) is the strongest federalist organization in any country. The thought and policy of this group underwent a considerable change during the first ten years of its existence and by 1957 it was not as strong numerically or as extremist in its position as formerly.[8] Opinion within its ranks has been divided over the question of the initial powers which the world federal state should possess. Disagreement has also been evident on the problem of whether the new government should come into force as soon as two or more states were willing to federate or wait until nearly all countries had acceded to federation, including all the major powers. In its early years, UWF was clearly 'abruptist,' that is, desirous of establishing 'world government now.' Its current policy is more long-range in nature and is centered around support of the United Nations and efforts to provide it with more authority.

The objective of UWF is an eventual 'world federation having powers limited to the prevention of aggression and control of armaments,' with universal disarmament 'enforced under proper safeguards through a system of world law applicable to all nations and to all individuals.' There has been an increasing emphasis placed on 'disarmament through the United Nations' with not as much discussion as in earlier years of sweeping powers for the world federal government. The UWF policy has centered around these points approved by its national convention:

> We commend all efforts to develop detailed plans for effective disarmament. We reiterate that such disarmament must be based on the following principles:
> (a) Disarmament must be complete, eliminating all national armed forces and armaments not necessary for internal order.
> (b) It must be enforceable on nations and individuals by the United Nations, through its inspectors, civilian police, courts and armed forces to insure compliance with disarmament regulations and to prevent aggression.
> (c) It must not be subject to veto.
> (d) It must be universal — undertaken simultaneously by all nations.
> (e) Machinery for peaceful settlements of international disputes, under law based on justice as between nations, must be available. . . .
> We believe that the disarmament program we advocate requires substantial changes in the UN Charter, among which are amendments affecting membership, voting in the Security Council and the General Assembly, the International Court of Justice, UN forces (under effective safeguards), increased authority of the General Assembly, revenue, and protection of every nation from UN interference in its domestic affairs and from UN interference with the constitutional rights of its citizens.

[8] Current membership is about 20,000, a considerable drop from a peak of 50,000 in 1949.

While the arguments of the world government enthusiasts have great appeal on the surface, a number of them are open to serious question. Those who still demand the immediate remaking of the United Nations into even a limited world government oversimplify the problem by not assessing fully the manner in which governments are made, nor do they recognize the basic meaning of sovereignty. All evil cannot be eradicated simply by revising the Charter or devising a new constitution. Constitutions follow upon a society which has grown used to common institutions, a community attached to certain norms and interests. It is from this communal society that governments and constitutions spring. The community is developed first, and the constitution, the laws, and the administration come afterwards.

The way in which the United States was created is often cited as an argument in favor of the theory of world federalism. When carefully scrutinized, this analogy breaks down. The thirteen colonies meeting in convention did not constitute thirteen separate sovereignties preparing to join together as one. They had fought a war together and possessed the same moral convictions, the same loyalties, a common heritage, and similar political institutions. When the Philadelphia convention created the United States, one common loyalty was exchanged for another. A social order was not built, a community was not created where none existed before. What was done in 1787 was to perfect the community that had already developed under the British crown and was made manifest in the common struggle during the Revolution. The colonial people existed as a community before the establishment of the United States, just as a world community must be created before the erection of a world state.

The concept of sovereignty is a legal one, devoted to the authority of the state in the field of law. It is not itself an instrument of power. Even if sovereignty were delegated to the world authority, power would remain within national borders in terms of industrial potential and natural resources. Wars are conflicts of power but not necessarily conflicts of sovereignties. History is witness to many civil wars wherein the transference of sovereignty to some central authority did not provide peace and order. Furthermore, national sovereignty is not entirely a fixation in the minds of politicians and academicians. Actually, it is rooted firmly in the daily behavior of citizens who give their allegiance to the authority of the state. Sovereignty cannot be delegated by governments unless habits are basically changed, unless the behavior tendencies of millions upon millions of people are directed toward a world, instead of a national, community.

If, in some desperate effort to solve the problems dividing the Soviets and the Western world, the United Nations were to be transformed into some form of world government with the General Assembly made a legislature based on the democratic principles of popular representation and majority rule, could it succeed in the absence of a real majority possessed of common values, interests, and goals? The answer is a categorical 'no' since the struggle between East and West would not dissolve merely because the setting was changed. The possibility of establishing a limited world government is at the present time as remote as it has been for centuries.

REGIONAL SYSTEMS

Increasing emphasis has been placed upon regional systems as a means of advancing security. In 1958, for example, the United States belonged to four multipartite, regional, collective self-defense organizations. Whatever enforcement authority can be mustered by the United Nations is intimately linked to regional blocs and military systems. The Korean military action as far as the United Nations was concerned was largely a NATO and Commonwealth effort. The blocs in the General Assembly for the most part speak for and represent the several forms and types of regional systems in existence. Most of the security arrangements devised by these regional organizations have resulted from the inability of the United Nations to provide an adequate system for the maintenance of peace and security. This being so, these arrangements in a sense reflect the disunity which exists in the United Nations and do not, in themselves, represent efforts to by-pass or undermine the unity originally prescribed for the Organization as a whole.

All but one of these security structures justify their existence, as far as their compatibility with the Charter is concerned, as collective self-defense organizations permitted under Article 51. The Soviet system has its basis primarily in Articles 53 and 107, which allow unimpeded action for regional arrangements directed against the renewal of aggressive policy of enemy states during World War II. Much of the European effort to accomplish development programs and closer-knit economic policies has arisen from the peculiarly local aspect of the problems involved and the inadequacy of United Nations leadership.

The Organization of American States is the embodiment, in most respects, of the regionalist's argument for a smaller organization, restricted in a geographical sense to states and peoples living in proximity to each other, which can offer the machinery necessary for meeting common problems effectively. The Organization of American States has not been confronted with any major crisis, nor is it likely to be, but it has demonstrated an ability to isolate danger spots and move decisively when the occasion demands. With a long history of economic and social collaboration based upon the familarity and tradition of shared experiences, the Latin American States, with the assistance of the United States, have managed to develop a degree of harmonious relationship unmatched elsewhere.

The weakness of the League of Arab States stands in direct contrast to the Organization of American States. Despite a common heritage and racial and religious similarity, the League has been unable to channel objectives in a common direction in an area of the world desperately in need of unity. It may be that with sufficient outside assistance and some adjustments of the troubles with Israel, the Arab League can supply the leadership necessary for the Middle East.

The North Atlantic Treaty Organization is as yet, fortunately, untested militarily. It has not been an easy task to develop the integration necessary for such a multi-national security organization or to obtain the combatant elements needed to make it an effective military force. The immense financial burden required for the support of military contributions to NATO by its European members has been an increasing problem. The Middle East crisis in 1956–57 caused a considerable rift among the principal members of the Atlantic community which will take time to heal. A major change came in April, 1957, when Paul-Henri Spaak, former Belgian Foreign Minister and a devoted believer in a united Europe, became NATO's Secretary-General, replacing Lord Ismay, a military man. The full impact of German contingents in NATO and a German General heading a NATO command is yet to be felt. In 1958, therefore, the future was not clear. Was NATO to be a limited, American protected area whose range of action and influence would be confined to Europe and would exclude common diplomatic action by its members in all other parts of the world? Or was it to be one of several areas, such as the Western Hemisphere, the Far East, or the Middle East, where the United States may construct or has already built defensive arrangements? Or will it become a community of at least theoretically equal members with similar traditions and aims, a partnership acting as a unit throughout the world?

Also uncertain is the path ahead for the Southeast Asia Treaty Organization. Presumably the Pacific counterpart of NATO, SEATO is much weaker, less compact, and widely spread over immense land and sea areas, with its continental members (Pakistan and Thailand) the weakest in the entire combination. Other military problems are easily discernible from a glance at a map of the area. The most obvious question that arises is what the Western world can actually do to protect the countries still exposed to communist threats in Southeast Asia without resorting to a conflict along the lines of that in Korea and Indo-China. Perhaps the only answer is to concentrate on an approach based on sound economic, social, and humanitarian activities rather than on military measures.[9]

The most important economic integration has come from the establishment of the European Coal and Steel Community and the Organization for European Economic Co-operation. Both have made great headway toward breaking down traditional barriers which have been such a divisive factor in Europe. Both concentrate on long-range planning and while they have objectives not necessarily identical, they indicate the building of a framework for co-operation which is not likely to develop within the United Nations. The greatest achievements have been made in the fields of intra-European trade and foreign exchange. Through the gradual reduction of restrictive trade practives and discrimination, and the advocacy of policies aimed at combating inflation and preventing wasteful industrial overlapping, both the Community and OEEC have moved Western Europe toward greater integration. It is obvious that such an arrangement offers great potential advantages, since all the countries involved are surrounded by tariff barriers and restrictions on the flow of funds, which are severe impediments to trade and economic development. The progress of the Common Market and Euratom will be watched with the greatest interest in this connection. Serious problems still remain, however, which can be solved only through patient and careful economic planning and diplomacy. Nations which still have commitments with overseas territories for preferential treatment, as the United Kingdom does with Canada and other dominions, pose only one of these problems.

The movement for the political unification of Western Europe has aroused a great deal of talk and much speculation but has not progressed beyond this stage. The Council of Europe, with its Consultative Assembly standing as a quasi-European parliament has been unable to do much more than support existing regional organizations and endeavor to bring them within its loose framework. As one of its members remarked, it is 'an Assembly in search of a job.' The true basis for a wider, genuine union has not been established. The drive for a European political union 'is a rational movement sponsored by intellectual and reasonable men of affairs, who are acting from a multiplicity of highly respectable motives' and 'appeals on the Continent, though not in Britain, to reminiscences of a great past.' [10] Nowhere is there significant evidence of a true desire on the part of Europeans to submerge their national entities in a wider political union.

[9] See, for example, Henderson, William, 'The Development of Regionalism in South-East Asia,' *International Organization*, Vol. 9, No. 4 (November 1955), pp. 463–76.
[10] Bonn, M. J., *Whither Europe: Union or Partnership?*, New York, 1952, p. 203.

Nationalism is not weaker today and is very likely stronger than it has been in the past decade. Whatever success the European movement has enjoyed is the result of external pressure and internal fears. This is not a sound foundation upon which to build a new structure. What is needed is the development of a common European patriotism which can cement together the peoples of a union after the external pressures have dissipated. Until nationalism is supplanted by 'Europeanism' there can be no true supranational European state. In the meantime, the economic and military arrangements already in operation, and the constant prodding of the Council of Europe for a closer working alignment, possibly under its aegis, will have to suffice until a common allegiance can arise from the greatness of Europe's civilization.

A WORLD COMMUNITY?

The central problem of international organization is the accomplishment of a stable peace between nations and this involves the whole question of security. This is dependent exclusively upon the unity of the great powers, a principle which 'is the very essence of the Charter' of the United Nations. It is nowhere stated in the Charter but this unity was presumed to exist when the United Nations came into existence. Fundamentally, unity can be brought into being through the processes of traditional diplomacy operating inside as well as beyond the confines of the United Nations. Before international organization can be strengthened at the political level there must be a mitigation of conflict and a narrowing of the areas of controversy so that the issues separating peoples can be minimized to permit the growth of interests which can unify them. In this way can come the building of the world community, that slow, evolutionary process of developing communal values and interests which is the primary requisite for the attainment of any world state. This is a task of supreme importance which has been discussed for centuries by those interested in developing true international government.[11] A world community involves the development of moral and political judgments shared by wider than national groups, the creation of something to be loyal to beyond that of the national state. Lessing, in the eighteenth century, touched upon this question when he observed that 'religious, class, and state divisions, the sovereignty of the national state, can be overcome only by the ideal of humanity.'

[11] The valuable work under way by the Center for Research on World Political Institutions at Princeton University should be consulted in this connection, especially its first study by Van Wagenen, Richard W., *Research in the International Organization Field, Some Notes on a Possible Focus,* published in 1952. See also Wright, Quincy, ed., *The World Community*, Chicago, 1948.

What is needed is to exploit more fully the possibilities inherent in the cosmopolitanism exhibited in private or nongovernmental organizations as well as the expansion of the public, specialized organizations. In a similar vein, various economic, social, political, and cultural groups within all countries must be encouraged to accomplish common group purposes which extend beyond individual borders. What is needed is a gradual substitution of national conflict by group conflict that can and does transcend national boundaries. Society within any nation is composed of groups, often competing with each other and conflicting in their interests. Such conflicts as arise, however, are essentially healthy and invigorating, stimulating to national society as a whole and do not lead to open warfare because such groups possess deeply rooted common values. It was just such functional group co-operation that was the strength behind the formation of the national state in general and the United States of America in particular.

International organization at its current stage of development can assist in encouraging the idea of the world community. If international agencies become numerous and widespread enough and answer to the needs of enough peoples, there can develop a loyalty to them and to a growing sense of world community of which they are a part. But a sense of belonging to and sharing a part of the life of a wider than national community will not come by legislating or decreeing it or by wishful thinking. There can be no timetable for bringing about the community, which comes first, and the authority, which comes second, in the same general process that has created the individual national state.

Clearly the development of international organization has come in response to the needs of mankind. The United Nations is the present manifestation of the natural legacy, passed from one generation to the next, of the continuous search for the warless world of peace and prosperity. Fundamentally, the League of Nations and the United Nations have had a common aim, to demonstrate that eventually all nations may develop mutual trust and resolve conflict. The League failed, possibly because it was ahead of its time. The United Nations today stands as the only institution that can mirror the opinions of the world and through world opinion forge a common sense of universal justice.

The gravity of the present world situation is emphasized because it is so difficult to see how our divided civilizations can reach a new unity. No realistic appraisal which measures the gulf separating the various ideological groupings from each other can dare to speak with confidence of developing a new universalism. But integration in society is rarely achieved through conscious and deliberate effort. Instead it is a gradual process resulting from the confrontation of society with intangible realities which point in the direction of a greater unity. International organization not only can serve as a means for the integration of mankind but also may assist in the substantiation of human values lest a cynical denial of the search for truth engulf humanity.

SELECTED BIBLIOGRAPHY

Chapter 1

Brierly, J. L., *The Law of Nations,* 4th ed. (New York: Oxford University Press), 1948.

Fenwick, C. G., *International Law,* 3rd ed. (New York: Appleton-Century-Crofts), 1948.

Haas, E., and Whiting, A., *Dynamics of International Relations* (New York: McGraw-Hill), 1956.

Kelsen, H., *The Law of the United Nations* (London: Stevens and Sons), 1951.

Kohn, H., *The Idea of Nationalism* (New York: Macmillan), 1945.

Lerche, C. O., Jr., *Principles of International Politics* (New York: Oxford University Press), 1956.

Levi, W., *Fundamentals of World Organization* (Minneapolis: University of Minnesota Press), 1950.

Martin, A., *Collective Security, A Progress Report* (Paris: UNESCO), 1952.

Mitrany, D., *A Working Peace System* (London: Royal Institute of International Affairs), 1943.

Morgenthau, H., Jr., *In Defense of the National Interest* (New York: Knopf), 1952.

—— *Politics Among Nations,* 2nd ed. (New York: Knopf), 1954.

Royal Institute of International Affairs, *Nationalism* (London: Oxford University Press), 1939.

Schwarzenberger, G., *Power Politics,* 2nd ed. (London: Stevens and Sons), 1951.

Wright, Q., *A Study of War,* 2 vols. (Chicago: University of Chicago Press), 1942.

—— *Problems of Stability and Progress in International Relations* (Berkeley: University of California Press), 1953.

—— *The Study of International Relations* (New York: Appleton-Century-Crofts), 1955.

PERIODICALS

Haas, E., 'Types of Collective Security,' *American Political Science Review,* Vol. 49 (March 1955).

Kissinger, H., 'Force and Diplomacy in the Nuclear Age,' *Foreign Affairs,* Vol. 35 (April 1956).

Rothwell, C. E., 'International Organization and International Politics,' *International Organization,* Vol. 3 (November 1949).

Symposium, 'The National Interest — Alone or with Others,' *Annals of the American Academy of Political and Social Science,* Vol. 282 (July 1952).

Wolfers, A., 'The Pole of Power and the Role of Indifference,' *World Politics,* Vol. 4 (October 1951).

Chapter 2

Baker, R., *Woodrow Wilson and the Peace Settlement,* 3 vols. (Garden City: Doubleday, Page), 1922.

Birdsall, P., *Versailles Twenty Years After* (New York: Reynal and Hitchcock), 1941.

Burton, M. E., *The Assembly of the League of Nations* (Chicago: University of Chicago Press), 1941.

Choate, J. H., *The Two Hague Conferences* (Princeton: Princeton University Press), 1913.

Davis, H. E., ed., *Pioneers in World Order* (New York: Columbia University Press), 1944.

George, D. L., *Memoirs of the Peace Conference,* 2 vols. (New Haven: Yale University Press), 1939.

Greaves, H. R. G., *The League Committees and World Order* (London: Oxford University Press), 1931.

Hall, D., *Mandates, Dependencies, and Trusteeship* (Washington, D.C.: Carnegie Endowment for International Peace), 1948.

Hembleton, S., *Plans for World Peace through Six Centuries* (Chicago: University of Chicago Press), 1943.

Hill, N., *The Economic and Financial Organization of the League of Nations* (Washington, D.C.: Carnegie Endowment for International Peace), 1946.

Howard-Ellis, C., *The Origin, Structure and Working of the League of Nations,* 2 vols. (Boston: Houghton Mifflin), 1928.

Hudson, M. O., *International Tribunals, Past and Present* (Washington, D.C.: Carnegie Endowment for International Peace), 1944.

Mangone, G., *A Short History of International Organization* (New York: McGraw-Hill), 1954.

Marburg, T., *The Development of the League of Nations Idea,* 2 vols. (New York: Macmillan), 1932.

Miller, D. H., *The Drafting of the Covenant,* 2 vols. (New York: Putnam), 1928.

Morley, F., *The Society of Nations* (Washington, D.C.: Brookings), 1932.

Mowat, R., *The Concert of Europe* (New York: Macmillan), 1930.

Ranshofen-Wertheimer, E., *The International Secretariat* (Washington, D.C.: Carnegie Endowment for International Peace), 1945.

Russell, F., *Theories of International Relations* (New York: Appleton-Century-Crofts), 1936.

—— *The Saar: Battleground and Pawn* (Stanford: Stanford University Press), 1951.

Stawell, F. N., *The Growth of International Thought* (New York: Holt), 1930.

Walters, F. P., *A History of the League of Nations,* 2 vols. (New York: Oxford University Press), 1952.

White, L., *International Non-Governmental Organizations* (New Brunswick: Rutgers University Press), 1951.

Zimmern, Sir Alfred, *The League of Nations and the Rule of Law* (London: Macmillan), 1936.

Chapter 3

Cecil (Viscount), *A Great Experiment* (New York: Oxford University Press), 1939.

Conwell-Evans, T. P., *The League Council in Action* (London: Oxford University Press), 1929.

Davis, H. E., ed., *Pioneers in World Order* (New York: Columbia University Press), 1944.

Hill, N., *The Economic and Financial Organization of the League of Nations* (Washington, D.C.: Carnegie Endowment for International Peace), 1946.

Hogan, W. N., *International Conflict and Collective Security: The Principle of Concern in International Organization* (Lexington: University of Kentucky Press), 1955.

Mander, L., *Foundations of Modern World Society*, 2nd ed. (Stanford: Stanford University Press), 1947.

Myers, D., *Handbook of the League of Nations* (Boston: World Peace Foundation), 1935.

Phelan, E. J., *Yes, and Albert Thomas* (London: Cresset), 1936.

Rappard, W., *The Quest for Peace* (Cambridge, Mass.: Harvard University Press), 1933.

Royal Institute of International Affairs, *International Sanctions* (New York: Oxford University Press), 1938.

Shotwell, J. T., *War As An Instrument of National Policy* (New York: Harcourt, Brace), 1929.

Shotwell, J. T., and Salvin, M., *Lessons on Security and Disarmament from the History of the League of Nations* (New York: King's Crown), 1949.

Smith, S. S., *The Manchurian Crisis, A Tragedy in International Relations* (New York: Columbia University Press), 1948.

Walters, F. P., *A History of the League of Nations*, 2 vols. (New York: Oxford University Press), 1952.

Willoughby, W. W., *The Sino-Japanese Controversy and the League of Nations* (Baltimore: The Johns Hopkins Press), 1935.

PERIODICALS

Eagleton, C., 'The Attempt to Define Aggression,' *International Conciliation*, No. 264 (November 1930).

—— 'The Attempt to Define War,' *International Conciliation*, No. 291 (June 1933).

Hubbard, U., 'The Co-operation of the United States with the League of Nations,' *International Conciliation*, No. 329 (April 1937).

Myers, D., 'Liquidation of the League of Nations Functions,' *American Journal of International Law*, Vol. 42 (April 1948).

Sly, J., 'The Genesis of the Universal Postal Union,' *International Conciliation*, No. 233 (October 1927).

Sweetser, A., 'The Non-Political Activities of the League of Nations,' *Foreign Affairs*, Vol. 19 (October 1940).

DOCUMENTS

League of Nations, *Commercial Policy in the Interwar Period,* Geneva, 1942, II. Economic and Financial, 1942, II. A. 6.

―――― *Economic Stability in the Postwar World,* Geneva, 1945, II. Economic and Financial, 1945, II. A. 6.

―――― *Food, Famine, and Relief,* 1946, II. Economic and Financial, 1946, II. A. 6.

―――― *International Institute of Intellectual Co-operation* (Paris: League of Nations), 1938.

―――― *Ten Years of World Co-operation* (Geneva: League Secretariat), 1930.

―――― 'The Development of International Cooperation in Economic and Social Affairs,' *Special Supplement to the Monthly Summary of the League of Nations* (Geneva: League Secretariat), August 1939.

United Nations, *Analysis of Provisions of Pacific Settlement Treaties,* Note by Secretariat, UN Doc. A/AC. 18/57, May 6, 1948.

Chapter 4

Byrnes, J., *Speaking Frankly* (New York: Harper), 1947.

Chase, E., *The United Nations in Action* (New York: McGraw-Hill), 1950.

Churchill, W., *The Grand Alliance* (Boston: Houghton Mifflin), 1950.

Dean, V., *The Four Cornerstones of Peace* (New York: Whittlesey House), 1946.

Evatt, H., *The United Nations* (Cambridge, Mass.: Harvard University Press), 1948.

Goodrich, L. N., and Hambro, E., *The Charter of the United Nations, Commentary and Documents,* rev. ed. (Boston: World Peace Foundation), 1949.

Hull, C., *The Memoirs of Cordell Hull,* 2 vols. (New York: Macmillan), 1948.

Wilmot, C., *The Struggle for Europe* (London: Collins), 1952.

PERIODICALS

Carnegie Endowment for International Peace, *International Conciliation,* see issues from 1940–1946.

Davis, N., Gilchrist, H., Kirk, G., and Padelford, N., 'The United Nations Charter with Explanatory Notes of Its Development at San Francisco,' *International Conciliation,* No. 413 (September 1945).

Goodrich, L. M., 'From the League of Nations to the United Nations,' *International Organization,* Vol. 1 (February 1947).

Kirk, G., and Chamberlain, L., 'The Organization of the San Francisco Conference,' *Political Science Quarterly,* Vol. 40 (June 1945).

DOCUMENTS

United Nations, *Documents of the United Nations Conference on International Organization, San Francisco, 1945,* 16 vols. (New York: United Nations Information Service), 1945–1946.

United States, *The United Nations Conference on International Organization; Selected Documents,* Department of State Publication 2490, Conference Series 83 (Washington, D.C.: U.S. Government Printing Office), 1946.

United States Congress, *Postwar Foreign Policy Preparation, 1939–1945,* Department of State Publication 3580, General Foreign Policy Series 15 (Washington, D.C.: U.S. Government Printing Office), 1950.

—— *Report to the President on the Results of the San Francisco Conference* . . . , Department of State Publication 2349, Conference Series 71 (Washington, D.C.: U.S. Government Printing Office), 1945.

Chapter 5

Bentwich, N., and Martin, A., *A Commentary on the Charter of the United Nations* (London: Macmillan), 1950.

Brierly, J. L., *The Covenant and the Charter* (New York: Macmillan), 1947.

Goodrich, L. M., and Hambro, E., *The Charter of the United Nations, Commentary and Documents*, rev. ed. (Boston: World Peace Foundation), 1949.

Haviland, H. F., Jr., *The Political Role of the General Assembly* (New York: Carnegie Endowment for International Peace), 1951.

Kelsen, H., *The Law of the United Nations* (New York: Praeger), 1951.

PERIODICALS

Coster, D. W., 'The Interim Committee of the General Assembly: An Appraisal,' *International Organization*, Vol. 3 (August 1949).

'Covenant of the League of Nations and the Charter of the United Nations: Points of Difference,' *Department of State Bulletin*, Vol. 3 (August 19, 1945).

Frye, W. R., 'Press Coverage of the UN,' *International Organization*, Vol. 10 (May 1956).

Goodrich, L. M., 'The Development of the General Assembly,' *International Conciliation*, No. 471 (May 1951).

Hovey, A., Jr., 'Obstructionism and the Rules of the General Assembly,' *International Organization*, Vol. 4 (August 1950).

Hyde, J. N., 'United States Participation in the United Nations,' *International Organization*, Vol. 10 (February 1956).

Kunz, J. L., 'Privileges and Immunities of International Organization,' *American Journal of International Law*, Vol. 41 (October 1947).

DOCUMENTS

United Nations, *Annual Report of the Secretary-General* (New York: United Nations Secretariat), *seriatim*.

—— *Repertory of Practice of United Nations Organs*, 5 vols. (New York: United Nations Secretariat), 1955.

—— *Report of the Preparatory Commission of the United Nations*, Doc. PC/20, December 23, 1945.

—— *Yearbook of the United Nations*, prepared by the UN Secretariat (New York: Columbia University Press), *seriatim*.

—— *The United States and the United Nations*, an annual report by the President to the United States Congress.

Chapter 6

Bentwich, N., and Martin, A., *A Commentary on the Charter of the United Nations* (London: Macmillan), 1950.

Brown, B. H., *Chinese Representation. A Case Study in United Nations Political Affairs* (New York: Woodrow Wilson Foundation), 1955.

Goodrich, L. M., and Hambro, E., *Charter of the United Nations, Commentary and Documents*, rev. ed. (Boston: World Peace Foundation), 1949.

Haviland, H. F., Jr., *The Political Role of the General Assembly* (New York: Carnegie Endowment for International Peace), 1951.

Houston, J. A., *Latin America in the United Nations* (New York: Carnegie Endowment for International Peace), 1956.

Koo, W., *Voting Procedures in International Political Organizations* (New York: Columbia University Press), 1947.

Riches, C. A., *Majority Rule in International Organization* (Baltimore: The Johns Hopkins Press), 1940.

PERIODICALS

Ball, M. M., 'Bloc Voting in the General Assembly,' *International Organization*, Vol. 5 (1951).

De Russet, A., 'Large and Small States in International Organization,' *International Affairs*, Vol. 45 (April 1955).

Eeckman, P., 'The Domestic Jurisdiction Clause of the Charter: A Belgian View,' *International Organization*, Vol. 9 (November 1955).

Engel, S., 'De Facto Revision of the Charter of the United Nations,' *Journal of Politics*, Vol. 14 (February 1952).

Goodrich, L. M., 'The United Nations and Domestic Jurisdiction,' *International Organization*, Vol. 3 (February 1949).

Hovey, A., Jr., 'Voting Procedure in the General Assembly,' *International Organization*, Vol. 4 (August 1950).

Howell, J. M., 'The French and South African Walkouts and Domestic Jurisdiction,' *Journal of Politics*, Vol. 18 (February 1956).

Klooz, M. S., 'The Role of the General Assembly of the United Nations in the Admission of New Members,' *American Journal of International Law*, Vol. 43 (April 1949).

Lee, D., 'The Genesis of the Veto,' *International Organization*, Vol. 1 (February 1947).

Liang, Yuen-Li, 'Abstention and Absence of a Permanent Member in Relation to the Voting Procedure in the Security Council,' *American Journal of International Law*, Vol. 44 (October 1950).

Moldaver, A., 'Repertoire of the Veto in the Security Council, 1946–1956,' *International Organization*, Vol. 11 (Spring 1957).

Morgenthau, H., 'The New United Nations and the Revision of the Charter,' *Review of Politics*, Vol. 16 (January 1954).

Padelford, N., 'The Use of the Veto,' *International Organization*, Vol. 2 (June 1948).

Rolin, H., 'The International Court of Justice and Domestic Jurisdiction,' *International Organization*, Vol. 8 (February 1954).

Rudzinski, A., 'Admission of New Members: The United Nations and League of Nations,' *International Conciliation*, No. 480 (April 1952).

DOCUMENTS

United Nations, *Repertory of Practice of United Nations Organs*, 5 Vols. (New York: United Nations Secretariat), *seriatim*.

United States Congress, *The Problem of Membership in the United Nations,* Staff Study No. 3, Subcommittee on the United Nations Charter, Committee on Foreign Relations, United States Senate, 83rd Congress, 2nd Session (Washington, D.C.: U.S. Government Printing Office), 1954.

────── *Representation and Voting in the United Nations General Assembly,* Staff Study No. 4, Subcommittee on the United Nations Charter, Committee on Foreign Relations, United States Senate, 83rd Congress, 2nd Session (Washington, D.C.: U.S. Government Printing Office), 1954.

────── *The Problem of the Veto,* Staff Study No. 1, Subcommittee on the United Nations Charter, Committee on Foreign Relations, United States Senate, 83rd Congress, 2nd Session (Washington, D.C.: U.S. Government Printing Office), 1954.

────── *How the United Nations Charter Has Developed,* Staff Study No. 2, Subcommittee on the United Nations Charter, Committee on Foreign Relations, United States Senate, 83rd Congress, 2nd Session (Washington, D.C.: U.S. Government Printing Office), 1954.

Chapter 7

Goodrich, L. M., and Hambro, E., *Charter of the United Nations, Commentary and Documents,* rev. ed. (Boston: World Peace Foundation), 1949.

Goodrich, L. M. and Simons, A. P., *The United Nations and the Maintenance of Peace and Security* (Washington, D.C.: Brookings), 1955.

Houston, J. A., *Latin America in the United Nations* (New York: Carnegie Endowment for International Peace), 1956.

Korbel, J., *Danger in Kashmir* (Princeton: Princeton University Press), 1954.

Wehl, D., *The Birth of Indonesia* (London: Allen and Unwin), 1949.

PERIODICALS

Black, C. E., 'Greece and the United Nations,' *Political Science Quarterly,* Vol. 63 (December 1948).

Collins, J. F., 'The United Nations and Indonesia,' *International Conciliation,* No. 459 (March 1950).

Eagleton, C., 'The Case of Hyderabad before the Security Council,' *American Journal of International Law,* Vol. 44 (April 1950).

Emerson, R., 'Reflections in the Indonesian Case,' *World Politics,* Vol. 1 (October 1948).

Hurewitz, J. C., 'The United Nations Conciliation Commission for Palestine,' *International Organization,* Vol. 4 (November 1953).

Hyde, J. N., 'Peaceful Settlement,' *International Conciliation,* No. 444 (October 1948).

Leonard, L., 'The United Nations and Palestine,' *International Conciliation,* No. 454 (October 1949).

Lowrie, S., 'The UN Military Observer Groups in India and Pakistan,' *International Organization,* Vol. 9 (February 1955).

Mohn, P., 'Problems of Truce Supervision,' *International Conciliation,* No. 478 (February 1952).

Richardson, C. B., 'The United Nations Relief for Palestinian Refugees,' *International Organization,* Vol. 4 (February 1950).

Rushbrook-Williams, L. F., 'Inside Kashmir,' *International Affairs,* Vol. 33 (January, 1957).

Wright, Q., 'International Organization and Peace,' *Western Political Quarterly,* Vol. 8 (June 1955).

DOCUMENTS

United Nations, *Annual Report of the Secretary-General, seriatim.*

―――― *Repertory of Practice of United Nations Organs,* especially Volumes 2 and 3.

―――― Secretary-General, *Summary Statement by . . . on Matters of Which the Security Council is Seized,* Doc. 5/3618, July 16, 1956.

―――― *United Nations Review,* formerly *United Nations Bulletin,* published by the UN Department of Public Information. Most numbers contain useful summaries and documentary materal of all questions before UN organs.

―――― *Yearbook, seriatim.*

―――― *Repertoire of the Practice of the Security Council 1946–51* (New York: UN Secretariat), 1954.

United States Congress, *Pacific Settlement of Disputes in the United Nations,* Staff Study No. 5, Subcommittee on the United Nations Charter, Committee on Foreign Relations, United States Senate, 83rd Congress, 2nd Session (Washington, D.C.: U.S. Government Printing Office), 1954.

―――― *The United States and the United Nations,* an annual report by the President to the United States Congress.

Chapter 8

Bentwich, N., and Martin, A., *A Commentary on the Charter of the United Nations* (London: Macmillan), 1950.

Goodrich, L. M., and Hambro, E., *Charter of the United Nations, Commentary and Documents,* rev. ed. (Boston: World Peace Foundation), 1949.

Goodrich, L. M., and Simons, A. P., *The United Nations and the Maintenance of International Peace and Security* (Washington, D.C.: Brookings), 1955.

Houston, J. A., *Latin America and the United Nations* (New York: Carnegie Endowment for International Peace), 1956.

Lie, T., *In the Cause of Peace* (New York: Macmillan), 1954.

Martin, A., *Collective Security. A Progress Report* (Paris: UNESCO), 1952.

PERIODICALS

Andrassy, J., 'Uniting for Peace,' *American Journal of International Law,* Vol. 50 (July 1956).

Eagleton, C., 'The Prevention of Aggression,' *American Journal of International Law,* Vol. 50 (July 1956).

Goodrich, L. M., 'Korea: Collective Measures Against Aggression,' *International Conciliation,* No. 494 (October 1953).

Goodrich, L. M., and Rosner, G. E., 'The United Nations Emergency Force,' *International Organization,* Vol. 11 (Summer 1957).

Haas, E. B., 'Types of Collective Security. An Example of Operational Concepts,' *American Political Science Review,* Vol. 49 (March 1955).

Kelsen, H., 'Is the Acheson Plan Constitutional?' *Western Political Quarterly,* Vol. 3 (December 1950).

Wolfers, A., 'Collective Security and the War in Korea,' *Yale Review,* Vol. 43 (June 1953).

United Nations, *Repertory of Practice of United Nations Organs,* Volumes 1 and 2.
———— *Repertoire of the Practice of the Security Council 1946–51* (New York: UN Secretariat), 1954.
———— *Annual Report of the Secretary-General, seriatim.*
———— General Assembly, Security Council. *Official Records.*
United States, *Korea, 1945 to 1948,* Department of State Publication 3305 (Washington, D.C.: U.S. Government Printing Office), 1948.
———— *United States Policy in the Korean Crisis,* Department of State Publication 3922, Far Eastern Series 34 (Washington, D.C.: U.S. Government Printing Office), 1950.
———— *The United Nations and the Problem of Greece,* Department of State Publication 2909, Near Eastern Series 9 (Washington, D.C.: U.S. Government Printing Office), 1947.

Chapter 9

Atomic Energy, Its International Implications (New York: Oxford University Press), 1948.
Goodrich, L. M., and Hambro E., *Charter of the United Nations, Commentary and Documents,* rev. ed. (Boston: World Peace Foundation), 1949.
Goodrich, L. M., and Simons, A. P., *The United Nations and the Maintenance of International Peace and Security* (Washington, D.C.: Brookings), 1955.
de Madariaga, S., *Disarmament* (New York: Coward-McCann), 1929.
Newman, J. R., and Miller, B. S., *The Control of Atomic Energy* (New York: McGraw-Hill), 1948.
Tate, M., *The Disarmament Illusion* (New York: Macmillan), 1942.
———— *The United States and Armaments* (Cambridge, Mass.: Harvard University Press), 1952.

Cavers, D. F., 'Arms Control in the United Nations: A Decade of Disagreement,' *Bulletin of the Atomic Scientists* (April 1956).
'Determined Efforts to Seek Agreement in Disarmament,' *United Nations Review,* Vol. 3 (August 1956).
Osborn, F., 'The USSR and the Atom,' *International Organization,* Vol. 5 (August 1951).
Wilcox, F. O., 'The United Nations and the Search for Disarmament,' *Department of State Bulletin* (July 16, 1956).

United Nations, Disarmament Commission, *Third Report* of the Subcommittee of the. . . . Doc. DC/83, May 4, 1956.
United States, *International Control of Atomic Energy: Growth of a Policy,* Department of State Publication 2702 (Washington, D.C.: U.S. Government Printing Office), 1946.

United States, *International Control of Atomic Energy: Policy at the Crossroads,* Department of State Publication 3161 (Washington, D.C.: U.S. Government Printing Office), 1948.

———— *International Control of Atomic Energy and the Prohibition of Atomic Weapons,* Department of State Publication 3846 (Washington, D.C.: U.S. Government Printing Office), 1949.

———— *Report on the International Control of Atomic Energy* (Acheson-Lilienthal Report), Department of State Publication 2498 (Washington, D.C.: U.S. Government Printing Office), 1946.

Chapter 10

Carlston, K. S., *The Process of International Arbitration* (New York: Columbia University Press), 1946.

Fleming, D. F., *The United States and the World Court* (Garden City: Doubleday), 1945.

Hudson, M. O., *International Tribunals, Past and Future* (Washington, D.C.: Carnegie Endowment and Brookings), 1944.

———— *The Permanent Court of International Justice 1920–1942* (New York: Macmillan), 1943.

———— ed., *International Legislation,* 9 Vols. (Washington, D.C.: Carnegie Endowment for International Peace), 1931–1950.

Lissitzyn, O., *The International Court of Justice: Its Role in the Maintenance of Peace and Security* (New York: Carnegie Endowment for International Peace), 1951.

PERIODICALS

Hambro, E., 'The International Court of Justice,' *International Affairs,* Vol. 30 (January 1954).

Hudson, M. O., 'Twenty-Fourth Year of the World Court,' *American Journal of International Law,* Vol. 40 (January 1946) — a comparison of the P.C.I.J. with the I.C.J. The first number of this journal each year includes a review article on the work of the Court during the preceding year.

Kelsen, H., 'The Draft Declaration of Rights and Duties of States; Critical Remarks,' *American Journal of International Law,* Vol. 44 (April 1950).

Rosenne, S., 'The International Court and the United Nations: Reflections on the Period 1946–54,' *International Organization,* Vol. 9 (May 1955).

DOCUMENTS

United Nations, *Survey of the Development of International Law and Its Codification by International Conferences,* UN Doc. A/AC: 10/5, April, 1947, reproduced in *American Journal of International Law,* Vol. 41 (1947), supplement.

Consult also Treaty Series of the UN; *Reports* of International Arbitral Awards issued by the UN; *Yearbook* of the I.C.J.; *Reports* of Judgments, Advisory Opinions, and Orders issued by the I.C.J., The Hague; and *Reports* of the International Law Commission.

Chapter 11

Hill, M., *Immunities and Privileges of International Officials* (Washington, D.C.: Carnegie Endowment for International Peace), 1947.

Lie, T., *In the Cause of Peace* (New York: Macmillan), 1954.

Loveday, A., *Reflections on International Administration* (London: Oxford University Press), 1956.

Phelan, E. J., *Yes, and Albert Thomas* (London: Cresset), 1936.

Ranshofen-Wertheimer, E., *The International Secretariat* (Washington, D.C.: Carnegie Endowment for International Peace), 1945.

Schwebel, S. M., *The Secretary-General of the United Nations* (Cambridge, Mass.: Harvard University Press), 1952.

The United Nations Secretariat (New York: Carnegie Endowment for International Peace), 1950.

PERIODICALS

Cohen, M., 'The United Nations Secretariat. Some Constitutional and Administrative Developments,' *American Journal of International Law*, Vol. 49 (July 1955).

Crocker, W. R., 'Some Notes on the United Nations Secretariat,' *International Organization*, Vol. 4 (November 1950).

Friedmann, W., and Fatouros, A., 'The United Nations Administrative Tribunal,' *International Organization*, Vol. 11 (Winter 1957).

Honig, F., 'The International Civil Service: Basic Problems and Contemporary Difficulties,' *International Affairs*, Vol. 30 (April 1954).

Jackson, E., 'The Developing Role of the Secretary-General,' *International Organization*, Vol. 11 (Summer 1957).

Kunz, J. L., 'Privileges and Immunities of International Organizations,' *American Journal of International Law*, Vol. 41 (October 1947).

Scott, F. R., 'The World's Civil Service,' *International Conciliation*, No. 496 (January 1954).

DOCUMENTS

United Nations, *Yearbook, seriatim.*

—— *Annual Report of the Secretary-General, seriatim.*

United States, *The Status and Role of the Secretariat of the United Nations*, Staff Study No. 12, Subcommittee on the United Nations Charter, Committee on Foreign Relations, United States Senate, 84th Congress, 1st Session (Washington, D.C.: U.S. Government Printing Office), 1955.

Chapters 12, 13 and 14

Cantril, H., ed., *Tensions That Cause War* (Urbana: University of Illinois Press), 1950.

Elder, R. E., *Economic Development: Special UN Fund for Economic Development (SUNFED)* (New York: Woodrow Wilson Foundation), 1954.

Goodrich, L. M., and Hambro, E., *The Charter of the United Nations, Commentary and Documents*, rev. ed. (Boston: World Peace Foundation), 1949.

Green, J. R., *The United Nations and Human Rights* (Washington, D.C.: Brookings), 1956.

Loveday, A., *Reflections on International Administration* (London: Oxford University Press), 1956.

Sharp, W. R., *International Technical Assistance* (Chicago: University of Chicago Press), 1952.

Von Goeckingk, J., *United Nations Technical Assistance Board: A Case Study in International Administration* (New York: Woodrow Wilson Foundation), 1955.

White, L., *International Non-Governmental Organizations* (New Brunswick: Rutgers University Press), 1951.

Woodbridge, G., ed., *UNRRA*, 3 vols. (New York: Columbia University Press), 1950.

PERIODICALS

Ascher, L. S., 'The Development of UNESCO's Program,' *International Organization*, Vol. 4 (February 1950).

Blelloch, D., 'Bold New Programme: A Review of United Nations Technical Assistance,' *International Affairs*, Vol. 33 (January 1956).

Claude, I. L., Jr., 'The Nature and Status of the Subcommittee on Prevention of Discrimination and the Protection of Minorities,' *International Organization*, Vol. 5 (May 1951).

Higgins, B., and Malenbaum, W., 'Financing Economic Development,' *International Conciliation*, No. 502 (March 1955).

Hoffman, M. C., 'Problems of East-West Trade,' *International Conciliation*, No. 511 (January 1957).

Lockwood, A. N., 'Indians of the Andes,' *International Conciliation*, No. 508 (May 1956).

Loveday, A., 'An Unfortunate Decision,' *International Organization*, Vol. 1 (June 1947).

———— 'Suggestions for the Reform of the United Nations Economic and Social Machinery,' *International Organization*, Vol. 7 (August 1953).

'Narcotic Drug Control,' *International Conciliation*, No. 485 (November 1952).

Neal, M., 'The United Nations and Human Rights,' *International Conciliation*, No. 489 (March 1953).

'The International Labour Organization Since The War,' *International Labour Review*, Vol. 67 (February 1953).

Tripp, B., 'UNESCO in Perspective,' *International Conciliation*, No. 497 (March 1954).

Vernon, R., 'Organizing for World Trade,' *International Conciliation*, No. 505 (November 1955).

Warner, E., 'The Expanding Role of ICAO as Civil Aviation Grows,' *United Nations Review*, Vol. 2 (October 1955).

'Why? What? How? Questions Answered on Technical Assistance,' *United Nations Review*, Vol. 4 (February, March 1958).

DOCUMENTS

United Nations, General Assembly and ECOSOC, *Official Records*.
——— *Repertory of Practice of United Nations Organs*, Vols. 3, 4, and 5.
United States, *An Appraisal of the United Nations Educational, Scientific, and Cultural Organization*, by the Delegation of the United States to the 2nd Extraordinary Session of the General Conference of UNESCO. Department of State Publication 5209 (Washington, D.C.: U.S. Government Printing Office), 1953.
See also the annual reports, regular publications and other documents of the various specialized agencies.

Chapter 15

Cheever, D. S., and Haviland, H. F., Jr., *Organizing for Peace* (Boston: Houghton Mifflin), 1954.
Finkelstein, L. S., *Somaliland under Italian Administration: A Case Study in UN Trusteeship*. (New York: Woodrow Wilson Foundation), 1955.
Goodrich, L. M., and Hambro, E., *Charter of the United Nations, Commentary and Documents* rev. ed. (Boston: World Peace Foundation), 1949.

PERIODICALS

Atyeo, H. C., 'Morocco, Tunisia and Algeria Before the United Nations,' *Middle Eastern Affairs*, Vol. 6 (August–September 1955).
Chieh, Liu, 'International Trusteeship System, Visiting Missions,' *International Conciliation*, No. 448 (February 1949).
Coleman, J. S., 'Togoland,' *International Conciliation*, No. 509 (September 1956).
Eagleton, C., 'Excesses of Self-Determination,' *Foreign Affairs*, Vol. 31 (July 1953).
Haas, E. B., 'The Attempt to Terminate Colonialism: Acceptance of the United Nations Trusteeship System,' *International Organization*, Vol. 7 (February 1953).
'International Responsibility for Colonial Peoples: The United Nations and Chapter XI of the Charter,' *International Conciliation*, No. 458 (February 1950).
Rivlin B., 'Self-Determination and Dependent Peoples,' *International Conciliation*, No. 501 (January 1955).

DOCUMENTS

United Nations, General Assembly, *Official Records*.
——— Trusteeship Council, *Official Records*.

Chapter 16

Bok, D. C., *The First Three Years of the Schuman Plan* (Princeton: Princeton University Press), 1955.
Bonn, M., *Whither Europe: Union or Partnership?* (New York: Philosophical Library), 1952.
Canyes, Manuel, *The Organization of American States and the United Nations*, 3rd ed. (Washington, D.C.: Pan American Union), 1955.

Florinsky, M., *Integrated Europe?* (New York: Macmillan), 1955.

Houston, J., *Latin America and the United Nations* (New York: Carnegie Endowment for International Peace), 1956.

Organization for European Economic Co-operation, *The Organization for European Economic Co-operation: History and Survey*, 5th ed. (Paris: OEEC), 1956.

Royal Institute of International Affairs, *Britain in Western Europe: WEU and the Atlantic Alliance* (London: Royal Institute), 1956.

———— *The Middle East—A Political and Economic Survey* (London: Royal Institute), 1954.

Sennholz, H. F., *How Can Europe Survive?* (New York: Van Nostrand), 1955.

PERIODICALS

Armand, L., 'Atomic Energy and the Future of Europe,' *Foreign Affairs*, Vol. 56 (July 1956).

Basch, A., 'The Colombo Plan: A Case of Regional Economic Co-operation,' *International Organization*, Vol. 9 (February 1955).

Bebr, G., 'Regional Organization: A United Nations Problem,' *American Journal of International Law*, Vol. 49 (April 1955).

Bertrand, R., 'The European Common Market Proposal,' *International Organization*, Vol. 10 (November 1956).

Eyck, F. G., 'Benelux in the Balance,' *Political Science Quarterly*, Vol. 54 (March 1954).

Fenwick, C. G., 'The Inter-American Regional System: 50 Years of Progress,' *American Journal of International Law*, Vol. 50 (January 1956).

———— 'Inter-American Regional Procedures for the Settlement of Disputes,' *International Organization*, Vol. 10 (February 1956).

———— 'The Organization of Central American States,' *American Journal of International Law*, Vol. 46 (July 1952).

Goormaghtigh, J., 'The European Coal and Steel Community,' *International Conciliation*, No. 503 (May 1955).

Gordon, L., 'Myths and Realities in European Integration,' *Yale Review*, Vol. 45 (September 1955).

———— 'The Organization for European Economic Co-operation,' *International Organization*, Vol. 10 (February 1956).

Haas, E. B., 'Regionalism, Functionalism and International Organization,' *World Politics*, Vol. 9 (January 1956).

Henderson, W., 'The Development of Regionalism in Southeast Asia,' *International Organization*, Vol. 9 (November 1955).

Karp, B., 'The Draft Constitution for a European Political Community,' *International Organization*, Vol. 8 (May 1954).

Kunz, J. L., 'The Idea of Collective Security in Pan American Developments,' *Western Political Quarterly*, Vol. 6 (December 1953).

Killen, E. D., 'The Anzus Pact and Pacific Security,' *Far Eastern Survey* (October 8, 1952).

Little, T. R., 'The Arab League: A Reassessment,' *Middle East Journal* (Spring 1956).

Merry, H. J., 'The European Coal and Steel Community, Operation of the High Authority,' *Western Political Quarterly*, Vol. 8 (June 1955).

Padelford, W. J., 'A Selected Bibliography on Regionalism and Regional Arrangements,' *International Organization*, Vol. 10 (November 1956).

――――― 'Regional Organizations and the United Nations,' *International Organization*, Vol. 7 (May 1954).

――――― 'Political Co-operation in the North Atlantic Community,' *International Organization*, Vol. 9 (August 1955).

Thomas, M. L., 'A Critical Appraisal of SEATO,' *Western Political Quarterly* (December 1957).

DOCUMENTS

Consult the annual *Reports* of each of the organizations discussed, their regular publications, and charters or constitutions. Full texts of charters and constitutions may be found in *International Organization* or *American Journal of International Law, passim.*

Chapter 17

Bonn, M. J., *Whither Europe: Union or Partnership?* (New York: Philosophical Library), 1952.

Clarke, G., *A Plan For Peace* (New York: Harper), 1950.

Corbett, P. E., *Law and Society in the Relations of States* (New York: Harcourt, Brace), 1951.

――――― *The Individual and World Society*, Publication No. 2, Center for Research on World Political Institutions (Princeton: Princeton University Press), 1953.

Deutsch, K. W., *Political Community at the International Level: Problems of Definition and Measurement.* Organizational Behavior Section, Foreign Policy Analysis Project, Foreign Policy Analysis Series No. 2 (Princeton: Princeton University Press), September, 1953.

Guetzkow, H., *Multiple Loyalties: Theoretical Approach to a Problem in International Organization.* Publication No. 4, Center for Research on World Political Institutions (Princeton: Princeton University Press), 1955.

Mangone, G. J., *The Idea and Practice of World Government* (New York: Columbia University Press), 1951.

Schiffer, W., *The Legal Community of Mankind* (New York: Columbia University Press), 1954.

Schuman, F. C., *The Commonwealth of Man* (New York: Knopf), 1952.

Van Wagenen, R. W., *Research in the International Organization Field. Some Notes on a Possible Focus.* Publication No. 1, Center for Research on World Political Institutions (Princeton: Princeton University Press), 1952.

Wilcox, F. O., and Marcy, C. M., *Proposals for Changes in the United Nations* (Washington, D.C.: Brookings), 1955.

Wright, Q., ed., *The World Community* (Chicago: University of Chicago Press), 1948.

PERIODICALS

Boasson, C., 'International Organization Examined and Appraised,' *World Politics*, Vol. 8 (July 1956).

Finkelstein, L. S., 'Reviewing the United Nations Charter,' *International Organization,* Vol. 9 (May 1955).

Lent, E. S., 'The Development of United World Federalist Thought and Policy,' *International Organization,* Vol. 9 (November 1955).

Mitrany, D., 'The Functional Approach to World Government,' *International Affairs,* Vol. 24 (July 1948).

Morgenthau, H., 'Political Limitations of the United Nations,' in Wright, Q., ed., *Law and Politics in the World Community* (Berkeley: University of California Press), 1953.

———— 'The New United Nations and the Revision of the Charter,' *Review of Politics,* Vol. 16 (January 1954).

Patterson, E. M., ed., 'World Government,' *Annals of the American Academy of Political and Social Science,* Vol. 264 (July 1949).

Roberts, O. J., 'Background for Atlantic Union,' *Bulletin of the American Association of University Professors,* Vol. 36 (Winter 1950).

APPENDIX

I. Covenant of the League of Nations (Selected Articles)

ARTICLE 10

The Members of the League undertake to respect and preserve as against external aggression the territorial integrity and existing political independence of all Members of the League. In case of any such aggression or in case of any threat or danger of such aggression, the Council shall advise upon the means by which this obligation shall be fulfilled.

ARTICLE 11

1. Any war or threat of war, whether immediately affecting any of the Members of the League or not, is hereby declared a matter of concern to the whole League, and the League shall take any action that may be deemed wise and effectual to safeguard the peace of nations. In case any such emergency should arise, the Secretary-General shall, on the request of any Member of the League, forthwith summon a meeting of the Council.

2. It is also declared to be the friendly right of each Member of the League to bring to the attention of the Assembly or of the Council any circumstance whatever affecting international relations which threatens to disturb international peace or the good understanding between nations upon which peace depends.

ARTICLE 12

1. The Members of the League agree that if there should arise between them any dispute likely to lead to a rupture they will submit the matter either to arbitration or judicial settlement or to enquiry by the Council, and they agree in no case to resort to war until three months after the award by the arbitrators or the judicial decision or the report by the Council.

2. In any case under this Article the award of the arbitrators or the judicial decision shall be made within a reasonable time, and the report of the Council shall be made within six months after the submission of the dispute.

ARTICLE 13

1. The Members of the League agree that whenever any dispute shall arise between them which they recognise to be suitable for submission to arbitration or judicial settlement, and which cannot be satisfactorily settled by diplomacy, they will submit the whole subject-matter to arbitration or judicial settlement.

2. Disputes as to the interpretation of a treaty, as to any question of international law, as to the existence of any fact which, if established, would constitute a breach of any international obligation, or as to the extent and nature of the reparation to be made for any such breach, are declared to be among those which are generally suitable for submission to arbitration or judicial settlement.

3. For the consideration of any such dispute, the court to which the case is referred shall be the Permanent Court of International Justice, established in accordance with Article 14, or any tribunal agreed on by the parties to the dispute or stipulated in any convention existing between them.

4. The Members of the League agree that they will carry out in full good faith any award or decision that may be rendered, and that they will not resort to war against a Member of the League which complies therewith. In the event of any failure to carry out such an award or decision, the Council shall propose what steps should be taken to give effect thereto.

ARTICLE 15

1. If there should arise between Members of the League any dispute likely to lead to a rupture, which is not submitted to arbitration or judicial settlement in accordance with Article 13, the Members of the League agree that they will submit

the matter to the Council. Any party to the dispute may effect such submission by giving notice of the existence of the dispute to the Secretary-General, who will make all necessary arrangements for a full investigation and consideration thereof.

2. For this purpose the parties to the dispute will communicate to the Secretary-General, as promptly as possible, statements of their case with all the relevant facts and papers, and the Council may forthwith direct the publication thereof.

3. The Council shall endeavor to effect a settlement of the dispute, and, if such efforts are successful, a statement shall be made public giving such facts and explanations regarding the dispute and the terms of settlement thereof as the Council may deem appropriate.

4. If the dispute is not thus settled, the Council either unanimously or by a majority vote shall make and publish a report containing a statement of the facts of the dispute and the recommendations which are deemed just and proper in regard thereto.

5. Any member of the League represented on the Council may make a public statement of the facts of the dispute and of its conclusions regarding the same.

6. If a report by the Council is unanimously agreed to by the Members thereof other than the Representatives of one or more of the parties to ths dispute, the Members of the League agree that they will not go to war with any party to the dispute which complies with the recommendation of the report.

7. If the Council fails to reach a report which is unanimously agreed to by the members thereof, other than the Representatives of one or more of the parties to the dispute, the Members of the League reserve to themselves the right to take such action as they shall consider necessary for the maintenance of right and justice.

8. If the dispute between the parties is claimed by one of them, and is found by the Council, to arise out of a matter which by international law is solely within the domestic jurisdiction of that party, the Council shall so report, and shall make no recommendation as to its settlement.

9. The Council may in any case under this Article refer the dispute to the Assembly. The dispute shall be so referred at the request of either party to the dispute, provided that such request be made within fourteen days after the submission of the dispute to the Council.

10. In any case referred to the Assembly, all the provisions of this Article and of Article 12 relating to the action and powers of the Council shall apply to the action and powers of the Assembly, provided that a report made by the Assembly, if concurred in by the Representatives of those Members of the League represented on the Council and of a majority of the other Members of the League, exclusive in each case of the Representatives of the parties to the dispute, shall have the same force as a report by the Council concurred in by all the members thereof other than the Representatives of one or more of the parties to the dispute.

ARTICLE 16

1. Should any Member of the League resort to war in disregard of its covenants under Articles 12, 13, or 15, it shall *ipso facto* be deemed to have committed an act of war against all other Members of the League, which hereby undertake immediately to subject it to the severance of all trade or financial relations, the prohibition of all intercourse between their nationals and the nationals of the covenant-breaking State, and the prevention of all financial, commercial or personal intercourse between the nationals of the covenant-breaking State and the nationals of any other State, whether a Member of the League or not.

2. It shall be the duty of the Council in such case to recommend to the several Governments concerned what effective military, naval or air force the Members of the League shall severally contribute to the armed forces to be used to protect the covenants of the League.

3. The Members of the League agree, further, that they will mutually support one another in the financial and economic measures which are taken under this Article, in order to minimize the loss and inconvenience resulting from the above measures, and that they will mutually support one another in resisting any special measures aimed at one of their number by the covenant-breaking State, and that they will take the necessary steps to afford passage through their territory to the forces of any of the Members of the League which are cooperating to protect the covenants of the League.

4. Any Member of the League which has violated any covenant of the League may be declared to be no longer a Member of the League by a vote of the Council concurred in by the Representatives of all the other Members of the League represented thereon.

II. Charter of the United Nations

WE THE PEOPLES OF THE UNITED NATIONS DETERMINED

to save succeeding generations from the scourge of war, which twice in our life-time has brought untold sorrow to mankind, and

to reaffirm faith in fundamental human rights, in the dignity and worth of the human person, in the equal rights of men and women and of nations large and small, and

to establish conditions under which justice and respect for the obligations arising from treaties and other sources of international law can be maintained, and

to promote social progress and better standards of life in larger freedom,

AND FOR THESE ENDS

to practice tolerance and live together in peace with one another as good neighbors, and

to unite our strength to maintain international peace and security, and

to ensure, by the acceptance of principles and the institution of methods, that armed force shall not be used, save in the common interest, and

to employ international machinery for the promotion of the economic and social advancement of all peoples,

HAVE RESOLVED TO COMBINE OUR EFFORTS TO ACCOMPLISH THESE AIMS.

Accordingly, our respective Governments, through representatives assembled in the city of San Francisco, who have exhibited their full powers found to be in good and due form, have agreed to the present Charter of the United Nations and do hereby establish an international organization to be known as the United Nations.

CHAPTER I

PURPOSES AND PRINCIPLES

ARTICLE 1

The Purposes of the United Nations are:

1. To maintain international peace and security, and to that end: to take effective collective measures for the prevention and removal of threats to the peace, and for the suppression of acts of aggression or other breaches of the peace, and to bring about by peaceful means, and in conformity with the principles of justice and international law, adjustment or settlement of international disputes or situations which might lead to a breach of the peace;

2. To develop friendly relations among nations based on respect for the principle of equal rights and self-determination of peoples, and to take other appropriate measures to strengthen universal peace;

3. To achieve international co-operation in solving international problems of an economic, social, cultural, or humanitarian character, and in promoting and encouraging respect for human rights and for fundamental freedoms for all without distinction as to race, sex, language, or religion; and

4. To be a center for harmonizing the actions of nations in the attainment of these common ends.

ARTICLE 2

The Organization and its Members, in pursuit of the Purposes stated in Article 1, shall act in accordance with the following Principles.

1. The Organization is based on the principle of the sovereign equality of all its Members.

2. All Members, in order to ensure to all of them the rights and benefits resulting from membership, shall fulfil in good faith

the obligations assumed by them in accordance with the present Charter.

3. All Members shall settle their international disputes by peaceful means in such a manner that international peace and security, and justice, are not endangered.

4. All Members shall refrain in their international relations from the threat or use of force against the territorial integrity or political independence of any state, or in any other manner inconsistent with the Purposes of the United Nations.

5. All Members shall give the United Nations every assistance in any action it takes in accordance with the present Charter, and shall refrain from giving assistance to any state against which the United Nations is taking preventive or enforcement action.

6. The Organization shall ensure that states which are not Members of the United Nations act in accordance with these Principles so far as may be necessary for the maintenance of international peace and security.

7. Nothing contained in the present Charter shall authorize the United Nations to intervene in matters which are essentially within the domestic jurisdiction of any state or shall require the Members to submit such matters to settlement under the present Charter; but this principle shall not prejudice the application of enforcement measures under Chapter VII.

CHAPTER II

MEMBERSHIP

ARTICLE 3

The original Members of the United Nations shall be the states which, having participated in the United Nations Conference on International Organization at San Francisco, or having previously signed the Declaration by United Nations of January 1, 1942, sign the present Charter and ratify it in accordance with Article 110.

ARTICLE 4

1. Membership in the United Nations is open to all other peace-loving states which accept the obligations contained in the present Charter and, in the judgment of the Organization, are able and willing to carry out these obligations.

2. The admission of any such state to membership in the United Nations will be effected by a decision of the General Assembly upon the recommendation of the Security Council.

ARTICLE 5

A Member of the United Nations against which preventive or enforcement action has been taken by the Security Council may be suspended from the exercise of the rights and privileges of membership by the General Assembly upon the recommendation of the Security Council. The exercise of these rights and privileges may be restored by the Security Council.

ARTICLE 6

A Member of the United Nations which has persistently violated the Principles contained in the present Charter may be expelled from the Organization by the General Assembly upon the recommendation of the Security Council.

CHAPTER III

ORGANS

ARTICLE 7

1. There are established as the principal organs of the United Nations; a General Assembly, a Security Council, an Economic and Social Council, a Trusteeship Council, an International Court of Justice, and a Secretariat.

2. Such subsidiary organs as may be found necessary may be established in accordance with the present Charter.

ARTICLE 8

The United Nations shall place no restrictions on the eligibility of men and women to participate in any capacity and under conditions of equality in its principal and subsidiary organs.

CHAPTER IV

THE GENERAL ASSEMBLY

Composition

ARTICLE 9

1. The General Assembly shall consist of all the Members of the United Nations.

2. Each Member shall have not more than five representatives in the General Assembly.

Functions and Powers

ARTICLE 10

The General Assembly may discuss any questions or any matters within the scope of the present Charter or relating to the powers and functions of any organs provided for in the present Charter, and, except as provided in Article 12, may make recommendations to the Members of the United Nations or to the Security Council or to both on any such questions or matters.

ARTICLE 11

1. The General Assembly may consider the general principles of cooperation in the maintenance of international peace and security, including the principles governing disarmament and the regulation of armaments, and may make recommendations with regard to such principles to the Members or to the Security Council or to both.

2. The General Assembly may discuss any questions relating to the maintenance of international peace and security brought before it by any Member of the United Nations, or by the Security Council, or by a state which is not a Member of the United Nations in accordance with article 35, paragraph 2, and, except as provided in Article 12, may make recommendations with regard to any such question to the state or states concerned or to the Security Council or to both. Any such question on which action is necessary shall be referred to the Security Council by the General Assembly either before or after discussion.

3. The General Assembly may call the attention of the Security Council to situations which are likely to endanger international peace and security.

4. The powers of the General Assembly set forth in this Article shall not limit the general scope of Article 10.

ARTICLE 12

1. While the Security Council is exercising in respect of any dispute or situation the functions assigned to it in the present Charter, the General Assembly shall not make any recommendations with regard to that dispute or situation unless the Security Council so requests.

2. The Secretary-General, with the consent of the Security Council, shall notify the General Assembly at each session of any matters relative to the maintenance of international peace and security which are being dealt with by the Security Council and shall similarly notify the General Assembly, or the Members of the United Nations if the General Assembly is not in ses-

sion, immediately the Security Council ceases to deal with such matters.

ARTICLE 13

1. The General Assembly shall initiate studies and make recommendations for the purpose of:
   a. promoting international cooperation in the political field and encouraging the progressive development of international law and its codification;
   b. promoting international cooperation in the economic, social, cultural, educational, and health fields, and assisting in the realization of human rights and fundamental freedoms for all without distinction as to race, sex, language, or religion.

2. The further responsibilities, functions and powers of the General Assembly with respect to matters mentioned in paragraph 1(b) above are set forth in Chapters IX and X.

ARTICLE 14

Subject to the provisions of Article 12, the General Assembly may recommend measures for the peaceful adjustment of any situation, regardless of origin, which it deems likely to impair the general welfare or friendly relations among nations, including situations resulting from a violation of the provisions of the present Charter setting forth the Purposes and Principles of the United Nations.

ARTICLE 15

1. The General Assembly shall receive and consider annual and special reports from the Security Council; these reports shall include an account of the measures that the Security Council has decided upon or taken to maintain international peace and security.

2. The General Assembly shall receive and consider reports from the other organs of the United Nations.

ARTICLE 16

The General Assembly shall perform such functions with respect to the international trusteeship system as are assigned to it under Chapters XII and XIII, including the approval of the trusteeship agreements for areas not designated as strategic.

ARTICLE 17

1. The General Assembly shall consider and approve the budget of the Organization.

2. The expenses of the Organization shall be borne by the Members as apportioned by the General Assembly.

3. The General Assembly shall consider and approve any financial and budgetary arrangements with specialized agencies referred to in Article 57 and shall examine the administrative budgets of such specialized agencies with a view to making recommendations to the agencies concerned.

Voting

ARTICLE 18

1. Each member of the General Assembly shall have one vote.

2. Decisions of the General Assembly on important questions shall be made by a two-thirds majority of the members present and voting. These questions shall include: recommendations with respect to the maintenance of international peace and security, the election of the non-permanent members of the Security Council, the election of the members of the Economic and Social Council, the election of members of the Trusteeship Council in accordance with paragraph 1(c) of Article 86, the admission of new Members to the United Nations, the suspension of the rights and privileges of membership, the expulsion of Members, questions relating to the operation of the trusteeship system, and budgetary questions.

3. Decisions on other questions, including the determination of additional categories of questions to be decided by a two-thirds majority, shall be made by a majority of the members present and voting.

ARTICLE 19

A Member of the United Nations which is in arrears in the payment of its financial contributions to the Organization shall have no vote in the General Assembly if the amount of its arrears equals or exceeds the amount of the contributions due from it for the preceding two full years. The General Assembly may, nevertheless, permit such a Member to vote if it is satisfied that the failure to pay is due to conditions beyond the control of the Member.

Procedure

ARTICLE 20

The General Assembly shall meet in regular annual sessions and in such special sessions as occasion may require. Special sessions shall be convoked by the Secretary-General at the request of the Security Council or of a majority of the Members of the United Nations.

ARTICLE 21

The General Assembly shall adopt its own rules of procedure. It shall elect its President for each session.

ARTICLE 22

The General Assembly may establish such subsidiary organs as it deems necessary for the performance of its functions.

CHAPTER V

THE SECURITY COUNCIL

Composition

ARTICLE 23

1. The Security Council shall consist of eleven Members of the United Nations. The Republic of China, France, the Union of Soviet Socialist Republics, the United Kingdom of Great Britain and Northern Ireland, and the United States of America shall be permanent members of the Security Council. The General Assembly shall elect six other Members of the United Nations to be non-permanent members of the Security Council, due regard being specially paid, in the first instance to the contribution of Members of the United Nations to the maintenance of international peace and security and to the other purposes of the Organization, and also to equitable geographical distribution.

2. The non-permanent members of the Security Council shall be elected for a term of two years. In the first election of the non-permanent members, however, three shall be chosen for a term of one year. A retiring member shall not be eligible for immediate re-election.

3. Each member of the Security Council shall have one representative.

Functions and Powers

ARTICLE 24

1. In order to ensure prompt and effective action by the United Nations, its Members confer on the Security Council primary responsibility for the maintenance of international peace and security, and agree that in carrying out its duties under this responsibility the Security Council acts on their behalf.

2. In discharging these duties the Se-

curity Council shall act in accordance with the Purposes and Principles of the United Nations. The specific powers granted to the Security Council for the discharge of these duties are laid down in Chapters VI, VII, VIII, and XII.

3. The Security Council shall submit annual and, when necessary, special reports to the General Assembly for its consideration.

ARTICLE 25

The Members of the United Nations agree to accept and carry out the decisions of the Security Council in accordance with the present Charter.

ARTICLE 26

In order to promote the establishment and maintenance of international peace and security with the least diversion for armaments of the world's human and economic resources, the Security Council shall be responsible for formulating, with the assistance of the Military Staff Committee referred to in Article 47, plans to be submitted to the Members of the United Nations for the establishment of a system for the regulation of armaments.

Voting

ARTICLE 27

1. Each member of the Security Council shall have one vote.

2. Decisions of the Security Council on procedural matters shall be made by an affirmative vote of seven members.

3. Decisions of the Security Council on all other matters shall be made by an affirmative vote of seven members including the concurring votes of the permanent members; provided that, in decisions under Chapter VI, and under paragraph 3 of Article 52, a party to a dispute shall abstain from voting.

Procedure

ARTICLE 28

1. The Security Council shall be so organized as to be able to function continuously. Each member of the Security Council shall for this purpose be represented at all times at the seat of the Organization.

2. The Security Council shall hold periodic meetings at which each of its members may, if it so desires, be represented by a member of the government or by some other specially designated representative.

3. The Security Council may hold meetings at such places other than the seat of the Organization as in its judgment will best facilitate its work.

ARTICLE 29

The Security Council may establish such subsidiary organs as it deems necessary for the performance of its functions.

ARTICLE 30

The Security Council shall adopt its own rules of procedure, including the method of selecting its President.

ARTICLE 31

Any Member of the United Nations which is not a member of the Security Council may participate, without vote, in the discussion of any question brought before the Security Council whenever the latter considers that the interests of that Member are specially affected.

ARTICLE 32

Any Member of the United Nations which is not a member of the Security Council or any state which is not a Member of the United Nations, if it is a party to a dispute under consideration by the Security Council, shall be invited to participate, without vote, in the discussion relating to the dispute. The Security Council shall lay down such conditions as it deems just for the participation of a state which is not a Member of the United Nations.

CHAPTER VI

PACIFIC SETTLEMENT OF DISPUTES

ARTICLE 33

1. The parties to any dispute, the continuance of which is likely to endanger the maintenance of international peace and security, shall, first of all, seek a solution by negotiation, enquiry, mediation, conciliation, arbitration, judicial settlement, resort to regional agencies or arrangements, or other peaceful means of their own choice.

2. The Security Council shall, when it deems necessary, call upon the parties to settle their dispute by such means.

ARTICLE 34

The Security Council may investigate any dispute, or any situation which might lead to international friction or give rise to a dispute, in order to determine whether the continuance of the dispute or situation is likely to endanger the maintenance of international peace and security.

ARTICLE 35

1. Any Member of the United Nations may bring any dispute, or any situation of the nature referred to in Article 34, to the attention of the Security Council or of the General Assembly.

2. A state which is not a Member of the United Nations may bring to the attention of the Security Council or of the General Assembly any dispute to which it is a party if it accepts in advance, for the purposes of the dispute, the obligations of pacific settlement provided in the present Charter.

3. The proceedings of the General Assembly in respect of matters brought to its attention under this Article will be subject to the provisions of Articles 11 and 12.

ARTICLE 36

1. The Security Council may, at any stage of a dispute of the nature referred to in Article 33 or of a situation of like nature, recommend appropriate procedures or methods of adjustment.

2. The Security Council should take into consideration any procedures for the settlement of the dispute which have already been adopted by the parties.

3. In making recommendations under this Article the Security Council should also take into consideration that legal disputes should as a general rule be referred by the parties to the International Court of Justice in accordance with the provisions of the Statute of the Court.

ARTICLE 37

1. Should the parties to a dispute of the nature referred to in Article 33 fail to settle it by the means indicated in that Article, they shall refer it to the Security Council.

2. If the Security Council deems that the continuance of the dispute is in fact likely to endanger the maintenance of international peace and security, it shall decide whether to take action under Article 36 or to recommend such terms of settlement as it may consider appropriate.

ARTICLE 38

Without prejudice to the provisions of Articles 33 to 37, the Security Council may, if all the parties to any dispute so request, make recommendations to the parties with a view to a pacific settlement of the dispute.

CHAPTER VII

ACTION WITH RESPECT TO THREATS TO THE PEACE, BREACHES OF THE PEACE, AND ACTS OF AGGRESSION

ARTICLE 39

The Security Council shall determine the existence of any threat to the peace, breach of the peace, or act of aggression and shall make recommendations, or decide what measures shall be taken in accordance with Articles 41 and 42, to maintain or restore international peace and security.

ARTICLE 40

In order to prevent an aggravation of the situation, the Security Council may, before making the recommendations or deciding upon the measures provided for in Article 39, call upon the parties concerned to comply with such provisional measures as it deems necessary or desirable. Such provisional measures shall be without prejudice to the rights, claims, or position of the parties concerned. The Security Council shall duly take account of failure to comply with such provisional measures.

ARTICLE 41

The Security Council may decide what measures not involving the use of armed force are to be employed to give effect to its decisions, and it may call upon the Members of the United Nations to apply such measures. These may include complete or partial interruption of economic relations and of rail, sea, air, postal, telegraphic, radio, and other means of communication, and the severance of diplomatic relations.

ARTICLE 42

Should the Security Council consider that measures provided for in Article 41 would be inadequate or have proved to be inadequate, it may take such action by air, sea, or land forces as may be necessary to maintain or restore international peace and security. Such action may include demonstrations, blockade, and other operations by air, sea, or land forces of Members of the United Nations.

ARTICLE 43

1. All Members of the United Nations, in order to contribute to the maintenance of international peace and security, undertake to make available to the Security Council, on its call and in accordance with a special agreement or agreements, armed forces, assistance, and facilities, including rights of passage, necessary for the purpose of maintaining international peace and security.

2. Such agreement or agreements shall govern the numbers and types of forces, their degree of readiness and general location, and the nature of the facilities and assistance to be provided.

3. The agreement or agreements shall be negotiated as soon as possible on the initiative of the Security Council. They shall be concluded between the Security Council and Members or between the Security Council and groups of Members and shall be subject to ratification by the signatory states in accordance with their respective constitutional processes.

ARTICLE 44

When the Security Council has decided to use force it shall, before calling upon a Member not represented on it to provide armed forces in fulfillment of the obligations assumed under Article 43, invite that Member, if the Member so desires, to participate in the decisions of the Security Council concerning the employment of contingents of that Member's armed forces.

ARTICLE 45

In order to enable the United Nations to take urgent military measures, Members shall hold immediately available national air-force contingents for combined international enforcement action. The strength and degree of readiness of these contingents and plans for their combined action shall be determined, within the limits laid down in the special agreement or agreements referred to in Article 43, by the Security Council with the assistance of the Military Staff Committee.

ARTICLE 46

Plans for the application of armed force shall be made by the Security Council with the assistance of the Military Staff Committee.

ARTICLE 47

1. There shall be established a Military Staff Committee to advise and assist the Security Council on all questions relating to the Security Council's military requirements for the maintenance of international peace and security, the employment and command of forces placed at its disposal, the regulation of armaments, and possible disarmament.

2. The Military Staff Committee shall consist of the Chiefs of Staff of the permanent members of the Security Council or their representatives. Any Member of the United Nations not permanently represented on the Committee shall be invited by the Committee to be associated with it when the efficient discharge of the Committee's responsibilities requires the participation of that Member in its work.

3. The Military Staff Committee shall be responsible under the Security Council for the strategic direction of any armed forces placed at the disposal of the Security Council. Questions relating to the command of such forces shall be worked out subsequently.

4. The Military Staff Committee, with the authorization of the Security Council and after consultation with appropriate regional agencies, may establish regional subcommittees.

ARTICLE 48

1. The action required to carry out the decisions of the Security Council for the maintenance of international peace and security shall be taken by all the Members of the United Nations or by some of them, as the Security Council may determine.

2. Such decisions shall be carried out by the Members of the United Nations directly and through their action in the appropriate international agencies of which they are members.

ARTICLE 49

The Members of the United Nations shall join in affording mutual assistance in carrying out the measures decided upon by the Security Council.

ARTICLE 50

If preventive or enforcement measures against any state are taken by the Security Council, any other state, whether a Member of the United Nations or not, which finds itslf confronted with special economic problems arising from the carrying out of those measures shall have the right to consult the Security Council with regard to a solution of those problems.

ARTICLE 51

Nothing in the present Charter shall impair the inherent right of individual or collective self-defense if an armed attack occurs against a Member of the United Nations, until the Security Council has taken measures necessary to maintain international peace and security. Measures taken by Members in the exercise of this right of self-defense shall be immediately reported to the Security Council and shall not in any way affect the authority and responsibility of the Security Council under the present Charter to take at any time such action as it deems necessary in order to maintain or restore international peace and security.

CHAPTER VIII

REGIONAL ARRANGEMENTS

ARTICLE 52

1. Nothing in the present Charter precludes the existence of regional arrangements or agencies for dealing with such matters relating to the maintenance of international peace and security as are appropriate for regional action, provided that such arrangements or agencies and their activities are consistent with the Purposes and Principles of the United Nations.

2. The Members of the United Nations entering into such arrangements or constituting such agencies shall make every effort to achieve pacific settlement of local disputes through such regional arrangements or by such regional agencies before referring them to the Security Council.

3. The Security Council shall encourage the development of pacific settlement of local disputes through such regional arrangements or by such regional agencies either on the initiative of the states concerned or by reference from the Security Council.

4. This Article in no way impairs the application of Articles 34 and 35.

ARTICLE 53

1. The Security Council shall, where appropriate, utilize such regional arrangements or agencies for enforcement action

under its authority. But no enforcement action shall be taken under regional arrangements or by regional agencies without the authorization of the Security Council, with the exception of measures against any enemy state, as defined in paragraph 2 of this Article, provided for pursuant to Article 107 or in regional arrangements directed against renewal of aggressive policy on the part of any such state, until such time as the Organization may, on request of the Governments concerned, be charged with the responsibility for preventing further aggression by such a state.

2. The term enemy state as used in paragraph 1 of this Article applies to any state which during the Second World War has been an enemy of any signatory of the present Charter.

ARTICLE 54

The Security Council shall at all times be kept fully informed of activities undertaken or in contemplation under regional arrangements or by regional agencies for the maintenance of international peace and security.

CHAPTER IX

INTERNATIONAL ECONOMIC AND SOCIAL COOPERATION

ARTICLE 55

With a view to the creation of conditions of stability and well-being which are necessary for peaceful and friendly relations among nations based on respect for the principle of equal rights and self-determination of peoples, the United Nations shall promote:

    a. higher standards of living, full employment, and conditions of economic and social progress and development;

    b. solutions of international economic, social, health, and related problems; and international cultural and educational cooperation; and

    c. universal respect for, and observance of, human rights and fundamental freedoms for all without distinction as to race, sex, language, or religion.

ARTICLE 56

All Members pledge themselves to take joint and separate action in cooperation with the Organization for the achievement of the purposes set forth in Article 55.

ARTICLE 57

1. The various specialized agencies, established by intergovernmental agreement and having wide international responsibilities, as defined in their basic instruments, in economic, social, cultural, educational, health, and related fields, shall be brought into relationship with the United Nations in accordance with the provisions of Article 63.

2. Such agencies thus brought into relationship with the United Nations are hereinafter referred to as specialized agencies.

ARTICLE 58

The Organization shall make recommendations for the coordination of the policies and activities of the specialized agencies.

ARTICLE 59

The Organization shall, where appropriate, initiate negotiations among the states concerned for the creation of any new specialized agencies required for the accomplishment of the purposes set forth in Article 55.

ARTICLE 60

Responsibilty for the discharge of the functions of the Organization set forth in this Chapter shall be vested in the General Assembly and, under the authority of the General Assembly, in the Economic and Social Council, which shall have for this purpose the powers set forth in Chapter X.

CHAPTER X

THE ECONOMIC AND SOCIAL COUNCIL

Composition

ARTICLE 61

1. The Economic and Social Council shall consist of eighteen Members of the United Nations elected by the General Assembly.

2. Subject to the provisions of paragraph 3, six members of the Economic and Social Council shall be elected each year for a term of three years. A retiring member shall be eligible for immediate re-election.

3. At the first election, eighteen members of the Economic and Social Council shall be chosen. The term of office of six members so chosen shall expire at the end of one year, and of six other members at the end of two years, in accordance with arrangements made by the General Assembly.

4. Each member of the Economic and Social Council shall have one representative.

Functions and Powers

ARTICLE 62

1. The Economic and Social Council may make or initiate studies and reports with respect to international economic, social, cultural, educational, health, and related matters and may make recommendations with respect to any such matters to the General Assembly, to the Members of the United Nations, and to the specialized agencies concerned.

2. It may make recommendations for the purpose of promoting respect for, and observance of, human rights and fundamental freedoms for all.

3. It may prepare draft conventions for submission to the General Assembly, with respect to matters falling within its competence.

4. It may call, in accordance with the rules prescribed by the United Nations, international conferences on matters falling within its competence.

ARTICLE 63

1. The Economic and Social Council may enter into agreements with any of the agencies referred to in Article 57, defining the terms on which the agency concerned shall be brought into relationship with the United Nations. Such agreements shall be subject to approval by the General Assembly.

2. It may coordinate the activities of the specialized agencies through consultation with and recommendations to such agencies and through recommendations to the General Assembly and to the Members of the United Nations.

ARTICLE 64

1. The Economic and Social Council may take appropriate steps to obtain regular reports from the specialized agencies. It may make arrangements with the Members of the United Nations and with the specialized agencies to obtain reports on the steps taken to give effect to its own recommendations and to recommendations on matters falling within its competence made by the General Assembly.

2. It may communicate its observations on these reports to the General Assembly.

ARTICLE 65

The Economic and Social Council may furnish information to the Security Council and shall assist the Security Council upon its request.

ARTICLE 66

1. The Economic and Social Council shall perform such functions as fall within its competence in connection with the carrying out of the recommendations of the General Assembly.

2. It may, with the approval of the General Assembly, perform services at the request of Members of the United Nations and at the request of specialized agencies.

3. It shall perform such other functions as are specified elsewhere in the present Charter or as may be assigned to it by the General Assembly.

Voting

ARTICLE 67

1. Each member of the Economic and Social Council shall have one vote.

2. Decisions of the Economic and Social Council shall be made by a majority of the members present and voting.

Procedure

ARTICLE 68

The Economic and Social Council shall set up commissions in economic and social fields and for the promotion of human rights, and such other commissions as may be required for the performance of its functions.

ARTICLE 69

The Economic and Social Council shall invite any Member of the United Nations to participate, without vote, in its deliberations on any matter of particular concern to that Member.

ARTICLE 70

The Economic and Social Council may make arrangements for representatives of the specialized agencies to participate, without vote, in its deliberations and in those of the commissions established by it, and for its representatives to participate in the deliberations of the specialized agencies.

ARTICLE 71

The Economic and Social Council may make suitable arrangements for consulta-tion with non-governmental organizations which are concerned with matters within its competence. Such arrangements may be made with international organizations and, where appropriate, with national organizations after consultation with the Member of the United Nations concerned.

ARTICLE 72

1. The Economic and Social Council shall adopt its own rules of procedure, including the method of selecting its President.

2. The Economic and Social Council shall meet as required in accordance with its rules, which shall include provision for the convening of meetings on the request of a majority of its members.

CHAPTER XI

DECLARATION REGARDING NON-SELF-GOVERNING TERRITORIES

ARTICLE 73

Members of the United Nations which have or assume responsibilities for the administration of territories whose peoples have not yet attained a full measure of self-government recognize the principle that the interests of the inhabitants of these territories are paramount, and accept as a sacred trust the obligation to promote to the utmost, within the system of international peace and security established by the present Charter, the well-being of the inhabitants of these territories, and, to this end:

a. to ensure, with due respect for the culture of the peoples concerned, their political, economic, social, and educational advancement, their just treatment, and their protection against abuses;

b. to develop self-government, to take due account of the political aspirations of the peoples, and to assist them in the progressive development of their free political institutions, according to the particular circumstances of each territory and its peoples and their varying stages of advancement;

c. to further international peace and security;

d. to promote constructive measures of development, to encourage research, and to cooperate with one another and, when and where appropriate, with specialized international bodies with a view to the practical achievement of the social, economic, and scientific purposes set forth in this Article; and

e. to transmit regularly to the Secretary-General for information purposes, subject to such limitation as security and constitutional considerations may require, statistical and other information of a technical nature relating to economic, social, and educational conditions in the territories for which they are respectively responsible other than those territories to which Chapters XII and XIII apply.

ARTICLE 74

Members of the United Nations also agree that their policy in respect of the territories to which this Chapter applies, no less than in respect of their metropolitan areas, must be based on the general principle of good-neighborliness, due account being taken of the interests and well-being of the rest of the world, in social, economic, and commercial matters.

CHAPTER XII

INTERNATIONAL TRUSTEESHIP SYSTEM

ARTICLE 75

The United Nations shall establish under its authority an international trusteeship system for the administration and supervision of such territories as may be placed thereunder by subsequent individual agreements. These territories are hereinafter referred to as trust territories.

ARTICLE 76

The basic objectives of the trusteeship system, in accordance with the Purposes of the United Nations laid down in Article 1 of the present Charter, shall be:

a. to further international peace and security;

b. to promote the political, economic, social, and educational advancement of the inhabitants of the trust territories, and their progressive development towards self-government or independence as may be appropriate to the particular circumstances of each territory and its peoples and the freely expressed wishes of the peoples concerned, and as may be provided by the terms of each trusteeship agreement;

c. to encourage respect for human rights and for fundamental freedoms for all without distinction as to race, sex, language, or religion, and to encourage recognition of the interdependence of the peoples of the world; and

d. to ensure equal treatment in social, economic, and commercial matters for all Members of the United Nations and their nationals, and also equal treatment for the latter in the administration of justice, without prejudice to the attainment of the foregoing objectives and subject to the provisions of Article 80.

ARTICLE 77

1. The trusteeship system shall apply to such territories in the following categories as may be placed thereunder by means of trusteeship agreements:

a. territories now held under mandate;

b. territories which may be detached from enemy states as a result of the Second World War; and

c. territories voluntarily placed under the system by states responsible for their administration.

2. It will be a matter for subsequent agreement as to which territories in the foregoing categories will be brought under the trusteeship system and upon what terms.

ARTICLE 78

The trusteeship system shall not apply to territories which have become Members of the United Nations, relationship among which shall be based on respect for the principle of sovereign equality.

ARTICLE 79

The terms of trusteeship for each territory to be placed under the trusteeship system, including any alteration or amendment, shall be agreed upon by the states directly concerned, including the mandatory power in the case of territories held under mandate by a Member of the United Nations, and shall be approved as provided for in Articles 83 and 85.

ARTICLE 80

1. Except as may be agreed upon in individual trusteeship agreements, made under Articles 77, 79, and 81, placing each territory under the trusteeship system, and until such agreements have been concluded, nothing in this Chapter shall be construed in or of itself to alter in any manner the rights whatsoever of any states or any peoples or the terms of existing

international instruments to which Members of the United Nations may respectively be parties.

2. Paragraph 1 of this Article shall not be interpreted as giving grounds for delay or postponement of the negotiation and conclusion of agreements for placing mandated and other territories under the trusteeship system as provided for in Article 77.

ARTICLE 81

The trusteeship agreement shall in each case include the terms under which the trust territory will be administered and designate the authority which will exercise the administration of the trust territory. Such authority, hereinafter called the administering authority, may be one or more states or the Organization itself.

ARTICLE 82

There may be designated, in any trusteeship agreement, a strategic area or areas which may include part or all of the trust territory to which the agreement applies, without prejudice to any special agreement or agreements made under Article 43.

ARTICLE 83

1. All functions of the United Nations relating to strategic areas, including the approval of the terms of the trusteeship agreements and of their alteration or amendment, shall be exercised by the Security Council.

2. The basic objectives set forth in Article 76 shall be applicable to the people of each strategic area.

3. The Security Council shall, subject to the provisions of the trusteeship agreements and without prejudice to security considerations, avail itself of the assistance of the Trusteeship Council to perform those functions of the United Nations under the trusteeship system relating to political, economic, social, and educational matters in the strategic areas.

ARTICLE 84

It shall be the duty of the administering authority to ensure that the trust territory shall play its part in the maintenance of international peace and security. To this end the administering authority may make use of volunteer forces, facilities, and assistance from the trust territory in carrying out the obligations towards the Security Council undertaken in this regard by the administering authority, as well as for local defense and the maintenance of law and order within the trust territory.

ARTICLE 85

1. The functions of the United Nations with regard to trusteeship agreements for all areas not designated as strategic, including the approval of the terms of the trusteeship agreements and of their alteration or amendment, shall be exercised by the General Assembly.

2. The Trusteeship Council, operating under the authority of the General Assembly, shall assist the General Assembly in carrying out these functions.

Chapter XIII

THE TRUSTEESHIP COUNCIL

Composition

ARTICLE 86

1. The Trusteeship Council shall consist of the following Members of the United Nations:

a. those Members administering trust territories;

b. such of those Members mentioned by name in Article 23 as are not administering trust territories; and

c. as many other Members elected for three-year terms by the General Assembly as may be necessary to ensure that the total number of members of the Trusteeship Council is equally divided between those Members of the United Nations which administer trust territories and those which do not.

2. Each member of the Trusteeship Council shall designate one specially qualified person to represent it therein.

Functions and Powers

ARTICLE 87

The General Assembly and, under its authority, the Trusteeship Council, in carrying out their functions, may:

a. consider reports submitted by the administering authority;

b. accept petitions and examine them in consultation with the administering authority;

c. provide for periodic visits to the respective trust territories at times agreed upon with the administering authority; and

d. take these and other actions in

conformity with the terms of the trusteeship agreements.

ARTICLE 88

The Trusteeship Council shall formulate a questionnaire on the political, economic, social, and educational advancement of the inhabitants of each trust territory, and the administering authority for each trust territory within the competence of the General Assembly shall make an annual report to the General Assembly upon the basis of such questionnaire.

Voting

ARTICLE 89

1. Each member of the Trusteeship Council shall have one vote.

2. Decisions of the Trusteeship Council shall be made by a majority of the members present and voting.

Procedure

ARTICLE 90

1. The Trusteeship Council shall adopt its own rules of procedure, including the method of selecting its President.

2. The Trusteeship Council shall meet as required in accordance with its rules, which shall include provision for the convening of meetings on the request of a majority of its members.

ARTICLE 91

The Trusteeship Council shall, when appropriate, avail itself of the assistance of the Economic and Social Council and of the specialized agencies in regard to matters with which they are respectively concerned.

CHAPTER XIV

THE INTERNATIONAL COURT OF JUSTICE

ARTICLE 92

The International Court of Justice shall be the principal judicial organ of the United Nations. It shall function in accordance with the annexed Statute, which is based upon the Statute of the Permanent Court of International Justice and forms an integral part of the present Charter.

ARTICLE 93

1. All Members of the United Nations are *ipso facto* parties to the Statute of the International Court of Justice.

2. A state which is not a Member of the United Nations may become a party to the Statute of the International Court of Justice on condition to be determined in each case by the General Assembly upon the recommendation of the Security Council.

ARTICLE 94

1. Each Member of the United Nations undertakes to comply with the decision of the International Court of Justice in any case to which it is a party.

2. If any party to a case fails to perform the obligations incumbent upon it under a judgment rendered by the Court, the other party may have recourse to the Security Council, which may, if it deems necessary, make recommendations or decide upon measures to be taken to give effect to the judgment.

ARTICLE 95

Nothing in the present Charter shall prevent Members of the United Nations from entrusting the solution of their differences to other tribunals by virtue of agreements already in existence or which may be concluded in the future.

ARTICLE 96

1. The General Assembly or the Security Council may request the International Court of Justice to give an advisory opinion on any legal question.

2. Other organs of the United Nations and specialized agencies, which may at any time be so authorized by the General Assembly, may also request advisory opinions of the Court on legal questions arising within the scope of their activities.

CHAPTER XV

THE SECRETARIAT

ARTICLE 97

The Secretariat shall comprise a Secretary-General and such staff as the Organization may require. The Secretary-General shall be appointed by the General Assembly upon the recommendation of the Security Council. He shall be the chief administrative officer of the Organization.

ARTICLE 98

The Secretary-General shall act in that capacity in all meetings of the General Assembly, of the Security Council, of the Economic and Social Council, and of the

Trusteeship Council, and shall perform such other functions as are entrusted to him by these organs. The Secretary-General shall make an annual report to the General Assembly on the work of the Organization.

ARTICLE 99

The Secretary-General may bring to the attention of the Security Council any matter which in his opinion may threaten the maintenance of international peace and security.

ARTICLE 100

1. In the performance of their duties the Secretary-General and the staff shall not seek or receive instructions from any government or from any other authority external to the Organization. They shall refrain from any action which might reflect on their position as international officials responsible only to the Organization.

2. Each Member of the United Nations undertakes to respect the exclusively international character of the responsibilities of the Secretary-General and the staff and not to seek to influence them in the discharge of their responsibilities.

ARTICLE 101

1. The staff shall be appointed by the Secretary-General under regulations established by the General Assembly.

2. Appropriate staffs shall be permanently assigned to the Economic and Social Council, the Trusteeship Council, and, as required, to other organs of the United Nations. These staffs shall form a part of the Secretariat.

3. The paramount consideration in the employment of the staff and in the determination of the conditions of service shall be the necessity of securing the highest standards of efficiency, competence, and integrity. Due regard shall be paid to the importance of recruiting the staff on as wide a geographical basis as possible.

CHAPTER XVI

MISCELLANEOUS PROVISIONS

ARTICLE 102

1. Every treaty and every international agreement entered into by any Member of the United Nations after the present Charter comes into force shall as soon as possible be registered with the Secretariat and published by it.

2. No party to any such treaty or international agreement which has not been registered in accordance with the provisions of paragraph 1 of this Article may invoke that treaty or agreement before any organ of the United Nations.

ARTICLE 103

In the event of a conflict between the obligations of the Members of the United Nations under the present Charter and their obligations under any other international agreement, their obligations under the present Charter shall prevail.

ARTICLE 104

The Organization shall enjoy in the territory of each of its Members such legal capacity as may be necessary for the exercise of its functions and the fulfillment of its purposes.

ARTICLE 105

1. The Organization shall enjoy in the territory of each of its Members such privileges and immunities as are necessary for the fulfillment of its purposes.

2. Representatives of the Members of the United Nations and officials of the Organization shall similarly enjoy such privileges and immunities as are necessary for the independent exercise of their functions in connection with the Organization.

3. The General Assembly may make recommendations with a view to determining the details of the application of paragraphs 1 and 2 of this Article or may propose conventions to the Members of the United Nations for this purpose.

CHAPTER XVII

TRANSITIONAL SECURITY ARRANGEMENTS

ARTICLE 106

Pending the coming into force of such special agreements referred to in Article 43 as in the opinion of the Security Council enable it to begin the exercise of its responsibilities under Article 42, the parties to the Four-Nation Declaration, signed at Moscow, October 30, 1943, and France, shall, in accordance with the provisions of paragraph 5 of that Declaration, consult with one another and as occasion requires with other Members of the United Nations with a view to such joint action on behalf of the Organization as may be necessary for the purpose of maintaining international peace and security.

ARTICLE 107

Nothing in the present Charter shall invalidate or preclude action, in relation to any state which during the Second World War has been an enemy of any signatory to the present Charter, taken or authorized as a result of that war by the Governments having responsibility for such action.

CHAPTER XVIII

AMENDMENTS

ARTICLE 108

Amendments to the present Charter shall come into force for all Members of the United Nations when they have been adopted by a vote of two-thirds of the members of the General Assembly and ratified in accordance with their respective constitutional processes by two-thirds of the Members of the United Nations, including all the permanent members of the Security Council.

ARTICLE 109

1. A General Conference of the Members of the United Nations for the purpose of reviewing the present Charter may be held at a date and place to be fixed by a two-thirds vote of the members of the General Assembly and by a vote of any seven members of the Security Council. Each Member of the United Nations shall have one vote in the conference.

2. Any alteration of the present Charter recommended by a two-thirds vote of the conference shall take effect when ratified in accordance with their respective constitutional processes by two-thirds of the Members of the United Nations including all the permanent members of the Security Council.

3. If such a conference has not been held before the tenth annual session of the General Assembly following the coming into force of the present Charter, the proposal to call such a conference shall be placed on the agenda of that session of the General Assembly, and the conference shall be held if so decided by a majority vote of the members of the General Assembly and by a vote of any seven members of the Security Council.

CHAPTER XIX

RATIFICATION AND SIGNATURE

ARTICLE 110

1. The present Charter shall be ratified by the signatory states in accordance with their respective constitutional processes.

2. The ratifications shall be deposited with the Government of the United States of America, which shall notify all the signatory states of each deposit as well as the Secretary-General of the Organization when he has been appointed.

3. The present Charter shall come into force upon the deposit of ratifications by the Republic of China, France, the Union of Soviet Socialist Republics, the United Kingdom of Great Britain and Northern Ireland, and the United States of America, and by a majority of the other signatory states. A protocol of the ratifications deposited shall thereupon be drawn up by the Government of the United States of America which shall communicate copies thereof to all the signatory states.

4. The states signatory to the present Charter which ratify it after it has come into force will become original Members of the United Nations on the date of the deposit of their respective ratifications.

ARTICLE 111

The present Charter, of which the Chinese, French, Russian, English, and Spanish texts are equally authentic, shall remain deposited in the archives of the Government of the United States of America. Duly certified copies thereof shall be transmitted by that Government to the Governments of the other signatory states.

IN FAITH WHEREOF the representatives of the Governments of the United Nations have signed the present Charter.

DONE at the city of San Francisco the twenty-sixth day of June, one thousand nine hundred and forty-five.

III. Abbreviations in Common Use

ANZUS	Treaty between the United States, Australia and New Zealand
BENELUX	Customs union between Belgium, the Netherlands, and Luxembourg
ECAFE	Economic Commission for Asia and the Far East (UN)
ECE	Economic Commission for Europe (UN)
ECLA	Economic Commission for Latin America (UN)
ECOSOC	Economic and Social Council (UN)
ECSC	European Coal and Steel Community (Schuman Plan)
EEC	European Economic Community
ERP	European Recovery Program (US)
EPU	European Payments Union
FAO	Food and Agriculture Organization
GATT	General Agreement on Tariffs and Trade
IAEA	International Atomic Energy Agency
IBRD	International Bank for Reconstruction and Development
ICAO	International Civil Aviation Organization
ICJ	International Court of Justice
IFC	International Finance Corporation
ILO	International Labor Organization
IMCO	Inter-Governmental Maritime Consultative Organization
IMF	International Monetary Fund
IRO	International Refugee Organization
ITU	International Telecommunication Union
NATO	North Atlantic Treaty Organization
OAS	Organization of American States
OEEC	Organization for European Economic Co-operation
PCIJ	Permanent Court of International Justice
SEATO	Southeast Asia Treaty Organization
SHAPE	Supreme Headquarters Allied Powers Europe (NATO)
TAB	Technical Assistance Board (UN)
UAR	United Arab Republic
UNCURK	United Nations Commission for Unification and Rehabilitation of Korea
UNEF	United Nations Emergency Force
UNESCO	United Nations Educational, Scientific, and Cultural Organization
UNICEF	United Nations Children's Fund
UPU	Universal Postal Union
UNRRA	United Nations Relief and Rehabilitation Administration
UNRWAPRNE	United Nations Relief and Works Agency for Palestine Refugees in the Near East
WEU	Western European Union
WHO	World Health Organization
WMO	World Meteorological Organization

INDEX

AREA AND POPULATION OF MEMBERS OF THE

UNITED NATIONS

Name of Country	Total Area (Square Kilometres)	Latest official estimate or census Date	Population	Date of U.N. Membership
Afghanistan	650,000	1 VII 1956	12,000,000	19 Nov. 45
Albania	28,748	1 VII 1955	1,394,000	14 Dec. 55
Argentina	2,808,492	1 I 1957	19,678,000	24 Oct. 45
Australia	7,704,159	30 IX 1956	9,479,000	1 Nov. 45
Austria	83,849	31 XII 1955	6,975,900	14 Dec. 55
Belgium	30,507	31 XII 1955	8,896,246	27 Dec. 45
Bolivia	1,098,581	5 IX 1956	3,235,251	14 Nov. 45
Brazil	8,513,844	1 I 1957	60,552,819	24 Oct. 45
Bulgaria	111,493	1 XII 1956	7,629,254	14 Dec. 55
Burma	677,950	1 VII 1956	19,855,560	19 Apr. 48
Byelorussian Soviet Socialist Republic	207,600	1 IV 1956	8,000,000	24 Oct. 45
Cambodia	175,000	1 VII 1955	4,358,000	14 Dec. 55
Canada	9,960,547	1 I 1957	16,344,000	9 Nov. 45
Ceylon	65,610	15 VI 1956	8,782,800	14 Dec. 55
Chile	741,767	31 VIII 1956	6,972,207	24 Oct. 45
China	9,736,288	1 VII 1948	463,493,000	24 Oct. 45
Colombia	1,138,355	5 VII 1956	12,939,140	5 Nov. 45
Costa Rica	50,900	31 XII 1956	1,013,200	2 Nov. 45
Cuba	114,524	28 I 1953	5,829,029	24 Oct. 45
Czechoslovakia	127,819	1 VII 1956	13,224,000	24 Oct. 45
Denmark	42,936	1 VII 1955	4,439,000	24 Oct. 45
Dominican Republic	48,734	1 VII 1956	2,608,329	24 Oct. 45
Ecuador	270,670	1 VII 1956	3,777,000	21 Dec. 45
*Egypt	1,000,000	1 VII 1955	22,934,000	24 Oct. 45
El Salvador	20,000	1 VII 1956	2,268,464	24 Oct. 45
Ethiopia	1,184,320	1955	20,000,000	13 Nov. 45
Finland	337,009	31 I 1957	4,315,000	14 Dec. 55
France	551,208	31 XII 1956	43,787,000	24 Oct. 45
Ghana	237,873	1 VII 1956	4,691,000	8 Mar. 57
Greece	132,562	31 XII 1955	8,007,000	25 Oct. 45
Guatemala	108,889	31 XII 1955	3,303,215	21 Nov. 45
Haiti	27,750	1 VII 1955	3,304,564	24 Oct. 45
Honduras	112,088	1 VII 1956	1,711,449	17 Dec. 45
Hungary	93,030	31 XII 1955	9,861,314	14 Dec. 55
Iceland	103,000	1 XII 1955	159,480	19 Nov. 46
India	3,288,375	1 VII 1955	381,690,000	30 Oct. 45
Indonesia	1,491,562	1 VII 1955	81,900,000	28 Sep. 50
Iran	1,630,000	1 XI 1956	18,944,821	24 Oct. 45
Iraq	444,474	1 VII 1955	5,200,000	21 Dec. 45

Name of Country	Total Area (Square Kilometres)	Latest official estimate or census Date	Population	Date of U.N. Membership
Ireland	70,283	1 VII 1956	2,895,000	14 Dec. 55
Israel	20,678	31 I 1957	1,883,000	11 May 49
Italy	301,226	1 VII 1956	48,223,000	14 Dec. 55
Japan	369,813	1 II 1957	90,050,000	18 Dec. 56
Jordan	96,610	1 VII 1956	1,471,315	14 Dec. 55
Laos	237,000	1 VII 1955	1,425,200	14 Dec. 55
Lebanon	10,400	1 VII 1956	1,450,000	24 Oct. 45
Liberia	111,370	1 VII 1955	1,250,000	2 Nov. 45
Libya	1,759,540	1 VII 1955	1,105,000	14 Dec. 55
Luxembourg	2,586	31 XII 1955	311,033	24 Oct. 45
Malaya	131,321	1956	6,000,000	17 Sep. 57
Mexico	1,969,367	1 VII 1956	30,538,050	7 Nov. 45
Morocco	410,805	1 VII 1955	9,723,448	12 Nov. 56
Nepal	140,753	7 VII 1954	8,431,537	14 Dec. 55
Netherlands	40,893	1 I 1957	10,956,000	10 Dec. 45
New Zealand	268,083	31 XII 1956	2,209,000	24 Oct. 45
Nicaragua	148,000	31 XII 1956	1,302,454	24 Oct. 45
Norway	323,917	1 I 1957	3,478,000	27 Nov. 45
Pakistan	944,824	1 VII 1956	83,603,000	30 Sep. 47
Panama	74,470	1 VII 1956	934,400	13 Nov. 45
Paraguay	406,752	1 VII 1956	1,601,000	24 Oct. 45
Peru	1,249,049	1 VII 1956	9,651,000	31 Oct. 45
Philippines	299,404	1 VII 1956	22,265,300	24 Oct. 45
Poland	311,700	31 III 1956	27,680,000	24 Oct. 45
Portugal	92,200	1 II 1957	8,879,000	14 Dec. 55
Romania	237,502	21 II 1956	17,489,794	14 Dec. 55
Saudi Arabia	1,600,000	1 VII 1952	7,000,000	24 Oct. 45
Spain	503,486	1 VII 1956	29,203,000	14 Dec. 55
Sudan	2,505,825		11,000,000	12 Nov. 56
Sweden	449,681	30 IX 1956	7,322,000	19 Nov. 46
*Syria	181,337	31 XII 1955	4,194,298	24 Oct. 45
Thailand	514,000	31 XII 1956	20,880,000	16 Dec. 46
Tunisia	125,180	1 II 1956	3,782,380	12 Nov. 56
Turkey	776,980	1 X 1956	24,797,000	24 Oct. 45
Ukrainian Soviet Socialist Republic	576,600	1 IV 1956	40,600,000	24 Oct. 45
Union of South Africa	1,223,783	30 VI 1956	13,915,000	7 Nov. 45
Union of Soviet Socialist Republics	21,618,800	1 IV 1956	151,600,000	24 Oct. 45
United Kingdom	244,016	30 VI 1956	51,215,000	24 Oct. 45
United States	7,827,976	1 I 1957	169,661,000	24 Oct. 45
Uruguay	186,926	31 XII 1955	2,631,783	18 Dec. 45
Venezuela	912,050	31 XII 1956	6,038,860	15 Nov. 45
Yemen	195,000	1 VII 1949	4,500,000	30 Sep. 47
Yugoslavia	255,804	30 XI 1956	17,932,000	24 Oct. 45

Source: Map No. 766 Rev. 1, United Nations, June 1957

* With the establishment of the United Arab Republic and the acceptance of its credentials on March 7, 1958, Egypt and Syria lost their individual membership.